AF715133

William M. Evarts

WILLIAM M. EVARTS

William M. Evarts

LAWYER, DIPLOMAT, STATESMAN

By

CHESTER L. BARROWS

SUBMITTED IN PARTIAL FULFILLMENT OF THE REQUIREMENTS FOR THE DEGREE OF DOCTOR OF PHILOSOPHY, IN THE FACULTY OF PHILOSOPHY, COLUMBIA UNIVERSITY

1941

THE UNIVERSITY OF NORTH CAROLINA PRESS

CHAPEL HILL

TO

My Wife

Preface

THE REPUTATION of a lawyer is ephemeral. His fame is temporary and dies with the juries he addresses. The court record gives abundant space to the judge's decision, but little to the lawyer. So it happens that the best legal minds are little known or remembered. There is a lack of biographical material upon great American lawyers, perhaps because of the difficulties of research. It is the purpose of the present work to depict William M. Evarts primarily as a lawyer and an advocate.

His public life as a statesman touches at important junctures the development of the nation and the city in which his fortunes were cast, and illuminates each episode in which he was involved. His diplomatic career also has large significance. The work of his predecessor, Hamilton Fish, and of his successor, James G. Blaine, has been set forth by skilled biographers; but Evarts' diplomacy in the State Department has been neglected.

By the layman Evarts is remembered chiefly as a wit and teller of stories. He was much more: orator, philosopher, and sage. Although his son, Sherman Evarts, has preserved his better-known speeches in three volumes, many of the best speeches and choicest stories remain scattered.

Evarts steadily refused to write or dictate reminiscences. William H. Winters of the New York Law Institute began a collection of materials, which has been of great assistance. Of greater value has been a collection of Evarts manuscripts furnished by Allen W.

Evarts. But most of the materials for this work have had to be gleaned the "hard way." Among others to whom the author is indebted are Henry Wardner, Mrs. Elizabeth Perkins, Professor Allan Nevins, and Professor Arthur C. Cole for their encouragement, supply of materials, or critical examination of the text.

George F. Hoar once said of Evarts, "If his biography shall ever be properly written, it will be as delightful as that of Sheridan or Sidney Smith for its wit and will be valuable for the narrative of the great public transactions in which he took part. Especially it will preserve to posterity the portraiture of a great lawyer and advocate of the time before the day of specialists when the leaders of the American Bar were great lawyers and advocates."

CHESTER L. BARROWS

March 6, 1941

Contents

William M. Evarts

1

The Years of Preparation

It was a January day in 1888. The usual bustle filled the corridors of the United States Capitol. Behind an unobtrusive door leading from the central rotunda into the Supreme Court chamber a drama was being enacted; yet there was no crowd of politicians or sightseers to witness it. A few spectators had tiptoed by the Negro attendant to the crimson-velvet-cushioned seats. But only the initiated fully understood that an important case was in progress.

The setting was impressive. This famous old Senate chamber, which had resounded to the oratory of Webster, Clay, and Calhoun, was now a hall of justice, devoted to the tangled problems of liberty and property. It was a small, semicircular room, a fine example of Greek symmetry, with Ionic columns supporting a central dome. Around the walls were marble pilasters and busts of deceased chief justices. Above was a small, unused gallery, and in the center of the balcony railing, over the chair of the chief justice, a gilt eagle looked down from a golden rod. The nine justices, in black silk robes, sat upon a raised platform behind a curtained bar. All were intent upon the speaker. Directly in front sat the seven counsel, three representing the State of California, and four retained by large railroad interests. The verdict in the case would decide, after a two-year legal battle, whether California could levy a tax upon the franchise of railroads incorporated by Congress. An important decision was in the making.

One of the counsel for the railroads was addressing the court.

In black frock coat, with old-fashioned turned-down collar and black cravat, he seemed an incarnation of the law. He was seventy years old, thin, of medium height, with massive head and sharp, aquiline features. He spoke easily, at times with subtle humor and again with a solidity and conciseness that carried conviction. With perfect diction and fine choice of words, never hesitating, and often using long sentences which piled clause upon clause with uncanny ingenuity, Senator William M. Evarts of New York argued his last case before the supreme tribunal. He urged a broad interpretation of the Constitution. Shaking his finger impressively, he said, "In the long run it [the Court] has made the Constitution an instrument elastic enough to provide for the country's growing pains."[1] He won his case. The victory seemed easy; merely another of his many triumphs and by no means his greatest. But behind his evident power, his mastery of logic and eloquence, lay years of study and a devoted love of the law; behind it, too, lay great natural ability, complete integrity, and fifty years of preparation.

The heritage of William M. Evarts was remarkable. On the paternal side he traced his descent from Welsh ancestors who had migrated to Connecticut about 1635. Three successive generations resided at Madison or East Guilford, Connecticut. The fourth of the line, one James Evarts, a farmer of uncommon public spirit, moved with his wife Sarah to Sunderland, in Bennington County, Vermont.[2] There in 1781 was born Jeremiah Evarts, father of William M. Evarts, and one of the finest New Englanders of his time. That this quiet village should have produced Ethan Allen and Jeremiah Evarts was enough to make it famous.

Jeremiah was a Puritan of the old school. Although he had studied law at Yale and practiced for a short time in New Haven, he did not find happiness in the calling. He had been stirred by a revival during student days, and the opportunity in 1810 of becoming editor of the Boston *Panoplist,* a paper devoted to orthodox Congregationalism, appealed to his literary and religious tastes. His analytic mind, his power of exposing sophistry, his unbounded industry, and his strong religious convictions made the *Panoplist* probably the best religious paper in the country during the ten years that he had charge of it. He wrote well, and the boldness of his ideas captivated many minds. His journal became a powerful source of strength for the old Puritan theology, assailed by the new Unitarianism in Boston.[3]

A contemporary says of Jeremiah, "He seemed to have commenced study in his youth with the fixed purpose of being prepared for usefulness and for being used." His strong mind glowed with a desire to do good. His writings, if collected, would fill several volumes. In launching a temperance movement in Boston at a time when drinking was almost universal, he met the objection that it would be impracticable with the retort, "It is right, therefore practical."[4]

His greatest achievements were in the missionary field. He was one of the founders of the American Board of Foreign Missions and was for years its corresponding secretary. His essays condemning the exploitation and removal of the Southern Indian tribes were regarded by John Marshall as "the most conclusive argument" he had ever read. But the tribes were removed in defiance of the Supreme Court. Overwork and a frail constitution brought Jeremiah to a premature grave in 1831. He left behind hundreds of friends, among them John Jay, Dr. Channing, and Ralph Waldo Emerson. To his son William he bequeathed a scholarly, disciplined mind, a prodigious memory, strong powers of reasoning, sound judgment, an appreciation of religious and civic responsibilities, and an even temperament unruffled by cares or adversities.[5]

The maternal heritage was equally remarkable. Jeremiah's wife, Mehetabel Sherman Evarts, was one of the famous Sherman family, a Puritan line that has produced many notables including Roger Sherman, William T. Sherman, John Sherman, Stuart P. Sherman, Chauncey Depew, and the Hoar family of Concord. Mehetabel was the daughter of Roger Sherman, signer of the Declaration of Independence. She first married Daniel Barnes, a West Indian merchant, who died six years later. For her second husband she chose

Jeremiah Evarts; and Timothy Dwight of Yale performed the marriage ceremony in 1804. She was a woman of high character, great beauty, and sprightly wit. Many famous men and women of the Revolutionary era were among her acquaintances; she had dined with John Hancock and knew Washington well. Her wit, of which her son inherited a full portion, was illustrated in girlhood days when Washington came one day to visit her father. She opened the door for him as he was leaving, and Washington said, patting her on the head, "You deserve a better office, my little lady." "Yes, sir," she replied with a courtesy, "to let you in."[6]

Boston in 1825 was scarcely more than a country town, although its forty thousand people and its famous mayor, Josiah Quincy, perhaps entitled it to be called a city. It was marked by thrift and enterprise. The harbor teemed with ships; the taverns did a thriving business; stage-coaches rattled in and out; illuminating gas was just coming into use. No city in America stood higher in wealth or cultivation. Boston Common could hardly be called a beauty spot; it was merely a field surrounded by a wooden fence and used as a pasture for cows, a playground for children, and a drill ground for the militia. On Beacon Street stood some of the finest houses in America.

Here, at No. 22 Pinckney Street, William Maxwell Evarts was born on February 6, 1818. His birthplace was a plain three-story brick house with arched alcove entrance, not pretentious, but respectable, and quite suitable to the limited means of Jeremiah Evarts. The street sloped down Beacon Hill to the Charles River only three or four blocks from the house.

The four other children were all older than William. Mary, the oldest, was destined to marry the Reverend David Greene, grandfather of Professor Evarts B. Greene of Columbia University; the second oldest, Martha, also married a clergyman, the Reverend Ebenezer C. Tracy; and the next two in order, John Jay and Sarah, died in early youth. When the news of another son reached Jeremiah Evarts in South Carolina, where he was engaged on one of his many missions, he recorded in his journal: "I commend the babe to protection of Heaven, and pray that its soul may be saved in the day of the Lord Jesus, however it may please God to dispose of its temporal estate."[7] He named the baby after his friend and classmate at Yale, William Maxwell, a Virginia lawyer noted for his wit and literary ability and in later years president of Hampden-Sydney College.

Little can be said of the boy's early childhood. If he showed any signs of genius, they were not recorded. But his education began at an early age. "When I was a boy in Boston," he said years after, "we had blankets on our bed with large letters on them 'G. R.'; and I took my first lesson in Latin . . . for I asked my mother what those letters meant and she said they were King George's blankets; but I said how does 'R' stand for King George, and she told me it was George Rex, and that was my first lesson in Latin when I was but five years old."[8] He was reared in an atmosphere of culture, and his lack of robustness turned him to books. His father's religious zeal and high position in the community as selectman, editor, reformer, and missionary impressed him. In his home he saw prominent men, who came to call on his father: Emerson, Channing, John Jay, and Jedidiah Morse. He attended one of the new primary schools which Boston boasted. Perhaps nothing impressed him more during these years than the visit of Lafayette to Boston in 1824. The school children were drawn up in two ranks on the Common to cheer the arrival of the Marquis. The boy was too young to understand the scene; but in later life he was proud to say that he was a contemporary of Lafayette and that the Marquis had stopped to greet him as a descendant of Roger Sherman.[9]

His first scholastic success came at the Bowdoin Grammar School on Derne Street, which he attended from his seventh year to his tenth. Benjamin Franklin had given the city one hundred pounds for medals to be awarded annually to the most deserving pupil of each grammar school. Young Evarts was one of the prize winners. The recipient had the additional honor of being a guest at a public dinner in Faneuil Hall, receiving the medal from the hands of the mayor and having his name entered upon the records of the city. On these occasions the city fathers did all the speaking and often drank more than was good for them. "That dinner given me," said Evarts, "was an important introduction to life . . . and if I have ever gained in my later life any credit for either eating or speaking at dinners, it has been owing to that early hospitality."[10]

In 1828 his father went to Washington and took the lad with him. The city was then little more than a rambling Southern town; but Evarts' ambition and imagination were fired by the trip and by the people he met. What ten-year-old boy would not have been proud to meet President Adams and John C. Calhoun? Calhoun was a great admirer of Roger Sherman and was well acquainted with Mrs. Samuel Hoar, Evarts' aunt. He took a liking to the boy, showing him the sights about town and introducing him to the President.[11]

Evarts in time entered the oldest school in America, the Boston Latin School. It stood on School Street, opposite King's Chapel, on the site now occupied by the Parker House, a three-story building of granite and brick surmounted by a belfry. It was a democratic institution; the sons of the rich and of day-laborers sat together, dressed alike, in winter wearing the prescribed black suit and white collar, in summer a long, clerical-looking calico gown. There was little snobbery, and the only distinction was that accorded the boy who stood at the head of his class.

But life at the Latin School was hard. Half the students dropped out by the end of the second year; indeed, the scheme of education had more disciplinary merit than anything else. Hours were long, vacations short. The pupils sat at long benches or "forms," and wrote with quills. The first year was spent in committing Latin words to memory, after which the grammar was taught as if it contained the eternal truths of life. There were no devices for making lessons easy or interesting and no improved grammars.[12] Speaking of this classical discipline years after, Evarts said, "I certainly was taught to say in the most perfect manner the longest list of Latin nouns and prepositions that I did not want to learn at all, became intimately acquainted with their whole pedigree and relations with large sums and words that I never expected to meet in my subsequent life at all; but having learnt that, I could learn other things very easily."[13]

Unlike most of his schoolmates, Evarts enjoyed life at the Latin School. Perhaps the reason lay in his marked talent for Latin. With a twinkle in his eye, drawing a handkerchief back and forth in his hand, he would reel off Latin while the class listened in astonishment. He seemed to master everything of a literary nature with ease and to take a pardonable pride in reciting. He was always at the head of his class and was a model of propriety, a little gentleman. Life had more in store for him than for any of his thirty-eight classmates, although several were to become professors at Harvard. Henry Ward Beecher, John Lothrop Motley, and Charles Devens, who were schoolmates but not in his class, were to become noted men.[14]

The monotony of school life was broken on Saturdays, when all the students went upstairs to Master Leverett's room to hear declamations. Every boy spoke from the platform once a month; to most this was an ordeal, but Billy Evarts found the task easy and in his last year won the prize for elocution. He began to acquire poise and self-confidence in speaking. He meanwhile heard Harrison Gray Otis and Josiah Quincy deliver orations at the Boston Bicentennial celebration, and his interest in public speaking was quickened.[15]

The death of his father, leaving a widow with three children and little money, threatened for a time to cloud his prospects. Fortunately Leverett, who was leaving the Latin School to open one of his own, recognized the boy's capabilities and agreed to give him free tuition at the new school. Although Evarts always regretted that he did not graduate from the Latin School, he had another year under an able master.

His prospect for going to college seemed dubious. But his uncle, the Reverend David Greene, who had become his guardian, was able to offer help, while Judge Simeon Baldwin, another uncle, had previously arranged with Jeremiah for an exchange of children which would enable young William to live at the Judge's home and attend Yale.[16] And so, as he later put it, he traveled "two hundred and forty miles by stage coach from Boston to New Haven to avoid going to Harvard University, which was across the bridge." Doubtless Yale was preferred because his grandfather and father were Yale men and because Yale still stood for the strict orthodox Congregationalism to which the Evarts family adhered.

One of his classmates, Thomas M. Day, gives a picture of Evarts on his way to college: "He was in Hartford on his way . . . and I was invited to meet him at the dinner table of Judge Williams, Ch. Justice of the Supreme Court of Conn. He married Delia Ellsworth, daughter of Oliver Ellsworth . . . Mrs. Ellsworth knew that I was intending to enter Yale in the same class . . . and invited me to meet my future classmate at her table. We were congenial from the first acquaintance. I think [he] had the rare knack of making *friends,* from persons before unknown."[17]

The Yale of 1833 was a modest college. It consisted merely of Old Brick Row, a straight line of severe, old-fashioned edifices along College Street between Chapel and Elm streets, and a grassy campus enclosed by the famous old wooden fence and sweeping elm trees. In short, the college was confined to one city block. Seven buildings composed Old Brick Row: South, Athenaeum, South Middle, Lyceum, North Middle, Chapel, and North. Behind the row was the Laboratory, used as a dining hall, and the tomblike Trumbull Gallery, built the year before Evarts arrived. None of these buildings could make any pretense to architectural beauty. The tuition was only thirty-three dollars a year, board was sixty-four dollars, and the total annual expenses about one hundred and ninety dollars.[18]

Evarts was doubly fortunate in being able to make his home with Judge Baldwin: he had congenial surroundings, and he listened to frequent discussions of the law. During his junior year he lived at No. 12 on the first floor of South College, and during his last year at No. 126 on the top floor of North College. These old dormitories, with their sagging beams, billowy floors, cracked walls, and musty odor were architectural monstrosities. The low ceiling could be reached with the hand, the floor was bare, the heat from the stove varied with the uncertain fuel supply, and dust and dirt were abundant. To go out into the corridor at night was risky, for the stairs were treacherous and unlighted. Bedrooms were dark, small, and unventilated.[19]

During his junior year Evarts roomed with William T. Bacon, six years older, who later became a clergyman and editor of the *New Englander*. During his senior year his roommate was Abel B. Robeson, later a physician in New York.

Billy Evarts now became plain "Bill." His ease in making friends increased. The spirit at Yale was democratic, and there was little tendency toward clannishness. Students gathered along the old fence at twilight after vespers to talk, laugh, and sing. No college boy could have been as well liked as Evarts was unless possessed of some spirit. During his junior year he was involved in a bit of disorderliness in the dining hall, which the faculty deemed sufficiently serious to justify a "second warning" and a letter from the president to his guardian.[20] Nor did Bill hesitate to attend the convivial meetings at the "Barons," an old-fashioned tavern which the students were strictly forbidden to visit. At these conclaves he seems to have first manifested that dry humor and sparkling wit so characteristic in later life.

Years before, it had become necessary for each class to organize a defense committee against the town rowdies, choosing a "bully" as leader because of his fighting qualities and making him leader in class affairs, and a "minor bully" as lieutenant. By Evarts' day these offices had undergone a transformation and were honors given the two most popular men of each class. They presided at class meetings and carried gold-mounted canes as emblems of office. Evarts was elected minor bully and, as Thomas Day wrote, "made a capital presiding officer, dignified and firm in preserving order, but easy of address and not rigid against fun or technicality."[21]

The class of 1837 boasted that it had more graduates who became eminent in public life than any previous class. Morrison R. Waite later became chief justice; Edwards Pierrepont became minister to England; Samuel J. Tilden, who left at the end of the first year, became governor of New York; Benjamin Silliman, Jr., son of the noted chemist, followed in his father's footsteps; and George Duffield became a well-known editor and composer of hymns.

Fifty years after graduation (1887) Duffield read a poem at a class reunion reminiscent of college days, in part as follows:

What class had better teachers, when our honored Prex was *Day,*
When *Jimmy Kingsley* Latin taught, and *Loomis* Algebra?
When our Prof. in Greek was *Woolsey,* and we studied dear Alcestis,
When *Porter* heard us Homer, who of teachers still the best is . . .
Nor *Goodrich* be forgot, who, learned in the Greek,
Could teach us better how to live than classic phrase to speak . . .
We were old Prex's favorite Class, the '37 boys,
His one paternal censure this, "no class e'er made such noise. . . ."
Our orator (our Joker, too), what need to breathe his name,
Already on the thousand tongues of universal fame? . . .
Bob Learned, was the fattest, and the least disposed to strife . . .
Or *Evarts,* South Hall, Junior year, had not escaped with life . . .
'Twas hard to say who laughed the most, when laughing was begun
But *Waite,* had still the loudest laugh, *Dutton* made the fun . . .
Uncle Sam, when days were dark, with lantern straight proceeded,
At once to Yale and Thirty-Seven, and found the men he needed.[22]

"Prex" was President Jeremiah Day, an uncle of Evarts, and an able leader and teacher. Though he was dignified and conservative, his serenity, modesty, and unselfishness endeared him to the students. James Kingsley not only taught Latin but inspired his students with a critical outlook. Theodore Woolsey, who later became president of the college, taught Greek and exerted a strong influence on college life. In the classes of these masters Evarts shone, as he had at the Latin School. His roommate, Bacon, believed him possessed of the best mind in the class, while Thomas Day later testified, "We all recognized his classical training and his thorough understanding of matters discussed."[23]

He was a brilliant debater and public speaker, the joy of Chauncey A. Goodrich, professor of rhetoric and oratory. Every student was urged to join one of the three debating societies, Linonia, Brothers in Unity, or Calliopea, each of which had its own quarters in the Athenaeum. Evarts joined Linonia, became its vice-president and secretary, and in later life ascribed to the training received from it much of whatever merit he might claim as a public speaker. Linonia was partly a fraternal and partly a debating club, dating back to 1753, which had a wholesome influence on student life. The faculty encouraged its Wednesday evening meetings by shorter lessons the next day.[24]

What modern college student would voluntarily read, in addition to prescribed work, more than twenty thousand pages of miscellaneous books and magazines during his sophomore and junior years? Evarts not only did this, but he took the trouble to record carefully just what he read. History, poetry, essays, novels—all were devoured with avidity. His purpose was not so much to gain information as to improve his writing. Boldness of style, ingenuity of illustration, and terseness of reasoning always pleased him. He could read Latin half as fast as English, and did not hesitate to undertake it. At the other extreme, Cooper's *Last of the Mohicans* delighted him and, like his father, he became indignant over the oppression of the red man. Believing that most Americans were ignorant of their own history, he pursued a course of reading to cure that fault in himself.[25]

He had in him the making of an editor. During his junior year he presided over a class meeting called to organize and edit *The Yale Literary Magazine,* which still lives. Bacon initiated the project, and Evarts was one of the five original editors. They began work with some doubts, fearing they might be adding one more to the list of seven short-lived periodicals which had been previously attempted. Nevertheless, they declared in their first number: "Our prospects are encouraging. Our subscription list fully equals our expectations—communications are abundant—and we have hardly heard one croaking voice foreboding failure."[26] The original office was at No. 12 South, where Evarts and Bacon roomed. It was Evarts who proposed the name and selected the Latin motto. By graduation day the original board had issued twelve numbers. In the last they wrote: "We take an interest in this child of many fathers . . . whose honor we have preferred to our own ease, and for whose nourishment we have not scrupled to ransack each nook and corner of this literary realm. . . . The office of the 'Editor' is no *sinecure* . . . and the life of an editor is not all 'a gilded show.' . . . The apathy and indolence of many of those who are best able to render the pages of the Magazine entertaining and useful, and the persecutions of those who have none of these gifts, are two things most trying to an editor's temper."[27]

Evarts had come to Yale with a strong religious background. Perhaps the rattle and bang of shutters hurriedly thrown back against brick walls at five o'clock in the morning as the bell roused a slumbering college for chapel, or the longer vesper service later in the day, had little to do with his spiritual growth. But he was a true son of Jeremiah Evarts and joined the church on confession of faith. In his journal he spoke of the "vanity of all earthly pursuits," and on the fly-leaf he jotted: "Seize the day, trusting as little as possible to tomorrow," and "Life gives nothing to mortals without great labor." Under his outer mask of jollity and good comradeship there was a serious-minded young man, determined to live with integrity.[28]

In his senior year he was elected to Skull and Bones, the oldest secret society, and to Phi Beta Kappa.[29] At graduation he stood third in a class of about one hundred and was chosen, together with Pierrepont and Waite, as a commencement orator. That politics was beginning to interest him was evident from his commencement oration on "Intellectual Development," a plea for independence in political thought, for he was disgusted with the machine politics of the Jackson administration. He was true to his New England Federalist heritage when he wrote in his journal: "The principles of the much-calumniated Federalists are clearly shown to be the only ones which can produce stability and prosperity under our present form of government. Unless recourse is had to those, and that speedily, real despotism will soon exist under the name of liberty. . . . The Jeffersonian dominion has remained almost unbroken since its first establishment in his person, and the depth of moral degradation to which it has brought our country, is truly sickening. . . . Officers are all mercenary—infidelity in religion, and radicalism in politics, are rapidly increasing—party spirit is becoming wider in its influence and stronger in its basis—and the opinion is openly avowed that no man of talent and great eminence can ever hope to fill the presidential chair."[30] With the same anti-Jackson viewpoint he spoke before a sympathetic audience at commencement, deploring a public opinion which tolerated the conditions then existing in Washington and calling for leaders with steadfast principles and higher patriotism to replace the spoilsmen.

In leaving Yale Evarts stood at the first important cross-roads of his life. He had a marked taste for literary work and the classics, a deep religious feeling, and a budding interest in politics. What should he do next? It cannot be said that he had fully determined upon the law as a career, but it is certain that he decided upon it soon after graduation. Influences in this direction had not been lacking. His father had been a lawyer and a man of statesmanlike qualities; the example of Judge Baldwin had counted; but probably the greatest influence came from the Hoar family. Samuel Hoar was one of the best lawyers in Massachusetts, and his son, Rockwood Hoar, Evarts' cousin, had just entered the Dane Law School at Harvard. During his vacations at Concord young Evarts had seen and heard much of the law. The career of Samuel Hoar would have been an incentive to any young man. For thirty years he monopolized the cases before the courts of Middlesex County. His simple, straightforward manner, his unaffected methods in the courtroom, his convincing appeals to juries, his rigid honesty—all tended to make him the conscience of his community. He had been associated with Daniel Webster in one case and had opposed Rufus Choate in another. With money he assisted many a worthy cause, and many a young man received a needed loan.[31]

It was customary to prepare for law school by study under a lawyer. So Evarts went to Windsor to combine law study under Horace Everett with school teaching for a year. Everett was an experienced lawyer and an able Whig member of Congress. A tourist to Windsor today may still see on the Evarts estate a small one-room shedlike building where Evarts made his first acquaintance with law books, and over the door still hangs the sign "Horace Everett." No better place than Windsor could have been found for study—a quiet, pretty little village in the Connecticut Valley in a delightful scenic setting. Perhaps already the young law student had resolved, if fortune favored, to build a home in these Vermont hills. And a stronger tie soon bound him to Windsor, for here he met Helen Minerva Wardner, daughter of Allen Wardner, a prominent banker of the village and at one time state treasurer.

A year of study equipped Evarts for entrance to the Dane Law School. No entrance examinations were required, the students merely giving evidence of good character and ability to pursue the course. He set off first for a short visit to Concord, which now indeed was his home, for his mother, unable after the death of Jeremiah Evarts to maintain the Boston home, had gone there to live. Undoubtedly this was one reason why he thought the Harvard Law School preferable to Yale. Moreover, not only was Rockwood Hoar at Harvard, but George Wardner, brother of the young lady he had met in Windsor, was in attendance.

The university in 1839 comprised seven buildings: Stoughton, Holden, Hollis, Harvard, University, Massachusetts, and Dane Hall. The last, built in 1832, was a two-story brick building, shaped like a letter T with portico in front supported by Ionic columns, and hidden behind sweeping elms. Only eighty or ninety students were enrolled in the law school, but this represented a remarkable growth over the mere handful there a few years before. Charles Sumner, George T. Curtis, and John L. Motley had graduated just before

Evarts arrived; Rockwood Hoar was in his class; Richard H. Dana, Jr., James Russell Lowell, and Elihu Washburne were one year behind him.[32]

Evarts formed an intimate and lasting friendship with Dana. Forced to drop out of law school two years earlier by impaired eyesight, Dana, despite his finely cultured background, had shipped as a common sailor to the Pacific, and had obtained material for his famous *Two Years Before the Mast,* one of the most successful books of its type ever written. Indeed, its success nearly turned Dana to a literary career, but law attracted him more. He became a great lawyer, a friend of seamen, and a representative of the best culture of his time. He and Evarts had much in common, and their pathways in life often crossed.

They were fortunate to find at the law school such masters as Joseph Story and Simon Greenleaf. Becoming intimately acquainted with these great teachers, they learned to understand the mental processes and the methods by which each had gained his success. Story had come to Harvard in 1829, heralded as second to none in knowledge of the law. It was largely his power and force that changed the school from one of local to national fame, broadened its aims, and increased its enrollment. His lectures, even upon dry topics, were given with such earnestness and eloquence and were so well illustrated that they seemed more like entertaining chats than formal discourses. His majestic presence, genial face, musical voice, and conversational mode of teaching won the admiration of his students. He seemed to lead the mind rather than drive it, and the hour often passed before he or his students were aware of it. He stimulated their ambition by holding before them examples of distinguished lawyers whom he knew. Story brought Greenleaf to Harvard in 1833. Not so brilliant or picturesque as Story, he was more deliberate, thorough, exact, and systematic. It has been said, "Story prepared the soil, and Greenleaf sowed the seed." At this time he was at work on his famous treatise on "Evidence," which he published soon after Evarts left Harvard. Under no better masters could a law student have received his initial training.[33]

Twice a year moot courts were held in the library, attracting a crowd of spectators. The students prepared their cases with care and Story presided, giving elaborate oral decisions. Dana was much impressed with one of Evarts' arguments. "The most successful speech," he wrote, "made during the whole time I was there was made before a jury of undergraduates, Judge Story on the Bench, by William M. Evarts. A law argument which he introduced into it, addressed to the Court, was the most complete, systematic, precise, eloquently spoken argument I have ever heard. . . . Judge Story always complimented liberally, but never went so far as in this instance. Indeed, Evarts has been a peculiar young man, at school, at college, and in his professional studies. If he does not become distinguished, he will disappoint more persons than any other young man whom I have ever met."[34]

With such training and reputation, Evarts left the law school to seek fame and fortune in New York. He had been given the diploma of LL.B., which bore the valued autographs of Story and Greenleaf. Would fortune attend him? Would he find happiness in a strange city? Could he live up to the ideals he had formed? These thoughts must have revolved in his mind as the stagecoach rattled over the post road.

2

A Start in the Law

Evarts found New York in 1840 a city of three hundred thousand people. It was bounded on the North by Fourteenth Street and was rapidly growing despite the hard times, the after-effects of the great fire of 1835, and the political unrest of the day. He arrived armed with letters of introduction to some of the best families; among them one from Joseph Story to Chancellor Kent describing him as a young man of "very uncommon talents and professional attainments . . . destined to take a very elevated rank in his profession."[1]

It was the eminent lawyer Daniel Lord, who gave Evarts his start. Evarts had first met him during college days at New Haven. But it was the casual suggestion of a comrade at the law school which now led him, on reaching New York, to seek a place in Lord's office. He was aided by a family connection and by his excellent credentials. As Evarts described it years after: "Mr. Lord was really the reason, the occasion, the opportunity, the means, by which I was permitted to be introduced to any degree of professional labor. . . . I remember very well the kindness with which he received me. . . . 'Well, Mr. Evarts, (he said) you have come to commence your studies and be a lawyer in New York,' and I replied doubtfully, perhaps as I supposed modestly, 'I have come to try.' 'Well, sir,' said he, 'if you have only come to try, you had better go back; if you have come to stay, we shall be glad to receive you,' and when I amended my answer by the information he gave me, that it was possible for me to stay, that I had come to be a lawyer, he received me cordially; and from that time to the time of his death he has been my friend, my supporter, and my guide."[2]

Daniel Lord at this time ranked with Charles O'Conor, William C. Noyes, and James T. Brady as one of the few really eminent lawyers in New York. Originality, strong reasoning powers, fidelity to clients, cheerfulness, and integrity marked the man. Among his clients were some of the most influential men of the city, such as John Jacob Astor. Though he took all types of cases, criminal law was not to his taste. Steadfastly refusing public office, he devoted himself to his profession though he was not indifferent to civic causes. He was at the peak of his fame in 1840.[3]

Evarts was fortunate in being taken into Lord's private office—for the outer office was already overcrowded—where he could observe at close range the methods of his mentor. Among other students in the outer office was John Jay, grandson of the Chief Justice. He and Evarts soon became intimate, and a life-long friendship resulted. Jeremiah Evarts had been a friend of Chief Justice Jay and had named one of his sons John Jay Evarts, a fact which gave the young law students something in common. Young Jay possessed one advantage over Evarts, for a marriage to the daughter of a rich New York merchant had already given him financial independence. Nevertheless, the lives of the two men were destined to run in parallel lines. As Evarts said long afterward, "There has been no moment either at home or abroad, either in politics or the movements of society, that we have not been boys together."[4]

Adjusting himself to life in a strange city was not altogether easy for Evarts. He felt that New York society was "frivolous and dissipated," and for a time he was lonesome. However, he soon found friends by joining the Column Club, an organization of young lawyers and law students, founded fifteen years earlier for literary and political discussion. It derived its name from the center column which supported the roof in the back room of Dr. Lyell's church on Worth Street, where the club was permitted to meet. It had some thirty members and an imposing list of officers bearing such resounding titles as archon, premier, and chief justice. At the mystic rites and debates on Saturdays the deliberations were serious and sometimes heated. The club also had frequent good times on the benches at the Battery or dining together at Delmonico's. Evarts soon became a popular member and formed lasting friendships with John Bigelow and Edgar S. Van Winkle.[5]

His apprenticeship completed at the age of twenty-three, Evarts was admitted to the bar on July 16, 1841, and two months later was also licensed to practice in Massachusetts. He was now ready for life—a young man of brilliant mind, courteous and well-bred, sparkling with wit and humor, fond of the good things of life, and possessed above all with zeal for his profession. He had been fortunate in his early legal associations, and realizing the fact he said many years afterward, "It seems to me as if I were indebted to others from the beginning to the end. I do not speak of how much I owe to my masters in the law school, Story and Greenleaf—but I may be permitted to say, too, that no young man can be better aided in the early days of his profession than I was. . . . I recognized the debt to all—the constant obligation; and when at last the seal shall be set to my life (until which we are admonished to call no man fortunate), I may well be deemed fortunate if any law student, if any young lawyer or any dying veteran of the profession shall feel even a moderate degree toward me as I do toward these my masters and my friends."[6]

Evarts' first year in New York happened to be that of an exciting presidential campaign. He watched the boiling political kettle with intense interest. Deeply distrustful of Jacksonian democracy, he naturally preferred the Whig party; and Daniel Webster was his especial hero. He had often seen Webster in Boston and had been introduced to him during his senior year at Yale.[7] It was therefore natural for him to take up his political pen in behalf of the Whigs. In a series of articles he supported Harrison for president and Seward for governor, writing upon such topics as the protective tariff and Democratic extravagance. His cleverness and insight attracted the attention of Whig leaders in the city.[8] He witnessed a campaign marked by frenzy and violence, which included a riotous attack by the Loco-Focos on Whig headquarters. Thurlow Weed launched *The Log Cabin* with young Horace Greeley as editor. Evarts was able to join other Whigs in celebrating victory.

But he was disgusted by the aftermath. The unexpected death of Harrison, the schism in the Whig party when Tyler refused to follow its principles, and the resignation of the entire Cabinet except Webster—these were the sorry fruits of the victory. Appreciating Webster's plight, Evarts, who had been encouraged by the warm reception given his first writings, contributed two articles to *The New World* in October, 1841. The first, entitled "Mr. Webster's Position," upheld Webster's decision to remain in office to complete the treaty negotiations with Great Britain on an issue in which the United States was "morally and legally" wrong (a reference, doubtless, to the failure of the United States to adhere to the Quintuple Treaty against the slave trade). Webster's position, wrote Evarts, was neither equivocal nor that of a disappointed man, and it would be approved by history.

The second article, entitled "Mr. Tyler and the Whig Party," was an unsparing criticism of Tyler for his departure from Whig principles. Describing him as an accidental president, whom the Whigs should never have put on the ticket, and as a man of "wrong-headed conscience" and "religious self-respect, verging upon contempt for others," Evarts pronounced him unfit for power. The party, he believed, should follow neither Tyler nor Clay, but a midde-of-the-road course with Webster, for the sake of party harmony.

Webster praised the articles, and Professor C. C. Felton of Harvard wrote Park Benjamin, editor of *The New World,* that Evarts' political pen had real power. The young lawyer was tempted to continue, but changed his mind. His political pen became silent.[9] He took little active interest in politics for the next six years. He retained his affiliation with the local Sixteenth Ward Whig committee, and in 1845 was made chairman. But he still had a reputation to gain in the law and, as always, his profession came first.[10]

Upon Daniel Lord's advice he opened his own law office at No. 60 Wall Street on October 1, 1841. Having an overflow of cases, Lord was generous enough to send some of them to Evarts.[11] Unlike most beginners, he did not have to wait for clients.

The following January brought a greater opportunity. Evarts had become acquainted with Charles E. Butler, a lawyer of his own age and member of the firm headed by J. Prescott Hall, a leading lawyer of the city. When President Tyler appointed Hall district attorney, the latter had to turn over his private practice to Butler. Needing a partner, Butler invited Evarts to join him, with Hall still acting as adviser. Hall was a Yale man, prominent in the New England Society, an eloquent speaker, and known to his colleagues chiefly as the editor of two volumes of Superior Court reports. Evarts hesitated, thinking he might do better alone. But after considering the matter for a day, he wrote Butler, "The advantages which I should derive . . . would be very great, and the opinion which you are pleased to express that such advantages would not be entirely upon my side, is very gratifying."[12] Thus a partnership of mutual value was formed and lasted for the next nine years.

Then came an extraordinary opportunity, which brought Evarts before the public eye. He was retained as junior counsel in the defense of the notorious forger Monroe Edwards in the most exciting criminal trial of the day—a *cause célèbre,* still remembered as one of the most remarkable forgery cases in the annals of the American bar.

The career of the dashing, handsome Colonel Monroe Edwards illustrated the old adage that fact is stranger than fiction. As a young man he had fallen into bad company in Texas. He had engaged with a shrewd, desperate adventurer named Holcroft in the illegal slave traffic, and had discovered from his scribblings during idle hours that he could forge any handwriting. Some petty forgeries, together with his profits from the slave traffic, enabled him to buy a plantation in Texas. Elegant, refined in manners, admired by the fair sex, he became the leading citizen of his county.

Seeking new worlds to conquer, he perpetrated an outrageous forgery upon a friend named Dart, thereby obtaining more money to buy slaves; but Dart had him sent to jail. The reckless Edwards jumped his bail; and, followed by the ever-faithful Kitty Clover, a Creole girl who loved him to the end, he quit Texas, losing his fortune and estate. He resolved to avenge himself upon the Texans by informing the British government of the illicit slave trade between Africa and the Southwest. With forged letters of introduction to distinguished British statesmen he reached London and secured an interview with Palmerston. He even borrowed money from Earl Spencer, Daniel O'Connell, and others. But his unsavory reputation caught up with him, and all doors were soon closed. He left for Paris, where by accident he encountered Holcroft, who had assumed the name of Charles Johnson. They at once renewed their old partnership.

His next escapade was the great forgery. Returning to Philadelphia in 1841, he devised a plan for forging notes drawn on Southern banks and cashing them in Northern banks. Needing the signature of a reputable Southern firm, he wrote Maunsell, White & Company, well known New Orleans cotton brokers, representing himself as "H. S. Hill," a wealthy Arkansas planter, and asking the name of their New York agent. He was delighted to receive an immediate reply, referring him to Brown Brothers. Over the forged signature of Maunsell, White & Company he wrote Brown Brothers, introducing himself as "John P. Caldwell," a wealthy Louisiana planter, and asking an advance of $25,000 on certain cotton which he declared was held by the New Orleans brokers as security. This letter, except for the mispelled word "fiew," was a masterpiece of forgery. It was written in the technical language of one broker to another and bore a postmark similar to that used at New Orleans. How he managed to get the letter into the office of Brown Brothers without sending it through the mails is uncertain. Probably an unscrupulous confederate named Child delivered it. By the same ruse he sought an advance of $25,000 from the firm of Corrie and Company in New York. Now needing an excuse if caught in possession of $50,000, he concocted a fictitious contract between himself and the slaver, Charles Johnson, purporting to show that Johnson had given him $50,000 to buy slaves in the West Indies. As an additional excuse, he displayed a large sum in bonds to Caroline Phillips, daughter of his landlady in Philadelphia, who was too much excited by his proposal of marriage to notice that they were counterfeits.

Then came his most daring step. The $25,000 from Brown Brothers consisted of seventeen drafts or checks on various banks in Baltimore, Richmond, and Norfolk, and had to be cashed. He boldly entered these banks, displayed the letter from Brown Brothers, and received cash. But he committed one grave blunder. He failed to destroy his counterfeit stamps and colored inks, or the shot-bag in which he had received the money from one of the banks. He kept these tell-tale articles in his trunk, positive that they would never be discovered.

The large reward offered by Brown Brothers for the apprehension of the forger suggested to Edwards a clever method of taking vengeance upon an old acquaintance named Powell, who had once betrayed him. Recollecting that Powell resembled him and that he was just embarking from Boston for Liverpool, Edwards sent an anonymous letter to Brown Brothers informing them that Powell was the forger and could be caught in Liverpool. But this attempt to throw the police upon the wrong trail proved fatal. Officers found Powell still in Boston and learned from him that Edwards was in Philadelphia. Thereupon Edwards was arrested, the telltale implements were found in his trunk, and he was promptly indicted for forgery.

He was sent to the Tombs in New York, to await trial in the Court of Oyer and Terminer, the highest court of criminal jurisdiction in New York County. But prison was nothing new to him. His wits had always saved him and he believed they could do so again. He would prove an alibi. He induced Child to enter his name on various hotel registers in New York under the dates on which "John P. Caldwell" was supposed to be cashing checks in other cities. Robert Emmett, son of the famous Irish lawyer, was retained as defending counsel. Fearing that Emmett might doubt his ability to pay counsel fees, Edwards in his prison cell boldly forged a letter purporting to prove that he had money in a New Orleans bank. Three other counsel were retained—John J. Crittenden, Thomas A. Marshall, and Evarts. Senator Crittenden of Kentucky was nationally prominent, and his family and that of Edwards were both from Logan County and well acquainted. As a boy Edwards had been a favorite with Crittenden. Marshall, likewise a Kentucky congressman, was at the height of his fame as a temperance orator and reformed drunkard. Evarts was a novice compared to these giants. But one newspaper spoke of him on the opening day of the trial as "a young and most promising lawyer . . . said to be the most promising in the country, and whose countenance speaks volumes for his intelligence and attainments."[13]

In order to delay the trial, Edwards even deceived Evarts, showing him a letter supposed to have come from Charles Johnson in Cuba, in which Johnson promised to give a deposition in Edwards' favor. A three months' postponement was granted to allow time for the deposition, but of course it never arrived.

A great crowd gathered about the Tombs on June 7, 1842, to catch sight of the notorious prisoner as he was taken to court. Not since the Colt murder six months before had the public been treated to such a spectacular case. A wave of forgeries which had recently swept the country had excited much indignation. Edwards was escorted by a phalanx of police. It was hard to believe he had spent eight months in prison. He resembled a bridegroom going to his wedding—smiling, dignified, fresh from the hands of the barber and tailor, and showing no trace of fear. To him the trial was only a triumphal climax. He felt no doubt of acquittal, for he had planned a skillful defense.

The prosecution was equally confident, and it had damaging evidence up its sleeve. The State had spared no expense in retaining able counsel. At their head was Ogden Hoffman, one of the most popular lawyers of the city, a skilled cross-examiner, fresh from his recent triumph in the Robinson murder case. Judge William Kent, son of the chancellor, presided. He had his hands full but conducted the trial firmly and impartially. The courtroom was wretched; inadequate tables were given the counsel, and the chamber was overcrowded, hot, and stuffy.

The prosecution promised to present an unbreakable chain of evidence to prove that "H. S. Hill," "John P. Caldwell," and Monroe Edwards were all the same man. One witness after another took the stand to identify Edwards as the man who had cashed checks at various times and places; bankers, brokers, and hotel keepers all recognized him as the self-styled "John P. Caldwell." As the evidence poured in, the defense counsel became increasingly nervous, looking anxiously at each other and wondering if their client had deceived them. They would have been justified in abandoning the case, but decided to see it through.

Their consternation increased when the initialed shot-bag found in Edwards' trunk was identified by a Baltimore bank clerk. The worst blow was the testimony of Richard Vaux, something of an expert on stamps and handwriting. He demonstrated that the stamp found in Edwards' trunk coincided perfectly with the one on the Maunsell letter to Brown Brothers, but not at all with the genuine stamp of the New Orleans postoffice. This revelation almost wrecked the defense. Emmett jumped to his feet to cross-examine Vaux and drew from his pocket the letter which Edwards had shown him as purporting to come from a New Orleans bank to show deposits to cover counsel fees, little dreaming that it was another forgery. Emmett handed it to Vaux for inspection. To Emmett's amazement Vaux demonstrated it was another forgery.[14]

The testimony ended, the counsel presented their arguments to the jury. The courtroom was thronged on the third day, the spectators curious to learn what kind of defense Crittenden and Marshall could offer. To their surprise young Evarts rose to give the opening address. He had spent more labor upon the preparation of the case than his colleagues, and Crittenden decided to give him the chance.

Evarts made the most of a bad matter. He pointed to various

disadvantages under which the defense had labored: the trial of a Westerner in a Northern court, the great money power behind the prosecution, the arbitrary confiscation of Edwards' money and papers, the failure to reveal the exact nature of the indictment till the day before the trial, and the public prejudice against Edwards. "Give a dog a bad name," he pleaded, "and anybody may kill him." He outlined Edwards' movements during the time he was supposed to have been engaged in the forgeries, concluding that Edwards was not at the places at the times charged. As for the stamps and inks, said Evarts, "It really doesn't seem to me either very strange or very criminal, for a gentleman so well provided in his wardrobe as our client, to have a marking apparatus."

There was applause and stamping of feet when Evarts sat down. Edwards' hopes rose even higher when the deposition of Caroline Phillips was read, explaining his possession of large sums of money. The summaries of the other counsel added little to the case. Marshall launched into a personal attack upon Colonel Webb, editor of the *Courier and Enquirer,* who had criticized him for participating in the case. Observing Webb in the courtroom, Marshall poured out his anger upon him, concluding with a dashing challenge to a duel—a challenge which was accepted, and which resulted in a severe wound for Webb. Ogden Hoffman was by far the ablest lawyer in the case, and his summary was the most important feature of the trial.

Despite the weight of the evidence against Edwards, some people felt that he would bribe some of the jury and escape. Philip Hone, the famous diarist, who sat through much of the trial and regarded Edwards as the "boldest faced villain and most impudent scoundrel" he had ever seen, was sure the jury would not convict. But justice was done. After an all-night session the jury rendered a verdict of guilty. Hone wrote: "I have never witnessed such general satisfaction in the conviction of a criminal as in this case. . . . Sober, grave citizens, men too of a kind, liberal feelings, stop and congratulate each other on the result."[15]

But one more act was added to the drama. Edwards maintained

a show of nonchalance to the end. Before pronouncing sentence, Judge Kent asked if he had anything to say. Evarts jumped to his feet and requested a few days' delay to enable the prisoner to make certain necessary arrangements for his family. When the petition was refused, Edwards addressed the court in defiant tone, shouting that the sentence made little difference to him. Judge Kent reprimanded him sharply and gave him ten years in Sing Sing, saying he would have increased the term if the law had allowed. During the next two years in prison Edwards made two attempts to escape, suffered a mental collapse, and died violently insane. He was buried in the potter's field.[16]

Although he lost his first important case, Evarts had no reason to be downcast. At the close of the trial Ogden Hoffman congratulated him upon his share in it, but advised him to keep clear of the criminal and confine himself to civil law.[17] With a few exceptions Evarts did not appear again in criminal cases. As Edwards had no money to pay counsel fees, Evarts was not reimbursed even for the expenditures he had made in preparing the case. But he had gained something more important than a money payment—a reputation as a promising young lawyer. The sale of fifty thousand pamphlet copies of the trial proceedings, published by the *Herald,* gave him no small advertisement.

To Mrs. Coleman, daughter of Senator Crittenden, Evarts said reminiscently years later, "I shall never forget that trial in connection with your father. I was a young man on the threshold of my career, and your father's reputation was firmly and widely established. . . . His cordial manner throughout the trial is most gratefully remembered by me, and at its close he asked me to take a walk with him. During the walk he took a slight review of the trial, complimented me upon my course during its progress and the ability he pleased to think I had manifested, and in conclusion, grasping my hand with warmth, he said, 'Allow me to congratulate and encourage you on the course of life you have adopted. I assure you that the highest honors of the profession are within your grasp, and with perseverance you may expect to attain them.' These words from Mr. Crittenden would have gratified the pride of any young lawyer and given him new strength for the struggles of his profession. I can truly say they have been of the greatest value to me through life."[18]

A year after the Edwards case, Evarts married Helen Wardner of Windsor. His prospects of success in his new law partnership quite justified the step. The ceremony was performed in St. Paul's Episcopal Church in Windsor on August 30, 1843. Not long thereafter he brought his bride to the house which he had purchased from Daniel Lord at 37 East Nineteenth Street, next door to Horace Greeley. It was an excellent neighborhood, for Union Square was then an aristocratic center, and the thickly settled part of the city extended only a few blocks above it.[19]

Mrs. Evarts was a handsome woman, intellectually a match for her husband and able to hold her own in any exchange of wit. She made a delightful home for him and their children. She was always warmly solicitous for her husband's welfare, and her experience as housekeeper and hostess for her widowed father stood her in good stead. She was not ambitious for social position but was capable of taking a commanding place in the circles in which she and her husband moved. In this Nineteenth Street house Evarts and his wife began to rear their large family. The first three children were born here—Charles Butler Evarts in 1845, Roger Sherman Evarts (who died in infancy) in 1847, and Allen W. Evarts in 1848. Evarts was always domestic in tastes, loving nothing so much as to be with his wife and children. However preoccupied with work he might be, Saturday night was always reserved for his family or for entertaining in his home.

Six years of hard work in the courts followed his marriage. He figured in no more spectacular cases; yet those that came his way were of increasing importance. Sometimes he won; often he lost, because his adversaries were lawyers of greater experience. He began to make acquaintances among the aristocratic merchants of the city. They were the men who made New York—men seen daily at the Merchants Exchange: William B. Astor, Moses H. Grinnell, John Ward, Robert Minturn, George Griswold, and A. A. Low. By degrees Evarts' ability won the attention of these merchant princes, but not until a decade had passed.[20]

During these six years Evarts made a few appearances in the federal courts. As early as 1845 he had a case in the Federal District Court for the southern district of New York. This tribunal, holding its sessions in a squalid house on Chambers Street, made up in dignity what it lacked in environment. Lawyers were required to appear in jet-black coats or dress suits, and Judge Betts presided for many years with a courtesy and learning that earned him the respect of the bar.[21] Significantly, this first case, involving a question of a damaged cargo of iron, lay in the field of admiralty law and resulted in a victory for Evarts.[22] Admiralty was then a thorny subject to most lawyers and so remained for many years; but for Evarts it held no terrors. He undertook a study of it which eventually gained him recognition as an authority. In the collision case of the steamer *Narragansett,* which Evarts lost in the District Court but partially won in the Circuit Court, he first encountered the great lawyer, Francis B. Cutting, and argued before the eminent judge, Samuel Nelson.[23]

Before the Court of Appeals was created in 1847 the highest court of the state was the Chancery Court of Saratoga, presided over by Reuben H. Walworth. Below him were the vice-chancellors in several districts of the state. It was in the first district, where Vice-Chancellors Sandford and McCoun presided, that Evarts had his most important early cases. This court, sitting in New York City, was overburdened with cases; justice was so slow that litigation sometimes dragged through three to five years. With the assistance of J. Prescott Hall, Evarts won his first case in this court in May, 1844, on a technical question of the rights of a mortgagee.[24]

Much of Evarts' subsequent legal eminence was due to famous will cases. Curiously enough, he lost all three of his earliest will cases in the court of the Vice-Chancellor.[25] In the first he encountered Henry E. Davies, prominent lawyer, Whig leader, and later judge of the Court of Appeals; in the second, the able attorney

Dudley Selden; and in the third, two formidable adversaries, John Anthon and Marshall Bidwell. The clients in all three cases were related, illustrating the fact that it is often by inter-relationships of wealthy families that a lawyer obtains his best clientele. In his most important case before the Vice-Chancellor, *Iddings* v. *Bruen,* a complicated suit involving a question of prior lien to the estate of the famous tea merchant, Tom Smith, Evarts was also unsuccessful.[26]

The Court of Chancery over which Walworth presided at Saratoga was held in one wing of his private home. Lawyers came to "Pine Grove" from all over the state. Without historic woolsack or insignia of judicial power, "Raw-Hide" Walworth, as some of the junior members of the bar called him, presided with a strong hand. Evarts appeared but once before the famous Chancellor. In behalf of Jesse Hoyt, a wealthy New York merchant, he sought an injunction to restrain certain defendants from publishing letters surreptitiously taken from Hoyt; but the Chancellor denied the injunction.[27]

The most important of all Evarts' cases during these early years, and his first in the new Court of Appeals, was *Walworth* v. *Farmers' Loan and Trust Company.* It was a novel case, attracting wide attention in business and legal circles. The issue was whether Hiram Walworth, clerk of the court and relative of the Chancellor, had a right to discharge the first mortgage on property held in trust by the court and so give validity to the second mortgage. Evarts presented an ingenious argument to show that a clerk could not discharge a mortgage on his own authority. The court agreed; but held that his act had been legalized when the owners of the property elected to proceed on the second mortgage.[28] Evarts was disappointed; but it was apparent from the judges' decision that the authorities cited by Evarts had greatly worried them.

Evarts also made frequent appearances in the Superior Court, the highest tribunal of New York City, which probably passed upon more important questions of commercial law than any other court in America. Chief Judge Thomas Oakley presided, ably assisted by the equally famous John Duer. Both were legal giants whose fame has passed into tradition. Judges of their ability seldom adorn the bench of a city court today. They made the court known all over the land and its reports became high authority.[29] But there was nothing spectacular about Evarts' early cases in this court. They related merely to drab problems of bankruptcy, contracts, and promissory notes. He met greater success, however, than in the other courts.[30]

By 1850 Evarts had completed the journeyman stage of the law and was ready to become master-workman. His ability was attracting older members of the bar; other lawyers were beginning to seek his assistance, and clients were no longer hesitating to pit him against more experienced adversaries. He had gone far for a young man of thirty-two. Of course, nationally he was still unknown; but in the city and state he had acquired a considerable reputation, partly by his ability as a lawyer, partly by his activities in public affairs.

3

An Introduction to Public Life

Although Evarts was preëminently a lawyer, the adventurous narrative of his courtroom experiences alone is far from constituting the most important part of his biography. It was through the public offices he held, the public addresses he made, and the leadership he exerted that he gained a place in American history.

The first public office came without seeking in 1849. Though he had laid aside his political pen forever in 1841, the prospect of a Whig victory in 1848 revived his interest. Both parties in New York were divided by the slavery issue into conservative and radical factions. His connection with the merchant princes, as well as his natural inclinations, led him to join the conservative Whigs. Already he had been admitted to the select group which gathered at Moses Grinnell's, and which included such prominent men as Marshall O. Roberts, Isaac Bell, Benjamin F. Silliman, Nathan T. Griswold, and Moses Taylor. He won some attention from Whig leaders by taking a minor part in the campaign for Taylor. The Whig victory brought him an appropriate reward. Through the influence of William H. Seward and R. M. Blatchford, the new administration appointed J. Prescott Hall district attorney for the southern district of New York, and Evarts became assistant district attorney, a post which he held until the end of 1853.[1]

The office of the district attorney was on the ground floor of the new City Hall on Chambers Street, while the District Court was on the floor above. Evarts did not give up his partnership with

Butler, but he found the duties of his new office increasingly burdensome. Hall's ill health, indolence, and interest in social diversions inclined him to leave much to his subordinate. The office was no sinecure, and it was relatively of greater significance than today. Evarts discharged his duties with energy and thoroughness. The chief questions that faced him grew out of the enforcement of the neutrality laws—a subject which introduced him to international law and harmonized with his study of admiralty law.

The first problem, in 1849, arose during the war between Denmark and the German Confederation over Schleswig-Holstein. When the German government purchased the American ship *United States* and armed it in the port of New York, it became Evarts' duty to watch it closely and keep Washington informed. For several weeks he was kept in doubt, fearing a breach of neutrality. Baron von Roenne, the German minister, finally gave assurances that the ship would not be used against Denmark and it was allowed to depart.[2]

A more exciting and perplexing problem was the stoppage of filibustering expeditions, fitted out to aid Cuban rebels in their struggle for freedom from Spain. The enforcement of neutrality, even as far north as New York, was difficult, for public opinion strongly favored the filibusters.

Three times Narciso Lopez raised ships, men, and money in the United States for expeditions intended to aid in liberating Cuba. The Round Island expedition was fitted out near Mobile in direct defiance of President Taylor's proclamation. Three transports were to carry the filibusters, and two of them, the *Sea Gull* and *New Orleans,* were chartered in New York. Suspecting that the vessels were to be improperly used, Evarts ordered Captain Isaac McKeever, commandant of the Brooklyn Navy Yard, to place marines aboard the ships. The *Florida,* another suspected vessel, was not seized because it was not yet ready for sea. No arrests were made, and the *Sea Gull* and *New Orleans* were shortly restored to their Cuban owners; but the temporary seizure effectually broke up the plans of the filibusters, and President Taylor commended the prompt action of the New York authorities. The second attempt, known as the Cárdenas expedition, was likewise a failure. It did not involve the port of New York except in so far as it required increasing alertness by Evarts.[8]

The third attempt of Lopez, the Bahía Honda expedition of 1851, raised real difficulties. Hall had become ill, so that full responsibility fell upon Evarts. Unaware that a spy named Burtnett was revealing their plans to Evarts and the Spanish minister, the filibusters made elaborate preparations in New York with the intention of joining other adventurers at Savannah and New Orleans. The first consignments of arms and men were to leave New York in the *Cleopatra,* which lay at the foot of North Moore Street. The *Nahantee,* stationed at the foot of Eighteenth Street, and the *William Roe* at South Amboy were to meet the *Cleopatra* just outside quarantine, where men, arms, and stores were to be transferred to the *Cleopatra.* Responsibility for getting the ship away safely rested with the owner, James O'Sullivan, and with two confederates, Captain Lewis, who was in charge, and Louis Schlessinger, who had recruited some two or three hundred Germans and Hungarians of military experience.

Realizing the popular hostility which a prosecution would encounter, Evarts did not act until he was sure of the evidence. Burtnett, the informer, wanted to give the affair a dramatic climax and advised that the *Cleopatra* be allowed to proceed to Savannah, where the whole expedition should be captured. Evarts rejected this plan. He had the *William Roe* detained at South Amboy on a technical flaw in her papers, and the *Cleopatra* for nonpayment of its purchase price. These cautious steps would not arouse the suspicions of the filibusters; yet they would prevent the ships from leaving port. However, when the debt on the *Cleopatra* was paid, Evarts had to act again. On the night of April 26, just as the ship was about to depart, he had warrants issued for the arrest of O'Sullivan, Lewis, and Schlessinger; and indictments were then brought against them on the basis of Burtnett's testimony. This broke up the New York expedition. Lopez, however, reached Cuba with the

New Orleans filibusters. He met disaster when the Cubans failed to come to his assistance and was executed in Havana.[4]

Now came the most difficult task—the prosecution of the filibusters in New York. In New Orleans three successive juries had acquitted suspected filibusters, and Evarts was therefore anxious to vindicate the government by a conviction in New York. Under the prodding of Judge Betts, who censured the New Orleans authorities for their laxity, the grand jury brought an indictment of ninety-seven counts. Evarts sought quick action. But the two able counsels for the defense, Francis B. Cutting and John Van Buren (son of Martin Van Buren), succeeded in delaying trial by claiming that the indictment did not come within the neutrality act of 1818, and that the crimes were not described with the definiteness required by law.[5]

The case finally came to trial before Judge Judson a year later. Since Hall was still ill, the government assigned Ogden Hoffman to assist Evarts; but Hall recovered just before the opening, so that Evarts played only the rôle of assistant. He took a leading part in presenting the case to the jury, urging that law enforcement should supersede sentimental feeling for the Cuban rebels. He displayed a surprising knowledge of international law. A spectator, A. Oakey Hall, later described him: "I recall the big head on the square shoulders, the nervous energy pervading every part of his gaunt countenance. . . . But I forgot the slender figure in listening to the fine robustness of his argument and the plumpness of his unanswerable logical positions."[6] After the trial had dragged through twenty-three days, the judge made an elaborate charge to the jury which left no doubt that the neutrality laws had been violated. But the jury split evenly and the filibusters escaped. It was "a lame and impotent conclusion," declared the *Herald,* "and there was sufficient evidence to convict."[7]

A lesser problem of neutrality meanwhile arose in the case of the *Kate Boyd*. This grew out of a war between Haiti and the Dominican Republic. The ship was loaded at New York with munitions, which were destined to be transferred to a vessel purchased by Haiti in Boston. The purchase of munitions was legal; but it was unlawful to buy a ship in one neutral port, and her armament in another. Evarts ordered the seizure of the craft and had her held on suspicion.[8]

The prosecution of crimes committed upon the high seas usually fall to a district attorney. Evarts dealt with several cases during Hall's illness. When James Bowen was charged with assault upon a ship's officer, the evidence left no doubt of his guilt, and Evarts easily won the case.[9]

More important was the prosecution of Edward Douglas, James Clements, and Thomas Benson for mutiny and murder on the high seas. The three young men mutinied against the other seven members of the crew of the *Glenn* on a return voyage from Valparaiso, killed the second mate, and took control of the ship; but the captain and the loyal majority of the crew soon got the upper hand and brought the mutineers to port in irons. Erastus C. Benedict and Luther R. Marsh were assigned to defend them; Evarts and Ogden Hoffman prosecuted. Hoffman positively declined to accept a retainer until he had, by his own examination, satisfied himself completely that the accused were guilty. A sharp legal battle followed. Marsh besought the jury not to be swayed by the "glittering scimiter" of Evarts or the "ponderous battle-axe" of Hoffman;[10] and he obtained a new trial in the Circuit Court on technical grounds. Lorenzo B. Shepard and George F. Betts then had charge of the defense. They succeeded in having Douglas tried separately. Evarts brought a ship model into court to aid him in describing what occurred on the night of the murder. The defense tried to show that Douglas had no part in the mutiny till after the murder of the mate; but Evarts and Hoffman insisted he was not only a confederate but the ringleader. After deliberating a half-hour, the jury returned a verdict of guilty. Judge Nelson sentenced the three mutineers to be hanged.[11] This proved to be the only case of capital punishment in which Evarts ever participated.

Except for an appointment in 1853 to the Commission of Charities and Correction, headed by Simeon Draper, and paying no salary, Evarts held no other public office for nearly twenty years.[12]

While in office Evarts did not wholly ignore politics. A conservative Whig, as were Rufus Choate, Edward Everett, and other able, patriotic men, he was a follower of Webster and Clay in supporting the Compromise of 1850 and an opponent of the radical faction in the party led by Seward and Greeley.

He made one striking speech in favor of the Fugitive Slave Law. The great mass meeting held at Castle Garden on October 30, 1850, was supposed to be nonpartisan; but actually it was a meeting of conservative Whigs and Democrats to endorse the Fillmore policy of compromise and approve the Fugitive Slave Law. The circular auditorium, where Jenny Lind had appeared under the management of P. T. Barnum just a few months before, was again crowded. Over the entrance was emblazoned the motto, "Liberty and Union, Now and Forever, One and Inseparable"; above the stage hung a large portrait of Washington and a streamer bearing the words, "One Country, One Constitution, One Destiny." A letter from Webster was received with wild cheers. Then followed speeches by three Whigs and three Democrats, all well-known lawyers, including Charles O'Conor and James W. Gerard, Ogden Hoffman, and James T. Brady.[13]

Evarts was the youngest and least known of the speakers. He explained the Fugitive Slave Law and defended its constitutionality. One popular objection to it, he explained, was quite baseless. It was not a violation of the rights of habeas corpus or trial by jury, for rendition was preliminary to the trial, as in the extradition of a deserting seaman. "A correct understanding of its provisions," he said, "must remove all such impression [of its subversion of liberty]. . . . Let us know and feel that he who strikes at *a* law, strikes at *the* law. . . ."[14] Evarts was sincere in believing that a fugitive slave could be tried only in the state from which he had fled, and that such state could rightly grant or refuse jury trial, as it pleased. His speech was undoubtedly too heavy, although not lacking in snatches of wit. He spoke under the difficulties of a long program, a large hall, and a noisy audience which was not particularly interested in the legal aspects of the Fugitive Slave Law. The address could therefore not be called successful. Nor were its results beneficial to him. He was sincerely for compromise; but it seemed outrageous to some that the son of Jeremiah Evarts could "equivocate" with slavery, and for several years the speech was cited as evidence that he lacked firmness in his attitude toward the South.[15]

Evarts, looking to Webster as savior of the Union and guiding star of the nation, hoped to see him elected president in 1852. The orator was often in the city, staying at the rooms reserved for him at the Astor House, where Evarts doubtless repeatedly saw him. Soon after the Castle Garden meeting, Evarts attended the New England Society dinner at the Astor House and heard Webster speak. It fell to Evarts to propose a toast. Noting the presence of Dr. Benjamin Brandeth, inventor of a famous pill, he raised a laugh by lifting his glass and saying, "To Daniel Webster and Benjamin Brandeth; the pillars of the Constitution."[16]

Preliminary to the Whig national convention of 1852, efforts were made by Webster's friends to arouse enthusiasm for him. Meetings were held in Boston and other centers. On March 5 a group of lawyers, headed by Evarts, Hiram Ketchum, and George Wood, planned a demonstration in Metropolitan Hall. George Griswold and Moses H. Grinnell furnished the necessary money. But there was little sentiment for Webster in New York, and instead of a crowded hall, as they expected, only a small audience appeared. Evarts had composed resolutions favoring Webster's candidacy, which he read and which were widely published. While the first mention of Webster's name evoked applause, little enthusiasm appeared during the subsequent speech-making. The audience was clearly divided in sympathy. "It looks like the finishing stroke to the distinguished Secretary of State," declared the *Herald*.[17]

At the Baltimore convention the Whigs nominated Scott instead of Webster; and disappointment hastened Webster's death soon after. Evarts felt that he had lost a friend and guide. He was present at the proceedings in the Circuit Court where eulogies of Webster were given by J. Prescott Hall and Judge Betts; and he was chosen one of twenty members of the bar to attend Webster's funeral at Marshfield.[18]

Evarts' reputation as an orator was becoming so well established that he was chosen centennial orator at Yale in 1853. He had always been counted among the most loyal alumni of the college. Presiding at his class reunion at the Tontine Hotel in New Haven in 1850, he had made the most effective speech.[19] The centennial celebration, held at commencement, was a notable occasion. A long procession, with undergraduates in front, followed by President Day, Evarts, the Governor and Lieutenant Governor of Connecticut, trustees, faculty, Linonians, and graduates, crossed the campus to the North Church, where Evarts delivered his address on "Public Life."

With more fervor than ever before, and evidently with Webster in mind, he set forth the three characteristics of an unselfish public life. First, he declared, the public leader must have a passion for social welfare; second, a social outlook, widening with each growing sphere of public action; and third, and most important, a willingness to make readjustments when society has outgrown any institution. Character counted most in statesmanship; for "he who hath not meditated upon God and the human mind, may possibly make a thriving earthworm, but will indubitably be but a blundering patriot and sorry statesman." "Let us understand," concluded Evarts, "that neither the selfish passions of vanity or ambition, the thirst for glory or the lust for power, nor a sentimental patriotism, nor a philanthropic enthusiasm, are a sufficient basis of a genuine, pure-spirited laborious *public life*."[20]

Among Evarts' friends, Dana congratulated him on the "masterly air" of his address; but George S. Hilliard was more critical. "I fear," he wrote, "you must have been too deep for your hearers. . . . I accept your definition of public life, and yet a mind and character like yours should not always act upon the public from a private sphere."[21]

Easily superior to the Yale speech was Evarts' address the following year, "The Heritage of the Pilgrims," at the annual New England Society dinner. Indeed, this speech was the first of perhaps the half-dozen best orations of his life.

Evarts was fond of the Society. When he first came to New York he had taken Daniel Lord's advice and joined it, soon becoming a life member and in time president. Its purposes were to promote friendship, to provide mutual assistance, and to hold an annual dinner to commemorate the landing of the Pilgrims. Despite the striking contrast between the frugal meals of the Pilgrims and the luxurious banquets of their prosperous descendants, the gatherings were praiseworthy affairs. As a rule the speeches were of a high literary finish, seasoned with delicious humor, though they sometimes showed an inordinate pride in New England ancestry.

As the day for his speech drew near, Evarts sought seclusion at Hall's summer home in Newport. As he left, one of the maids inquired why such a crazy man was allowed in the house. "She heard me," explained Evarts, "repeating sentences to see if they jumped right."[22]

The grand dining room of the Astor House was in gala attire. At one end of the hall hung portraits of Washington, Franklin, and Webster, and at the other an engraving of the landing of the Pilgrims; on the tables were pastry models of Webster and Plymouth Monument. The menu was in the best Astor House style and by no means followed the Maine law. Brief speeches by President King of Columbia, Judge Charles P. Daly, David Dudley Field, and Seward were all applauded.[23]

Then Evarts arose for an analysis of Puritan life and character and an encomium of its virtues. He looked beneath the surface and found the unusual spirit of the Puritan fathers to be the result of religious conviction, unselfish brotherhood, and a sense of liberty. "In an age," he said solemnly, "when faith has grown colder, when religion is much less a matter of public and general thought . . . these elevations of spirit seem, to man, inconsistent with the calm, sober performance of duty which marked the conduct of these men. Some stigmatize them as vagaries of vulgar fanaticism, others pardon them as the extravagancies of a generous enthusiasm, but *we* acknowledge them as an essential element in the agencies which were to operate great social and political revolutions at home, and found and build up a nation abroad. . . . If the virtue and power, to which today we pay homage, survive in the sons of the Pilgrims, doubt not their influence will soon penetrate and pervade the whole general mass of society throughout the nation, fear not but that *Equality of Right, Community of Interest, Reciprocity of Duty* will bind this whole people in a perfect, a perpetual union."[24]

It was a good speech, perhaps too serious for present-day tastes, but deeply thoughful. "We have no hesitation," wrote a critic, "in saying that this production is worthy of being read over, and over, and over again; we would rejoice to have it studied by all the young men of our country."[25]

After Webster's death it took something extraordinary to reawaken Evarts' interest in politics. But the Kansas-Nebraska Act of 1854 aroused thousands, embittering the slave issue, hopelessly splitting the Whig party, and leading multitudes to the Republican banner. Evarts called it an act of blindness. He presently became less conservative and inclined toward the Seward wing of the party; but he would not go as far as John Jay, the Abolitionist, who devoted his pen and fortune to the cause.[26] Welcoming the formation of the Republican party, he approved its stand against the extension of slavery in the territories. He could count himself among the pioneer Republicans of New York, for he was active in the formation of the party in 1855 and was one of the self-appointed committee of seven which organized it in the Eighteenth Ward.[27] However, he was not popular with the extreme element of the party, for they could not forget his Castle Garden speech.

All eyes were focused on Kansas, where the principle of squatter sovereignty was about to precipitate bloody strife. When Eli Thayer came to New York to seek aid for the New England Emigrant Society, Evarts was present at a meeting of some thirty merchants and lawyers at George Blunt's house to hear his appeal. The way to beat slavery, said Thayer, was to beat it in the territories. When he had finished, Evarts rose and remarked: "Ever since my Castle Garden speech, you know I have been called a Hunker Whig. Now, what reason you had to suppose that such a man would care whether slavery were extended or restricted I do not know. Therefore, I do not know your reasons for inviting me to attend this meeting. But you did invite me and I have come. I am glad that I am here and I thank you for calling me. I have heard many speeches, on many occasions, upon the slavery question; but never till now have I listened to any practical elucidation of the subject. Like thousands of others I have been waiting for an opportunity to contend successfully against slavery without violating the laws or sacrificing the Constitution and the Union. Such an opportunity is now presented. I rejoice in it and shall embrace it. Now, though I am called a Hunker Whig and though I am poor, for I am not worth four thousand dollars, I joyfully give my cheque to the Emigrant Aid Company for one thousand dollars."[28] Twenty-four years later, Thayer wrote Evarts reminiscently, "Your eloquent words, supported by your prompt and generous action, just at the time when such words and such action availed most for Kansas, entitle you to a big place among her early friends."[29]

Evarts' conversion was again clearly demonstrated the following spring. The Republicans launched their campaign of 1856 with a great mass meeting on April 29 at the Broadway Tabernacle. Evarts was active in arranging for it and drafted the carefully worded invitation. When Benjamin Butler stepped forward to open the meeting, the Tabernacle was crowded to capacity. No banners or music were needed; the cause alone was sufficient to draw a huge audience. Evarts had prepared resolutions, denouncing the repeal of the Missouri Compromise, the situation in Kansas, and the policy of the Pierce administration. They were unanimously approved.

But a hurried change in program had to be made. Of the four out-of-state congressmen expected to speak, only one had arrived. Another orator was needed. Evarts had expected to move the approval of the report of the New York delegation sent in February to a preliminary Republican national convention; but he had not expected to make a speech. Hurriedly jotting down a few notes, he appeared on the platform and delivered a fervid appeal against slavery which proved the best address of the evening.

He pictured the alarming growth of the slave area since 1789 and warned his audience that, if this continued, soon no free area would be left. "It is for you to protest *now*," he exhorted, "or your acquiescence will be pleaded with your children for further concessions by them. . . . In my judgment the slavery interest is no more entitled to the control and protection of the federal government than the financial and tariff interests. . . . The party of slavery is necessarily a geographical party . . . but free labor can live anywhere. Ours, then, is the comprehensive party." The climax of his speech was the story of the slave mother who fled across the Ohio with her child, and when about to be recaptured, killed the babe rather than permit it to be returned to slavery. "Are the *slave women* of Kentucky," he shouted, "of nobler blood than the *free men* of New York?"[30]

Joseph Choate called this impromptu oration "a capital speech," and declared that Evarts was fast developing into "a great man." Rockwood Hoar sent his congratulations, and deplored the lack of similar Republican spirit in Massachusetts.[31]

A month later, news of the brutal attack of Preston Brooks upon Senator Sumner roused intense feeling. Again, on May 30, Broadway Tabernacle was packed. Every seat was taken, while others stood in the aisles, and thousands outside held a meeting in the street. Indignation ran high, and Evarts, who presided, strove valiantly to keep the audience within prudent bounds and to prevent the meeting from becoming an Abolitionist rally. He read resolutions, phrased in moderate words, expressing sympathy for Sumner, condemning Brooks's attack as brutal and cowardly, and calling for the expulsion of Senator Butler of South Carolina from the Senate. They were approved with a wild cheer, as were the speeches of Daniel Lord, Samuel Ruggles, Edwin Morgan, and President King of Columbia. At the close, the audience called loudly for Henry Ward Beecher, who was on the platform. Fearing Beecher would inflame the audience, Evarts hurriedly declared the meeting adjourned. But the audience would not be balked, and Beecher at last stepped forward and spoke—fortunately in a judicious vein.[32]

The campaign was exciting. Of the Republican candidates—Seward, Chase, McLean, and Frémont—Evarts favored the aged and colorless Judge McLean. But the prize fell to Frémont, the pathfinder. Though disappointed, Evarts collaborated with other Republican leaders in advising Frémont upon his letter of acceptance.[33] The issue was more important than the candidate. By October excitement was intense, and pulpit and press gave vent to strong feeling.

At the height of the campaign a great Republican rally was held at the Academy of Music. Ex-Governor Robinson of Kansas, Senator Wilson, and Evarts were the principal speakers. Once more the audience overflowed the hall. Frémont sat in a box, watching the proceedings intently. Evarts' speech may not have been as fervid as his extemporaneous effort in April, but it was better reasoned, longer than any other political speech he had ever made, and probably the best of his early utterances.

He belittled the Southern threats of secession if Frémont were elected, and analyzed the political situation cleverly. A vote for Frémont, he declared, was a vote for freedom; a vote for Buchanan was a vote for slavery. "We would rather have a man living all his lifetime under the influence of Slavery, and yet who favors Freedom, than a man living all his life under the influence of Freedom, and who prefers Slavery." If the Republican party were revolutionary, it was only in so far as it sought to set things right side up rather than upside down, and to wrest control from a minority that had held the possession of the government for some years. "Now, gentlemen," he said in closing, "there is a trial going on before the people. And the tribunal is the assembled majority of the free citizens of the United States. The culprit is the Democratic party, taken red in the guilt of all the crimes, of all the shames, of all the sorrows of Kansas. . . . If the Democratic party escapes your verdict, you are convicted as no better than it. . . . The issue is put, the indictment is drawn, the Republican party is the chief prosecutor, the proof is complete, the evidence is all in, the prisoner confessed, and now the question is whether [they] . . . have made us all slaves. All the pomp and pageantry of Freedom is but as sounding brass and tinkling cymbals, if the spirit of liberty is so far decayed among us as to have this great treason unrebuked."[34]

When the election went against the new Republican party, Evarts was sufficiently optimistic to prophesy that Buchanan would trim his sails to Northern sentiment.[35] For him personally the defeat was probably a boon. He might have accepted public office under Frémont at the expense of his profession, in which he was to make a real mark during the next four years.

4

A Legal Gladiator

A STRANGER meeting Evarts on the streets of New York in 1857 would have decided at once that he was a lawyer. He was not tall; but his thin angular figure, broad shoulders, and narrow waist gave an impression of height. His head and face were striking—long-skulled, with square, prominent forehead; a long hooked nose; large, deeply-set gray eyes; the chin square and decisive; cheeks hollow and wasted; and complexion sallow.

In manner he was placid but earnest, and at times he could show a deliberate and very pleasing grace. But usually he seemed to throb with nervous energy. His voice was clear, sharp, and ringing, not loud or musical, but deep and earnest—the voice of an orator. His gestures were few but effective. He never seemed in haste, yet never hesitated. He had none of the grand Websterian manner, but he gave an impression of reserve strength; and the precision of his speech, with his total absence of pretense, inclined men to listen when he spoke. His natural dignity repelled any familiarity from strangers, but among friends he unbent in the most cordial fashion. When his face lighted up with an attractive smile and he gave free play to his natural wit, he was a fascinating personality.

He was first and last a lawyer and found in his profession ample scope for an intellectual and moral influence upon his generation. He had great learning and a comprehensive grasp of legal principles, while his wit and keen perception made him a formidable adversary. In the face of able rivals he rose so rapidly that at the age of forty his victory was won. In 1857 Union College conferred upon him the degree of Doctor of Laws.

The qualities that marked Evarts as a lawyer were the ability to make the clearest and most convincing presentation of a case; the power to gain victory by sheer intellectual force, courage, and energy; an ever-present resourcefulness to take advantage of the weak points of the opponent and of every neglected opportunity; a disposition to enter court, not with superior air or purpose of confusing judge or jury, but to aid both court and client in finding a just solution and so enhance the development of law; anxiety to avoid unwise or unnecessary litigation; readiness to set an example of unselfishness and moderation, to overlook petty technicalities, and to reject opportunities for personal advantage at the expense of justice; frankness, sense of humor, and regard for the honor of the profession. He was a hard and conscientious worker. His daily accomplishments would astonish the average man. He studied unremittingly and acquired an astounding amount of legal learning. He read some law every day throughout his active life. His unusual endurance, despite frailty of body, was a large factor in his success.

He was always the old-fashioned type of lawyer, not only in the simplicity of his dress, but in refusing to become a specialist. All law was his field and he was willing to undertake any type of case. He preferred constitutional law, and perhaps no other American, except Marshall and Webster, had more of the important cases in this field. In dealing with constitutional questions, he was expected to advise upon public affairs and to make sacrifices for public welfare. If he could ever be called a specialist, it was in giving legal opinions. By 1860 corporations were increasingly seeking his opinions, and it became quite the fashion in Wall Street to say, "Let us take Evarts' opinion."

He did not need to resort to the smaller arts of his profession. His grasp of principles, power of analysis, retentive memory, and fund of classical, literary, and historical knowledge enabled him to meet any situation. He grasped a case with a concentration and rapidity that excited the wonder of clients. He saw the situation before the narration of events had been completed; he quickly classified it and unerringly applied the proper legal test. He seemed to analyze the most involved complications and pierce at once to the heart of the most plausible sophistry. Like a skillful general, he always massed his forces at the vital point. "Evarts cut into a legal problem," said A. Oakey Hall, "as one would cut into a pineapple —laying aside deftly the skin and rind and getting at once at the pulp and juice of the controversy, and then sugaring it with a clear style."[1]

He showed equal power in arranging and presenting a case. He could untangle the greatest confusion of facts and evidence and bring them into harmony with the principle upon which the case rested. His written briefs and oral arguments were conspicuous for their thoroughness. It was not his nature to rest content with one point; he used every possible argument which honesty permitted. It was not unusual at the end of a day to see him discussing points with his partners, seeking every possible suggestion. A passable argument was not sufficient, and this explains why some of his cases, though no longer possessing any intrinsic significance, are still valuable as models to the law student.

It was before appellate tribunals that he was at his best. As Moorfield Storey puts it, "He was better fitted to address the court *in banc* than to persuade a jury. He was too self-controlled to forget himself in his case, nothing came white-hot from his lips, and his words as we read them now do not produce the impression which only intense convictions will make on a jury or a popular audience."[2] He preferred oral argument to the use of written briefs, feeling it to be more effective. He did not rely upon exhaustive notes, but used them only to refresh his memory.

Evarts was a lawyer of philosophic mind. He treated cases in a large way, taking time to demonstrate the science of jurisprudence as it applied to the case in hand, and thus lifting it to a higher plane. He liked the unexplored regions of the law, and was often asked to share in its novel or untravelled regions. That is why he preferred civil cases, where principles alone were involved and the appeal was to reason rather than emotion. His lambent humor saved many of his arguments from being dull. By apt allusion or illustration, by anecdote or play of fancy, he interested the court and frequently set his auditors laughing. He resembled Rufus Choate in this, knowing instinctively how to relieve the monotony. He was always considerate of his opponents in the courtroom. His unfailing courtesy won the admiration of bench and bar, and he had a way of attacking adversaries without wounding them. His closest friends were lawyers.

For many years he enjoyed an excellent income from his profession. He followed the Websterian principle that a lawyer should never cheapen his services. As his cases became more important, his fees became heavier. Among his clients were bankers, merchants, and insurance companies in and about Wall Street. Such clients could pay well. Evarts was known in later life to charge as much as twenty thousand dollars for an opinion. Indeed, his fees were as high as those of any lawyer of his day. At the peak of his career he was credited with a steady income of seventy-five thousand dollars.[3] It is related that once, being retained in a prominent will case, he requested a retainer of five thousand dollars; but his client misread the note and sent him a check for twenty-five thousand, which Evarts returned with thanks.[4] Evarts once explained, with a twinkle in his eye, that the legal profession was long-suffering and unpopular—long-suffering because it involved more trials than any other profession, unpopular because it was the means of bringing more judgments upon people than all of the rest of the community; that the privations of the profession were so great that rich men were not attracted to it; and the next best thing was to make rich men out of the lawyers.[5]

The firm of Butler and Evarts underwent important changes in the fifties. On January 1, 1852, Charles F. Southmayd was added as a third partner, Hall meanwhile retiring as adviser. Southmayd proved a most valuable asset for thirty years. A New Englander, he had received no law-school training, but had been nicknamed "chancellor" at the early age of seventeen in Judge Hurlburt's office. He mastered all the leading cases, a feat then quite possible for a diligent student. It is said that he knew Kent's *Commentaries* almost by heart. After he had unravelled a complicated case for the Astor family in 1842, they became his clients for years. Evarts first encountered Southmayd as adversary in the case of *Iddings* v. *Bruen*. Southmayd's partner, Alexander S. Johnson, was soon after elected to the Court of Appeals, whereupon Evarts and Butler seized the opportunity to add Southmayd to their firm.

Southmayd was six years younger than Evarts and his precise opposite in some respects. He cared for nothing but the law, giving all his time to it. He revelled in knotty problems, and if a difficult will or contract had to be drawn, it was usually left to him. It was said that never did one of his pleadings, trusts, wills, or deeds miscarry. He prepared many of Evarts' briefs. He was always at his desk, and clients flocked to him with confidence. In consultation he was invaluable, but he hated to go to court and seldom did so. He furnished the advice, while Evarts and Butler executed it. Not that Southmayd lacked ability to meet the give and take of the courtroom; on the contrary, he was a match for Evarts in repartee and it was a great treat to hear them chaffing each other. He preferred the rôle of soliciter and the life of a scholarly recluse, thereby furnishing an element which strengthened the firm.[6]

The office was presently moved from Wall Street to four rooms at No. 2 Hanover Street. Of approximately a thousand lawyers practicing in the city, a large majority were located on Wall, Nassau, Beaver, Pine, and William streets or on Broadway, so that the move to Hanover Street took the firm outside the charmed circle; but business improved. Measured by modern standards, the office was primitive. It boasted two or three clerks, but no stenographers. There was no railing such as marks off the simplest office today, and not even a separate office for each partner. To have employed a general bookkeeper would have been deemed unprofessional; each partner kept his own accounts. Documents were written out in longhand and when copies were required, infinite labor by clerks or students was necessary. The goose quill was appropriately the lawyer's emblem; but steel pens appeared by 1860. Documents were bound by "red tape." Suits were brought to trial in a peculiar manner. When the calendar was called, it was watched by an office boy who warned the counsel in time to reach court if the place of trial were near enough; if it was not, lawyers might spend hours waiting for a case to be tried.

In 1855 Joseph Choate came to New York to seek his fortune with the following letter in his pocket:

> "My Dear Mr. Evarts
>
> "I beg to incur one other obligation to you by introducing the bearer, my friend and kinsman to your kindness.
>
> "He is just admitted to our bar, was graduated at Cambridge with a very high reputation for scholarship and all worth, and comes to the practice of law, I think, with extraordinary promise. He has decided to enroll himself among the brave and magnanimous of your bar with a courage not unwarranted by his talents, character, and ambition and power of labor.
>
> "There is no young man whom I love better, or from whom I hope more or as much and if you can do anything to smooth the way to his first steps the kindness will be most seasonable and will yield all sorts of good fruits.
>
> "Most truly
> "Your servant and friend
> "Rufus Choate"[7]

Evarts did smooth Choate's first steps, paving the way to his fame and fortune and a law partnership which lasted forty years. Recalling the day he entered Daniel Lord's office, he said to Choate, "Join the New England Society and come into my office."[8] Choate served first as clerk, then as scrivener, and then became a junior to Evarts in the preparation of his cases. He was amazed by Evarts' power of assimilating facts and mastering cases. When Evarts found that he could depend upon Choate's preparatory work, he often went to court relying entirely upon it. Choate, who found in Evarts a congenial and stimulating associate, once said: "I owe him more than words can tell." From the polished Butler and the erudite Southmayd young Choate also learned much.[9]

Choate had been born and bred in Salem, Massachusetts. Beneath the sunny disposition and geniality that usually marked him there lay the austerity of a New England Unitarian and a power of caustic criticism. These two characteristics—outward attractiveness and inward firmness—explain his success. He was slender, with a massive, well-poised head, dreamy expression, and humorous eyes. Indifferent to dress, appearance, or surroundings, he seemed to do his work without effort and seldom got excited. Indeed, his easygoing nonchalance unsuited him for public life, and his aristocratic views and dislike of politics made him unacceptable to politicians. One statesman in a law firm, he used to say, was sufficient! He was greatly admired, for he could sway a jury or rouse the enthusiasm of an audience. Yet he was not a man of intimacies and always seemed to live apart.[10]

Choate left in 1858 to try a partnership with William H. Barnes. In the same year Butler also retired, and was given a farewell dinner by his partners at the Astor House. It was most unusual for a lawyer to retire at forty with a competent income, yet Butler achieved that result. However, he soon found retirement at his Stockbridge farm too tame and renewed his connection with the firm, though his name was no longer used.[11]

For six months, January 1 to June 1, 1859, the firm went under the name of Evarts & Southmayd. But Evarts then persuaded Choate to return, informing him that the earnings were about twenty thousand dollars a year, and that his share would be fifteen per cent. For the next twenty-five years, therefore, the firm name was Evarts, Southmayd, and Choate.

One other change took place. Jeremiah Evarts Tracy, Evarts' nephew, in time became an assistant in the office. Fresh from Yale with his law degree, he proved a valuable addition. His mother, Martha Sherman Tracy, was Evarts' sister; his father, Ebenezer C.

Tracy, was editor of the *Vermont Chronicle.* Young Tracy ultimately became a leading realty lawyer of the city.

Various changes occurred in Evarts' family life during the fifties. His mother, who resided with him, died at the age of seventy-seven and was buried with Jeremiah in the family lot in New Haven. Nine more children were born, bringing the total to twelve, and completing a large, happy family. William Evarts, later an assistant district attorney, was born in 1851; Hettie S. Evarts, Mary Evarts, Helen M. Evarts, and Elizabeth H. Evarts were born respectively in 1852, 1854, 1856, and 1858; the twins Sherman and Prescott Evarts were born in 1859, the former becoming a lawyer and the latter an Episcopal minister; Louisa W. Evarts was born in 1861; and Maxwell Evarts, who most resembled his father in appearance, was born in 1862.

The house on East Nineteenth Street was no longer adequate. Evarts sold it for $6,150 to William Allen Butler, who resold it for $8,000; six years later still it went for $13,000. "The moral is," said Butler, "that if you happen to own property in a growing part of the city, unencumbered by mortgage, it is best to hold on to it."

The new home which Evarts rented at 231 Second Avenue, on the corner of Fourteenth Street, served him for the remainder of his life. It was in a fashionable neighborhood. Near by was Stuyvesant Square, surrounded by fine houses. Evarts liked the new house. It was a brown-stone mansion, standing a trifle back from the street, with flowers and grass about it—a substantial house, homelike and simple in architecture. The library to the left of the entrance hall had the most conspicuous place; opposite was the dining room, a stately room with oaken furniture and family plate on the sideboard. Broad, well-waxed oaken stairs led up to the drawing room, which was well furnished and heavily carpeted. Evarts liked this home so well that years afterward, when the neighborhood was no longer fashionable, he refused to migrate uptown.

He had acquired a summer home which he loved even more. To escape the heat of New York summers and the cares of business, he found a delightful retreat in Windsor, Vermont. This little village of two or three thousand people, with its main street winding along the bank of the Connecticut River, had three churches, a courthouse, a sawmill, a gristmill, and a coeducational seminary. The houses were neatly kept, some being indicative of wealth. Horace Gray's garden was one of the finest in the county. The sunny slopes of the Cornish hills lay on the eastern side of the river; wooded heights rose to the west; and to the south, three miles from the village, old Mount Ascutney towered some three thousand feet. From its summit Windsor resembled a riverside park.

One object marred the panorama—the state prison near the center of the town, on the site of the old prison of 1809. "It is a beautifully conducted institution," explained Evarts to guests. "None but the most worthy are admitted, and disorderly and intoxicated persons, it seems, are not allowed. Owing to the great demand, we are unable to supply quarters for all, and so we take the worst; but as the worst of a Vermont population corresponds to the cream of a New York legislature, some idea can be formed of our high standard as jailers."[12]

There was a large tract of land west of the main street, long known as "Paradise" because of its beauty. At one corner of this area, just a few steps from the center of the village was the house of Edward Curtis, which Evarts purchased in 1846. Windsor was then difficult to reach, the nearest railhead being at Fitchburg, from which people journeyed to Windsor by coach; but by 1849 the railroad reached Windsor. How and when Evarts became acquainted with Curtis—a New York lawyer, regarded by Henry Clay as "Webster's man" but by Van Buren as an intriguer who controlled Webster—is uncertain.[13]

Evarts' purchase proved the beginning of a large estate. He soon bought the house next door, which became known as the "Giants" and was used often to accommodate his visitors. In 1857 he bought another segment of "Paradise" from Sylvester Hubbard. The estate was given the name "Runnemede," an allusion to the famous Runnymede near Windsor, England, where King John signed the Magna Charta. For, in 1777, in the Constitution House, adjacent to Evarts' estate, another Magna Charta had been executed—the Constitution of Vermont, the first American instrument specifically to prohibit slavery.[14]

Meanwhile, in 1853, Edwin Stoughton, a New York lawyer, had purchased property near by, developing an estate known as "Blow-Me-Down." Stoughton was of good Vermont stock, about Evarts' age; he already had won recognition at the New York bar. The friendship between the two lawyers ripened into a close attachment, and out of it developed many benefits for both.

Evarts' house was on rising ground, set slightly back from the street, a rambling structure, neither ornate nor imposing, but suggestive of taste, comfort, freedom, and the quiet of country life. He maintained this estate not only as a summer retreat but as a farming enterprise. As his means increased, he spent a considerable part of his income to maintain and improve it. Runnemede became a popular resort, not only because of its natural beauty but because of the open-handed friendliness of its host, who manifestly delighted to entertain those who came to see him.

During the fifties Evarts was developing that fraternal spirit toward fellow-lawyers which so distinguished his later career. New York still had no bar association; indeed, no guild spirit whatever existed. Half of the bar did not know the other half, and lawyers were inclined to keep each other at arm's length. But an *esprit de corps* was slowly emerging. Evarts was among the leaders in encouraging it.

Occasionally lawyers and judges met to pay tribute to a passing veteran of the bar. For example, when Nicholas Hill, an old-school lawyer, died in 1859, memorial proceedings were held in the Federal Circuit Court room with Judge Nelson presiding, and Evarts, O'Conor, and Brady spoke. Again, in 1860, upon the death of George Wood, a meeting was held in the New York Supreme Court room at which Evarts, Lord, and Noyes spoke.[15] Evarts seemed to have a certain facility for speaking on these solemn occasions and was often called upon.

During the fifties Evarts practiced in the Court of Appeals, the State Supreme Court, the Superior Court, the Court of Common Pleas, the Federal District and Circuit Courts, and the Supreme Court at Washington. None of these tribunals had yet become sullied by unprincipled judges or lawyers, and cases were pleaded with confidence that they would be decided upon their merits.

The Court of Appeals was the most influential state court in the country. Lodged in the Old Capitol at Albany, a plain, rectangular, two-storied stone building overlooking the Hudson, it would have resembled an old-fashioned college dormitory had it not been for the six Doric columns in front and the cupola surmounted with a wooden Themis. It was difficult to conceive how so small a building could house the legislature, governor's staff, other state officials, the Common Council of Albany, several courts, and county and local offices. In one of the legislative chambers, the Appeals judges, dressed in black gowns, held session from ten to two. They lived at Congress Hall, the one satisfactory hotel near the Capitol, ate at the same table, and mingled freely with lawyers who might be in town. It was the ability of the judges, together with the variety and importance of the cases brought before them, that gave the court its high reputation. But there were defects. The docket was overcrowded, causing delays of justice; some of the judges were on circuit in the Supreme Court and so able to review their own decisions; their eight-year term was much too short; and the fluctuating personnel caused instability in decisions. Of the judges—Jewett, Bronson, Ruggles, Gardiner, Foote, Selden, Davies, Comstock, Denio, and Johnson—the last three stood out prominently. Comstock was the ablest and delivered decisions in several of Evarts' cases. He probably rendered more influential opinions than any other justice who ever sat on the court. Hiram Denio was not brilliant, but no judge possessed greater public confidence. Alexander Johnson was of broader cast of mind and perhaps the most impartial member of the bench. During its early history a frequent lack of harmony was displayed in the opinions of the court. Dissents were common. But it became more harmonious as its composition became more stable.[16]

The State Supreme Court for the New York district was situated in a building fronting Chambers Street near City Hall. It likewise had a roster of able judges. But the Superior Court of the city, in the same building, was of higher grade. Beside Judges Oakley and Duer, there were such lesser lights as Woodruff, Bosworth, Hoffman, and Campbell. Evarts was fond of Woodruff and once said of him: "He regarded the career of human life, not as a game, but as a discharge of duty, and the constant observance of duty through life as the best and highest success permitted to man."[17] The Court of Common Pleas was the oldest in the country. It was not a petty court, but handled important cases and had finality in certain types. Charles P. Daly, who served as judge for forty-one years, was an institution in himself.

It was surprising how few lawyers practiced in the Federal Circuit and District Courts. The former was almost a close corporation with not more than a dozen lawyers practicing regularly. Evarts appeared increasingly in both. In the Circuit Court Judge Nelson gained a national reputation, and his opinions carried great weight.

Evarts first appeared in the Supreme Court at Washington in 1857, although admitted to practice in 1846 on the motion of Daniel Webster.[18] Taney, Nelson, Grier, Curtis, Campbell, McLean, Wayne, Daniel, and Catron then composed the Court.

It happened that his first case, *Taylor* v. *Carryl,* was of more than ordinary importance—a conflict of federal and state jurisdiction. Upon demand of creditors a sheriff seized the bark *Royal Saxon* in Philadelphia and under state authority sold it to the plaintiff. Meanwhile, the crew sued in a federal court for wages due them and were granted an attachment. Assuming his authority to be paramount, the federal marshal sold the ship to the defendant.

Evarts appeared for the plaintiff in support of state authority; John Cadwallader and Samuel Hood, two Pennsylvania lawyers, appeared for the defendant. Cadwallader had a national reputation and Evarts' prospects were none too bright. Furthermore, in a recent case the Court had upheld federal admiralty authority in a sweeping manner. However, the Court was beginning to veer from the nationalistic trend which Marshall had emphasized; it was the year of the Dred Scott decision, and Taney leaned toward State Rights. Cadwallader argued that a state had no jurisdiction over maritime liens for seamen's wages. Evarts replied that the sale of a ship for debts by a sheriff was like that of any other property within a state. After the case had been argued twice, the decision was close, five to four in favor of the plaintiff, with Taney strangely dissenting. In substance, the Court held that the admiralty jurisdiction of the federal courts, although exclusive on some subjects, was concurrent on others, and was concurrent in this case.[19]

Oddly enough, Evarts thus won his first case in the Supreme Court as an advocate of State Rights, which was quite contrary to his political philosophy. He did not appear again before the Court till 1862.

5

Rivals at the Bar

IT WAS DURING the decade 1853 to 1863 that Evarts first earned fame as a lawyer. He appeared in all types of cases, some important and some trivial, arguing at times against lawyers of whom no record can be found, and at times against real giants of the bar.

Among the latter was William Curtis Noyes. He may not have ranked in public esteem with Charles O'Conor or David Dudley Field, but Evarts never opposed a higher type of lawyer. Self-made, deeply religious, diligent and untiring, with an exhaustive and authoritative knowledge of cases and an original mind, he possessed character and power of logic rather than glittering talents in declamation. He was highly versed in corporation and commercial law and was much sought after on Wall Street. As a great scholar, he assisted David Dudley Field in the preparation of the New York Penal Code, revelling in Field's valuable private library of seven thousand volumes in the rear of his Fifth Avenue mansion.[1]

Noyes and Evarts had several interesting battles. The first of these was the case of *Hartt* v. *Harvey* in the State Supreme Court. Dr. Cheever, pastor of the Church of the Puritans and a radical Abolitionist, created a schism in his church by his fiery sermons and became the most talked-of clergyman in the city. Evarts greatly admired him. When a lawsuit was instituted to determine which faction had legally elected the trustees of the church, Evarts represented the original trustees and Noyes the rival group. The court sustained Evarts' contention that the election officials, after certifying the first group and then discovering some ballots illegal, could not give the offices to the second group.[2]

The Schuyler frauds resulted in one of the most celebrated cases of pre-war years. Robert Schuyler, president of the New York and New Haven Railroad, issued two million dollars worth of surplus stock without consent of the stockholders, hoping that the re-issue of supposedly cancelled certificates would never be discovered, for the company books were not accessible. But when an explosion occurred in the stock market, Schuyler resigned in disgrace and absconded, bringing ruin on many others. It became Noyes's duty, as counsel for the company, to have Schuyler indicted and the fraudulent stock declared void. Evarts, Daniel Lord, and Francis B. Cutting, representing the holders of the new stock, sought to show that they had purchased it in good faith.

"I do not think," said Evarts, "our Bar ever presented so singular a scene as the trial of the New Haven Railroad Case, in which speaking almost literally, Mr. Noyes was on one side and all of the rest of us on the other. It was a wonderful trial of a man's resources and of his temper, and when any of us were exhausted on our side, there was always a fresh hand to take it up for us; but he stood the constant combatter of all of us in succession."

The stock was declared void, and Noyes thus saved the company from paying immense claims. But it was an unwise decision, holding in substance that a corporation was not responsible to individuals for acts of its agents. Noyes died before the case reached the Court of Appeals, where the decision was reversed in favor of Evarts and his colleagues.[3]

Noyes was at his best in the Rose Will Case. John Rose had left $300,000 for the education and employment of poor children of the city, conditional upon the raising of an equal amount within five years; if it were not obtained, half the bequest would go to the American Colonization Society and half to general charity. The testator's brother, Henry Rose, contested the will. Was such a conditional bequest to charity legal? Evarts supported the bequest; O'Conor appeared for the Colonization Society; and Noyes represented Henry Rose. Noyes proved master of the situation. "There was nothing," said Evarts, "that he had not considered, and nothing that he did not know that was . . . substantially valuable in the doctrine of charitable uses." The Court of Appeals declared the bequest void.[4]

The West Washington Market Case offered still another clash between Evarts and Noyes. Since it had a wide public interest, it was fully reported in the press. The area along the Hudson waterfront at the foot of West, Vesey, and Dey streets became so valuable that for years a filling-in process had created new land, extending the shore line till it reached far out beyond the original line granted the city by the charter of 1730. Did this redeemed land belong to the state or the city? Assuming control, the city rented it to market-men who built their sheds and stalls upon it; but of the $250,000 expected in yearly rentals only about a third found its way into the city treasury. The state, claiming title, leased the land to Messrs. Taylor and Brennan at an annual rental of $5,000. When the city and the market-men resisted this state intervention, Taylor and Brennan brought suit for damages and rentals unlawfully withheld from them, and won a verdict for $600,000 in 1859. But there arose a suspicion of collusion between Taylor and Brennan and the city corporation counsel, Richard Busteed. The latter signed agreements for mutual suppression of suits, left Taylor and Brennon in possession of the land, and refused to defend the rights of the market-men. It appeared that in doing this Busteed had surrendered the rights of the city to one of the most valuable sites.[5]

The climax came in December, 1859, when the questions of collusion and of the title were given a thorough airing before Judge Ingraham in the State Supreme Court. The city was represented by Noyes, Bronson, McKeon, and Gilbert; Brennan and Taylor were represented by Edmonds and Platt; Evarts appeared for the state. On behalf of the new corporation counsel, Greene C. Bronson, the counsel for the city, argued that fraud and collusion had been practiced. Noyes presented a strong case for the city, though he was constantly interrupted by questions from Evarts. Noyes's main contention was that Busteed had no power to bind the city by agreements. In reply, the counsel for Taylor and Brennan insisted that Busteed's conduct had been commendable if he believed that title really rested with the state.

Aspersions had fallen upon Evarts for participating in the drafting of one of Busteed's agreements. But the aged corporation counsel, Bronson, completely exonerated him. "If I had not known him," said Bronson "to be incapable of doing anything that was not above reproach, the noble argument made by him yesterday, even though against me, would have convinced me of it." Indeed, Evarts' "noble argument" for the state was in loftier vein than the other pleas. He defended the integrity of all the men connected with the case, declared that Busteed had been free to act as he thought best, insisted the qustion was not of fraud but of title to the property, and declared that the title vested in the state because the land was originally under tidewater. Judge Ingraham, however, refusing to decide the question of title, restored the rents from the property to the city. He denied the power of Busteed to bind the city by agreements and declared them void. On the other hand, he refused to entertain a charge of fraud. Evarts thus lost his case; but soon afterward a compromise was reached between the city and the state whereby Taylor and Brennan received $300,000 for dropping all further claims for rents.[6]

The friendly rivalry between Noyes and Evarts was terminated in 1864, by Noyes's death. He had overtaxed his strength, having revised the last pages of the New York Penal Code only the night before he was stricken. At a meeting of the bar a few days later, Evarts, O'Conor, Field, Brady, and others spoke in tribute to him; and Evarts justly remarked that "God has given nothing to mortals in this life of much value without great labor."[7]

David Dudley Field was another great rival of Evarts at the bar. In his prime Field probably had more millions of dollars depending upon his legal shrewdness than any other lawyer. He was one of a famous family, his brother Cyrus being the great inventor, while his brothers Stephen J. and Henry M. Field won distinction as lawyer and author respectively. His father had roomed with Jeremiah Evarts at Yale. Field, who was older than Evarts, and had been practicing law a dozen years before the latter came on the scene, had built up an extensive practice, from which he was accumulating a fortune. He was a man of strong feelings, imperious nature, and great intellectual power. In appearance he was tall, erect, decided in movement and speech, and courteous and graceful in bearing. Few men in New York were better known and few so little understood. To most observers he seemed cold and stern; but a warm personality lay beneath his chill exterior, and in private life he was companionable. Few lawyers could deliver keener thrusts and his earnest, positive manner, free from impassioned oratory, was hard to resist. He liked to break precedents, to argue before unfriendly courts, and to extract favorable decisions from unwilling judges. But his chief fame rested upon his work as a legal reformer. Day and night he toiled for eighteen years upon the tremendous task of codifying the laws of the state, so absorbed in it that any attention to his practice seemed miraculous. Yet he called it a mere "healthful diversion." He wished to be remembered as author of the legal code of New York, and was often ridiculed for this praiseworthy ambition.[8]

Evarts found it difficult, in their few early encounters, to defeat him. In an insurance case, in which Evarts tried to show that the company was not liable because no watchman had been on duty Field defeated him.[9] They met again in the case of the disputed chamberlainship, which aroused keen public interest. Mayor Fernando Wood had removed Stout as city chamberlain for refusing to pay out certain moneys, and appointed one Platt to succeed him. When the city comptroller, Robert T. Haws, refused to recognize Platt's appointment, the issue was brought into court, Field appearing for Platt and Evarts for Haws. Evarts contended that Stout's removal was without a stated cause, and that the consent of the aldermen to the removal had been given at an illegal meeting. But in trying to prove that a court could interfere with the mayor's removal power, Evarts was supporting an outmoded doctrine, which the Court of Appeals refused to sustain.[10] The rivalry between Field and Evarts became sharper in later years, but never to the extent of destroying their mutual esteem.

The noted Brooklyn Ferry Case brought a battle of wits between Evarts and John W. Edmonds, an ex-judge and lawyer of the old school, who had studied law with Martin Van Buren. Evarts defended the city in a suit brought by the state to secure an injunction preventing the five ferry lines between Manhattan and Brooklyn from combining in one corporation, forming a monopoly, and raising fares. Evarts' task was to prove that only two of the ferry lines were self-supporting, and that the others would fail unless a combination were effected; to show that it was not a question of monopoly, but of public benefit; and to demonstrate that the franchise to the ferry lines was a property right vested in the city from earliest times. The State Supreme Court upheld his position declaring it to be the duty of the legislature, not the court, to decide whether a rate was oppressive, and refusing to consider the question of monopoly.[11] The case marked a milestone for Evarts in that it was the beginning of his connections with large public service corporations.

On the other hand, in the case of *People* v. *Bowen,* he represented the state in a suit brought to challenge the validity of the charter of the Metropolitan Gas Light Company. Two new adversaries faced him: John Slosson, former judge of the Superior Court, and Waldo Hutchins, an able corporation lawyer. Evarts had the weaker side of the case. He sought to show that the company had been created by a special enactment, contrary to the constitution, and that it was a monopoly, using the streets without compensation to the city. Today such an argument would seem ludicrous. The Court of Appeals held that the legislature had complete discretion in creating a public utility corporation by either general or special act.[12]

The Trinity Church Case, one of the most interesting of all, brought Evarts a new rival, Charles Tracy, and also a new colleague, Amasa J. Parker. Tracy, a corporation lawyer, was son-in-law of J. Pierpont Morgan. Parker and Evarts were counsel for the Church. Parker had served in Congress, and had been twice defeated for governor. He was prominent in educational circles, one of the founders of the Albany Law School, and a former judge of the Court of Appeals. He often encountered Evarts later in the courts. In colonial days Trinity Church had received from the Crown a lease of a huge estate on Broadway between the Battery and Fourteenth Street. After the Revolution the state temporarily acquired the land, but the Church soon recovered possession. In time the property became worth millions, including houses, shops, theatres, depots, and some of the most valuable buildings in the city. A Trinity Church lease, with its peculiar privileges, was one of the most desirable titles in the city.

In 1856 the state sued to recover title to two lots known as the Church Farm; and if the suit succeeded, it might ultimately recover all of the property. Tracy argued that the state had succeeded to the rights of the Church after the Revolution, and that the statute of limitations did not apply to churches. Evarts and Parker insisted the statute did apply, that the state had not proven its title, and that the rights under the royal grant had been confirmed by the New York Constitution. The court upheld the title of the Church, declaring that since the state had not been able to show adverse title for forty years, the presumption was in favor of Trinity.[18]

While Evarts was appearing in these cases, which kept him in the public eye, he was encountering new rivals in the fields of admiralty law and marine insurance. The case of the *Ocean Bird* aroused a strong anti-Spanish feeling in the city. Graham, owner of the vessel, and his creditors both claimed possession when the ship arrived from Cuba with a Spanish crew. Graham went aboard with a federal marshal to take possession; Captain Viademonte, acting for the creditors, retained Evarts in a suit to recover possession. Both Graham and Viademonte appealed for public support in the press. For a day or two excited crowds hung about the pier at Tenth Street. After several hearings before Judge Betts the creditors were declared the rightful owners, a decision which increased anti-Spanish sentiment. Fearing mob violence, Evarts went aboard ship with a large police force; but no trouble ensued and the ship put to sea.[14]

Two expert admiralty lawyers whom Evarts encountered were Charles Donahue and Erastus C. Benedict. Despite his odd appearance—short, fat, cross-eyed, and with mincing step—Donahue had a large practice and a high reputation. In a collision case, involving two ships off Sandy Hook, Evarts defeated him. But Donahue turned the tables in a case involving the question of the right of a captain to refuse to carry excess cargo.[15] Benedict, the author of several treatises on admiralty, and known to the public as an educational leader, was associated with Evarts against Donahue in a case relating to the damage of a cargo of iron by rust, which they lost.[16]

In marine insurance cases Evarts never engaged a more able adversary than Francis B. Cutting, a great master of commercial law. Much older than Evarts, he had a lucrative practice before the latter came to New York. He was a tall, handsome man of commanding presence, strong intellect, and graceful accomplishments, whose brilliancy would have turned him to politics but for his love of the law. He had already acquired a considerable fortune and was prominent socially.

Cutting had a little the better of their battles. In the novel case of the *Albatross,* Evarts and Daniel Lord represented the owner, Simeon Draper, and won the case. The Court of Appeals held that the insurance company was liable when the ship foundered even though the nominal captain was not an experienced navigator.[17] But in another marine insurance case, relating to damage suffered by a cargo of hides, Cutting won a complete victory for the insured. Evarts, Cutting, and Alexander Hamilton, Jr., a man of seventy-five, were colleagues in a marine insurance case, but sought in vain to show that an insurance policy did not cover a certain voyage from Brazil to New Orleans on which a cargo of coffee had been lost.[18]

When a great fire broke out in 1853 in the publishing house of Harper & Brothers, caused by a match accidentally thrown into a pan of camphene, Evarts represented the publishers in an important insurance case. The policy exempted the insurance company from liability for fire caused by the *use* of camphene; but Evarts insisted that the provision referred only to the employment of camphene as lighting material. The Court of Appeals agreed, refusing to exempt the insurance company from liability.[19]

Not a few of Evarts' cases were shipping problems, bringing him among other prominent clients, Marshall O. Roberts, Cornelius Vanderbilt, and William H. Aspinwall. As one of his many enterprises Commodore Vanderbilt seized the opportunity afforded by the gold rush to run a steamship line from New York to Nicaragua, and by reducing fares made this Isthmian route popular. In the Roving Commission Case Evarts was retained by Vanderbilt to defend him from the charge of disposing of certain property fraudulently. It was a question of securing an order from the court to take testimony from certain witnesses in Nicaragua and California. The application was refused. Nor was Evarts successful in defending Vanderbilt's ships from double fees levied upon them at the port of New York.[20]

William H. Aspinwall, head of the Pacific Railroad and Panama Steamship Company, was one of the richest men in New York. In one case Evarts strove to show that he was not personally liable, as a stockholder of the Mexican Ocean Mail and Inland Company, for a contract to build wagons for its transportation service. He lost the case; but he never won an easier victory than in prosecuting the suit of the Union Mutual Insurance Company, of which Aspinwall was director, against a debtor.[21] Here Evarts first encountered Charles A. Rapallo, a truly able lawyer, later Judge of the Court of Appeals. Overcoming the handicap of a meager education, Rapallo had developed a large practice and had become a scholarly recluse, disdaining politics, and giving all his talents to the law.

In another case on behalf of Aspinwall he first faced William Allen Butler. There was no finer gentleman at the bar, but Butler was too fond of literary pursuits to reach the top of his profession. He was a son of the distinguished Benjamin F. Butler, a nephew of Daniel Lord, and a man of wealth. Today he is best remembered for his famous poems, "Nothing to Wear" and "Two Millions," and the satirical "Mrs. Lumber's Raffle."[22]

Evarts' cases relating to ordinary business transactions, such as promissory notes, contracts, prior liens, mortgages, assignments of property, and wills have little intrinsic interest except where a client or adversary proved important. He was generally successful in his cases relating to promissory notes and bills of exchange. In one of these, *Lysaght* v. *Phillips,* Jeremiah Larocque, one of the best known of the older generation of lawyers, was his opponent. In this particular suit Evarts' client was a British admiral, and the court sustained the argument that his right to collect on a bill was not impaired by an agreement between the previous acceptors of the bill not to do so.[23] Evarts secured an increasing number of British clients; for example, in *Dodge* v. *Wilbur* he successfully defended the agent of a bankrupt London firm from personal liability on a bill of exchange.[24]

Edwards Pierrepont, his Yale classmate, was his rival in the Willetts case in the Court of Appeals. Pierrepont, who lived on Fifth Avenue, was one of Evarts' closest friends. He had served a term as judge of the Superior Court. The case was of especial interest because Pierrepont was acting for Morrison R. Waite, the third of the Yale triumvirate, and a promising lawyer in Toledo. The question at issue was whether certain New York creditors, represented by Evarts, or a Toledo bank, of which Waite was receiver, had a prior lien upon another bank. The victory went to Evarts.[25]

Another new rival was Aaron J. Vanderpoel, of whom it is said that he tried more cases than any other lawyer of his day. This plain, practical-minded attorney, trained in the office of William

Curtis Noyes, was founder of the firm of Vanderpoel and Hall, which enjoyed a large business as counsel to city officials. His partner, A. Oakey Hall, an aggressive young lawyer, was rising rapidly in city politics. Evarts also met old John Anthon, founder of the New York Law Institute and author of several legal works—an indefatigable attorney who could try four or five cases a day without weariness. In a lien case Evarts stood alone against Anthon and three colleagues and defeated them.[26]

But *Hoyt* v. *Thompson* was the most important lien case in which he engaged. This was the second time that Evarts had argued a case for the wealthy merchant Jesse Hoyt. The question was whether Hoyt or Thompson had prior lien to a $60,000 bond which the Long Island Railroad had transferred for a debt, and Evarts won the suit in the Court of Appeals. After Thompson's death the case reappeared, with Edward P. Cowles, partner of the well-known legal writer Barbour, as Evarts' opponent. This time the decision was reversed in Cowles's favor. When the executor of Thompson's estate refused to pay Cowles his two-thousand-dollar fee because of other claims on the estate, Evarts took the matter to court on Cowles's behalf and had the fee paid.[27]

James W. Gerard, grandfather of the famous ambassador to Germany in 1917, was another leading attorney of the city. O'Conor regarded his powers of persuasion as "marvelous." Gifted with the polish and wit of his French ancestry, and the soul of geniality, Gerard was almost irrresistible in winning juries. "Never attack your adversary with a bludgeon," he once said; "run him through with a rapier." But Evarts was successful in his encounters with Gerard in several contract cases.[28]

It was also in a contract case that Evarts met his old Yale friend, Benjamin D. Silliman, in the Court of Appeals. Evarts contended that a steamboat company was liable to the owner for loss of goods when a steamer en route from New York to Stonington was destroyed by fire. He won the case in the Superior Court, lost it in the State Supreme Court, and gained a final victory in the Court of Appeals.[29]

A more unusual case was that presented by Mrs. A. D. Wetmore's marriage contract. Before her marriage to Charles F. Wetmore and just before coming of age, this wealthy woman had made an agreement with him whereby she was guaranteed her own property in the form of a trust fund after marriage. The marriage proving unhappy, she claimed that the laws of New York gave her immediate possession of her property regardless of the trust fund, and demanded that the ante-nuptial agreement, which had been made in New Jersey, be set aside. Evarts argued her cause in vain. After she had separated from her husband, Evarts interceded to obtain from Wetmore permission for her to see her daughter at Newport.[30]

One of the best jury lawyers in New York was William Fullerton, who had been admitted to practice the same year as Evarts, and had been in partnership with O'Conor. Although usually amiable, he could be most caustic on cross-examination. Like Evarts, he found his hobby in costly farming. In their first encounter, a contract case between an American ship-owner and British brokers, Fullerton won the verdict.[31] But in an embezzlement case, *Paddon* v. *Williams,* Evarts defeated Fullerton.[32]

The Phelps Will Case was the greatest battle Evarts ever fought with Daniel Lord. They had already met in the Schuyler Fraud Case and two marine insurance suits, and the score between them stood about even.[33] Anson G. Phelps, with his son-in-law, William E. Dodge, had formed a firm which expanded from merchandising into manufacturing, mining, and railroading. Around its copper-manufacturing plant in Connecticut rose the town of Ansonia. Phelps accumulated great wealth and became noted for his philanthropy. His will granted an annuity to his wife, gave $100,000 to each child who might be living ten years after his death, and provided $600,000 for religious and benevolent purposes. The residue was to be divided equally among his children and grandchildren ten years after his death. As the widow and one child died before the end of ten years, their share fell into the residue. Two of the daughters then sued for annulment of the ten-year clause in order that the residue might vest immediately in the next of kin.

The case finally reached the Court of Appeals, where Lord represented the executor in support of the will; Marshall S. Bidwell and William Tracy represented the benevolent interests; Evarts, John K. Porter, and William Allen Butler represented the contesting daughters. Very ingeniously, Evarts tried to show that Phelps's purpose was to provide for an accumulation of his estate over a period of ten years, in order to increase the amount to be distributed to his heirs. He submitted elaborate figures to demonstrate that the accumulation would about equal the amount paid out immediately in debts and legacies, leaving at the end of ten years a sum approximately equal to the estate at the time of death. Evarts' figures were strong evidence of Phelps's purpose. He then showed that the laws of New York forbade such accumulations, and argued that the will should therefore be annulled. In giving the opinion of the court, Judge Selden praised Evarts' ingenuity; but he held that Phelps's purpose was to dispose of his income annually as it accrued, rather than over a period of ten years, and that such purpose was legitimate.[34]

From a survey of Evarts' cases during the decade 1853 to 1863, it appears that he won some three fourths of them, that increasingly he was retained in problems of large public interest, and that he was matching his wits successfully with those of the ablest lawyers.

6

Battles with O'Conor

EVARTS never faced a more formidable foe than Charles O'Conor. The two men were alike in their ability, their devotion to the law, and their incessant industry; but in everything else, they differed. Yet, the two men liked and respected each other. In early life O'Conor had overcome seemingly insurmountable difficulties. His father, escaping from Ireland during the uprising of 1798, came to New York, where young O'Conor was born in 1804. After the premature death of his mother, the boy had only the shadow of a home. His father was of the decayed gentleman type, shiftless, and usually to be found in the company of ne'er-do-wells. The boy first came in contact with the law at the age of thirteen, when his father got him the job of office boy with a friend who professed to practice. Although he never had more than six months' schooling, he read eagerly and got some instruction from his father. Finally, a lawyer, Joseph Fay, saw genius in the lad and took him into his office. Thereafter his progress was rapid. In 1825 the Court of Common Pleas broke its regulations by admitting him to the bar.

But O'Conor's troubles were not over. He had no office or law books. He finally rented some makeshift quarters and borrowed money to buy a library of one hundred and sixty volumes. Then came ten years of severe struggle for recognition. Often he went without food. Yet during the first year he astonished the bar by defeating Thomas Addis Emmet, the outstanding advocate of the day; and he won his first case in the Chancery Court. Of O'Conor's early struggles Evarts once said, "Never let us forget the truth that the discipline of poverty and necessity is the best assurance for the making of a great lawyer. . . . Mr. O'Conor, endowed by nature with prodigious gifts of intellect . . . with the added power of industry, that if it was not born in him was burnt into him by ten years of poverty and struggle at our Bar, had everything in his favor to make a great lawyer."[1]

When asked to what he attributed his success, O'Conor replied with one word, "Study." From the first he devoted himself to his law books, denying himself all pleasures. Study became the absorbing passion of his life and made him almost a recluse. He even refused to marry till far advanced in years. After reaching the peak of success, he still was an unremitting student. Judge Daly described O'Conor as he appeared in 1835: "I vividly recall how he looked, tall, spare, and very erect, a highly intellectual face, lustrous piercing eyes, flowing, raven-black hair, and a sharp, penetrating high voice, that was always well sustained, and by which each word was slowly articulated, with a distinctness that was unusual. I recall the great impression which his voice and his whole manner made upon me, especially his voice, which vibrated through and filled every part of the courtroom. This telling voice and riveting look of the eyes remained long with him, when his hair was gray, his figure slightly bent."[2]

In court O'Conor was always alert, armed at every point, ready for every surprise, and irresistible in marshalling his forces. On the day of battle he was proud and confident, with every position guarded and ready to take immediate advantage of any slip. He was an expert pleader and knew by heart every line of Chitty's treatise. Samuel J. Tilden, who perhaps knew him best, declared that he had a more precise knowledge of the law than any other living American.

His physical endurance was astonishing; a man, said Choate, "whose physique seemed to be made of gutta-percha and steel springs." His only exercise was the long walks he took at night, thinking over the problems of the next day. In 1855 he moved to

Fort Washington, and occasionally walked all the way down town to his office. For years he refused to buy a carriage. Indeed, in his later life he became a crank on rules governing his health.

The Goodyear Rubber Case and the Forrest Divorce Case brought him prominence. He defended Mrs. Forrest against the efforts of her celebrated actor husband to divorce her. Forrest prosecuted the case with a reckless expenditure of money. O'Conor had the popular side as champion of a wronged woman and won her a $64,000 alimony; but his fee of $40,000 cost him most of the popularity he had gained.

He cared little for public office, an early failure to be elected alderman perhaps having discouraged him. He twice refused the lucrative federal district attorneyship, but did accept it in 1853, just as Evarts' term expired. Tilden confided to John Bigelow in 1853 that he did not believe O'Conor suited to public office, saying, "Mr. O'Conor is a man . . . of great mental activity—indefatigable, vehement and sarcastic in controversy—remarked at the bar as able rather than wise, and remarkable for want of tact. . . . Add, inexperience in politics, very limited acquaintance with its subjects, its questions, its history, its methods, or its men—unsettled convictions, a tendency to capriciousness, and as little as can be found of that capacity which enables a man instinctively to act with others or make them act with him, and you have the political aspects of his character. . . . This opinion is the result of many years observation. It was confirmed when I was associated with him in the Convention that formed the present constitution of this State, and, in intercourse constant and never unfriendly."[3]

There was something forbidding about this austere, combative Irishman—something disagreeable in his pale face, piercing eyes, thin compressed lips often twitching at the corner of the mouth, square jaw, careless dress, scholastic manner, and cold, relentless nature. But there was a happier side. James C. Carter, closely associated with him for years, believed that his pugnacious air was only a cover used to bewilder adversaries, and that actually he was generous and warm-hearted. There is no doubt of his generosity.

He once remarked that it was always his habit to give away most of what he earned. Probably it was his own early struggles that made him so ready to give to the poor and unfortunate, and even to suffer imposition. He hated injustice. During the revolutions of 1848 in Europe he wrote, "So long as a King is left upon his throne there will be no justice in the Earth." Such was the man who became Evarts' chief rival at the bar.[4]

"How I came to be personally acquainted with Mr. O'Conor," said Evarts, "I scarcely recall. Probably it was without any formal introduction and by some kind of notice on his part, in some litigation in which I had appeared as an antagonist, or as a subordinate. . . . Whenever he carried the day triumphantly, he carried it off by open and manly strength, skill, and courage, and whenever he was overborne in the contest—not often, to be sure, by personal triumph, but by the law and decision—he was always ready and frank and generous in admitting that the strength and skill of his opponents had gained the victory. . . . He was preëminently a man without vanity . . . absolutely hostile to every form of humbug."[5]

Their first encounter was in a contract case in the Superior Court in 1853. To Evarts it must have been a thrilling experience. He faced a man fourteen years older, who had already been practicing twenty-eight years and was in his prime. The issue was whether the defendant had contracted to buy some iron which the plaintiff had shipped from Liverpool. O'Conor succeeded in showing that no contract had existed, but the court ordered a new trial.[6]

Three years later Evarts, O'Conor, and Samuel J. Tilden appeared for the defendant in a disputed election case involving the comptrollership. The plaintiff was represented by John W. Edmonds and James T. Brady. Flagg, the defendant, had claimed election as comptroller on the Tammany ticket, while Giles, the Know-Nothing candidate, asserted that the returns from one district were fraudulent. Evarts and O'Conor said little, leaving the burden of the defense to Tilden, who produced elaborate mathematical tables from the tally sheets to prove that, in view of the vote admittedly cast for other officers, and the large Irish element in the district, it would have been impossible for Flagg to have lost. At the close of Tilden's argument, one of the jury proposed that each juryman write the name of the candidate elected on a slip and drop it into a hat; and this resulted in a unanimous verdict for Flagg.[7]

Evarts met defeat at the hands of O'Conor in several early cases, none of them of great importance.[8] He also won several victories. In one of these, a lien case, he not only defeated six opposing counsel, one of whom was O'Conor, but secured a reversal of the lower court.[9]

The Irish Presbyterian Church Case and the Atlantic Cable Case were more important. O'Conor represented the Church and Evarts represented Henry C. Bowen, editor of the *Independent,* with whom the Church secretary had made a contract to sell some Church property. The trustees of the Church denied the authority of the secretary to act, asserting that they had not ratified the sale and that the property was worth much more than the price offered. Evarts replied that the contract was made under corporate seal, signed by the proper officers, and therefore binding. The court agreed with this view.[10] Cyrus W. Field and Peter Cooper were interested spectators in the State Supreme Court at the trial of the Atlantic Cable Case. The cable company, with Evarts and David Dudley Field as counsel, was sued for refusal to compensate the owner of the steamer which was laying the cable to Trinity Bay in Newfoundland. O'Conor and Cutting represented the plaintiff. The company claimed that the crew of the steamer had so bungled the enterprise that the cable broke, whereby it was released from obligation to pay. The trial dragged through many days, and before a decision was reached a settlement was made out of court.[11]

In the Gridiron Case Evarts and O'Conor were associated in opposition to William Curtis Noyes, William Allen Butler, and John Van Buren. When the legislature authorized the defendants to construct a horse-drawn railway on Seventh Avenue, the adjacent property owners sought an injunction to prevent it, contending that the act was unconstitutional as an appropriation for private use and grant of exclusive privilege in a public street. Evarts and O'Conor, acting for the railway, contended that the legislature could use the streets for any public purpose without compensation to abutting owners because a street was public property. The court divided, but upheld the railway.[12]

There were three struggles of first-rate importance between Evarts and O'Conor: the Metropolitan Police Case, the Parish Will Case, and the Lemmon Slave Case, each more significant than its predecessor. The first of these cases grew out of an extraordinary struggle between local and state authorities over the control of the city police system. For years the city government had been corrupt, and the police had become tools of politicians. The aldermen allowed the police to befriend rogues; prisoners were discharged after arrest; crime went unpunished. A protest to the legislature brought improvement. The police were placed under the mayor and were required for the first time to wear uniforms. Reform, however, did not last; the old corruption returned and once more the people looked to the legislature for help.[13] Mayor Fernando Wood wielded dictatorial power with baneful influence. Criminals were shielded, and bribery was common. The worst class of voters carried city elections and supported Wood. His associates were so low, said Evarts, that when taking the right side of a moral question, Wood excused himself with the remark, "We must sometimes pander to the religious sentiment of the community."[14]

In 1857 the legislature created the Metropolitan Police Board, headed by Simeon Draper, thereby virtually transferring control of the police to state authority. Mayor Wood, however, became defiant, gathered the old police around him, refused to relinquish his authority, and threatened the new board with violence. The city was treated for a time to the novel spectacle of two police systems contending for mastery. When the worst elements, eager for plunder, supported Wood and gained temporary control, New York was threatened with a reign of terror. On the critical day, June 16, the Seventh Regiment was mobilized and restored order. Wood was forced to resort to law rather than terrorism. He sought an injunction against the new police board.[15]

In the preliminary legal skirmish Evarts was one of eight lawyers acting for the state. The court not only refused the injunction, but denied Wood a writ to oust the new board. Then came a battle in the Court of Appeals over the constitutionality of the act of 1857, fought out between Evarts and Cutting as attorneys for the state, and O'Conor and Edmonds for the city. O'Conor was so sure of victory that he had promised it to Fernando Wood.

Evarts unquestionably played the chief rôle in the case. "Never before or since," wrote A. Oakey Hall later, "have I listened to such rare illustrations, such subtle distinctions, and such an aggregation of constitutional lore as scintillated in his elaborate and persuasive speech. The Albany court room was crowded. Before the argument began I polled the consensus of lawyers whom the importance of the litigation between city and state had attracted, and scarcely one believed that our contention would succeed."[16]

Apparently the act of 1857 was really unconstitutional. But Evarts had an ingenious argument. He showed it was not a violation of home rule because the five counties affected could defeat it by refusing financial support. In substance it was a proper use of the state police power. Meeting O'Conor's objections point by point, he argued that the act was not an encroachment on the mayor or judiciary; it was not an invasion of the Bill of Rights; it did not create a new authority unknown to the Constitution; it did not destroy city or county governments or create new subdivisions of the state; it was not a seizure of private property without compensation; and it did not divest the voters of the right to elect their local police officers. "If the State," said Evarts, "could create a police force for the whole State, it could create one for parts of the State."

The court upheld the validity of the act by a vote of six to two. Of the six approving judges, five were Democrats, a fact which proved that the decision could not have been partisan. Denio wrote the opinion in terms that were obviously based upon Evarts' argument.[17]

On learning of the decision, the mob element of the city rose on July 3 in a rebellion that smacked of the Paris Commune. Taking advantage of the temporary weakness of the police, they built barricades, attacked the new police, and for several days terrorized the city. The Seventh Regiment happened to be in Boston but hurried back; and on July 5 Evarts and Dana watched the entire force drawn up on Broadway preparing to quell the last disturbances.[18] The new police system not only proved more efficient than the old, but helped to save the city in 1863 during the draft riots. But the new board faced suits brought by the old police, who claimed that their removal was unjust and illegal. At its request, Evarts submitted to the board a legal opinion, holding that if a policeman had been removed for cause, he had no claim to reinstatement, but that what constituted due cause was a question for the legislature.[19]

The board was then flooded with suits for back pay by discharged policemen, which, if they succeeded, would cost the city millions. Evarts participated in several of these suits, the most important of which was the McCune Case in the Court of Appeals. Evarts, Field, Noyes, and Vanderpoel appeared for the state; while Brady and Nicholas Hill represented McCune. Evarts sought to show that McCune's refusal to accept duty or swear allegiance to the new board constituted insubordination; but the court decided that, under the act of 1857, the old police had been automatically transferred to the new force without their affirmative acceptance.[20]

The Parish Will Case was the most important that Evarts ever dealt with in that field, and except for the Lemmon Slave Case, was his greatest battle with O'Conor. He would not have appeared in it but for the death of Ogden Hoffman in 1856. It seems to have been upon the recommendation of Daniel Lord, a witness to the Parish Will, that he was selected to replace Hoffman as counsel for Mrs. Parish.[21]

Henry Parish and his brother Daniel were partners in one of the largest dry-goods establishments of the city. With his wife, the former Susan M. Delafield, Henry lived in a palatial mansion on Union Square. On July 19, 1849, a stroke of apoplexy left Henry an invalid. Up to that day there was no abler business man in New York. He was rich, well liked, just, and honorable. But the stroke left him a helpless wreck, unable to express himself except by vague signs and incoherent groans. He was confined to his house and dependent upon his wife for everything.

He had made a will in 1842, leaving a large sum to his wife, giving special bequests to others, and providing that the residue, if any, should go to his brothers Daniel and James. In 1849, about a month after the stroke, he added a codicil, giving more to his wife; in 1853 he gave her additional property; and in 1854 the third codicil gave her nearly all of his estate and revoked the residuary clause. Furthermore, he appointed as executor, in place of his brother Daniel, Joseph Delafield, his wife's brother. The influence of the wife upon an invalid husband appeared obvious. Was she using undue influence or, as death neared, did Henry Parish feel his increasing devotion to her and, knowing that his brothers had enough in their own right, wish to give her his fortune? Did he know what he was doing when he made the three codicils, or was he an imbecile?

The brothers contested the codicils and retained O'Conor as counsel; Evarts and Cutting defended Mrs. Parish. But at the beginning of the trial Cutting suddenly broke down and the whole burden fell upon Evarts. Unquestionably he had the difficult side.

The celebrated case first came before the Surrogate in 1857. The testimony filled five huge volumes and required months of tedious work.[22] One volume was devoted to expert medical testimony. Evarts and O'Conor had to cut through this maze of evidence given by relatives, friends, doctors, lawyers, servants, tradesmen, and business acquaintances. Out of it all they produced opposing theories as to Henry Parish's sanity.

Evarts' theory was that Henry Parish, although physically an invalid, was mentally capable of making the codicils; that his intent was to leave the bulk of his fortune to his wife and a small, indefinite residue to his brothers, who really had no need of it; that this was his original intent in 1842 and continued to be up to his death; that he made the codicils because his fortune was increasing and he wished his wife to benefit from the increase; and that he revoked the residuary clause because he feared that his wife might die, and the brothers would get everything.

In support of this ingenious hypothesis, Evarts pictured Henry Parish as still master of his household, still receiving friends as before, and still in affectionate harmony with his wife; he painted Daniel as an unscrupulous brother, trying to wrest Henry's fortune from him; he accused the contestants of perverting the testimony and confusing physical with mental incapacity; he gave illustrations of Parish's sanity; he indignantly denied any coercion by Mrs. Parish, describing her as a dutiful wife attentive upon a dying husband and incapable of tricking so many witnesses over a period of six years. The issue, he declared, was not money, but the good name of the widow.[23]

Like Evarts, O'Conor appealed to reason. Parish's intent, he said, was to give his wife an adequate income for life and leave the bulk of his fortune to his brothers. He pictured Parish as a helpless imbecile, wholly changed in nature as well as in course of life, and subject to the wiles of a selfish, domineering wife, who kept the brothers away from the house, forced him to make the codicils, made him appear sane to observers, and for six years played this unscrupulous game. Turning to Evarts, O'Conor said: "The proponent . . . seeks to establish in effect that Henry Parish lived for nearly seven years . . . in a state of moral perversion; that in this closing period, his whole moral nature . . . was changed without provocation to vindictive hatred. . . . We seek to write a biography of honor, . . . to close it at a date when God, in His wise Providence, permitted the mind of Henry Parish to lose its power."[24]

The Surrogate compromised. He probated the will and first codicil but rejected the last two codicils. He held that Parish's mental faculties had been impaired, but not beyond testamentary capacity, and refused to hold Mrs. Parish guilty of undue influence.[25] In terms of money this meant that the brothers would receive $757,000 instead of $36,000. Evarts advised an appeal. The case reached the Court of Appeals, where it was twice argued, and finally settled in 1862. Mrs. Parish had meanwhile died, but her executors continued to retain Evarts. In this final struggle Evarts was assisted by John W. Edmonds and Alexander Johnson, while O'Conor was associated with John K. Porter.

The death of Mrs. Parish doubtless explains why O'Conor spoke more vehemently against her than before. Evarts, knowing that he was fighting a losing battle, denounced the Surrogate for his "odious and pernicious" compromise. He attacked O'Conor with a fury he had never before displayed for insinuating that some of the defense witnesses were dupes of Mrs. Parish. He condemned O'Conor also for distorting the evidence to stress the unpleasant relations between husband and wife.[26]

The argument of John K. Porter must have dispelled the last doubt in the mind of the court. He was a partner in the famous law firm of Cagger, Hill, and Porter, a man of warm-hearted personality, irresistible before a jury, and a strenuous fighter. Porter's argument was probably the best. Mercilessly and exhaustively, he marshalled the facts and analyzed the evidence to prove the fraudulent intent of Mrs. Parish. He painted a shameful story of an avaricious wife, describing how she coerced her husband to get his property in her name, how she kept him prisoner, how she opened an account at the bank a month after he was stricken, how she allowed him to grope about the house in the hope that he would kill himself, and how he feared her.[27]

The court voided the will and the three codicils, declaring that Parish must be deemed to have died intestate and therefore the widow's share would be one third. Concluding that Parish was not of sound mind, the court laid down the rule, which became a precedent, that a "testator must, at the time of executing the will, have had sufficient capacity to comprehend the condition of his property, and his relations toward the persons who are, or might be, the objects of his bounty, and the scope and bearing of the provisions of his will." But the rule, while in accord with established medical doctrine, did not directly assert that *all* of those whom physicians classed as imbeciles were incapable of making a will.[28]

Evarts had waged a hard fight, and might find some comfort in the dissent of two of the judges. Selden, the chief justice, held Parish to be competent, declaring that any other decision would be equivalent to admitting that Mrs. Parish had played the role of a "demon."

The Lemmon Slave Case, argued in the Court of Appeals in 1860, dwarfed into insignificance the previous battles between Evarts and O'Conor. It was more than an ordinary legal contest, for the issue involved the whole position of slaves brought into the North. It did more than any previous case to establish Evarts' reputation as a lawyer.

The facts were few and simple. In 1853 Jonathan Lemmon and his wife brought eight slaves from Virginia to New York and lodged them in temporary seclusion in a house on Carlisle Street, intending soon to take them to Texas. When their presence was discovered, Judge Paine of the Superior Court was asked to issue a writ of habeas corpus for their release. At once the question was raised: Was a slave, in transit through a free state, automatically free or still under the laws of the slave state of the owner? The Kansas-Nebraska Bill had not yet revived the slavery issue, nor had the Dred Scott decision been pronounced.

The courtroom at City Hall was crowded by spectators anxious to see what Judge Paine would do. The Lemmons were represented by Henry D. Lapaugh; the slaves by two Abolitionists, John Jay and E. D. Culver. While admitting that precedent supported the right to carry slaves through a free state like other merchandise, Judge Paine nevertheless granted the writ on the ground that international law did not recognize slavery or the right of passage with slaves. It was one of the first decisions of its kind and ran counter to all American precedent. The slaves were set free, and a fund subscribed to send them to Canada. Sympathizers with the South raised another fund to indemnify the Lemmons for the loss of their property.[29]

Meanwhile, a furious newspaper controversy had arisen all over the country. Greeley's *Tribune* grew belligerent in supporting Paine's decision. To Southerners it seemed an Abolitionist encroachment upon their rights and an unblushing theft of slaves. If the judgment were not reversed, New York might expect retaliation. The Virginia legislature assisted the Lemmons in appealing their case; the New York legislature also intervened, and Governor King appointed E. D. Culver and Joseph Blunt to assist Ogden Hoffman with the defense. Hoffman's death gave Evarts an opportunity, for the Governor appointed him to the vacancy.

In January, 1860, seven years after the case arose, it came to trial in the Court of Appeals. Evarts, Blunt, and Chester A. Arthur represented New York State; O'Conor and Lapaugh appeared for the Lemmons. Arthur was a young man just beginning his legal career in Culver's office. He took no part in the argument but assisted in the preparation of the case. Anticipating a great battle between O'Conor and Evarts, a large audience was on hand, including many lawyers.[30]

O'Conor knew that he must prove slavery right under the federal Constitution. Unequivocally he avowed that it was the duty of every American to support the Constitution. There was no doubt of his sincerity. "I insist that negro slavery is not unjust; it is just, wise, and beneficent," he had shouted at a mass meeting a few weeks before.[31] Like many of Irish blood, he felt an instinctive animosity toward the Negro. He challenged anyone to find in the Bible a line that implied slavery was wrong and declared it to be "an indispensable element in our growth and prosperity."

O'Conor's application of the law was shrewd. No judge, he asserted, could outlaw slavery under the Constitution; Lord Mansfield had possessed no right to forbid it in England in the classic Somerset case. The New York law of 1857 forbidding slavery was "unconstitutional and revolutionary," a violation of the commerce clause of the federal Constitution and of the privileges and immunities of citizens passing from one state to another. In short, Judge Paine's decision was "inconsistent with the peace of the country and the rights of other States."[32]

Evarts could speak on the slavery issue with the same conviction. He had become a strong foe of slavery, stating his views in no uncertain terms the previous year at the laying of the cornerstone of the Forefathers' Monument at Plymouth, and at two political rallies just before the trial.[33] When Evarts arose to reply to O'Conor, the courtroom was crowded to capacity. The legislature had adjourned, apparently on purpose to hear him.[34]

It was an argument worthy of careful study. The issue, he said, was whether Virginia could prescribe the condition of slaves in New York. Slavery could not exist in New York unless some decree to the contrary could be found in the federal laws and Constitution, or in the New York laws and Constitution, or in international law and comity. This was the foundation of Evarts' argument.

First, he said in developing this thesis, there was nothing in the federal laws or Constitution which protected a slave in New York. The Constitution had no concern with the domestic institutions of the states. The privileges and immunities clause did not mean that a Virginian entering New York brought with him the privileges enjoyed in Virginia; he had only those enjoyed by the citizens of New York. The fugitive slave law did not apply because the slaves in question were not fugitives.

In the second place, there was nothing in the Constitution or laws of New York that permitted slavery. The law of 1857 forbidding slavery was admittedly *ex post facto;* yet it made clear the attitude of the state. Slavery did not come under the principle of interstate commerce; it was a matter of the police power of the states. The decisions of the Supreme Court were uniform on this point, and even the Dred Scott decision, upon which O'Conor rested, upheld this principle.

Third, international law and comity did not protect slaves in transit; on the contrary, international law declared that slavery rested on force and local law, and had no force when a slave was brought into a free state. Natural law, likewise, abhorred slavery, and the Virginia Bill of Rights decreed that "all men are by nature free and independent."

In reply to O'Conor's prophecy that the Union would collapse if slavery were not upheld Evarts made a counter-prophecy, declaring: "This catastrophe will be, not the overthrow of the general and constituted liberties of this great nation, not the subversion of our common government, but the destruction of this institution, local and limited, which will have provoked a contest with great forces of liberty and justice, which it cannot maintain, and must yield in a conflict which it will, then, be too late to repress."[35]

O'Conor had the last word. He ridiculed the dangers which Evarts pictured as certain to arise from allowing the transit of slaves through a free state. "It is for the stranger and wayfarer that we plead," O'Conor exhorted, "for him we claim a right of passage—and we claim no more." He warned that the Supreme Court would give the right if the Court of Appeals denied it. He accused Evarts of making the most of a friendly audience, and concluded, "Negro slavery cannot be abolished."[36]

Evarts won his case by a vote of five to three. Justice Denio, in delivering the opinion of the court, followed closely Evarts' reasoning, holding that the laws of New York forbade slaves in transit; that since Congress had not acted on the matter, it was strictly a state problem; and that even temporary slavery could not exist unless sustained by positive law.[37]

Evarts won on the merits of his case, not because he spoke before a sympathetic court and audience. He had skillfully turned the doctrine of State Rights against O'Conor, and he argued with power and brilliancy. Of course he had taken an extreme position in asserting that slavery could not exist without a local law supporting it. But he had been given a splendid opportunity to deal with great principles to which his mind naturally inclined. He had defeated the greatest lawyer of the day; he had clarified the anti-slavery sentiment; he had unintentionally prepared the way for his own return to politics.

7

A Party Earthquake

THE POLITICAL KETTLE boiled furiously as the campaign of 1860 approached; and Evarts kept one eye on his profession and the other on politics. His admiration for Seward had increased. Just how or when he first became acquainted with Seward is uncertain, but his regard grew into a genuine, life-long friendship, which produced important consequences for both. He believed that Seward was the man to meet the approaching crisis.

Just a month after the Lemmon Case, Evarts played a small part in launching Seward's candidacy for president. He appeared at the Republican Union "festival," held by the Eighteenth Ward organization at the Gramercy Park house to endorse Seward, and made a brief, ringing speech, declaring that the party was fighting slavery not as a social institution, but as a political power. His sentiments were echoed by Dr. Henry Bellows, David Dudley Field, George Opdyke, and others. The caustic *Herald* described it as another "shriek of freedom" for the leader of the "irrepressible conflict."[1]

The story is told of Seward that while travelling through a rural section as governor, mounted on the box of the stage-coach to enjoy a cigar, he began talking with the inquisitive driver, who did not recognize him. After asking Seward whether he were land-agent, preacher, salesman, or newspaper man, and always getting "No" for an answer, the driver mustered up courage and asked him what his business was.

"Governor," replied Seward tranquilly.

"Governor of what?"

"Governor of the State of New York."

"Get out."

"Well, I can convince you of it," said Seward, "for here's a man on the road with whom I am acquainted." As the coach passed by, he called, "Good morning, Mr. Bunker; I want to ask you a question. Am I not the governor of New York?"

"No, by thunder," was Bunker's reply.

"Who is, then?" asked Seward somewhat startled.

"Thurlow Weed."[2]

For thirty years Thurlow Weed, editor of the *Albany Evening Journal,* was a political power in the state. His love of wire-pulling was notorious. First as Whig and then as Republican, he played the rôle of Warwick, making senators and governors, dictating to state conventions, distributing patronage, and directing legislation. Not that he was dishonest or selfish; he did not use politics for his own purse or advancement. But he loved power and had a way with men. Tall, with a slight stoop and a benevolent air, he could easily be taken for a scholarly man. He paid liberally for favors and was a friend of the unfortunate. From his headquarters at No. 11 Astor Hotel he exercised a political control that some presidents might envy; here the state patronage was dispensed, and slates of scheming politicians were smashed.[3]

Weed and Seward had been allies since 1830, and through Weed's influence Seward had become governor and senator. Greeley's *Tribune* had also been of great assistance to the Auburn leader. But in 1854 Greeley resigned as junior partner of the "firm" of Seward, Weed, and Greeley. For all his labors Greeley had never been rewarded with public office, and when the coveted lieutenant governorship was not awarded him, he wrote Seward a petulant complaint and thereafter became his political foe, supporting Frémont for the presidential nomination in 1856. Why Seward did not reward him no one can now say.[4]

Seward's prospects brightened greatly after the Rochester speech on the "irrepressible conflict" focused attention upon his candidacy.

But he had other opponents than Greeley within his own party. Some of the former Democrats who had joined the Republican party could not forget that he had been a Whig; others disliked his early opposition to the Know-Nothings; still others resented his intimacy with Weed. Radicals like Wendell Phillips doubted the sincerity of his anti-slavery speeches; conservatives were alarmed by his prediction of the "irrepressible conflict." How serious the disaffection might be was unknown at the time of the Chicago national convention.

Evarts was among the many Americans who believed the party would rally to Seward at Chicago.[5] Even Greeley conceded that he would probably be nominated. In April Evarts was honored with the chairmanship of the New York delegation, which was pledged to Seward and determined to see him named. There were seventy delegates, among them William Curtis Noyes and John A. King. Weed had made a tactical error in not including Greeley, who managed to appear as delegate from Oregon. The delegates varied from such idealists as George William Curtis to prize fighters and ward bosses like Tom Hyer. Perhaps Evarts was made chairman to offset the unsavory reputation of some of them.

Gay and confident, they rode west on the Michigan Central with Seward flags flying. At each of the several stops the inhabitants turned out in large numbers with brass bands and cannon. Evarts and several others made brief speeches from the train. "Everybody felt fraternal," wrote the *Herald* reporter. "Moses H. Grinnell and Tom Hyer, Matthias Green and William Evarts, outsiders and insiders, all ate the same luxuriant sandwich, swallowed the same quart of dust, were singed with the same cinders, enjoyed the same festive doughnut, nibbled the same African cracker, gnawed the juicy railway-station beef, hung in epicurean delight over the delicious pie, and exerted their imaginative faculties upon the rural coffee and provincial whiskey. It was a touching, dusty scene. All your famous equalizers—dirt and politics, hunger and thirst—did the work of fraternization, and extremes touched."[6] In Chicago a huge crowd was on hand to welcome the dust-covered politicians.

Although it was generally believed that Seward would be nominated, a strong undercurrent against him was already manifest. Conservatives and Radicals were putting their heads together. The Pennsylvanians had promised the Illinois delegates to support Lincoln for vice-president in return for votes for Cameron for president. Greeley was working for Bates of Missouri, and the Ohio men for Chase. But Weed was in high feather, managing the perfect New York machine, with Governor Morgan and Henry J. Raymond as his lieutenants and Evarts as spokesman. At his headquarters at the Richmond House he talked confidently of Seward's nomination, claiming that his opponents could not unite. He treated Chicago to mammoth processions, orators, bands—all to manufacture enthusiasm for Seward. But the young Wisconsin delegate, Carl Schurz, was not the only Seward adherent who felt his enthusiasm chilled by this display, by the inexhaustible supply of cigars and champagne, and by the behavior of Tom Hyer, who headed the professional applauders.[7]

The Seward men realized that all was not well. They heard delegates, supposedly loyal, argue that the New Yorker's nomination would mean party suicide in November.[8] For the first time Evarts realized the possibility of defeat. He saw contingents thousands strong carrying torches and banners for "Old Abe." He admired Lincoln, but had no acquaintance with him and did not believe that the West could produce the right man for such perilous times.

The delegates assembled in the Wigwam, a large, ugly, hastily-built structure, capable of seating ten to fifteen thousand people and filled to capacity by an excited throng. The first day was spent in organizing. The Seward forces were hopeful of nominating their candidate on the second day; but when for some reason the clerks reported that they had not been provided with tally sheets for recording the votes, the convention adjourned.

That night the opposition forces were very busy. Greeley was on the point of throwing up the sponge; but his adherents, particularly David Dudley Field, insisted that all was not lost. The editor went from one caucus room to another at the Tremont House, seeking to form alignments that would stop Seward. Much was done to harmonize antagonistic elements, and several delegations were convinced that Seward could not carry their states in November. Evarts and Weed became disturbed as news of defections reached them. Weed even telegraphed a cipher message warning Seward to be prepared for disaster.[9]

As chairman of the New York delegation, Evarts had the privilege of nominating Seward on the third day. Since the modern custom of making nominating speeches was unknown, this gave him no opportunity to address the convention. The other nominations followed rapidly—Lincoln, Wade, Cameron, Bates, McLean, Reed, Chase, Dayton, Sumner, Frémont, and Collamer—a total of twelve candidates. Office-seekers in the gallery shouted vociferously at every mention of their favorite's name.

During the balloting Evarts worked strenuously. In *Twenty Years of Congress* James G. Blaine describes his activities: "Seldom if ever in the whole field of political oratory have the speeches of Mr. Evarts at Chicago been equaled. . . . He pleaded for the Republic, for the party that could save it, for the great statesman who founded the party and knew where and how to lead it. He spoke as one friend to another, and the great career of Mr. Seward was never so illumined as by the brilliant painting of Mr. Evarts."[10]

Delegates of the first two states, California and Connecticut, went for Seward and brought a great cheer; but when Illinois cast the first vote for Lincoln, the applause became a whirlwind and the Wigwam rocked with enthusiasm. Evarts' face whitened, but he hid his emotions. His hopes rose when it became apparent that no one would win on the first ballot. Indeed, there was still a chance for Seward, who led with 173½ votes to 102 for Lincoln, with the other votes scattered. Since 233 were needed to win, there appeared the possibility of a long deadlock.

But the opposition to Seward rapidly grew. Lincoln's supporters urged that their candidate would be stronger with the electorate;

and a sudden shift of Pennsylvania to Lincoln on the second ballot was a stunning blow. The vote on this ballot stood 184½ for Seward to 181 for Lincoln. Amid terrific tension, the third ballot was taken, resulting in a stampede to Lincoln, who received 231½ against only 180 for Seward. The Illinoisan needed two more votes. Then the chairman of the Ohio delegation rose to announce a change of four votes from Chase to Lincoln, giving him the nomination. A cannon roared the news of the Middle West's triumph.[11]

It was a crushing blow to the Seward men. Weed burst into tears. Evarts gamely rose to his feet, quicker than a score of others who sought recognition, and made his way forward. Mounting the secretary's table, with evidence of great emotion, his lip quivering, his face sad, he said: "The State of New York by a full delegation, with complete unanimity of purpose at home, came to this convention and presented for its choice one of its citizens, who served the State from boyhood up, who labored for it and loved it. We came from a great State, with, as we thought, a great statesman, and our love for the great Republic, from which we are all delegates, the great American Union, and our love for our statesman and candidate, made us think that we did our duty to our country and the whole country in expressing our love and preference for him. For, gentlemen, it was from Governor Seward that most of us learned to love Republican principles and the Republican party. His fidelity to the country, the Constitution and the laws; his fidelity to the party and the principle that the majority governs; his interest in the advancement of our party to its victory, that our country may rise to its true glory, induces me to speak his sentiments, as I do, indeed, the opinion of our whole delegation, when I now move you, as I now do, that the nomination of Abraham Lincoln of Illinois, as Republican candidate for the office of Chief Magistrate of the American Union, be made unanimous."[12]

If Weed had been more discreet and if Greeley had not worked against Seward, the result might perhaps have been otherwise. As Frederic Bancroft puts it: "Lincoln's nomination was the triumph of availability and local enthusiasm, assisted by unexpected circumstances, over great merit and greater popularity."[13]

Like Seward, Evarts was deeply hurt. But as he left the Wigwam with George William Curtis, he said, "Well, Curtis, at least we have saved the Declaration of Independence."[14] He referred to the clause which Curtis had insisted upon placing in the platform, declaring that "all men are born free and equal."

Evarts did not sulk in his tent; he supported Lincoln's campaign. There was much to be done, for Lincoln was little known in New York. One is astonished to read in the *Herald* just after the nomination the following description: "Abram Lincoln is an uneducated man—a vulgar village politician, without any experience worth mentioning in the practical duties of statesmanship, and only noted for some very unpopular votes which he gave while a member of Congress. In politics he is as rabid an abolitionist as John Brown himself, but without the old man's courage."[15]

A month after his return from Chicago, Evarts, together with Curtis and General Nye, spoke at a great Republican rally in Cooper Union. Greeley appeared on the platform, greeted by cheers and hisses. R. M. Blatchford, who presided, said in introducing Evarts: "When William M. Evarts mounted the table with a convulsive heaving of the chest, with sorrow in his heart and with tears in his eye, and made that beautiful speech, I would rather have made it than to have been the author of Anthony's speech over the dead body of Caesar." Reviewing the work of the convention, Evarts revealed that Seward could have been nominated for vice-president if the New York delegation had not believed that this would weaken the ticket. "The principles of Seward were the principles of Lincoln," he declared. "We are going to see to it that the Republican strength of 1856 and 1858 is exhibited in an enlarged and vehement volume in the vote of 1860."[16]

Early in August, Seward, Weed, Blatchford, and other Republican leaders visited Windsor to urge that Evarts take an active part in the campaign. It is probable that he was asked at this time to become a candidate for the vacancy created in the Senate by Seward's resignation.[17] It was at Auburn, Seward's home, that Evarts delivered his principal speech of the summer. The *Times* gave the address its entire front page. It was a well-reasoned statement of the political situation, conservative, irresistible in logic, and vivid in imagery. An audience of ten thousand listened intently for two hours.

The issue, asserted Evarts, was liberty and union. The Abolitionists stood for liberty at the expense of union; the Breckinridge Democrats for slavery and disunion; the Bell followers subordinated liberty to union; but the Republicans stood for liberty *and* union. "It is a monstrous absurdity that a government which rules a territory does not include dominion over slaves"; however, that was a matter for the Supreme Court. "The real sectionalism of this country," he concluded, "is the predominance of a particular interest that seeks its own aggrandizement. . . . Our fathers planted this tree of constitutional liberty to flourish forever, to dominate with its protecting shade over the whole continent, from ocean to ocean, to be a shelter from generation to generation of men that should be true to the principles of liberty . . . but I tell you that it has not produced as good fruit of late as it used to do. It is not anything you do to the boughs, but it is stirring up the roots and extending the free soil from which they must derive their nourishment that it is to reproduce and amplify forever the growth, the beauty, the flower and fruit which belongs to its nature."[18]

Evarts presided when Seward made his last speech of the campaign in the ballroom of the Palace Garden on Fourteenth Street. Some six thousand people had squeezed into the inadequate hall, while others surged about the entrance. Seward was late, and Evarts had an uncomfortable time allaying the impatience of the audience. He tried to introduce other speakers, but the crowd clamored for Seward. There were some shouts for Greeley, but Evarts would not heed them. Seward was finally greeted with a great ovation and delivered a spirited denunciation of the South. A spectator might well have believed that he was the candidate. At the close, the

Wide-Awakes were on hand with torchlights to escort him to his hotel.[19]

Lincoln carried New York by five thousand, and Edwin D. Morgan became governor. The situation immediately became more acute. The press might find space on the front page for international prize fights and the visit of Prince Albert, but secession was the absorbing topic. Evarts, up to his ears in important litigations, was deeply disturbed. He realized that the crisis had come and was ready to stand with Seward for the Union. When news of the great drought in Kansas and the sufferings of the free-soilers reached New York, he led in the creation of a committee to raise money and supplies for the stricken area. He refused to join some of the business men in a move for conciliation with the South. He was willing to repeal the personal liberty acts because they violated national law, but he would make no further concessions.[20]

Presiding over the annual dinner of the New England Society in December, which lacked its usual festive spirit, Evarts said: "While wisdom lasts, be sure the days will not be shortened, nor the wealth of territory impaired, of the great American Republic which has succeeded to the lesser Puritan Commonwealth." With grim humor Evarts explained that Mayor Wood was not present because "he had taken a wife and could not come." The toast to President Buchanan was coldly received, as was also a letter from John Botts of Virginia pleading for conciliation. Unexpectedly, Seward and Hannibal Hamlin, the vice presidential candidate, stalked in before the meeting was over and were greeted with great applause. "No more important meeting than this New England dinner has taken place for a long time," declared the *Herald*. "It may well be called . . . a revolutionary banquet."[21]

All this time political ambition was growing in Evarts, for the opportunity to succeed Seward in the Senate fascinated him. His friends were urging him to seek the office; Rockwood Hoar begged him to seize this opportunity to help uphold the laws and Constitution against Southern attack. Evarts hesitated. He wrote Dana that he was being "floated" from his "safe moorings in the law and carried off on the uncertain tide of politics. . . . A wife and nine children ought to save a man, yet John Rogers died at the stake. I cannot keep my head clear of the subject anyway, and am obliged to talk more or less every day about affairs and prospects." He finally announced his candidacy on January 1, 1861.[22]

He was well qualified for the office—a lawyer of rare ability, a leading Republican, an excellent debater and speaker, accustomed to the best society, and always a welcome figure on public occasions. He possessed nearly every gift and grace that nature could bestow. But there were drawbacks; he was not a politician in the usual sense; he had never sat in a legislative body; and still more important, he was too independent to please the political bosses.

Although an overwhelming Republican majority sat in both houses of the legislature, it was divided into Weed and Greeley factions. Weed's recent pronouncement in favor of compromise with the South, together with Greeley's eagerness for revenge upon Weed, had increased the split, setting the scene for a bitter feud, with the senatorship as the prize and Weed's long dictatorship hanging in the balance. Evarts was thus precipitated into a fierce factional dispute. Greeley was his chief opponent; of the other candidates only Judge Harris, a Lincoln supporter, whose hopes lay in a split between Evarts and Greeley, was dangerous.

Three weeks before the election Evarts was unquestionably the favorite. But this fact led Greeley and Harris to concentrate their fire upon him. They circulated copies of his Castle Garden speech of 1850 to prove that he was for compromise, while Evarts' friends retaliated by circulating copies of his Broadway Tabernacle speech of 1856 and his argument in the Lemmon Slave Case. But the main difficulty lay in Evarts' independent attitude. He would not solicit votes. He left that to Weed.[23]

A week before the election Weed became discouraged by the growing opposition. But Evarts' friends came to the rescue, pushing his candidacy so vigorously during the next few days that Weed took heart. He summoned his lieutenants from all over the state, including the Republican State Committee, and Evarts found himself supported by as skillful a corps of managers as could be found. Among them were Simeon Draper, Robert T. Haws, Moses H. Grinnell, and A. Oakey Hall. A wave of minor office-holders poured in from every corner of the state. It is estimated, declared the hostile *Tribune,* "that the whole number of men collected from all parts of the State for Mr. Evarts for the purpose of influencing, dragooning, and controlling the members of the Legislature in his behalf during the past week has not been less than one thousand. . . . Never were the halls and parlors of the hotels or the lobbies of the Legislature thronged with such a feverish and intense activity."[24] As a result, Evarts once more became the favorite in the race. But the Greeleyites, led by Charles A. Dana, and inspired by the slogan, "Down With the Dictator," were capturing both those who could expect nothing from Weed, and those independents who hated bosses. They circulated a report that Lincoln preferred Greeley, which it was difficult to explode before the balloting began.[25]

Three days before the caucus the contest was at fever heat. Both sides radiated confidence, but actually were nervous, striving to win over some twenty-five doubtful legislators. Like a pendulum the contest wavered back and forth. Evarts was busy at Congress Hall, sending out agents chosen by Weed. The political bee had stung him hard, and he was out to win—but only if he could do so fairly. A. Oakey Hall relates that at a meeting of the Evarts men the day before the caucus, a plan was proposed to bring pressure by the discreet use of money; but Simeon Draper objected. "No use, gentlemen," he said, "for if it were done and successful, such are the supremacy of Mr. Evarts' principles, that when he discovered the means, he would not accept."[26]

Seldom had such excitement been witnessed in Albany as on that Saturday night when one hundred and sixteen Republicans met to nominate. The lobbies and galleries of the caucus chamber were filled with agents and spectators. They even swarmed out upon the main floor, where they did not belong. Though Evarts felt sure of victory, his foes were confidently betting he would lose. He sat quietly smoking with Weed and Governor Morgan in the executive chamber. To win it was necessary to poll fifty-nine votes. On the first ballot Evarts had forty-two, Greeley forty, Harris twenty, and thirteen were scattered. Weed, intensely nervous, issued rapid orders to his agents, who were hurrying back and forth to the caucus chamber, and became still more excited when the second ballot was taken. This time Greeley had forty-two, Evarts had fallen to thirty-nine, and Harris had risen to twenty-two. On hearing the result Weed sent a message asking Harris to drop out, but without result. The Harris men would have thrown their votes to Greeley anyway. Five more ballots were cast without a break in the deadlock. On the eighth ballot Greeley jumped to forty-seven, with Evarts still at thirty-nine. It then dawned on Weed that the faithful lieutenants upon whom he had relied in many successful battles, had, like himself, been duped, and he asked Evarts whether he should throw his votes to Harris. Evarts requested one more ballot. It showed no change, but it was rumored that the Harris men had decided to throw their votes to Greeley on the next ballot. Pale and trembling, Weed called his agents. "Tell the Evarts men to go right over to Harris," he said. The order was carried out and Harris was elected.

In any ordinary campaign Weed's powerful organization could not have been defeated; but this was no ordinary fight. The manoeuvre which defeated him and Evarts had taken place the night before, when twenty legislators pledged themselves to Greeley, and each promised to convert another. Although these forty votes failed to give Greeley the senatorship, they created a balance which won for Harris. The smashing of the Weed machine was the great object of the opposition, and in that sense the nomination was a repetition of what had happened in Chicago. Greeley might rejoice at his revenge, but he really wanted the senatorship. He was never kind to Evarts thereafter, constantly criticizing him in the columns of the *Tribune*.[28]

Evarts had fallen a victim to the Weed-Greeley feud. It was his misfortune that he made the greatest effort of his life for public office at the very hour the Weed machine collapsed. His disappointment was keen. He blamed his defeat upon Weed's inopportune attempt to conciliate the South at a moment when the threat of Charleston's guns was rousing the fury of the North. This, said Evarts, "combined with envies and jealousies of some of my *seniors,* who thought my elevation too sudden for me, an instinctive activity of all dishonest and corrupt interests to oppose me & some local feelings," were the causes of defeat.[29] Like Erskine, the great English lawyer, he had lost an election because a party earthquake occurred at the time of a national emergency.

He had learned to meet the sting of defeat at Chicago, and did not brood unduly over it. It was no time for brooding. A war was at hand. He appeared at the second annual "festival" of the Republicans at the Astor House soon afterward, and speaking in an atmosphere charged with excitement, called for action against the seceding states and declared that "the pacification of the country" was the principal duty of the incoming administration.[30]

His defeat for the Senate proved providential, for a seat in that body would not have offered him the best opportunity for service in wartime. Nor would his pocketbook easily have permitted him to exchange his professional income for the salary of a senator. Just as fate seemed to deal him a hard blow, the national crisis afforded him new opportunities of service for his country at home and abroad. The news of Sumter opened a new chapter in his career.

8

Defender of the Union

GRAVE DOUBT existed as to the course which the government of New York City would take just after the firing on Fort Sumter. Mayor Fernando Wood sympathized with the secessionists. "I was one of five men," Evarts related years after, "that on Tuesday after the firing on Sumter met in a private office in Pine Street to feel the pulse of the people, and to call a public meeting, and we did not know whether we dared to do it, lest the fewness of the number should be counted and the game be lost; and then we did not dare take the Academy of Music, for fear our shrunken columns would display the poorness of the patriotism of New York."[1]

But the patriotism of the vast majority of New Yorkers quickly asserted itself. "Not for fifty years," declared the *Times* on April 16, "has such a spectacle been seen as that glorious uprising of American loyalty which greeted the news that open war had been commenced upon the Constitution and the Government of the United States. . . . Party dissensions were instantly hushed; political differences instantly disappeared. . . . Men ceased to think of themselves or their parties—they thought of their country and of the dangers which menaced its existence."[2]

On the morning of Thursday, April 18, the Sixth Massachusetts Regiment arrived from Boston on its way to protect Washington. It breakfasted at the Astor House. A huge crowd was on hand to watch it depart. The troops poured out of the hotel, amid dead silence, and even the command, "March" could be plainly heard;

but when the band struck up *Yankee Doodle,* the pent-up enthusiasm broke into a great roar. Down Broadway they marched, with the Colonel, the Mayor, and Evarts at their head, while an endless surging cheer followed them. Describing the event in after years, Evarts said, "We thought we would see whether United States soldiers would be interfered with in New York. We met them at the station. We marched them down Broadway to the ferry. . . . There was no trouble, nothing but cheers."[3]

A great patriotic mass meeting was needed. Some thirty prominent men—among them Evarts, Hamilton Fish, John A. Dix, Peter Cooper, Simeon Draper, R. M. Blatchford, and William Allen Butler—planned it for the twentieth. Evarts circulated a subscription to raise funds to send the Seventh Regiment to Washington, and more than three thousand dollars was immediately pledged. Meanwhile, news of the attack on the Sixth Massachusetts Regiment by a Baltimore mob aroused feeling to a fiery pitch. At least two hundred thousand people filled Union Square and the adjoining streets on the twentieth. The buildings were decked with bunting; five stands had been erected for orators; bands were playing; and the heroes of Fort Sumter added a touch of grimness to the scene. Evarts was one of twenty orators. "I regard this," he said, "as a business meeting, commencing the greatest transaction this generation has ever seen. . . . A question for us to decide is whether we are worthy children . . . and whether our descendants shall curse us as we bless our fathers. You are here to write a history which your children will glory in."[4]

The overwhelming response to the speeches resulted in the appointment of a Union Defense Committee to aid the government in prosecuting the war. It comprised twenty-one members, with John A. Dix chairman and Evarts secretary. Its first meeting on the twenty-second appointed a Committee of Correspondence, including Evarts, Fish, Pierrepont, and Cisco, to communicate with federal and state authorities. The Union Defense Committee was essentially an emergency organization to hurry troops and supplies to the battle area. Within a short time it accomplished wonders, not hesitating to adopt any measure that seemed necessary.[5]

Governor Morgan also appointed Evarts, Blatchford, Grinnell, and George D. Morgan as a special commission with extraordinary powers to act as adjunct of the War and Navy Departments in organizing regiments and forwarding supplies. To obtain direct authority from the government, Evarts, Pierrepont, and Weed set off for Washington on a hazardous trip by boat and rail and accomplished their purpose.[6]

Evarts' service on the Union Defense Committee brought him in close contact with Hamilton Fish, who succeeded Dix as chairman in May. The two men were already well acquainted. Fish lived only a few blocks from Evarts on Second Avenue near Ninth Street, and Evarts had visited him in his summer home at Garrison-on-the-Hudson. When, in June, ugly rumors of scandal became current, Fish threatened to resign from the committee. Evarts begged him to remain, and he did, on condition that its work no longer be kept secret.

The committee armed, equipped, and transported troops. It placed in the field sixty-six regiments; it chartered steamers, one of which captured eight Southern vessels; it furnished relief to many families. As the emergency lessened during the summer of 1862, its work was taken over by the federal government.[7]

Meanwhile Evarts was retained by the government to prosecute the celebrated case of the *Savannah* privateers, the first to bring into the courts the questions of secession and the belligerent rights of the South. It was the type of case in which Evarts was at his best. The Confederate privateer *Savannah* had left Charleston in May, 1861, had captured one Northern merchant vessel, but was herself captured in June by the Union warship *Perry*. Her arrival in New York brought crowds to the Battery. The crew of thirteen "pirates" were taunted as they were paraded through the streets to the Tombs, and a demand arose that they be hanged.[8]

The government was embarrassed. The United States had always permitted privateering in wartime and had not joined with other nations in the Declaration of Paris of 1856 abolishing it. Seward had offered to adhere to the Declaration in 1861, but withdrew from this position when Europe appeared unfriendly. Lincoln's proclamation declaring Confederate privateers to be pirates, and therefore subject to the death penalty, could obviously not be applied without risk of bloody reprisals. The Earl of Derby declared in the House of Lords that privateering was not piracy, that international law never so regarded it, and that the United States could not claim belligerent rights for itself while denying them to the Confederacy. But Lincoln was determined and the North supported him. Feeling in the South was intense. A Charleston paper declared that if such prisoners were hanged, every Northerner that fell into Confederate hands would be subject to a similar fate, and Jefferson Davis notified Lincoln that retaliation would follow.[9]

In October the case came to trial in the Circuit Court before Judges Nelson and Shipman. Many lawyers were attracted by the unusual issue, and a great crowd came to catch sight of the "pirates." These spectators manifested a keen interest in the counsel. For the government appeared Evarts, District Attorney E. Delafield Smith, Samuel Blatchford, and Ethan Allen.[10] The two first-named were old friends. Some years before, when Smith was corporation counsel, Evarts was surprised to find him in Dr. Hall's church one Sunday morning, singing with all his heart. Whispering to a friend, Evarts said, "Why, there is Smith singing 'I want to be an angel.' I knew he wanted to be district attorney, but I didn't know he wanted to be an angel." The remark was later repeated to Smith, who retorted, "No, I have never mentioned the matter to Evarts, knowing that he had no influence in that direction."[11]

The defense lawyers were Daniel Lord, James T. Brady, and J. Larocque. Lord had been a Yale classmate of the father of one of the crew. Brady, who appeared for Captain Baker of the *Savannah,* took the leading part in the defense. This popular Irish lawyer, of ardent, poetic, generous nature, was the Chevalier Bayard of the bar, the delight of audiences and juries. He dealt mainly with the criminal law, and his forte was trying desperate cases from which other lawyers shrank. He lacked the steady application of O'Conor or Evarts, but in his peculiar field was more effective than they, and during his thirty-four years at the bar he saved fifty-one men from the gallows. In defending the *Savannah* prisoners he was at his best.[12]

The indictment was brought under the Federal Act of 1790, punishing piracy and robbery on the high seas with death. The evidence was not disputed, the defense freely admitting the facts. The question was whether the prisoners were absolved from allegiance to the United States by acting under the commission issued by Jefferson Davis. This question, in turn, depended on the larger issue of the right of secession or revolution. It required an exploration of the whole field of political philosophy and the nature of the federal government.

Brady's position resembled that of John Adams in defending the British soldiers after the Boston Massacre. He contended that the crew, acting in good faith under the commission of Jefferson Davis and seeking only to capture prizes under the rules of war, were not personally responsible. As for the right of secession, he said, "I reach the conclusion that the *power* to secede and the *power* to organize a Government existing, there is no power on earth which, on any rule of law, can interfere with it, except that of war, conducted on the principles of civilized war." France and England had recognized Confederate belligerency; Lincoln himself in 1848 had asserted that a people had the right of revolution if a government did not suit them. The act of 1790 applied only to American citizens, and four of the privateersmen had never been citizens. In short, a war existed and privateersmen had the right to use force without being called pirates.[13]

When Evarts rose to reply, he had the advantage of a friendly audience. He had taken but a small part in the early phase of the trial, having been retained only the day before it began. He spoke the greater part of two days, seven and one-half hours altogether. This was too long an argument; and though he gave a masterly summary of the rights of the government, it was far above the level of the average jury, rather befitting the Supreme Court. He spoke with his usual ease, deliberation, and fairness. Though he lacked the physical grace of Brady, he presented a better-reasoned argument.[14]

The motive of the prisoners, he said, was "robbery at sea" with a view to personal gain and profit, not patriotism for the Confederacy. The fact that some of them were not citizens was evidence of this fact. Since the government had not recognized the belligerent rights of the Confederacy, the courts could not do so. The prisoners could not shield themselves behind a Confederate commission, because the law of 1790 expressly denied that rebellion could be pleaded as a defense against piracy.

The right of secession and revolution, continued Evarts, was no defense. Secession was "utterly inconsistent with the theory of our government, and utterly unimportant, as a practical right, for any supposable or even imaginable case." No state could leave the Union; and, added Evarts, "I once heard from the lips of Mr. Calhoun himself this recognition." The American Revolution had rested upon a long train of specific grievances, whereas the South possessed only the two unsound claims that it no longer had majority control and that Congress had encroached upon slavery. The conviction of the prisoners need not result in their death, for the President could pardon them. But acquittal would mean an overthrow of the will and power of the government.[15]

Judge Nelson believed the prisoners guilty under the law of 1790. The jury and spectators listened breathlessly for a half-hour as he delivered his charge to the jury. One juror asked him whether a civil war was to be held as existing and whether the prisoners were to be considered as having taken property for their own use; to which the judge answered in the negative. After an all-night session, the jury failed to agree, with eight for conviction and four for acquittal. Some jurors felt that the death penalty was too harsh; others were influenced by Brady's argument; perhaps Jefferson Davis' threat to execute an equal number of Union prisoners had some influence.[16] It was a fortunate outcome, for Lincoln's theory could not have been enforced easily.

Evarts had no reason to feel downcast. With law, precedent, and common sense against him, he had done well to win over eight of the jurors. He declared afterwards, "I had seven counsel with seven separate speeches against me, and I had to reply (1) for the prosecution, (2) for the Government, (3) for the Republican party, (4) for the Free States, (5) for the Nation, (6) for the principles of constitutional Government, (7) for the human race, and all this though I had a fee for only one of those interests." To the district attorney, to whom he submitted his bill for $1,250, he wrote: "You are so well aware of the great burden of responsibility of this trial to those who acted for the Government against the most numerous array of able counsel I have ever known combined in any cause, that I need say nothing as to the reasonableness of the charge. . . . The sum I have named is not more than half what I should charge a private client for professional services of equal labor and responsibility."[17]

The labor in this case, together with other duties, so exhausted Evarts that he was confined to his house for a week—a most unusual experience for him. His willingness to submit to additional responsibilities during the first year of the war seemed to leave him no peace at all.[18]

The gloomiest year of the war, 1862, was one of added burdens. The future seemed dark. McClellan was preparing the Army of the Potomac, but refused to strike at Lee. Evarts tried to be optimistic at the New England Society dinner in December, 1861. "Let us never doubt," he declared, "we will have adequate energies to secure this continent to liberty."[19] But the feeling spread that the war was not being conducted with proper vigor.

Evarts shared in this feeling. He looked with misgiving upon Lincoln's inexperience, doubting his ability to meet the crisis. He believed that Seward, the Secretary of State, should take charge, and wrote him confidentially: "A chafing people, a Congress filled with malcontents and empty of leaders, a Cabinet with disturbed plans and purposes, a long accustomed freedom from any sharply critical situations in our foreign affairs, [are] hard to handle. . . . I hope you will feel strong enough to attempt what I am sure your friends feel as important to the completeness of your fame in the history of the 'Great Rebellion' some Clarendon is to write . . . the formation of a public-spirited Cabinet, framed to the issues that have come in *since* the election. The whole country is longing for this."[20]

When it seemed likely that Gideon Welles would resign as head of the Navy Department, Evarts urged Seward to have Richard Henry Dana appointed. He meanwhile wrote Dana in criticism of Lincoln: "It has been a fixed opinion with me from the beginning that the conduct of this affair *must* come into the hands of a younger man between 50 and 60 years of age."[21] To Weed, who was in Europe, he wrote, "Governor Seward and diplomacy have thus far carried away all the credit which has fallen to anybody in the disastrous course which our affairs have taken." Weed agreed, replying, "I am sure this war wisely entered upon and energetically carried on, would have been virtually concluded now."[22]

But although Evarts distrusted the administration, he did not air his views in public. He supported the government loyally at mass meetings and rallies. Just after Grant's victories at Forts Henry and Donelson, he addressed an excited mass meeting at Cooper Institute. Old General Scott appeared, and was given a great ovation. Evarts exhorted the government to a more vigorous prosecution of the war and compared the Confederates to the mutinous half of a crew who were willing to sink the ship in order to get their half. Upholding Lincoln's use of the war powers, he remarked, "It is always constitutional, in the human frame, when fever or disease invades it, to meet the enemy by the most vigorous poisons, that would be unconstitutional in time of health." The same night, at a Republican rally at Irving Hall, with Greeley and Raymond as the other speakers, Evarts declared, *"War,* to sustain the Constitution, however different from peace in its *methods,* is just as constitutional." He added a slap at profiteers: "Next to the crime of taking money to betray your country, in its danger, is the offense of extorting money for defending it in its necessity."[23]

When, on the night of May 16, the Academy of Music was packed from floor to dome to hear the radical Tennessee editor, Parson Brownlow, Evarts took the place of Governor Morgan as presiding officer. But he could not subscribe to the radical parson's desire to "lick England and France," and exterminate all Southerners after the war.[24]

Evarts' speeches were patriotic, not political. He had no time for politics. Manton Marble could not interest him in establishing a new journalistic mouthpiece for Thurlow Weed. Indeed, when he came back from Europe in 1863, Weed retired from politics. Nor was Evarts at all interested that summer in the talk in Democratic and conservative Republican circles of making him candidate for lieutenant governor on the ticket with Seymour.[25]

While he was giving time, money, and labor to the war, his wife was active in the formation of the Women's Central Association of Relief. Speaking of women's part in the war, he later said that they "had all of the heroism of the men, for whatever of toil and hardship the men bore, the women bore; for the women bore the men."[26]

In still other ways Evarts served the cause. He presided at the initial meeting which launched the New England Soldiers' Relief Association and became its president. Its purposes were "to provide the necessary means, and to provide suitable care, attendance, and accommodations for the sick, disabled, and wounded New England soldiers, as they pass through the city on their way homeward from war." The Association, which coöperated with Dr. Bellows, head of the United States Sanitary Commission, was especially active during the spring of 1862. Soldiers were provided with sleeping quarters, food, clothing, and medical attendance at 194 Broadway. During the first year and a half it ministered to some twenty-eight hundred needy soldiers. Evarts was most active during the initial stage of organization. He also furnished Dr. Bellows with legal advice in the dissolution of the Sanitary Commission at the end of the war.[27]

Evarts was one of the original sixty-seven members of the Union League Club of New York. Though he had little time for participation in its political and relief work, he frequented its headquarters in the Jerome Mansion at Madison Avenue and Twenty-Third Street. When Jay Cooke launched a drive for a new branch of the national bank, he presided at the supper given to the committee in charge and assisted in the drive.[28]

Meanwhile he was retained by the government in the famous Prize Cases. These were not a criminal prosecution like the *Savannah* Privateers Case, but precipitated a struggle over constitutional law in the Supreme Court. The cases arose from the capture and condemnation in prize court of Confederate blockade-runners. Evarts seemed unusually fortunate in being retained in such prominent cases; indeed, no other American lawyer enjoyed so many opportunities for distinction in the great public cases of the period from 1861 to 1877.

He represented the government from the very outset in the Prize Cases. The blockade-runner *Hiawatha* was brought into New York and other prizes into prize courts in Florida and Massachusetts. As the district attorney was engaged elsewhere, Evarts was retained in the condemnation proceedings, which he won in the District Court. Similar decisions were rendered in the case of the other vessels, and thus the government confiscated property of great value. The claimants appealed, and Evarts, appearing in the Circuit Court, won another verdict from Judge Nelson. Reporting the result to Attorney General Bates, Evarts wrote: "The controversy in these cases has been maintained, on the part of the claimants, with great vigor and ability, through a numerous array of counsel, including among them our most eminent lawyers. I am quite convinced the views of the relations of the Government to the Rebellion . . . which I have had occasion to present . . . are the correct exposition of the public law. I am sure that the importance to the Government . . . of maintaining these views cannot be over-estimated."[29]

It was evidently Seward who prevailed upon Bates to retain Evarts in four cases which were now lumped together and appealed to the Supreme Court for final settlement. Evarts had seldom appeared before this tribunal and was anxious to do well. He was gratified to find that Dana, who had won a prize case in Massachusetts, was his colleague.[30] Dana made a great argument—some thought the best of his career.

Daniel Lord proved to be the leader of the defense. He took the position that the vessels had been captured in 1861 before Congress officially declared war; that the President's declaration of a blockade was not tantamount to war; and that there could hence be no valid blockade or prize jurisdiction.[31]

In the *Savannah* case Evarts had argued that belligerent rights did not exist and that the crew were pirates. Ironically, in the Prize Cases his task was to show war did exist and the President could declare a blockade and exert prize jurisdiction. He laid before the court an elaborate brief.[32] His two-day argument centered upon four propositions. First, he declared, when all peaceful means failed to stop a rebellion, the government could apply all warlike means to crush it. Force had to be met with force. The struggle then raging was not a private war, but a full public war. One nation could not be at war with another while the second was at peace with the first. The President was the sole judge of an emergency threatening to overthrow the government, and could decide what means should be taken to prevent it. Second, he argued, the capture of enemy prizes in a rebellion was lawful, for otherwise a Boston merchant could fit out a ship to carry contraband to Charleston. Third, captured property could be condemned without the approval of the owners. Anything carried in trade by the enemy became lawful prize. And finally, and most important, a government does not have to plead at the bar for the right to preserve its own existence. "No other Government," said Evarts, "ever urged such a plea . . . for if, in truth, the law of the Government is at variance with its power, . . . its fate can be neither uncertain nor remote."[33]

Many distinguished lawyers were present two weeks later to hear Justice Grier read the opinion of the Court. The Court held that a civil war did not have to be declared, and it vindicated Lincoln's use of war powers, including the condemnation of prizes. "They cannot ask a Court," said Grier, "to affect technical ignorance of the existence of war which all the world acknowledges to be the greatest civil war in the history of the human race, and thus cripple the arm of the Government and paralyze its power by subtle definitions and ingenious sophisms."[34] Four justices, including Chief Justice Taney, dissented, feeling that Lincoln had exceeded his powers previous to the declaration of war by Congress in July, 1861. Most jurists today would probably agree that the use of power by the President in anticipation of subsequent ratification by Congress is bad practice.

The verdict had been expected. Evarts was greatly pleased. He received a five-thousand-dollar fee.[35] But what was more important, he had enhanced his reputation as an authority on international law, thus opening the way to his appointment as counsel for the government in questions of neutrality abroad.

9

Legal Agent Abroad

LINCOLN and Seward were much worried by what most Americans regarded as Great Britain's unfriendly neutrality during the war. As early as 1861 they felt it necessary to send agents abroad to counteract the propaganda of energetic Confederate agents. Archbishop Hughes of New York, Bishop McIlvaine of Ohio, and Thurlow Weed were hurried to England or France to make speeches, contribute to the press, or sell United States bonds. William H. Aspinwall and John M. Forbes were sent to purchase two ironclads known to be under construction at Laird's shipyard; but they found the situation unfavorable, and had to avoid any steps which might prejudice the American cause.[1]

The government had two classes of foreign agents. First, there were those sent by some department of the government to accomplish a specific purpose and roving diplomats like Thurlow Weed irregularly accredited by the State Department. This group was of high character. Second, and of more dubious value, were the "poaching diplomat," accredited to some government, but seeking a wider field of activity, and the "volunteer diplomat," not accredited at all, who assumed himself to have a divine mission.[2]

When in March, 1863, Seward heard that the *Florida,* built in Great Britain, had gone to sea and captured the American merchantman *Jacob Bell,* with a cargo valued at a million and a half dollars, he told the American minister, Charles Francis Adams, that the incident portended the destruction of the whole American merchant marine. On learning a few weeks later that the *Alexandra,* another Confederate cruiser, was nearly ready to leave Liverpool, and that still others were being built, he instructed Adams to try judicial proceedings to prevent the departure of the vessels.[3]

Seward felt that someone with a comprehensive understanding of neutral rights should be sent to advise Adams upon legal technicalities. He telegraphed Evarts on April 12 to come immediately. As a result of this conference, Evarts found himself a week later aboard ship for England as special agent of the State Department, with instructions "to institute nothing and do nothing except what he [Adams] might think it useful for him to do" and to win as many friends abroad as possible.[4]

Evarts carried letters of introduction to British leaders and statesmen, including Earl Spencer, Lord Cavendish, Sir John Coleridge, Anthony Trollope, Lord Monteagle, Sir Henry Holland, the Archbishop of Canterbury, the Bishop of London, Thomas Baring, Richard Cobden, John Bright, William E. Gladstone, Baron Rothschild, Roundell Palmer, and others. George Bancroft furnished him with letters to political and literary friends. Other letters smoothed the way before his arrival. For example, Charles Sumner wrote the Duchess of Argyll: "Mr. Evarts . . . is a very eminent lawyer, without a superior in the country, and has been dispatched to do all he can, in consultation if possible with your law officers or with others, to arrest the guilty vessels. . . . He has been in public life, and is a purely professional man. I think his visit will do good; and I am so much interested in it that I shall give him a letter to the duke, and also to Mr. Gladstone."[5]

Adams did not regard Evarts' presence as an interference. On the contrary, he believed that it would relieve him of technical legal questions. He received the newcomer cordially and put him in touch immediately with those engaged in preparing evidence against the suspected vessels. Evarts felt pleased with the prospect and wrote Seward that the British government seemed to feel its responsibility to remain neutral.[6]

Evarts went to England with a high opinion of British society.

As a sophomore at Yale he had read Richard Rush's narrative of diplomatic experiences in London. Quickly becoming acquainted with many people of importance, he drove a two-horse brougham about the city to leave his card at many doors and received invitations in return. He discussed the case of the *Alexandra* with British lawyers. Sir Henry Holland, a man of seventy-five, formerly the Queen's physician, who was widely informed, fond of conversation, and much like Evarts in temperament, took a keen interest in him. They went to Parliament to hear Gladstone and Palmerston, and to Exeter Hall, where Evarts sat on the platform and listened to political speeches. "There was no halting or scraping," he recorded in his diary. "They were as glib and fluent and as free from ideas as our own."

He breakfasted with Gladstone, Mrs. Gladstone, the Bishop of Sutherland, Thackeray, and Cobden. He became intimate with Roundell Palmer, the British Attorney General; Thomas Baring, head of the famous banking house; and Thomas Hughes, author of *Tom Brown's School Days.* He seemed acceptable to all, and Cobden confided to him that his visit was already "doing good" and that the people were pleased with him. Cobden wrote Sumner: "Mr. Evarts is the right man in the right place. He is an able international lawyer; quite a match for anyone here in his own special walk. His manners are quiet and impressive. He is mixing very much in our best society and I hear him spoken of with great respect."[7]

Evarts formed a lifelong friendship with Lord Coleridge, the British Chief Justice, who liked him immensely. "He strikes me," Coleridge wrote, "as a very able man, full of good sense and moderation, and, yet, capable of putting the American case in a very strong and cogent way to our Government. . . . It certainly speaks well for Mr. Seward that he should pick out and employ such an agent. . . . I hope for the best efforts from *sensible* men on both sides of the water. . . . He [Evarts] is a little hard, perhaps, but very clever, reasonable, and a gentleman."[8]

Evarts found another intimate friend in young Henry Adams,

who was acting as secretary to his father. Although there was a difference of twenty years in their ages, another lifelong friendship was formed. Adams quickly took to Evarts, regarding him as the best of the flock of the authorized emissaries. They frequented legal circles together, discussing with British lawyers and relating anecdotes of bench and bar. They talked confidentially of the war, and of the need of political reform at home; and Adams noted that Evarts still felt the loss of the senatorship and was somewhat "soured on his political luck."[9]

"If you could have seen Evarts and me," wrote Adams to his brother after a trip to Cambridge University, "after dinner at one of the little colleges, conducting a noisy and jovial game of whist, with cigars and brandy and soda-water, and a clergyman and fellow of an adjacent college known as Jesus, for our partner, you would have smiled. . . . You recollect, no doubt, that he wears his hat so that a plumb line dropped from its center would fall about twelve inches behind his heels. His speech is Yankee and his aspect shouts American with stentorian lungs. Fortunately his conversation and his mind make up for the peculiarities of dress and appearance, so that I was always relieved when he took off his hat and opened his mouth."[10]

Evarts' enjoyment of his mission was lessened by only one irritation. Confederate agents were trying to misrepresent his relations with the American minister, while Northern busybodies talked indiscreetly. The former even went so far as to publish statements in the British press that Evarts had been sent to override Adams. For example, the London *Standard* reported, "He [Evarts] is a particular friend of W. H. Seward. The latter, it is known, has lost all confidence in Mr. Adams, who, but for his name, would have been recalled long ago"—a slander which Seward hastened to deny. Adams felt these thrusts, but his friendly relations with Evarts remained unchanged. "It cannot be denied," he wrote, "that ever since I have been here the almost incessant interference of government agents of all kinds has had the effect, however intended, of weakening the position of the minister. Most of all it happened in the case of Mr. Evarts, whom the newspapers here have all insisted to have been sent to superintend my office in all questions of international law. I doubt whether any minister ever had so much of this kind of thing to contend with."[11]

Never forgetting the main purpose of his mission in the swirl of social activities, Evarts impressed upon those whom he met the aims and position of the North in its struggle with the Confederacy. He found himself in a labyrinth of intrigue, with the attitude of those most responsible for British policy still uncertain. Palmerston appeared hostile and Lord Russell friendly, but both were unreliable; Gladstone's behavior was highly ambiguous, so that no one could tell where he stood.

But Evarts was optimistic. To John Bigelow, who had become consul-general at Paris, he wrote, "I find the government more awake to the dangers of their stickling for 'freedom of British commerce' than I had feared they would be."[12] Yet he was surprised to learn that, despite the *Trent* affair, Palmerston admired Seward. Disraeli told him the Conservative party would not make political capital out of the war. As for the ironclads that were being fitted out in Liverpool and in the Clyde, he was assured they would never go to sea. He noted that the swing of the war in favor of the North was having its effect, and that British opinion was beginning to understand more clearly the aims and resources of the North. "They begin to think it worth while," he wrote, "to consider whether the chances of our triumph do not involve uncomfortable results to them unless they are ready with a friendly reception for our success."[13]

Evarts' chief task was to give the American minister legal advice in the case of the *Alexandra.* The British government finally decided to detain the vessel and order a prosecution of the owners for breach of neutrality. In so doing, the ministry realized it would encounter opposition and incur great unpopularity if the prosecution should fail. The evidence against the steamer, which was being built at Miller's shipyard in Liverpool, made clear a hostile intent. Evarts aided the British lawyers in preparing the prosecution.[14]

The case came before Chief Baron Pollock on June 22. Contrary to expectation, the verdict was for the defendants. The whole British bar was astonished, and Evarts was chagrined. The Chief Baron charged the jury that British neutrality laws aimed to prevent hostilities in *British* waters only, and so forbade armament in port; but once outside British waters, a vessel could be armed. In other words, British shipbuilders could supply the Confederates with all the warcraft they could buy, if they were not armed within British ports.

Evarts' only hope was to secure a reversal of the decree. Since the courts had adjourned for the summer, he felt it of little use to stay in England. Most of the influential people had left London for the season. Already he had stayed longer than he had originally planned. Adams recommended that he return to America and come back to England when the courts reopened. Evarts left on July 17, breakfasting before his departure with Henry Adams, Cyrus Field, and Richard Cobden, who discussed the political situation and, as Adams put it, "fired a parting shot at Gladstone."[15]

Evarts reported to Seward, and also saw Lincoln. He urged the President to visit Europe some day and see the great men who were applauding his policies; whereupon Lincoln replied that he would feel embarrassed to meet men of such great classical learning because he had no training of the kind.[16]

Soon after his return, Evarts heard that Sir Henry Holland had come to America and was visiting George Bancroft. He asked Bancroft to bring Sir Henry to Windsor, adding, "I will show you the ignoble pen from which, in the shape of *pork,* your elegant pen has received some of its sense and strength." Sir Henry came and enjoyed Evarts' hospitality immensely.[17] Returning to England soon after, Sir Henry kept Evarts informed, telling him that Disraeli was striving for amicable relations with America.[18]

While trying to catch up with his law practice, Evarts followed British affairs closely. Although the British government had promised not to allow the ironclads to leave port, news of the *Alexandra* was not heartening. The case was brought into the Court of Exchequer, with Chief Baron Pollock again presiding. To the consternation of the government he refused to permit a re-argument, declaring that he had not charged the jury at the previous hearing as was supposed. Sir Henry doubtless hit the mark when he wrote Evarts, "The Chief Baron, whose incompetence for his place is obvious to all but himself, has been *eating up* his own words."[19] The case was closed unless another appeal was made.

In December, 1863, Evarts left New York upon his second mission, which kept him abroad five months. He found British opinion more favorable to the North. "The rebellion," he reported to Seward, "is now tiresome to the public mind. Its success has disappointed expectations, and its failure is accepted as a possible solution of the puzzle."[20] But the British government was unready to make any great change of policy. Finding no immediate action could be taken in the *Alexandra* case, Evarts went to Paris, where a new difficulty had arisen.

A few months before, a stranger had appeared at the American consulate in Paris and for 20,000 francs sold evidence to Bigelow to prove that several ships were being built for the Confederates at Nantes and Bordeaux with the permission of the French government. The matter was promptly called to the attention of Drouyn de l'Huys, French foreign minister, who expressed surprise and called the construction a breach of neutrality that would not be tolerated. It became apparent, however, that the word of Napoleon III and his foreign minister could not be relied upon, and the work on the ships continued.[21]

Seward asked Evarts to go to Paris to talk with French statesmen and lawyers, and Bigelow urged him to hurry, as the moment seemed propitious. Evarts was received cordially. Bigelow declared that he qualified for his French duties as Ezekiel did on his mission to Tel-abib, by eating.[22] Evarts realized that caution was needed, for while the complications with Great Britain were diminishing, serious trouble with France might revive European hostility. Seward had dealt sharply with Great Britain, but with France he was moderate and friendly.

Evarts' immediate object was to prevent the departure of the *Rappahannock* from Calais. This vessel had escaped from an English port in an unfinished condition, with workmen still outfitting it and had been at Calais six weeks. Dayton, the American minister, had protested, but Drouyn de l'Huys had taken no steps.[23] Evarts had already met the French foreign minister at Brussels. He was received cordially by him, and presented the facts on the *Rappahannock,* asking a pledge that the vessel be detained. He argued that the war would end speedily with a Northern victory. The foreign minister, who seemed impressed, confessed that France had violated neutrality by admitting Confederate cruisers, promised to take the same steps against them that Great Britain had taken, and engaged to make a new investigation of the *Rappahannock*.[24]

Evarts' one-hour interview apparently did some good. Drouyn de l'Huys observed his pledge, and the *Rappahannock* remained at Calais for the duration of the war. Pleased with his success, Evarts sent two suggestions to Seward. First, he recommended that Seward should seek directly from the French government a withdrawal of recognition of Confederate belligerency; and second, that several American warships should be posted in the Channel to destroy any Confederate privateers that dared emerge, thus giving France and England proof of American power on the sea.[25]

But Seward was more concerned with Great Britain, knowing that Napoleon would probably follow the British lead. He replied to Evarts: "We want to know whether, if we have a difficulty on one side of the Channel, we must expect an enemy on the other—two enemies instead of one. Circumstances favor a good understanding with the Cabinet at London. We could clear up all difficulties if Great Britain should be willing."[26]

By mid-February, 1864, Evarts was back in London, where he found that nothing more could be done in the *Alexandra* case. He also found the political situation precarious, with the ministry so sensitive to attacks upon its courage that further change in its policy toward the Confederacy would be unlikely. Any decisive alteration might overthrow it. He talked the situation over with Vernon Harcourt, an able young lawyer whose advice upon questions of international law was much relied upon by the British government. Harcourt counselled a direct demand that Confederate cruisers be excluded from British ports, which Evarts relayed to Seward. But at this stage Seward felt the British government too "hard-pressed" and more likely to listen to conciliation.[27]

With the opening of the spring session of Parliament, Evarts found a new way to impress British opinion. Having made the acquaintance of a young member of Parliament named Shaw-Lefevre, whose sympathies were with the North, he furnished him with Confederate correspondence and other data which Lefevre used for an effective speech.

While waiting for an appeal of the *Alexandra* case, Evarts enjoyed a hasty tour to Italy, but was back in April. The House of Lords rejected the *Alexandra* appeal, ignoring the merits of the case entirely. Future trouble for Great Britain might have been avoided if the Lords had permitted an interpretation of British neutrality laws. The ship was allowed to leave port but was seized and condemned at Nassau by the British authorities, thus rendering no aid to the Confederacy.[28] "I am quite clear," Evarts wrote Seward, "in the opinion that in neither England nor France is there any danger of unfavorable disposition from their present attitude toward us. . . . I shall have the good fortune to leave England with all armed ships disposed of and no new ones threatened."[29]

Just before his departure, he attended the dinner given by Cyrus W. Field at the Palace Hotel in celebration of the renewal of cable communication between Great Britain and America after a lapse of six years. Field presided, and Bright, Adams, and Evarts were the chief speakers. "The press and telegraph," said Evarts, "are both useful servants only so long as they are servants of truth. May truth preside at either magnet, and may falsehood be forever buried in the intermediate ocean."[30] He accompanied John Bright on a visit to the gutta-percha works, where he saw the cable being made at the rate of ten miles a day.[31]

After listening to a libel suit relating to Lord Cardigan's responsibility for the charge of the Light Brigade, and attending a breakfast to the Italian patriot, Garibaldi, Evarts left for New York with Cyrus Field.[32]

For his second mission Evarts received $7,500; but of greater value to him was the experience gained. He steadfastly refused to discuss the two missions, feeling that they involved confidential matters. He really cared little for the game of diplomacy, although Henry Adams declared that he played it in "a large and liberal way."[33] There can be no accurate measurement of the value of his work in London and Paris, but beyond doubt he did all that was expected of him. It would be an exaggeration to say, as did one admirer, that he accomplished more "than a formidable fleet could have done."

Perhaps a London correspondent to the *New York Tribune* best summarized his work. Evarts, he said, "has dedicated almost the whole of his time and fine abilities to the task of explaining to European statesmen the real character of the American civil war, and indoctrinating them with correct ideas of its antecedents and inevitable issues. In this he has so admirably seconded our able representative, Mr. Adams, that I hear high praise of him, contributing immensely to the revulsion of feeling against the Rebels. . . . His brilliant wit and conversational powers rendered him deservedly popular. . . . He could not have worked harder or been more successful. I take his generally regretted departure to be the sign that all is satisfactory in our foreign relations. The Rebels here and their sympathizers use the most uncomplimentary expressions whenever his name is mentioned, and attribute the stoppage of Laird's rams entirely to him and Mr. Adams."[34]

10

Post-War Problems

HAD EVARTS SOUGHT a diplomatic post upon his return home, Seward might have found one for him. But his ambitions were linked with his profession, which had suffered during his absence. Nor had he any thought of a return to politics. The campaign of 1864 got under way just after his return, and he heartily supported Lincoln's re-election, giving some time to speeches during the last few weeks—his earlier distrust of the President having completely disappeared. But he wished no elective office for himself.

The end of the war was not yet in sight, and pessimism was still rife in the North. Many felt with the Democratic candidate, General McClellan, that a compromise peace should be patched up. Evarts sharply condemned this faintheartedness. "The struggling boat's crew," he wrote the Union Club at Yale, "that goes for an immediate cessation of hostilities with the rapids above Niagara, may resume them, but it will be at the bottom of the Fall."[1]

At a great Cooper Union rally in October, just after Sheridan's victories in the Shenandoah, an enthusiastic audience greeted him on his first public appearance since returning from abroad. His theme was liberty; he called it the issue of the campaign and accused the Democrats of betraying it.[2]

The day before election, a great outdoor meeting was held in Wall Street; bankers, merchants, mechanics, and day laborers rubbed shoulders, all intent upon electing Lincoln and saving the Union. The huge crowd thronged about the front of the customhouse, where a speakers' stand had been erected, and packed the adjacent streets as far as the eye could see. Short speeches were made by Richard H. Dana, Moses H. Grinnell, and David Dudley Field, and by Evarts, who was wildly cheered as he exclaimed, "On the result of this election hangs the independence of the South. The South knows it; England knows it; and the French Emperor knows it. . . . We are children, or worse, if . . . we hesitate to know and to act."[3]

Lincoln easily carried the election, although his margin in New York was close. Evarts attended the great victory banquet at the Metropolitan Hotel, and on being asked to say a word about American diplomacy, he described the victory as ending the last hope of America's foreign enemies.[4]

A few nights later, Evarts had a better opportunity to speak of American diplomacy. The eminent historian and reformer, Professor Goldwin Smith of Oxford, loyal supporter of the North, arrived in New York and was feted at the Union League Club. Some seventy guests were present to welcome him, including Peter Cooper, Parke Godwin, William Cullen Bryant, Horace Greeley, and Henry J. Raymond. They all listened with satisfaction as Smith assured them:—"All Englishmen who have any regard for the honor of England . . . reprobate and abhor the conduct of those shipbuilders and merchants of Liverpool, whose ignoble cupidity . . . has brought the nations to the verge of a desolating war." Evarts, after complimenting Smith upon his warm friendship for the Union, prophesied that democracy would bring the two nations closer together. "We have passed that period," he said, "when family compacts of kings, the *entente cordiale* of cabinets, the written stipulation of treaties could wholly or greatly determine the relations between the nations."[5]

When Chief Justice Taney died on October 12, 1864, a host of candidates for the vacant position appeared. Three Cabinet members, Chase, Blair, and Stanton, wanted it; Associate Justice Swayne had hopes; Judge William Strong of Pennsylvania was an aspirant; and the friends of Edward Bates urged that he be chosen. Montgomery Blair considered himself the rightful heir because Taney had been a close friend and admirer of the Blair family.[6]

Evarts, too, had friends who felt him abundantly qualified for the high office. Unquestionably he was the best lawyer of them all. The Court of Appeals unanimously signed a petition to Lincoln, urging his appointment and declaring, "He is preëminent for his refinement, courtesy, and dignity of his manner, and these qualities are not undeserving of consideration in a man who is to occupy the place heretofore filled by a Jay, Ellsworth, Marshall, and Taney."[7] Naturally, Evarts wanted the appointment. To abandon a great law practice for the salary of a chief justice would mean a financial sacrifice, but the position was the highest goal of the profession. He wrote Dana: "The Ch. Justiceship is, it seems to me, for the next ten years a place of great political importance over and above its simple judicial authority. . . . A good deal of interest has been spontaneously shown here to me in the place on public grounds, by persons of the *highest* political influence. This has been gratifying to me, for public grounds are the only ones that I can for a moment justify myself in allowing any weight to. . . . Aside from Gov. Chase I am justified in thinking that many things concur to make me a very prominent, if not the most prominent candidate."[8]

But Chase felt himself the better qualified of the two. "Evarts," he wrote, "is a man of sterling abilities and excellent learning and a much greater lawyer than I ever pretended to be. The truth is, I always thought myself much over-estimated. And yet I think I have more judgement than Evarts, and that tried by the Marshall standard, [I] should make a better judge; while he might, tried by the Story standard."[9]

At Washington Evarts' nomination was urged by Hoar, Richard Henry Dana, and Governor Andrew of Massachusetts. The Supreme Court was unanimously favorable. Hoar wrote him that Taney, just before his death, had said that Evarts would be the best appointee. "What I want," confided Hoar, "is to have Chase and Stanton the Kilkenny cats, and have you come in as an innocent third person—on grounds aside from politics."[10]

For a time Evarts' candidacy gave promise of success; but he lacked the large following of Chase. Not even Seward supported him, preferring Blair—which did not lessen Evarts' friendship for Seward. Sumner urged Chase's appointment in the Senate. Long before Taney's death, Lincoln had declared he would appoint Chase if the opportunity arose, partly because he knew and admired him, and partly because he felt that Chase would uphold emancipation and the Legal Tender Act. To be sure, a rupture between Chase and Lincoln had occurred in 1864 when Chase tried to obtain the Republican nomination for the presidency; but Lincoln had the magnanimity to forgive him. It was finally understood that Lincoln would appoint Chase, and that if he refused, Evarts would be second choice. Chase of course accepted.[11]

This was a sharp disappointment to Evarts. Once more high office had eluded his grasp. Judging from Chase's record during the nine years he held the office, marked by some able decisions but also by some grave errors and a general weakening of the Court, one might conclude that Evarts, with a much longer career before him, might have given the office more stability and prestige during a most difficult period of its history.

The end of the war came in sight soon after the election. Grant, Sheridan, and Sherman forced the Confederacy to surrender, and the people of New York City decided to celebrate on March 6. Evarts was one of a committee to plan the occasion. A half-holiday was declared, and the city gave itself over to rejoicing, with a mammoth parade up Broadway and a great mass meeting in Union Square.[12]

But the war left Evarts one unhappy reminder. His oldest son, Charles, who had left Yale in 1863 to become a lieutenant in the First New York Cavalry and who served a year under Sheridan in the Shenandoah, was incapacitated by a fall from his horse, was obliged to leave the service, and was never again in good health. He recovered sufficiently to graduate from the Columbia College of Mines in 1867 but found it necessary to retire to his father's farm in Windsor.[13]

In the midst of the rejoicing over Lee's surrender came news of Lincoln's assassination. Evarts was chosen one of a committee of thirteen to represent the city at Lincoln's funeral in Washington —the service at which he first saw General Grant. On returning, he paid a fine tribute to Lincoln in a short address at the New York Historical Society. "No more wonderful career than that of Abraham Lincoln," he said, "is told in sacred history or furnished in romance. He has been a direct example of what any one may come to under our constitution."[14]

To honor the Yale men who had served in the war a committee of forty-six, including Evarts, planned a great celebration on the campus for July 26. It proved one of the greatest days in Yale history. After presiding over the alumni meeting, Evarts took the place of honor with President Woolsey in the procession of students, faculty, and alumni which marched to Center Church to hear a patriotic address by Horace Bushnell. Then came the dinner at Alumni Hall in a martial setting, with Evarts presiding over five hours of speechmaking—despite his admonition that no one should talk more than ten minutes. It was probably at this dinner that Evarts began to earn a reputation as a toastmaster. His wit sparkled constantly. For example, just after President Woolsey had spoken, the applause caused a pyramid of confectionary on the table to totter and fall. There was a moment of embarrassment, but Evarts jumped to his feet and said, "We must all admit, gentlemen, that President Woolsey has been more attractive by his eloquence than was Pericles, upon whose lips the bee settled, for a whole avalanche of sweet things has now settled upon him. We must agree that, since the world began, no speaker, probably, ever received so *candied* a tribute to his oratory." Before the dinner broke up, a committee, including Evarts, was appointed to plan a Yale war memorial; but it was not till many years later that the plan was carried out. Evarts attended commencement next day and, with Justice Swayne of the Supreme Court, received the degree of Doctor of Laws.[15]

The significance of Appomattox was strongly impressed upon the philosophic mind of Evarts. At the New England Society dinner that winter he pointed out that no longer could the people of Charleston defy the Constitution as when they had ejected Samuel Hoar for trying to test the rights of imprisoned Negroes. "Our Constitution is sufficient," he concluded, "to maintain the peace of the nation and the liberty of black and white."[16] At the Boston Latin School he spoke more solemnly before a cultivated audience at the dedication of a war memorial. "It was," he said, "the unique case of a civil war in which the vanquished, as well as the victor, increased its freedom. . . . We have learned that war *for* war is neither fanciful nor poetical. . . . Peace, having its victories as well as war, has its disasters, its duties, its sacrifices, its burdens."[17]

War benefits few people, but it brought Evarts a large number of cases which would not have otherwise arisen. Scarcely had he reached home before he was back in the courts. The cost of extra counsel to the government during the war was nearly a half-million dollars. To Evarts alone, fees for occasional legal aid to the government amounted by 1867 to more than forty-seven thousand dollars.[18]

The Kohnstamm Criminal Fraud Case, which attracted wide attention, engaged him first. With James T. Brady he sought to defend Kohnstamm from the charge of having made a fraudulent claim against the government. Such claims had become a veritable "racket" toward the close of the war, and the Attorney General was anxious to win this test case. Edwards Pierrepont had been retained as prosecutor. The court was crowded during the five-day trial. The defense tried to prove that Kohnstamm was being made a scapegoat by the government to cover up frauds of its own officials. But the prosecution produced unimpeachable evidence to show that vouchers and bills had been forged. Kohnstamm was convicted and sentenced by Judge Nelson to ten years in Sing Sing.[19]

The Dix Case, soon afterward, was ridiculous. As commander of the New York area in 1864, General Dix had closed the offices of several newspapers, whereupon the state charged him with violation of the freedom of the press and false arrest. The case was tried before a select audience in the Court of General Sessions, with Evarts and Pierrepont appearing for the federal government in defense of Dix, and A. Oakey Hall for the state. Evarts showed the absurdity of holding Dix personally liable and argued for the right of the government to protect itself against insidious propaganda in wartime. Before a decision was reached, it was discovered that the newspapers in question had been maliciously hoodwinked into printing the objectionable articles. The editors were released and later obtained a decree awarding them one cent.[20]

The celebrated Opdyke-Weed libel suit in January, 1865, was the most sensational case in which Evarts was engaged since he defended Monroe Edwards. He disliked trials involving a public scandal and would not have undertaken the defense of Thurlow Weed but for his desire to help his old friend. Crowds came day after day to the little room of the Supreme Court in Manhattan to listen to the tale of war profiteering there unfolded.

The case grew out of a long, bitter feud between George Opdyke, wartime mayor of New York, and Thurlow Weed. For some time Opdyke had criticized Weed after his fall from power, and Weed, upon his return from Europe during the war, decided to hit back. He published articles in the *Albany Evening Journal* and *Commercial Advertiser* accusing Opdyke, as mayor, of selling the office of surveyor of port for ten thousand dollars; of executing secret contracts with the government for the sale of shoddy clothing for soldiers, thereby making more money than "any fifty sharpers, Jew or Gentile, in the city of New York"; of presenting improper demands for indemnity from the county for the destruction of his gun factory during the draft riots; and of taking advantage of the financial embarrassments of John C. Frémont to obtain an undue share of his Mariposa mining property in California.[21] Opdyke sued for libel.

Excitement ran high on the opening day of the trial. Many politicians expected to see the Republican party turned inside out; others expected to see Opdyke and Weed wash their dirty linen; still others were interested in the counsel, David Dudley Field and ex-Judge Emott for Opdyke, and Evarts and Pierrepont for Weed. Field had advised Opdyke to sue Weed for libel and fifty thousand dollars damages. The object of the defense was to prove the truth of Weed's alleged libels and to show that Opdyke was motivated by avarice in office and by the suit for damages.

Emott opened the case for the plaintiff, declaring, "Either George Opdyke is a heartless, corrupt, perjured scoundrel, or the author of these publications is a libeller, attacking a man's dearest possession with the most defamatory aspersions that human malice can invent." Pierrepont opened the defense with such clever comments upon Opdyke's wartime manipulations as to make him appear the accused.

It took a fortnight to examine witnesses, and public interest increased daily as the evidence became more intricate and spicy. Fierce skirmishes occurred every day between Evarts and Field, and the case well deserved its title of "the lawyers' joust." Although seldom upset in a courtroom, Evarts at times became angered by the tactics which Field used to secure the admission or denial of evidence. Try as he would, Field could not prevent inside information from coming to light to show how the city had been made to pay for the riots, and to reveal other shady manipulations on the part of Opdyke. Field was the more astute, but Evarts often won in their verbal tilts.[22]

When Evarts placed Frémont on the stand to relate the story of the Mariposa affair, excitement was intense. Frémont gave a straightforward account. He told how millions had been frittered away; how he had been chief owner of the ten-million-dollar mining estate till pressing debts forced him to accept Opdyke's aid;

and how Opdyke, Field, and others got control of Mariposa in return for promises to pay off his debts. Field cross-examined him heartlessly, and forced from him a reluctant admission that no unfair advantage had been taken of him. But it was finally shown that Opdyke and his confederates had gained control as trustees of two and a half million dollars worth of Mariposa stock, had virtually refused to restore it, had finally demanded that Frémont sell a large part of it to them at twenty-five cents on the dollar; and that Frémont had consented to this sharp bargain rather than lose all his holdings by lawsuits.

Evarts charged Field with extorting large fees from Frémont, to which Field retorted, "My friend Evarts would not accept such an offer if it were made. He would not take a large fee, not he!" With equal sarcasm Evarts replied that Opdyke's promise to give the fifty thousand dollars in damages to charity if he won the case, was a joke, because little would be left after counsel fees were paid. The spectators relished these clashes immensely and enjoyed comparing the methods of Evarts and Field. The latter, like an athlete, went straight to the mark with no flights of fancy; the former, proceeding more leisurely, with thoughts flowing like a winding river, held the court room in suspense waiting to catch the last word.[23]

In his final appeal to the jury Evarts flayed Opdyke relentlessly, as if he were the accused. He contrasted the public services of Opdyke and Weed; he showed that Opdyke's criticisms of Weed in the *Evening Post* were as libellous as those charged against Weed; he insisted that Weed's public-spirited purpose had been to unmask Opdyke's record as mayor; he uttered an appeal for the freedom of the press, which brought a burst of applause from the spectators; he described Frémont as a good Samaritan who thought he was among friends and not thieves; and he closed with a caustic attack upon Opdyke, describing him as "a slippery speculator and a man eager to make money and gain political preferment." Turning to the jury, he said, "If you like this kind of public man, and think that evil has been done in this community by the comments and denunciations of the defendants, clothe the plaintiff, as he asks you, in the purple and fine linen of your applauding judgment, put the golden chain of your favorable verdict about his neck, carry him from this courtroom on your Ajax shoulders, blow your sycophant trumpets for him:

"Sound him victorious
Long to reign over us
Opdyke the glorious."[24]

A clever eyewitness not inaccurately described Evarts' plea poetically:

"Here let us leave the Speaker, in his great matchless art,
The burning fire of eloquence to truth he did impart,
For his speech before that Jury will sure outlive the day,
When the living men who heard it, will long have passed away."[25]

The jury wrestled long over their verdict and finally failed to agree. Opdyke's suit thus failed. Weed was on hand to receive the congratulations of his friends, who had raised seventeen thousand dollars to pay his cost of the trial.[26] Thus ended a litigation which opened the long Reconstruction chronicle of graft and scandal.

Another sensational case involving dubious war contracts soon followed. Isaac Henderson had been dismissed as navy agent for accepting commissions on contracts let by the government. Henderson protested his innocence, and William Cullen Bryant defended him in the *Evening Post,* of which Henderson was part owner. A suit was brought by the government against Henderson, and the case was tried before Judge Nelson in the Circuit Court. The government was represented by District Attorney Dickinson, Caleb Cushing, and ex-Judge Bosworth. It was charged that Henderson had failed to purchase navy supplies at the lowest market price as required by law; that he had retained ten per cent for himself, and that he had split part of the profit. But evidence against Henderson was lacking, and Evarts was able to show he had not been guilty of fraudulent intent. The jury acquitted Henderson without even leaving their seats.[27]

Evarts had some connection with the notorious claim of Benjamin W. Perkins, who alleged that he had made two contracts to furnish Russia with war supplies. One contract was recognized and satisfied; but the other, which Perkins claimed to have made verbally with Stoeckl, the Russian minister, was denied. Perkins managed to enlist the aid of Evarts, who prepared a brief in support of the claim, on the basis of which Seward pressed it. But Russia steadfastly repudiated it as fraudulent.[28]

Describing Evarts as a lawyer in 1865, the *New York Herald* in its chatty way remarked: "Socially he is of the New England and Emerson type—the intellect largely predominating over the passions; so that while he has many affinities and excellent capacities for friendship, he has not that demonstrative, semi-Irish warmth which begets and fosters any particular closeness of intimacy. He is more a thinking machine than an animal. . . . Mr. Evarts occupies a position commanding respect, influence and power. Still in the prime of life, and with fortune and fame already conquered, the future will hold up for him a splendid possible career for advancement."[29]

His first step in this "advancement" was to take up a number of cases in the Supreme Court arising out of the war. The Court now had only three justices of the pre-war era: Wayne, Nelson, and Grier. The other six—Chase, Clifford, Swayne, Miller, Davis, Field—were less experienced but were all men of strength and learning. Most of Evarts' post-war cases before this tribunal were prize cases centering upon the question of the *intent* of the voyage.

First, there was the case of two alleged slave ships, held by the government on suspicion of making a voyage to Africa to engage in the illicit traffic. It was in this case that Evarts encountered J. Hubley Ashton, Assistant Attorney General, with whom he was soon to be closely associated. Ashton won the case by proving the voyage had all the earmarks of a slave enterprise.[30]

The *Dashing Wave* and the *Sir William Peel* cases related to ships seized by Union cruisers during the war at the mouth of the

Rio Grande on suspicion of engaging in trade with the Confederacy. Evarts represented the British owners and Ashton the government. In both cases Evarts was able to persuade the Court that illegal trade had not been intended, despite the suspicious look of the circumstances.[31] The *Magicienne* had likewise been seized on suspicion of blockade-running, but was released for want of evidence. Seward admitted that the government was at fault and agreed to an arbitration of damages. He appointed Evarts to act for the United States; Edward M. Archibald, British consul at New York, represented Great Britain. The sum of $8,645 was finally awarded as damages.[32] This was Evarts' first experience with international arbitration.

Other cases in the Supreme Court related to permits to vessels engaged in the cotton trade during the war. In that of the *Sea Lion* Evarts was unable to protect British owners who held a license from Admiral Farragut to engage in such trade at Mobile, although there was a strong dissenting opinion in his favor. But the doctrine that the President alone could license such trade, which defeated Evarts in the case of the *Sea Lion,* won him the case of *Hall* v. *Coppell.*[33]

The indiscriminate seizure of property in the Confederacy led Congress to pass the Abandoned and Captured Property Act, which provided that confiscated property should be sold and the proceeds put in the treasury; and that within two years after the war any claimant could sue and recover if he proved his ownership and loyalty. Evarts represented many claimants under this act, particularly in the Dennistoun Cotton Case, the Colton Salvage Case, and the so-called Confiscation Cases.[34]

The case of the *Meteor,* by far the most significant of Evarts' post-war litigations, again afforded him an opportunity to define neutral rights and obligations. He was retained by John M. and Robert B. Forbes, who, together with a dozen prominent New York business men, had built the *Meteor* during the Civil War for government use, but to their disgust were unable to dispose of the vessel because they were suspected of intent to violate American neutrality by trying to sell the ship to Chile, which was then at war with Spain. The *Meteor* was a long, graceful craft of fifteen hundred tons, built at Portsmouth and brought to New York in 1864. It was hoped that she would even capture the *Alabama*. With the end of the war in sight, the government refused to buy her and the owners found on their hands a vessel that had been constructed mainly for war use. As John M. Forbes said, "No patriotic effort ever encountered a more decided douche of cold water."[35] It represented an investment of two hundred thousand dollars.

In 1865 Forbes negotiated indirectly with Chilean agents, but the price asked was too high and the negotiations ceased. Forbes then decided to send the ship to Panama and sell it to any purchaser who might appear. To avoid a breach of neutrality, legal advice was sought and the Forbes brothers were told there was nothing unlawful in sending the vessel, armed or unarmed, to a neutral port for sale. To make sure, however, they removed all guns from the deck.

As the ship was about to leave New York, the Spanish minister protested to Seward, and the *Meteor* was ordered held for investigation. On board were found a few rifles, six months' provisions, and a crew of fifty-seven men. The cargo was consigned to Panama, but some of the crew said the real destination was Chile. The true reason for holding the ship was probably political; Seward was pressing the *Alabama* claims against Great Britain and could hardly afford to risk a breach of American neutrality laws.

The Forbes brothers retained Evarts and Choate to protect their rights. Appealing to the District Attorney, Evarts protested that their purpose had been merely to sell the ship at Panama, and that its detention was costing his client fifteen hundred dollars a day. Forbes went to Washington and secured the release of the *Meteor*, but on returning to New York found that Seward had reconsidered and ordered it held.[36] An appeal was taken to the District Court for release under bond—a legal remedy usually allowed. Evarts argued the matter vigorously before Judge Betts, condemning the interference from Washington. Betts admitted the hardship, but refused the bond.[37] The only recourse was a regular trial in the same court, but this was not granted with a jury, as Evarts had requested.

Confident that the law was on his side, Evarts did not even trouble to produce witnesses, which proved an error. The government had many witnesses and their testimony filled a good-sized volume. The issue centered upon the interpretation of the neutrality act of 1818, which forbade any person knowingly to be concerned in "*furnishing, fitting out,* or arming any vessel, with *intent* that such ship or vessel be employed in the service of any foreign prince or state." Evarts contended that such fitting out must show an *intent* to engage in war, that there must be proof of personal guilt by the owners, and that the burden of such proof was on the government. Ridiculing the evidence submitted by the government as based upon "mere suspicion, insinuation, aspersion, and surmise," he declared there was no contract with the Chilean government, nothing but a commercial adventure. He emphasized Wheaton's well-known dictum: "An American merchant may build and fully arm a vessel, and supply her with stores, and offer her for sale in our own market. . . . In such case, the extent and character of the equipment is immaterial. The *intent* is all."[38]

After a vexatious delay, Judge Betts condemned the *Meteor* as a war craft whose owners had planned to use it to violate neutrality. He declared that the evidence left no doubt of the intent. Apparently he could see no difference between the *Meteor* and the *Alabama.* Betts was undoubtedly influenced by the administration at Washington; but, as Dana said, "Why should it have been conceived necessary to sacrifice the *Meteor,* to overrule good law, to create a new necessity requiring to be met by new statutes of untried efficiency, simply for the purpose of creating a precedent which is after all no precedent?"[39] A bill was immediately introduced in Congress to clarify the act of 1818, requiring the owner of a vessel to be proved guilty of actually furnishing an armed craft to the belligerent. The measure passed the House, but never emerged from committee in the Senate.[40]

But the case was not yet ended. After the lapse of six months, during which the *Meteor* had depreciated to half its former value, Judge Betts released it under bond. This step was made possible by the removal of the objection of the State Department. Not satisfied with a release, Forbes appealed to the Circuit Court. Evarts repeated his argument and secured from Justice Nelson a complete vindication. Reversing Betts's decision, Nelson declared: "I do not see any breach of the act [of 1818], either in fact or by the way of intention. I cannot decide this case by conjecture and suspicion."

It was now the turn of the government to appeal. The case reached the Supreme Court in 1868, but was quashed, partly because Evarts had become attorney general and opposed its prosecution.[41] Forbes sought indemnity in the Court of Claims and eventually received seventy-six thousand dollars, which was but a small fraction of his loss. He doubtless stated the truth when he said, "The owners of the *Meteor,* all of whom went into it from patriotic motives, were loyal and true men. Their names are a sufficient guarantee against any attempt to do an illegal and mean act."[42]

11

The Defense of Andrew Johnson

Evarts had watched the struggle between Johnson and Congress with growing alarm, keenly aware that it was splitting the Republican party. He could not agree with the Radicals, who were bent upon vindictively punishing the South; nor could he approve of the Conservatives, for although they rightly wished a speedy restoration of the Union, many of them had a suspicious friendship for the Democratic party. To him the feud between Congress and the President spelled ruin for the party, and he placed the blame at the President's door.[1]

He made his position clear at a great Republican rally held in Cooper Union in October, 1867. Standing before a huge audience, with a banner inscribed "Andrew Johnson: Traitor, Renegade, Outcast," unfurled above his head, he described Johnson as a "President without a party," and declared that if he did not possess sufficient energy to pacify the country and uphold the rights of the Negro, Congress would do it at the next session. He joined in the now widespread demand for Grant as president, and warned against the return of the Democrats. Apparently he favored the Radical faction of the Republican party.[2]

The Radicals were generally victorious in the scattered state elections of 1867. Congress interpreted the results as a signal for pressing impeachment charges against Johnson, despite the President's impotence in the face of a two-thirds hostile majority. There was malice in this Fortieth Congress and a determination by Radical leaders—Sumner, Wade, Stevens, Butler—to avenge themselves upon Johnson for his vetoes. They might better have been content to tie his hands and leave him in helpless peace for the fourteen months of his term; but partisan hatred dictated otherwise. They might arouse public opinion against him to eject him from office and put Ben Wade in his place, and to distribute the consequent political plums among themselves.

They accused Johnson of conspiring to seize military power; but they were the real conspirators. The judiciary committee of the House had conducted an elaborate inquiry in 1867 for evidence to arraign the President for "treason, bribery, or other high crimes or misdemeanors." Evidence not being available, Congress passed over Johnson's veto the Tenure of Office Act, making the removal of Cabinet officers subject to the consent of the Senate. It was a deliberate challenge, for it stipulated that any infraction would be punishable as a "high misdemeanor."

Johnson met the challenge squarely. Knowing that his Secretary of War, Edwin M. Stanton, was intriguing with the Radicals, he asked him several times to resign and finally suspended him, appointing General Grant *ad interim*. When the Senate refused to concur in the removal of Stanton, Grant left his office. Johnson then sent Stanton a letter displacing him, and gave an official commission to General Lorenzo Thomas in his stead. Stanton immediately announced that the office was still his, swore out a complaint against Thomas, had him arrested, and barricaded the doors of the War Office after Thomas was released on bail. In the eyes of the Radicals Johnson's second attempt to get rid of Stanton constituted a breach of the Tenure of Office Act and ground for impeachment. Public opinion was whipped up, with Greeley's *Tribune* leading the assault upon the President.

An indictment was drawn in eleven articles, framed to win popular support and the approval of the Senate, which was to sit in judgment. The framers had no thought of justice. Indeed, the whole procedure of the House in bringing the indictment was defective: there was no preliminary hearing and the resolution to impeach did not go, as it should have done, to the Committee on the Judiciary, but to the Committee on Reconstruction, led by Thaddeus Stevens, bitterly hostile toward Johnson.

The first eight articles pertained to the attempted removal of Stanton, charging the President with *intent* to violate the Constitution and Tenure of Office Act. Articles 4, 5, 6, and 7, known as the "conspiracy articles," accused him of conspiring with General Thomas to hinder a duly appointed officer from performing his duties, thus violating the Conspiracy Act of 1861. The ninth, or Emory article, accused him of *intending* to induce General Emory to violate an army act of 1867. The tenth, or Butler article, charged him with making "inflammatory and scandalous harangues" to bring Congress into disrepute; but this long article made no mention of the violation of any law. The eleventh, or omnibus article, prepared by Stevens, repeated the previous ten in new terms, adding that the President had referred to Congress as "a Congress of only part of the States, thereby denying, and *intending* to deny, that the legislation of said Congress was valid." It was believed that this article might catch senatorial votes which others would not, especially since it was to be voted upon first. If Johnson were convicted under it, he could be removed without any vote on the other articles.[3]

The articles could really be condensed to four accusations: that Johnson had attempted to remove Stanton; that he had asserted an improper authority over the army; that he had refused to coöperate with Congress; and that he had criticized Congress. No charges of corruption were made because no evidence could be found. The framers knew full well the weakness of the indictment; they trusted to partisanship to convict him. And the six managers who were to conduct the prosecution—Butler, Bingham, Boutwell, Logan, Williams, and Stevens—expected to play the same heroic rôle that Burke had played at the trial of Warren Hastings.[4]

The indictment raised three questions: first, did the removal power vest in the President alone or jointly with the Senate? Second, could a vacant office be filled indefinitely by *ad interim* appointments? Third, and most important, was it permissible for the President to violate an act of Congress which he considered unconstitutional with the purpose of securing a judicial decision as to its validity?

On March 4, 1868, the managers filed into the Senate and presented the indictment. Chief Justice Chase, foreseeing grave difficulties, sent a communication to the Senate declaring that the proceedings must be regarded as a "trial" before a "court." The following day he went in person to take the oath to "do impartial justice"—an oath which each senator was also required by law to take. Chase was sincere, but a majority of the senators were not. Even Ben Wade, who would become president if Johnson were found guilty, had the bad taste to take the oath and sit in judgment in the Senate.

Meanwhile, the Cabinet had concerned itself with the problem of the President's defense. It was unanimously agreed that Henry Stanbery, the Attorney General, should act as the leading counsel. He resigned office immediately to devote himself to the task. It was also agreed that other counsel should be found. Benjamin Curtis, who had built up a great law practice in Boston after his resignation from the Supreme Court, was also selected, and reluctantly accepted, regarding the task as an unpleasant duty.[5]

There was much disagreement as to the other counsel for the President. David Dudley Field was mentioned, but Seward objected. O'Conor was proposed, but he was acting at the time as counsel for Jefferson Davis, which was enough to exclude him. Jeremiah Black was a great lawyer and close friend of Johnson; but at the time he was counsel for American claimants to the guano island of Alta Vela in the Caribbean, and he felt that he would embarrass the administration, which was inclined to support the claim against the Dominican Republic. His refusal to share in the defense, therefore, was apparently due to his good taste rather than to a break with Johnson over the Alta Vela affair, as some historians have asserted.[6] William S. Groesbeck, a comparatively unknown Cincinnati lawyer, and Thomas A. Nelson of Tennessee, least known of all but gifted with a rough eloquence and deeply devoted to Johnson, were agreed upon.

The choice of Evarts as the fifth counsel was not decided upon without difficulty. Rodman Price, a friend of the President, had recommended him as the type of man who should be chosen. Black had urged Johnson to select a leading Republican lawyer as a strategic move. But Seward's influence seems to have been the determining factor in the selection of Evarts. The obvious objection was the speech which Evarts had made against Johnson only four months before. Gideon Welles, Secretary of the Navy, who scarcely knew Evarts, regarded him as a "cold, calculating selfish man . . . destitute of enthusiasm or magnetic power." It was finally agreed by all except Welles that Evarts would be a good selection if he would forget politics and enter heartily into the defense. At a Cabinet meeting on March 9 Seward remarked that he had taken the liberty to telegraph Evarts to come to Washington; to which Johnson replied that he could not yet guarantee his employment: Evarts was in the midst of an important trial, but hurried to Washington, where he assured Stanbery he would exert himself to the utmost and the matter was thus settled.[7]

Of course part of the press was quick to criticize Evarts' appointment. The *Independent,* a Radical organ, called him "a hireling counsel" who had betrayed his party to "shield a renegade President from the righteous and avenging judgment of the American people," who had "pawned his honor for a lawyer's fee and was summoned to the President's defense, not because he was a shining light in the legal profession, but because he was an influential leader of the Republican party."[8] But there were other important publications which defended Evarts' course. The *Nation* declared that he was rendering neither a political nor a patriotic service, but was acting in a purely professional capacity. *Harper's Weekly* justified his acceptance on three grounds: first, as a lawyer he could not decline to defend a political foe any more than he could refuse to defend even a murderer; second, the fact of his previous opposition to Johnson in politics would lend an air of impartiality to the trial;

and third, no lawyer could well refuse an invitation to share in one of the most memorable trials of history.[9]

Precisely what motives impelled Evarts to undertake the case are not known. His high regard for Seward was certainly one factor. Of course the fee of $2,025, which was paid to each of the five counsels, was not an inducement.[10] Nor could a desire to figure in the public eye have been a motive: this was contrary to Evarts' nature, and spectacular trials did not appeal to him. Perhaps he felt the same altruistic impulse which inspired Denman to defend Queen Caroline. But the case certainly offered a great opportunity for any lawyer and he made the most of it.

The "Great American Farce" began on March 13. All Washington was agog, everybody talking of the trial, speculating upon its outcome, and eager to obtain one of the precious little admittance cards. Police were stationed at every door of the Senate Chamber to exclude disorderly elements. Within was a brilliant scene. The élite of Washington crowded the galleries, more than half of them ladies, while every available inch of floor space was filled with chairs. The Chamber was too small for such a spectacular event. The gallery which surrounded it would seat only a thousand people. The senators were placed in three semicircular rows, behind small wooden desks. In front, on the rostrum, sat Chief Justice Chase, clothed in his black robe of office. On his right was one table for the defense counsel and to his left another for the managers. As one eyewitness described the scene, "No such assemblage of legal talent, no such exalted official personage, no such gravity of criminal charge, had ever before given incident and interest to the history of the Republic."[11]

The managers were the center of interest. Old Thad Stevens sat at their table in a half-reclining attitude, his brows knitted, his face lowering and corpselike in color, his lips twisting nervously; a searching expression in his eyes. He was "like an apparition from the tomb," cold, relentless, fanatical, merciless. Butler, dressed in swallow-tail coat, was radiant in expression, keenly alive to the important rôle he was about to play. Bingham, Wilson, Boutwell, and Williams were quiet and grave. The managers were surrounded by admiring friends, whereas the defense counsel at the other table—Stanbery, Curtis, and Nelson—sat alone and received no expressions of sympathy. Evarts was absent, occupied in framing a reply to the charges.[12] To the disappointment of the spectators, the President did not appear; nor did he lower the dignity of his office by attending at any later stage of the trial.

Stanbery at once rose, and asked for forty days in which to prepare an answer to the indictment. It was a fair request, for the prosecution had spent an entire year gathering evidence. But Ben Butler sprang to his feet and exclaimed hotly, "Forty days! As long as it took God to destroy the world by a flood." Bingham demanded that the President's answer be filed at once. Stanbery quietly replied that a cause so important should not be treated "as if it were a case before a police court, to be put through with railroad speed on the first day the criminal appears." He asked for a reasonable time. Nelson, who excitedly seconded him, declared vehemently that such an injustice as the managers contemplated would not be perpetrated upon the meanest criminal in a court of law. The Senate finally granted ten days for preparation.[13] This short shrift not only worked a hardship on the defense, but indicated the prejudiced attitude which they might expect. Evarts, who had hoped for a much longer time, hurried back to New York to cancel several engagements in the courts. The defense counsel went to work feverishly to be ready on the appointed day.

On March 23 the trial was resumed, and Evarts appeared for the first time. Again the galleries were filled. Curtis and Stanbery took turns reading the answer to the first nine articles; while Evarts, in a louder tone which all could hear, read the answer to the tenth and eleventh articles. The President and all of the counsel had shared in framing the answer to the first nine, but the response to the last two was the work of Evarts alone. The counsel had wrestled for five hours the previous day over the rejoinder to the omnibus article, and Johnson was still dissatisfied but let it stand as Evarts had written it.[14] It recited in detail the story of Stanton's removal, and denied that any violation of the Constitution or other high crime had been committed by the President.

Evarts then made a tactical error by appealing for another thirty days. Logan roared in stump-speech fashion against delay; but Evarts retorted with quiet sarcasm, "The honorable Managers give us more professional credit than we are entitled to when they assume that our standard of our duty and our means and our needs for properly performing it, are necessarily to be measured by theirs." Butler demanded that a day be fixed, shouting, "We'll be here!" The Senate finally voted to give six more days. Since Evarts had been accustomed to a rapid preparation of cases, he felt confident of preparing this one within the allotted time.[15]

On March 30 the trial got under way. As leading manager, it fell to Butler to open for the prosecution. He was conscious of the responsibility. Indeed, it was preëminently his duty to make out the case for the prosecution, since there would have been no impeachment but for the work of himself and Stevens. Butler was determined to pillory the President before the defense even opened. "I came to conclusion," he had said, "to try the case as I should a horse case. I know how to do that."[16]

He advanced a few steps from the managers' table and made a speech of three hours' duration. Since he knew he could not convict the President on legal grounds, he resorted to a bitterly partisan attack. He compared the arraignment of Johnson with the trial of Warren Hastings. He defined an impeachable offense as one "subversive of some fundamental or essential principle of government, or highly prejudicial to the public interest." He denied that the Senate was a court, and declared the trial to be an "inquest of office" by a Senate which was a law unto itself. He denounced Johnson for his intemperate criticisms of Congress, and described him as "the elect of an assassin," forgetting that Lincoln's assassins had also plotted to kill Johnson. In short, Butler's extravagant speech was a declaration that the Senate could oust the President whenever two thirds desired to do so. He evaded the legal issue under the cloak of abuse. "The speech," said the *Herald,* "has not even the advantage of sophistry; its arguments are lame and beggarly; its quotations are worthless and can aid the defense only; its charges fall to the ground from their own weakness. . . . As a legal argument, it scarcely rises above the level of the pettifogger's balderdash."

During the following week witnesses for the prosecution were put on the stand. Evarts was alert, protesting against improper forms of questioning and bad evidence. Butler monopolized the examining, strutting self-assertively and handling the witnesses as he pleased.[17]

The managers were taking full advantage of the lack of precedents in impeachment procedure. The most recent case—that of Judge Humphreys in 1862—had been something of a fiasco. Chase started out by lecturing the Senate for framing rules of procedure before it had organized as a court, and tried to conduct the trial impartially. But the Senate took a defiant position. When Evarts insisted that the Chief Justice, like all judges, should decide on the admissibility of evidence, the majority overruled him and reserved the power to itself. The defense, in alarm, saw their case begin to crumble before it started.

Chase did not let himself become wholly impotent. Despite the limitations placed upon him, he strove valiantly to see that justice was done. Speaking in later years of Chase's part in the trial, Evarts said: "The charge against him, if it had any shape or substance, came only to this: That he brought into the Senate, in his judicial robes, no concealed weapons of party warfare, and that he did not wrest from the Bible, on which he took and administered the judicial oath, the commandment for its observance."[18]

On April 3 and 4 Evarts took sole control of the defense, jumping constantly to his feet to object to evidence produced by the managers or to cross-examine their witnesses. He had several sharp clashes with Butler on the admission of evidence, and the Senate's decision was of course usually adverse to him. He cross-examined Grant in a manner which was orthodox, but which offended the

General, and it is possible that Grant never fully forgave him for the grilling. He and the managers also clashed sharply over the admission of the testimony of a Cleveland editor who was hostile to Johnson. Evarts objected to the testimony on the ground that the editor had lost his original notes, and so could not reproduce the exact words which he quoted from Johnson. Chase sustained his objection, but the Senate admitted the evidence.[19]

Although the prosecution called twenty-five witnesses, they proved nothing except that Johnson had removed Stanton and appointed Thomas, that he had held conversations with army officers, and that he had made several indiscreet speeches. There was no evidence of high crime. There was no allusion to the much-advertised charge of Johnson's habitual drunkenness because there was no proof. The managers rested upon an assumed statement of facts and upon rumor and hearsay. They must have known that fifty-four of the senators were lawyers, familiar with the tricks of the profession and capable of distinguishing between sophistry and logic. But they trusted to a political verdict.

On April 5 Evarts happened to dine with Butler, Boutwell, Sir Edward Thornton, the British minister, and John Palfrey, the historian. Butler confessed that he wished he was on the other side of the case, whereupon Evarts said, half whimsically, that he too would like to change sides.[20] He probably meant that he feared the defense would fail.

On April 9 the defense opened its case with an able argument by Curtis. It caught the attention of every lawyer and struck the first real blow for the President. Curtis possessed a scholarship, courtesy, and an air of judicial fairness that had been lacking when the managers held the floor. He presented a closely-woven technical argument, saved from dryness by its clarity. He indulged in no oratorical tricks, not even a change of voice. He was not expected to ridicule the managers: that was to be left to Evarts. Nothing, said Curtis, has been shown to warrant impeachment, much less conviction; Johnson had not wilfully misconstrued the Tenure of Office Act, but held it unconstitutional, as many senators did at the time of its passage. While Curtis was speaking, some of the Radical senators had the bad taste to leave the Chamber, refusing to listen.[21]

A week was given to the examination of defense witnesses, with Evarts and Curtis doing most of the questioning. The object was to show the lawful *intent* of the President. This was done with great skill. The first important witness was General Lorenzo Thomas, who delighted the galleries with his naïve account of how he had demanded the War Office from Stanton. But Butler so befuddled him on cross-examination that the General's testimony was of little value. There was a great flurry when General Sherman was put on the stand. Cool, cautious, and deliberate, he gave the few brief answers expected of him to show that the President had not attempted to seize military control of the government. There followed a long, heated argument on the admission of his evidence; but again the Senate overruled Chase, and the testimony was rejected.

During Sherman's examination, Ben Butler constantly interrupted him, criticizing Chase for allowing him to testify at all. Evarts, unable to endure Butler's heckling, finally turned to him and rapped out: "This is a very peculiar case. Whenever the evidence is sought to be made applicable to it, it is a crime of the narrowest dimensions. . . . I apprehend that this learned court of lawyers and laymen will not permit this fast and loose game of limited crime for the purpose of proof and unlimited crime for purposes of accusation."[22]

The rejection of Sherman's testimony led many to believe that the prospect for the defense was hopeless. The President's counsel were themselves greatly disconcerted, and Chase was plainly angered by the tactics of the Radicals. But at least it had been shown that the President had offered the War Office to a man who would be nobody's tool. In despair, the defense turned to documentary evidence, hoping that this would be admitted. Their object was to show how the President usually made appointments. But when Evarts sought to introduce a presidential message relating to the appointment of Thomas, Butler shouted out that the defense "dare" not expect to have it admitted. Evarts replied that the defense might be superior when it came to rules of law and fact, but the prosecution was certainly the best authority on "measures of daring."[23]

Previous to April 15 there seemed no hope of saving Johnson. But the methods of the managers were ruining their own cause. A change of opinion became noticeable in the Senate and among the spectators. The fortunes of the hard-fought battle over impeachment began to shift in favor of the defense; the feeling rapidly grew that Johnson was being treated with rank injustice, and that he had been innocent of wrong intent.[24]

The burden carried by Evarts increased. Stanbery had overworked, and after ailing for several days was forced to drop out entirely till the very close of the trial. Evarts thus became leader of the defense. Wishing for time to procure information which only Stanbery possessed, he asked for a short adjournment. This request brought a tirade from Butler which went beyond the bounds of decency. After Butler had finished, Evarts rose and said: "I have never heard such a harangue before a court of justice. . . . All these delays seem to press upon the honorable managers except at the precise point of time when some of their mouths are open occupying your attention with their long harangues . . . and now twenty minutes by the watch with this harangue." Had Evarts known that Butler, at that very moment, was employing spies to break into his room at the Willard Hotel to search for correspondence bearing on the case—a fact of which Butler shamelessly boasted later—his remarks might have been more caustic.[25] The adjournment was refused.

The resources of the defense were now almost exhausted. But with public opinion shifting somewhat in their favor, they decided to place more witnesses on the stand, hoping that some of the testimony would be admitted. Gideon Welles had long desired an opportunity to show that the Cabinet had advised Johnson to veto the Tenure of Office Act as unconstitutional. Butler objected strenuously to Welles' testimony, asserting that the President should not be allowed to hide behind his Cabinet. Chase admitted the evidence, but the Senate promptly rejected it. Trying again, Evarts offered to show through Welles that the Cabinet desired a test of the constitutionality of the Tenure of Office Act; but again the testimony was thrown out. Three other Cabinet members, Seward, Browning, and McCulloch, were on hand to testify; but it seemed useless. Seward was much relieved, for he did not wish to go on the stand, though he was ready to do so if Evarts called him.[26]

There was general surprise on the eighteenth, when Evarts abruptly announced that the defense had finished. This decision struck many as a mistake when there were obviously other witnesses to be called. The managers were pleased and confident as the trial reached its closing phase. Nothing was left but the final arguments of counsel, which the managers were sure would give the final touch to a victory already won.

But Evarts still had hope. He wrote Pierrepont optimistically, "The President will not be convicted for two reasons. . . . The first is the weakness of the case on the evidence, and the second, the preference of certain politicians for the present situation to the change proposed. My present impression is that the best the impeachers can hope for is to divide the Senate about equally, but of this I am not, of course, as sure as of the failure of two-thirds."[27]

Just before the final arguments began, Evarts resorted to a bit of strategy to assure the Senate of Johnson's honest intentions. He proposed to the President that General John M. Schofield, a popular warrior of high character, be appointed to the much-disputed position of Secretary of War in order that the country might know that Johnson was seeking only the public welfare, and would even appoint a Radical. The idea originated with certain Republican senators, and Johnson approved it. The main question was whether Schofield would accept the nomination or not. On the afternoon of the twenty-first, Evarts saw him at the Willard Hotel and proposed the plan, showing him that if Johnson were convicted, it would be chiefly from a fear of what he might do if left in office; that this fear could best be allayed by putting a man of Schofield's high reputation into office; and that, indeed, Schofield would be doing the country and all concerned a great service. Schofield replied that he must consult Grant first. Grant was suspicious, but so confident of Johnson's conviction that he acquiesced. Returning to Evarts' room the same night, Schofield then announced that he would accept the office. The President duly forwarded the nomination to the Senate, and although it was not approved till after the trial, it seemed to have a reassuring effect upon some of the senators.[28]

The closing arguments began on the twenty-second, four by the managers and four by the defense counsel. Much was expected from Boutwell, the first speaker for the prosecution. A large audience was on hand to hear him, but went away disappointed. He read a very tiresome speech, and the galleries became restless and noisy during the three hours that he held the floor. Not only did he fail to rise to the occasion, but he exposed himself to ridicule by his extravagant statements. He introduced charges not found in the indictment or supported by evidence.

Nelson was the first speaker for the defense, and the poorest. He did better than Boutwell; but his style lacked polish and showed that he had prepared hurriedly, with little thought of arrangement or even grammar, and without any real effort to analyze the legal issues. But Nelson was fond of Johnson and spoke as one friend for another, refuting scurrilous charges against Johnson's motives and character.

Then came Groesbeck's unexpected masterpiece—a truly great speech, which raised him from the position of an unknown lawyer to that of the most-talked-of man of the hour. For sheer emotional power, it was the best of the eight speeches. In sharp contrast with Nelson's rough style, he spoke with grace and eloquence, dealing almost exclusively with the legal issues. The galleries followed him eagerly; the senators stopped chatting to listen; and during his peroration there was absolute silence. "Is this Senate," he asked, "prepared to drag a President in here and convict him of a crime because he believed as every other President believed, as the Supreme Court believed, as thirty-eight of the thirty-nine Congresses believed?" At the end Groesbeck sank into his seat exhausted, but aware that he had struck a telling blow for the President.[29]

It was Thaddeus Stevens' turn next. He had prepared a speech with care and made the most lawyer-like argument of all of the managers. Too feeble to stand, he spoke from his seat for a half-hour, and when his voice became inaudible, Butler took his manuscript and read it rapidly. Although free from the political buncombe of the other speeches of the managers, Stevens' speech at times flared with hatred of Johnson, describing him as a "wretched man standing at bay, surrounded by a cordon of living men each with the axe of an executioner uplifted for his just punishment." Yet Stevens virtually confessed the weakness of his case when he said, "No corrupt or wicked motive need instigate the acts for which impeachment is brought." It was Stevens' last effort; four months later he was dead.

Williams' spread-eagle argument, which he read, added little to the prosecution and there was manifest impatience on the twenty-eighth before he finished. The galleries wanted to hear Evarts.[30]

An intellectual treat was in store. It was expected that Evarts would be the last speaker for the defense and that the case might hinge upon the impression he made. The galleries were crowded. They hardly expected a speech of fourteen hours, on four consecutive days. Evarts should have cut it shorter, although it was then customary among lawyers to make long arguments. It was one of the best forensic efforts of his career. Just as he was arranging his papers to begin, Butler caused a commotion by springing up to explain his connection with Jeremiah Black and the Alta Vela affair, upon which Nelson had cast aspersions. Angered by Butler's remarks, Nelson rose and said something about a duel. Order was finally restored, and a dead hush fell upon the chamber as Evarts began.[31]

Evarts looked the part of an orator as he stood by the counsel's table. His slender, straight, massive head, long hooked nose and projecting chin gave him the face of a Cicero. His voice had little volume, but was so well managed, the enunciation so perfect, rarely rising above a conversational tone, that it was a pleasure to listen. He spoke easily, at times forcefully. His words were seldom stirring, for his appeal was to common sense and reason. He spoke extemporaneously, with little use of notes. He gesticulated freely. His favorite attitude was to place his left hand in the back pocket of his frock coat, while the right, holding the gold-rimmed eyeglasses, came down toward the senators at every emphatic word. His whole manner bespoke perfect ease, mastery, and deliberation. Nothing could hurry or disconcert him. His introduction seemed a trifle labored, as if it had been memorized, but glided naturally into passages that could not have been memorized. He had a great array of references and each day he cleared the table and arranged the manuscripts carefully. Not less than a dozen large envelopes filled a bulky portfolio, the envelopes spread out in the precise order in which they would be used. As the argument advanced, each in turn was opened and its contents used; but there was no delay or hesitation.[82]

That Evarts could have held the interest of the audience for four days, after all the previous speech-making, was proof of the fine quality of his argument. He knew how to change his pace, to combine the solid and the trivial, the serious and the comic. Nothing could be more adroit than his quotations from the speeches of senators or the arguments of the managers. When he finished a train of argument, he neatly summarized it in a terse, epigrammatic sentence. The galleries delighted most in his cutting sarcasm and sparkling wit, and his speech was full of such passages. He approached these hits with mock solemnity and an exaggerated courtesy toward those whom he was about to assault, and on reaching the point, his face would beam, causing the audience to roar and yet taking some of the sting out of his jibes. Most impressive of all was the force and charm of his personality. As one historian puts it, "The contrast between his presence and that of Butler is a striking illustration of the importance of character when a great cause is tried at the bar."[33]

He spoke first of the grave importance of the trial and the magnitude of the unforeseen results which might flow from it. If the President were removed, he said, there would be no constitutionally elected President; the nation would have a chief executive chosen by the Senate, not one by the people. Then, turning his fire on the indictment, he declared:

> "The people, hearing this tremendous enginery of impeachment, . . . this power which has lain in the Constitution like a sword in its sheath, is now drawn, . . . wish to know what the crime is the President is accused of. They understand that treason and bribery are great offenses, and that a ruler guilty of them should be brought into question and deposed. . . . But they wish to know what the crimes are. They wish to know whether the President has betrayed our liberty or our possessions to a foreign state. They wish to know whether he has delivered up a fortress or surrendered a fleet. They wish to know whether he has made merchandise of public trust and turned authority to private gain. And when informed that none of these things are charged, imputed, or even declaimed about, they seek further information and are told that he has removed a member of the Cabinet. 'Well, but how comes it to be a crime?' they inquire. Why, Congress passed a law, for the first time . . . to control by law this matter of removal from office; and they provided that if the President should violate it, it should be a . . . high misdemeanor; and now he has . . . undertaken to remove a member of his Cabinet, and he is to be removed himself for that cause. He undertook to make an *ad interim* Secretary of War, and you have made for you an *ad interim* President in consequence."[34]

Evarts devoted the first day mainly to Butler's contention that the Senate, sitting to try impeachments, was not a court. "Nobody," he said, turning to Butler, "is wiser than the intrepid Manager who assumed the first assault on this Court, and knew that the only way he could prevent his cause from being turned out of court was to turn the court out of his case. . . . The Constitution makes this a court; it makes its proceedings a trial; it assigns a judgment; it accords a power of punishment. . . . We may assume, then, that so far as words go, it is a court and nothing but a court . . . if this is not an altar of justice which we stand about . . . it is an altar of sacrifice . . . to the divinity of party hate and party rage. If this is not a court, it is a scaffold." Evarts was pleading with those senators who had a sense of justice and propriety. And in his final remarks on the first day, he declared: "The moth may consume the ermine of that supreme justice whose robes you wear; rust, Senators, may corrode the sceptre of your power; nay, Messrs. Managers, time shall even devour the people whose presence beating against the doors of the Senate-house, you so much love to vaunt and menace, but of the word I have spoken 'heaven and earth shall pass away and no jot or tittle of it fail.' "

In the fading light of that late afternoon the audience listened thoughtfully as Evarts pleaded for truth, honesty, duty, and justice. He spoke more like a minister of the Gospel than a lawyer. Perhaps the spirit of Jeremiah Evarts was upon him in this struggle of right over wrong.[35]

Next morning, as he prepared to go to the trial, Seward called at his hotel and flinging up his hands enthusiastically, exclaimed, "Ah, Mr. Evarts, the country is safe." But Seward was overconfident. The Radicals were still sure of conviction. The *Tribune,* which had abused the President throughout the trial and sought to poison the public mind against him, belittled Evarts' speech, pronouncing it a disappointment to his friends, long-winded, and an attempt of a "word-monger" to say "pretty things."[36]

But the fact was that the audience which heard Evarts on the second day was larger than the first. Every inch of standing room was taken and many were turned away. The solemnity of the first day was temporarily laid aside and Evarts gave the audience much to amuse them. He described the tactics of the managers as "Chinese methods of concussion," consisting of "a great braying of trumpets, sounding of gongs, and shouts and shrieks in the neighborhood of the opposing forces. . . . The air was filled with epithets, the dome shook with invective. Wretchedness and misery and suffering and blood, not included within the record, were made the means of this explosive mixture. And we are surveying the concussion, and after all, reduced to the humble and homely method of discussion, which belongs to attorneys whose intellects have been sharpened but not enlarged by the practice of law. . . . If the President is here no longer exposed to attacks upon the same principle upon which men claim to hunt the lion and harpoon the whale, then indeed, much that has been said by the honorable managers . . . falls harmlessly in your midst."[37]

The best hit of the trial was made by Evarts at Boutwell's expense. Boutwell had waxed poetic, describing a supposed hole in the sky near the Southern Cross into which the President should be hurled. But as he spoke, Evarts turned to Curtis and said, "I'll put Boutwell in that hole so that he never will get out again." He proceeded to do so. Declaring that Boutwell was the only person who knew where this unappropriated island in the skies, reserved for convicted Presidents, was to be found, Evarts recommended that he execute the judgment, describing the exploit with devastating irony:

> "With the President made fast to his broad and strong shoulders, and, having essayed the flight by imagination, better prepared than anybody else to execute it in form, taking advantage of the ladders as far as ladders will go to the top of this great Capitol, and spurning then with his foot the crest of Liberty, let him set out on his flight, while the two houses of Congress and all the people of the United States shall shout *'Sic utur ad astra.'* But here a distressing doubt strikes me; how will the manager get back? He will have gone far beyond the

> reach of gravitation to restore him, and so ambitious a wing as his could never stoop to a downward flight. Indeed, as he passes through the constellations, that famous question of Carlyle by which he derides the littleness of human affairs upon the scale of the measure of the heavens, 'What thinks Boetus as he drives his dogs up the zenith in their race of sideral fire?' will force itself on his notice. What, indeed, would Boetus think of this new constellation?"[38]

Never before or after did Evarts exercise his gift for wit on a stage so conspicuous or with such withering results. It was an exquisite retort to the extravagant language of all of the managers. There was a roar of laughter at its close, even the Chief Justice smiling as he rapped for order. Boutwell sat through the jibe with flushed face, trying to smile but looking uncomfortable. That night his discomfiture was the joke of all Washington. In his *Reminiscences,* written long after, Boutwell devoted a whole chapter to the trial, but did not mention Evarts once. The *Tribune* sought to cover up his defeat by remarking that Evarts had devoted his second day to getting his audience into good humor.[39]

But actually Evarts had done much more than this. He devoted most of the second day to the Tenure of Office Act, showing that its authors had attempted to revolutionize the whole process of removal, that the President had a right to test its constitutionality, and that he owed no apology to Congress for violating it. He cited at great length instances in which a law had been challenged to secure a judicial interpretation of it. Much interested in this part of the argument, Charles Francis Adams wrote Evarts: "My grandfather (John Quincy Adams) had felt the disposition of the Senate to dictate to him too keenly, not to entertain great fears of its tendency to usurp executive powers. The present events are doing a great deal to confirm his reputation as a writer upon government."[40]

On the third day Evarts was more concise and forceful, picking up all the diffuse arguments of the managers, and, as the *Herald* put it, "rolling them inward to a given center from the numerous points on the wide circumference of the debate"; forming a "perfect pyramid of combustible sophistries, legal crochets, clap-trap arguments, and no end of inflammable rhetoric"; and then, "slowly and deliberately applying the fatal fuse, he set the whole superstructure of the Radical Managers in a blaze . . . the flames hissing and crackling with alarming effect."[41]

That Evarts should have devoted three of his four days to the political and personal aspects of the trial, rather than its legal issues, shows that he understood the kind of jury that he was addressing. He pointed out that Johnson had been chosen from a minority wing of the party, and argued that he should not be impeached because he stood firm by those ideas he was known to hold from the start. He pictured the difficulties which would face the President of the Senate if he entered the White House at this critical moment; he pointed to the dangers of an omnipotent Congress; and he declared that a conviction of the President meant a veritable revolution accomplished under the cover of the law.

Most amusing on the third day was the skill with which he turned the tables on the managers for criticizing Johnson's intemperate speeches. Insisting that the demand for courtesy of speech was a rule which worked both ways, he quoted from the *Congressional Globe,* the coarse and abusive language used by Butler and Bingham in debate, and as he quoted the audience roared with laughter. Bingham appeared unconcerned, but Butler was plainly annoyed. The *Tribune* seemed to think that Evarts should be censured for dragging in such material.[42]

Evarts' well-aimed blows were exposing the flimsiness of the managers' case. Welles recorded in his *Diary* on the third day: "Mr. Evarts' speech is interesting and able, and men and women of all parties are greatly interested in it. There is an impression that the radical cause is growing weaker, and indications that the radical leaders have apprehensions. The arguments of the President's lawyers have alarmed them, and have shown them that they have no case, that though they have deceived themselves into the belief that they can deceive the country, there are truths which cannot be covered up and will endanger their future."[43]

The most effective part of Evarts' argument came on the last day. Reviewing carefully the record of the passage of the Tenure of Office Act, he revealed its ambiguity as applying to Cabinet members held over from the Lincoln administration, and the emphatic statement of certain senators that the act was not intended to limit the power of removal with respect to such hold-overs. He likewise pointed out that certain senators had signed a memorial during the war calling for the removal from the Lincoln Cabinet of certain undesirable members. And then came his great final plea for Johnson. It may have lacked the electric power of Groesbeck's peroration, but it was none the less effective. He called upon the Senate to give Johnson the same impartial treatment that it would accord Lincoln if he were brought before it for the same offense. Describing Johnson, he said:

> "Bred in a school of Tennessee democratic politics, he had always learned to believe that the Constitution must and should be preserved; and I ask you to recognize that when it was in peril, and all men south of a certain line took up arms against it, and all men north ought to have taken up arms in politics or war for it, he loved the Constitution more than he loved his section, and the glories that were promised by the evil spirit of rebellion. He is no rhetorician and no philosopher. The Constitution is to him the only political book that he reads. The Constitution is to him the only authority that he obeys. His mind may not expand; his views may not be plastic as those of many of his countrymen; he may not think we have outlived the Constitution, and may not be able to embrace the Declaration of Independence as superior and predominant to it. But to the Constitution he adheres. For it and under it he served the state from boyhood up,—labored for and loved it. For it he has stood in arms against rebellious forces of the enemy; and to it

he has bowed three times a day with more than eastern devotion."[44]

Toward the close, Evarts grew tired and his voice became subdued, but there was power and pathos in his words. He warned the Senate not to overthrow a coördinate branch of the government, lest the people ask, "Where is thy brother?" He concluded, "We could summon from the people a million of men and inexhaustible treasure to help the Constitution in its time of need. Can we summon new resources enough of civil prudence and restraint of passion to carry us through this trial, so that whatever result may follow, in whatever form, the people may feel the Constitution has received no wound?"[45]

Senators of both parties congratulated Evarts. But the extreme Radicals were incensed as they saw their purpose failing. In their hot resentment, they declared that they would read Evarts out of the party. Butler called him a "pseudo-Republican who had stolen the livery of Heaven in which to serve the devil." Indeed, the extremists spent a good part of a day in collecting data on Evarts' political record, including extracts from his Cooper Union speech against Johnson.[46]

But even the hostile press did not conceal its admiration for Evarts' argument. The *Tribune* admitted that his speech on the last day was "eloquent" and "commanded undivided attention." The *Nation,* while condemning it as dwelling mostly in "the regions of higher expediency," yet declared that Evarts had dexterously turned the weapons of the managers against them and overwhelmed them with ridicule and a display of superior learning. Theodore Tilton, editor of the *Independent,* who was soon to have stronger reasons for disliking Evarts, declared that his argument "meandered pleasantly along . . . and contained incidental remarks upon nearly all subjects, except the one under consideration." Most of the press gave Evarts high commendation. *Harper's Weekly* praised him, but pointed out that a President could, under the plea of testing the constitutionality of a law, refuse to obey it after two thirds of both houses had overridden his veto.[47]

Encomiums poured in upon Evarts from many sources. Seward pronounced his argument worthy of a place in history with the best forensic efforts in the trial of Warren Hastings. Curtis, who had been compelled by illness to retire before the close of the case, wrote that his speech was "statesmanlike and profound" and "likely as anything said by the counsel for the Prest. to have confounded those Senators who might be disposed to take . . . a light view of the case." Charles Francis Adams assured him: "The reign of passion seems to be coming to an end. You are entitled to every credit in having done such good work in checking its fury." An admiring cousin from Virginia wrote, "While I perceive the overpowering argument, I am more struck and pleased with the elevated moral tone—the grand stand for truth and justice. It is refreshing to find any one who can rise above the spirit of these times into a purer region. . . . I do not know that there is a word or a line your sainted father would disapprove."[48]

Unlike the other speakers, who had gone off to rest after their efforts, Evarts remained to listen to Stanbery, who was really too ill to speak but did so because of his sense of duty. Though the former attorney general soon had to give way to a substitute who read much of his speech, he insisted on returning for the peroration. Knowing Johnson better than any other man in Washington, he could speak best for his official record. "I have seen the man tried, as few are tried," he said feelingly, "[yet] stand firm as a rock against all temptation to abuse his own powers. . . . No man could have . . . more sublime patience. Sooner or later, however, I knew the explosion must come. . . . With all his faults the President has been more sinned against than sinning."[49]

Bingham closed the case for the prosecution. He called Evarts' argument "eternal," yet himself occupied three days. With loud voice and confident air, he delivered the most illogical, abusive, and partisan speech of the whole trial.[50]

The final decision was now at hand. Thirty-six votes were required to convict Johnson; nineteen to acquit him. The first ballot was not taken till May 16, and during the interval an avalanche of Radical pressure fell upon the doubtful senators; particularly on seven Republicans—Fessenden, Grimes, Ross, Henderson, Trumbull, Fowler, and Van Winkle. Yet they, together with twelve Democrats, had the courage to vote for acquittal in the face of the storm. This vote, however, was on the eleventh article alone.

During the next ten days the pressure upon the refractory senators increased. The Radicals hoped above all else to convert Ross, because he had voted with them on some questions. He was told that his state, Kansas, would repudiate him if he stood for acquittal. Indeed, he could not make up his mind till just before the vote. On May 26 came the dramatic roll-call, with interest again centered upon Ross. The vote was on the first three articles of the their ballots for acquittal. To avoid a complete verdict of acquittal, no vote was taken on the remaining articles—a trick which disgusted Evarts.[51]

Each senator was allowed to file an opinion, giving reasons for his vote. Trumbull declared in his statement that the President had the right to remove Stanton; that no proof of guilt had been shown; and that, if a precedent were set for removing the chief magistrate on insufficient grounds, no President would be safe when confronted by a hostile two thirds in Congress. Grimes and Henderson took the same view. Henderson, who had opposed impeachment from the first, declared, "I would as soon have voted to condemn an innocent man to death as to vote to impeach Johnson on the articles that were presented." For their temerity, the little group of senators were denounced by the Radicals, and none of them was reelected to Congress.[52]

The acquittal was a triumph of right over wrong. Time has vindicated both Johnson and those who voted in his behalf. Eventually Sherman, Blaine, and even Sumner admitted that the impeachment had been unjustified. Nearly all historical investigators have taken that view.

What weight should be given to Evarts' share in attaining this happy result? No accurate answer to this question is possible because of the numerous factors involved. But coming at the close of the pleadings, his argument, if not the best, was perhaps the most effective. His work during the trial gained for him national recognition as a shrewd reasoner, a profound lawyer, a great interpreter of constitutional law, and an orator of the highest rank. The most immediate consequence of his labors was his return to political life at Washington.

12

In the Johnson Cabinet

JOHNSON RENOMINATED Stanbery for attorney general, but in a spirit of resentment the Senate rejected him without giving reasons. Stanbery was glad to retire, writing Evarts, "They have done me a great service and if they are satisfied, so am I." When Curtis refused the vacancy, the President upon Seward's advice turned to Evarts, though doubtless with much reluctance. Evarts' acceptance strengthened Seward's position in the Cabinet during the remaining eight months of the administration.[1]

For a time it appeared that the Senate might reject Evarts. Butler appeared before the Judiciary Committee, to which the nomination had been referred, and launched a furious attack upon him. But the committee had the good sense to strike Butler's tirade from the record and report favorably. The Senate thereupon ratified the appointment by a vote of twenty-seven to seven, with Wade and Sumner among the opposition.[2]

The choice was pleasing to moderates of all parties. Evarts was well equipped for the office. But it would do little to improve his reputation, and in view of Evarts' well-known opposition to Johnson's policies was bound to raise a question. Gideon Welles considered Evarts' acceptance unwise, declaring, "The finger of Seward is in this." Rockwood Hoar warned Evarts that it was unwise for a counsel to go into partnership with a grateful client, but trusted that God would deliver him from the evils that would surround him.[3] There were other reasons why Evarts might well have refused. The shortness of the term would be an interruption of his law practice scarcely worth while; public opinion would misunderstand his acceptance, causing him a loss of prestige and destroying any chance he might have of political preferment with the Grant administration that was to follow.

What then led him to accept the office against the advice of some of his closest friends? Did the loss of the senatorship and chief justiceship, which still irked him, lead him to grasp at this office as a substitute? The fact is that he regarded it as a duty to accept. He wrote Dana: "As for a personal career in politics, I have never felt at liberty to plan for one, and I have less inclination for it than ever. I came here to do my duty in a difficult and dangerous juncture of the Government. I shall do it, and return to my business of farming and lawing, and leave to the newspaper correspondents the conduct of my affairs."[4]

He took over his new duties on July 20. Visitors poured in to congratulate him on the first day, and on the second he attended the first Cabinet meeting. He brought his family to Washington and leased a house in a fashionable neighborhood at the corner of Fourteenth and H streets.[5]

The New York Bar Association wished to honor him with a public dinner. "We are quite sure," read the invitation, "that we give expression to the general sentiment of the profession and the country, when we say, that your acceptance of the post, at serious sacrifice to yourself, reflects the highest credit upon you as a citizen, and evinces a patriotic spirit which may well challenge invitation." The dinner took place at the Astor House with some four hundred present. They marched arm-in-arm by twos into the banquet hall, Evarts and O'Conor leading the way, General Grant on the arm of Judge Davies, Admiral Farragut with Edwards Pierrepont, and General Banks with A. T. Stewart. The Radicals had planned a counter-dinner to give Grant an excuse for absence, for the General had declared he would not attend if certain Cabinet members who had testified against him at the impeachment trial were present. But he came, realizing that he would otherwise commit a gross breach of etiquette. After all, he was friendly with Evarts. When introduced, he made a speech of one sentence.[6]

The dinner proved a brilliant success. Evarts was delighted to find among the guests the aged Vice-Chancellor McCoun, before whom he had argued his earliest cases. To the congratulations that were showered upon him he responded modestly. He described his new office as professional, not political; and with the profession as his theme, he gave free rein to his wit. It was like the canvas-back duck, he said, which did not dive for its food, but waited till the other ducks brought the food to the surface and then took its share. By his story he illustrated the difference between office work and converting a jury. A tailor entered a law office on a hot summer day and asked the lawyer how he could work in such weather: to which the lawyer replied that he was only looking over some papers. Sympathetically the tailor responded that on such hot days he too could do ordinary sewing, but when it came to buttonholing he had to have good weather and a clear mind.[7]

Evarts' relations with President Johnson quickly became cordial, but they were never intimate. They were different in political views and cultural background. Johnson admired Evarts, especially his gift of after-dinner speaking; Evarts thought highly of Johnson as a man, although not always approving the conduct of his office. "My intercourse with President Johnson," he wrote in after years, "gave me an opportunity for service to my country I ever enjoyed. President Johnson, during the whole time of my acquaintance with him, impressed one with the dignity of his manners, the sincerity of his patriotism, and his unfailing confidence in the spirit and purposes of the great body of the American people. I shared in the fullest degree in this estimate. Upon a just and candid estimate of President Johnson's conduct in difficult times, he will surely be placed by the general judgment of his countrymen, among those who have deserved the most and best of the Republic."[8]

Evarts was on cordial terms with all of the Cabinet except Gideon Welles. For Welles, regarding Evarts as a man who "accommodated himself pretty readily to any party or any set of principles" as he would to his clients and as "a stiff, sharp logician," distrusted him. The old Secretary of the Navy complained frequently of Evarts' absences from Cabinet meetings and of his professional engagements in New York.[9] True, Evarts was often away on his own professional work; but then, attorney generals had always engaged in private practice because their salary was so meager. Welles's prejudice was not personal; it was a dislike of all lawyers in public life.

With three Cabinet members Evarts was on very familiar terms. He liked Orville H. Browning, Secretary of the Interior, an able lawyer, orator, and friend of the oppressed. Browning had acted as attorney general *ad interim* after Stanbery's resignation. Still better did he like General Schofield, a genial, sympathetic, approachable, and unostentatious man. Schofield found serious problems in the War Office and frequently turned to Evarts for advice in legal matters. He one day asked Evarts if he could give the law offhand on certain points; to which Evarts replied that he could if the points concerned the common law, but if they involved questions of statute law, he would have to consult his books.[10]

Seward, of course, was most intimate with Evarts. Welles once remarked that he believed Evarts had the superior mind. It was a period of important foreign negotiations, and from Seward Evarts acquired information that was later of great value to him. The Darien Canal project was an illustration of the close relationship between them. A treaty was negotiated with Colombia giving the United States complete control of the Darien route across the isthmus. Seward and Evarts went to New York to organize a company to construct the canal. The stockholders met at Peter Cooper's house and Seward, ably seconded by Evarts, spoke enthusiastically of the project.[11]

Evarts' residence on fashionable H Street became a social center during his last two months in office. He acquired the same reputation for hospitality that he enjoyed in New York and Windsor. The reception he gave on January 20, 1869, was the most brilliant of the season. President-Elect Grant, Vice-President-Elect Colfax, congressmen, senators, representatives of the bench and bar, the army and navy—indeed, most of the wealth and fashion of Washington—drove up in their carriages. Mrs. Evarts and her charming daughters greeted the guests with unaffected cordiality. The whole family had a great knack for entertaining. At this reception Grant enjoyed Evarts' wit, as did Admiral Farragut and General Hancock. Ben Butler was present and in excellent spirits, ready for banter with anybody, vowing that he did not carry political feuds into social life.[12] The dinner party in February at Evarts' home in honor of the Supreme Court was another splendid affair. Besides the justices, three of the Cabinet, several senators, General Garfield, and General Thomas were guests. A mammoth bouquet of rare flowers, its fringe of violets arranged to form the words: *Justitia fiat, Ruat prandium,* attracted attention.[13]

The delightful acquaintance between Evarts and Henry Adams was renewed. Adams had returned from England to enter journalism. Happening to meet him on the street in New York, Evarts invited him to come to Washington and stay with him. Adams accepted, as did Moorfield Storey, another young man ambitious for a literary career, when similarly invited. Both found a cordial welcome.[14]

When Evarts took Adams to call upon the President, Johnson was not particularly interested in a reformer educated in two or three foreign countries; but he received the young man cordially and gave him "a little lecture upon constitutional law." Adams began to scrape acquaintance with congressmen and newspaper men and to write articles for periodicals, obtaining information from Evarts, and confessing his guilt in stealing ideas from him. Through Evarts he got access to the archives of the State Department to begin his historical research. Describing Evarts in after years, Adams said, "Generous by nature, prodigal in hospitality, fond of young people, and a born man of the world, Evarts gave and took liberally without scruple, accepted the world without fearing or abusing it. He laughed where he could; he joked if a joke were possible; he was true to his friends and never lost his temper."[15]

In the Cabinet discussions upon the policies of the administration, Evarts stood for two principles. First, he believed in fair treatment of both races in the South. The efforts of Secretary of War Schofield to preserve order in the South and secure fair elections for the newly enfranchised voters, were cordially assisted by Evarts. He also strongly opposed the numerous suits which Radical congressmen were urging for the confiscation of Southern property, and he urged Johnson to recognize the new governments in the South, erected under military supervision, in order to avoid falling into another impeachment trap which Congress was setting for him.[16]

In the second place, Evarts believed in a restoration of the balance between the legislative and executive departments. He vigorously opposed any surrender to the Radicals in Congress. One day he bluntly asked the Cabinet if Congress were to be permitted to take over the executive branch of government, and advised Johnson to rebuke the Radical leaders for their encroachments.[17]

But his chief rôle was that of mediator between Congress and the President. He sought to restrain Johnson and yet restore the balance. He knew the temper of the Radicals well. Johnson had confidence in him and followed his advice more closely than he had Stanbery's. Evarts was not as obnoxious to the Radicals as other members of the Cabinet and thereby had some success as pacificator. Even old Thad Stevens, arch-Radical of them all, on the day of his death welcomed Evarts at his bedside and spoke of him highly.[18]

Evarts was the last attorney general to leave office before the organization of the Department of Justice in 1870. Not only was the legal business of the government scattered and uncoördinated, but an excessive amount of labor was expected of the attorney general. Beside giving legal opinions he was expected to appear in cases in the Supreme Court. His staff comprised only two assistants and nine clerks. Samuel Hoar, oldest son of Rockwood Hoar and just out of Harvard, was appointed pardon clerk, and W. F. Peddrick became chief clerk.[19]

An illustration of Evarts' characteristic discretion in making appointments is furnished by his filling of a vacant judgeship in Vermont. There were numerous aspirants. Evarts, much to the disgust of a certain New York lawyer, nominated the youngest and least known. "Don't trouble yourself about Evarts," said a friend to the lawyer, "he lives half the year in Windsor and understands the situation. He knows that he can fish up any trout-stream in Vermont, and catch a better man for a judge than he could find in your big city with Lord Rosse's telescope and a search-warrant."[20]

During his short term Evarts rendered about forty legal opinions, which for pithiness, style, and value compare favorably with those of any predecessor. The most widely discussed, perhaps, was his opinion on the eight-hour law for laborers employed by the government. Many workers preferred a ten-hour day if they were given a slight increase in pay. When the War Department reduced wages in proportion to the shortened day, a great protest arose from organized labor, and a committee of workingmen asked the President to seek Evarts' opinion. Evarts sustained the War Department, holding that the eight-hour law placed no restriction upon wages. Although legally correct, the decision was most unpopular, and when Grant became President, an order was issued forbidding any department to reduce wages in proportion to the reduction in hours.[21]

Evarts' most important opinions related to the power of the President to appoint and remove under the Tenure of Office Act. To check the vast fraud and corruption in the office of the internal revenue commissioner, Evarts held that the President could not compromise cases of internal revenue frauds, but must submit them to the attorney general or the secretary of the treasury. Regarding Rollins, the head of the Internal Revenue Bureau, as a "stool-pigeon" for the Radicals, Johnson sought to get rid of him. When he resigned, Congress dared the President to appoint a successor and threatened impeachment again. Johnson wished to accept the challenge and, against Evarts' advice, accepted the resignation as unconditional. In the controversy which followed, opinion was about equally divided as to the wisdom or unwisdom of the President's course. Johnson finally sought Evarts' opinion and it was generally expected that Evarts would declare the office vacant under the Tenure of Office Act. But Evarts held that Rollins could retain the office till his successor had been confirmed by the Senate. Legally the opinion was sound; politically it saved Johnson from a trap; but it left Rollins in office to the end of the term. Although Evarts avoided any opinion upon the constitutionality of the act, it could be inferred that he believed it to be void, and that the removal power should vest exclusively in the President.[22] He rendered other opinions on appointment and removal which likewise sustained the power of the President.[23] In one army case, however, he held that the President had no right to restore the commission of a resigned army officer.[24]

Opinions were required upon government subsidies to the Union Pacific Railroad, upon claims against the government, upon mail contracts, upon courts-martial, and upon the use of the army to assist sheriffs and marshals in the execution of the law.[25]

A topic which filled the newspapers from 1865 to 1868 was the prosecution of Jefferson Davis for treason. As counsel for the government, Evarts had a leading part in this unhappy affair before and during his attorney generalship.

From the day that Davis was imprisoned in Fortress Monroe the Radicals had called loudly for his death. This was not because he had been the Confederate President, but because he was believed to have been connected with the plot to assassinate Lincoln. Johnson and Seward, both of whom were objects of the assassination plot, at first favored the prosecution. Indeed, in 1865, the Cabinet had at first been inclined to favor a charge of murder, but finally decided that a charge of treason, with a civil rather than a military trial, would be better because it would permit a judicial decision declaring secession to be treason. Attorney General Speed retained as prosecutors John H. Clifford, former Attorney General of Massachusetts, Lovell H. Rousseau, a Kentucky congressman, and Evarts. It was agreed that Davis should be brought before the Circuit Court in Richmond, with Chief Justice Chase and District Judge Underwood presiding.

Then a succession of delays arose. Chase, opposed to the prosecution, refused to hold court in an area still subject to military law. A year of inaction followed. In April, 1866, Speed called the counsel to Washington to frame a hastily made indictment; but still Chase refused to try the case. Clifford withdrew, believing there was little probability anyway of convicting Davis before a Virginia jury. The resignation of Speed and the accession of Stanbery to office caused further delay.

Meanwhile Davis had retained Charles O'Conor and James T. Brady to defend him. O'Conor tried for two years to secure Davis' release on bail. Though the Radicals balked his efforts, he took heart when he saw the half-heartedness of the government. In fact, no one showed much energy in the prosecution. Rousseau dropped out; Lucius Chandler, district attorney at Richmond, was dubious about the indictment; Stanbery seemed indifferent, leaving the counsel to do as they wished; and to his dismay Evarts found by the spring of 1867 that he alone was responsible for the prosecution, and that a hearing on the question of bail was to come before Judge Underwood within two weeks. Realizing the embarrassment of the government, O'Conor decided to force the issue, demanding that Davis either be given an immediate trial or freed on bail.

Evarts and many others believed that bail could not be given in cases of treason. General surprise was felt, therefore, when Judge Underwood granted it, fixing the sum at one hundred thousand dollars, which was supplied by Horace Greeley, Cornelius Vanderbilt, and Gerrit Smith. Davis was released. Then came the question of a trial. Reluctantly Evarts appeared before Underwood and admitted that the government was not ready for the trial. It was not at all his fault that O'Conor thus scored a double victory.[26]

To strengthen the prosecution Evarts and Chandler secured the services of H. H. Wells, an expert criminal lawyer, and R. H. Dana. Stanbery began to show some interest, but insisted that Evarts should take full charge. Quite disgusted, Evarts said to Dana, "It may be that the trial will take place at the end of November, more likely in May next, and likely as either, not at all."[27] He agreed with Dana that there should be no trial unless Chase presided. While waiting, Evarts and Dana began to prepare a new indictment. Chandler and Wells were set to work to find new evidence, and in November Evarts and Dana went to Richmond to examine what they had found. Their work was highly unsatisfactory and endangered the whole case, because by law an indictment had to issue within three years after the offense. Evarts wrote Chandler some sharp letters.[28]

Dana had by this time become convinced that the prosecution should be abandoned. "Why," he asked, "should the United States voluntarily assume the risk of a failure, by putting the question of the treason of Jefferson Davis to a petit jury of rebel vicinage? Who can warrant that one man on the jury may not be a sympathizer with Davis, or be persuaded by fear or other influence to disagree?" Evarts agreed with him, and replied, "If you will draw a letter to the Attorney General . . . that the Government will do better to proceed no further in the cause, and send it to me with your signature, I will add mine to it."[29] Dana did so, but Evarts withheld the letter for a time because Stanbery had resigned and the impeachment case had begun.

By March, 1868, Chandler and Wells brought the evidence they had been collecting to Washington and a lengthy new indictment was drawn. A grand jury approved it in the Richmond Circuit Court, with Davis absent. Instead of bringing the indictment under an act of 1862, which applied only a fine and prison penalty, the government brought it under an act of 1790 which carried the death penalty, thus making conviction more difficult.

Just as it seemed that a trial was at last to begin, the impeachment case in Washington interrupted the proceedings. O'Conor was alarmed by the possibility that Ben Wade might become president, and advised Davis to jump his bail if the impeachment succeeded. He blamed Seward for the many delays, referring to him as "a cowardly snake-in-the-grass official" who pretended to be "very innocent and indifferent." But later that spring O'Conor, greatly relieved by the failure of impeachment, readily agreed to a postponement until fall.[30]

When Evarts became attorney general, the responsibility for the prosecution fell completely on his shoulders. Johnson was against it; Seward was for it. Evarts had no difficulty in getting Dana to address a "spontaneous" letter to him to be read in Cabinet meeting. Here Dana set forth at length the reasons why he believed the prosecution should be dropped, declaring, among other arguments: "The risks of such an absurd and discreditable issue of a great State trial are assumed for the sake of a verdict which, if obtained, will settle nothing in law or national practice not now settled, and nothing of fact not now in history, while no judgement rendered thereon do we think will ever be executed." Evarts read the letter to the Cabinet, expressing full agreement with it, and recommended that the President issue a proclamation of general amnesty and "close out the rebellion." Johnson agreed, as did also Browning and McCulloch; but Seward and Welles opposed. It was finally arranged that Evarts should prepare an amnesty proclamation and present it at the next meeting. But Johnson hesitated to issue it, forcing Evarts to keep up the appearance of a prosecution and to seek a delay of the trial till a new administration should be in power.[31]

O'Conor now saw an opportunity to end these wearisome delays and save Davis. He warned Evarts that he was about to seek a suppression of the indictment under the Fourteenth Amendment, which prescribed disability from office as the punishment for those in Davis' position. The case was heard on November 30, 1868, in the Richmond court. Chase approved O'Conor's argument, and Underwood opposed it. The case was therefore certified to the Supreme Court for final decision. It was pending there on December 25, when Johnson finally issued the amnesty proclamation.[32]

Amnesty came as a relief to Evarts. He knew the Supreme Court would quash the indictment, but he wished to avoid the appearance of a defeat for the government. He therefore agreed with O'Conor to drop the prosecution if the matter were not pressed in the Supreme Court. O'Conor readily assented, and just before Evarts left office he entered a *nolle prosequi* and Davis was set free. The case had cost the government $21,950, of which Evarts had received $10,540 as counsel. To be sure, he lost an opportunity to appear in another great state trial; but the task would not have been congenial. His efforts in having the case dismissed were for the best interests of the country.[33]

Evarts appeared frequently in the Supreme Court during his eight months in office, often with his assistant, J. Hubley Ashton. A new series of prize cases had arisen from the war, and had to be prosecuted.

The case of the *Georgia* was the most important. This Confederate cruiser had sought refuge in Liverpool, and had been purchased by Bates, a British citizen. The ship went to sea under a British flag but was captured by a Union cruiser as a prize. Bates claimed that it was neutral property; Evarts contended it was a lawful prize and the Court upheld him.[34] The Court likewise sustained him in the blockade-running case of the *Diana* and in the Confiscation Cases.[35] In the Braine Piracy Case Evarts refused to apply the amnesty proclamation to a pirate who tried to hide his crime under the cloak of an act of war.[36]

He won still other victories. The Floyd Acceptances Case, involving a government contract with the famous Western express company, Russell, Majors, and Wadell, occupied press headlines for a time. Two Western land claim cases and one concerning rebates on customs duties were not as important. The case of *United States* v. *Rosenberg,* in which Evarts' opponent was his Windsor neighbor, E. W. Stoughton, and which related to forged certificates, was one of the two or three cases Evarts lost in the Supreme Court.[37]

But the Legal Tender Cases were by far the most important litigations. The issue was the validity of the Legal Tender Act of

1862, under which Congress had issued irredeemable paper as legal tender for debts. The general expectation was that the Supreme Court would sustain the act, which had already been upheld in seventeen states. The issue was squarely raised in the case of *Hepburn* v. *Griswold*. Evarts and Benjamin R. Curtis argued for the constitutionality of the law, while Clarkson N. Potter and J. A. Townsend were opposed. Evarts knew he would have to rest upon the doctrine of implied powers, and was puzzled to find a course of reasoning that would prove convincing. He discussed the case often with Henry Adams as they drove, dined, and walked together, using Adams as an anvil on which to hammer his ideas by encouraging him to debate the subject.[38]

A spectator described the trial as "an intellectual banquet." Curtis spoke first in his usual lucid style, occupying not more than an hour. Townsend and Potter consumed two days in reply, stressing the injustice of legal tender notes and the attitude of the framers of the Constitution toward them. Potter overloaded his argument with illustrations, some of them of doubtful analogy.

Evarts' argument abounded in learning and clever illustration. Except that he was too deliberate at times, causing the attention of the Court to flag temporarily, his argument was a model of excellence. As one listener put it, "There was something so stirring in the many eloquent illustrations and appeals of the Attorney-General, that we could not but feel that very likely they would effect a lodgement in the sternest legal minds."[39]

"My first proposition," said Evarts, "is that to determine what shall be the money of the country . . . belongs to the government." It was not a question of private right or liberty; it was one of government policy. Moreover, he argued, "I submit that this exercise of authority by Congress is no encroachment upon . . . the State Governments." The relations of debtor and creditor, the coining of money, and issuing of bills of credit—all this belonged to Congress, not the states. The records of the Convention of 1787 showed that the control of the currency was to lodge solely in Congress.[40]

The gist of his argument centered upon his third point—that the issue of legal tender notes was an implied power of Congress. It was justified for precisely the same reason that Marshall had justified a national bank, Congress possessing this power just as it possessed the right to regulate currency and declare war. The framers did not list it among the delegated powers because they knew its pernicious character in normal times. "We have eighty years of government," he said, "without resorting to this as a means in aid in any necessity. It was only when we come to a civil war . . . that this exceptional and excessive expedient . . . has been resorted to. . . . I am . . . an admirer of the State constitutions, their vigor, energy, and protection. But you might as well say that the sick man argued wisely who recounted to his physician that he had passed through the diseases of childhood and had never taken calomel as a reason under the congestive fever of the marshes, why he should submit to no other stronger doses than had saved him from the mumps and chickenpox."

He pictured the dire emergency of 1862, the pressing need for money, the fear that the government might actually collapse. Under these circumstances, the act was an absolute necessity, and no adequate substitute had ever been proposed. The government might have gone even further, taken the taxpayer by the throat and exacted his last farthing. If it could levy a draft and tear men from their homes, it could issue legal tender to "float the ship of state over the breakers." And what followed? "Taxes were possible to be paid; services and supplies were possible to be obtained; and the faith of the people in their Government did give an intrinsic value to the promise to pay in gold and silver when the Government should be able to pay."[41]

It was not until fourteen months later, when Grant was president, that the Court rendered an opinion. Contrary to the general expectation, and in flat opposition to his earlier attitude as secretary of the treasury, Chase held the act unconstitutional as applied to debts contracted before 1862.[42] It was a four-to-three decision, with two vacancies in the Court. It aroused great hostility in Congress; the country still needed the greenbacks, for it was far from ready for a specie basis.

Evarts' argument, to which the government counsel recurred, still had force. Two new justices were appointed, and in the case of *Knox* v. *Lee* in 1871 the Court reversed itself, upholding the Legal Tender Act. This new opinion was a vindication of the position taken by Evarts, but he doubted the wisdom of such a rapid shift of opinion by the Court. In a public address three years later he remarked: "The signal spectacle of the Court, which had judged over Congress and Secretary, now judging over itself, gave rise to much satire. . . . I concede it to be a subject of thorough regret that the just result was not reached by less uncertain steps. . . . But a large reason and wider prudence . . . drew the Court from the perilous edge of *law-making*."[43]

After all, Evarts' experience in the Johnson Cabinet was brief. The last meeting of the Cabinet on the morning of March 4, 1869, was interesting. Grant had flatly refused to ride up Pennsylvania Avenue in the same carriage with Johnson. Several of the Cabinet felt that the President could not with self-respect appear at the inaugural ceremony; but Evarts, Seward, and Schofield believed that he should. Evarts played the rôle of conciliator to the last. The President left the matter in doubt till the next morning. As the Cabinet assembled at the White House, most of them anxious to attend the inaugural, they looked askance at the President. Evarts kept his overcoat on and Seward asked if all were ready to attend. But Johnson ordered them to sit down and finish certain matters of business. At noon, after the inaugural was over, he rose and bade them farewell as they rode away in their carriages.[44]

A few days later, regretting that he was unable to attend a dinner given in honor of Johnson in Baltimore, Evarts sent an open letter, declaring that he would always appreciate Johnson's tolerance in appointing him, and would forever feel a personal obligation toward him.[45]

Rumors had been current that Grant was to retain Evarts in the Cabinet. The two men were on cordial terms despite Grant's Radical leanings and his clash with Evarts during the impeachment trial. Evarts, Moses H. Grinnell, and General Wickham were guests of Grant at a private dinner just before the retiring attorney general left Washington. Speaking of his contacts with Grant during his last months of office, Evarts said, "We were thrown into the most agreeable social relations. . . . So far as I was concerned, the relations between the incoming President and myself were of the kindest description." There are indications that Evarts would have accepted a Cabinet post if offered.[46] But it may have been just as well that he did not join an administration which soon came to be known for its notoriously low standards.

The year 1868 had been crowded with events for Evarts. He had defended Johnson, prosecuted Jefferson Davis, argued the Legal Tender Cases, and become a national figure in politics. It marked also the twenty-fifth anniversary of his marriage. Congratulating him, Rockwood Hoar wrote, "Like most of your doings in life, the marriage may now be safely pronounced a decided success—I am inclined to think the most brilliant success of all."[47]

13

Reformer

EVARTS AT ONCE returned to New York to resume his practice. He was astonished and dismayed by what had happened during his absence. The city had fallen into the clutches of the most dishonest ring in its history. Notwithstanding the pressure of his work, he decided to fight for civic reform. Corruption had grown so alarmingly since the mayoralty of Fernando Wood that nothing but an immediate wakening of the electorate could save the city.

In the New York Constitutional Convention of 1867, Evarts had already shown his strong interest in judicial reform. The Union League Club had appointed him a member of its committee to prepare for this convention. One hundred and sixty delegates had assembled at Albany on June 4, 1867, and for eight months had wrestled with difficult governmental problems. Evarts, Horace Greeley, George W. Curtis, Samuel J. Tilden, and Edwards Pierrepont had been delegates-at-large from New York City, and the convention had been of high quality, and its debates of a high order. It proved to be one of the best state conventions ever assembled.[1]

In the convention of 1867 the reform of the Court of Appeals was the chief question. This tribunal was overburdened with work; the eight-year term of the judges was too short; and the personnel of the court changed too frequently. Evarts was one of the judiciary committee of fifteen to which this problem was referred. No abler committee could have been chosen—all its members were judges or lawyers of high repute. Its report proposed that the judges of the Court of Appeals should be elected by districts and hold office for good behavior to the age of seventy.[2]

The convention quickly agreed to certain minor recommendations made by the committee; but the questions of short or long tenure, and of the election or the appointment of judges, created a sharp division. Public sentiment had reacted strongly against the elective method, so popular when the Constitution of 1846 was written. The convention decided to leave the issue to the voters. The other great issue, that of tenure, provoked the best debate of the session. On December 5 an amendment was offered to the committee report, calling for a fourteen-year term instead of life tenure to seventy. Speeches for and against the amendment followed, resulting in what the *Times* described as "the most brilliant day in the history of the convention." Daly and Evarts made the best pleas for life tenure.[3]

In view of President Franklin D. Roosevelt's proposed reform of the tenure of Supreme Court judges, Evarts' words have a modern implication. "Taking them as men," he said of the judges, "we are yet to endeavor to protect and fortify them as much as possible against the weakness of human nature. . . . What is low in them, we are to endeavor to raise and support; what is strong in them, we are to cherish, defend, and preserve. . . . Public office is for public service, and not for private advantage. . . . I . . . have . . . a very earnest conviction that the experience of both England and of this country . . . built upon the plan of judicial tenure during good behavior . . . give the best judges. . . . I say the State must make its best offer to a man of this intelligence. . . . She must offer him a career commensurate with the talents, and the character, and the duty that belong to him as man. She shall not offer him a broken life; she shall not require him to exchange for the public service, for half of his life, a personal career his talents and his character assure him for a whole life. . . . If there be any influence that is worse than any other, . . . it is this feeling that it is of no great consequence at any time what is done by anybody in regard to any office, because it is not to last long, and there will be opportunity to correct the error."[4]

It was a challenging plea. But life tenure seemed to many then, as now, dangerous. When a compromise was submitted, making the judges reëligible for a second term of fourteen years, Evarts rose to object. Life tenure, he insisted, was not dangerous for the Court of Appeals. Not one judge had ever disgraced it. Men might as well argue that the marriage tie should not be permanent because of the possibility of a bad wife. "We must choose," he concluded, "and if the principle of responsibility is to outweigh the principle of independence, then we must have short terms and frequently recurring elections."[5]

Evarts was greatly stirred by the issue. He asked Greeley to publish his speech in the *Tribune* to educate public opinion. But he was disappointed. Three times the convention rejected life tenure, the vote on the last ballot being forty-five to fifty-one. It was evident that the rural Republican delegates had joined the Democrats in opposing it. A fourteen-year term was finally agreed upon.[6]

The convention of 1867 was so protracted that Evarts' attendance became irregular. One day Greeley grew exasperated with the delays, and left for two or three weeks. Finding the same delegate speaking when he returned, he exclaimed, "My God, hasn't that man got through yet?"[7] Evarts served on the committee of revision, and was chairman of the committee on the Preamble and the Bill of Rights. Except in dealing with judicial reform, his work was incidental. He spoke against the disenfranchisement of those engaged in the rebellion, against giving the governor the right to veto items in bills, and against the delegation of financial powers to counties and municipalities.[8]

At the subsequent referendum the voters, by a close margin, rejected all the work of the convention except judicial reform. The failure of the new Constitution was probably due to the preoccupation of the electorate with the readjustments of Reconstruction.

The corruption shown by various judges in New York City

offered a sorry contrast to the generally high character of the state judiciary. Unscrupulous judges and lawyers throve under the patronage of the Tweed Ring, which had been fixing its tentacles with an ever increasing grip since 1865. During the mayoralty campaign that year Evarts first voiced his disgust with the situation. Speaking at a Union party rally, he urged the election of Marshall O. Roberts. The city, he declared, ought to have a new form of government, which should be a model for the other cities of the nation. His hits at the three factions in the Democratic party were greatly appreciated. But Tammany was too strong and elected John T. Hoffman by a close margin. Elated by his victory, Hoffman boasted that the city, washed by its two rivers, could congratulate itself upon its virtue in choosing him; to which Evarts retorted at a New England Society dinner with the apt quotation:

> "The River Rhine, as is well known,
> Washes the city of Cologne;
> But tell me all ye nymphs divine,
> What power shall wash the River Rhine?"[9]

Four years later, at another New England Society dinner in 1869, Evarts began his labors for the reform of the city bench and bar. In the midst of a gay, impromptu speech, he suddenly became serious. "The lawyer is driven from politics," he said, "because there is no politics. They have suffered an eclipse—not total, to be sure, but annular; nothing but a *ring* visible. . . . A great duty, a heavier labor is before us. It is to meet and combat, in every station that affects the popular welfare, corruption. . . . This community can be rescued from the vilest servitudes."[10]

The first step in reform was the creation of the Bar Association. In 1869 two hundred lawyers, with Evarts' name at the head of the list, petitioned for an association. At their first meeting, the signers planned a constitution, and chose an executive committee of sixteen, with Evarts as chairman. The committee issued a call to a select list of lawyers, known to be in sympathy with the movement, to meet to ratify the constitution and complete the organization. The aims, declared the committee, were to fix standards of admission to the bar, to increase the term of judges and mitigate their influence in politics, to procure a suitable building and a library, and to restore the "glory and dignity" of the bar. "We mean to come together as a body," continued the committee, "to look the question fairly in the face, and if we find that we have been tainted by the influence of the times to undertake ourselves the work of purification, to revive a past renown, and to give new life to traditions we believe only to be dormant, not extinct." The organizers were at first careful to disavow any intention of political reform.[11]

To perfect the organization a meeting was called on February 1, 1870, and a committee of nine was appointed to prepare a constitution and by-laws. Discussion of professional ethics kept the meeting to a late hour. Notable points were made by Evarts, Pierrepont, Stoughton, Nicoll, Tilden, Emott, Eaton, and Edmonds. Evarts appealed for an honest and absolutely fearless organization. "I can remember," he said, "when, for a lawyer to come out from the chambers of a judge with an *ex parte* writ that he could not defend before the public, before the profession and before the Court, would have occasioned the same sentiment toward him as if he came out with a stolen pocket-book. . . . If an institution contains corruption, and if the line is not drawn closely to sever it at once from the sound body, however honest may be the purpose of the worthy members, the plague-spot is in the body, and the *whole is sick*."[12]

The Bar Association was soon spurred to more aggressive action. It offered a large reward for the apprehension of certain assailants who had attacked Dorman B. Eaton. It adopted a constitution, elected Evarts its first president, and chose an executive committee and a committee on admissions. It was a great honor for Evarts, one which he would not have accepted, had the election not been unanimous. He remained president for nine consecutive years.[13]

Continuing its efforts, the Association set up a standard of requirements for admission to the bar, and ultimately got a law through the legislature giving the Court of Appeals authority to fix requirements for admission to the bar. A building at 20 West

27th Street was purchased, and the first meeting in the new quarters was on June 28, 1870. Evarts was generous in contributing money and law books; and when, in 1875, a fine new mansion for the Association was built at 7 West 29th Street, his firm was one of the few large contributors. Among the more valuable of his gifts to the library were fifty-one volumes of *British and Foreign State Papers,* one hundred and thirty-two volumes of the *Chronicles of Great Britain and Ireland During the Middle Ages,* thirty-six volumes of Cobbett's *Parliamentary History,* two hundred and seventy-four volumes of Hansard's *Parliamentary Debates,* and thirty-one volumes of documents relating to the Geneva arbitration of 1872.[14]

It required skill, tact, and leadership to conduct the affairs of the Association during these formative years. Evarts' reëlection for the longest period that any president has as yet served speaks for his success.

The bar turned its guns upon Boss Tweed, Pete Sweeney, Slippery Dick Connolly, and Elegant Oakey Hall, who had been plundering the city for five years. In the city elections of 1868, marked by every conceivable fraud, the Ring had gained control of the municipal government, inaugurating a reign of plunder. Tweed was bold and unscrupulous; Connolly was needed for his knowledge of finance; Sweeney, the chamberlain, was the brains of the Ring; but Hall, the mayor, was different—a man of good New York family, versatile, cultured, and influenced by ambition rather than greed.

The Ring controlled judges, district attorneys, grand juries, the Common Council, finances, department heads, police, election officials—in short, everything connected with county and city government. It worked through subordinate rings, the chief of which was the combination of George G. Barnard, Albert Cardozo, and John McCunn, all judges of local courts. Barnard had turned from reform to graft, as a result of disappointed ambition, to become the most vicious of the three; Cardozo was learned and industrious, but utterly lacking in respect for the law; McCunn was ignorant and out for plunder. Upon this triumvirate the Ring could depend for legal protection. To complete his control, Tweed got himself elected to the state senate and ultimately gained control of the legislature. By February, 1870, he was bold enough to seek a new city charter designed to centralize power in the Ring.

The people were indifferent, failing to understand the gravity of the situation. During the fall of 1870 some public sentiment was aroused and a fusion ticket put in the field; but Tweed boldly defied the opposition and asked, "What are you going to do about it?" Hall was reëlected mayor. Evarts had a typical experience at the polls. On giving his name to the election clerk, he was told that Mr. Evarts had already voted. "Has he, indeed," said Evarts. "I hope he voted right."[15]

Describing the predicament of New York some years after, Evarts said: "What a strange situation we had gotten into and what a strange set of pot-bellied tyrants this great city was subjected to. Without genius, without courage, without fame, they contrived to bestride this great community like a colossus; and certainly for some years we did not do, or think we could do, anything but peep about to find ourselves dishonorable graves."[16]

His first real effort against the Ring was a speech at Cooper Institute on April 6, 1871. This was addressed to a mass meeting held to protest against the new twenty-two-million-dollar tax bill which the triumphant Ring was about to force upon the city. Voicing general indignation, Evarts said: "The truth is, gentlemen, that a meeting like this is but a symptom of what occupies the public mind throughout the whole country—of deep, serious concern about the very institutions upon which our liberty rests. . . . You can have it [liberty] stolen from you whenever you do not arrest the thief. You can have it murdered before your eyes when you are too cowardly to intercept the assassin. . . . It is no longer a matter of pride to be a New Yorker; it is a matter of deep disgrace. . . . I do not wonder that the Democratic masters scoff and sneer at the virtue of the Republican party which they have measured and bought. . . . I cannot express my contempt for the people that throw away in open day the power of taxation on the cringing argument that if we complain, somebody else will tax us more. . . . I propose that at the next election we will have some representatives who are satisfied with being representatives, and not placemen."

This mass meeting marked the beginning of a genuine public revolt. The speeches of Henry Ward Beecher and Dr. Bellows were also thought-provoking. The *Times* flared with the headlines: "The People Aroused." The Bar Association redoubled its efforts. Although aware that it had no power except that of a voluntary union of lawyers, and that its existence could be cut off by a Tweed-controlled legislature, its leaders went ahead fearlessly.[17]

Evarts helped to stop a legislative monstrosity in May. A bill passed the legislature increasing the patronage of the Supreme Court, extending its jurisdiction, and removing it from control by the Court of Appeals. The real purpose of the Ring was to gag the press and public. The Bar Association met hastily to protest, and Evarts raised a laugh when he said: "If the father of this bill is known to anyone present, I hope he will state it. It is doubtful if the Legislature knew they had passed it." Evarts headed a delegation to Albany to urge Governor Hoffman to veto the bill. He showed that the bill placed the people at the mercy of a judge's caprice, and Hoffman killed it.[18]

In July the *Times* began its startling revelations of the way in which the city had been mulcted of many millions of dollars. At a great mass meeting in September, Choate, with a scroll in his hand, shouted, "This is what *we* are going to do about it." Unrolling the scroll, he read twelve resolutions calling for a complete accounting by the Ring, a repeal of the new city charter, and punishment of the guilty. A committee of seventy, representing the general citizenry and led by Tilden and Havemeyer, was chosen to coöperate with the Bar Association in carrying forward the reform movement. Connolly's office was investigated and he was replaced by Andrew H. Green; legal proceedings were started against the Ring; and the *Times* redoubled its denunciations.[19]

Having been on a short pleasure trip to Europe during the late summer of 1871, Evarts took no part in these events. On returning in September, he found that his son Allen had joined an organization of young reformers and that public opinion was rising. The important object was to defeat the Ring at the November elections.[20] He appeared thrice before large audiences to denounce the Ring.

At Chickering Hall on October 20 he said, "I believe the people of the city of New York now thoroughly understand the length and breadth of the evil, the nature of the remedy, and that they have the courage, the constancy and the intelligence firmly and persistently to apply the peaceful remedies, that are to restore to the honest people of this city the management of their own affairs. . . . We must not underestimate the strength of Tammany. . . . Carry your Legislature, and you have the halter around the neck of every corrupt judge and every timid district attorney."

At Cooper Union a few days later, with Horace Greeley presiding, Evarts was the principal speaker at a huge Republican rally. The hall was jammed to the doors; a band and fireworks outside enlivened the scene. Not even a severe storm could keep the people away. Evarts spoke with great earnestness. "If a nation is either so stupid or so cowardly that it will not use the weapon under its control, it deserves to fall. . . . I say to you that there is no crime of treason under any government, written in any book, or in the bloody scaffolds that history shows us, that deserves so deep a curse, and so swift a retribution as the corruption of a free people. . . . These men laugh at you; they tell you in so many words that they will repeat, and repeat—miscount and miscount. . . . All persons of this city who, with the explicit evidence of these frauds before them, do not seek to redress and punish them by taking part against the criminals are their accessories after the fact. . . . Lovers of liberty in countries across the Atlantic, who are straining their eyes to see what is to come of all this, will conclude that the beacon of liberty has hidden its light forever." It was a stirring appeal, spoken, as the *Times* declared, "frankly and fearlessly."[21]

The legal proceedings against the Ring were put in charge of a

Bureau of Municipal Correction, which became a branch of the attorney general's office. O'Conor, who was made chief prosecutor, selected Evarts, Wheeler H. Peckham, and ex-Judge Emott as associates. Though charges were brought against Tweed, it was realized that the power of the Ring made success doubtful. A warrant for Tweed's arrest on October 28 was met by an immediate grant of bail.[22]

Evarts made his third speech just before the election, addressing a monster rally at Cooper Institute sponsored by the committee of seventy. Choate and Tilden also spoke. Excitement was greater than ever, and there was now no doubt of the attitude of the voters. Over the rostrum were emblazoned the words: "What are we going to do about it?" There was a note of victory in Evarts' brief speech. He begged the voters to turn out in such numbers that a deliberate miscount would be impossible. "The ballot is that which distinguishes a free government from a despotic one," he exhorted. "We must not be told flatly and squarely by these despots that we may vote as we please, and they will count as they please."[23]

No election was ever fraught with more vital consequences, or more anxiously awaited. In both the Republican and Democratic parties the better elements voted for reform. The Ring was defeated, and the fact that Tweed was reëlected to the Senate meant little.

The Ring quickly collapsed in the face of the triumphant onslaught. Tammany Hall was not lighted on election night. Sweeney fled to Europe. A committee of the Bar Association brought charges against Barnard, Cardozo, and McCunn. Cardozo resigned; the other two were impeached and removed. In short, a smashing victory was won. It was a striking illustration of the effectiveness of the ballot, without appeal to violence.

Just after the election Evarts left for Europe on an important mission to Geneva, returning in October, 1872. He found that the Ring no longer existed; but Tweed was still defiant and able with powerful legal support to ward off all proceedings against him. Reform was not complete as long as he was at large. Another election was at hand with Havemeyer running for mayor on the reform ticket against O'Brien, the Tammany candidate. At a great noonday meeting in front of the Subtreasury Building on Wall Street, Evarts cautioned the people against O'Brien's promises of reform. "An invitation to ride in the saloon car of Reform," he said, "does not mean a surrender of the engineership to his care."[24] Again the voters approved true reform by electing Havemeyer, and it remained only to smash Tweed.

Two months later, Tweed was brought before Judge Noah Davis. Many people suspected that he had "fixed" the jury, and that his counsel, David Dudley Field, William Fullerton, and young Elihu Root, would save him. Much to the disgust of Judge Davis, he did gain a respite. But a second trial took place without a jury, and Davis sentenced Tweed to twelve years in jail with a $12,000 fine. Evarts took no part in either trial; but a few days later, accompanied by the eminent British lawyer, Rothery, who was visiting him, he was spectator at a most unusual scene. Tweed's counsel, insisting that Judge Davis was biased, had petitioned him to refuse to appear in the case. Angered by this reflection upon his fairness, Davis now reprimanded Tweed's counsel; but Field was not present, having discreetly gone to Europe.[25] It was not till 1875 that Tweed was finally convicted by O'Conor in the famous Six Million Dollar Suit.

Evarts played a secondary rôle in the smashing of the Ring, for at the critical period he was absent on an important mission in Europe; but his speeches, his legal advice, and his moral support as president of the Bar Association were valuable factors in the outcome. His work probably explains why in 1873 he was elected president of the Union Club, one of the oldest, most exclusive and aristocratic clubs of the city.[26]

His rôle in the equally famous episode of the Erie Frauds was likewise intermittent because of interruptions. The story of the struggle of Cornelius Vanderbilt with Daniel Drew, Jim Fisk, and Jay Gould has been often told. It was early in 1868, just before the

Johnson impeachment trial, that Evarts first became connected with this legal battle. With bold effrontery the three conspirators—Fisk, Gould, and Drew—brought suit against the Chicago, Rock Island, & Pacific Railroad, of which they were stockholders, for committing the same offense of which they were most guilty: issuing illegal stock. They hoped to gain control of the railroad by stopping the issue of stock and securing the appointment of a receiver. They were represented by David Dudley Field and John K. Porter; while the defendants retained Evarts, Charles Tracy, William Fullerton, and Aaron J. Vanderpoel. Evarts' aim was to wrest the case from the clutches of Judge Cardozo and have it transferred to the Circuit Court. But Cardozo gave a verdict in favor of the conspirators and refused a removal to the federal court.[27] The episode illustrated anew the corrupt alliance between the judiciary and the grafters.

Evarts' next connection with the Erie was more important. In 1867 the Erie directors had agreed to guarantee the interest on five million dollars worth of bonds of the Boston, Hartford, & Erie Railroad, a bankrupt corporation under the control of an unscrupulous group headed by Robert H. Berdell. This Berdell mortgage was really a purchase by the Erie of five million dollars worth of the Boston, Hartford, & Erie bonds, and another pig-in-a-poke transaction. In 1868 the Boston road sought to sever its connection with the Erie, and was satisfied when the Erie purchased all of its bonds at eighty per cent of their par value, paying for them in part by Erie acceptances. J. C. Bancroft Davis, representative of the Boston road, consulted Evarts as to the value of the acceptances under the Berdell mortgage. Evarts gave a professional opinion, for which he received an extraordinary fee—the largest, it is said, of his career—holding that if the Erie did not make good on the acceptances, the Boston road could sue for an accounting and restoration of the bonds.[28]

The third scene was enacted three years later. Jim Fisk was now at the peak of his power, living in flashy style, managing his Opera House on Twenty-Third Street in swaggering manner, with his uniformed body-guard and troupe of coarse beauties. As Evarts said, he was "driving the four-in-hand of riches, packed with courtesans."[29] British investors, who had purchased millions of over-issued Erie stock and received no dividends, watched the plunder of the Erie by Gould and Fisk with dismay. They retained Evarts and Rockwood Hoar and sued in the Circuit Court for an accounting, restraint of further stock issues, and appointment of a receiver. Over a hundred charges were brought against Gould and a great legal battle ensued. David Dudley Field and Benjamin R. Curtis represented Gould.

There were two issues. Could the stockholders sue directors, and did the Circuit Court have jurisdiction? In the first round Judge Blatchford gave a verdict for the British stockholders. Then followed a suit to force Gould to turn over his books to a master for inspection. Again Evarts was victorious, and Gould acquiesced in a new receivership. But Gould had managed to keep part of the stock from falling into the receiver's hands. This led to another suit, and once more Judge Blatchford decided in favor of the British stockholders, requiring that the stock be registered.[30]

But the fight was not quite over. During Evarts' temporary absence in Europe Judge Blatchford gave a most unpopular decision in favor of Gould and went out of his way to reprimand Southmayd, who was acting in Evarts' place, for "addressing his argument to the newspapers." Gould still managed to hold a fifth of the stock demanded by the British stockholders. Evarts locked horns again with Field over this issue. Gould was forced to disgorge, at last, a defeat which closed his four years of plunder of the Erie, and resulted soon after in his dethronement as head of the road. Evarts might well feel that he had played a part in the result.[31]

There was a sequel. Peter H. Watson, new head of the Erie, continued to employ some of Gould's methods, and the stock fell to its lowest point. A bill was introduced at Albany to concentrate power in the hands of an Erie clique. Representing the stockholders, Evarts argued against the bill before the Senate Judiciary Committee, but it nevertheless became law. When he then sought signatures to a petition for the repeal of the law, unscrupulous enemies, posing as stockholders, signed the petition and then informed the committee that Evarts had urged them to forge their names. However, in July, 1874, a complete exposure of the company's financial methods resulted in a new suit against it. Evarts appeared before the Attorney General at Albany to prepare the ground for a prosecution, but Watson resigned and the policy of plunder ceased.[32]

The Erie litigations threatened the career of David Dudley Field and involved Evarts in a delicate situation. Samuel Bowles of the *Springfield Republican* criticized Field for defending Tweed, Fisk, and Gould; and Francis C. Barlow published a letter revealing Field's dubious relations with Fisk. Barlow presented charges against him to the Bar Association, accusing him of using illegal processes. These charges shook public faith in Field's honesty. Members of the bar criticized him mercilessly, and the press attacked him for months. The career of a smaller man would have been blasted immediately. As president of the Bar Association, Evarts was embarrassed. A majority of the members were clearly for expelling Field, and the committee on grievances, to which the charges had been referred, favored expulsion. Evarts presided over a meeting to consider this report. After others had spoken, he rose and in a strong appeal, tempered by moderation, good sense, and impartiality, advised against the action, showing that in the long run the bar would hurt itself. He averted a direct vote on the report by having it tabled. He did not escape criticism for his leniency, but the subsequent career of Field proved that a great lawyer was saved from dishonor.[33]

With the fall of Tweed, Fisk, Gould, and their associates in 1873, New York seemed to enjoy the prospect of good government. Attending the first annual dinner of the Chamber of Commerce at Delmonico's in May—a brilliant affair with most of the wealth of the city represented—Evarts spoke hopefully of the future. "One tithe of the energy and public spirit," he said, "by which a few merchants in disguise threw the tea overboard in Boston harbor will enable us to throw overboard from the Ship of State a great many encumbrances that are unsatisfactory and disagreeable. We in our country seem to have assumed that a good government, secured by the merits of our ancestors, was as permanent a possession of our race as all the gifts of climate and grateful soil; but we still find that all freedom can do for men, is to enable them, possessing the spirit and courage of freemen, to defend themselves against aggression at home and abroad."[34]

But scarcely had the Tweed Ring and the Erie conspirators been laid to rest when the Canal Ring, which had been fattening upon spoils for years, reached the peak of its manipulations by 1874. Millions of dollars had been wasted through corrupt contracts and collusive deals. The Ring controlled not only the legislature but the county governments along the canal route.

Representing the commercial interests of the city, Evarts, George Opdyke, and Frank Moulton went to Albany to protest against a pending constitutional amendment which, if passed, would virtually end the canals as a state-supported enterprise. Evarts argued that the canals could operate successfully with low tolls if the extravagance and corruption in the management ceased. Although there was no immediate result, Evarts received the thanks of the New York Produce Exchange for the "deep interest manifested by him in whatever concerns the welfare and commercial standing of the Metropolis."[35] It was Governor Tilden who finally crushed the Canal Ring in 1875.

The time had come to give New York City a new charter. Evarts had been agitating for it for years. Governor Tilden was sympathetic, and upon his recommendation the legislature created a commission to recommend an improved plan of government for all of the cities of the state. It was composed of eminent lawyers or well-known men, consisting of Evarts, E. L. Godkin, Samuel Hand, John A. Lott, Joshua M. Van Cott, James C. Carter, Oswald Ottendorfer, William Allen Butler, Simon Sterne, and Henry F.

Dimick. At its first meeting on December 15, 1875, Evarts was elected chairman.

For an unpaid commission, each member occupied with manifold interests, the task was appalling. There were innumerable problems, such as municipal finance, corruption of boards and officials, relations to state and national government, the degree of home rule, and the particular problems of each city. Indeed, agreement upon a charter seemed impossible. Although the labor was divided among the members of the commission and protracted meetings were held weekly, it became apparent at the end of four months that the work could not be finished within the required time. Evarts asked for an extension of time.

After many weeks of work the commission finally submitted to the legislature an elaborate plan with six essential features: first, home rule for cities under general laws enacted by the state; second, concentration of executive power in the mayor; third, an elected board of aldermen with all legislative power except such as related to finance and taxation; fourth, a board of finance elected by tax and rent payers; fifth, a detailed plan for securing economy and efficiency in financial administration; and sixth, limitations upon borrowing and indebtedness. The commission did a careful piece of work, which Lord Bryce pronounced "classical" and the *Tribune* described as "the ablest and most important report that has been submitted to the Legislature in years." Evarts had a large part in it, and his advice was invaluable.[36]

But the legislature was so slow to move that a citizens' meeting was called at Chickering Hall on April 7, 1877, to urge action. Several members of the commission, including Evarts, spoke and the audience registered a hearty approval of the report. The legislature, said Evarts, should not reject it unless it devised something better. The legislature finally acted favorably, but the approval of the subsequent legislature, required by law, was not forthcoming. It was unfortunate that such a worthy reform, after acceptance by one legislature, should then have been buried by another. It was the provision for a board of finance that wrecked it, for the requirement that the board be chosen by taxpayers was misconstrued as a discrimination against the propertyless.[87]

Reviewing the decade just considered, one greatly wonders that Evarts found time for any reform work at all. That he did make time in the midst of his many professional activities speaks well for his character as a citizen.

14

Counsel at the Geneva Arbitration

WHILE IN THE JOHNSON CABINET, Evarts had watched with alarm the smouldering hostility between Great Britain and the United States. He hoped that Seward would find a solution. The return of the Conservatives to power in England brought more friendly relations, culminating in the Johnson-Clarendon Convention of 1868. But Seward denounced this as not made in full conformity with his instructions. Evarts likewise assailed it in Cabinet meeting, charging that under it the *Alabama* claims would probably amount to only eight million dollars, while the British would demand a hundred millions for their cotton and other property destroyed during the war.[1]

By the close of 1870 the relations between the two countries were near the breaking point. Charles C. Beaman had been set to work to prepare a detailed list of claims for damages caused by the escape of Confederate cruisers from British ports. The list was published in March, 1871.[2] Great Britain became worried. She might be drawn into the Franco-Prussian War; and then as a neutral the United States might let forth a swarm of cruisers like the *Alabama* to vex her commerce. Negotiations between Hamilton Fish and John Rose finally bore fruit in the famous Treaty of Washington of May, 1871, creating a tribunal of five arbitrators to sit at Geneva and adjudicate the *Alabama* claims.

Under this treaty, it was first necessary to choose an American arbitrator and agent. Grant and Fish quickly agreed that J. C.

Bancroft Davis, Assistant Secretary of State, should be the agent to prosecute the American case. With the help of Beaman, Davis set to work, hoping to have the case ready for the opening session of the Tribunal in December. The choice of the arbitrator was not equally easy. Fish proposed Charles Francis Adams, but Grant opposed this. William B. Lawrence was rejected because a Democrat; Pierrepont because he knew little international law; Cushing because he was busy elsewhere; and Evarts because Grant was suspicious of him. The President finally accepted Adams, who proved a fortunate choice.[3]

The choice of counsel to aid Bancroft also caused difficulty. Men familiar with international law, acquainted with diplomacy, and known in British circles were needed. Davis suggested Evarts, Cushing, and George Bemis. Cushing was agreed upon easily. Although seventy-one, he was an able diplomatist of wide experience, versed in international law, a tireless worker of encyclopedic knowledge, and a master of language.[4]

Not forgetting that Evarts had urged his appointment as secretary of state, Fish now urged Evarts' appointment as counsel. Grant replied that "under no circumstances" would he appoint Evarts, and gave the second place to William M. Meredith; but ill health forced Meredith to decline. The pressure for Evarts increased; Robert Schenck, the American minister to London, Rockwood Hoar, Fish, Davis, and others urged his appointment upon Grant, who seemed cold to the proposal. Explaining this coldness, Fish wrote Schenck: "In truth Evarts' great ability has not reconciled the Republicans to his taking a position in the Johnson Cabinet *after* defending him as counsel. The professional act was excusable—they won't forget the other—which was a mistake against which many of Evarts' best friends to *my personal* knowledge warned him." Again Grant gave way to Fish. Evarts and Benjamin Curtis were asked to become counsel, but Curtis declined.[5]

A third attorney was unnecessary, but Davis insisted. It was Delano, Secretary of the Interior, who urged upon Grant "a Mr. Waite of Toledo," of whom the rest of the Cabinet had never heard.

Evarts also urged the appointment, more ready to accept his own appointment if Waite became his colleague. Waite's career thus far could not match that of Cushing or Evarts. He was a lawyer of merely local reputation. His appointment was a surprise to the bar and to himself, for he had no inkling of it until he received a telegraphic announcement. "I need not tell you," he wrote Evarts, "that it gives me the greatest of pleasure to be associated with you in this honorable employment. The appointment came upon me very unexpectedly, but it is none the less acceptable on that account."[6]

The three counsel formed a splendid legal array. Cushing was the most experienced in diplomatic precedent and international law; Evarts was not far behind in either field and was better versed in American constitutional and statute law. Furthermore, he was better known to the British bar. He was more truly representative than the other two; behind him were leading New York merchants who were personally interested as claimants against Great Britain.

A few of Evarts' friends were dubious. They intimated that Grant's purpose was to get him out of the way during the coming presidential campaign. "Everybody is glad," wrote J. H. Ashton, "that the Alabama business should be put in your hands. And yet I, for one, wish it did not involve the necessity of your leaving the country at this juncture. A good many eyes are on you now that can't look so far, and see so far, as Geneva."[7]

Bancroft Davis had the American case ready by December. None of the counsel except Cushing had any part in it. Listing five classes of claims against Great Britain and asking for the payment of a gross sum to the United States, it was unduly severe and aggressive, accusing Great Britain of deliberate unfriendliness. Its worst feature was a demand for indirect claims, which were wholly contrary to precedent and would be difficult to arbitrate.

Soon after Evarts went to Washington to consult with Fish, he earned the unhappy title of "the counsel who lost his case before he opened it." Upon leaving the State Department with a copy which was still a secret document, he managed somehow to drop it from his carriage. Search proved fruitless, but someone found it who knew its value and disposed of it for a price at the British legation. Only a few persons were aware of the mishap till after the case became public. While it had no serious consequences, it was naturally a source of great mortification to Evarts.[8]

Bancroft Davis submitted the case to the Cabinet and to several experts, including Richard Henry Dana, for their opinions. Disgusted with it, Dana wrote Evarts, "Everything depends on the *conception of our case* and the mode of putting it. . . . When Mr. Bancroft Davis sent me the printed 'case' . . . the little hair I had left stood on end in consternation. . . . It was as if, for the battle that was to decide the fate of an empire, the government had left a junior staff officer to plan the campaign. . . . I returned it to him unopened. . . . I hope there is yet time for you to re-open the case, and prepare it according to your own conception." Dana did not stand alone in this critical attitude. Not even Fish believed that the United States had any right in law to the indirect claims and confessed to Evarts that he did not know how to deal with them. He finally instructed Evarts to say little about them, adding with a laugh that he might use them in his peroration "as bars on which the spread eagle might perch."[9]

The third week in December, Waite arrived in Washington and devoted himself to mastering the case. Meanwhile a rumor spread over the country that Evarts had openly criticized it, but he quickly spiked this falsehood.[10]

When the case became known in England, a storm arose which threatened to wreck the arbitration before it began. In contrast with the document drawn up by Bancroft Davis, the British case, which was the work of Lord Tenterden, the British agent, and the two British counsel, Roundell Palmer and Mountague Bernard, was a simple and dignified presentation of law and fact. Whereas the American case sought an indemnity for the depredations of thirteen Confederate cruisers, the British denied any responsibility except in the cases of the *Alabama* and *Florida,* and insisted that due precautions had been taken to prevent the escape of even these two vessels.

Early in February the British press became hysterical. The Gladstone ministry tottered. When it was discovered that the indirect claims had not been *expressly* included in the Treaty of Washington, the clamor redoubled and the United States was accused of bad faith. Evarts watched with alarm the growing storm.

The American counsel received their instructions and were ordered to join Bancroft Davis, who was already at Geneva. They were told to act together in all matters and to seek the award of a lump sum. Grant had already recommended to Congress that each counsel receive ten thousand dollars besides his expenses, and the salary of a secretary.[11] Evarts selected W. F. Peddrick, his former chief clerk in the attorney general's office, to act as his secretary.

When the time came for Evarts to sail he was given a rousing send-off. A dinner was tendered him at the Union Club by Blatchford, O'Conor, Dix, Choate, Astor, Pierrepont, and others. Taking an optimistic view of his task, he told the New England Society a day or two before he sailed that there was much to hope from a nation which, just emerging from a victorious war, was willing to settle a dispute by arbitration. He left for Liverpool with his wife and several sons and daughters.[12]

In England he found fierce antagonism to the American claims. Minister Schenck asked him to stay in London with him a few days to help allay the hostile sentiment. He talked with Schenck, Adams, Sir John Rose, and others, seeking some expedient for ending the indirect claims. While talking with Adams and William E. Forster, the able Parliamentarian, at Maurigny's Hotel, he suggested that the arbitration proceed despite British refusal to consider the indirect claims. "How can we," asked Forster, "when we are determined not to pay any award on them?" To which Evarts replied, "But you might let this be clearly understood." Adams approved the idea and all present began to see a possible way out.[13] Evarts proved of such service in London that, after reaching Geneva, he was called back in February to continue his efforts toward peace. Even as late as April, when he was on the continent, Sir John Rose begged him to return again to England; but he was then busy preparing for the meeting of the Tribunal.[14]

Neither Fish nor Davis was able, because of public sentiment, to consider a withdrawal of the indirect claims. But Evarts believed that Grant could and should withdraw them. He dared suggest to Davis that the President be put in a position where he would find it expedient to do so, saying that the British could probably be persuaded to make an agreement excluding the indirect claims. But Davis took offense at the suggestion and became suspicious of Evarts.[15]

The American counsel met in Paris to prepare the counter-case, which had to be submitted to the Tribunal by April 15. Evarts and his family took quarters on the Avenue Joséphine, near the American embassy where Davis was staying. The counsel preferred Paris to Geneva because of the greater ease in communicating with Washington and London.[16]

In Paris Evarts visited the studio of the French artist, M. Desmarcq, who was at work upon a large painting of the signing of the Declaration of Independence. As a grandson of Roger Sherman, he tried to describe to the artist just how that statesman had looked. In came J. M. Read, also a descendant of a signer and he too began to give instructions to the artist. Finally Schenck entered. The bewildered artist asked if he too had an ancestor among the signers and when Schenck replied that he had not, the relieved artist exclaimed, "Thank God for that."

Evarts attended a dinner party at which one of the guests was the American dentist, Dr. Evans, who had gained notoriety by assisting Empress Eugenie to escape from Paris during the recent Prussian siege. Evans seemed insistent upon boasting of his intimate relations with French royalty. Standing it as long as he could, Evarts finally leaned forward across the table, and speaking so that all could hear, said in half-quizzical manner, "Well, doctor, we certainly owe you a debt of gratitude. For us it is a great thing even to see a king or prince; but it seems that they have all opened their mouths to you."[17]

On April 15 the counter-cases were filed with the Tribunal. The American counter-case was a brief statement, accompanied by a huge mass of documentary evidence. The counsel had taken part in preparing it, and Davis found they did not always agree with him. Cushing insisted upon including many old controversial papers dating back to his attorney generalship. In opposing the indirect claims he took positions which Davis felt would weaken the counter-case. Exasperated, Davis wrote Fish that Evarts was acting "like a spoiled child."[18]

While the filing of the British counter-case offered no assurance that the arbitration would go on, it was a hopeful sign. It was a lengthy document, accompanied with a great mass of evidence, and confined to the direct claims. British opinion was now so hostile to arbitration that Tenterden had to file a public protest with it, but privately told Davis that he hoped the arbitration would continue.[19]

Days of doubt and uncertainty followed. As June 15, the date on which the arguments were to be presented to the Tribunal, drew near, it appeared that Great Britain would default. Fish wrote Schenck, "I suppose Great Britain really intends to break away from the treaty—like the man who held the wolf by the ears, it is hard to hold on. . . ." On the same day Lord Russell rose in Parliament and demanded a vote against arbitration. Davis wrote Fish despondently that the American counsel were "depressed," and that Evarts was "nervous" over the situation. Indeed, Evarts felt it useless to prepare an argument unless there was certainty of a hearing.[20]

Under such unfavorable conditions he left Paris with his family and the other counsel for Geneva. All were downcast en route. It seemed as if all their work was to go for nothing. On June 15 Davis delivered the American argument to the Tribunal. But Tenterden, instead of submitting a British argument, moved that the Tribunal adjourn for eight months during which the controversy might be settled by diplomacy. It was a shrewd move, but Davis was prepared to meet it. He substituted a motion for a two-day adjournment to consider Tenterden's proposal, which was granted.[21]

Something had to be done quickly. Adams, ably supported by Evarts, saved the situation. The New Englander recommended to Davis that he arrange with Tenterden for submission of only the direct claims. Davis did so, but Tenterden protested that he had no instructions and certainly would not take any such action unless the arbitrators agreed. The same night Davis hurried to see Evarts, urging him to press the matter with Palmer. Tenterden meanwhile discussed the matter with the British counsel. Then he went to Davis' hotel, roused him from bed, and proposed to accept the plan upon three conditions: first, that any decree of the Tribunal upon the indirect claims should be held extrajudicial; second, that Lord Cockburn, the British arbitrator, should not be required to express any opinion upon the indirect claims; and third, that both governments should accept the new plan.

The American counsel conferred most of the following day. It was decided that Evarts should try to induce Palmer to omit the first two conditions. Evarts made headway with Palmer, and the situation brightened before the day closed. Adams came forward with a plan whereby the Tribunal should merely decline jurisdiction over the indirect claims. Evarts drew up a draft of the proposal, and by the nineteenth Cockburn, Tenterden, and the British counsel agreed upon it. The Tribunal made its formal declaration next day, with Cockburn absent. Thus, after four days of negotiation, the arbitration was saved. Evarts played the rôle of diplomat rather than that of counsel, and did much to smooth rough places.

The American counsel were greatly relieved; they now had a chance to work for one of the greatest causes ever committed to lawyers. Although Fish had opposed the scrapping of the indirect claims, he seemed delighted with the turn of affairs.[22] Most historical accounts give Adams the credit for securing the happy result. The credit belongs to no one person. Evarts had persistently opposed the indirect claims and had worked for their exclusion ever since stepping foot in England. Adams won over the three neutral arbitrators; but Evarts and Davis carried on the four-day negotiation with Tenterden and Palmer. Evarts was the one member of the American delegation personally acquainted with the British and highly regarded by them; Cushing and Davis were viewed with suspicion, and Waite was unknown.

The next step was the submission of the British Argument. Little work had been done upon it, and when it was submitted on June 27 it showed the marks of hasty preparation. Palmer confessed to Evarts that the British were not ready to go before the Tribunal and asked for a postponement to September. The Tribunal refused. Then Palmer tried to get Evarts to agree to a resubmittal of both cases, now that the indirect claims were excluded; but Evarts replied that it would be unfair to the American cause. The British were clearly worried by their failure to prepare. On June 27 Tenterden asked the Tribunal to permit further arguments, but was refused. Regarding these requests as impudent, Fish instructed Davis to allow "no privileges or favors of any kind."[23]

Cockburn was especially anxious for a recess. He had come to Geneva with little knowledge of the case, sure that no arbitration would occur. He sought a ten-week delay. The American counsel objected, arguing that it would give the British an unfair advantage, enabling them to go home and obtain new sources of information, a privilege the American counsel could not enjoy. The Tribunal compromised, granting a two-week recess till July 15. During the recess Evarts returned to Paris for a few days.[24]

All was not work at Geneva. Waite and Evarts found time for amusement. They were often together, Waite enjoying Evarts' wit immensely. There was plenty of social activity among the American delegation. Dinners and dances were much in evidence at the Evartses, Davises, and Adamses. There had to be some play to relieve the tension; as Henry Adams said, "All the men, young and old, who have been here, have been tremendously worked and swear diabolically." At these gay affairs Evarts was usually in his chatty mood. But one evening, when Mrs. Adams was his partner at a dinner at the Davises' hotel, she could not get a word out of him, he seemed so absorbed in his wife's appearance as she sat opposite in a new handsome gown.

The British delegation, on the contrary, were most seclusive, living together at their own hotel and doing no entertaining. Tenterden was quite popular and Lady Palmer was gracious and hospitable, but Cockburn was impossible.[25]

Evarts increased his reputation for wit and brilliant conversation. At the dinner table his raillery was irrepressible and he enjoyed it as much as others. He had that rare power of laying aside immediate cares and enjoying himself thoroughly. The smile that played around his lips before some keen thrust became a well-known signal. At least one of his stories at Geneva has been preserved. It related to one of his daughters when a small child. He had sent a donkey to his farm in Windsor, and she, having never heard a donkey bray and believing it must be due to homesickness, said sympathetically, "He won't be homesick when father comes." Evarts always regarded this as a compliment and evidence that he was good company.

The sessions of the Tribunal were held in the "Salle des Conferences" of the ancient Hôtel de Ville, a room since called the "Salle de l'Alabama" and bearing today upon its walls a tablet commemorating the momentous transaction of 1872. It was a small room, but adequate for the purpose. Ordinarily it was used for sessions of the Swiss Congress. Dark red curtains hung at the three French windows looking out upon the Botanical Gardens, and the rest of the room was decorated in harmony with the draperies, giving it a dull and formal appearance, in keeping with the curved judicial bench erected on a low platform in front of the windows. Facing the platform was a semicircle of desks enclosing several tables where sat the counsel. Upon the platform behind the judicial bench sat the five arbitrators.[26]

The President of the Tribunal, the aged Count Sclopis of Italy, tall, stout, noble, and commanding in appearance, firm and independent in character, was a member of the Italian Senate and surpassed his colleagues in learning and reputation as a jurist and author. His fame made him the unanimous choice for presiding officer, although custom would have given the distinction to Jacob Staempfli, the Swiss arbitrator who sat at his right. Staempfli, a self-made man of marked ability, had held almost every important office in the Swiss Government and was thoroughly prepared, having carefully studied the official documents months before.

At the left of Sclopis sat the short, round-shouldered, studious looking Baron d'Itajuba of Brazil, the least vigorous of the arbitrators. At either end of the judicial bench sat the British and American arbitrators, Sir Alexander Cockburn and Charles Francis Adams. Cockburn came to Geneva with a record to be proud of. He had been a member of Parliament, solicitor general, attorney general, and lord chief justice, an office he held for twenty years. His charges to juries were models, and his decisions were noted for their classical excellence. He was a man of varied accomplishments, a sportsman and society man of the best type. He probably had more legal learning and a quicker mind than the other arbitrators; but he brought to Geneva an aggressive superior manner and a temperament ill suited to diplomacy. He was enraged by criticism. Convinced that the United States was seeking an unfair advantage, he hoped to prevent an arbitration.[27] Adams was the arbitrator most interested in the outcome. For years he had worked to bring Great Britain to an accounting. A favorable verdict would vindicate his efforts.

At the semicircle of desks in front of the arbitrators sat the counsel. Evarts' thin, sharp face contrasted strongly with the round, almost clerical face of Palmer. It was a great array of legal talent—Evarts, Cushing, Waite, and Davis on one side; Palmer, Bernard, and Tenterden on the other.

The proceedings centered upon the direct claims under the following three rules agreed upon in the Treaty of Washington as tests of violated neutrality: "A neutral Government is bound, first, to use due diligence to prevent the fitting out, arming, or equipping within its jurisdiction of any vessel, which it has reasonable grounds to believe, is intended to cruise, or carry on war against a power with which it is at peace; and also to use like diligence to prevent the departure from its jurisdiction of any vessel intended to cruise, or carry on war so above, such vessel having been specially adapted, in whole or in part, within such jurisdiction to warlike use. Secondly, not to permit or suffer either belligerent to make use of its ports or waters as a base of naval operations against the other, or for the purpose of the removal or augmentation of military supplies, or arms, or the recruitment of men. Thirdly, to exercise due diligence in its own ports or waters, and as to all persons within its jurisdiction to prevent any violation of the foregoing obligations and duties."[28] It was in the light of these rules that the cases and counter-cases had been framed and that the arguments were now presented.

The American Argument was a long document of thirteen chapters. Evarts had written the first, second, eleventh, and twelfth chapters. In the introductory chapter he had outlined the nature of the questions at issue and sought to define their scope. In the second, he reviewed British policy during the war, declared neutrality unjustified, and accused Great Britain of acting as arsenal, navy yard, and treasury for the Confederacy. In the eleventh chapter he placed the burden of proving due diligence upon Great Britain. In the twelfth, which was his best chapter, entitled "The Failure of Great Britain to Fulfill Its Duties," he wrote, "We cannot fail to note the entire absence from the proofs presented to the Tribunal of any evidence exhibiting any desire or effort of the British Government to impress upon its staff of officials . . . or any duty of vigilance to detect, of promptitude to declare, of activity to discourage, the illegal outfit or dispatch of vessels in violation of international law." One position in this chapter was unsound. Evarts was not correct in arguing that the British government failed to protest the return of Confederate cruisers to British ports.[29]

Evarts' four chapters were ably argued, but not easy to read because of long, involved sentences. In the second chapter, for example, the first and third sentences contained ninety-seven and one hundred and two words respectively. It is little wonder that the translators who sought to put it into French protested the difficulty of the task. But Evarts coolly remarked, "That shows the poverty of the French language."[30]

The arbitration actually began on July 15. Staempfli suggested that the case of each cruiser be considered in the light of the three rules. Cockburn disagreed, proposing all the cruisers be considered together in the light of international law. Fortunately Staempfli's more definite plan was adopted.

First came the case of the *Florida*. After three days had been given to it, Cockburn insisted the British counsel should be allowed to submit further argument. He became angry and excited and Sclopis reprimanded him. His motion was denied. Even Tenterden became disgusted with Cockburn's poor sportsmanship and complained that it was damaging to the British cause.[31]

D'Itajuba, who was friendly to the British, asked for a reconsideration of Cockburn's motion and Palmer was allowed to present reasons why further argument should be heard. The American counsel protested. But it was fortunate for Evarts that further argument was allowed; it made possible his main contribution. It was decided that the British should submit additional written argument, with the right of the American counsel to reply, orally or in writing, upon three questions: first, the general question of due diligence; second, Confederate cruisers entering British ports; and third, the supplying of coal to Confederate cruisers in British ports. Davis approved further argument, declaring, "I thought we had nothing to lose by an argument in which we had the reply, in the hands of such masters as General Cushing, Mr. Evarts, and Mr. Waite."[32]

Palmer filed a new written argument on July 29. It was not confined to the three questions, but covered the whole American Case, ingeniously planned to show that the accusations against Great Britain should be viewed only in the light of British municipal law. It became the chief point of the British defense.

Evarts' great opportunity came on August 5 when he rose to reply to this argument. He chose to speak in English, which Sclopis and D'Itajuba could not understand at all and Staempfli imperfectly. Why he chose an oral argument is not clear. He knew of course that the arbitrators would read it in translation. Perhaps it was the effect upon Cockburn and upon public opinion that motivated him. He knew the risk of cross-examination from Cockburn, but relied upon his wits to save him. At all events, it was the only oral argument presented.[33]

Like Palmer, he decided to cover the whole scope of the controversy. First, he denied that "due diligence" should be measured by British municipal laws, particularly the Foreign Enlistment Act of 1819. Reading from the Treaty of Washington, Evarts showed that the intent was to interpret the three rules in the light of international law, not British law, and that Palmer was trying to bring these rules to a "vanishing point."[34]

Second, he denied Palmer's doctrine that Great Britain was not liable for cruisers returning to British ports once they had received their commissions. He held that the British government was obligated to seize such a cruiser the moment it entered a British port.

At this point Cockburn began to prod Evarts with shrewd questions which would have disconcerted a less poised mind. Must the British government seize such a ship, he asked, if unaware of the original belligerent intent? Yes, retorted Evarts, it was the duty of British officials to keep informed of such intent. Under the rule of hospitality the country visited could not be "predominated over" by the country receiving hospitality. Furthermore, the Confederacy was not a recognized sovereign and therefore the visiting cruiser was completely subject to the government of the country visited.

Third, Evarts denied Palmer's theory that the fitting out of vessels in neutral waters without armament was not a violation of international law. He quoted numerous authorities to prove the contrary and showed that they applied all the more strongly to insurgents. "How long," he asked, "could such violation of the neutrality of Great Britain have been exercised by belligerent France without a remonstrance?"

Fourth, he denied that a belligerent could use stress of weather as a subterfuge to gain supplies in a neutral port. It was nothing more or less than disguised warfare. But, asked Cockburn, how was the neutral to know whether a vessel seeking asylum in port was intended for a destructive mission? It could not know, replied Evarts, but it could thereafter deny further hospitality to that vessel.

In substance, Evarts concluded his first day's argument by showing that the carrying of armament from a British port to equip a Confederate ship outside of British waters was more than a mere commercial transaction. "It was," he asserted, "a direct furnishing of a cruiser with armament from your port. It might as well have been accomplished within three miles of your coast."[35]

There was no bitterness in Evarts' words. He was on the best of terms with the British counsel, particularly Palmer, who visited him often in Geneva. On the very day after his argument Evarts was a guest at a dinner given by the Palmers. Rivalry was forgotten and arbitrators, agents, and counsel spent a pleasant evening.[36]

On the second day, Evarts returned to his main point: that Great Britain could not hide under the Foreign Enlistment Act. "What would be thought," he asked, "of a cruiser of the United States lying off the port of Liverpool . . . awaiting the arrival of a tender . . . by prearrangement, with an augmentation of her battery and the supply of her fighting crew? . . . If your law . . . was not adequate to our rights, then our argument is that your law needed improvement."

At the close Evarts turned to the Tribunal and said solemnly, "When you pass upon the question whether this is a violation of the second rule, you pass upon the question, under the law of nations, whether an obligation of a neutral not to allow a hostile expedition to go forth from its ports can be evaded by having it sent forth in parcels, and having the combination made outside of its waters. You cannot decide in this case, and between these parties, without establishing by your award, as a general proposition, that the law of nations proscribing such hostile expeditions, may be wholly evaded, wholly set at naught by this equivocation and fraud practiced upon it; that this can be done, not by surprise . . . but that it can be done *openly and of right.*"[37]

Evarts had made a fine argument. Describing it to Fish, Davis wrote, "Evarts' speech of yesterday pressed them [the British] very hard. Roundell Palmer and Mountague Bernard sat before the Arbitrators making constant gestures of dissent, and the peppery old Chief Justice kept interrupting, but the more he interrupted, the harder Evarts bore down." Indeed, Evarts had been interrupted by Palmer seven times, by Tenterden three times, and by Cockburn twenty-seven times; but was always ready with a keen but good-natured answer.[38] It was not Evarts' eloquence that counted; it was his reasoning and logic which raised havoc with the British Case. There doubtless does not exist a better exposition of the duties of a neutral.

Cushing followed with an able written argument, comparing American and British neutrality laws. He lacked Evarts' balance and was inclined to be more prejudiced and resentful toward Great Britain. Then came Waite's short but effective written argument on British liability for allowing Confederate ships to coal in British ports. It was doubtless the greatest achievement of his life, bringing him high office and a doctorate at Yale. The work of the counsel was concluded on August 23 when Palmer was permitted to argue the question of British responsibility for the entry of the *Florida* into Mobile, to which Evarts replied with a short written argument.[39]

On the same day the Tribunal proceeded to vote. It held Great Britain liable for losses caused by the three cruisers *Alabama, Florida,* and *Shenandoah,* Cockburn alone dissenting. That night the Hôtel Beau Rivage was the scene of a splendid dinner given by Davis in honor of the arbitrators, followed by a brilliant ball.[40]

There were still two questions for the Tribunal: should interest be allowed and how much should the damages be? Palmer presented a written protest against the granting of interest and the three American counsel submitted a joint reply. Despite Cockburn's protest, interest was allowed at seven per cent reckoned from 1864.

Just how the Tribunal arrived at the final gross award of fifteen and a half million dollars is obscure. It was done in secret session and was evidently a compromise between two extremes. Cockburn exploded when he heard the result but apologized.[41]

The final scene on September 14 was impressive. The chamber was crowded. For the first time the general public of Geneva were admitted. Mrs. Evarts, Mrs. Davis, and the wives of some of the arbitrators were present. The Council of Geneva had come in their black robes. Evarts looked happy. All awaited the arrival of Tenterden and Cockburn, who were late. After the secretary had read the award, Sclopis rose and said with evident emotion, "We carry away with us the testimony of our consciences that we have not failed in our duty. We fervently hope that God may inspire all Governments with the constant and effectual idea of maintaining . . . the chief of all benefits—peace." Applause rang through the hall and a salvo of artillery was fired from the castle of La Treille. The arbitration was over.[42]

Evarts and his wife and daughter Hettie reached Paris on the seventeenth. He might feel proud of his part at Geneva. Davis gave all of the counsel high praise in his official report to the State Department. From Fish came the official thanks of the President.[43]

Evarts had a large share in the satisfactory result. He had urged the doctrine that a government could not avoid its duties to another nation by reason of any constitutional limitations which it might have chosen to adopt. The Tribunal accepted this doctrine and it became a part of international law so far as the United States was concerned. It was and is the only doctrine under which nations can live with reasonable security during wartime. Evarts bore the chief burden in proving the failure of Great Britain to observe due diligence. From the start he saw the significance for future arbitration and future rights of neutrals. For the student of international law his argument still remains a model. In the opinion of Joseph Choate, Evarts' success at Geneva was the "finest laurel" that he ever won and "the most notable professional achievement that ever fell to the lot of an American advocate."[44]

15

The Aftermath of Geneva

THE GENEVA ARBITRATION had important consequences for Evarts. Not the least of these was the enduring friendship he and Sir Roundell Palmer formed. When Sir Roundell and Lady Laura returned to England to open their new home at Blackmoor, Evarts and his wife were their first guests. In this hospitable atmosphere the two lawyers found that they were even more congenial than they had at first supposed. After leaving, Evarts wrote his host, "I think we may feel that our personal relations to each other have not been without benefit to the greatest interests of these two powerful nations. . . . I shall always remember that I was in England when your first fire was lighted in your great hall-chimney; and I shall never feel that your public service, or domestic prosperity, are wholly foreign or distant to me."

That Palmer's regard for Evarts was equally high was shown in the description of the American which he included in his memoirs years after: "In person spare, in countenance refined and intellectual, in conversation sincere and candid, with a good deal of dry humor, he stood very high in the estimation of us all, and not the least in my own. He was a good lawyer and a skillful advocate, and he also had the qualities of a statesman; his manners were simple, and in his domestic relations he was very happy. Altogether he was a man of whom any country could be proud."[1]

Palmer was rewarded for his work at Geneva by elevation to the peerage with the office of Lord Chancellor. Cushing was appointed minister to Spain after Grant had refused to consider either Evarts or Curtis for the post.[2] Waite was soon to be rewarded with the chief justiceship. But Grant seemed to overlook Evarts. It was evident that the President felt suspicious of the former Attorney General's independence in politics.

Though Evarts reached New York as the campaign of 1872 was reaching its peak, he took little part in it, for he had no enthusiasm for either Grant or Greeley. Attending the last great Republican rally at Cooper Institute, he sat on the platform and heard Blaine and Boutwell speak. When unexpectedly called upon to say a few words, he expressed confidence in Republican victory, but did not mention Grant.[3]

Grant should have given Evarts some mark of recognition for his services at Geneva. The vacancy which was shortly created in the Supreme Court by the resignation of Justice Nelson afforded an opportunity, but Grant appointed Ward Hunt of New York. Evarts' friends, headed by William Cullen Bryant, invited him to be the guest of honor at a dinner at the Union League Club; but he declined, replying that the invitation was itself a sufficient testimonial of appreciation for his work.[4] There can be little doubt that he felt Grant's indifference keenly. Introducing Elihu Washburne, the American minister to France, at a reception at the Union League Club in December, he declared that the negligence of the American people in rewarding their public servants might result in leaving the country without servants worthy of reward.[5] A few nights later he made a speech at the New England Society dinner which irritated the Grant administration. Describing the work at Geneva, he declared, "We have made it apparent to the proudest nation of the world . . . that there must be a peaceful accounting for errors and wrongs"; but he made no mention of Grant or Fish. Instead, he paid a warm tribute to Seward, who "was able without war . . . to establish the principle of arbitration." Davis sent Fish a copy of Evarts' speech, criticizing it sharply. Unquestionably Evarts intended no slur upon Fish, for they were on good terms and Evarts had complimented him upon his successful diplomacy.[6]

Apparently the Geneva episode was closed. Evarts returned to his practice and won another prize case in the Supreme Court.[7] But the award made by the Tribunal presented a difficult problem of distribution, and raised in particular the question whether the insurance companies were entitled to a share. Evarts accepted a retainer as attorney for several insurance companies and went to Washington in January, 1873, to urge their claim before congressional committees. Bancroft Davis was quick to criticize him for "lobbying," but actually he was merely serving a client and aiding in a solution of the legal issues involved.

The pressure of the various claimants threatened to develop into a public scandal.[8] Some members of Congress believed that claims should be presented in the regular federal courts; others desired a special court; some preferred a commission to receive appeals; some favored and some opposed the demands of insurance companies; and still others would give a preferred place to mutual insurance companies because they had not been able to profit from high war rates. These conflicting views gave birth to the Butler bill in the House, providing for a special court to settle the claims. A similar bill in the Senate forbade the court to consider the claims of insurance companies unless the claimants could prove that their losses exceeded their gains. Senator Edmunds, chairman of the Judiciary Committee, had charge of the bill; while Senator Thurman, who favored the insurance companies, was his chief opponent. Caleb Cushing was on hand, fighting the companies.[9]

Evarts had valuable first-hand evidence to offer. He wrote Edmunds before going to Washington that, although he knew an avalanche of criticism would fall upon him, he was determined to let Congress know what views had been taken of the question at Geneva. He first appeared before the House Judiciary Committee, of which the hostile Butler was chairman. After pleading before this body, Evarts circulated a memorandum among the congressmen and senators explaining the rights of the companies. It was so forcible a document that Senator Thurman read extracts from it in an argument to the Senate. Evarts made it clear that the government had acted as agent for the claims of the companies throughout the proceedings at Geneva.[10]

The Butler bill went to conference and emerged on March 3 in entirely new form, providing that the Geneva award was to be invested in government bonds and held for future disposition. In disgust, Evarts wrote Dana: "I have felt most keenly the public dishonor of the course of our Gov't in regard to the Geneva award and the necessity of controversy with its highest authorities to prevent the consummation of the shame. I have known that the purpose was *meditated* with greater or less distinctness from the time the treaty was brewing, but, alas! I did not believe it could take form and endure the light, and am rudely awakened to find the *whole* force of the Government bent on this business."[11] At the next Congress Evarts appeared again before Butler's committee, this time representing larger interests than before. The committee listened attentively for an hour. He denounced the "perfidious" plan of leaving the distribution entirely to government discretion. Morally and legally, he asserted, the rights of the underwriters should be recognized. "The indemnity is in the hands of the United States, to be paid to the owners, their representatives or assigns. No part of it can be paid to anyone else; no part of it belongs to the United States. . . . If the United States should retain it, nothing but the general immunity of the government from judicial pursuit could protect it from accountability to the insurer, at law."[12]

Evarts drew up a new memorandum; and, using it in the Senate debate, Thurman argued that the fact that the *total* profit of the insurance companies during the war was high furnished no grounds for denying their claim for *particular* losses. He showed that two thirds of the five million dollars claimed was asked by mutual insurance companies, which could not profit from high rates; and he insisted upon the right of subrogation, which Cockburn and Palmer had both admitted at Geneva. Senators Bayard, Schurz, and Conkling also spoke for the insurance companies. But their view of the subject was rejected by the close vote of thirty-two to twenty-seven.[13]

Evarts had no further connection with the ridiculous and unjust policy of Congress. It was not till July that a court began the task of adjusting the claims, adjourning in 1876 after only a small sum had been awarded the insurance companies. It looked as if the claimants might all die before they got their share of the award. When Congress discovered in 1882 that ten million dollars were still undistributed, it revived the special court and allowed certain types of claims not entertained at all at Geneva; yet it still excluded the insurance companies. By 1885 the award had been finally distributed. Congress might with more justice have followed the course urged by Evarts. There can be no doubt that the insurance companies had a proper claim to the value of the property on which they had paid a total loss.[14]

If Evarts had not won attention in England by his work at Geneva, he would doubtless not have been retained by British clients in the famous case of the *Springbok* in 1873. This offered another great opportunity to appear in a suit which was long cited as a precedent. Whereas in the Geneva arbitration he had defined the obligations of a neutral, his task now was to insist upon neutral rights. In essence the question raised was one of the *intent* of a neutral to violate the blockade. He had appeared in numerous suits against blockade-runners in the Supreme Court, but never in one of such far-reaching significance.

The peculiar feature of the case, which distinguished it from other prize cases, lay in its relation to the doctrine of continuous voyage. Great Britain had applied this doctrine during the Napoleonic era against American neutral shipping carrying cargoes from the French Indies to the United States and thence to France, insisting that the trip was essentially one continuous voyage and therefore illegal in war time. But British authorities seized American ships on the second leg of the voyage between the United States and France.

When during the Civil War the United States was a belligerent and Great Britain a neutral, the federal government extended the doctrine to prevent cargoes of contraband goods reaching the Confederacy from England by the way of the Bahamas. Nassau became a notorious center of transshipment, and American naval officers were instructed to seize British vessels if there appeared reasonable evidence of intent to run the blockade. The *Bermuda,* on its way from Bermuda to Nassau with munitions, was captured and condemned. The *Stephen Hart,* on its way from London to Cuba, with a contraband cargo consigned to Confederate agents, offered a clear-cut case and the ship was condemned. The *Gertrude,* en route from Nassau to New Brunswick with contraband and false papers, was likewise taken as prize. All of these cases had a bearing upon that of the *Springbok*.

In 1862 the *Springbok* left London with a valuable cargo, bound for Nassau. She was captured when nearing her destination, brought to New York, and condemned as a prize by Judge Betts in the District Court. The judge based his decision upon the following grounds: (1) the owners of the cargo were Isaac, Campbell & Company, the owners of the *Stephen Hart,* and *Gertrude,* and the brokers were the same as in the case of the *Stephen Hart;* (2) the arrival of the *Gertrude* at Nassau created grave suspicion of intended transshipment to the Confederacy; (3) and the *Springbok's* papers were unsatisfactory. In substance, Betts's decision meant that the moment a vessel left a neutral port with contraband aboard, it was liable to capture even if it had a neutral destination.[15]

The British and French press criticized Judge Betts severely. "It is the *bona fide* destination of the vessel," declared the *London Globe,* "not the ulterior destination of her cargo, that justifies capture." The British owners appealed to the Supreme Court. By a five-to-four decision the Court sustained Betts's condemnation of the cargo, although the ship itself was released. The judges held that the presence of a few cases of swords and bayonets and certain defects in the bills of lading were evidence of intent to break the blockade. In the rush of war-time litigation the Court did not give the case the consideration it deserved, a fact proved by the vagueness of Chase's decision and the failure to record the dissenting opinion or the arguments of counsel. Authorities on international law called the decision an unwarranted support of belligerent power. Explaining the Court's action, Justice Nelson later admitted that the Court was not familiar with the law of blockade, and was influenced by anti-British sentiment.[16]

By the Treaty of Washington a Mixed Commission was established to settle claims growing out of the war. While Evarts was at Geneva, the owners of the *Springbok* filed their claims with this commission and retained him to present their case. In accepting, Evarts wrote, "My fee for the management of the case and the argument will be £400 in addition to the retainer you paid me. . . . I am unable to give you any encouragement of success before the 'Mixed Commission.' The claims do not seem to have been very prosperous, and in this case of ours we have considerable obstacles in the way. But, if you so decide, I will do the best I can."[17]

The commission had removed its hearings from Washington to cooler and more fashionable Newport. The situation was certainly not promising. Frazier, the American commissioner, considered it his duty to oppose every British claim regardless of its merits, and he was sedulously aided by Hale, the American agent. Gurney, the British commissioner, appeared weak, assenting too easily to American claims. Count Corti of Italy, the third commissioner, lacked knowledge of international law and was not on good terms with Gurney. At the outset Evarts suffered a blow when the commission refused to allow him to present an oral argument, which it should have done under the terms of the treaty.[18]

With the assistance of J. M. Carlisle, counsel for the British government—a man almost blind—Evarts went to work at Newport upon an elaborate brief. It was probably the best he ever wrote. Carlisle proved of great assistance. Evarts attacked the decision of the Supreme Court on three grounds: (1) it disregarded the essential principles of prize jurisdiction; (2) no adequate ground appeared for condemning the vessel; and (3) the Court had misconstrued the facts, depending upon conjectures instead of awaiting proofs.[19]

Evarts' exposition of neutral rights was masterly. A prize investigation, he pointed out, must be limited to "what the evidence discloses"; otherwise neutral commerce would be subjected to the "unchecked and speculative cupidity of belligerents." It was not the doctrine of continuous voyage which he criticized; it was the use of surmise as to the vessel's destination instead of actual proof. If the extraneous evidence before a court was inadequate, further proof should be taken. He showed that authorities on international law supported this principle.

The Supreme Court, Evarts continued, erred in believing that an attempt had been made to conceal the cargo. The failure to list all of the cargo was due merely to ordinary British trade regulations in colonial commerce. It also erred in invoking the evidence in the cases of the *Gertrude* and *Stephen Hart* and in inferring an intent to violate the blockade, from the nature of the cargo, which was only one per cent contraband. In short, the Court jumped to conclusions upon "a hypothesis of continuous voyage," permitting what must inevitably amount to a paper blockade of neutral ports.

Most important of all, concluded Evarts, this decision would endanger the future interests of the United States as a neutral. If the decision of the Supreme Court were allowed to stand, the commerce of neutrals would be placed to an intolerable degree at the mercy of belligerents. The verdict amounted to "an enlargement of the domain of good prize of war to the theatre of neutral trade between neutral ports, upon the fiction of possible continuous voyage."[20]

Thus Evarts showed that what the Court had regarded as a suspicious case of blockade-running was really an innocent commercial voyage. Authorities have praised his argument highly. John Bassett Moore declared, "It has never been my good fortune to read a better argument in a prize court and I do not expect ever to see a better one. . . . No one but a great lawyer with a profound apprehension of the principles of international law could have made such an argument."[21]

But, as Evarts feared, the cards were stacked against him. In a hurried decision the Mixed Commission denied the claim of the owners of the cargo, giving no reason. Undoubtedly the British commissioner took his cue from the British Foreign Office, and joined his two colleagues in upholding this far-reaching interpretation of belligerent rights because it would in the long run favor Great Britain as a belligerent. The rights of the owners were deliberately sacrificed for the sake of fixing a precedent. "I am vexed at the decision," Evarts wrote his client, "which, I think, must have passed wholly upon secondary, if not quite extraneous considerations. If the Commission had allowed an oral argument, I should have felt more secure of an opposite result."[22]

Once more the leading authorities—Gessner, Twiss, Phillimore, Baker, Woolsey, Wharton, Calvo, Bluntschli, Parels, Fauchille, and Hall—criticized the decision. "There can be no question," declared the *Herald,* "that the doctrine . . . would be most disastrous to neutral trade. . . . No nation would have any security that its neutrality would be respected while the doctrine of 'continuous voyage' enforced by British squadrons and cruisers all over the globe menaced and harassed its commerce."[23] And so it proved. In 1877, at a meeting of the leading authorities on international law at Antwerp, a resolution was passed denouncing the doctrine of the Supreme Court. Again in 1882 the decision of the Mixed Commission was condemned as a "novel theory," and it was recommended that the United States abandon its stand as a dangerous precedent.

The most complete proof that Evarts had taken a prudent position came when the United States once more played the part of a neutral during the World War. Many valuable American cargoes consigned to neutral ports were intercepted by British cruisers on the ground that their ultimate destination was Germany. Great Britain stretched the doctrine of continuous voyage to an extreme limit. In the case of the *Kim* the British court rode roughshod over the principles which Evarts had asserted, holding, "The true test is the ultimate destination of the goods."[24] In this they merely followed the American tribunals.

Two months after the decision of the Mixed Commission, Evarts defended neutrality in quite a different manner. The Ten Years' War had broken out in Cuba in 1868, and was marked by every conceivable cruelty. The Cubans, ill-prepared for their struggle for independence from Spain, expected aid from sympathetic Americans; but the United States was neutral and took precautions to prevent assistance to Cuban rebels.

Evarts had no sympathy for filibusters. He had had experience with them in earlier years. But in 1869, soon after leaving the Johnson Cabinet, he acted as counsel for some suspected filibusters in the case of the *Quaker City*. Edwards Pierrepont, federal district attorney, created a sensation when he ordered the arrest of the leaders of a junta in New York who were believed to be backing the Cuban cause. Among those indicted by the grand jury were José Morales Lemus, who called himself minister from the Cuban Republic; José M. Basora, Dominican consul at New York; José Mora, a wealthy New York merchant; and Colonel William O'Ryan. Evarts was counsel for Lemus. Before a crowded courtroom he complained that the bail demanded was excessive, and secured a reduction. In the trial which followed the government was unable to produce sufficient evidence to convict the prisoners, and the jury and public opinion were distinctly on Evarts' side.[25]

Four years later, in November, 1873, the *Virginius,* an American ship long engaged in carrying arms to Cuban rebels, was captured by the Spanish, brought into Santiago, and four of the crew, including the noted Colonel O'Ryan, shot. Five days later came a thunderbolt. It was learned that Captain Fry and thirty-six men had been executed as pirates, in a most savage manner, despite the fact that some were of American citizenship. The atrocity was due to the reckless and fanatical character of the Spanish authorities at Santiago. The *Virginius* had long been marked for doom, but it was unfortunate that she fell into the hands of the most bloodthirsty of local authorities. A wave of indignation swept the country. Meetings were called to protest. The Cabinet approved Fish's ultimatum demanding the restoration of the *Virginius,* release of the survivors, a salute to the American flag, and punishment of the Santiago authorities. Meanwhile preparations for war began.[26]

It is regrettable that Evarts had not been appointed minister to Madrid after his return from Geneva. The bellicose manner in which General Sickles behaved served only to pour oil on the flames. The Spanish government became defiant. Evarts had watched the situation with alarm. When the war had first broken out in Cuba he had written Rockwood Hoar that a "storm was brewing" which would have serious consequences for the United States.[27] He knew that such situations called for the right kind of diplomacy.

While the war was at its peak on November 17, a great mass meeting was called in Steinway Hall in New York, where General Banks and Congressman Cox were the chief speakers. Rain and snow could not keep away the eager throng that soon filled the hall. An overflow meeting was held near by in Tammany Hall. It was fortunate that Evarts was chosen to preside. Amid the confusion and excitement, the hisses for Fish and derisive cat-calls for Spain, Evarts found his task difficult. The reading of Governor Hendrick's telegram, calling for armed intervention in Cuba, set the crowd wild. Reports of the meeting vary, but all agree that Evarts' speech was the great event of the evening. The *Nation* called it the only speech worth listening to.

He pronounced the atrocity "one of the most horrible transactions" of history, wholly inexcusable, and a violation of the treaty with Spain. Even admitting that the crew of the *Virginius* were pirates, they should have been given a trial. He raised a tremendous cheer when he said, "We are a law-abiding people, and we insist upon it that other nations shall abide by the law in dealing with us. We intend to have redress and absolute security that no such outrages shall ever again be repeated during the future life of our nation." While the audience was cheering wildly, Evarts revealed that his real aim was moderation. "We understand," he continued, "that vengeance and bloodthirstiness are not necessary exhibitions of a nation's triumph and power. . . . Our duty . . . is plain. . . .

If it is true, as seems entirely probable, that the power of Spain no longer controls the action of the Cubans, if it be true that these people have all the responsibility of irregular warfare, we will see to it that they do not have all the immunities of regular authorities. We are not to be driven from one recourse to another, but we are to obtain, peaceably no doubt, such amends for the past and such protection for the future as will make the American people resume their quiet and renew their pride, satisfied that neither are to be disturbed in the future."

It was thus that Evarts turned a dangerous meeting into one which showed commendable moderation, although some of the other speakers furnished "ginger hot in the mouth." As the *Tribune* remarked next day, Evarts is "one of those men whom no commotion from the center of gravity could upset and one who could not be illogical if he tried."[28] Soon after, Fish reached a satisfactory settlement with Spain. Evarts congratulated him, but prophesied that future relations between Spain and Cuba would have to be watched closely.[29]

When Chief Justice Chase died in May, 1873, Evarts was recognized throughout the country, and especially by the legal profession, as one of the likeliest of the candidates to succeed him. Other able men had their supporters—Curtis, Hoar, Trumbull, Groesbeck, and Miller—but Evarts possessed superior learning and talent.

Senator Sumner favored Rockwood Hoar, but he had no influence with Grant, who had already dismissed Hoar as attorney general. When it became plain that Hoar would not be considered, Evarts exclaimed bitterly, "The inexorable rule of unfitness, it seems, must be insisted upon even to exclude a friend"; to which Hoar replied, "If fitness governs, you will be the foremost, and if it does not, I should be sorry to think I was in competition on any other principle."[30]

Fish felt that Evarts' acceptance of office under Johnson was still an "insuperable objection," and that the Senate would not confirm his nomination if it were made. Senator Conkling, who had already refused the office, could be expected to oppose Evarts' nomination. It was becoming evident that Evarts' independence in politics was an obstacle to his advancement. For this and other reasons Caleb Cushing was rejected by the Senate, although his appointment to the post in Spain was approved.[31] The nomination of Attorney General Williams followed—an unpardonably second-rate choice. The New York bar protested. Williams was a politician of unsavory reputation. "The general feeling of the public," asserted the *Independent,* "is that the President might and should have done better, with such men as Evarts, Cushing, Curtis, and Hoar,—to say nothing of the present members of the Supreme Court."[32] Williams withdrew under fire.

The final nomination of Morrison R. Waite was a surprise, for he could not be ranked among the leading lawyers. It evoked neither great opposition nor warm enthusiasm. To pass over Evarts and appoint Waite, on the basis of his services at Geneva, was a strange distinction. But it had no effect upon the personal friendship of the two men. However Evarts might feel toward Grant, he was sincere in writing Waite: "I congratulate you . . . on being a candidate. . . . If it costs you no more time, thought or desire than it does me, you will have the clear gain of honor without drawback of loss or burden."[33] Evarts had become accustomed to political disappointment and did not feel keenly his failure to become Chief Justice. Appointment to the post would have meant a greater financial sacrifice than in earlier years, when the income from his profession was not so large. He liked to tell the story of Chief Justice Taney's daughters, who, on hearing their father had been nominated, exclaimed, "Then we shall be obliged to take in washing."[34] Recalling that his grandfather, Roger Sherman, had a distinguished career in the Supreme Court, he may have felt that a family could hardly expect two members to reach that high office. It may be noted here that at about this time he determined that Roger Sherman's portrait should occupy its rightful place in Independence Hall. He secured an artist, James Earl, and the portrait was soon after presented to the city of Philadelphia.[35]

An incidental result of Geneva was the marriage of Evarts' daughter, Hettie, to Charles C. Beaman in the summer of 1874. It was at Geneva that the romance had begun. Beaman, a man of thirty-four, already possessed a reputation as a lawyer and an authority on international law. After leaving the Harvard Law School his interest had been aroused by problems of neutrality and his prize essay on "The Rights and Duties of Belligerent Vessels in Neutral Waters" and his article on arbitration in the *North American Review* had attracted much attention. His book, *National and Private Alabama Claims and Their Amicable Settlement,* published in 1871, was pronounced the most comprehensive treatment of the subject. The aid he gave Bancroft Davis in preparing the American case, and his appearance before the Mixed Commission in the case of the *Texas Star,* added to his reputation.

Evarts was very fond of Beaman. They were much alike in energy, common sense, intellectual ability, cheeriness, and dry wit. After the wedding party returned home from the church in Windsor, Beaman sat down at the piano in a jovial mood and sang with great gusto, "I Would That I Was Single Again." Next morning Evarts was heard coming down stairs making a horrible noise. The family rushed to see what was the trouble, exclaiming, "Why, father, we didn't know you could sing." Evarts replied, "Well, I never knew it myself until I heard Beaman."[36]

16

Thirty Years of Law

THOUGH INTERRUPTED by public services, Evarts' legal career during the thirty years following the Civil War grew increasingly significant. The decade from 1866 to 1876 was professionally the most active of his life. It would be impossible to trace all of his cases, for some remain undiscovered because they were never reported; but the greater ones have a real interest.

More than a third of all of his cases in the post-war years were argued in the Supreme Court at Washington. Wearing the customary black frock coat and speaking with his usual deliberation, he always appeared at his best in this decorous chamber. He could plead with an earnestness that compelled interest; the justices would cease twitching in their chairs and thumbing their briefs to listen intently. Evarts liked this court, its courtesy, its judicial atmosphere, its freedom from the arrogance of manner so often found in lower tribunals. He once said of it, "What other place is there in the frame of society and government, of which we have any history or any observation, that is equal to that of a tribunal that can pronounce irreversible decrees? No king, no magistrate, no parliament, no congress, on certain great topics of judicial control and decision, can overrule or reverse the decrees of this tribunal. Nothing short of a new constitution of the great nation that has grown up under the Constitution, by a change of its own sovereign decrees, can reverse these public judgements of this Court."[1]

Another third of Evarts' cases were in the Court of Appeals.

This tribunal was unparalleled in the variety, excellence, and importance of the body of state decisions which it laid down. Following the reorganization of 1870 the new justices—Sandford E. Church, William F. Allen, Rufus W. Peckham, Martin Grover, Charles A. Rapallo, Charles J. Folger, and Charles Andrews—inspired confidence from the outset. The court became a model for other states and its decisions were closely followed. It met at first in one of the legislative halls of the old Capitol, where, amid furnishing of the most severe simplicity, the ungowned judges held court from two to six in the afternoon. Evarts could catch the morning train to Albany and return in the evening. With the opening of the new Capitol in 1879, the court had the finest quarters in the country. These were situated on the third or main floor; an impressive chamber, finished in red oak, portraits of former judges on the walls, an elaborately adorned bench, a great fireplace, high windows commanding a panorama of the Hudson Valley, a bronze statue of Chancellor Livingston—all contributed dignity to the court. A tall clock in the corner was the only unpleasant reminder for lawyers. Across the hall was a special room for waiting attorneys, with portraits of famous lawyers, among which that of Evarts ultimately found a place. It was in this court that Evarts argued some of his greatest cases.[2]

In the lower courts—the New York Supreme Court, the Superior Court, and the Court of Common Pleas—Evarts appeared less often. These courts, housed downtown in Manhattan in a new building erected at great cost by the Tweed Ring, were much alike, and till after 1871 were of low standards. After the collapse of the Ring great improvements were made in these courts, and a regime of corruption was ended.

Before the war Evarts had not been very successful in will cases, usually finding himself on the weaker side. In the notorious Gardiner-Tyler suit in 1866 he once more had the difficult side. Like the Parish Will Case, it raised a question of undue influence. It concerned three persons: the wealthy widow, Mrs. Gardiner of Staten Island; her forty-seven-year-old son David; and her daughter, Mrs.

Julia Tyler, a strong-willed woman of thirty-five who was the widow of ex-President Tyler. David managed his mother's estate of "Castleton" for years and improved it. By her first will his mother gave him the estate, dividing the rest of her property between him and Julia. When Tyler died, leaving his widow, Julia, a Virginia estate of decreasing value, she decided to go to "Castleton" and live with her mother. This started the trouble. Julia soon acquired a strong influence over her invalid mother and made David's life unbearable, causing him to leave home, and dictated offensive letters to him signed by the mother. Her constant pleas of poverty finally induced the mother to write a new will. On her deathbed, four hours before her decease, she allowed her daughter to dictate the second will to the family lawyer, signed it after it was read to her, had the doctor pronounce her capable of making a will, and died. This will divested David of his rights; it gave "Castleton" to Julia and divided the rest of the property equally between Julia and David, but in such a manner as to give Julia the income from David's share during her lifetime. Was this will the true intent of the mother or the work of a scheming daughter?

David successfully contested the will in the Surrogate's court, and Mrs. Tyler appealed to the state Supreme Court with Evarts as counsel. He secured a reversal in her favor on errors of fact. On further appeal, however, the Surrogate was sustained by the Court of Appeals. The court declared that Julia had misrepresented the facts to her mother and that there was a strong presumption of undue influence.

Subsequently, Evarts secured an amicable settlement between David and Mrs. Tyler and acted as administrator of her property. When she became financially distressed and a neglectful government failed to provide a pension, she worried Evarts with repeated requests for money, asking him also to seek a pension for her and a political appointment for her son. He lent her money, taking as security the proceeds of the sale of her Staten Island property and the trust deed on her Virginia estate, both of which together did not cover the loan.[3]

Facing O'Conor in the Lovett Will Case, Evarts found quite a different problem. In disposing of his two-million-dollar estate, George Lovett had left equal annuities to his daughter Augusta Gillender, who had a child named Helena, and to his daughter Mary Kingsland, who had nine children; providing that after the death of the two daughters the estate should be so divided among the ten grandchildren that Helena should get a fourth, and the other nine grandchildren an equal share of the remaining three fourths. The will raised intricate points of inheritance law. Augusta retained Evarts to defend her interests in the Court of Appeals; O'Conor appeared for the Kingsland children. Evarts argued that Lovett's purpose was to give Augusta control of the estate during her lifetime, outside of the two annuities, so that it might accumulate for the grandchildren. The court agreed that this was the intent, but held such accumulation contrary to law and decided that the estate should vest at once in the grandchildren.[4]

Again in the Stanley Will Case it was Evarts' misfortune to be on the difficult side. This was a case of great interest to lawyers because of the important problems of charitable bequests which it involved. William Stanley of Hartford bequeathed his real estate in the business section of Hartford to the South Ecclesiastical Society, with the proviso that it should never be sold. The property became very valuable as the years passed and the legislature felt justified in authorizing its sale. Colt, the purchaser, was sued by the Stanley heirs for breach of the will. The case reached the Supreme Court with Evarts acting for the heirs and Benjamin R. Curtis for Colt. Evarts contended that the will had been broken and the property should revert to the heirs; Curtis insisted that Stanley had intended to create a trust, not to set up a condition which should work a forfeiture if broken. In giving the Court's opinion, Justice Nelson declared that Stanley's purpose was to benefit the Society, not limit it, and that the lapse of time and change of conditions justified the sale of a charitable bequest.[5]

Beginning with the suit of *Slosson* v. *Lynch,* Evarts met with better success in his will cases. It involved a pre-marital agreement between man and wife, whereby, if she died childless, her property should go to the next of kin. Evarts argued that the next of kin included three grandchildren of her deceased brother; Daniel Lord contended that it meant her two sisters. The State Supreme Court upheld Evarts' interpretation.[6]

This was Evarts' last encounter with Daniel Lord, who died soon after in 1868 at the age of seventy-three. At a meeting of the bar in the District Court room, Evarts, O'Conor, William Allen Butler, and others paid tribute to Lord's long career. With deep emotion Evarts said: "He was as quiet and simple, as honest and straightforward, and as constantly laborious and faithful as if work was all there was to life. . . . Although he never held judicial or official station, nor was honored by political distinction, we must feel [his life] has been a life as worthy to be lived, as useful and as influential, as any of those lives which have been more elevated in the career of public influence. . . . He never overlooked the fact that the profession of the law was not in, and of itself, the pursuit of gain, . . . that its rewards were in the service of the public. . . . His example, his life, is not affected by any decay, nor fretted by any corrosion. It is complete; it is secure."[7]

The Phelps Will Case in the Connecticut Supreme Court and the Colton Will Case in the Supreme Court at Washington offered little of significance. Both, however, were victories for Evarts.[8] But the Stokes Will Case in 1881 was a *cause célèbre*. James Stokes, head of the famous business firm of Phelps, Stokes, & Company, left a six-million-dollar estate. By the will and first codicil he provided for his widow and divided the residue equally among his seven children and one grandchild. By a second codicil, which caused the litigation, he discriminated against his daughter, Mrs. Dora S. Dale, placing her share in a trust fund which would revert to the other heirs after her death. Mrs. Dale challenged this codicil on the ground that her father lacked testamentary capacity and had been coerced by his sons, Anson, James, Thomas, and William. Evarts was retained by Anson, the executor, to uphold the will and codicils. Twenty years before, Evarts had failed in an attempt to break the will of the elder Anson Phelps. Now, against such adversaries as George F. Comstock, Theron G. Strong, and Francis N. Bangs, would he succeed in defending the instrument?

Bangs was a new opponent, but one whom Evarts often encountered in later years. Although eccentric, careless of dress, quick-tempered, and often rude, Bangs was an able, keen-witted lawyer who acquired one of the largest practices in the city and ultimately became president of the Bar Association. Before a jury he won many seemingly impossible verdicts, while before an appellate court he pleased the judges with his simplicity and brevity.

The Stokes Case dragged through six years in the courts, and the testimony filled five large volumes. Innumerable witnesses were examined and lawyers spent months on their summaries. The preliminary struggle was an attempt by Mrs. Dale to force Anson to produce accounts and papers for inspection by her counsel; but Evarts secured a defeat of her petition.

The case was tried on its merits before Surrogate Rollins. Evarts' summary took three days. He pictured James Stokes as living a quiet, sober, uneventful life, looking after his family business, and helping manage the affairs of his church. The second codicil, he argued, was intended to keep the estate within the possession of his own kin; for Mrs. Dale's child had died and her own health was precarious, creating the possibility that her share might fall to Mr. Dale, something Stokes was most anxious to prevent. The charge that Stokes lacked testamentary capacity was based on physical, not mental condition. The lack of a sound mind, said Evarts, could not be proven by "little instances of the want of memory, by little instances of the want of temper, by little instances of the want of courtesy."

Evarts' argument breathed with witty sallies, directed chiefly at the opposing counsel. To illustrate the fact that absent-mindedness was common to the greatest men he told the story of Sir Isaac Newton and Dr. Stukely. The doctor called to see Sir Isaac, but the servant dared not call him from his study. The doctor sat down to wait while the servant spread the table for dinner. After an hour of waiting the famished doctor ate the tempting chicken, asking the servant to prepare another dish. Sir Isaac appeared and asked the doctor's pardon while he ate dinner. He sat down, declaring that he was faint with hunger, lifted the cover, beheld the bones of the fowl which the doctor had eaten, rose and said apologetically, "I actually had forgotten that I had dined." Bangs scoffed at the story, declaring that absent-mindedness was a matter of habit. "It is not in the proof," rejoined Evarts. "Neither is his dinner," retorted Bangs, while the courtroom rang with laughter.

When Evarts produced documentary evidence to prove that Stokes was fully competent to transact business, Bangs replied that it was only routine business and laid great stress upon Stokes's bursts of temper. Evarts retorted with the story of the Earl of Coventry, who tried to break his wife of the habit of using rouge. At a public dinner he noticed rouge on her face and chased her around the table and rubbed it off, but she persisted in a habit which so poisoned her that death ensued. Was this burst of temper, asked Evarts, a sign of lack of intelligence?

Evarts turned the tables neatly upon a witness—a physician who had declared Stokes demented—by pointing out that he had not hesitated to give Stokes detailed instructions for his health, which only a man of sound mind could have comprehended. As for the charge of undue influence by the sons, all were rich in their own right and as for the special gift to the favorite son William, "If a man worth six millions of dollars cannot extend help to a son to the extent of his love . . . without all the rest of the family treating it as a robbery of their expectations, why what is the use of having families and wealth and affections?"

Evarts won a complete victory, for the court upheld the will and second codicil. Evarts had no connection with the aftermath. After Mrs. Dale died, her husband continued a bitter, groundless contest, which in itself proved that Stokes must have known what he was doing in making the second codicil.[9]

The Hoyt Will Case, soon afterward, created greater interest. Jesse Hoyt, a self-made grain merchant, left a seven-million-dollar estate. He bequeathed an ample income to his daughter Mary, but provided that the rest of the estate and her income after her death should go to her uncles or their children. Mary sought to break the will, claiming that her uncles had placed her in an asylum just before her father's death and had used undue influence upon her father, who lacked testamentary capacity.

Three factors roused public interest in the case: its long duration in the courts, the eccentricities of Mary Hoyt, and the eminence of the lawyers. Roscoe Conkling acted for the daughter till his death, and then Benjamin F. Butler and Roger A. Pryor became her counsel. Evarts was leading counsel for the executors and uncles, and with him stood Choate and Elihu Root. Much of the groundwork of the defense, such as securing evidence and preparing briefs, fell to Root, whose capacity for labor and ability to nail down points with logical precision were rapidly earning him fame as a lawyer.

Evarts appeared only in the first phase of the case, and his main contribution was a masterful closing argument before Surrogate Rollins. As in the Stokes Case, his task was to show that the testator had been of sound mind and intelligent purpose. He reviewed the testimony of numerous witnesses to prove Hoyt's high character and mental capacity; he demonstrated that he was master in his household, knew what was going on, and showed originality and prudence in business. Hoyt had idolized Mary, but he knew that a woman of forty-three was most unlikely to marry, and therefore assigned the bulk of his fortune to his brothers and their children to maintain the family's name and prestige. If he left too much to Mary, unscrupulous men would seek her in marriage. It was she, not Jesse Hoyt, who was of unsound mind, and her father had known it when he made his will. Her lawyers insisted she was not insane, yet refused to bring her into court where she could be observed by all.

Evarts' reasoning was so irrefutable that he won his case. The Surrogate upheld the will and declared Hoyt to be of testamentary capacity. But he avoided delivering any judgment on Mary's sanity, merely describing her as an obstinate, violent, and eccentric woman. Evarts had no part in the final scenes. Choate and Root successfully reargued the case in the Court of Appeals. Mary then attempted a million-dollar suit against the executors, which was dropped when a general settlement was concluded seven years after the commencement of the case.[10]

Evarts' contract cases were of course numerous and of infinite variety, but they lacked the intriguing human interest of his will cases. The case relating to the Brooklyn Bridge was the only one of public significance. He had a share in saving the project for building the bridge at a time when its continuation appeared doubtful. Construction had begun in 1870 with the approval of the legislature and Secretary of War. An act of 1875 limited the expenditure to eight million dollars, of which Brooklyn was to pay not more than two millions in any one year and New York not over one million in any one year. In 1878 Kelly, comptroller of New York City, refused to issue bonds for the million dollars due that year, asserting that the bridge was unsafe and an obstruction to navigation, and that the total expense would exceed eight million dollars. With Evarts and A. J. Vanderpoel as counsel, the Bridge Company sought to compel performance of the contract. Kelly was represented by George F. Comstock. Evarts contended that the maximum fixed by the legislature was not to be so construed as to defeat the project, and that the War Department had pronounced the structure safe and unobstructive. The Court of Appeals sustained him, and ordered the bond issue. To the great joy of the Brooklyn people, work was resumed.[11]

If Evarts' contract cases had little intrinsic interest, they were notable for the lawyers concerned. In *Moore* v. *Huntington,* in the Supreme Court he defeated W. W. McFarland, a dramatic type of lawyer who would have suited the rôle of a tragedian. In the Rutland Marble Case Evarts and Senator Edmunds defeated Benjamin Curtis in the same court. In *Drake* v. *Taylor* he was beaten in the Circuit Court by Clarence A. Seward, adopted son of the great statesman.[12]

Southmayd hated to go to court and seldom went. But in the case of the *Delaware & Hudson Canal Company* v. *the Pennsylvania Coal Company* he accompanied Evarts, and fought tooth and nail against Stephen P. Nash. This was one of the earliest clashes between Evarts and Nash. This churchman-lawyer, counsel for Trinity Church, earned a high reputation and became a power for good in the Bar Association. Evarts and Southmayd succeeded in demonstrating to the Supreme Court that the coal company had never made a contract with the canal company.[13]

Increasingly, Evarts appeared in cases relating to corporate stock. William H. Aspinwall was his client in two of these suits, one of which he lost to Edwin B. Stoughton and the other he won against Charles A. Rapallo.[14] The thoroughness with which he treated a legal problem was illustrated by the case of *Carpenter* v. *Danforth*. Although a simple case concerning the purchase of stock by a director from a shareholder, Evarts' brief covered eighteen major legal points and twenty major points of fact. He won the case easily.[15]

Twice Evarts acted for the Western Union Telegraph Company. There was a strong popular feeling that it had watered much of its stock, but in the Court of Appeals he successfully defended it against a charge of fraud and overcapitalization. In Washington he appeared before the Senate Committee on Post Offices and Post Roads to protest against three bills proposed for placing the telegraph under government ownership and operation.[16]

When Jay Cooke's banking house in Philadelphia crashed in the panic of 1873, the government sued for priority of payment from Cooke's assets. Evarts tried to show in Cooke's defense that certain British bankers were his partners and jointly liable for the debts in question; but the Supreme Court held Cooke solely liable.[17]

Evarts' marine insurance cases were as numerous as ever, interspersed as usual with collision cases and cases of marine contract.[18] One of these last, the case of the *Moses Taylor*, raised the question whether a maritime contract to transport a passenger from New York to San Francisco could be enforced by the California courts or belonged exclusively to the federal courts. Evarts and Pierrepont argued successfully for the latter view. The case became an important precedent, depriving state courts of a large class of cases.[19]

It was Evarts' good fortune to be connected with one of the most discussed extradition cases in American law—indeed, the only one in which the President ordered the delivery of a fugitive in the absence of an extradition treaty. Don José Arguelles, a Cuban official, sold illegally a large number of slaves and fled to New York to enjoy the fruit of his ill-gotten gains. When promptly arrested by a federal marshal upon order of Secretary Seward and at the request of the Havana authorities, and put aboard ship to be returned to Cuba, he charged the marshal with kidnapping him and had him indicted under New York law. Much excitement arose. As the United States had no extradition treaty with Spain, Seward's action seemed high-handed and was much criticized. A trial took place in the Court of Sessions, with Evarts, James T. Brady, and Clarence A. Seward representing the government. Their object was to secure a removal of the case to the federal courts, and they relied mainly upon a federal statute permitting arrests by executive authority. Amasa J. Parker and A. Oakey Hall, representing the state, contended that the statute was a war measure not applicable to the case. Judge Russell refused to remove the case, but ultimately it reached the Supreme Court and the statute in question was declared unconstitutional. While the court deliberated, Seward acted. He had Arguelles returned to Cuba, was thanked by the Spanish government, and defended his course in a long argument before a congressional committee.[20]

Evarts' defense of James Watson Webb, editor of the New York *Courier and Enquirer,* in the nasty *Caroline* scandal, was quite outside of the ordinary run of his cases. On reaching Brazil, to which he had been appointed minister by Seward, Webb revived a claim to the *Caroline,* a Peruvian ship condemned in a Brazilian seaport as unseaworthy, and sold. The American insurers, upon whom the loss fell, failed to recover the vessel and assigned their claim to

Lemuel Wells, who failed to interest the State Department in supporting his claim to the ship against the Brazilian government. Webb pressed the claim vigorously and the Brazilian government reluctantly paid five thousand pounds to the United States. After Hamilton Fish became Secretary of State an investigation convinced him that the money should be repaid to Brazil, and President Grant so ordered. But it was now found that Brazil had paid Webb £14,252, which he defiantly refused to repay or account for, simply claiming that he made large payments to Brazilian officials to secure his claim. This plea that he had practiced bribery seemed a ridiculous excuse. Attorney General Hoar denounced Webb publicly and started a prosecution, while the Brazilian government declared Webb dishonest. Fish was positive that the minister had been guilty of extortion. When Webb returned from Europe to face the charges and retained Evarts as counsel, the latter advised him that he had a substantial defense, and a trial followed in the District Court. Despite the efforts of the prosecution, Judge Blatchford refused to compel Webb to name the Brazilians to whom he had given money. The jury seemed bent on a verdict of acquittal, but the judge's charge led some of the members to change their mind and no agreement was reached. Webb left the court a free man, although many believed him guilty. Evarts' defense had been no small factor in the result.[21]

Evarts also appeared in two of the California land cases arising out of the territorial acquisitions from Mexico. In *De Haro* v. *the United States* he was associated with Montgomery Blair and Jeremiah Black, while the government was represented by Henry Stanbery and Caleb Cushing. The case required a thorough knowledge of Mexican land grants prior to the conquest of California and the subsequent action of the United States toward Mexican property owners. Ramon and Francisco de Haro had been granted lands by Mexico, which became of immense value as the city of San Francisco developed. The grant was confirmed by American land commissioners and the District Court. The heirs of the De Haros enjoyed sixteen years of occupancy before it was discovered that one of the original papers, signed by the Mexican governor, was spurious. This meant that the De Haro claim reverted solely to a provisional license given by the Mexican government, and raised the question whether it was equivalent to a grant. The document appeared authentic and was listed among the grants made by the Mexican Secretary of State. But the District Court of California rejected it, holding it to be a mere license to occupy the premises until the common lands were surveyed. In the Supreme Court Evarts presented a strong argument to prove that the license gave the De Haros a title, but the court upheld the California decision.[22]

In the case of *Frisbee* v. *Whitney* the controversy was over valuable California lands which included a city, town, navy yard, and depot of the Pacific Mail Steamship Company. Frisbee based his claim to a quarter-section of these lands upon an early grant to his father-in-law, Vallejo, which had been confirmed by the land commissioners. When the court invalidated the grant, a rush for the lands took place. Whitney entered the property which Frisbee had claimed, had an armed clash with him, and brought suit, claiming that the land had become public domain, subject to preëmption, and that his entrance had given him superior title despite a subsequent act of Congress which accorded Frisbee first option. Evarts appeared in the Supreme Court for Frisbee, arguing that he was the real possessor, that Whitney was an intruder, and that Congress had perfected Frisbee's title. The court so held and Evarts received a thousand-dollar fee from his client.[23]

In the field of patent law Evarts acted for important clients. One group of them were the heirs of Charles Goodyear. Like other great inventors, Goodyear suffered from encroachment upon his patents; capitalists robbed him remorselessly and bankrupted him with protracted litigation, so that he died prematurely under the burden of debts and worries. His heirs continued to experience legal difficulties. In one case Evarts and Stoughton represented the heirs in the Supreme Court; for the defendant, the Providence Rubber Company, Cushing and Black were counsel. Goodyear accused the company of infringing his patent by making rubber products for the army and navy and rubber bulbs for syringes. The company replied that Goodyear's original patent was void, that its extension had been procured by fraud, and that Goodyear had granted the company a license. The case was argued with great learning and ability, and the twelve hundred pages of testimony were carefully sifted. All the more important was Evarts' decisive victory, the court pronouncing Goodyear's patent to be "impregnable." In another case Evarts defended the Phoenix Rubber Company in a suit brought by the Goodyear heirs. The inventor had assigned to the company a license to manufacture and sell pontoons and rubber blankets in return for royalties, but the company failed to render an accounting. On technical grounds, Evarts was able to demonstrate that the president and agents of the company could not be forced to appear as witnesses.[24]

Rumford and Hecker, two names familiar to every cook and housewife, also became involved in patent litigation. Rumford had received a patent for a baking powder, and for some years sold acid to Hecker, who made large profits from the sale of self-rising flour. When Rumford obtained a reissue of his patent, Hecker asserted that it applied to a different product, and that he could therefore manufacture baking power without further obligation to Rumford. The latter sued for infringement of his patent in several states. In the New York Circuit Court Hecker sought an injunction to restrict the suits to one state and one suit, and as counsel for Rumford, Evarts secured a defeat of the injunction. Then, in the Circuit Courts of Rhode Island and New Jersey, he argued the merits of the case, displaying quite a mastery of chemistry and contending that there was no essential difference between the products of the two companies. Replying pungently to the claim that the Rumford process had been anticipated by a man named Lawes, who had found a mixture for making manure, Evarts said: "It would certainly be extraordinary if, while he was making manure, he had by chance got a mixture that would make good bread." Evarts won his case.[25]

Patent cases usually involve a knowledge of technical apparatus, making them a difficult subject for the general lawyer. Evarts lived before the day of the specialized patent lawyer. In the case of *Mitchell* v. *Tilghman* he had to make a careful study of the chemical nature of acids, fats, and glycerine; in the Amoskeag-Garner Case he had to learn much of calicoes and prints; and in the Higgins Case he had to study the intricacies of weaving.[26] The Burdett-Estey Case required a mechanical knowledge of organ-making. In the Supreme Court Evarts argued that certain changes made by Estey in his organs, such as a different width of reed-boards and size of valve-openings, did not add any feature that could be called an infringement of existing patents.[27] Evarts won all of these patent cases.

He acted for the government or for private clients in many revenue cases, but was not always successful. Loopholes in the revenue laws made evasion easy and caused trouble for the federal treasury. His professional opinion was asked and he was retained in the Rycock wine cases, the champagne cases, the Swiss silk cases, and others, which dealt chiefly with undervaluations at the port of entry.[28] His humor did not desert him even in such prosaic litigations. In one case dealing with the grading of colored sugars, he wrote in his brief, referring to the Bible story of Jacob and Laban, "If Jacob had spotted the cattle after they were brought forth, by a skillful application of paint, his title might well have been considered doubtful."[29]

The Claflin Smuggling Case in 1875 caused much excitement among the New York merchants. Horace B. Claflin, philanthropist, pillar of Beecher's church, and head of one of the largest commercial houses in the world, was indicted for selling six smuggled cases of silks imported from France, valued at thirty thousand dollars. Since it did not seem possible that Claflin could be guilty, public sympathy was with him. Evarts and Elihu Root, who defended him, succeeded in showing that the indictment was vague and that no intent to defraud had been proven.[30]

As would be expected, Evarts engaged in some important tax litigations. Particularly interesting was the Cotton Tax Case, soon after the war, which divided the Supreme Court. Congress had taxed all cotton three cents a pound. This seemed like a discrimination against the South, especially as Thaddeus Stevens was sponsor of the tax. Could Congress tax the staple of one section? After two arguments the case came up in 1871 for a final hearing. Evarts and Benjamin R. Curtis represented the taxpayers; Attorney General Hoar appeared for the government. Evarts insisted that it was a direct tax, not apportioned as required by the Constitution; that it amounted to an illegal export tax on cotton; and that if it were an indirect tax, it lacked the uniformity required by the Constitution. Chase was ill when the decision was rendered and the other justices divided equally. Evarts lost his case.[31]

Among other tax problems which Evarts faced were such questions as the following: Could the federal government tax brokers or manufacturers of clothing for soldiers? Could a state tax aliens brought into the port of New York, all vessels passing quarantine at New Orleans, brokers who imported merchandise, passengers transported from California to Nicaragua, or non-resident traders?[32]

The Virginia coupon cases were more important. Virginia had repudiated millions of dollars of her bonded indebtedness by forbidding the use of matured coupons as payment for taxes. The first real test of her action came in the case of *Poindexter* v. *Greenhow*. Evarts headed four counsel for the coupon-holders, while Virginia was represented by Francis S. Blair and Robert T. Merrick. Poindexter had given the tax-collector twelve dollars in coupons, which the collector refused, seizing a desk in Poindexter's office in lieu of the tax. Had the state violated a contract or was it exempt from suit under the Eleventh Amendment? The Supreme Court held that it had violated a contract and that the coupons were receivable for taxes. The court, in a most unusual construction, against which four justices dissented, drew a distinction between a suit against a state and against an officer of a state seeking to recover damages under an unconstitutional act.[33]

Evarts' greatest tax litigations were the famous Bank Tax cases. His arguments were of high order and not unlike those of Webster in the classic case of *McCulloch* v. *Maryland,* for he fought in behalf of the exemption of banks from state taxation. During the war the Supreme Court had stood firm against all attempts by the states to tax federal securities. But the issue rose again after the war.

First came the case of the Bank of the Commonwealth. When the state levied a tax upon the capital stock of this bank, it joined with other banks which had the bulk of their resources in federal securities in resisting the tax. Evarts, Lord, Silliman, Emott, Bradford, and Fancher represented the banks; Brady, Kernan, and Develin appeared for the state. Evarts contended that since such securities could not be taxed in the possession of individuals, they could not be taxed in a bank, even though the bank was chartered by the state; and the Supreme Court held the tax void.[34]

But meanwhile Congress granted the states the right to tax national bank stock locally, providing the tax was no greater than that assessed on other capital. New York seized the opportunity to tax, even where the entire stock of a bank was in the form of federal securities, and the Court of Appeals sustained its action. The National Bank of Utica, which had purchased its securities previous to the act, claimed a breach of contract, and a committee representing the national banks of the country brought a test case before the Supreme Court. Evarts, Sedgwick, Reynolds, and Tremaine represented the banks; Kernan and Parker were counsel for the tax officials.

Evarts pictured the destructive effect of the tax, declared it void as a tax upon bank property, insisted that there was no difference between a tax upon the aggregate stock of a bank and upon the stock of each shareholder, and asserted that the act of Congress had been violated by taxing the national banks at a different rate from the state banks. Changing Marshall's famous phrase slightly, he said, "If a State has the power to tax, there is no limit." A copy of his argument was sent to all of the national banks, and they were urged to do everything possible to resist the tax. Once more Evarts won. Justice Nelson gave the opinion of the Court, holding the tax void on the sole ground that it was not levied at the same rate as on other capital.

The legislature hastened to cure this defect, and once more the issue had to be fought out in the Supreme Court. Confident that the Court would sustain him, Evarts repeated his argument. To his dismay, Justice Nelson treated the case in summary fashion and upheld the tax. Three justices, however, dissented. The Court thus settled the principle that a tax on shares of stock was not a tax on the property of the bank, but on the private property of the stockholders and hence was a lawful form of taxation. Evarts received a fee of $7,250 for his work in these cases. Although defeated, he helped strengthen the doctrine held today that a state cannot tax federal securities as property of a national bank.[35]

A review of Evarts' record during the thirty years following the war reveals that as a commercial lawyer he was engaged mainly in the field of wills, contracts, and insurance; that the greater number of his cases were in the Supreme Court; and that he won a decided majority of them. In the field of patents, taxation, and revenue he had even more cases, and was even more successful. There was another field, however, in which he was earning larger fees and greater reputation—the field of corporation law.

17

Great Railroad Cases

AMERICAN economic history has no more romantic chapter than that which describes the rise of the network of railroads after the Civil War. As the best years of Evarts' professional career paralleled this development, it was inevitable that he should be drawn into many railroad cases, and should become to some degree a specialist in the field. Apart from his actual appearance in cases, he spent a great deal of time advising clients how to keep out of trouble. He probably earned more in this advisory capacity than from litigations. Although evidence on this point is lacking, it is certain that his opinions were much sought after and always well compensated.

There are two distinct narratives to be told: first, his conspicuous work in litigations attending the rise of rapid transit in New York City; and second, his relations with railroads in general, particularly the great lines of the West.

The chief legal issue in the city's railroad problem was whether abutting property owners were being deprived of their rights by the construction of street railways. This problem had never been fully settled before the war, but the general rule was that a surface railway could be built without compensation to or consent of the majority of the abutting owners. Evarts had appeared in one of these early cases just at the close of the war, *Osborne* v. *the Brooklyn City Railroad,* representing a property owner of Greene Avenue who claimed that a horse-drawn street railway was an interference which entitled him to damages because he owned to the middle of the street. Needless to say, if this contention had been upheld by the courts, street railways could never have come into existence. Evarts lost the case, Judge Benedict holding that Osborne owned only to the line of the street and must prove special damage, differing from that of other owners, to support an individual suit against a street railway.[1]

The advent of the elevated railway complicated the problem. At the close of the war it was apparent that surface railways and omnibuses could not meet the demand for rapid transit. Under legislative permission a company was created to operate a rope or cable elevated line. The West Side and Yonkers Patent Railway Company was organized, and the first half-mile of elevated railway in the world was constructed, as an experiment, from Battery Place along Greenwich Street to Ninth Avenue. It was operated by a cable wound around a drum driven by a steam engine placed beneath the sidewalk. The elevated structure was supported on one-legged columns about fourteen feet high placed at the curb. On its trial trip the first train started and stopped with such violence that the false teeth of President Ackerman were dislodged, nearly choking him. But the road was regarded as a great success and a wonderful feat of engineering. A protest, however, came from abutting property owners, who sued in the Circuit Court, with Edwin Stoughton and Clarence A. Seward as counsel. Evarts had the distinction of defending the first elevated company of history. In harmony with precedents for surface lines, he argued that the legislature had the power to incorporate such a railway and that, in the absence of proof of special damage, the property owners had no ground for demanding compensation. Judge Blatchford so held.[2] Despite its victory, mechanical difficulties soon overtook the railway, and it was sold by the sheriff at auction in 1870 for $960 to a rival, the New York Elevated Company.

The public demand for rapid transit increased. Editorial columns were devoted to it. All sorts of solutions were proposed: subways, elevated lines, an increase of surface lines, and even suspended tubes with trains driven by air pressure. The legislature authorized the New York Elevated Company to take over the West Side road, and in 1872 the Gilbert Elevated Railway Company was authorized to operate a tubular line propelled by atmospheric pressure, while other franchises were granted by special acts. When the usual evil results of special legislation ensued, a constitutional amendment was enacted in 1874, forbidding incorporation except by general law; and the famous Rapid Transit Act of 1875 created a commission, appointed by the mayor, to determine the necessity for new lines, locate the routes, and fix upon plans of construction. No line could be built without consent of the local authorities and a majority of abutting owners; but in the absence of such consent, application could be made to the New York Supreme Court to appoint special commissioners whose approval could be accepted in lieu of that of the property owners. Under this act, the Gilbert Company abandoned its tubular plan and turned to the construction of a steam elevated line on Sixth Avenue.

Alarmed by the prospect, the surface lines and property owners decided to challenge the constitutionality of the Rapid Transit Act. The chief opposition to the Gilbert Company came from the Sixth Avenue Surface Railroad, which had been operating since 1854 and naturally opposed an elevated line. It sought an injunction in the Superior Court in June, 1876, to restrain the Gilbert road from an invasion of its franchise. This important test case before Judge Sedgwick brought forth a great array of lawyers: Evarts, Choate, Butler, and Comstock for the Sixth Avenue Surface line; Porter, Carter, Green, and Lowry for the Gilbert Elevated Company.

Evarts realized that he held the unpopular and difficult side of the case. He had to prove some special right in the street and some special damage resulting from the erection of the superstructure over the street. The special right would be the contract which his client had with the city for the use of Sixth Avenue; the special injury would be the nuisance created by the elevated, obstructing the street and causing noise and smoke. His argument was given wide publicity in a pamphlet entitled *Great Speech of Hon. William M. Evarts on Rapid Transit.* He painted the injurious effect of an elevated line supported on girders only fourteen feet above the street, the competition which would ruin the surface railway, the injury that would be done the avenue if it were obstructed with posts, endangering traffic and increasing the hazard from passing fire apparatus. He brought into court an elaborate model of Sixth Avenue, with tracks, cars, horses, elevated road, and fire engines, to demonstrate how much congestion would result in the street. He showed the injurious effect the structure would have upon the property owners, depreciating their property values and driving them away. Comfort was to be sacrificed to rapid transit for commuters; the city was to be made less fit to live in so that it might be more accessible to those outside. As for the act of 1875, it did not grant the right to build this type of railway, and even if it did, the act was unconstitutional because it was contrary to the amendment of 1874 forbidding special charters. But Judge Sedgwick denied the injunction, and Evarts lost his case.

Yet the battle was not over. When the Supreme Court appointed commissioners to condemn the property needed for the elevated road, Evarts fought the move first in the Supreme Court and then in the Court of Appeals. The *Herald* doubtless voiced popular opinion when it declared: "Suits in the Court of Appeals ought not to discourage the supporters of Rapid Transit. . . . Nothing is easier than for litigious corporations willing to spend money in a desperate contest to maintain suits in the courts. They have too much at stake to spare expense and did the best thing they could in subsidizing Evarts to advocate their rotten cause. . . . We do not grudge him his large fees, we have too much confidence in the Court of Appeals to believe that it will be swayed from justice and law by any ingenious arts of advocacy." Evarts repeated much of his earlier argument. He insisted that the act of 1875 was unconstitutional, that an elevated steam railway exceeded the requirement of "public use as a street," and that such schemes were an interference with health and private property.

The Court of Appeals unanimously decided against him, and upholding the Rapid Transit Act, declared that the Gilbert line was free to complete its road, that the consent of the property owners was not necessary, and that the road could not be considered the result of a special act.[3]

Then six years later came the next case. Both the Gilbert road, which had changed its name to the Metropolitan Elevated Railway, and the older New York Elevated Railway found themselves in financial difficulties; and they sought the help of the Manhattan Railway Company. By a tripartite agreement, the two former roads agreed in 1882 to lease their property and rights to the Manhattan Company, which would complete and operate them, thus providing a more unified transit system and preventing a collapse. But it soon appeared that the cost of this undertaking ran far beyond the estimates, while the income fell below expectations. Bankruptcy overtook the Manhattan Company, and it defaulted on bonds and dividends. To save it, the other two lines made concessions, chiefly in a reduction of the rentals paid them by the Manhattan. But since these concessions were made by the directors and never approved by the Metropolitan stockholders, the latter brought suit in 1884, charging the directors with a fraudulent conspiracy and asking the dissolution of the tripartite agreement. Another impressive group of lawyers appeared: Evarts, Field, and Vanderpoel for the Manhattan; Carter and Barlow for the Metropolitan. Evarts succeeded in showing that no fraud had been intended, and that the directors had acted for the best interests of the roads. The tripartite agreement was sustained.[4] It was a just decision and ended a long and malicious attack which had filled the columns of the press for months.

Meanwhile Evarts had become legal adviser of the ill-starred Cable Railway Company. Under an act of 1882, this company was to operate twenty-nine new surface or elevated routes at a five-cent fare, using cable-cars similar to those which had already proved a success in Chicago. In giving his legal approval of the charter, Evarts held that it permitted any means of locomotion except "animal power." When an act of 1884 forbade the opening of further surface lines, Evarts advised the company that it did not apply to their project; but it appeared that it had been lobbied through the legislature by the horse-car roads for the express purpose of blocking the Cable Company enterprise. The Second Avenue Railroad Company, a surface line, challenged the authority of the Cable Company, asserting that the act of 1884 repealed that of 1882, and that the Cable Company had exceeded its time limit.

An interesting suit was fought out in the Court of Common Pleas. The Cable Company sought an injunction to restrain the Second Avenue Company from projecting a new line on First Avenue, where the Cable Company was planning one of its units. Some fifteen horse-car railways were interested in the outcome; for if the injunction were granted, their future was doomed. Judge Daly refused the injunction. The case then went to both Special and General Term of the Supreme Court, where Evarts argued for a reversal. He contended that the act of 1884 did not repeal that of 1882 or give the Second Avenue Company a concurrent right. Before a decision was rendered, the Second Avenue Company withdrew and paid all costs of litigation. But the victory for Evarts proved temporary.

The existence of the Cable Company was now challenged by the city authorities and property owners. Although it had the backing of many prominent citizens, it was charged with having failed to comply with the act of 1882. With F. R. Coudert, C. A. Hand, and W. H. Peckham as counsel, the property owners brought suit at General Term, where Evarts, C. P. Shaw, and R. Sewell defended the company. The court held that the company had caused a depreciation in property values, that it had failed to fix a time limit for completion, and that the act of 1884 had ended its existence. The Court of Appeals sustained this decision; and when the company applied to the legislature for aid, the proposed act was defeated.[5]

Meanwhile, in the Court of Appeals, Evarts had battled with David Dudley Field in the most famous of his elevated railway cases: *Story* v. *The New York Elevated Railway Company*. The case raised again the question whether the streets could be used for an elevated railway without compensation to abutting owners. The

Court of Appeals had divided three to three on the issue, one judge absent, but it was now ready for a re-argument before a full bench. Many lawyers were present, interested in the flood of litigation that would follow if Evarts won his case for the property owners.

The facts in the case were simple. Rufus Story owned two lots on Front Street and could trace his title back to two grants made by the city in 1773. These grants contained a covenant requiring that traffic along the street be forever kept open. This gave Story ground for his suit. He contended that he had a right of easement in the street, which was obstructed by the elevated line, and that he was therefore entitled to damages.

It rested with Evarts to break the precedents and show that the property owner had some rights. Pitted against John E. Parsons, an able champion of great corporate interests, Evarts for two hours held the undivided attention of court and spectators. One lawyer declared, "It was by far the best argument that I have ever heard addressed to a court." The subject gave Evarts opportunity for a remarkable display of learning and wit. He argued that the creation of an elevated road without compensation to Story was a breach of contract, that is, of the grant which the city had made in 1773, while it was also a taking of property without due process of law and a violation of the equal protection of the law. An abutting property owner had a *property* right or fee in the street, and an elevated road was a subversion of that right.

The court upheld him by the close vote of four to three. Benjamin F. Tracy rendered the opinion, holding that the deeds of 1773 amounted to a covenant which gave Story an easement in the air, light, and access to the street, the deprivation of which entitled him to damages.[6] Although the decision opened the way to other suits, it would apply only where property owners could show a similar covenant with the city. Thanks to Evarts, the property owner had received his "day in court."

In the larger field of national railroad development Evarts was equally active. As he watched the growth of pools, rebating arrangements, and other practices which aroused a demand for state and federal regulation, his ingrained conservatism and his political and economic philosophy aligned him on the side of private rights. Not that he approved of monopoly or ignored the demand for social justice; his activities as a reformer disprove that. But he was a typical nineteenth-century lawyer, believing in freedom of enterprise, in the rights of property, in due process of law, and in the American business man. He was well aware of the dubious methods of the railroads, their financial juggling and unscrupulous rivalry; he knew that laws were often insufficient and courts helpless; he realized that unscrupulous lawyers were prospering from railroad abuses. But it is a remarkable fact that not one scrap of evidence in all his manifold railroad litigations connects him with shady practices.

In 1865 he won his first minor railroad case.[7] Then came a series of suits relating to the Ohio & Mississippi Railroad. This Ohio corporation claimed it had a contract with the Indianapolis & Cincinnati Railroad, an Indiana corporation, for interstate traffic and splitting of receipts. But in 1866 the right of a railroad chartered by a state to operate across state lines was a novelty, and the Indiana road denied that any such contract existed. The case attracted great attention because of the principle involved. Evarts represented the Ohio road; Thomas B. Hendricks, later vice-president, and George E. Pugh, a brusque type of lawyer, represented the Indiana road.

Evarts' task was to prove that a railroad could carry on business in another state without the legislative consent of that state. He showed that this was possible under the principle of comity, and that contracts for through traffic would be a boon to transportation. Denouncing the provincial attitude the states were still taking toward interstate commerce, he said: "I am sure this learned Court will not seek for doubtful interpretations of the law on such vague, uncertain topics as . . . public policy." But the decision went against him. The court declared that the contract lay beyond the power of the parties making it. This judgment satisfied current opinion, but it obstructed interstate commerce.[8]

The case of *Cincinnati* v. *Morgan* in the Supreme Court brought on a struggle between Evarts and Henry Stanbery. The question was one of a lien on the Ohio & Mississippi Railroad, and Evarts, representing Morgan, found himself on the easy side of the case. He ridiculed the claim of the city as "a lien by argument of Mr. Stanbery" and won his case.[9]

State bond issues for railroad construction flooded the market after the war, the terms of many of them requiring legal interpretation. Southmayd evinced more talent than Evarts in such matters. Extremely cautious, distrustful of anything speculative, refusing steadily to shake hands with Jim Fisk or Jay Gould, he became a trusted adviser of investors on bond issues.[10]

Evarts gave two notable opinions on bond issues in the early seventies. As the Blue Ridge and the Greenville & Columbia railroads in South Carolina were not prospering, the legislature approved a consolidation, which was authorized to issue bonds, and to execute a mortgage to Henry Clews to secure their payment. The opinions of Evarts and D. H. Chamberlain, Attorney General of the state, were sought as to the right of the state to waive its lien without consent of the bondholders so as to make the new mortgage a prior lien. Evarts approved the waiver as in the best interests of the public. He was in no way connected with the subsequent "Bond Ring" headed by Governor Scott, which managed to bribe the legislature to release the railroads from all liability for the six million dollars worth of bonds.[11]

The history of certain Minnesota bond issues was equally distressing. An ambitious program of railroad building had been followed by collapse and repudiation of bonds. The holders, many of them New Yorkers, fought repudiation unsuccessfully for years. Feeling the honor of the state at stake, Governor Marshall proposed in 1870 to sell public land to pay the bondholders. To assist him the Eastern investors secured from Evarts and Benjamin R. Curtis an opinion pronouncing repudiation to be a violation of the obligation of contracts. "No man," declared Evarts, "can dwell upon the features of the scandalous history of debt repudiated and trusts betrayed by the State of Minnesota without indignation." But the voters of the state rejected the proposal two to one.[12] Soon afterward, Evarts represented Selah Chamberlain, the largest bondholder, in a suit in the Supreme Court. He expected the court to deny his attempt to recover from the railroads their unsold lands or money received for lands sold; but he hoped to brand the state as a defaulter. And so he did, for Justice Field denied the claim, but condemned the state for its lack of good faith. Minnesota finally paid the bondholders fifty cents on the dollar.[13]

Beginning in 1873, Evarts was engaged in great litigations relating to the transcontinental railroads.[14] He first represented the Union Pacific in an appeal to the Department of Justice for the right to extend its line. By a change of plan Congress left the Central Branch of the Union Pacific without a connection, granting the route to Denver to another line. Evarts and Benjamin R. Curtis argued the necessity for a Western connection before the Solicitor General, but their plea failed.[15] Then came the famous *Crédit Mobilier* scandal, the government being defrauded of millions by a construction company which built the Union Pacific. The Poland investigating committee of Congress implicated such men as Brooks, Garfield, and Colfax, in shady relations with the *Crédit Mobilier,* while the Wilson investigating committee reported the financial condition of the road to be serious. Congress authorized Attorney General Williams to sue the stockholders of the Union Pacific for recovery of alleged fraudulent profits which the *Crédit Mobilier* had made out of construction contracts. Suit was brought in the Circuit Court of Connecticut. The defendants, some one hundred and fifty individuals or corporations, were scattered all over the country, but were represented as a group by Evarts and Benjamin R. Curtis. They demurred to the complaint, and the demurrer was sustained by the court, which declared that the government had not proved sufficient interest to support a suit. Indeed, the prosecution was shamefully mismanaged by Attorney General

Williams, who should have recovered its lost millions. An appeal was taken to the Supreme Court, where Evarts argued the question of jurisdiction. The Court declared that it had jurisdiction, but that the railroad had met the requirements of its charter and the government could recover nothing.[16]

Problems of state taxation of railroads brought Evarts more litigation. The Peniston Case, which is often cited in treatises on taxation, squarely raised the question whether a state could tax within its border the property of a railroad chartered by Congress. On behalf of the Union Pacific, Evarts argued that the railroad was an instrumentality of the federal government and could not be taxed by a state. The Supreme Court, with three justices dissenting, held that the tax affected federal power only remotely, and that a line had to be drawn somewhere. But Evarts won the Maguire Case for the Union Pacific, showing that a Missouri tax on railroad earnings was specifically forbidden by Congress till certain conditions were met.[17]

The most conspicuous of Evarts' railroad cases were the granger litigations of the seventies. The farmers of Illinois, Iowa, Wisconsin, and Minnesota, victimized by the rapacious railroads and grain elevator companies, forced the passage of state laws to correct abuses and obtain reasonable rates. But the laws amounted to little because the railroads defied them or the courts voided them. The panic of 1873 aroused the farmers to desperation, and they resolved to fight for state control of rates. When the Potter Law of 1874 in Wisconsin asserted the right to regulate rates through a commission clothed with autocratic powers, the heads of the St. Paul and the Northwestern railroad systems declared the law confiscatory and sought Evarts' opinion.[18] He agreed that the law was confiscatory and a violation of the obligation of contracts. "The question of the reasonableness of fares and freights as between the public and the common carriers," he said, "is a *judicial* one, solvable only before a court or jury, and upon actual circumstances of each disputed transaction at the time it arises."[19]

In the fall of 1876 the granger laws reached the Supreme Court.

A great legal battle loomed up. Would the "due process" clause of the Constitution protect the railroads as against the police power of the states to protect their citizens? Would the Court step in and assert some degree of federal control? The State Freight Tax Case of 1873 left no doubt that the Court believed that Congress would regulate under the commerce clause. But it was generally believed that the Court would not uphold the granger laws. Observers were therefore greatly astonished when, in the famous case of *Munn* v. *Illinois,* involving the fixing of maximum rates by the state for the storage of grain in elevators, the law was sustained. In giving the opinion, Chief Justice Waite said: "When . . . one devotes his property to a use in which the public has an interest, he, in effect, grants to the public an interest in that use, and must submit to be controlled by the public for the common good."[20] This classic decision introduced the "doctrine of public interest."

Evarts was not in the Munn Case, but appeared soon after in a granger case of equal importance, *Peik* v. *The Chicago and Northwestern Railway Company.* Associated with him were Edwin B. Stoughton and Charles B. Lawrence for the railroad. The question was whether Wisconsin could regulate rates under the Act of 1874. Being something of a gentleman farmer himself, Evarts may have cherished a secret sympathy for the Midwestern farmers; but no inkling of it appeared in his argument, nor were his general economic views favorable to them. The distinguishing point in the case lay in the fact that the Wisconsin railroads had consolidated with others in Illinois, giving their business an interstate character. Furthermore, a land grant to one of the Wisconsin railroads had stipulated that the government might use the road free from toll. Upon these two points Evarts was able to argue that the regulation of rates by Wisconsin was a violation of the obligation of contracts and of due process of law, and a flat interference with interstate commerce. Although he rested on strong ground, he may have anticipated defeat because of the Munn Case. Sure enough, Chief Justice Waite ignored the interstate character of the problem, declaring it must await the action of Congress. He held that Wisconsin could regulate rates just as if consolidation had not taken place and that no breach of contract had occurred.

In three other granger cases, all of them corollaries of the Peik Case, Evarts launched ingenious new attacks upon the constitutionality of the Wisconsin law. It was of no avail: Waite had chosen the path of public interest and continued to pursue it.[21] If Evarts was on the unpopular side in the granger cases, at least he was right in declaring that the regulation of railroads was properly a problem for Congress. Little did he know that he was to have a share in the much needed legislation by Congress ten years later.

Not long after the granger cases, Evarts tried to save the town of Montclair, New Jersey, from the consequences of its early extravagant purchase of railroad bonds. Montclair had been incorporated by the legislature in 1868 as a town separate from Bloomfield because of its eager willingness to purchase the bonds of a proposed railroad. But the panic of 1873 rendered the bonds worthless. Determined to recover from the town, the bondholders organized and fought for their rights so tenaciously that legal expenses became an annual item in the Montclair budget. The issue finally reached the Supreme Court, where Evarts appeared for the town and Barker Gunmere, father of a former chief justice of New Jersey, represented the bondholders. Evarts rested upon the act of incorporation of 1868, claiming that it exempted the town from liability; but it appeared that the authors of the act had phrased it ambiguously, and the Court construed it as placing the liability upon the town.[22]

When Henry Villard was projecting his famous Northern Pacific line, he sought Evarts' opinion on several legal problems. This was during the most ticklish period of Villard's great adventure, just after he had formed his notorious "blind pool," promising investors great returns without telling them how their investments were to be spent. Specifically, he wished Evarts' advice upon the validity of a bond issue and upon contracts with branch roads.[23] Evarts also had some connection with the development of the great railroads of the Southwest. He appeared before a Senate committee to plead against the rescinding of a land grant to the Texas and

Pacific Railroad. Though Congress had forbidden a union with any other "competing line," the road had joined the Southern Pacific. Evarts made it clear that the consolidation was supplemental rather than competing and that it sought to carry out the very purpose that Congress intended. His plea was successful and the lands were not forfeited.[24]

The Farley-Hill suit furnished a dramatic conclusion to Evarts' cases. James J. Hill conceived his great idea for a new Northern transcontinental when he purchased the bankrupt St. Paul and Pacific Railroad, thereby establishing a through line for his own St. Paul, Minneapolis, and Manitoba line. Jesse P. Farley, who held the unusual position of manager and receiver of the St. Paul and Pacific, awoke to the fact that he might make millions out of the situation. He claimed that he had given Hill the necessary information about the bankrupt road; that he had originated the idea of the purchase and coöperated with Hill in executing it; and that he had received a promise of a share in the stock of the new company. When Hill denied the claim as preposterous, Farley sued for his share of the profits. It required thirteen years of bitter struggle in the courts to settle the issue, which was twice fought from the Circuit Court in St. Paul to the Supreme Court in Washington. At the first trial a mass of testimony was taken. Farley, explaining that his double interest as manager and receiver had forced him to keep the matter secret, declared that Hill had defrauded him of fifteen million dollars.

Evarts did not appear in the case till it first reached the Supreme Court, when he represented Hill, with Senator George F. Edmunds as his adversary. Their arguments left the judges in uncertainty, and a re-argument followed. The Court then refused to render a decision because of errors by the lower court and certain irregularities in the defense. This outcome proceeded from the suggestion of Farley's counsel, but was doubtless satisfactory to Evarts. With the later phase of the case Evarts had no connection; but the Supreme Court finally dismissed Farley's suit, and thus vindicated the position Evarts had taken.[25]

Justice Gray, who wrote the decision in this case, was on familiar terms with Evarts and relished his humor. Having just married and occupied a new house in Washington, he took pride in showing Evarts over it. As the inspection ended, Evarts asked who was the architect. Gray replied that Hornblower had drawn the plans, but that he had meddled so much with them that Hornblower refused to sponsor his own handiwork. "Ah," exclaimed Evarts, "then you will put on the cornerstone: 'Hornblower *fecit;* Gray *interfecit.*' "[26]

18

The Defense of Henry Ward Beecher

THE CHARGE that Henry Ward Beecher—the eloquent Brooklyn preacher—had been an adulterer and ought therefore to be hurled from the exalted pedestal upon which he had long stood, shocked and grieved the American public. The press was agog over the great Brooklyn scandal during the first six months of 1875. Of all the spicy episodes of the day—the prosecution of Tweed, the exposure of the Whiskey Ring, and the attack on the *Crédit Mobilier*—it was the most sensational.

It was odd that Evarts should become the chief bulwark in defending the fair name of the pastor. He did not like such cases. But his sympathy was aroused by Beecher's peril, and when asked to aid him, he accepted and threw himself unreservedly into the task. The *Brooklyn Eagle* later remarked: "The most wonderful matter in the Tilton-Beecher case, apart from the character and career of the defendant, has been the amount, variety, and quality of the work which Mr. Evarts has put into it."[1]

The development of the Beecher scandal extended over several years, and its history involves a narrative of complicated and contradictory evidence. Henry C. Bowen, a wealthy merchant and pillar of the Plymouth Church, had brought Beecher to Brooklyn, established him as editor of the *Independent,* a religious journal which Bowen had founded, and introduced him to Theodore Tilton, a promising reporter twenty-two years younger than Beecher. Tilton had great journalistic ability, soon becoming assistant editor and helping to increase the circulation of the *Independent* rapidly. Many famous men contributed to it, including Evarts, and it became the leading religious journal of the country. Beecher grew fond of Tilton and did all that he could to advance him. When Beecher went abroad in 1863, Tilton became editor.[2]

The rift began in 1866, when Beecher aligned himself with President Johnson while Tilton became a Radical. No longer did Tilton publish Beecher's sermons in the *Independent.* Indeed, Beecher resigned from the staff of the paper the following year. When Tilton became connected with the feminist movement and expressed its advanced ideas in the columns of the *Independent,* eliciting a protest from many of its readers, Beecher accepted the editorship of a rival weekly, the *Christian Union.* Self-esteem was the most potent factor in Tilton's nature. His rapid rise had given him an overpowering conceit and ambition. He had great talent and knew it; he was an athlete, orator, and poet in one, and well versed on nearly all subjects. But his radical ideas alarmed Bowen, who induced him to resign as editor of the *Independent,* continuing as a contributor, and accept the editorship of the *Brooklyn Union.* Like Beecher, he had a host of friends, and up to 1870 his success was remarkable.[3]

Previous to that year Tilton had no open break with Beecher. Indeed, he really admired Beecher. At the New England Society dinner in 1869, with Evarts present, Tilton said publicly, "I must not forget to remember the illustrious pulpiteer of Brooklyn Heights, to whom I am bound by many tender ties of gratitude, chief of which is that he married me—and I hope it is valid—I think it is."[4] Tilton's home on Livingston Street was always open to the preacher, who was a frequent visitor. Here he met Mrs. Elizabeth Tilton, a woman of thirty-two. She had been married ten years and was a good wife and mother, a woman of literary tastes, affectionate disposition, and emotional nature. She had listened to Beecher's sermons for fifteen years, and almost worshipped him.

The breach between the two men opened in July, 1870, when Mrs. Tilton made a confession to her husband which Tilton later set forth in a sworn statement to the church in the following words: "On the evening of October 10, 1868, or thereabouts, Mrs. Elizabeth R. Tilton held an interview with the Rev. Henry Ward Beecher, at his residence, she then being in tender state of mind, owing to the recent death and burial of a young child; and during this interview an act of criminal commerce took place between the pastor and this parishioner, followed also by similar acts on various occasions." Tilton followed this up in the next issue of the *Independent* with an editorial under the caption, "The Wreck of a Life," which did not mention Beecher but undoubtedly referred to him.[5] In reply, Beecher in due time declared, "Concerning all my visits it is sufficient to say that at no interview which ever took place between Mrs. Tilton and myself did anything occur which might not have occurred with perfect propriety between a brother and a sister, between a father and a child, or between a man of honor and the wife of his dearest friend; nor did anything happen which she or I sought to conceal from her husband."[6]

By December, 1870, Tilton found both his business and his domestic affairs at a desperate crisis. His wife had left him upon Beecher's advice; but, as Beecher later explained, not with any thought that he was the cause of Tilton's woe. Bowen was trying to get rid of Tilton and break the contract he had with him. Tilton decided to act. He told Bowen the whole story and Bowen faced Beecher with the charge. Beecher denied everything, called Tilton "crazy" and delighted Bowen with some information about Tilton which the newspaper-owner could use to get rid of him. Thus, the first of Tilton's efforts to "strike Beecher at the heart" missed its mark.

A few days later, however, he took the second step. He obtained from his wife a written confession of adultery. Great mystery still surrounds this remarkable note, for neither the original nor any copy of it was ever produced in court. Then came the third step. Tilton confided in Frank Moulton, who earned the title of "mutual friend" by carrying messages back and forth between Tilton and Beecher; and Moulton brought about a meeting between the two on December 30, but was not present in the room when they conversed. This meeting is likewise mysterious, for different versions of it were later given in court. Beecher said merely that Tilton charged him with improper advances to his wife; Tilton said that he had charged Beecher with "sexual intimacy," and that Beecher had staggered from the room moaning, "This will kill me." All that is certain about the interview is that Tilton read a document supposed to have been his wife's confession, and tore it up without placing it in Beecher's hands.

If Tilton's actions in December were strange, Beecher's subsequent behavior was still stranger. With Tilton's permission he visited Mrs. Tilton that same night and induced her to write a letter of retraction, in which she repudiated her confession. On the next day Tilton sent Moulton to charge Beecher with being the cause of his removal by Bowen from all connection with the *Independent.* Finding Beecher in a contrite mood, Moulton got him to dictate a letter to Tilton, which was taken down by Moulton and signed by Beecher without a rereading, humbling himself before Tilton "as before his God," and begging forgiveness for being the cause of his unhappiness. This letter became the most important document at the trial.

Thus the history of the case showed a complicated series of charges, denials, confessions, retractions, and letters of contrition. It is strange that Beecher should have given his confidence to Moulton, whom he scarcely knew. Yet, according to the testimony, he confessed adultery to Moulton and to Mrs. Moulton, and entrusted Moulton with intimate letters which were later used against him. At Moulton's suggestion he even mortgaged his home in order to furnish Tilton with money to launch a new journal, *The Golden Age.*[7]

The next thread in the tangled skein was a tripartite agreement made by Beecher, Tilton, and Bowen in April, 1872. They undertook to settle all differences among themselves, to withdraw all charges, and to close the whole matter. Beecher explained that he signed the agreement, not from a sense of guilt, but out of a feeling that he had innocently been the cause of Tilton's misfortunes. How he could have signed unless he had a conviction that he had done wrong is inexplicable. It was as if three schoolboys had agreed not to spread dirty stories about each other.

A new element shortly entered the picture. Mrs. Victoria Woodhull, who had just established a radical feminist paper, *Woodhull and Claflin's Weekly,* had learned of the scandal from Tilton and decided to violate his confidence by exposing it in her paper. She poured forth the amazing story, declaring that her object was to make Beecher confess and stop the attacks which Plymouth Church was making upon her. Although the *Weekly* had an enormous sale, the public was not inclined to believe her story. Benjamin F. Tracy, a pillar of the church, soon had her in jail, and got Tilton and Moulton to show him all the letters. He reported that there was not sufficient evidence to convict Beecher.

Tilton then entered the fray again. He penned his famous "True Story" of the scandal and allowed the *Weekly* to publish it anonymously, thus breaking the tripartite agreement, and he published a notice in a Brooklyn paper that more would follow. In June, 1873, Beecher wrote Moulton that he found life hardly worth living and that his nerves were on the "ragged edge," a letter which proved important. He demanded a church investigation, which was eagerly granted. When Tilton appeared before the church council and repeated his charges, Beecher simply replied that his differences with Tilton had been settled. The council took Beecher's side and expelled Tilton from the church. It was the last meeting of Beecher and Tilton till they confronted each other in court.[8]

If the church had left Tilton alone, there probably would not have been any trial. But Leonard Bacon, a church leader, denounced him in a series of lectures at Yale, whereupon Tilton published his "True Story" under his own name. At Beecher's request another church committee made an investigation. Mrs. Tilton appearing before it, declared Beecher innocent, while Tilton brought in a mass of testimony to prove him guilty. Not only did the committee exonerate Beecher, but before his whole congregation of some three thousand he spoke in self-defense and was given an almost unanimous vindication. But there were many who doubted his innocence. Dr. Fairfield, an Ohio clergyman, wrote a daring attack upon him, based on the evidence given the committee; to which Robert Raymond, a church leader, replied with a defense. The press was flooded with questions and comments, and the scandal became a public possession.

Tilton had one recourse left, to sue Beecher for alienation of his wife's affections. In July, 1874, he published a specific charge of adultery in the *Argus,* and Moulton presented a similar one in the *Graphic.* He then brought suit, a civil process known as an action in crim. con. (criminal conversation), asking one hundred thousand dollars damages.[9]

An intensely interesting drama was then enacted in the Brooklyn City Court. Day after day for six months crowds came to watch the unfolding of the scandal. Ambassadors, judges, millionaires, and bishops sat alongside of butchers and bakers, equally interested in the spectacle. For two hundred and twelve days the court was a mecca for the curious and the morbid. The press kept pace daily with the latest events, and cartoons of the prominent actors in the trial were sold on the street. The case was the common topic of conversation, but opinion was much divided.

The courtroom was far too small, a rectangular chamber with flat ceiling and very poor acoustic qualities. It had none of the trappings of modern courtrooms. At one end was the bench; at the other were seats for the spectators, with a gallery above. Extra chairs in the middle of the room increased the congestion. The jury sat at the right of the bench, while in front of the jury box were two low tables for the counsel who were elbowed by reporters and so crowded that they could scarcely work. Every seat was taken, and often the chairs squeezed in the narrow space behind the judge were occupied, while other spectators stood in the aisles or at the rear. This little courtroom, intended only for ordinary routine cases, became a buzzing hive of curious humanity.

Judge Neilson did not wish to preside, but did so with common sense and firm hand. He would not allow the counsel to change his rulings by argument and was quick to rebuke disorder. There were times when the crowd escaped his authority and proceedings became too informal, but he always regained control and no one ever questioned his impartiality.[10]

The lawyers were watched closely, and significance was attached to their every word and action. Evarts, Porter, Tracy, and Shearman appeared for the defense; Beach, Fullerton, Pryor, and Morris for the plaintiff. Evarts was of course the leading counsel on his side. Beecher was a great admirer of Benjamin F. Butler but had been unable to obtain his services. Although unaccustomed to this type of case, Evarts was in fine fettle, in the prime of his powers, unperturbed by the excitement, and bent on saving Beecher.

A reporter describes Evarts at the start of the trial in somewhat uncomplimentary terms: "His clothes will be shabby before long if he does not get a new suit. . . . He is half-way between a wizen-faced musty old gentleman and one of the fine, precise, yellow veterans who have long hung in portrait galleries since men wore stocks three inches broad. Mr. Evarts wears such a neckerchief now, and blue cloak with broad velvet collar. His voice comes up from somewhere in his depths as though hoisted out of a cellar where he had a great deal more of it stored away; and there is an interval between the opening of his mouth and the outcome of any sound. . . . In manner he is quick and testy, but he does not waste time in purposeless bickerings. He apparently expects to gain every point he makes, and takes it hardly when he fails, dropping into his chair. . . . His diction is almost perfect and he speaks slowly and distinctly, no matter how much stimulated by opposition and anger. He interrupts the Court with a presumption and frequency that would disturb a less even-tempered man than Judge Neilson."[11]

Evarts was no Benjamin F. Butler. He struck no attitudes, but relied upon force of logic and his original way of stating his ideas to carry him through. He did not declaim, but conversed; he did not gesticulate, but used the familiar forefinger to emphasize his points. His manner was like that in the Johnson trial: a cool, rational approach, contrasting sharply with the excitability and emotionalism of his colleagues and opponents.[12]

Next to Evarts, John K. Porter was the main cog in the defense. His theatrical demeanor and indefinable magnetism fascinated the jury. He was soon to win even greater publicity by securing the acquittal of Orville H. Babcock, President Grant's secretary in the Whiskey Ring scandal. Tracy did well during the early stages of the trial but was handicapped by illness at its close. "Tearful Tommy Shearman," clerk of the church and confidant of Beecher, a short, nervous, fussy little man with Jewish features, ably assisted in preparing the case. He was devoted to Beecher and refused a fee for his services.

The defense rested its argument upon the thesis that Beecher was the victim of a cunning conspiracy by Tilton and Moulton to drive him from his pulpit and ruin him. To substantiate this theory Beecher's counsel had the advantage of knowing all the essential evidence beforehand, not only because Tracy had seen all of the documents, but because Tilton had submitted the evidence to the church council. Evarts and his associates had six months to prepare, with all the evidence before them and unlimited funds supplied by the church.[13]

The leading lawyer for Tilton was William A. Beach, a conspicuous figure at the bar for forty years. Tall, athletic, and impressive in his double-breasted coat, he gave an air of military precision to all he said or did. Unlike Evarts, he was lacking in humor and always deadly in earnest. He had gained fame in the "Five Million Dollar Suit" of the Erie Railroad against Vanderbilt, and in the conviction of Edward Stokes for the murder of Jim Fisk. He spoke well, often with bitter, scalding sarcasm. In spectacular trials he had had a much greater experience than Evarts.[14]

William Fullerton was also to be feared. This portly elderly lawyer was regarded as the keenest cross-examiner of the day. His conversational manner, suave demeanor, gentle tone, and coaxing attitude caught witnesses off guard. He stood with notes in one hand and eyeglass in the other, putting questions in a low voice which disgusted Evarts, and leading the witness into an ambush. Evarts made sharp attacks upon him, sometimes causing him to flare up in anger, and leading to a battle of repartee which delighted the spectators.[15]

Roger Pryor and Morris were also invaluable to the prosecution. The former, an ex-Confederate general of excellent record and a typical Southerner in appearance and manner, was a thorough master of legal authorities and most useful as advisory counsel. Morris, who prepared Tilton's case, had figured for twenty years in nearly all of the great criminal cases in Brooklyn courts. He proposed a simple, direct proof of adultery, but Tilton refused to brand his wife as an adulteress and held his counsel to Beecher's own declaration, "She is guiltless, sinned against, bearing the transgressions of another."

The trial was long. When it began there were days when the ice in East River prevented the arrival of the lawyers from Manhattan by ferry; before it ended one of the jurymen fainted from the heat of the June sun. About two hundred and fifty documents were introduced and analyzed. Much of the testimony was irreconcilably contradictory. Printed in small type, the testimony filled three thousand foolscap pages.[16]

The issue hinged upon two opposing interpretations of certain letters of Beecher, Tilton, and Mrs. Tilton. According to the plaintiff's interpretation, Beecher was a self-confessed adulterer who resorted to desperate expedients to cover his guilt; according to the defendant's interpretation, he was a noble, innocent man, who had risked his reputation to protect the good name of Mrs. Tilton and repair an unintended injury to Tilton. Were Beecher's letters confessions or merely outpourings of a sensitive man under the delusion of a supposed injury to a friend?

The trial began on January 11, 1875. The police handled the crowd with difficulty and only ticket-holders were admitted. Every seat was filled when Judge Neilson rapped for order. Morris opened with a ten-hour speech. In an adroit manner he tried to show that Beecher had confessed, and that his correspondence revealed desperate attempts to conceal his guilt. His impassioned peroration left the audience tense; but as he sat down, Evarts rose and drawled, "Your Honor, now that the business of the trial is about to begin—would it not be well to have the tables arranged a little better?" It was a neat stroke, from peroration to prosaic furniture. But Evarts was sincere; during the first week he kept insisting upon more room for the lawyers.[17]

Moulton, the first witness for the prosecution, suave and courteous, seemed to have all the innumerable details of the scandal at his command. His calmness and confidence made him popular, and Fullerton conducted the direct examination with great success. Evarts had a slight acquaintance with Moulton, having appeared with him before a legislative committee to seek the reduction of canal tolls. He threw questions at him thick and fast, worrying the witness, and refusing to be shaken off. It was Porter, however, who conducted the main cross-examination of Moulton. Not altogether pleased by the way his associate handled the task, Evarts suggested many of the questions.[18]

That Evarts was feared was shown by an incident at the close of the session on January 13. Beecher stepped to the table where the opposing lawyers sat and said laughingly to Beach that if he escaped the paws of two such lions as Beach and Fullerton, he would believe he was innocent. To which Beach replied, pointing to Evarts, "You forget the Daniel standing among the lions, and closing their mouths."[19]

One January morning Evarts came threading his way into court, his tall hat as usual resting carelessly on the back of his head, and remarked to the jury with a laugh that he did not believe his fee paid him for walking across the river on loose ice. The story is told that once during the trial the ferry floated about the river for more than an hour in the fog, and that Evarts organized a mock trial on board to while away the time. He was occasionally late but was a man for whom the courts waited.[20]

A day seldom passed that he did not make some dry joke. During the impanelling of the jury he was struggling with Beach over the admission of a jolly-looking German whom Beach wanted but Evarts did not. Evarts asked the German the meaning of the words *literature* and *condone*. Without hesitation the German replied that *literature* meant a letter and *condone* meant part of a continent. After the laughter subsided, Beach still insisted the witness was competent to understand the "gentleman on the other side." Like a flash Evarts retorted, "But, your Honor, we want him also to be able to understand the gentlemen opposed to us." Even the judge had to laugh. On another occasion, in trying to give the definition of a *faux pas,* Evarts said, "I do not know the exact meaning, but I do know it is not a *pas seul*." Again, when the defense counsel found it necessary to consult with Beecher on Sunday and the pastor objected that it interfered with his church duties, Evarts reminded him that the Lord had approved the lifting of an ass out of a pit on the Sabbath. "Quite true," exclaimed Beecher, "and if there has ever been a bigger ass than I am, I do not know of it; of course I will come."[21]

When the prosecution sprang a surprise by calling Tilton to the stand, Evarts jumped to his feet, declaring that the law did not permit husband and wife to testify against each other. It took two days to settle this question. Evarts' point was that what the law did not permit directly could not be done indirectly. Beach admitted the principle but denied its application. Evarts produced a great array of authorities and complained that it would be a hard rule that would permit Tilton to testify and not his wife. The direct examination of Tilton lasted three days, the witness displaying an oratorical manner and an audacity and self-consciousness that could proceed only from a strong ego.[22]

Evarts' cross-examination of Tilton was one of the most striking episodes of the trial. It lasted nearly a week—a battle of wits between an egotist and an expert strategist. Evarts had doubtless not forgotten Tilton's article in the *Independent* under the caption, "The Soilure of a Fair Name," in which Tilton accused him of base motives in acting as counsel for President Johnson. On the other hand, at the New England Society dinner in 1869, Tilton had spoken highly of Evarts, comparing him to James Otis as a defender of the rights of the people.[23]

In cross-examining Tilton, Evarts assumed an inoffensive air, which gave the witness confidence and made him talkative. For hours Evarts kept up an easy, long-range fire, wearing a perpetual smile. His object was to set before the jury Tilton's views of himself, of Beecher, of society, of religion, of philosophy, of everything. Adultery was never mentioned. Tilton answered questions about politics, woman's rights, and free love. It was all a skirmish before the real attack. Then shifting to a cold, curt manner, Evarts produced a love poem written by Tilton, entitled "French Without a Master," which he read in sarcastic tone, each verse receiving due emphasis, concluding with the following lines which he read with a mock emotion that rocked the court with merriment:

"Sweetheart, no! you cannot go!
Let me sit and hold you so.
Adam did the same to Eve!
Aimer, aimer, c'est à vivre."[24]

As he proceeded to dig into the alleged confession of Mrs. Tilton, the tripartite agreement, the "True Story," and Tilton's relations with Mrs. Woodhull, the witness grew uneasy under the grilling. It was apparent that Evarts' purpose was to show Tilton's character in the worst light, and give the impression that the charge of adultery was due to his misfortunes and his desire for vengeance. When Fullerton took up the re-direct examination of Tilton, Evarts nagged him persistently, contesting every step of the way. Fullerton could hardly ask a question without meeting an objection, and finally declared he would offer a reward for a question that would be acceptable to Evarts. Thus Evarts succeeded in making the defense prominent at a time when the prosecution was supposed to hold the stage.[25]

Mrs. Moulton was the third important witness. She related how

Beecher had confessed his guilt to her and insisted that it be kept secret. Evarts tried to shake her testimony by making her rehearse it over and over, but failed. It was evident that this shy woman believed Beecher to be guilty, and her testimony made a deep impression.[26]

This concluded the important evidence for the prosecution. Tracy made the opening address for the defense, launching into a fierce attack upon Tilton. "We propose," he warned, "to dissect him first in the interest of truth, and bury him afterward in the interest of decency." Then came the parade of defense witnesses, most of them called to prove Tilton's questionable relation with women, the discord in his own household, his responsibility for the Woodhull publications, and his vengeful motive. There was no lack of witnesses, and much of the testimony of the prosecution was contradicted. Evarts did little of the examining, merely coming to the rescue when a witness was hard pressed by Fullerton's cross-examination.

Beecher was, of course, the star witness for the defense and his testimony was awaited with keen anticipation. When at last he was placed on the stand, with Evarts doing the questioning, excitement ran high. The trial had not told on him thus far and he looked ruddy and happy, often laughing at the sallies of the counsel. But his wife, who accompanied him to the courtroom, looked sad and anxious. Beecher knew that an ordeal awaited him. But he appeared at ease when he took the stand, betraying no fear. He refused to take the customary oath, declaring it contrary to his scruples, but did make an affirmation in the New England form. Evarts questioned him for a week and Beecher responded perfectly, compelling alternate laughter and tears. At times he flushed, trembled, and even wept. He relived the scenes in detail, and even gave vivid imitations of characters. Evarts did not hurry him and conducted the examination with such skill that Fullerton had few opportunities to object. Beecher explained that he consented to the "letter of contrition" to restore peace with Tilton and signed it without seeing what Moulton had written. The "ragged-edge letter," he explained, was due to a despondent spirit, not a bad conscience. He declared that he had not confessed adultery to Mrs. Moulton or anybody else. As a climax, Evarts asked Beecher three questions, worded differently, but all inquiring in effect whether he had had improper relations with Mrs. Tilton. The questions were put so well that audience and jury got the full benefit of Beecher's emphatic "No" in reply to each.[27]

Fullerton's cross-examination was a nightmare to Beecher. Charles O'Conor pronounced it the ablest he had ever heard conducted. For four days Fullerton gave the pastor no rest, seeking in every way to confuse and embarrass him. Beecher faltered on some questions and made indirect replies to others. Eight hundred and forty-nine times he responded with "I don't know," or "I can't recollect," or similar vague replies. But actually Fullerton did not make much headway.[28]

One day, during a lull, Evarts was handed a caricature of himself which some reporter had sketched. Instead of showing irritation, he handed it to Beach and to the judge and jury, and it went the rounds of the reporters. Again, while a bank cashier was testifying that he remembered receiving a deposit check, Evarts produced a slip of paper which had accompanied the check and which contained the words, "Spoils from new friends for the enrichment of old." Evarts handed the slip to the jury, showing that the pinholes in it corresponded with those in the check. Beach moved solemnly that the pinholes be stricken out; Evarts replied dryly that "some ray of light would come through the holes."[29]

When the defense had finished with its witnesses, the prosecution made the mistake of putting Bowen on the stand. He was plainly nervous. His hostility to Beecher led Evarts to cross-examine him with unusual harshness, and Bowen's face whitened under the ordeal. He became confused, contradicted himself, and on the whole gave testimony which was more a handicap than a help to the prosecution.

By May 13 all of the testimony was in. Judge, jury, and counsel felt relieved. Even Evarts had become wearied. Speaking at a Yale

Alumni Association meeting early in May he said, "The Beecher trial . . . is much longer than the moral law. That trial does not require a superfluity of flesh, and in that heated courtroom an absence of flesh is a blessing. I think that after the trial I shall recover my usual soundness and vigor."[30]

A study of the testimony leaves the reader in doubt. The *New York Times* insisted the evidence was much clearer if construed in the light of Beecher's guilt, and the *Sun* stated seven reasons why Beecher should be held guilty; on the other hand, the *Brooklyn Eagle* and many other newspapers were convinced that the minister was innocent.[31]

On May 19 the counsel began their closing summaries. First came Porter, who spoke for five days, despite the heat, with dramatic effect and almost too vigorous invective. But when he had finished, Beecher's fate was still in doubt. It would plainly require a great effort to save him, for the sympathy he had won in the early stage of the trial was changing to doubt.

Evarts presented the longest argument that he ever delivered, an eight-day summary of the evidence for the defense. The *Eagle* asserted that the case rested entirely with him and that the verdict of history would be his statement of it. When he rose on May 27 to speak, not a seat was empty, hundreds occupied stools in the aisles, and even the steps to the rostrum and the window sills were filled. At the gallery doors spectators stood on tiptoe and pushed each other aside to catch a glimpse of him. He opened his packages of notes, made a bow to the judge and jury, and spoke slowly, carefully, and distinctly, the audience listening so intently that his lowest tones could be heard in the farthest corner.[32]

The counsel for the defense watched Evarts eagerly, knowing he was their last hope. Beecher listened with rapt attention, at times showing great emotion. Evarts stood stiff as a billiard cue, emphasizing his words with a characteristic swing of the arm. Much of his argument was dry and complex, but the bulk of it was well arranged and well expressed, and punctuated with a wit which relieved the tension. At points it was too scholarly for the jury; at others it was clear as crystal to the lowest understanding. The thirty stenographers agreed that he spoke slowly but was most difficult to follow because of his many intricacies, parenthetical remarks, and collateral statements. Latin quotations were not lacking, although Evarts was careful to translate them. The jury listened carefully and seemed impressed.[33]

Taking a fling first at the scandal-mongers, Evarts said: "Everybody has been trying everybody else. . . . All the scoffers and infidels have been trying the Christians. . . . In every quarter where the wicked classes make their meetings, and hold their gossips with a sneer and a smile, the scandal was accepted. . . . When this great preacher comes to give his account, at the last judgement, of the many talents that have been confided to him, the hard Judge named in the parable will find no fault in him."

Evarts' purpose was to prove a conspiracy, deliberately conceived and executed by Tilton through his wife. "He knew she was as pure as gold," he declared, "but he had sworn he would strike Reverend Beecher to the heart, for interfering in his business interests and taking part in his domestic discords." In a combined attack on Beecher and the institution of marriage, Tilton was willing to make his wife appear an adulteress. "The intellectual traits," admonished Evarts, "that have framed this charge are as contemptible as the odious moral traits that have prompted it." Like Samson Agonistes, Tilton was pulling down the pillars of the temple of his religion and family upon his own head. It was in this vein that Evarts, at the beginning of his argument, turned the spotlight of condemnation away from Beecher upon Tilton. Before the first day was over he had made several strong legal points. He showed that an action in crim. con. required conviction of adultery beyond all reasonable doubt; that it was better that ten cases go unpunished than that one be unjustly punished; and that Tilton had lived with his wife four years after her supposed confession despite the law forbidding husband and wife to live together after adultery if legal proceedings were to follow.[34]

The crowd that came to hear Evarts on the second day was even greater; indeed, it was the largest outpouring yet seen. The judge objected that twice as many people were present as there should be, but took no steps to eject them. Sympathy was unquestionably now with Beecher, and Tilton had few friends. Although Evarts still hurled Cicero at the jury, five or six lines at a time, he became more practical. He directed his argument at the foreman of the jury who had already betrayed a belief in Beecher's innocence and reflected Evarts' moods perfectly. Evarts devoted most of the day to the conspiracy theory. It was envy, he asserted, which motivated Tilton. "Envy frets itself because of the prosperity of others and pines at their superiority." He charged Tilton with weaving a web of hypocrisy and falsehood. "They thought the boldness, the heinousness, the elaborateness, the circumstantiality of the charge, including picked items of evidence, selected pieces of Mr. Beecher's handwriting," was sufficient to "strike death in the public judgement."[35]

On the third day Evarts sought to prove that discord in the Tilton household was another cause of Tilton's hatred of Beecher. Analyzing Tilton's denial in the light of his testimony, Evarts declared: "He invents, contrives shallow pretenses that, looked at by themselves, won't stand the penetration and discomfiture of a truthful interpretation. . . . Three hundred and five things we wanted to know that Mr. Moulton did not recollect; and I don't think it would be too much to say that you could sometimes almost see Mr. Tilton fetch and carry their memories."[36]

Evarts spent most of the last four days in a detailed analysis of the evidence, and particularly the events of 1870. He ridiculed the idea that Mrs. Tilton could have confessed adultery in July of that year. "Only think of it," he exclaimed, "a woman thirty-five years old that has had six children," and Beecher, "at the age of fifty-six, after he had had nine children, and a wife that he had been faithful to from the time they were both seventeen years of age. . . . I do not think we lawyers, or you jurymen, or the Judge on the bench, would listen long to such a story of violent consummation against chastity, . . . and yet the rhetorician [Tilton] thinks he has put a white robe of chastity over his wife by putting such a narrative into her mouth, that he has covered Mr. Beecher with the double guilt of paramour and mistress, and made his wife a saint. . . . This story is the veriest trash that was ever written."

Tilton had described it as a case of "transcendental adultery," which gave Evarts a cue for one of the best hits of the trial. He told the story of two clergymen who, returning from a church convention on a Mississippi steamboat, were discussing transcendentalism. An interested layman ventured to ask the meaning of the word. "Well," said one of the clergymen, "that question is more easily asked than answered." Then pointing to the shore, the clergyman continued, "Do you see that bluff here on the river?" "Yes." "Do you see how pierced it is with swallows' holes?" "Yes, I see that." "Well, now," said the clergyman, "you take away all the bluff and leave nothing but the swallows' holes, and that is transcendentalism." Thus Evarts concluded there was nothing but fiction in Tilton's story of his wife's confession.[37]

For four days Evarts traced chronologically the events of the scandal, taking each letter and explaining how it fitted into the narrative. The jury, despite their desire to go home, were greatly interested. Evarts was completely master of all the details, relying only upon a colleague to hand him an authority or quotation as he needed it.

On June 8, the last day of his argument, it was decided that Evarts should finish even though the court sat overtime, and it was not till half-past six that the last words fell from his lips. The fascinated crowd stayed to the end. Among the spectators was Harriet Beecher Stowe, seated beside her brother.

Evarts' closing words were stirring. In a low voice, with deep earnestness, he said to the jury: "In giving your verdict for the defendant, Mr. Beecher, you give a verdict of safety and honor to the two families of Mr. Beecher and Mr. Tilton. You uphold the wife, you save the family of Mr. Tilton, and you save him in his permanent and definite honor. . . . Your verdict for the plaintiff strikes into the heart of his wife, and to the destruction of his children; breaks the heart of this noble wife of Mr. Beecher, and destroys the honor of that family; strikes a blow at the credit of our communities; brings dishonor upon the name of our Christian religion, . . . and, in fact, is a blow at the dignity and credit of human nature and the civilization and purity of American life. . . . You cannot doubt, you do not doubt, but if any one of you does doubt, that doubt itself must give the verdict for Mr. Beecher."

And he went on: "When you have this character [Beecher's] woven in lineaments that no man doubts of, and in this life in its whole period from boyhood to the present day, . . . you do not need to spend much time in finding out that the scarlet guilt of adultery, and the coarse, selfish pursuits of seduction do not match with the generous heart, the loving kindness, and the nobility of Henry Ward Beecher." As for Tilton, he "comes, in the arrogance of his nature, and the extravagance of his selfishness and egotism, to discard all the principal and supporting elements of useful life, to reject Moses and the prophets, to trample upon Christ and the apostles. . . . He puts himself almost in the condition of one morally insane. . . . This morbid self-worship with which Mr. Tilton has elevated himself above the restraint of religion, of morality, of duty to wife and children, and to society . . . is the final and conclusive application of how what seems so strange in his career finds in it the natural development of moral alienation from faith and duty. . . . In your verdict you will find, and we shall find with joy, that truth matches all around."[38]

As Evarts finished, the spectators broke into a storm of applause. Beecher appeared much affected and rushed through the crowd to Evarts, who was being congratulated by his colleagues. The speech was certainly one of the most remarkable pleas ever delivered in a court of law. But its power lay not in a direct facing of the facts, but in the ingenuity, adroitness, and consummate art of the speaker. It played around the vital points instead of grasping them; it explained away with endless refinement; it did not completely satisfy the auditors that Beecher was innocent.

On the following day Beach began his summary. He spoke more rapidly than Evarts, with a perfect style, but was at times so positive in tone that the hostility of the listener was aroused. He criticized Evarts for speaking so long, but outdid him with an address lasting ten days. He did not launch into such a tirade against Beecher as the defense had delivered against Tilton; on the contrary, he admitted that Beecher had led a most useful life. Toward the close he intimated that the jury had been improperly approached. Evarts laughed aloud, jumped to his feet and protested. It was finally agreed this charge of bribery should be dropped till after the verdict, and it was never pursued further. There is reason to believe that Beach believed Beecher innocent. During the last stages of the trial he wished to abandon the case, and declared afterward: "I felt, I feel now, that we were a pack of hounds trying in vain to drag down a noble lion."[39]

There was a striking contrast between the arguments of Evarts and Beach. Evarts was fertile in suggestions, inferences, and word pictures; Beach was more direct. Evarts showed dexterity in burying from sight testimony that was in his way and weaving a plausible story out of scanty materials; Beach untangled the web of concealment and held it up to a clear light. But Evarts left the greater mark on the jury by appearing as judge rather than advocate.[40]

Judge Neilson's charge to the jury was restrained and fair, yet favored Beecher. He placed the burden of proving adultery on the plaintiff and instructed that evidence of guilt should be such as to convince the mind of a cautious man. And he added, "In a case of this character a man grown old in prayer and pious deeds has *prima facie* the benefit of a presumption which a mere man of the world has not."[41]

As the jury was retiring, Evarts and Tilton came face to face. Evarts immediately extended his hand, saying, "I hope there is no animosity, Mr. Tilton?" The plaintiff shook hands and replied politely, "No, not a bit"; but his manner was cool.[42]

The jury deliberated for a week, much divided in opinion. It was a week of anxious suspense. The court assembled daily. Evarts came and went, spending most of his time at the Mansion House near by. Crowds hung about the courthouse, watching the windows where the jury was in conference. Many rumors spread about the city. Evarts was optimistic, certain that Beecher would be saved. The jury, hot and haggard, took fifty-two ballots; on one ballot they stood eleven to one for acquittal and on another seven to five. Finally they informed the judge that no agreement could be reached. It later became known that the jury had deadlocked at nine to three for acquittal.[43]

Beecher, thus legally exonerated, returned to Plymouth Church and preached for many years. Mrs. Tilton, broken in spirit and health, died soon after the trial. Tilton went into voluntary exile, living in Paris, playing chess, writing poetry, and entertaining a small circle of friends with his innate charm and wit.

Just what Evarts thought of Beecher's innocence is not known. But he wrote the pastor soon after the trial, "Do not hesitate to regard the result as a complete triumph of the truth. A few days will show the dissent is but the emphasis of the real verdict." In taking a case so distasteful and one which could offer him no adequate compensation for the time required or add much to his reputation, Evarts must have been motivated either by a belief in Beecher's innocence or a desire to save him in the best interests of the church and society. During a lecture tour two years later, Beecher wrote Evarts that he felt largely indebted to him for his acquittal.[44]

Unquestionably the *Herald* was correct in saying: "It was in the end, Evarts who saved Beecher, Evarts who stood alone amid a waste of auxiliary lawyers, fighting the case for the defense." He bore the physical and mental strain with ease. While his associates and opponents had been absent at one time or another because of ill health he had remained at his post throughout the six months. But he was glad to seek a rest at Windsor after the case closed. The *Windsor Journal* reported: "William M. Evarts comes out of the severities of the Brooklyn trial, looking hearty and vigorous as if his task had been nothing unusual."[45]

19

Achievements in Oratory

ALTHOUGH EVARTS' CHIEF TITLE to fame naturally rests upon his attainments as a lawyer, he applied his professional skill and his natural gifts so widely to public affairs and other fields of service that he exerted a broad influence upon his time. Especially did he distinguish himself by his achievements in oratory.

A true orator is more than a powerful master of rhetoric. He must possess intellect, a philosophic mind, wit, character, religious conviction, a generous outlook upon life, and high ideals of public service. Evarts had these qualities in generous measure. His intellectual equipment was such that few could match him on the public platform or in the courtroom. He grasped a situation with a power of absorption which excited the wonder of his friends. Joseph H. Choate called him the quickest-witted man he had ever met.[1] His capacity for acquiring, ordering, and presenting facts was prodigious.

Nor was he lacking in ethical insight. He once said, "Let us know and feel that all the triumphs of eloquence and of intellect are vain and useless . . . unless they tend in some degree to the welfare of our fellow-men, in which service we were born, and to which service we should, to the last, adhere."[2] In the courtroom or upon the platform he almost always lifted the subject to a high plane. From the day he delivered his first oration on "Public Life" at Yale to his last public appearance in 1895 he harped upon the importance of unselfish public service. The orator requires, he said, "energy, labor, truth, courage, and faith. These make up the ultimate wisdom to which the moral constitution of the world assures a triumph."[3] This idealism did not make him popular with the crasser sort of politicians, but it won the admiration of thoughtful citizens.

Taking Cicero as his model, Evarts imposed upon himself the task of mastering the whole art of speech. He read widely and could pour his ideas out of a full mind. His utterances were at times complex, but their logic was irresistible. While he could be as terse as Carlyle, he was usually inclined to employ long, cumulative sentences in the style of Rufus Choate. George F. Hoar once said, "Gladstone had, what is rare, and what no famous American orator that I know of, except Choate and Evarts have had—a tendency to diffuse and somewhat involved speech, and at the same time a gift of compact epigrammatic utterances on occasion."[4] The gravity and deliberation of his manner, emphasized by the sustained shaking of his forefinger above his head as he approached a climax, carried conviction. He could well be compared to Seward in tone of voice and manner of speech. Men hearing him for the first time were often surprised that such a clear, silvery voice could proceed from such a fragile body.

There were those who rated him cold, forgetting that logic is cold; there were those who believed that he was no orator because he seldom excited the emotions. He held that the best plea was the one which compelled reason. James A. Garfield said of him, "It seems to me that the greatest quality of Mr. Evarts' mind is sanity."[5] His confidence, ease of manner, resource and readiness, earnestness, breadth of learning, and perfect command of language won admiration but did not strike fire. He refused to excite himself, speaking slowly, distinctly, and easily, each sentence symmetrical, his face immobile except for an occasional smile.

But if Evarts was not an impassioned or inspired orator, he was a very good one. Some of his contemporaries—George William Curtis, William Cullen Bryant, James Russell Lowell—were as effective as he, and perhaps surpassed him. Oratory was never a prime aim of his life; it was a natural gift to be used on occasion.

Although his orations are listed in all books on eloquence, it cannot be said that he was incisive or penetrating. He knew simply how to adapt words to the occasion, to feel the pulse of his audience, and to express his thought in clear and at times eloquent language. Anyone reading his *Arguments and Speeches,* as edited by his son Sherman, may think them neither profound nor eloquent. But reading his speeches and hearing them were experiences as far apart as heat is from cold. He had his limitations as an orator; but if his merits had not greatly outnumbered the limitations, he would not have been selected to speak on innumerable impressive occasions, and would certainly not have been Centennial orator in 1876.

The fact that his oratory was a bit too stilted and intellectual, was a natural result of his classical training. He could not make a speech without giving some evidence of the fine discipline of the Boston Latin School and Yale. Proud of this classical background, he was a bit old-fashioned about it. Attending a banquet at the Boston Latin School in the late seventies, at which Edward Everett Hale presided and Wendell Phillips, Ralph Waldo Emerson, and President Eliot were leading speakers, he declared in a reminiscent mood that it was a mistake to allow education to drift away from the old emphasis on disciplinary values. "I have felt," he said, "in my experience as a scholar, and have always endeavored to teach my boys, that if a young person can be taught to do well what they don't wish to do at all, then you may trust them to do well pleasant things that they prefer."[6]

Evarts' fame for wit has been more enduring than his reputation for great orations on set subjects. He had developed since early days at Yale a fund of stories and knack of telling them which made him a favorite at after-dinner speaking. There is scarcely a book of contemporaneous biography that does not contain one of his witticisms. Herbert Bowen declared, "He probably said more clever things than any American who ever lived, with the exception of Benjamin Franklin; but he kept no record of his witty sayings, and no one else could keep one for him; so he will get from posterity five smiles to Ben Franklin's one hundred." And Senator Hoar added, "You could never challenge him or provoke him to an encounter without making an abundant and sparkling stream gush forth. He never came off second best in an encounter of wits with any man."[7] It would require a sizeable volume to hold all of the good things that came from his lips. Unfortunately his reputation for wit became so great that writers have indiscriminately ascribed to him many stories and puns that he did not tell. For the biographer it is therefore difficult to separate the stories he really told from those of mere hearsay.

The ease with which he drew upon his reservoirs of humor and epigram was astonishing. His was a genial wit, seldom venomous, although it could be biting if circumstances warranted. He seldom smiled. However much others might roar with laughter, his face remained grave. But occasionally he signalized the approach of something good by a queer relaxation of the lines about the mouth, and the faintest suggestion of a smile.

At public dinners, especially as toastmaster, he was superb. Henry Cabot Lodge called him the most brilliant after-dinner speaker he had ever heard, describing his wit as "phosphorescent," flashing constantly, with apparently little effort. James C. Carter went further, asserting that Evarts "created a revolution" in the art of after-dinner speaking.[8] Our present day has seen a decline in the art. The toastmaster still faces shirt-fronts and cigars; but too often publicity, advertising, coarseness, or some ulterior motive mars the speechmaking of the evening.

Many of Evarts' after-dinner speeches were delivered at Delmonico's, where public functions were a winter specialty. His wit also flowed freely at a monthly dining club, founded by Whitelaw Reid, Levi Morton, and others, which met at the Union League Club. Among those often seen in this congenial group were James Gordon Bennett, John Jay, Clarence King, and William H. Hurlburt. He also joined another group at the Century Club, which included John Jay, James C. Carter, Andrew D. White, George W.

Curtis, E. L. Godkin, John Pierpont Morgan, and Chester A. Arthur.[9]

For years Evarts' wit enlivened the annual dinners of the New England Society. At one of these dinners Mark Twain turned the laugh on him. He had just finished an amusing speech, when Evarts rose, shoving his hands down into his trouser pockets, and laughingly remarked, "Doesn't it strike this company as a little unusual that a professional humorist should be funny?" Mark Twain waited till the laughter subsided and drawled, "Doesn't it strike this company as a little unusual that a lawyer should have his hands in his own pockets?"[10]

Evarts could also rise to an emergency and speak extemporaneously with great ease. Once at a Century Club dinner, he listened as one distinguished speaker after another—George Bancroft, Ralph Waldo Emerson, Oliver Wendell Holmes, and Richard H. Dana—spoke in honor of the seventieth birthday of William Cullen Bryant, and was surprised when unexpectedly called upon. Gathering his ideas from those who had already spoken, he cleverly wove them into a tribute to Bryant that was as effective as the prepared speeches.[11]

His dexterity as toastmaster was proverbial. In the absence of Professor Agassiz, he acted as chairman at a dinner at Delmonico's to John Tyndall, the famous British scientist. He remarked that he could not understand why a lawyer should be asked to preside over a meeting of scientists unless it was to avoid jealousies by choosing the leader from a profession noted for doing other people's business better than they could do it themselves.[12]

If the occasion required, he could also speak with great solemnity. A most impressive dinner, attended by such notables as William Cullen Bryant, Peter Cooper, A. T. Stewart, and President Woolsey, was once given in honor of the inventor, Samuel F. B. Morse. Evarts may have recalled the advice which his father Jeremiah had given to Morse in 1812: "I hope you will let politics alone for many reasons, not the least of which is a regard for the internal tranquillity of your mind. I never knew a man made happy by studying politics; nor useful, unless he had great duties to perform as a citizen." Addressing Morse, Evarts said, "I never turn my eyes to the wall in my parlor that I do not attribute to your accomplished pencil the only preservation of the features of my father and your friend." And dwelling upon the contributions of inventors, he continued, "Man begins by repining at his own weakness and envying the superior power of brutes . . . but there comes the crowned procession of inventors, that teach us that a good God, in giving man reason, has given him all these powers. . . . Man has only to reach out his hand and take the good gift that God stands ready to give."[13]

Beside the requisite mental and moral characteristics, Evarts had the physical exterior of an orator. In his late fifties especially he looked the part. Henry Holt described him as "a strikingly handsome man" with "the most markedly intellectual face" he had ever seen. The stock and high collar, the clean-shaven but attenuated face, the careless-falling hair, the hawk-like nose, the gray glittering eyes, and the odd gestures of the body and head—all were suggestive of individuality and distinction. He had a curious resemblance to Cicero. The marble bust of that great orator in the Yale library was often mistaken for an image of Evarts. One New York newspaper published a burlesque article upon the resemblance, declaring with ironical exaggeration: "When Mr. Evarts last visited Rome and walked in the Forum, the guides crossed themselves, and the very street urchins fled terrified before him, as if, in fact, one of the marble Ciceros of the Capitoline Museum or the Palace of the Conservators had stepped down from his pedestal. As between Cicero and Caesar, the weight of evidence is that Mr. Evarts looks like Cicero."[14]

But on the street Evarts lost his dignity of mien, for to the last he clung to his habit of wearing his tall hat, tilted on the back of his head. Gillam, the cartoonist, liked to depict him with this "vintage of 1825," cocked at an acute angle. Evarts resented the caricatures, declaring that he did not wear old hats and that he spent much on new ones, as he could prove by his hatter. It wasn't the hat, but the way he wore it, that was striking. He presented an odd appearance walking along the street on a cold day, with coat-collar turned up around his ears and tall hat pushed far down on the back of his head.[15]

Evarts' speeches fall into four general classifications: professional arguments in court, political speeches, commemorative orations, and occasional addresses, the last including after-dinner speeches. His commemorative orations gave him his chief fame as an orator. He delivered six, two of which have already been mentioned: the oration on "Public Life" at Yale in 1853, and that on "The Heritage of the Pilgrims" in 1854. The third was his eulogy of Chief Justice Chase, delivered at the invitation of the alumni of Dartmouth College on June 24, 1874, at the commencement exercises at Hanover. Since Evarts had been a rival of Chase for the chief justiceship, it is odd that he should have been invited; but he knew Chase well, greatly admired him, and had often practiced before him in the Supreme Court. The little town of Hanover presented a gay scene; throngs had poured in from all the surrounding country and many alumni were present. Evarts was popular in the vicinity, for Windsor was only a few miles away.

His oration was not a mere eulogy of Chase; it was a delineation of his character and an estimate of his place in history. "His views of the Commonwealth," began Evarts, "were essentially Puritan. . . . Mr. Chase asked but one question to determine his course of action, 'Is it right?' . . . He was among the first of the competent and practical political thinkers of the day to penetrate the superficial crust which covered the slumbering fires of our politics, and to plan for the guidance of their irrepressible heats so as to save the constitutional liberties of the nation. . . . He must be awarded the full credit of having understood, resolved upon, planned, organized, and executed . . . the formation of the Republican party. . . . I hazard nothing in saying that the management of the finances of the Civil War was the marvel of Europe and the admiration of our own people." As for the chief justiceship, there was no doubt that Chase wanted it and was fitted for it. He had maintained the great traditional position of the Court at a time when it was divided between the old and the new politics. "The force of his reason, the clearness of his perception, the candor of his opinions," assured "his rank with eminent judges of our own and the mother country." As for his disappointed ambition for the presidency, "It was not in the fortune of Mr. Chase's life to take the flood at any tide, in the restless sea of politics."[16]

Evarts' oration received favorable comment everywhere. The *Tribune* considered it marked by "a just and generous discrimination exceedingly rare among public men at any time," and called it "a noble eulogy . . . second to none of those remarkable funeral orations which have been made during the past year." George William Curtis called it "masterly . . . done with a stately rhetoric which became the theme." But Rockwood Hoar felt that Evarts had been too generous, for he believed that Chase was "insincere, selfish, and intriguing."[17]

In September, 1876, Evarts was invited by a committee under Hamilton Fish to deliver the dedicatory speech at the unveiling of the Seward statue in Madison Square. Two hundred and fifty subscribers had given one hundred dollars each, and the services of a well-known sculptor had been secured. The marble statue, about twenty feet high, represented Seward in a posture of deep thought. John Bigelow presented the statue on behalf of the subscribers, Mayor Wickam accepted it, and Evarts' address followed. No one was better fitted to recount Seward's achievements. Evarts had known him intimately for twenty years, and to speak for him was "an office of affection and duty." He described Seward as the Senator before the war who distinguished between abolition and compromise on the slavery issue. As Secretary of State, he won the admiration of America and Europe. As leader of the Republican party, he had "as much to do with its foundation, with its discipline, with its instruction, with its triumph, and with all the great transactions in which it led." Seward was a man of judgment and foresight, but a man much abused and misrepresented. "Great was he in intellectual ability, great in moral qualities, great in opportunities which served him, great in perils that he encountered, great in the triumph of his politics, and great in the prosperity of his statesmanship."[18]

Two months later, Evarts gave the dedicatory address at the unveiling of the Webster statue in Central Park. Since America in his time had produced no other statesman, except Seward, that Evarts more admired, it was fitting that he should have been selected. This statue, given the city by George W. Burnham, a wealthy and public-spirited business man, stood on West Drive near the Seventy-second Street entrance to the Park. The figure of Webster stood erect, head and shoulders thrown back, right hand in the breast of the coat, as if he had just concluded some powerful passage in an oration. A speakers' platform had been erected and a band furnished music. Benches in front of the statue accommodated about a thousand invited guests, while as many more stood. Two addresses were delivered, one by Evarts and one by Robert C. Winthrop.

Standing beneath the statue which towered above him, Evarts made one of his best orations. "I congratulate you," he began, "upon this evidence that public spirit does not fail in the republic." Pointing upward to Webster, he exclaimed, "There he stands, as he stood for a lifetime of assured fame, in the full blaze of a whole people's attention, crowned by his Maker with glory and honor—as he stood in the courts, in the Senate, in the popular assemblies, at the helm of state, amid the crowds that followed his steps. . . . I can bear testimony that without arrogance, yet full of dignity, he never sought to enhance, but always to lessen, the imposing influence which his mien and fame impressed on everyone. The kindliness of his manner and his affectionate attention to every claim made upon his duty or his favor, none who knew him will ever forget. . . . His countrymen maligned him; but it was his country that he loved, and he would not curse it for anybody's cursing him. . . . No man . . . has held such a share of influence in the popular assemblies, in the counsels of the party, in the State, or in the Senate, or in the discharge of the duties of minister of State. . . .

He combines the intellectual, the moral, and the personal traits . . . which gave to one Grecian above all others of his countrymen—Pericles—the title of Olympian. . . . If I were to name two men whose services were incomparably above that of all others in making this new experiment of free government and of a paper constitution, . . . I should say that to the great Chief Justice Marshall, and to the great forensic, popular, parliamentary defender and expounder of the Constitution, Daniel Webster, we owe what we now enjoy. . . . Shall it not be pardoned to affection, if we say that the associations with those who survive seem to us but little, compared with the memory of him whose friendship we remember, and whose fame we rehearse."[19]

If Evarts' orations on Seward and Webster were excessively eulogistic and quite lacking in critical discrimination, the reason is obvious. He idolized both men beyond their merits. His address on Chase, whom he did not place in the same rank, was noticeably more critical.

In preparing such public addresses, Evarts usually made a brief outline. He did not, as most speakers do, resort to a verbatim manuscript. He spoke as clearly and fluently with an outline as do many orators who read their speeches. If the address was of more than ordinary importance, he might have at hand another paper with a list of striking statements or quotations to be used at the appropriate moment. For example, he had prepared for the Webster speech the following pungent maxims, though he did not use all of them:

1. The whims of men form notable policies—but steadiness is predicable of the movements of a people.

2. If we do not wish to make the presidency a throne or a shrine, we cannot endure that it should become a pillory or a counting room.

3. Whatever madness inflames the suffrage, the people must feel the scourge.

4. Public life is a situation of power and energy. He trespasses against his duty who sleeps upon his watch, as well as he that goes over to the enemy.[20]

Evarts' grandfather, Roger Sherman, had taken a part in the writing of the final draft of the Declaration of Independence. Evarts had this immortal draft in front of him when he delivered his greatest oration at Philadelphia on July 4, 1876, at the Centennial anniversary celebration.

This celebration was one which he himself had helped to arrange. A year before, at Steinway Hall in New York, he had urged upon an audience of some three thousand the importance of holding the Centennial ceremonies in Philadelphia rather than New York. A few months later he received from the Centennial Commission the invitation to be orator of the day. He replied that he fully appreciated the honor but had misgivings as to his ability. Despite long experience, he was hesitant about this speech, and the responsibility weighed upon him. He insisted that Choate should go to Philadelphia with him and sit on the platform near by, so that if he broke down, Choate could take his place. For such an emergency he had to have a manuscript ready. Needless to say, no such emergency arose.[21]

He was puzzled how to set about the task, but finally chose as a subject, "What the Age Owes to America." This would obviously afford him an opportunity to survey the past century. Anticipating his choice, the *Herald* queried, "How often it has been said . . . that Franklin and Washington would not know their own land, were they to come to the earth and take their places in Independence Square with the huzzaing thousands who are to listen to the eloquence of Mr. Evarts?" When asked how long he expected to speak, Evarts replied, "I spoke for four days in the Johnson Impeachment trial, two days before the Geneva Tribunal, and for eight days in the Beecher trial; no time limit has been set for the centennial oration, but there is an implied understanding that I shall get through before the next centennial."[22]

Despite the terrific heat, the Quaker City was filled with gay crowds on July 3, ready to surrender to the spirit of national pride. Thousands more poured into the city hourly by train; hotels and boardinghouses were packed; the metropolis seemed a mecca for all America. Horses might drop in the street from the heat, but it did not daunt the crowds. The Grand Army paraded that morning, with its old, tattered battle flag; in the evening a torchlight parade marched up Chestnut Street amid cheering multitudes; and at midnight the Liberty Bell rang out from the State House with the same tones that had roused the city a century before.

Scarcely had the crowds dispersed to catch a little sleep before dawn brought out a fresh multitude. At sunrise, from the Centennial grounds in Fairmount Park, the Keystone Battery fired a salute. Then the guns from the men-of-war in the river roared, chimes rang from the churches, and whistles from locomotives and steamboats joined the chorus. At nine o'clock a military parade passed Independence Hall, reviewed by General Sherman, the Secretary of War, Prince Oscar of Sweden, the Emperor of Brazil, and other dignitaries.

At ten o'clock the imposing ceremonies began in Independence Square, where some fifty thousand people were packed under a broiling sun, while another hundred thousand filled adjoining streets. A huge platform, seating more than three thousand, had been built across the north side of the square, sloping gently down toward the front with the speakers' stand occupying the center. All the seats on the platform were occupied by invited guests, sheltered from the sun by a canvas canopy. Directly opposite, at the other end of the square, was another platform with Gilmore's hundred-piece band and a chorus of three hundred voices. The dense crowd, although packed like sardines, was good-natured and patriotic, and its enthusiasm did not wilt as the thermometer mounted into the nineties. It watched eagerly as prominent figures appeared on the platform. The presidential nominee, Governor Hayes of Ohio, received a storm of cheers; Generals Sherman and Sheridan were also loudly applauded. The absence of President Grant received much unfavorable comment, for he had not sent even a letter of congratulation or regret.

The ceremonies began with the overture "The Grand Republic." General Hawley, President of the Centennial, then introduced Vice-

President Ferry as presiding officer of the day. The chorus sang the ode composed by Oliver Wendell Holmes for the occasion. The original manuscript of the Declaration was then held high before the crowd, and a mighty shout went up as they beheld the yellow parchment. The grandson of Richard Henry Lee read it, Bayard Taylor read a national ode, and then Evarts was introduced as orator of the day. Other speeches followed by Beecher, Charles Francis Adams, Winthrop, and Storrs.[23]

Evarts' oration was not the usual Fourth of July speech, but a philosophical discourse, brilliant rather than pictorial. It reviewed a century of progress with comprehensive grasp. Speaking first of the framers, the orator declared them fortunate, "first, in the clearness of their title and in the world's acceptance of their rightful claim. Fortunate next, in the enduring magnitude of the State they founded and in the beneficence of its protection of the vast interests of human life and happiness which have here had their homes. Fortunate, again, in the admiring imitation of their work which the institutions of the most powerful and advanced nations more and more exhibit; and last of all, fortunate in the full demonstration of our later time that their work is adequate to withstand the most disastrous storms of human fortunes, and survive unwrecked, unshaken, and unharmed."[24]

With historic insight Evarts contrasted the American Revolution with the Puritan and French Revolutions. "The English experiment," he said, "stumbled in its logic by not going far enough," while the French philosophers "came to a greater disaster by overpassing the lines which mark the limits of human authority." All the more remarkable was the "marvelous wisdom of our ancestors, which struck a line between too little and too much; which walked by faith indeed for things invisible; which dared to appropriate everything for the people which belonged to Caesar, but to assume for mortals nothing which belonged to God."

What were the results of the Declaration during the succeeding century? First, it gave promise of a long national life. "With our territory unmutilated, our Constitution uncorrupted, a united people, in the last years of the century, crowns with a new glory the truths of the Declaration of Independence by the emancipation of a race."

Second, the spirit of the people had not lessened. Public office might have suffered, patriotism might have drooped, selfishness might have eaten into the heart of the commonwealth; but "the greatest lesson of all is the preponderance of public over private, of social over selfish, tendencies and purposes in the whole body of the people, and the persistent fidelity to the genius and spirit of popular institutions of the educated classes, the liberal professions, and the great men of the country."

And third, the strength of the American political system had not abated. "All modifications of European politics," said Evarts, with little realization of what was coming in the twentieth century, "accept the popular principles of our system, and tend to our model." Nor did he realize that "freedom of conscience . . . freedom from military power . . . freedom of the press," or the original principles which "still inspire the laws, live in the habits of the people, and animate their purposes and their hopes," would be widely discarded in Europe sixty years later.

His peroration was a happy prophecy for the future of the Republic: "Unity, liberty, power, prosperity—these are our possessions today. . . . The spirit of the nation is at its highest—its triumph over the inborn, inbred perils of the Constitution has chased away all fears, justified all hopes, and with universal joy we greet this day." But reverence for the past gives way to responsibilities for the future. "Under the double trust . . . let us take heed to our ways, and . . . resolve that the great heritage we have received shall be handed down through the long line of advancing generations, the home of liberty, the abode of justice, the stronghold of faith among men, which holds the moral elements of the world together, and of faith in God, which binds the world to His throne."[25]

It was thus that Evarts vaunted American democracy at a time when war clouds were rising in Europe, and extolled the political genius of the men who, a century before, had proclaimed the right of the people and their fitness to govern themselves.

20

The Battle for Hayes

EVARTS WAS SO DEEPLY DISGUSTED by the scandals of the Grant administration that by 1875 he had become an open critic of the President. He selected as the first object of attack the policy of "bayonet rule" in Louisiana; and when a mass meeting was called in January to protest against Grant's use of federal troops to purge the legislature of Democrats, he appeared and made the leading speech. Although the meeting was announced as nonpartisan, the Democrats were in the majority and there were frequent shouts of "Down with Grant!" "You are assembled here," declared Evarts, "to teach every political party that there are limits . . . which no political party can safely surpass . . . I think the President of the United States is to be held responsible. . . . The fundamental right of a legislature to control, to determine the qualifications and the constitution of its own body, is of the very essence of legislative government."[1]

Shortly after, at a dinner to Carl Schurz, who had just been defeated for senator and was about to depart for a European tour, Evarts presided and in introducting Schurz boldly described the Grant administration as one of spoilsmen.[2]

The fact was that the Republican party was splitting into three elements. The Stalwarts supported Grant and hoped to see him elected for a third term; the Independents or Reformers stood for Civil Service reform and honest government; and a group more difficult to define, later called Half-Breeds, usually sponsored reform but were more prone than the Independents to compromise for the sake of expediency and to put their own interest above that of party or country. In 1876 Evarts could be classed as an Independent.

Seldom does political independence make a candidate more available for public office, but it did so for Evarts in 1876. A host of aspirants for the presidency had appeared. Evarts said that the party reminded him of "an army whose terms of enlistment had expired—a field full of stragglers." During the three months before the Republican convention assembled at Cincinnati, not a little sentiment for him appeared. The *Tribune* urged his nomination. Some of his friends felt that he should marshal the Liberal-Republicans and Independents and lead them to victory, while others believed he could win as many Democrats as Republicans. "Perhaps the Democrats," Henry Adams wrote, "will go the Republicans one better and offer us Evarts." The *New York Reporter,* speaking for the commercial interests, declared, "We fear no contradiction in asserting that were this brilliant lawyer-statesman . . . the nominee, merchants and bankers of this and other great business centers would at length feel confidence."[3] But Evarts made no effort to enter the presidential race, and Rutherford B. Hayes was nominated after a sharp fight among the three elements of the party.

In August a considerable demand appeared that Evarts be nominated for the governorship. The same three factions existed in the state: Conkling, boss of the state Republican machine, sponsored the Stalwart candidate, Alonzo Cornell; Evarts represented the Reformers; and Edwin D. Morgan, although a Reformer, was less distasteful to the party machine. Again Whitelaw Reid set the *Tribune* to work for Evarts and urged him to take the lead. But Evarts shrank from the race and took a noncommittal stand, allowing his friends to urge his candidacy, but saying nothing. Just before the Saratoga convention he told Reid that he would not accept, for he believed that his nomination would only widen the breach between Conkling and the Reformers.

Nevertheless, a three-cornered struggle developed in the convention among the Cornell, Morgan, and Evarts men. In advance, it had been expected that Conkling's machine would win for Cornell, but the Evarts delegates were more numerous than anticipated, and it was important to choose a candidate acceptable to Hayes. Evarts saw that while he could not win, he might prevent the Stalwarts from winning. Therefore, when Edwin A. Merritt, a well-known reformer, assured him of one hundred votes, he permitted George William Curtis to nominate him. Morgan then won on the first ballot, receiving 242, and 126 for Evarts.[4] This was the result which Evarts had anticipated, and he was not disappointed. Under the circumstances, the large vote he received was a moral victory. The important fact was that he had frustrated the Stalwarts and forced a compromise. Moreover, as Curtis put it, "Without a word of any kind from him, without the solicitation of agents or adherents, without any of the usual methods of candidates . . . the name of this eminent citizen . . . rose spontaneous . . . in this political crisis. It was one of the noblest and most striking tributes to a high personal character in our political history."[5]

Evarts, who really did not want to be governor, wrote Reid philosophically: "The politicians beat the lawyer. All things work together for the good of them that fear God." To which Reid replied, "Blessed are the meek, for they shall inherit the earth. I had no idea that you could string together so much good Scripture in favor of the meekness, not to say the joy, with which you greet the Saratoga outcome."[6]

The presidential campaign did not at first interest Evarts greatly. He scarcely knew Hayes and decided to keep silent. Waite, who knew Hayes well, urged Evarts to support him; but Evarts knew that if he did, this would be interpreted as a bid for office.[7] At the last minute, however, realizing that Hayes was in danger of losing New York, he broke his silence and responded to a petition to speak. This petition, signed by some two hundred prominent New Yorkers, sought his views especially upon the millions of dollars worth of claims which Southerners had filed with Congress, in the hope that such claims might be paid if Tilden should win the election.

A great and enthusiastic audience mustered to hear him at

Cooper Institute. His political independence had made him popular, and when he was introduced, the crowd rose and cheered, waving hats and handkerchiefs. His speech, the first of any importance since the Centennial oration, was a clever analysis of the political situation. It contained some stirring passages and some flashes of wit. He aroused his audience, and if he had desired, he might have fired them to even greater feeling.

He contrasted Tilden and Hayes. Although Evarts had coöperated with Tilden in the prosecution of the Tweed Ring and esteemed him personally, he regarded some of his policies as dangerous and had never thought highly of his war record. As for Hayes, his fine record in the war and as governor were sufficient. Evarts believed that Hayes was more sincere on Civil Service reform than Tilden, and that the Republican party was in a better position to effect reform than the Democrats would be after long exclusion from power.

On financial questions the Republicans stood for sound money, resumption of specie payment, and payment of the national debt; Evarts pointed out that the Democrats wavered, preferring paper money. Still worse was the Democratic stand on the Southern question. "There is one thing," said Evarts, "that can stand neither the curse of God nor men, and that will be the desertion of the freedmen by leaving them a prey to the rebels." Reminding his audience of Tilden's letter in 1860, calling the Union a loose confederation and advising the people not to fight for it, Evarts concluded: "Governor Tilden won't change his political opinions. . . . And now they ask us to bring back the same people, defeated and divided. A nation will never go back!"[8]

If there was too much waving of the "bloody shirt" in Evarts' speech and too much denunciation of Tilden, at least it was more moderate in tone than the Republican press. Its merit lay in the independence which marked some of his statements.[9] The election was close. Tilden carried New York. On the morning after the election it was believed that he had carried the country. But there were doubts about the nineteen electoral votes from Florida, South

Carolina, Louisiana, and Oregon. Hayes needed all nineteen to win; Tilden needed but one.

The disputed election brought Evarts a great opportunity. As counsel for the Republican party in the hearings before the Electoral Commission, he added much to his reputation. While Congress debated for two months, those great principles which Evarts had extolled at the Centennial received a severe test. Charges and counter-charges flew back and forth; and unless a solution could be found before March 4, there was danger of civil war. Demagogues tried to inflame public feeling, and bands of minute-men were enrolled, sworn to seat Tilden at all costs. Both parties sent "visiting statesmen" to advise the local returning boards in the three disputed Southern states. Grant had the magnanimity to telegraph Evarts a special invitation to go with the Republican delegation to New Orleans. Evarts coolly refused, though his name appeared by error on some of the lists of visiting statesmen.[10] It was with relief that the nation learned of the creation of the Electoral Commission in January.

After studying the debates in the Constitutional Convention of 1787, Evarts concluded that the framers had intended the President of the Senate to count the votes. He felt that the Electoral Commission was a dangerous experiment, divesting the President of the Senate of his rights; and he supplied Garfield with arguments against the Electoral bill. In his speech in Congress Garfield warned that the Commission might have all the vices of a state returning-board, that its method of appointment was irregular, that its jurisdiction was too indefinite, and that a dangerous precedent was created. Evarts, who sat listening in the gallery, was dismayed to see the bill pass.[11] He doubtless foresaw that the Commission would become a political rather than a judicial tribunal.

The rules of procedure permitted each party to employ counsel, with the privilege of presenting oral or written arguments. On January 26 ex-Governor Dennison of Ohio, an intimate friend of Hayes, called upon Evarts in Washington to ascertain whether he would act as chief counsel for the Republican party. "The work," said Dennison, "will of course be one of love without fee." Evarts replied that he would serve for a moderate fee, and two days later received an appointment from the National Committee, leaving the question of payment unsettled.[12] Rockwood Hoar was considered as one of his associates, but rejected. The other Republican counsel finally agreed upon were Edwin Stoughton, Stanley Matthews, and Samuel Shellabarger. The Democratic counsel were more numerous and probably more experienced: Charles O'Conor, Jeremiah Black, Richard T. Merrick, Ashbel Green, William C. Whitney, George Hoadly, Lyman Trumbull, Matthew Carpenter, and John A. Carpenter. O'Conor lent prestige to the cause but was suffering from the illness that had seized him during the Tweed prosecution.

The Commission met on February 2 in the same vaulted hall where the Johnson impeachment trial had been held. As at that time, it was found that the chamber was too small for the general public, so that admission was by ticket to privileged persons. Fifteen chairs for the Commission had been crowded behind an improvised bench. In front was a long table with the counsel sitting at either end. Individually, the members of the Commission were remarkable—all lawyers of recognized ability—and their record justified the hope that they would do impartial justice. Evarts spoke of the Commission later as "composed of as great material and of as good men as were ever collected in the country."[13] Justice Clifford, who presided, sat in the center; to his left were the Republicans: Bradley, Miller, Edmunds, Morton, Frelinghuysen, Garfield, and Hoar; to his right the Democrats: Field, Strong, Bayard, Thurman, Abbott, Hutton, and Payne.

There was little in the proceedings of the Commission that was picturesque or dramatic. Evarts rose at the opening to inquire whether the presiding officer or the whole Commission would decide questions of procedure. Clifford replied that he would not presume to act without the consent of the majority of the Commission.[14]

The battle first centered upon the three certificates from Florida.

Certificate No. 1, which gave the vote of the state to Hayes, was signed by Governor Stearns and apparently met all legal requirements. But if the state returning-board had not rejected some of the ballots, the popular vote would have been for Tilden. Certificate No. 2, signed by the state Attorney General, gave the vote to Tilden. Certificate No. 2 had been obtained by the most questionable means. The Democratic legislature had brought *quo warranto* proceedings in a circuit court against Republican electors; the court had declared the Tilden electors duly chosen; and Governor Drew, who had succeeded Stearns, issued Certificate No. 3 in favor of Tilden. Thus the Commission faced the task of deciding whether to give preference to a certificate on the basis of its face value, or go behind it to seek evidence as to its true or fraudulent nature. This raised a crucial question: Did the Commission have the power to go behind a certificate and receive additional evidence? On its settlement depended the choice of the President.

Evarts hastened to object to going behind the certificates for further evidence. In his pocket he had a letter from James Root, a member of the Republican National Committee, outlining an argument on this very point.[15]

The Republican view was that each state was the judge of its own elections, and neither Congress nor any body created by it could properly go behind the certification of a governor to examine the details of a canvass. It would simplify the work of the Commission and probably give the vote of Florida to Hayes. The Democratic position was that the Commission had complete power to go behind the returns to discover fraud and decide what the true vote had been. Thus, by a peculiar reversal of politics, the Republicans advocated strict construction of the Twelfth Amendment.[16] With precedent lacking, the Commission hesitated; but it finally decided to allow counsel to argue the preliminary question—a procedure which took five days. Merrick and Black argued for the Democrats; Matthews, Stoughton, and Evarts replied for the Republicans; and O'Conor concluded for the Democrats.

Merrick made probably the most logical argument for the Democrats. He contended that a federal court had the right to go behind election returns if a state legislature declared a certificate void. He insisted that the Commission was a judicial tribunal, appointed to examine all of the evidence. Probably he was correct; at all events, his conclusion was the most just and logical. Stanley Matthews replied for the Republicans in a speech which Evarts described as making an "immediate impression." But the fact was that Merrick's speech worried the Republican counsel, and they managed to give Evarts two nights and a day to reconnoiter the Democratic position and select the best points for attack. This was done by occupying the time with arguments by Matthews and Stoughton.[17]

When Evarts rose to speak, everyone felt that a crisis had been reached and that much depended on his ability to make the worse appear the better reason. The chamber was jammed, and the hall outside filled by a throng who could not get in. Since only three hundred and fifty could be accommodated, those present considered themselves fortunate. There hangs today in one of the upper corridors of the Capitol a painting by Mrs. Fassett representing Evarts addressing the Commission.[18]

He flung down the gauntlet by declaring that the Commission could not go behind the certificate of a governor. But foreseeing that this position might be used against him in the case of the Oregon certificate issued by a Democratic governor, he added that the Commission could go behind a certificate to examine whether it falsified the record on which it was based. He argued that *quo warranto* proceedings to interfere with an election were never intended by the framers of the Constitution. "It is an absolutely novel proposition," he said, "that judicial power puts its little finger into the political transaction of choosing anybody to an elective office. You will find that an attempt to bring judges . . . into the working of this scheme of popular sovereignty . . . will make it . . . intolerable."[19]

The Democratic members of the Commission bombarded Evarts with a fusillade of questions. All his courage and audacity were needed to enable him to face the onslaught.

"Suppose," queried Justice Field, "the canvassers had made a mistake in footing up the returns, and suppose that mistake changed the result of the election, and that they discovered it before the electoral vote was counted, would there be no remedy?"

"No," replied Evarts.

"Then," said Field, "a mistake in arithmetic, in adding up the figures, may elect a President of the United States and Congress be powerless to prevent it?" Evarts did not reply because the question was not asked him directly.

"Suppose," continued Field, "the canvassers were bribed, and suppose they entered into a conspiracy to count a fraud, and in pursuance of that bribery and conspiracy altered the returns, declaring elected persons not chosen by the voters, and had transmitted the vote to the Senate, but before that vote had been counted the fraud was detected and exposed, would there be no remedy?"

"No," repeated Evarts. "Whatever fraud there is must be discovered and protested against before the Board of Canvassers makes its returns." "But," persisted Field, "suppose the members of the board were themselves conspirators?"

"It makes no difference under the law," replied Evarts.

"If this be sound doctrine," rejoined Field, "it is the only instance in the world where fraud becomes enshrined and sanctified behind the return of its authors."

Evarts did not venture any further explanation. But Field tried one more question: "Suppose the canvassers were coerced by force, suppose men put pistols to their head and threatened to blow out their brains if they did not perjure themselves, would there be no remedy?"

Again Evarts answered, "No." He maintained that neither fraud, nor error, nor force justified Congress in reversing the action of a state returning-board. Had he faltered under these questions, which exposed the weakness of his argument, his cause might have been lost.[20]

There was nothing dramatic about his argument, and he recognized that humor was out of place. He offered close, unornamented, legal reasoning; he appealed to no feeling and roused no passion, as many expected he would. Most of the audience were disappointed, for they had expected to hear a great oration. His style was severe, technical, and deliberate. Without notes, he spoke slowly, apparently thinking out his argument as he progressed, but actually its coherence proved it had been well prepared. Garfield believed that Evarts lacked his usual force and fervor, and Stanley Matthews agreed that he lacked point and force.[21]

The simple fact was that Evarts was at his best when he had a great cause in which he could sincerely believe. The seating of Hayes seemed to him a worthy cause; but the grounds of appeal were circumscribed, partisan, and dubious. It was not a cause which involved the performance of justice in a court; it was a hard political game played through to a hard—and as we now know, unfair—end. It must have been distasteful to Evarts whether he felt the Republicans in the right or in the wrong. An effort to decide the presidency by an ingenious straining of the law could not call forth his best talents. If there was anything he hated, it was an interference with the purity of the ballot-box, and he knew that there had been impurity on both sides. He had added little to what Matthews and Stoughton had already said, for he had simply carried the doctrine of the inviolability of state certification to an extreme.

The following day was Evarts' sixtieth birthday. He was entertained at the home of S. B. Chittenden, a Brooklyn congressman. Some of the guests hinted that he might be the next Secretary of State if Hayes won. Someone also suggested that Hayes be President, and Tilden Secretary of State. Evarts laughingly retorted, "It is well enough for Governor Hayes to give away his own office if he thinks he ought to; but, I'd like to know what right he has to take mine."[22]

By a strict party vote of eight to seven, the Commission decided on February 8, "That no evidence will be received or considered by the Commission which was not submitted to the joint convention of the two Houses by the President of the Senate, except such as relates to the eligibility of F. C. Humphreys, one of the electors."[23]

Testimony was then taken on the Humphreys case. When the Democratic counsel were so bold as to put the Attorney General of Florida on the stand, Evarts promptly objected, and the Commission rejected the testimony. The Democratic counsel contended that Humphreys was ineligible because he was an office-holder in the custom-house, and that his resignation from this post was invalid on technical grounds. In reply, Evarts showed that the right of resignation was unrestricted and that, even if Humphreys did hold the office, the Commission could not make a search for his title because each state was judge of its own elections. By another vote of eight to seven the Commission upheld the eligibility of Humphreys.[24]

With the preliminary question settled, the Commission heard arguments upon the three Florida certificates. But this presented little that was new. Evarts took each certificate in turn. He showed that No. 1, signed by the Governor, complied with all requirements. No. 2 lacked such signature and so was void. No. 3, based on *quo warranto* proceedings, was described by Evarts as "a posthumous certificate of post-mortem action, never proceeding from any vital or living college of electors."[25] The Commission repeated its eight to seven vote, upholding No. 1 and giving the four electoral votes of Florida to Hayes.

A better hope for the Democrats existed in the case of Louisiana. Thousands of votes had been thrown out by the Republican returning-board on the ground of fraud, and this gave Tilden's followers reason to believe that the Commission might go behind the returns. Once more there were three certificates: No. 1, signed by Kellogg, Republican carpetbag Governor, who was supported by federal troops; No. 2, signed by McEnery, Democratic Governor, who was supported by state troops; and No. 3, similar to No. 1, which had been sent to Washington to correct a supposed error in No. 1.

On February 15 Evarts spoke for more than two hours on the Louisiana case. This proved his longest and most important contribution and his best argument. The crowded chamber listened to a discourse based on seemingly impregnable law and logic. Much of it was devoted to a refutation of Democratic charges. After making a careful analysis of the Louisiana election laws, he concluded that nothing could be done to purge the list of electors named in No. 1 because Congress had passed no regulations on the subject of eligibility of electors; nor could an elector be disqualified because he held a state office. If fraud existed, it was for the state, not the federal government, to deal with it.[26]

Speaking with more feeling because he knew he was on surer ground, he said, "If you give the great power of the Federal Union a judgement in the matter of how the State has performed its duty, you give the judgement that the wolf had over the lamb." "If the Federal government assumed the task of going behind the returns to purge the election in every local district, it would initiate an enormous change in the plan of American government."[27]

There was much in Evarts' last point. Indeed, he had argued so cogently that, as he sat down, several Democrats were heard to admit that he had demolished their case. But the Commission's usual vote of eight-seven was based rather on partisan grounds than on any conviction that Evarts had presented the Republican case in a stronger light.[28]

The Democrats had one more card to play—the attempt to win one of the three electoral votes from Oregon by turning the Republican argument into a boomerang. Evarts had foreseen this possibility, and in the Florida case had held that the Commission could go behind the returns to discover whether they falsified the record on which they were based. The three Republican electors—Odell, Cartwright, and Watts—admittedly received a majority vote; but the Democratic Governor had refused Watts his certificate on the ground that he held office as a postmaster, and issued it to Cronin, a Democrat who had not received a majority. Watts resigned as postmaster and joined Odell and Cartwright in signing Certificate No. 1, which was for Hayes but lacked the signature of the Governor. Cronin, declaring that two vacancies existed in the electoral college, proceeded to fill them with Republicans, and sent Certificate No. 2 to Washington with two Republican and one Democratic vote—enough to give the election to Tilden. Cronin's certificate had the endorsement of the Governor, but did not meet the requirement that only electors receiving the highest number of votes be certified.

Evarts' final argument was delivered on February 22. He had approved going behind the returns and took a leading part in examining witnesses and proving that Cronin did not have a majority. He contended that Odell, Cartwright, and Watts had acted properly. Failing to secure the Governor's certification, they had obtained an abstract of the vote from the Secretary of State and sent it to Washington; thus supplying the fact upon which the Governor's certification would lawfully rest. "The Governor," said Evarts, "had no right to issue the Cronin certificate and Cronin had no right to form a new electoral college. He might better have called for a new election. Did you ever hear that the exclusion of a member of the board . . . authorized him to go and fill the board and go on with the business? . . . If you adopt the rule that the majority constitute the college, you put yourself under the principle which governs all corporate action."[29]

Again the Commission decided in favor of Hayes. No argument took place over the electoral vote of South Carolina, and once more the state was awarded to Hayes.

But the struggle was not quite over. Congress would have to approve the decision of the Commission. A group of Southern Democrats planned a filibuster to delay the inauguration of Hayes until they could gain from him a pledge to withdraw federal troops from the South and restore home rule. To prevent the filibuster, several conferences of political leaders were held on the twenty-sixth. One met in Evarts' room at Wormley's Hotel, but it is not certain whether Evarts was present. In a conversation with Penn, a Louisiana Democrat, Evarts had remarked that Hayes would do the right thing by the South, and this opened the way for the meeting. Among those present were John Sherman, James A. Garfield, Henry Watterson, Stanley Matthews, and ex-Governor Dennison, while one witness later swore that Evarts was there. The result was a "bargain" whereby the Democrats agreed to abandon the plan for a filibuster if Hayes agreed to withdraw the troops. It was not a corrupt bargain; on the contrary, it was dictated by the most laudable motives.[30] The way was now cleared and Hayes was inaugurated on March 5.

The rightfulness of the decision of the Commission will always be disputed. Books are still arguing over the question, though nearly the whole weight of opinion holds that Tilden was entitled to the presidency. The Republican argument that the Commission could not go behind the returns, although legally strong, was unjust in operation. Even from a legal aspect it was not impregnable: Congress did go behind the returns in a senatorial election in 1873, and the Commission did likewise in the Oregon case. The better moral case lies with the Democrats, and there can be little doubt that at least the electoral vote of Florida should properly have gone to Tilden. The proceedings and result were governed by political, not judicial, considerations.

The fact remains, however, that a national crisis was met without resort to force. The dispute gave opportunity for a remarkable illustration of the civil capacity of the American people. As Evarts afterward said, "By an exhibition of wisdom and courage, by a comprehensive and circumspect estimate of the gravity of the situation, the people of the country exhibited a control over themselves in an emergency . . . that bespoke the greatness of the Nation."[31]

Evarts bore a heavy share of the burden as leading counsel for the Republicans. He was the only counsel to argue in all three cases of Florida, Louisiana, and Oregon. But he did not escape criticism from those who felt that his rôle was inconsistent with his independence in politics and his reputation as a lawyer. But the attacks were unjust. Although some of his arguments were open to question, there was no more reason to criticize him than O'Conor or any of the other counsel, or Justices Miller and Strong, two distinguished jurists who sat on the Commission and adopted Evarts' views. He might feel that he had taken an important share in the solution of a perilous problem.

21

At the Right Hand of the President

EVARTS' APPOINTMENT as Secretary of State was not merely a reward for his services as counsel. Hayes had recorded in his diary even before the Electoral Commission met that Evarts was the man for the post. Though he did not know Evarts well, he recognized his ability, independence in politics, and knowledge of foreign affairs, and he was aware of the general satisfaction that his appointment would give. Moreover, Hayes foresaw trouble with the Conkling machine in New York and wanted a leader of the reform faction to fight the Stalwart spoilsmen of New York. The appointment was strongly urged by Schurz, who had much influence upon Hayes. Waiting till the Electoral Commission had completed its task, Hayes sent Sherman to proffer the appointment, and Evarts accepted it.[1]

A storm of opposition immediately arose among the oligarchs in the Senate. Why should an Independent, who had defended Johnson, criticized Grant, and refused steadily to participate in the intrigues of political bosses, be given the chief place in the Cabinet? Was this not a direct defiance of Conkling and a breach of senatorial courtesy? Conkling had warned Hayes by circulating a petition in the New York legislature in favor of the appointment of his henchman, Tom Platt, as postmaster general, and by writing Hayes that New York Republicans would not support a man "who had received wealth and honor from an Administration" which "he had publicly abused and vilified, and whose record as a Republican has been more than doubtful."[2]

But Hayes did not bend before the storm. The flood of letters he received, begging him to stand firm, was evidence that he had made a good appointment. Conkling, Blaine, Cameron, and Butler led the attack upon the nomination. A personal dislike for Evarts actuated all these men except Blaine, who preferred another candidate but confidentially told Garfield that, were he President, he would appoint Evarts.[3] First the oligarchs tried persuasion, sending delegations to Hayes to urge candidates whom they preferred. Then they attempted a campaign of delay and obstruction, hoping to bulldoze the President. On March 7, seven of Hayes's Cabinet nominations were referred to seven different committees which had not yet been organized. It was an unprecedented and studied insult, offered with a view to delaying confirmation.[4]

On the following day a nonpartisan and informal meeting of business men was held on the steps of the Subtreasury Building in New York to register disapproval of the senatorial tactics. Led by John Jay and John A. Stevens, the gathering passed resolutions upholding the right of the President to select his own Cabinet. Indeed, the Senate mutineers soon began to waver in the face of rising public indignation. The revolt lasted only three days, when the recalcitrant senators broke lines to accept the nomination. Evarts was approved by a vote of forty-four to two, with a good many senators not voting. Piqued by the refusal of Hayes to find a place for his son in the Cabinet and not relishing the prospect, as chairman of the Foreign Relations Committee, of coöperating with Evarts, old Simon Cameron resigned from the Senate.[5]

Hamilton Fish continued to serve in the State Department for a week while ratification was pending. But on the morning of March 12 Hayes and Fish signed Evarts' commission and at noon the new Secretary was sworn in and introduced to the members of the staff.[6]

Congratulations poured in upon him. Richard H. Dana wrote that he could hardly trust his eyes when he looked upon such a "Cabinet of gentlemen." John Jay declared that he expected to see Evarts elevate the whole tone of foreign diplomacy, a reflection doubtless upon Grant rather than Fish. The press was uniformly favorable. "The country," asserted the *Nation,* "will be well served." With untimely ill-grace, Beecher declared, "He will make an excellent Secretary of State if he can be held down to practical and practicable things, and I believe that Hayes is the man to get the most good and usefulness out of him."[7]

Whitelaw Reid's estimate hit the mark. "He has an intimate knowledge," said Reid, "of the subjects with which the department must be chiefly concerned. He is already known and esteemed in the countries with which we chiefly desire to stand well . . . his personal intercourse with foreign representatives could not fail to increase the respect of foreigners. . . . It would rally to the Administration a great many independents whose sympathies have always been with the Republican party, but who have been able to give it under its recent management only a halting and uncertain approval."[8]

Evarts was pleased by the long-delayed recognition, but aware that it meant a four-year interruption of professional life. He wrote Pierrepont: "How shall I make official life comport with my habits and life of independence and with the essential interests of my family I do not know. I would gladly have seen some one else take the place but there seemed to be no one obvious for it and it might have been critical for me to decline it." Nor was the financial sacrifice to be overlooked. A salary of ten thousand dollars was only a fraction of what he could earn as a lawyer.[9] But the appointment was an honor which few men would refuse, and a logical climax to years of diplomatic experience.

As adviser to Hayes, Evarts was an important factor in the domestic policies of the administration. Some observers feared he would try to take the leadership. Garfield, who never quite relished Evarts' independence, attributed to him some of the perplexities of the administration. "Evarts is so full of theory and his own cogitations," wrote Garfield, "that he reaches no practical conclusions. I fear his dreamy doctrines have captivated the President and led him into many of his unfortunate ways that have done much to alienate his friends."[10] But Garfield was wrong. There is absolutely no evidence that Evarts tried to force his views on the President.

The relation between Hayes and Evarts was one of mutual trust and esteem. A friendship was cemented which endured till Hayes's death. They became intimate, often taking walks together, especially at night before retiring. If Hayes rested strongly on Evarts' legal mind and good judgment, it was because he trusted him; but his decisions were his own.[11]

Evarts was fortunate in being a member of one of the best and most harmonious of Cabinets. Sherman, Schurz, and Evarts were the most influential members and had the most to say. Two elements, conservative and liberal, can perhaps be distinguished, with Key representing the former and Schurz the latter. Evarts, although usually in harmony with Schurz, occupied a half-way position. Sherman, McCrary, Devens, Key, Schurz, and Evarts were good men; but Thompson, Secretary of the Navy, proved of doubtful quality. Cabinet meetings, held at noon on Tuesdays and Fridays in a high-studded room of the White House, were marked by free discussion and good fellowship. There were no acrimonious disputes and few delays in getting things done. Evarts' wit flashed at times, but he gave strict heed to the business in hand.[12]

Thurlow Weed was right when he wrote Evarts that the new administration would soon be embarked on "a sea of difficulties." First, there was the Southern question. Carpetbag governments, supported by federal troops, still persisted in South Carolina and Louisiana. But just before leaving office, Grant shifted from his unwise policy of coercion and in part redeemed himself by refusing to permit federal troops to be allowed at the polls. During the week that Hamilton Fish served in the Hayes Cabinet he urged upon the President the advisability of moderation toward the South and of the withdrawal of the troops. Furthermore, the President was pledged by the Wormley Hotel agreement.[13]

Evarts had a part in bringing about the withdrawal of the troops. When Stanley Matthews wrote Chamberlain, the Republican Governor of South Carolina, that it would be a good thing for the country if he resigned, Evarts appended a friendly but noncommittal postscript, saying: "I have read this letter and conversed with Colonel Haskell and Senator Gordon on the subject, so interesting to us all. I should be very glad to aid in the solution of the difficulties of the situation, and especially to hear from you speedily."[14] The postscript gave Matthews' letter an administration sanction. Chamberlain was indignant and replied, "There are better ways than this to conciliate and pacify the South." He showed the letter to Senator Corbin, who exhibited it dramatically in the Senate. Blaine pounced upon it eagerly, declaring, "I do not propose at the beck of Mr. Stanley Matthews or Mr. Evarts to say that the public good requires that he [Chamberlain] shall retire for the public good." But Chamberlain, who never intended the letter to become public, realized the hopelessness of his situation and wrote Evarts, "I have absolute confidence in your wisdom and patriotism." It soon became clear that Evarts and Matthews had acted from the highest motives, offering friendly advice without desiring to dictate the Governor's resignation.[15]

Three weeks later a solution was reached. Both Chamberlain and his Democratic rival, Wade Hampton, were invited to the White House. Evarts acted as host, taking Chamberlain to breakfast and Hampton to dinner, and entertaining the Confederate General till late in the evening. A lucrative post having been promised Chamberlain, he resigned, the troops were withdrawn, and South Carolina was restored to home rule.[16]

The Louisiana problem was not so easy. When Hayes decided to send a nonpartisan commission of five to New Orleans to investigate, Evarts wrote careful instructions for it. The commission was directed to discover which of the two governments in the state had the confidence of the people. Soon after reaching New Orleans, it reported to Hayes that Nicholls, the Democratic Governor, commanded more popular support than Packard, the Republican carpetbagger. Evarts immediately telegraphed a cipher message, instructing the commission to watch for the most opportune moment when the federal troops could be withdrawn without violent result.[17]

Meanwhile enemies of the administration placarded Washington with posters bearing the headlines: "William M. Evarts, Before the Electoral Commission, February 1, 1877," followed by an extract from the address in which he had argued for the protection of the Negro in Louisiana.[18] This unjustified attack failed of its purpose. Evarts had uttered his plea at a time when the Nicholls government had made no promise to abide by the Constitution or give the Negro any rights—a promise which now had been given the visiting commission.

By April 21 the commission reported that cordial relations had been restored between the two factions. Three days later Hayes withdrew the troops.[19] Of course Evarts was included in the tirades of abuse that were heaped upon Hayes by the Stalwarts for restoring the Democrats to power. In Boston Wendell Phillips described the Secretary as a man without principles—a man who "reminds one of the Protestant riots in London, when men chalked on their closed shutters 'no popery' to conciliate the mob." Evarts was in complete sympathy with Hayes's generous and wise policy, and stated publicly that if Tilden had been elected, the problem would not have been thus rapidly solved.[20] He realized, however, that it was accomplished at the cost of a widened breach in the Republican party.

Hayes soon decided upon a series of tours in the East and South to further good will and harmony, and Evarts accompanied him on most of these journeys. In June a few days were spent in Massachusetts and Rhode Island. The presidential party, including Evarts, Devens, and Key, travelled to Boston, brief speeches being made en route from the platform of the palace car. They were met by Governor Rice and his staff, reviewed a parade, and attended an informal reception at Faneuil Hall. Evarts took the opportunity to steal off for a few hours at a class reunion at Yale, where he presided over a little group of thirty-five, concluding the day with an enjoyable evening at Silliman's home.[21]

Another tour in August took the President through Vermont and New Hampshire. The Vermont people had long anticipated the President's visit to the Bennington Centennial. A huge crowd was on hand. A great parade culminated in exercises at a pavillion on the historic site of the battle. When it came Evarts' turn to speak, he raised a laugh by uttering only one sentence. "It is only fair that I should warn you," he said, "that although I am very slow to begin a speech, I am much slower to end it, and I know your only safety is in my retiring before I commence." But he spoke at length that evening at the banquet. He recalled that he was on home ground, only a few miles from Sunderland, the birthplace of his father.[22]

It was a proud day for Evarts when Hayes visited Windsor. Never was Runnemede more honored than on August 18, when Hayes, Devens, Key, Rockwood Hoar, Senator Morrill, and others slept under his roof. The party was met at Claremont and driven to Windsor in the family barouche behind a "four-in-hand." That afternoon some three thousand people of the countryside came to shake hands with the President. From the piazza brief speeches were made by Hayes, Evarts, Key, and Devens; the band played; and three cheers were given for the President. Hayes attended church with Evarts the following day, and that afternoon they went for a drive. Although the weather was hot, Hayes enjoyed the stay. Evarts told him that his visit was likely to remain the chief topic of local pride for a generation.[23]

The principal purpose of the tour was to conciliate the South by an appeal to Northern audiences. Evarts was adept in saying the right thing. Speaking from the steps of the State Capitol at Concord, he remarked: "A wise historian has said that war ends well when it ends in reconciliation. There is no nearer or better or surer justification of the immense sacrifice of the lives and property of our countrymen North and South than that thereby the bonds of Union are cemented." At Manchester, speaking from the rear platform of the train, he declared that he did not think much of irreconcilables in the South and still less of those in the North. And he added, "It is said of us Yankees that we are meddlesome, but that is not true. If there is any one thing characteristic of a Yankee, it is the carefulness with which he tends to his own business; but then he considers everybody's business his own business." He told the story of the proposal of the Massachusetts legislature to reward Stark, the hero of Bennington, by giving him a suit of clothes taken from a captured British privateer. Fortunately no such ridiculous gift was made; for, said Evarts, "Nothing could justify any such transaction unless the legislature was *stark* mad or John Stark was *stark* naked."[24]

The presidential party visited the South during the fall of 1877, covering a circuit of some three thousand miles. Evarts and two of his daughters were in the party. They encountered a round of parades, banquets, and speeches. Everywhere Hayes and Evarts urged reunion and economic recovery. Stops were made at Nashville, Chattanooga, Knoxville, Atlanta, Lynchburg, and Charlottesville, at all of which Evarts adapted his remarks to the occasion. At Nashville he spoke highly of Stonewall Jackson; at Charlottesville, of Jefferson.[25]

Several days were spent in Richmond. Addressing a crowd of ten thousand that stood out in the rain to welcome their arrival, Evarts said, "I should have regarded the people of Richmond as the most intelligent in Virginia, had I not discovered that they do not know enough to go inside when it rains." As the President was concluding a speech at the fair grounds to a crowd of some thirty thousand, he introduced Evarts as usual, but to his dismay turned around to find the Secretary missing. Suddenly Evarts appeared, crying, "The lost is found." The crowd gave him such an ovation that he was astonished, and exclaimed with biblical solemnity: "There is more joy over the finding of one Cabinet minister who was absent than over the three that had not gone astray."[26]

Hayes's work in healing the sores caused by the war was an important achievement of his administration. He urged that national interests ought to supplant all merely sectional and selfish desires. As Evarts put it in a speech at Chattanooga: "We know we can do great mischiefs to one another, we know we can cultivate great discords here upon battlefields on which we differed, and forget the most glorious memories of our noble institutions and the splendid future which belongs to us as our common birthright all over the land—and knowing that, let us be satisfied under our Government . . . let us live in amity."[27]

During the Baltimore & Ohio Railroad strike of 1877 Evarts gave the President helpful advice. It was the first strike in which violence on a national scale required presidential intervention. At the request of the Governor of West Virginia Hayes promptly sent troops, but the disturbances spread, and additional soldiers had to be sent to Baltimore, Pittsburgh, and other points.

At the peak of the crisis Evarts cautioned the President against any arbitrary use of force. "Men are not to be court-martialled for a difference of opinion," he said. When General Schofield raised the question whether federal troops could be moved against a mob before the Governor issued a call for help, Evarts replied, "It will be given him in that hour what he will do."[28] Having issued a proclamation of warning against further disorders, Hayes sought Evarts' opinion as to how far he could go in the use of troops. In an important state paper Evarts declared: "It is for the President to determine . . . at every stage of the continuing domestic violence, what means he will employ . . . to accomplish the purpose of the protection of the State. Especially, it must be considered entirely within the President's military discretion to determine to what point he should limit the use of the forces under his authority as a mere aid to the local magistracies in, or the chief magistracy of the State, or at what point he should assume the command of all the forces available for the protection of the State. . . . Whatever, then, a State might do towards protecting itself, were it not denied an army and navy and their employment, the United States, clothed with these military powers and methods stripped from the States, *may* do, *must* do, if need be, towards protecting the State. In applying, then, the great means at its disposal to the great end proposed to it, the Government of the United States is subject to no limitations, under the Constitution, or in the nature of public obligations, except that its employment of these means towards this end should be reasonable, appropriate and adequate."[29]

Evarts was not alarmed by the disorders. He believed the nation would learn the lesson that a larger army was needed, and that federal troops were superior to state militia. Hayes deserved credit for his firm action, which ended the strike by August. En route to Windsor, Evarts wrote him that everybody was delighted with the handling of the "domestic violence." He suggested that in the future the settlement of labor troubles be left to a commission appointed by the President.[30]

Throughout this first year in Washington rumors constantly cropped up of a reorganization of the Cabinet in which Evarts would be one of those replaced. Hayes actually had no such intent. Behind these rumors, of course, were political enemies in Congress, who persistently criticized the President, describing him as a dreamer and a mere child in matters of party management.[31] Evarts does not appear to have been greatly disturbed.

With the currency problem, which occupied the spotlight during Hayes's second year, Evarts had little concern. Like the President, he was a sound-money man and regarded the Bland-Allison Silver Purchase bill as a menace to the credit of the nation. The Cabinet held a lively discussion of the bill on February 26, 1878. Evarts approved of Hayes's purpose to veto the measure, and disagreed flatly with Thompson's argument that the President should not take such action unless a bill was unconstitutional. Although the veto was overridden, Evarts found one redeeming provision in the new law, that advocating an international monetary conference. He hastened to prepare a circular letter to the American representatives abroad, inviting all powers to join the United States in seeking the adoption of a common ratio for gold and silver. Reading into this liberally-worded circular a thought that Evarts did not intend, his enemies asserted that it was a better argument for silver than the silver men themselves could make.[32]

In defense of Hayes's purpose to resume specie payment on January 1, 1879, Evarts made his first address to a New York audience since taking office. He proposed to counter the arguments of inflationists and set at rest the fears of a run on the treasury. The *Herald* announced sarcastically that "the most charming optimist in the country" would "give an account of how admirably matters are going on in the best of all possible worlds, and we shall be disappointed if he does not send his audience home wondering how it is that any of them ever grumbled at the hard times or wickedness of politicians." But Evarts received a hearty welcome at Cooper Institute. His audience had little interest in what he had to say of the Southern question or Civil Service reform, but manifested great concern in the money problem. He reviewed the history of the greenbacks, justified them as a war necessity, and insisted that they were promises which must be redeemed at full value. He ridiculed the fallacies of fiat money, "fattening on moonbeams," as he called it, and asserted that labor should never be paid in depreciated money.[33] That the resumption of specie payments proved a boon to the country is a well-known historic fact.

After the disastrous mid-term elections of 1878, the administration found itself politically isolated. Southern Democrats (despite their indebtedness to Hayes), Stalwarts, Half-Breeds of the Blaine stamp who disliked Hayes's concessions to the South, inflationists, spoilsmen, and others—all refused coöperation. They had not succeeded in proving Hayes's title to office illegitimate, but they would at least tie his hands for the rest of his term, override his vetoes, and shift power to Congress. A famous cartoon of the day, hostile to Hayes, illustrated his fading power. Entitled, "Hayes' Great Cabinet Trick—Uncle Horace materializes," it depicted Hayes as a medium, bound hand and foot in a box which Evarts and Schurz are opening. Out steps the ghost of Horace Greeley, crying: "Let us cast behind us the wreck and rubbish and worn-out contentions and bygone feuds. Hurrah for universal amnesty and impartial suffrage! . . . My magnetism is getting weak; join hands and turn out the gas. Hallelujah! Goodnight!"[34]

Evarts was deeply aroused when the Southerners proposed to repeal the law permitting the use of the army to police federal elections. It seemed to him that the Southerner wanted to have his cake and eat it too. To be sure, he declared at the President's request, in the annual message of 1878, "It is the right of every citizen, possessing the qualifications prescribed by law, to cast one unintimidated ballot honestly counted." He did not approve of soldiers at the polls. But, as he said at Cooper Institute soon afterward, referring to the proposed repeal: "Under the cover of . . . that proposition . . . was hidden an insidious attack upon the power of the American people. . . . Look at the State of Mississippi." He believed that repeal would lead to suppression of the Negro vote.[35] Hayes promptly vetoed the bill; but an army appropriation was finally passed with an amendment specifically forbidding the use of money for the support of troops in police work at the polls.

During the debates on the election bill Evarts appeared one day in the gallery of the House to hear Garfield speak. This appearance of a Cabinet member in Congress was immediately denounced by Blackburn, a member from Kentucky, who charged that Evarts came to overawe the House. The speech was greeted with derisive laughter by the Republicans. Indeed, Evarts once had a vigorous discussion with Hayes upon the right of Cabinet members to be heard in Congress, in which he declared that no such right existed.[36]

Evarts' indignation increased when Congress tried to play the rôle of a righteous House of Commons by refusing appropriations for operating expenses of the government. In the *Tribune* he published a statement ridiculing the comparison of Hayes with Charles I. "The House of Commons," he said, "sought to bring the King to terms, not by refusing appropriations, but by refusing to levy taxes. . . . Here, the Democrats proposed to have all the taxes collected as usual and then prohibited the President from spending the money for carrying out the people's Government." When Congress finally gave way before an adverse public opinion Evarts derisively described the Democratic retreat as "a remarkably well developed case of the small end of the horn."[37]

Aside from Evarts' connection with the general policies of the administration his relation to the party feud in New York offered some interesting episodes. He once said to Hayes, "New York politics have always been excessively troublesome to administrations of every party. How much to do about them, or how much to let them alone, is a puzzle."[38] In this instance it was the Conkling machine, not the Democratic organization, which furnished the puzzling problem.

From the outset Evarts was a target for Stalwarts and Democrats alike. The leading Democratic officials of the state conspicuously absented themselves from the nonpartisan reception given him at Albany just after his appointment. Not even his friend John Bigelow, Secretary of State, appeared. But Evarts took this boycott philosophically, chatting pleasantly all the evening.[39]

Hayes needed a strong counter-organization in New York which would offset the Conkling machine. Members of the reform element were numerous, and included eminent men like Curtis. But most of them had little political influence. The *Herald* was probably right in asserting that Evarts could not carry a single election district. He was the last man in the world to aid in building up a counter-machine. Yet wild rumors were afloat that he would lead a movement to revive the old Whig party.[40]

Actually, there was one step he *would* take. He would encourage a semiofficial newspaper which supported the administration. New York had friendly journals like the *Tribune,* but none that really spoke for the administration. Indeed, Reid of the *Tribune* was as quick to criticize as praise. Jonas M. Bundy, who had long served under William Cullen Bryant on the staff of the *Evening Post* and had struck out for himself by establishing the *Evening Mail,* offered the services of his struggling paper, seeking financial assistance in return. To prove the value of his editorials he sent Evarts samples from his pen and outlined his views of New York politics. "Mr. Conkling," he wrote, "has ruled the State for years through *fear,* not love, or respect, or admiration. The number of friends personally devoted to him can be counted on the fingers: Cornell, Platt, and a few others. His influence depends simply on the power of rewarding friends and punishing enemies. . . . The one thing necessary . . . is to remove the pressure—this incubus of fear . . . by showing to all that Mr. C. is no longer the dispenser of power and patronage: in short, that it is safe to oppose him. This can easily be done by preferring in all appointments of Postmasters, of Int. Rev. officers, of Custome House officials, of Marshals, and scores of miscellaneous functionaries, those who are known as friends of the Administration. . . . A diffused general public sentiment, while an excellent and necessary thing, yet requires organization in order to be effective."[41]

Evarts personally contributed to the *Mail* and induced other New York friends of the administration to do so. Bundy promised to be diligent and displayed a contagious optimism which pleased Evarts. The Secretary thought highly of Bundy, believed his pen more pungent than that of any other editor. Bundy had also an equally sincere regard for Evarts and looked upon him as a likely candidate for president in 1880. There was, however, a suspicious note of deliberate flattery in some of his letters to Evarts. Furthermore, Evarts was at times annoyed with Bundy's persistency in deluging him with letters and requests for money.[42]

The Secretary recognized that Bundy could be of real assistance. "He has capacity and fidelity," he wrote Pierrepont, "and can see an inch beyond his nose. The reason his paper is a valuable instrumentality is that it is not overgrown with pride and conceit and jibbery—that it is not suspected of enlistment—that it takes very little money to support it and has a great repute, moral and intellectual to build upon. If we let it go down we shall regret it. Bundy deserves our aid, but it is his services, not services to him, that I insist upon maintaining."[43]

The political sky was serene in New York during the summer of 1877. Conkling was away in Europe. Samuel Bowles believed that Conkling's power was waning, and that there would be no trouble, provided Evarts "had sense enough not to set up a gang." Evarts also was optimistic. But Reid believed the party on the verge of collapse. He visited Evarts at Windsor that summer and impressed upon him the seriousness of the situation.[44] Time proved that Reid was right.

Conkling's cohorts gave him a royal welcome upon his return. He had forgotten and forgiven nothing. His hatred for Hayes was deep and he never spoke of him in public without a sneer, referring to him often as "His Fraudulency the President." Nor had he forgiven the appointment of Evarts. Four days after his return there appeared in his organ, the Utica *Daily Observer,* the following attack: "Mr. Evarts' mercenary character is fully established. His avarice and ambition are continually running a race, but always with the same result—a dead heat. . . . A small fortune and first place in the Cabinet were sops thrown to the twin demons of avarice and ambition which beset him. . . . It would not be safe to offer him a hundred thousand dollars to appear as the attorney of a claim against the State Department."[45]

The attack was resumed at the Rochester State Convention. In the opening speech Tom Platt pronounced Evarts a "demagogue," dangerous when given power. Conkling's denunciation of the Hayes administration was the most dramatic event of the gathering. Rising to his full six feet, shaking his wealth of wavy hair, his eyes sparkling and his voice betraying his emotion, the Senator spoke for an hour, venting his wrath upon Hayes, Evarts, and Curtis. The battle was on.[46]

Conkling's attack upon Evarts exceeded all the bounds of decency. To picture the Secretary as a "Mephistopheles," molding New York politics to suit himself, with the ultimate purpose of reaching the Senate or presidency, was a ridiculous exaggeration. "From the time Hayes came into office and appointed a *Democratic* Cabinet," declared Conkling, "the principal labor of *little Evarts* and the rest has been to withdraw the Republican support from me. . . . I am sure nobody counts Evarts a Republican."[47]

When asked what he thought of the Senator's hostility, Evarts replied, "Mr. Conkling chooses to oppose. I can only say that I am sorry. He has had a great opportunity, for he might have made himself a leader in the Senate in the great work of nationalizing the Republican party." If Evarts cherished any personal animosity toward Conkling, there is little evidence of it. He was disgusted with Conkling's dictatorship and machine methods and had nothing but contempt for his attacks. One day a distinguished English jurist remarked to Evarts that he had just heard Conkling speak in the Senate and believed that he must be a formidable adversary in the courts. Evarts replied dryly that he had never seen Conkling in a court.[48]

The New York customhouse controversy brought the struggle to a focus. Evarts' part in it, although not fully known at the time, was important. The customhouse was the keystone of Conkling's political edifice—the greatest source of political patronage in the country. It had long possessed an unsavory reputation. Hayes appointed a commission, headed by John Jay, to investigate. Its report exposed a great deal of inefficiency, petty graft, and loss of revenue; recommended a reduction of personnel; and urged greater economy of operation. The investigators held the spoils system responsible for the evils. Hayes thereupon issued his famous order forbidding office-holders to take part in political activities—an order which applied both to Chester A. Arthur, the collector, and to Alonzo Cornell, the naval officer. As chairman of the Republican State Committee, Cornell ought to have resigned from the customhouse; but both Arthur and he refused, no doubt at Conkling's command. His patience exhausted, Hayes finally decided to remove them.[49]

Evarts was largely responsible for influencing Hayes to make the removals, although Schurz and Curtis also urged it. The Secretary was utterly disgusted with the situation. "God help a party," he wrote Whitelaw Reid, "whose agitations are all about Customs officers." Hayes delayed a Cabinet meeting till Evarts could be present to discuss the removals, and at this session Evarts took the initiative in recommending the appointment of Theodore Roosevelt and L. Bradford Prince as successors of Arthur and Cornell. When the nominations reached the Senate, he was held responsible for them. Declared Hamilton Fish, "Everybody who knows anything believes they were the work of Mr. Evarts, and he it is to whom all the animus refers."[50]

Conkling took the nominations very seriously, for he was convinced that there was a plot by Hayes and Evarts to wrest his leadership from him. He had the names referred to the Committee on Commerce and when the committee reported unfavorably, he led the long debate that followed. He placed the blame at Evarts' door, accusing him of trying to build up a machine of his own in New York. The Senate stood by him, rejecting the nominations by a vote of twenty-five to thirty-one.[51]

But Conkling's victory was short-lived. In arrogantly flouting the administration, he was weakening the party as well as himself. The people of New York were becoming weary of the struggle. Hayes sent the Senate the nominations of General Merritt and Silas Burt to fill the vacancies, two men whom Evarts heartily approved. To Conkling's discomfiture, the Senate confirmed them by a vote of forty to thirty. Although this was a victory for the administration, Hayes admitted that the whole episode had been badly mismanaged and that the purposes of the President should have been made clearer to the public.[52]

Evarts felt no bitterness toward Conkling during the controversy. On the contrary, he sought to play the rôle of conciliator. Bundy admired and praised him for this, avowing that he had "healed up many old sores, prevented any new ones from breaking out, avoided all irritation, and went on the principle of enduring all things for the sake of party harmony." But as the controversy waxed hot, Bundy changed his views. He urged Evarts to assert his full influence in New York, build up an organization against

Conkling, and take the lead of the party. This Evarts refused to do. "I believe the way out of the malignant politics of N. Y. State," he wrote Hayes, "is by frank and open treatment of both sides, if necessary, in each other's presence."[53]

It may be true, as John Sherman later charged, that "but for Evarts Pres't Hayes would never have had the New York Custom House controversy." But the fact is that six members of the Cabinet approved the removal of Arthur and Cornell. It was a daring step for Evarts to advise, and a courageous thing for Hayes to do.[54]

The *Mail* became quite a popular paper by the close of 1878. Few people knew of Evarts' connection with it. For a time the existence of the paper was imperiled by a struggle for control between the two owners, Clark Bell and Dr. W. H. White. Bundy sided with White, who finally, with the aid of H. B. Stebbins, H. B. Claflin, and J. Seligman, bought out Bell—all three of these backers having been induced by Evarts to come to the rescue. Evarts backed Bundy strongly, urging him to "keep up his spirit and fight." By 1879 the journal was on its feet financially, and new helpers were found, such as Edwards Pierrepont and Elliot C. Cowdin. The chief support, however, came from Cyrus W. Field, who had great admiration for Evarts. Field bought the *Mail,* paid its debts, and two years later consolidated it with the *Evening Express,* retaining Bundy as editor.[55]

Bundy declared, "If I can send the *Mail* into every county in the Union for twelve months, I will do more toward shaping the next presidential campaign and its issues than any other Editor." But there is no evidence that Evarts encouraged more than a defense of the Hayes administration. His critics were fond of attributing to him an ambitious desire for higher office. At a New England Society dinner in 1878, Blaine rose to respond to the toast, "New England Character," and made a sly thrust at Evarts. "There are many great men in New England," he said, "who aspire to a seat in Congress, first in the House and then in the Senate, and thence forward or backward to the Cabinet, and then under the inspiration of the strong air and mountain scenery of Vermont aspire still higher."[56]

While during his last two years in office Evarts unquestionably shifted his political ground, it was not from any hope that it would carry him to the White House. After the customhouse fracas he became increasingly conciliatory toward the Conkling Stalwarts. Bundy noted the change and questioned it. "I find," he wrote, "that you are actually gaining the warm admiration of some of the pronounced Conkling men, who have gone so far as to talk of you for Governor or Senator." Indeed, as the gubernatorial campaign of 1879 got under way, the Stalwarts under the leadership of William E. Chandler began to flirt with the Hayes administration, with a view to capturing its support for their candidate, Alonzo Cornell.

Previous to the Saratoga convention the administration made no effort to assist Cornell. Why should it support the very man whom it had ejected from the customhouse? Nothing could be more distasteful to Evarts, who was deeply worried. He discussed the matter earnestly with old Thurlow Weed and wrote Curtis that he believed Levi Morton would be more agreeable to all three factions of the party.[57]

A bitter feud ensued at Saratoga, where the Reformers and Half-Breeds united on Morton, their combined strength almost equaling that of the Cornell Stalwarts. Little real enthusiasm was felt for Cornell, but "gag" methods gave him the victory. In a letter to Evarts, Curtis summarized the result: "In 1877 I saw Conkling spit in the face of the Administration with two-thirds of the Convention behind him. In 1878, with seven-tenths, I saw him never his mouth shut from insult. In 1879 I have seen him, his majority reduced to seven votes, praise the Administration . . . while the Convention cheered the name of Hayes."[58]

Cornell's nomination was extremely embarrassing to Hayes. If the President refused to support Conkling, the Democrats would carry the governorship and perhaps the national election in 1880; if he supported Conkling he would antagonize the reformers. In this dilemma, wisely or unwisely, he decided that party unity was the primary goal. He would support Cornell. Evarts was downcast, although he agreed that this was the wisest course. "A real brave and impressive nomination," he wrote Reid, "would have enabled us to shake the Democratic party to pieces in the whole country and close the politics of the Rebellion. But we must submit to the frog-in-the-well process of another series of campaigns. However, if it were best that everything should be done in a day, God would not have taken six to make the world."[59]

As he expected, the Reformers and liberals of the party were astonished and disgusted. To them it seemed that Hayes was restoring the party to the Stalwarts. From the Independent organization Evarts received a notification that any support of Cornell by him would be "a direct blow at the permanent interests of the party," and that he should either preserve "a significant silence" or explain why he would recommend "a man who was removed from his office a year ago in order that it might be honestly and efficiently administered."[60]

With such warnings from old friends sounding in his ears, Evarts hesitated. Rockwood Hoar advised him to forget New York politics and make "a national appeal." General Sherman proposed that Hayes and Evarts go on a speaking tour to the West. Hayes liked the idea, but Evarts believed that it would convey an impression that the administration was frightened. With reluctance, Evarts finally agreed to speak for Cornell *once* in New York. This was not a concession to the Republican National Committee or even to pressure from Hayes; it was certainly not an ambitious bid for Stalwart support for himself; it was simply his own reluctant agreement that party unity came before personal feeling. John Sherman, who consented to make several speeches in Ohio, complained that Evarts should not be let off with one address. "Well, Mr. Sherman," retorted Evarts, "when the people of New York wish my views on public questions, they arrange for a meeting in Cooper Institute or some other place. I make the speech and it is read." This hint that his speeches got full publicity and Sherman's did not was regarded by Sherman as "a refined specimen of egotism." Young John Hay, who was seeking a diplomatic post, was also sent off to Ohio to speak for the administration.[61]

Evarts' one speech on October 21 at Cooper Institute came exactly ten days after Arthur had agreed to cease his attacks upon the administration. Indeed, it was Arthur, together with Morton, who called for Evarts that evening at the Brevoort House on their way to Cooper Institute. They found every seat filled. But no music or fireworks had been provided, and the usual decorations were lacking. As they entered, a pamphlet denouncing the Conkling machine was thrust into their hands. Arthur, Morton, and Blaine entered first and were greeted with cheers. When Evarts appeared, the audience rose to its feet, cheering and waving hats. Morton presided, and Evarts rose to deliver what Oakey Hall described as a "full dose of ingenious treason."[62]

He sought to get his audience in a proper frame of mind by dwelling first upon the right of suffrage and "majestic power of the people." Liberal Republicans then listened with amazement as he launched into an attack upon reformers who proposed to desert Cornell by "voting in the air." He made only brief mention of Cornell, however, first by a veiled apology for a candidate who might not be acceptable to the whole party, and then by referring to him as "a citizen without reproach" and a "representative of Republican principles." It was apparent that he justified a vote for Cornell solely on the ground that it would place New York in the Republican column in 1880. The speech was mainly an ingenious and entertaining description of the other candidates—Robinson, Potter, and Kelly—whom he compared to horses in a race, "some with and some without jockeys."[63]

His address met a mixed response, mostly unfavorable. "It is surprising," declared the *Herald*, "that he can so far abdicate his self-respect as to come here and speak for Cornell." Henry Adams, in alarm, believed that Evarts was handing the party back to Grant. Dorman B. Eaton asserted that the people would not be turned aside from reform by "diplomatic oratory." The *Nation* pronounced his speech "indecent," and Curtis called it "unspeakable." Curtis had visited Evarts at Windsor two months before and was on most cordial terms with him, but he could not stomach the Cooper Union speech. He wrote in *Harper's Weekly:* "Mr. Evarts, musing on the folly of voting in the air, may remember the arrow of which the poet sings, which was shot in the air and found in the heart of an oak. It is the hearts of oak, not bending reeds, that make and save parties."[64]

Cornell won the governorship, largely because of divisions in Democratic ranks. The result was a victory for Conkling and his machine. It gave the party sufficient unity to enable it to carry the state for Republicanism in 1880, thus achieving the main purpose of the Hayes administration. Although many reformers like Curtis were alienated, most of the reform faction saw the situation from Evarts' point of view and voted for Cornell. As the leader of the Republican Reform League said to Evarts: "Your coming, and that of Secretary Sherman, to help Cornell through, decided our League not to join in 'scratching' and thus save the ticket. One blast from our bugle would have made a wreck of Cornell."[65]

It is useless to debate whether the Hayes administration should or should not have supported Cornell. With the party torn by factions, unity was indispensable. In a letter to Hayes, written after leaving office, Evarts remarked: "I sometimes was inclined to think that the troubles in New York which your administration had to meet were aggravated by jealousies and repugnancies which I drew upon it. But the three weeks of General Garfield's possession of the presidency have relieved me from any such impression. The maintenance of the true constitutional authority of the President was the real matter in controversy."[66]

22

Life in Washington

Evarts did not conduct the office of Secretary of State with the puritanic seriousness of Hamilton Fish, who preceded him, or with the reckless aggressiveness of James G. Blaine, who followed him. He took the problems of office as he found them, refusing to become hurried or flustered. The burden of office did not weigh heavily on him. He was still the old-fashioned diplomat who had mingled with British aristocracy during the war. He had learned how to live, and he refused to allow politics or diplomatic problems to disturb unduly that way of living.

He maintained three homes: one in Washington, one in New York, and one in Windsor. The temporary home in Washington at 1507 K Street, which he leased at five thousand dollars a year, was an excellent house in a fine residential district, very near where Hamilton Fish had lived. Here, with his wife and four unmarried daughters, he entertained many guests. He insisted upon retaining the Second Avenue home in New York, but during his absence had his furniture stored at Sypher's, where for years his antique mahogany suites were spoken of with admiration.[1]

He loved the summer retreat at Windsor best of all. What Henry Adams once said of Timothy Dwight's fondness for this region might be said also of Evarts: "The uttermost depths of his nature were stirred only by affection for the Connecticut Valley. . . . After all, where was human nature more respectable than in this peaceful region? What had the United States then to show in scenery and landscape more beautiful or more winning than that country of meadow and mountain?"[2]

He had developed the finest farm in the country, of which he was so proud that he had one of its best scenes painted on canvas by Howland in 1877. There were two houses on the estate. The low, white, rambling, unpretentious house, hidden from the street by fir trees, was suggestive of comfort. It had changed but little with time. The wooden blinds, the brass knocker on the door, the oddly figured wallpaper, the old but highly prized furniture—all were reminiscent of the past. If he had an overflow of guests, which often occurred, they were lodged in the other house, the "Giants." Here was a handsomely decorated billiard room and an office which the family called the "State Department," because Evarts sought refuge there when he had work to do.

The grounds were beautifully and tastefully planned. To the rear of the houses stood a greenhouse, with a splendid flower garden, the walks of which were hedged with high pointed hemlocks symmetrically trimmed. Back of the garden spread waving fields of grass and corn, and in the distance were the stables and barns, indicating farming on a large scale. Altogether Evarts owned some six hundred acres on both sides of the Connecticut, of which about a third was under cultivation. In the stables were six or eight horses and all sorts of vehicles, from a "four-in-hand drag" to a "basket-phaeton." Some of the barn-lofts held a hundred tons of hay.

Charles Evarts, who managed the estate, wrote his father in the fall of 1877: "The crops are magnificent and the cattle superb. I have had numbers of people remark that they never saw such a splendid crib of corn. . . . I wish you might see the produce we are now harvesting."[3] Evarts paid much attention to the raising of livestock, and in 1875 had won nearly all the first prizes at the Claremont fair. He also raised swine and at one time had nearly five hundred sheep. In sending George Bancroft a supply of pork in 1876, he perpetrated one of his best-known but most atrocious puns. "I hope," he wrote, "you will find as much useful aliment for the body and mind in *this* product as in former years from the same *pen*. If you continue to give it preference, for a scholar's breakfast, over the grass-fed beef or mutton, it will give a new meaning to the high-sounding pretension on, 'The *pen* is mightier than the sword.' "[4]

Across the pastures lay the trout pond, covering twenty acres. Here were several rowboats and all the requisite appliances for trout fishing, but the fish were unusually difficult to catch because well fed. The pond originated from a myriad of springs, and Evarts believed the source lay in a subterranean lake.

Although the farm was well managed and large quantities of its products were sold, Evarts got little return on his investment. He whimsically remarked that he made it pay by "crediting the farm with everything taken off of it and charging nothing put on." To guests at his table he said, pointing to the milk and the champagne, "Take your choice; they're both refreshing, and they cost me the same."[5]

Charles C. Beaman and Edwin W. Stoughton, both near-neighbors, were often at Runnemede. Guests came and went in large numbers. The hospitality of the host was proverbial. Some of the most famous people of the day found delight in the homelike atmosphere, the sunlight, the paintings, the books, the country air, and the refinement and culture. The problem of caring for so many guests, even with two houses, was not simple. When Hettie Evarts married Beaman in 1874, fifty guests had to be given hospitality for two days and nights; but everything ran off smoothly and there was no end of fun and jollity.[6]

A visitor today at Runnemede will find in the library a small bust of Evarts made by the famous sculptor, Augustus St. Gaudens. When in Rome in 1872, Evarts visited the studio of the young artist, who was then on the threshold of his career, gave him his first commission for copies of the busts of Cicero and Demosthenes, and somewhat reluctantly promised to sit for a bust of himself later. St. Gaudens came to America and worked in New York on the bust, which proved a success. It was sent to the exhibit of the

National Academy of Design in 1877, but because of some disagreement of the committee, was not displayed. Through Evarts' assistance the young sculptor received commissions from Stoughton, Pierrepont, Elihu Root, and others, and his fame soon spread. Evarts treated him somewhat testily, but was fond of him and predicted for him a brilliant future. Beaman also became the young man's friend; and some years later, after gaining recognition as a great artist, St. Gaudens followed Beaman's suggestion and made his home at Aspet in the Cornish hills near Windsor. It is here that he did his best work.[7]

The life of the best Washington society had a gaiety in the late seventies which has been well pictured in Henry Adams' novel *Democracy*. Evarts moved in this society with grace and ease. He regarded his relations with the ministers of foreign countries as requiring a constant display of courtesy and much effort in entertaining. Adams wrote, "The Evarts are very cordial and civil, and the State Department magnificently hospitable." The Secretary paid much attention to the forms and proprieties of diplomacy. He could, however, break a tradition, as he did by wearing a frock coat instead of the usual dress suit at a New Year's reception at the White House.[8]

He was prominent at White House functions, and with Mrs. Evarts frequently dined with the President. At receptions he was always noticeable, always dignified and good-natured, always perfectly at ease. Social affairs at the White House were kept on a much more urbane level by Mrs. Hayes than by Mrs. Grant, though the new mistress of the White House was decidedly puritanical. Dancing was not permitted at the inaugural celebration, the billiard table was banished to the attic, and liquors were frowned upon. But her austerity did not prevent Mrs. Hayes from becoming one of the most popular presidential wives.

Evarts found her quite a match for him during the visit of the Russian Grand Dukes Alexis and Constantine. The Secretary received the royal guests with great formality at the door of the White

House, conducted them to the Blue Room, where the President and Cabinet in full dress waited to greet them, and introduced them. A great state dinner was given that evening in their honor, attended by the President and several high officials. Wishing to impress the Grand Dukes with American good will and knowing Mrs. Hayes's rule against serving wine, Evarts asked for an exception in this case. When she refused, he took the matter into his own hands and wine was served. But the glasses of the President and Mrs. Hayes were untouched, and it was the last time that wine was served in her presence. Indeed, a few days later, a temperance society, known as the "Mrs. Rutherford B. Hayes Temperance Society," was formed in Washington.[9]

At a diplomatic dinner of the period, a lady asked Evarts if drinking so many different wines did not make him feel seedy next day. "No, madam," he replied, "it's the indifferent wines that produce that result."[10]

The Secretary of State was expected to give a number of formal entertainments. Evarts' residence was adequate for evening receptions on a limited scale, but not for large affairs. It was the custom to hold these in a rented hall in the city. Hamilton Fish had tried in vain to obtain a new building for the State Department which would have an adequate hall. Evarts at first sought to use the hall in the old State Department, paying all the expenses; but after a time he fell back on the old custom of using rented quarters.[11]

At White House receptions Mrs. Hayes insisted upon marshalling the ladies in a stiff line in order of rank. She stood at their head, usually in a decorous, square-necked evening gown; next to her, in garnet satin or black velvet, came Mrs. Evarts with white lace cap; next, towering head and shoulders above the others, stood Mrs. Sherman; and then the other Cabinet ladies. All this was deadly to sociability. But generally speaking, society was informal. Henry Adams wrote, "We run in at all hours to see everybody; we make formal calls on the President, the Cabinet, and the Diplomats." The drawing-rooms of the Cabinet members were open to any who might choose to call. On New Year's Day they gave costly receptions—a custom at its height under Hayes—marked by much chatting and promenading. Everybody went to the White House at noon and then rushed by carriage to the homes of Cabinet members, where festivities continued until late at night, with rich and poor alike enjoying the day.[12]

No Old-World ambassador more thoroughly appreciated the diplomacy of the dinner table than Evarts. His inexhaustible fund of stories and humor served him well. Probably no Secretary of State was better gifted for the lighter side of diplomacy. He was a model host and usually the center of attraction at every gathering. Said John Hay, "He had the rare faculty of saying at the dinner-table the best things that were said there—invariably something that was quoted everywhere for days and even years afterward—and giving the impression while saying it that he had better things in reserve if he really cared to produce them." It is little wonder that the President and Mrs. Hayes often consulted him on social matters and even asked him to submit memoranda for guidance in White House entertaining.[13]

The President had many a laugh at his sallies. In a Cabinet meeting Hayes announced one day that he intended to make several new appointments in the foreign service. Surprised that he had not been consulted, Evarts said after a pause, "Mr. President, I have never had the good fortune to see the great *western reserve* of Ohio, of which we have heard so much." At first Hayes did not grasp the point, but the Cabinet did and all laughed heartily. Hayes always relished Evarts' quotation from Talleyrand when a mediocre candidate was appointed to an important office: "To have done and said nothing is a tremendous power, but it ought not to be abused." One day Hayes was amused when the Secretary, alluding to the squeaky oratory of a member of Congress, declared, "His voice is admirably adapted to the reading of fine print."[14] The public liked to exaggerate Evarts' habit of using long sentences. One morning the *Herald* stated, "William M. Evarts the other day began to tell a man that his coat tail was on fire. Before he got through the first half of the sentence three barns, twenty tons of hay and nine billy goats were burned up, not counting the coat tail."[15]

He was fond of *bons mots.* One day as he was about to enter his office, observing an unusually large number of persons waiting to see him, he exclaimed, "This is the largest collection for foreign missions I ever saw!" Edward Bok relates that at a great dinner party a lady seated next to Evarts asked him whether a woman was not the best judge of other women. "Ah, madam," he replied, "she is not only the best judge but the best executioner." When Andrew D. White was dining at Evarts' house, he noted that the dinner plate was marked with the words, *Facta non verba.* It seemed a peculiar motto for a lawyer. Evarts did not explain, but remarked that two congressmen had just dined with him and when one asked what the motto meant, the other replied, "They mean victuals, not talk."[16]

Evarts once rallied Bishop Potter of New York, whom he knew well and greatly admired,[17] upon the aristocratic character of his diocese, calling him the "Apostle to the Genteels." One of his best *bons mots* was uttered in 1880 at a dinner celebrating the one hundred and fiftieth anniversary of the founding of Baltimore. Speaking in the gayly decorated banquet hall of the Baltimore Academy of Music, Evarts pointed out that, although the original site of the city was purchased for ninety hogsheads of tobacco, values were quite different then, and regarded by a lawyer on the rational basis of *quid pro quo,* it could not be denied that ninety hogsheads of tobacco made a very good *quid.* He scored another laugh when, speaking of avocations, he declared that a hobby was better than a horse because a rider had to get off his horse at times, but a man could ride his hobby forever.[18]

John Hay was fond of telling the story of a journey with Evarts on a New England train. They had been riding for hours, apparently without getting anywhere. Suddenly they stopped at a little station and Hay rushed out to find something to eat. He returned with a paper bag full of large greasy doughnuts. Evarts eyed them a moment, thinking first of his digestion, and exclaimed solemnly, *"Timeo Danaos et doughnots ferentes."*[19]

As master of ceremonies at a dinner given by New York business men at Delmonico's to Sir Thomas B. Potter, the noted British free trader, Evarts said: "When I remember that we are being entertained by the Rev. Henry Potter; that we were invited to meet Sir Thomas Bayley Potter; when I observe at my right Clarkson N. Potter and at my left the Rev. Eliphalet Nott Potter, I am reminded of the young country gentleman who was unexpectedly summoned to supply a city pulpit. The church was imposing and the congregation so fashionable that when he rose to make the opening invocation he found himself a good deal flustered. The result was that, to the consternation of his hearers, he led off with the petition: 'O Lord, help us never to forget that Thou art the clay and we are the potters.'" Later Evarts proposed a toast: "Americans in England and Englishmen in America," adding as he glanced at Potter to the right of him and Junius Spencer Morgan to the left, that the true American was "something between the two." Then, turning to Potter, he said, "Abstruse students have instructed your people at tedious lengths upon the checks and balances of the American Constitution. I wish you, sir, to spread the knowledge through England and Europe that you have visited the American States and learnt what they are—oysters, green turtle, canvas-ducks; these are the checks to our American Constitution!"[20]

Evarts took time from his official duties for two dedicatory addresses. The first, in October, 1877, was at the laying of the cornerstone of the new Seventh Regiment armory at Fourth Avenue and Sixty-sixth Street in New York. He rode up Fifth Avenue in a military parade with Mayor Ely and other notables. At the designated site a great platform had been built, holding some four thousand persons, with a separate enclosure for the speakers. The surrounding streets and roofs of adjacent houses were crowded with spectators. The glittering bayonets and picturesque uniforms of the Masonic Order added to the spectacle. Evarts pictured the services of the regiment during the emergencies of the city's history from Abolition days to the riots of 1871, describing it as the "breakwater against casual and short-lived storms of public violence, . . . constant and at all times ready to enlist for the actual defense of the . . . law. . . . Discretion, moderation, obedience to the civil authority—these have been the traits that have marked the services of the regiment . . . these have made it the defender of all classes, of all opinions."[21]

The other dedicatory address, just at the close of his term, was delivered at the unveiling of the Egyptian obelisk, known as Cleopatra's Needle, in Central Park. He had taken a part in the acquisition of the obelisk. The Khedive had proposed to make the gift to the United States in 1869, but it was not till 1878 that it was delivered. Of the many obelisks carried away from Egypt, it was probably the only one voluntarily given, except one presented to England in 1819. It had stood at the Temple of Heliopolis near Cairo and was one of the many erected by Thutmoses III. Later it had been transferred to Cairo to grace the triumph of the Caesars, probably six years after Cleopatra's death. The difficult task of transporting it to New York was assigned by Evarts to Commander Gorringe. Commodore Vanderbilt paid the cost of transportation, amounting to about one hundred thousand dollars, and after nine months' labor the obelisk was ready for dedication.

When the committee in charge asked Evarts to speak he hesitated, but W. H. Hurlburt, editor of the *World,* prevailed upon him. "I am quite ill," wrote Hurlburt, "at the notion of your now declining to make that oration which all the dead Pharoahs are sitting up in their mummy cases to hear—not to mention a million or two of your own people." The ceremonies took place in the Metropolitan Museum, with many notables present. "An obelisk cannot work its passage across the Atlantic," said Evarts, describing the difficulties of transportation. He traced the history of the monument and touched upon the events that had occurred since its erection. "If these obelisks," he exclaimed, "could only perceive everything on which their shadow falls, what great teachers they would be! How they would humble the pride of the short-lived race of men that creeps about at their feet! . . . These obelisks may ask us: 'Can you expect that you will exist forever? Can you think that the soft folds of luxury are to wrap themselves closer and closer around this Nation and the pith and vigor of its manhood knowing no difficulties? Can age creep over you and your Nation, knowing no decrepitude?' These are questions that may be answered in the time of the obelisk, but not in ours."[22]

Evarts' office was in the south wing of the State, War, and Navy Building near the White House. Hamilton Fish had labored under the handicap of ridiculously inadequate quarters in the old Orphan Asylum building, far out on Fourteenth Street, where, in a cramped little room on the second floor, he conducted the foreign affairs of the nation till 1875, when the new office was opened.[23]

The staff under Evarts comprised the first assistant secretary of state (Frederick Seward and then John Hay), the second assistant (William Hunter), the third assistant (Charles Payson), the chief clerk, the chief of the Diplomatic Bureau, the chief of the Consular Bureau, the chief of the Bureau of Indexes and Archives, the chief of the Bureau of Accounts, the chief of the Bureau of Statistics, the translator, thirty-nine clerks, the chief engineer, and some thirty workmen.[24]

The appointment of Frederick Seward, son of the famous statesman, proved a happy one. Thin, of medium height, always wearing a skull-cap to hide the scars he had received in 1865, he had followed his father in a diplomatic career. Already he had served eight years as first assistant and welcomed the renewed tenure which Evarts offered him. But his health failed and in the fall of 1879 he was forced to resign. John Hay at first declined the vacancy, for, only thirty-eight and possessing an independent income, he hesitated to accept the responsibility; but Whitelaw Reid induced him to accept. Ill health dogged him from the beginning, and with difficulty Evarts induced him to finish the term. Both Seward and Hay proved valuable and were often left "sitting on the lid" during the Secretary's absence.

William Hunter, the second assistant secretary, became one of the most famous civil servants of our history. Entering the State Department in 1829 under Jackson as a clerk, he showed such diligence that by a special act of Congress he was elevated to the second assistantship in 1866. Having served a dozen secretaries of state, he was familiar with all details of departmental work; in addition, he was faithful, industrious, a great linguist, and noted for his prodigious memory.[25]

The diplomatic and consular service unquestionably needed reform when Evarts entered office. Congress had discussed the question of changes for years without action. Appointments to both services were largely made for political or personal reward. The consular service was inefficient, with small-calibered men holding their posts as sinecures, while the spoils system had fixed itself like a leech upon the foreign service.

Hayes insisted that reform must be "thorough, radical, and complete" in all of the departments. At the first meeting of the Cabinet, Schurz and Evarts were asked to formulate rules to govern subordinate appointments. But reform was difficult in the face of divided party opinion on the subject, and many of Hayes's friends were sceptical. Thurlow Weed confided to Evarts that Hayes would find a wide difference between theoretical and practical reform. Hamilton Fish exclaimed: "Civil Service reform! Bosh! We shall see what we shall see. . . . It is a showy horse to trot out but a hard one to keep in the harness." Knowing that its success depended largely upon public support, Evarts exhorted at a New England Society dinner, "It is for you to say . . . whether or no the paths of our public life shall be clean."[26]

Schurz was a more ardent reformer than Evarts; indeed, he was the most uncompromising leader of reform. He formulated, with Evarts' approval, a set of Civil Service regulations based on merit and efficiency. Each Cabinet officer was made responsible for applying these regulations to his own department, and Schurz set the example in the Department of Interior.[27]

"It seems to me very desirable," said Evarts, "that whoever is appointed, should take the office with a full recognition of the earnestness of the Government in its views of the Civil Service and with a sincere purpose to carry them out." But in applying reform to his own department, he encountered difficulties. He had to take account of political considerations, appeals from friends, and long-established custom. Evarts soon confessed perplexity. Speaking of reform at Cooper Union in 1878, he said: "All parties will profess it. All citizens will desire it, and in the perfection of abstract contrivances each will vie with the other; but, alas! the rub comes when you seek to apply it to any actual named occupant of an office."[28]

He did not hesitate to recommend a relative or friend for office if worthy of it. For example, he endorsed his cousin, Jeremiah Evarts, for a position in the customhouse at Chicago and appointed his son, Prescott, to succeed Charles H. Russell as his private secretary. Such appointments were above criticism; but some other men were named of whom he had little knowledge. Notwithstanding his announcement that no appointments would be made in his department until the troops had been withdrawn from the South, his office was crowded during the first month. For every first-class mission, he had at least ten applicants, and the disproportion was even greater for lower-grade positions. By the end of the first week in July more than seven thousand applications had been filed for consulships—with but one vacancy; whereupon Evarts announced that he intended to fill all desirable consulships by promotion or on a merit basis. Within a year fifty-four promotions had been made.[29]

Some applications had their humorous side. Evarts was amused and pleased when an aspirant from a remote town in the Northwest wrote frankly, "I have no excuse to offer for intruding upon your leisure or consuming the public time except a pardonable desire to live elsewhere." Wearied by the pressure for consulships, Evarts proposed one day to carve on his office door; "Come ye disconsulate," and on the other side Dante's line from the description of Hell, "Abandon hope, all ye who enter here."[30]

Evarts satisfied neither reformers nor spoilsmen. Vice-President

Wheeler asserted that he showed a lack of frankness toward office seekers, allowing them to cherish vain hopes when he should have given a positive refusal. The Edgerton episode was a case in point. Lycurgas Edgerton asked Evarts to appoint a certain Neil to a consulship. Evarts allowed himself to be drawn into a prolonged correspondence during the summer of 1878 with the persistent Edgerton, who even had the presumption to appeal over Evarts' head to the President. "Whether Mr. E. will ever stop writing, no man can tell," Evarts grumbled to Hayes, adding that no more attention should be paid to him. But Evarts' replies to Edgerton's uninvited letters encouraged the man to still greater explosions, including an accusation that Evarts was using his letters to defame his character. All patience exhausted, Evarts finally broke off the correspondence.[31]

A strong element of humor entered into Evarts' treatment of office seekers. When a popular young author came to seek a consulship, Evarts congratulated him on his reputation, but added: "Although you have laurels on your brows, I suppose you cannot browse on your laurels." Again, a consul in the tropics wrote that he suffered from the climate and desired a transfer; whereupon Evarts sent him to northern Sweden, where he suffered still more from the cold till Evarts relented and gave him a post elsewhere. Somewhat mordant was his rebuff to a German named De Ahua, who was obsessed with the notion that the State Department owed him a living. Eluding the watchman one day, he got into Evarts' office and pleaded for a job, arguing that he had come to America to fight for the country and must support his family. Evarts replied that the government could not take care of him. Then, said De Ahua, there was nothing left but to starve to death; to which Evarts genially retorted, "It is not necessary that you should live."[32]

Evarts was sincere in his efforts to improve the service. He sought repeatedly, but in vain, for an increase in the salaries in the diplomatic service. Ministers were not able to live on their pay in a style suited to their positions. The highest salary paid an American minister abroad was $17,500, whereas Sir Edward Thorton,

British minister in Washington, received £6000. In his trips abroad Evarts had observed the bad effects of the niggardly appropriations for the foreign service—the inadequate upkeep of foreign legations and the virtual reservation of the higher positions in a most undemocratic way, to men of wealth. But he was unable to induce Congress to make more generous appropriations.[33]

He wished to make the diplomatic service a career. He did promote a few ministers to higher posts, something quite unusual. But his ideal of a career service was not to be realized for decades. When he offered Richard Henry Dana, 3rd, an important post as secretary of legation, the young man was tempted to abandon his law career, but finally decided otherwise and wrote Evarts: "Could the civil service reform be assured for a longer term than four years and were diplomacy a career in this country, I should not hesitate to accept so high a start in so honorable a cause, but as it is, am I not right in saying that the position leads to nothing?"[34]

Evarts was well qualified for the position of Secretary of State and discharged the duties of the office with constant dignity and occasional brilliancy. He showed that sanity of judgment and serene outlook on affairs which had always characterized him. A skilled diplomatist by nature, he moved familiarly among men of ability, matching his wits with theirs, conscious of his power, but never making a display of it. In the petty intrigues of diplomacy he was not expert, but he could hold his own in the discussion of great international questions. His state papers and diplomatic notes were unsurpassed in draftsmanship. "The grave and dignified expressions used by him in every public document," declared the editor of a British law journal, "have sometimes incurred the ridicule of the American public, who—were they in England—would look for humor in a Royal proclamation; but we, in England, feel more inclined to say that Mr. Evarts' style was 'caviare to the general.'"[35]

In diplomacy he was cautious. As Senator Hoar declared, "Mr. Evarts was a man of equanimity and good nature, never thrown off his balance by any exigency in diplomacy, in political affairs, or in his trial of causes. Any person who has the occasion to follow him in his diplomatic discussions will be impressed with the far-sighted wisdom and caution with which he took his positions. . . . He was careful never, for the sake of present success, to commit the country to any doctrine which might be inconvenient in the remote future."[36]

Office routine, however, bored him and he left details to subordinates. In contrast to Hamilton Fish, who tried to read every paper that passed through his office, who thought no hour too late for work, and who demanded unremitting obedience and industry, Evarts could not be called an efficient executive. He took a large view of his responsibilities and neglected details in his preoccupation with general policies. He was often charged with procrastination. Schurz once declared impatiently that it was difficult to get him to report on any matter referred to him. When Hayes one day chided him for his slowness, Evarts replied, "You don't sufficiently realize the great truth that almost any question will settle itself if you only leave it alone long enough."[37] The fact is that Evarts was dilatory in replying to official correspondence, and too much inclined to protracted interviews and discussions. In his fondness for conversation he might forget the more drab duty of precise instructions to agents abroad. He once told Andrew D. White with a twinkle in his eye, "There are just two rules at the State Department: one that no business is ever done out of business hours; and the other is, that no business is ever done *in* business hours."[38]

Hamilton Fish and Bancroft Davis criticized Evarts sharply. Fish's criticisms sprang partly from what he heard of a lack of discipline in the Department, partly from his resentment of the general tendency of the Hayes administration to disparage the Grant administration, and partly from a feeling that Hayes and Evarts never sufficiently recognized the constructive accomplishments under Grant.[39] Davis was irked by Evarts' refusal to promote his son, who was in the diplomatic service.[40] But certainly Evarts did not deserve Fish's very acid comment at the close of his term: "I congratulate the country for its safety. . . . It feels now that there will be experience and discretion—a knowledge of the proprieties of diplomatic intercourse and correspondence, which it feared were not among the many, very strong, and excellent qualities of the Head of the Department."[41]

Evarts was also much criticized for continuing to practice law after taking office. Several important cases had been pending when he was appointed, particularly the Rapid Transit cases, and he felt that he owed it to his clients to finish them. The press immediately pounced upon him, ignoring the fact that the expenses of the Secretary of State are greater than for other Cabinet officers. Fish, a man of wealth, had probably spent fifty thousand dollars a year in excess of his stipend. Once more Fish was critical, writing Davis that Evarts had scarcely been in office a month to master his duties, yet had found time to go to New York to plead cases. Evarts soon allayed this criticism. It was only during the first few months of office that he argued frequently in the courts. During the last three years he did not appear more than five or six times, and in 1879 he even resigned as president of the Bar Association, feeling unable to discharge the duties of the place.[42]

To say that Evarts lacked the efficiency of his predecessor, to admit that he was dilatory in correspondence and at times negligent of routine, to concede that he should never have appeared in the courts at all—is not to say that he did not administer his duties with fair success. Most of the great diplomatic questions had been settled by Seward or Fish; Evarts wisely refused to give undue emphasis to new ones. By his moderation and sagacity he may have rendered a greater service than by attempting those brilliant strokes of diplomacy which the Senate and public opinion seemed to expect. He sought the ways of conservatism and conciliation without bluster or aggressiveness. It was of great advantage to him that he knew Europe and its problems. He once said, "Men who have not travelled and become familiar with the men and management of public affairs in other countries can never be adequate to the conduct of international relations. They are constantly dealing with *facts* in their knowledge of their own country, and with *illusions,* drawn from their imaginations, as to the foreign nation."[43]

If he had a philosophy of diplomacy, he never better expressed it than at a dinner at Delmonico's two years after he left office. "Saying common things and doing common things make up human life," he remarked, "and being able to say them and do them with propriety, with ease, with elegance, with justice, makes the difference in private life between good manners and bad; and makes the difference between governments, and their subjects or citizens, of oppression or of confidence and allegiance; makes in diplomacy the difference between a bad foreign secretary, a bad foreign minister, a bad foreign consul, and a good one. . . . And it is better by far that the friction of common life and of public life should be lubricated by this oil and cheered with this wine, than that it should be embittered and soured even when the substance and sense are all meant to be right."[44]

23

Defending the Rio Grande

"THE FIRST DUTY of a Government is to protect life and property. . . . The Government of the United States has determined to perform it to the extent of its power. . . . It is not solicitous about the methods or ways in which the protection shall be accomplished, whether by formal treaty stipulation or by informal convention; whether by action of judicial tribunals or that of military force. Protection in fact of American lives and property is the sole point upon which the United States is tenacious."[1] These words, directed at the Mexican government, gave the clue to Evarts' Mexican policy. For three years the Secretary waged a difficult but vigorous diplomatic contest with a shrewd and determined Mexican government. Difficulties with our neighbor to the South proved one of his most vexatious problems, and at times brought the two countries to the verge of war.

The background of the dispute can be stated briefly. After the Civil War Mexico was peaceable and grateful to the United States for helping to oust the French; Juarez and Lerdo ruled well, although they were unable to prevent border raids of bandits and cattle thieves along the Rio Grande. But Lerdo precipitated a revolt by refusing to give up the presidency at the end of his term and was driven from power in November, 1876, by the popular Porfirio Diaz, who was overwhelmingly elected president the following January. No other man in Mexico had so much prestige, so strong a popular support in all quarters of the Republic, and so much capacity to administer. All who were tired of anarchy turned to him.[2]

Hamilton Fish had dealt cautiously with Diaz during the closing months of his office. Diaz showed his good faith by paying the first installment upon debts due the United States. But difficulties soon grew up: raids of bandits and Indians across the border; smuggling in the so-called Free Zone south of the Rio Grande; and other border complications. Diaz was too much occupied in cementing his own position to heed these border troubles. He expected the Grant administration to recognize him, as was customary when a *de facto* government proved its ability to maintain itself; and apparently recognition was about to be given when Fish left office.[3]

But Evarts refused recognition. He decided to wait until Diaz gave fuller assurance that he would meet his international obligations. He preferred to watch events and see what action the Mexican Congress would take at its forthcoming session. He wanted to be sure Diaz could maintain a stable administration.[4]

On March 9 Lieutenant Colonel Shafter, who was in command on the border, reported new raids and recommended pursuit of the marauders across the Rio Grande. Not the slightest attempt, he reported, was being made by the Mexican government to stop the depredations; on the contrary, the bandits found refuge in Mexican towns and a market for their stolen goods. The only thing to do, he declared, was to attack them in their lairs. The sending of American troops across the frontier to punish robbers and recover stolen property was not a new proposal. Fish had sought permission to do this from President Juarez in 1870 and had warned Mexico that troops might be sent without permission, but had never taken action.[5]

Evarts decided it was time to act. He instructed John W. Foster, the able minister to Mexico, to drop a hint to the Mexican government; and Foster, in a frank conversation with Vallarta, the Mexican foreign minister, suggested that Diaz send troops under a tactful and responsible officer to coöperate with American troops in maintaining order on the border. Vallarta called the plan excellent, but protested that Diaz could not spare sufficient troops for such a purpose. Moreover, he insisted that the United States should first recognize the Diaz regime. Thus Evarts' first attempt to obtain Mexican acquiescence in the "doctrine of hot pursuit" failed. Further border raids in April led General Sheridan to recommend pursuit without consent if necessary.[6]

By its refusal to recognize Diaz, the Hayes administration laid itself open to the charge of seeking war. Not only Mexicans but political enemies at home were quick to charge Hayes and Evarts with desiring a conflict. While nothing could be further from their purpose, there actually was an element in the United States that would have welcomed war: speculating contractors, unemployed drifters, men who wanted adventure, and lawless and reckless people generally. Foster was greatly alarmed, for he had become convinced that these jingoists were seeking to divert attention from home problems by trying to add another slice of territory to American soil. Thus Evarts found his policy distorted into a bid for war and a support of American investments in Mexico.[7]

Foster, who knew Mexico well, feared that Evarts was on the wrong track in antagonizing Diaz, and suggested tactfully that much might be gained by granting recognition. After explaining the difficulty of his own unofficial position, he added: "I regard General Diaz as the only hope of the country. . . . Lerdo's restoration to power would only be the signal for outbreaks in all directions. . . . Should the President and you think it opportune to make a formal recognition of Diaz . . . I probably would be able to bring about an earlier settlement than otherwise."[8]

But Evarts was not ready to concede recognition. On the contrary, he was losing patience with Diaz and beginning to doubt his sincerity. While admitting that it was customary to recognize the regularly inaugurated President without too close a scrutiny of the methods by which he had gained power, he believed, as did Woodrow Wilson later, in a watchful waiting policy until assured that the election of Diaz was approved by the Mexican people and that his administration would meet its obligations to the United States.

On May 16, following new border outrages, Evarts wrote Foster in grim terms, "There have been raids and depredations upon the Texas frontier; theft, murder, arson, and plunder; violation of post-offices and custom-houses, incursions by armed men to destroy life and property; cattle-stealing has become a profitable occupation; military officials posted to protect the frontier are said to have protected the robbers; forced loans have been demanded, and American citizens have been compelled to submit to unjust and unequal exactions. . . . For each and all of these acts, many of them committed, if not with the sanction, at least in the name of the Mexican Government, not one single man, so far as is known to this government, has been punished. . . . It is natural that Mexican statesmen should urge upon you the argument that the restoration of official relations . . . would open the way toward such an adjustment. But it is natural, on the other hand, that the Government of the United States should be disposed to believe that some guarantee of such an arrangement should be made the condition precedent to any recognition, rather than to trust to the possibility that it may ultimately follow."[9]

On the same day, Evarts talked with Generals Sherman and Ord, and all three agreed that the raiders should be pursued beyond the Rio Grande. By coincidence, Vallarta now notified Evarts that Diaz would send troops to the border to coöperate in suppressing marauders; but this dispatch did not arrive in time to prevent a new drastic step.[10] Backed by the press and public opinion, Hayes issued his famous order of June 1 to General Ord, instructing him to pursue marauders across the border, punish them, and recapture stolen property. On learning that Diaz was sending troops to coöperate, Evarts interpreted Hayes's order to mean that if Mexican troops were present and prepared to intercept the marauders, Ord was to leave that duty to them. Thus "hot pursuit" became the policy, but it was to be used with discretion. It could be justified on the ground that, as Evarts' report to Congress in 1878 showed, its object was the friendly and mutual protection of both countries from border raids.[11]

Some critics compared the new policy to Grant's imperialist designs in Santo Domingo; others tried to show that it was without precedent. But a precedent had been created in 1860, when the War Department ordered Robert E. Lee, then commanding in Texas, to pursue bandits across the border if necessary. At that time Mexico had acquiesced, but the Civil War had postponed action.[12]

The new policy really needed no apology, for it was a vigorous course which the government should have adopted long before when border raids first began. The United States had always taken an attitude of forbearance toward Mexico on the theory that the republic was weak; but if Mexico could not punish her own bandits, it was time that the United States acted. The use of a few troops for pursuing marauders along a sixteen-hundred mile frontier could scarcely be interpreted as showing an American desire for conquest. Evarts hoped that Diaz would understand and coöperate.

But Diaz faced difficulties. Scarcely had the new order been issued when Diaz had to quell a Lerdist rebellion headed by General Escobedo. A band of Lerdists was driven across the river into Texas, eliciting another protest from the United States. Diaz knew that if he yielded to Hayes he would be discredited in the eyes of his countrymen and the old anarchy would start boiling again; if he got into war, Mexico would suffer. He decided upon a course which would satisfy his countrymen, yet to some extent comply with American demands. On the one hand, he strengthened his own position by encouraging the popular clamor against the United States, taking the opportunity to unite all factions against the United States. Vallarta declared that Mexicans were being treated like "Kaffirs of Africa" and that the sovereign rights of Mexico were being ignored. On the other hand, Diaz sent General Treviño to the frontier with a competent body of troops to punish marauders and coöperate with Ord. Treviño seems to have been instructed not to be officious or to hinder Ord; yet, if American troops crossed the border, to "repel force with force."[13]

War hysteria rose high in Mexico, where Foster reported that the government was convinced that Hayes was seeking war and territory. One Mexican newspaper charged that Hayes was trying to divert attention from his irregular election; another declared that American filibusters and speculators were intriguing to restore Lerdo. To allay misunderstanding, Evarts sent a long memorandum which he hoped Vallarta would consent to publish. It contained five points: first, that the instruction to General Ord was not a new measure; second, that the border depredations were not committed by Americans; third, that Mexico had done nothing to prevent them; fourth, that Mexico had frequently admitted its inability to perform its duty on the frontier; and fifth, that the instructions to Ord were misinterpreted by the Mexican government. But Diaz refused to make Evarts' statement public.[14]

Foster was embarrassed by the arrival of certain Americans with or without credentials from Evarts. Simon Stevens claimed he was Evarts' confidential agent and presented a card bearing Evarts' signature, declaring that he had seen all of Foster's dispatches at the State Department and knew the cipher used by it. Foster suspected that his real errand was to secure a railroad project, and refused to introduce him to Diaz. To Foster's relief a note came from Evarts instructing him not to rely upon the oral statement of such travellers and adventurers. But Señor Vallejo and his son-in-law, General John B. Frisbee, arrived as observers armed with proper credentials from Evarts. Frisbee had been a client in one of Evarts' important California land cases and apparently misled Evarts as to the purpose of his visit to Mexico. But the New York *Herald* exposed his plan to secure railroad concessions across northern Mexico for the Southern Pacific Railroad.[15] Such intrigues increased Mexican hostility and irritated both Evarts and Foster.

Political enemies, particularly in Congress, likewise embarrassed Evarts. Defending his position against these critics, Evarts declared: "Politicians may endeavor for their own purposes to make a handle out of the Mexican policy, but the facts are against them. There has been no invasion of Mexican soil by our troops, but Mexican soldiers have crossed to our soil and fought a skirmish, in which several men were killed." When Blaine accused Hayes in the Senate of seeking to divert attention from domestic problems, Evarts denied this and added that he was in the habit of telling the truth—a reply which carried a sting.[16]

In August a band of Mexicans made a raid into Starr County, Texas. American forces drove them back across the Rio Grande and arrested some of them. Diaz did not appear concerned. Indeed, his position had recently been much strengthened by recognition from Germany, Italy, and Spain, and he used the opportunity to increase the pressure for recognition of his government from the United States.[17]

Evarts began to shift his ground. He instructed Foster to ascertain exactly what terms Mexico would give in return for recognition, but made it clear that any agreement "must deal explicitly and clearly with the question of the use of military force to pursue offenders and recapture stolen property." Believing that Washington was yielding, Vallarta declined to settle any of the pending questions, and was most positive in his refusal to make a treaty for the reciprocal crossing of the border. In September Foster reported that he could make no headway except for a vague promise that the question of pursuit might eventually be arranged. Vallarta was playing a clever game and outmanoeuvring Evarts. He knew that he had much to gain and little to lose by refusing concessions to the United States. Foster, still feeling that Evarts misunderstood the situation, asked permission to come to Washington and explain it, but the Secretary told him to remain at his post.[18]

Evarts was undoubtedly ready to grant recognition in return for a treaty on reciprocal crossing, but he believed Diaz was not yet strong enough to protect the border and that his government was leading a "hand-to-mouth existence" because of financial weakness. Troubles on the border continued. In October an American force crossed the river in pursuit of marauding Indians but, on the approach of Mexican troops, retired.[19]

Congress decided to take a hand. While censuring the "temporizing" policy of Hamilton Fish, it was suspicious of Evarts' policy, and both houses decided to investigate. The House Committee on Military Affairs began to take testimony, while Conkling urged a Senate committee to follow the scent, hoping it would lead to Evarts' discomfiture. The House Committee on Foreign Affairs also spent months upon the problem. Evarts, appearing before it, denied that the administration was seeking war or territory; but he admitted that recognition might have to be given before all questions in dispute could be settled. He argued for a closer understanding between Congress and the President, reminding the committee that it could not know all the facts. Justifying this policy, he said, "If I were to express an opinion as to the effect of nonrecognition thus far upon the Mexican administration at home, it would be this, that it has already given more hope of stability to Diaz than if recognition had been made, and produced more actual and serious efforts on the part of Mexico to . . . discharge its duties to this country on the frontier."[20]

The year 1877 closed without further change. Hayes said in his annual message that he desired cordial relations with Mexico, but could not overlook the actual occurrences on the border or his duty to protect American lives and property. At the same time, Evarts, speaking at the New England Society dinner, declared emphatically, "Nobody that is powerful desires to quarrel with it [United States], and nobody that is powerless is it possible for us to quarrel with."[21]

In January, 1878, Foster was called to Washington to testify before the House committee. He declared boldly that Diaz was hoping for a split between the President and Congress and insisted, as Evarts had done, that close coöperation between the two branches of government would do much to strengthen the American position. He also urged recognition, arguing that Diaz had done more than any predecessor to preserve order; that continued troubles on the border were due more to his inability than his neglect; and that he had given a "very respectable administration." Foster unquestionably influenced Evarts in the direction of recognition. Although Evarts at first seemed indisposed to talk with the minister, he was impressed when Foster asserted that American policy was tending to unite Mexico, that Arizona Indians were causing as much trouble on the border as Mexican bandits, and that the rescinding of the instructions to Ord would be a wise step.[22]

In March, after Diaz had captured Escobedo, Evarts decided to change his policy. He sent Foster back to Mexico with instructions to grant recognition, and at the same time to make every effort to secure a settlement of disputed questions. It was not pressure from Congress that brought about this change because the House committee did not report till after recognition was granted on April 9.[23] Foster was given a cordial reception in Mexico, and found his position much more satisfactory. To Washington came a Mexican minister, Zamacona, whom Evarts regarded as a "very plausible smooth talker." All seemed to be going well and the Secretary wrote Whitelaw Reid optimistically, "There is no danger of war with Mexico or other grave event in our foreign relations, or I should have no time or heart for the minor affairs of life."[24]

But his troubles were not yet over. Diaz had wrung from him an important concession, and proposed to get another—the rescinding of the instructions to Ord. He did not want American troops on Mexican soil under any circumstances. Accordingly, when Foster again sought a settlement of the pending questions, the Ord instructions were waved in his face as a reason for refusal. Diaz was playing a shrewd game, asking much and giving nothing in return. It did seem possible, however, that the privilege of reciprocal crossing might be given if the instruction to Ord was rescinded.[25]

During the summer conditions became chaotic again along the border, which American troops repeatedly crossed in pursuit of bandits. Outwardly Evarts tried to appear calm, replying to a reporter who questioned him on the Mexican situation, "What is the use of boiling with indignation in mid-summer, with the thermometer disputing possession with the nineties?" But inwardly he was becoming impatient. Foster was having a hard time in Mexico again and wrote in disgust: "I have been met by delays, postponements, denials of justice, or absolute rejection of the just demands of my government, and up to the present date I have not been able to obtain a satisfactory settlement of a single one of these questions." His position became unbearable when the anti-American spirit reached its climax on September 15. At a Mexican anniversary celebration, held in a large theater, he was forced to listen to the reading of a fiercely anti-American poem which roused the audience to frenzy. Foster was convinced that war was near and wrote Evarts that the time had come for "plain language and vigorous measures."[26]

Diaz was evidently depending upon the support of American commercial interests to forestall war and develop trade with Mexico. Mexican agents, including Zamacona himself, were painting alluring visions of trade with Mexico, while in Mexico City a delegation of Chicago business men criticized Evarts' hostility to the republic.[27]

By the close of 1878 the pressure on Evarts to make further concessions was redoubled in many quarters. Foster was getting nowhere; new sources of dispute were appearing; Mexico was disclaiming responsibility for all crimes on the border: Americans were being forbidden to settle on the island of Ciare in the Gulf of California; increasing discriminations against Americans in Mexico were reported, for they were forbidden to hold real estate, subjected to forced loans and military service, and expelled without explanation. Evarts protested against these abuses in vain.[28]

The spring and summer of 1879 saw little improvement in the situation. To be sure, Zamacona, whose family was popular in Washington society, gave Evarts a reception in February which was one of the greatest social events of the season, but this meant little. Evarts' correspondence with the Mexican government was stiff and uncompromising. When Nuñez, the new minister to Washington, accused him of taking isolated cases as a gauge of Mexico's failure to punish border marauders, Evarts replied caustically that if cases of prompt punishment were as numerous as isolated cases of neglect, the selection of the latter would not have been made.[29]

But actually the worst was over by 1880. A new insurrection of the Lerdists at Vera Cruz was crushed by Diaz and marked the end of the internal disorders. The Mexican government became more prompt in repressing border troubles, and the number of raids decreased. Foster reported that popular hostility was dwindling and commercial relations with the United States improving. He believed that Diaz was sincere in his friendship now that his own position was well established. Evarts welcomed the change, as did also the President. There is no truth in the statement of H. H. Bancroft that Foster would have fomented hostilities, and that even Hayes was not averse to such a course.[30]

General Grant, who was touring the world, reached Mexico at an opportune time and was cordially received; and in March Foster and Grant returned home together. When Foster asked for a transfer to a European post, Evarts felt he was "well entitled" to it, promoting him to the post of minister to Russia. The two had not always seen eye to eye, but their personal relations had been cordial. Evarts fully appreciated the value of such an able representative in Mexico under such trying circumstances.[31]

Hayes and Evarts now decided to withdraw the Ord instruction. This was another concession to Mexico in return for good deportment, which it took courage to make. Many were ready to denounce it as an act of weakness. During the two and a half years the order had been in operation, there had been some ten to fifteen punitive expeditions into Mexico; yet no military clash between Americans and Mexican troops had occurred.[32] During the summer of 1880 Diaz offered to negotiate an agreement for the reciprocal crossing of the frontier, for a rising of Apache Indians made this desirable. Evarts appeared on the point of gaining his objective; but the Mexican Senate refused to ratify such an agreement for more than three months—a reservation which was not acceptable to Evarts. Such was the situation when he left office. It was not till 1882, when Diaz was temporarily out of office, that such a treaty was made for a short term, subject to renewal.[33]

During his last year in office Evarts had to deal with other Mexican problems, though none as serious as the border raids. Under a convention of 1868 a claims commission had been set up and had considered more than a thousand claims of the citizens of the two countries. Of the total awards decided in favor of Americans nearly a third related to the La Arbra and Weil claims. Benjamin Weil was awarded $480,000 for the seizure of his cotton by Mexican soldiers in 1864, and the La Arbra Mining Company $672,000 for the confiscation of its mine. The peculiar feature of the Weil case was that the commission was willing to entertain a claim for losses incurred in a prohibited transaction—the export of cotton from the Confederacy. The Mexican government approved the findings of the commission but claimed the right at some future time to show that both claims were fraudulent and based on affidavits of perjured witnesses.

Evarts at first believed the claims lawful and urged Congress to empower him to distribute the award to the claimants. But when the Mexican government produced new evidence to show the claims were fraudulent, he asked William H. Trescott, a most accomplished diplomat, to investigate and report. Trescott advised a reexamination of the claims, but Congress decided that the matter was closed and Mexico was unable to get a case before the American courts. Evarts then began a disbursement of the money as installments reached him from Mexico. He reported to Hayes that no proof of fraud could be found, and that a reopening of the case would reflect upon the commission. Charges of fraud continued after Evarts left office and finally, in 1900, the Court of Claims held that both claims had been obtained by fraud and a large sum was repaid to Mexico. Evarts was in no way liable for this result. He did not suspect fraud and approved only what appeared to be a fair award.[34]

Altogether, Evarts encountered a difficult problem in Mexico and was really defeated in his contest with Diaz. The "iron man" of Mexico refused to be persuaded or coerced into making agreements upon any of the points at issue. Evarts was forced to reverse his policy and to grant important concessions. But he could later find some comfort in the fact that the Garfield and Arthur administrations did little better.[35] And he could reflect, too, that he had succeeded fairly well in his main purpose: the ultimate protection of American life and property on the border. Mexico was shown for the first time that this was no longer a matter of indifference to the United States. His insistence upon the right of pursuit set a definite precedent, and when, fifty years later, President Wilson found it necessary to send out punitive expeditions under General Pershing, Evarts' very words were used by the President to set forth American policy.

24

War Clouds in Latin America

WHILE HIS anxieties over the Mexican problem were diminishing, Evarts was compelled to pay increasing attention to Isthmian affairs. He was confronted with the alternative of approving or opposing the construction of a canal at Panama under French auspices. Although plans for a waterway had long been discussed, for the first time a European power now actually took steps to connect the two oceans. Grant had regarded the need for a canal as so urgent that he had been willing, if necessary, to permit some European power to undertake the work. At the close of his term Hamilton Fish carried on unsuccessful negotiations with Nicaragua for a route, but rejected plans for a Panama canal as impractical.[1]

Meanwhile the success of Ferdinand de Lesseps at Suez had roused French interest. At Paris a scientific society, with Lieutenant Wyse as its moving spirit, discussed the possibilities of a canal across Panama. Wyse, after inspecting the route, sought a lease from Colombia; and, fearing the United States might develop a canal in Nicaragua, Colombia gladly granted a concession to him, with the proviso that the United States might share in its advantages. Obtaining a charter for a company from the French government, Wyse then sought the assistance of De Lesseps in securing capital. De Lesseps ingeniously brought the matter before the International Scientific Congress at Paris in 1879, so as to give the project the appearance of an international undertaking; but this was a packed body, consisting mainly of French delegates, and it approved the scheme as expected. In December De Lesseps was at Panama surveying the route, and France was wild with enthusiasm.[2]

To many Americans this seemed an attempt to steal a march on the United States and an encroachment upon the Monroe Doctrine. Did the treaty of 1846 between the United States and Colombia not guarantee the neutrality and free transit of the Isthmus, including the right to build a railroad and protect it? Was a canal under French auspices not inconsistent with this treaty? With rival American companies making surveys for a canal, was not this sudden appearance of the French on the scene most offensive?

If public opinion had been divided on the Mexican question, it was united on this problem. That the United States had a prior interest in any Isthmian canal was the conviction of virtually all Americans. Congress passed resolutions against the French enterprise; a committee of the House began an investigation, and recommended to Evarts the prompt acquisition of naval stations on both coasts of Panama.[3]

President Hayes was more disturbed than Evarts. Every member of the Cabinet agreed that American interests were paramount, and that under the circumstances the nation would not hesitate to assert its rights. Evarts set to work collecting all possible information on the subject.[4] On March 8, 1880, Hayes sent a special message to Congress, which was virtually a report by the State Department written by Evarts, and as such his greatest state paper. Quite in contrast to the hysterical tone of debates in Congress and the rising popular excitement, it was written in temperate vein. Reviewing the historical background, Evarts asserted that the United States had a paramount interest in any Isthmian canal and must exert a "potential control" over such waterway. "No contract could ever be entered into between private projectors and the Government of Colombia except in contemplation of this position. . . . The United States cannot consent to the surrender of this control to any European power. . . . An interoceanic canal . . . will be . . . virtually a part of the coast line of the United States."[5]

The message put an end to a vast amount of loose talk in and out of Congress. Couched in inoffensive language, it outlined a vigorous American policy. Congress approved the stand, and the hearings before the House committee took on a new importance. James B. Eads of St. Louis, who was fathering a project for a canal across the Isthmus of Tehuantepec, appeared before the committee, as did also a group of American capitalists interested in a Nicaraguan route. De Lesseps, shrewd as ever, came to New York to allay distrust and testified to the committee. He tried to convince Hayes that his company was a private affair, not a government project; but Hayes replied that whatever its character, American influence must predominate. The Milwaukee *Sentinel* made the ridiculous charge that Evarts naturally opposed the canal because he had once been counsel for the Panama Railroad. Actually, however, the railroad was promoting De Lesseps' scheme, hoping to sell its stock before impending financial collapse.[6]

France did not protest against the American stand. On the contrary, the French government assured Evarts that it was not backing De Lesseps; for Paris was impressed and wished to avoid trouble. The French minister to Colombia was instructed to refuse his support to the project, and when a French consul at Panama showed excessive cordiality toward De Lesseps, he received an official rebuke. But, on the other hand, the French government rejected Evarts' proposal that France join the United States in a guarantee of the neutrality of the canal. Furthermore, French investors became increasingly interested in Panama. Led on by De Lesseps and a venal Parisian press, they were deluded into the belief that the United States had approved De Lesseps' project, and French capital poured into the coffers of the company.[7]

Evarts meanwhile had difficulties with Colombia. He sent Ernest Dichman to reopen the legation at Bogota, which had been closed for two years, and Dichman advised that the treaty of 1846 be abrogated; but Evarts was not ready to go so far. He would, however, make it clear to Colombia that the treaty meant nothing if a canal could be allowed to pass into the hands of a foreign power. "This government," he declared, "cannot consider itself excluded, by arrangements between other powers or individuals to which it is not a party, from direct interest, and if necessary a positive supervision and interposition in the execution of any project which . . . would materially affect its commercial interests, change the territorial relations of its own sovereignty, and impose upon it the necessity of a foreign policy, which, whether in its feature of warlike preparation or entangling alliance, has been hitherto sedulously avoided. . . . In all language that this Government has ever used, in all the action that it has ever proposed, in reference to an oceanic canal, it has expressed not only its willingness, but its anxiety that such an enterprise should be for the benefit of the world's commerce, and in no proposition that it has ever made has it sought for its citizens or its commerce special advantages."[8]

It was in vain that Evarts sought a new understanding with Colombia. Convinced that he was trying to define the treaty of 1846 to suit himself and to fix the conditions under which it should be enforced, the government at Bogota steadily refused even when Evarts asked permission to establish coaling-stations at Panama. Colombia not only refused but demanded withdrawal of the two American war vessels that were hovering in the vicinity.[9]

Opposition also came from Great Britain, where it was felt that a canal under exclusive American jurisdiction would violate the Clayton-Bulwer Treaty of 1850, which provided for joint control of any Isthmian waterway. Evarts would have welcomed any honorable means of abrogating the treaty. George Williamson, expert on Isthmian affairs, suggested to him that Britain's continued occupation of the Mosquito Coast and Belize gave a good excuse for denouncing it; and Evarts himself hinted to Congress that, inasmuch as the treaty with Colombia had preceded that with Britain, the latter might be considered as not applying to Panama. This was a suggestion which the British government was not slow to attack. The House passed a resolution approving abrogation, but Hayes and Evarts felt the country had enough problems with Great Britain without creating new ones. Evarts did, however, warn London against acquiring naval stations on the Bay or Gonzales Islands, or at other points near the Isthmus.[10]

As time passed, Evarts became increasingly suspicious of De Lesseps. Samuel Ward warned him that the engineer was a swindler trying to play the rôle of the "great matador in the isthmian bull fight." It became evident that De Lesseps was a very shrewd promoter when he conceived the idea of creating an American organization to purchase supplies in the United States for the use of the French company at Panama. Secretary of the Navy Thompson had the bad taste to accept the headship of the organization with a salary of twenty-five thousand dollars, asserting that his influence would help to Americanize the undertaking. Greatly displeased, Hayes instructed Evarts to seek Thompson's resignation from the Cabinet. Evarts then bluntly wrote him: "The President regards your message through me as placing your resignation at his disposal, and decides at once to accept it to relieve you of all embarrassments on the subject." Thompson resigned without ill will. Evarts suggested the appointment of William C. Wickham of New York to the vacancy, but Hayes gave the post to Nathan Goff of West Virginia.[11]

Why should the United States not outwit De Lesseps by building its own canal? This possibility did not escape Evarts. He became interested in the concession which Diaz had given to Eads for his proposed canal across the Isthmus of Tehuantepec; and he also negotiated with Nicaragua and Costa Rica for a canal route, but without result.[12]

Toward the close of his term, when Colombia became more friendly, he asked for a protocol to the treaty of 1846 which would give the United States the right to disapprove of any canal project. But Colombia regarded this as an attempt to reduce her to vassalage in her foreign relations, and the Colombian minister refused even to discuss the proposal. Just as the minister was about to leave Washington, Evarts made a new suggestion that the two countries have the use of any canal at Panama on an equal basis, and that strategic points be fortified and occupied jointly in emergencies, but only by Colombian troops in peace time. The Colombian minister, Vila, accepted the idea, and signed the protocol; but on his return home he was accused of treason, and the agreement was never ratified.[13]

At the time Evarts left office the French company had not begun the construction of the canal, but it appeared that work would soon start. Evarts' last action was to remind Colombia that the treaty of 1846 was still binding, and that the consent of the United States was necessary before any canal was built.[14]

Upon succeeding to the State Department, Blaine followed the same policy of insisting upon a canal under American control; but he went further by seeking a modification of the Clayton-Bulwer Treaty. The dispute with Great Britain and Colombia continued into the administration of Theodore Roosevelt, by which time the French company had failed, and De Lesseps had been proved a swindler. The Clayton-Bulwer Treaty was abrogated by agreement, and Colombia was forced to acquiesce in the building of an American canal across independent Panama.

Hamilton Fish's remark that Evarts left the canal problem in a "mess" was unjust.[15] The Secretary cannot be credited with originating the doctrine of paramount interest in an Isthmian canal, but he asserted it more vigorously than had theretofore been done. He helped to crystallize opinion in favor of the doctrine; and though he did not keep the French out, or secure the modification of the Clayton-Bulwer Treaty, he helped lay the foundation for the accomplishment of these objects.

Opposition to foreign intervention was a fundamental policy of Evarts in all Caribbean relations. Though he did not invoke the Monroe Doctrine in any emphatic way, he made it clear to European powers that they should not seek territory in this area.

He had to be on guard against British encroachments. When the Ministry headed by Disraeli cast covetous eyes on the guano island of Morant Cays, which Evarts held to be American by right of discovery, a long diplomatic correspondence ensued. Again, when Great Britain became more aggressive in the old Venezuelan boundary dispute and Venezuela appealed to the United States, Evarts warned the British government. Still more emphatically, he admonished Great Britain for trying to enlarge its colony of Belize at the expense of Guatemala. "It is believed," he declared, "that this policy [Monroe Doctrine] is sanctioned by the public here, which would submit to sacrifice for its success."[16]

He likewise tried to promote peace between the republics on the Caribbean and various European countries. When difficulties arose between Germany and Nicaragua he proffered mediation and had important documents in the files of the State Department put at the disposal of Nicaragua. Through his good offices he assisted in the restoration of cordial relations between Venezuela and the Netherlands. He sent C. A. Logan as special envoy to offer American support to any plan that would terminate the endless disputes between Central American countries. When a German chargé at Guatemala described this mission as an attempt by the United States to absorb Central America, Evarts demanded and received a prompt disavowal.[17]

In Venezuela the American minister, Thomas Russell, had been dismissed for an unwise remark. Evarts threatened Venezuela and won his point by having Russell restored, but wisely decided to send another minister. When later a revolution broke out in the republic, Evarts refused recognition till order was restored. The chief cause of unrest in Venezuela lay in the debts to foreign nations. Evarts offered a solution whereby an American agent would receive and disburse amounts due to creditors, but after two years of correspondence Venezuela rejected the plan.[18]

More serious was the problem of preserving American neutrality in the waning conflict between Spain and Cuba. On the one side Evarts had to deal with an overabundance of Spanish pride, and on the other with American sympathy for the Cuban rebels. The Spanish government, recalling his speech on the *Virginius* affair in 1873, expected a hostile attitude from him. But he genuinely favored a neutral stand, exchanging many notes with the Spanish minister at Washington, which made this plain. He was fortunate in having at Madrid the genial James Russell Lowell, who was well fitted for his task and popular in Spain. His official dispatches to Evarts showed both political sagacity and a delightful humor. Evarts must have been amused by his unusual epistles, containing witty jests, vivid descriptions of Spanish life, and even poetry.[19]

One difficulty with Spain lay in the vexatious interference by Spanish officials with trade between Cuba and the United States. Fines, penalties, and technicalities became so exasperating that Evarts warned Madrid they were becoming "well-nigh unbearable" to American shippers.[20] Another irritation arose from the acquisition of American citizenship by Cubans who returned to Cuba to use this status as a cloak to escape penalties visited by Spain upon insurgents. Evarts had a long correspondence with the Spanish minister over the test case of Dominguez. He conceded that when fraud was involved in naturalization, the Mixed Commission, created in 1871 to adjust claims, could go behind the naturalization papers to inquire how they had been obtained; but the State Department, he asserted, would not invalidate a certificate of naturalization.[21]

The main problem, however, centered in neutral rights and duties. Evarts secured the payment of a ten-thousand-dollar indemnity for the seizure by the Spanish navy of three American whaling vessels on the suspicion of carrying supplies to the insurgents.[22] Although the Spanish government complained at times, Evarts was vigilant in the observance of neutrality, promptly investigating all alleged breaches. For example, in the case of the *Estelle,* built at Fall River supposedly for the insurgents, he detained the vessel till sure of her legitimate character.[23] Although the war ended in 1878 with the defeat of the Cubans, banditry and disorders continued in the Island till 1880, and required the continued vigilance of Evarts to prevent hasty action by American sympathizers with Cuba.[24]

There were those who regarded Evarts' attitude toward Spain as unduly patient and long-suffering. "Less *mental* and *more physical* force would accomplish more," wrote one impatient critic. "I would in the interest of the whole American people plant the American flag permanently upon the island of Cuba and remove the cause. . . . Such a course would not only thrill the American heart with pride, but would be a fair Evarts' notice to all other nations that we cannot always submit to having our citizens' rights imposed upon."[25] But it was precisely such blustering that Evarts always avoided. He preferred the path of conciliation and "appeasement." He did not believe that a Spanish-American War was inevitable, and he realized that Spain had the sympathy of both continental Europe and Great Britain, which was not true in 1898.

In trying to play the rôle of pacificator in the War of the Pacific, Evarts ran afoul a problem which, despite his good intentions, weakened his prestige as a diplomat. This war, between Chile on the one side and Peru and Bolivia on the other, lasted from 1879 to 1883, giving great anxiety to three administrations in Washington.

By a treaty of 1866 Bolivia ceded to Chile territory south of the twenty-fourth parallel with the understanding that both countries were to have equal rights to the guano beds and minerals between the twenty-third and twenty-fifth parallels. The Chileans proceeded to make fortunes from the nitrate beds. Differences arose over the treaty, but in 1874 the twenty-fourth parallel was established as a permanent boundary. Meanwhile, Peru secretly allied herself with Bolivia. In 1877 Bolivia levied an illegal tax upon nitrates exported by the Chilean Nitrate Company of Antofagasta; and when the company protested, Bolivia seized its property. Chilean troops occupied Antofagasta and the War of the Pacific began on February 14, 1879. Peru speedily joined her ally Bolivia. From the outset Chile held the upper hand. With a population much smaller than that of her combined enemies, she used her much larger navy and better-trained army with great success.

Once more it became Evarts' task to defend American neutrality. When Chile blockaded the coastal towns of Peru, raising the question of the rights of neutral citizens in a blockaded port, he gave notice that American lives must be protected during bombardments; but when a Chilean fleet under a flag of truce was fired upon by Peruvians and the fleet returned the fire, he conceded that Americans could make no claim for loss. He insisted that a blockade must be real and that American ships could enter a port not fully blockaded. He admitted the right of Peru to search suspected vessels, but warned the belligerents against the seizure of neutral vessels.[26]

When Chile proposed to destroy all Peruvian ports, Evarts declared that Chile would be "held to a strict measure of accountability"—the very words used by Woodrow Wilson in the *Lusitania* note of 1915. When, in the desperation of defeat, Peru set adrift boats containing explosives on the chance that they might destroy Chilean ships, Evarts protested against this dangerous mode of warfare. And when Bolivia, lacking ports of her own, sought to fit out privateers in American waters, Evarts promptly objected.[27] Throughout the conflict he displayed vigilance and legal acumen in upholding neutral rights.

But his efforts to mediate between the belligerents brought him little but criticism. The text "Blessed are the peacemakers" did not seem to apply to him. Perhaps if he had accepted the proposal that he join Great Britain and Germany in mediation the result might have been different; but he disliked any European influence in South America.[28] The settlement of a war of this sort, leaving intense hatreds behind it, required unusually delicate diplomacy. Evarts decided to make the attempt. Much depended on the character and ability of the three American ministers to Chile, Peru, and Bolivia—Osborn, Christiancy, and Pettis. Unfortunately they were not only small men, but were jealous of each other's progress, quarreling openly, and dooming mediation before it started.[29]

In the early summer of 1879 Horace N. Fisher, Chilean consul at Boston, arrived at the scene of war, claiming to hold a commission from Evarts, and began unauthorized discussions of peace. Pettis visited each of the belligerent governments and tried in a blundering way to obtain a promise of arbitration. When he failed,

Evarts neither approved nor disapproved his attempt. Pettis blamed Fisher for his failure, but Christiancy laid the blame at Pettis' door. The result served only to exasperate the three belligerent governments and make them less inclined to accept mediation.[30]

By the summer of 1880 Chile had gained the upper hand, controlling all the disputed territory and much of southern Peru. The gross vandalism displayed by the Chileans in the occupation of Lima, their wanton destruction of buildings and civilian property, the carrying away of priceless records and books, roused such deep resentment in Peru that there was little likelihood that the Peruvians would consent to any peace based on territorial cession. They looked to Evarts, who was known to oppose territorial cession as a condition of peace, for support.

The Secretary decided that the time had come for mediation. He believed that victors and vanquished would both welcome it. Pettis wrote him that all three belligerents "at heart would thank anybody to tell them how, or even point them to the way."[31] Again Evarts trusted the three ministers to make all the preparations for a peace conference. But by the time the conferees met on the American man-of-war *Lackawanna* in the Bay of Arica on October 22, 1880, the Chileans had gained such a sweeping success that they were in a position to demand all of the disputed province of Tarapacá, much Bolivian territory, the dismantling of Peruvian forts at Arica, and the payment of an indemnity.

The *Lackawanna* conference was held in an atmosphere of mutual distrust and misunderstanding. The two defeated countries had been led to believe that no territorial cession would be asked, and felt outraged when they learned of Chile's demands. Still other reasons existed for failure. The three American ministers, lacking definite instructions from Evarts, played the rôle of mere observers instead of mediators. Christiancy had blundered by giving Chile the impression that Peru would cede territory, and Osborn did still more by announcing that the United States would not act as arbiter if the conference invited it to do so. Evarts hastened to rectify this error, informing Osborn that Hayes would welcome arbitration;

but the damage had been done. The chief reason for failure grew out of Chile's demand for territory, Peru positively refusing any cession. The conference broke up and the three ministers concluded the farce by quarreling among themselves as to the best way to inform Evarts of the outcome.[32]

Just before leaving office Evarts once more tried to end the war. After the fall of Callao and Lima and the flight of the Peruvian president, he believed that Peru would accept any terms. On behalf of the *Société Générale de Crédit Industriel et Commerciel,* representing creditors of Peru, the Comte de Montferrand and P. Suarez hastened from Paris to see Evarts and urge American arbitration to save the country from an anarchy which would mean the loss of all foreign investments. Advising Evarts to act, William H. Trescott said, "If you cannot just now take what would be a great step in advance, could you not at least open the way and indicate the course for your successor?" Evarts approved the French plan, because it would enable Peru to offer Chile a war indemnity that would probably be acceptable. But he felt it improper for the United States to take the position of an international trustee until the belligerents agreed that it should do so. Thus, at the close of Evarts' term, the government was committed to an attitude of friendly remonstrance with Chile against the dismemberment of Peru until Peru had been given a chance to negotiate with her creditors on terms that would enable her to offer Chile an adequate war indemnity. Evarts had failed in the *Lackawanna* mediation, but he should be credited with putting the government on record as anxious to prevent the conquest of one South American country by another.[33]

Blaine, however, discontinued the mediation. The war dragged on until 1883, when Peru ceded Tarapacá to Chile and consented to a Chilean occupation of the provinces of Tacna and Arica for ten years, at the expiration of which time a plebiscite would decide their future. It was not till 1929 that a final settlement gave Arica to Chile and Tacna to Peru, with Bolivia's demand for an outlet to the sea ignored.

Of the three Secretaries of State—Evarts, Blaine, and Frelinghuysen—who tried to end the war, Evarts blundered the least in his efforts at mediation. His impartiality contrasted sharply with Blaine's outspoken hostility to Chile and Frelinghuysen's wish to sacrifice both Tacna and Arica to Chile.

Evarts believed that an effectual way of scattering war clouds lay in developing trade with South America. Great Britain had long almost monopolized this trade, but by 1877 American exports were rapidly expanding. The Secretary, as a representative of the commercial interests of New York, had a sincere interest in this development.

Indeed, the encouragement of foreign trade was one of the cornerstones of Hayes's policy. At the annual banquet of the New York Chamber of Commerce in 1877 Hayes, Evarts, Schurz, Devens, and other distinguished men of both parties spoke upon American trade. "What," asked Evarts, "can keep down the commerce of such a nation with such resources? . . . Nothing but bad laws. . . . Tariffs must be simple; duties must be collected. . . . We must have ships either by buying or building them. . . . A good deal more, I think, may be done in the future . . . to make our representatives to foreign nations, whether ministers or consuls . . . coöperators . . . [in] diffusing our commercial intercourse."[34]

Although Evarts favored a protective tariff, his interest while in office was neither in protection nor free trade, but in what he called "full trade." "The vast resources of our country need an outlet," he declared, "I hope through trade conventions with foreign governments to further extend the markets for our products. To do this we must offer privileges if we expect equal benefits in return." He felt that American trade had suffered because of the lack of decision. "It is for us to enter into the harvest-field and reap it," he remarked. "We must not stand first on one leg and then on the other, undecided as to which foot we shall put forward in our progress to that great harvest-field. If we wish to build ships, let us build them; if we wish to buy ships, let us buy them; if we wish to sell our raw material, let us sell it; if we wish to sell the products of our industry, let us sell them."[35]

Reciprocity of trade is usually associated with his successor, Blaine, but Evarts also advocated it. He sent an important circular to all consuls in Latin America in 1878, declaring: "It is believed the period has now arrived when it should be wise for all the nations of this continent to consider more carefully than heretofore how they may best enlarge their trade with each other. . . . The United States are in a condition to supply cheaply and easily many products and manufactured articles, suitable to their wants, to all or nearly all of the Spanish American Republics . . . receiving in return natural products. . . . It is desired by the Department that its Diplomatic and Consular officers should devote attention to the question of methods by which trade with the United States can be most judiciously fostered."[36]

After collecting information from consular agents, Evarts sent a large body of information to Congress with recommendations upon a wide variety of topics; the need of adapting goods to the taste of the Latin Americans; capitalization on Latin American preference for American goods; the development of steam transportation, which was the chief factor in British success; and the immediate creation of direct and frequent mail connection. When a trade journal devoted to the improvement of trade with Latin America was launched in New York, he offered aid to the editor.[37]

He also set about the improvement of the consular service, which for years had been the object of ridicule. Bad as it was, Grant had made it worse by unwise appointments, even justifying some of his bad appointments on the ground that it was well to get such men out of the country! In trying to get an increase of consular salaries, Evarts was no more successful than with diplomatic salaries. Since the fees collected by consuls and turned into the Treasury greatly exceeded the cost of the service, there was little justification for the niggardliness of Congress.[38]

But Evarts made headway in other reforms. Most important, he introduced a new system of consular reports. Fish had discouraged the publication of such reports, issuing them annually in one volume too late to be useful to business men. Many reports were not published at all, while others were curtailed in order to keep the annual volume within reasonable limits. In 1878 Evarts began calling for more frequent reports, covering every branch of trade and industry in every foreign country. On April 11 he made the greatest effort the State Department had ever made to utilize the consular corps as a fact-finding agency. He dispatched his "Labor Circular" to consuls of leading cities, instructing them to report conditions of labor, wages, costs of living, money systems, and business habits.[39] In 1880 he followed this up with the following order: "You are . . . requested to prepare and forward to this Department reports upon all subjects which may be calculated to advance the commercial and industrial interests of the United States." He thus succeeded in establishing a system of monthly reports, the first appearing in October, 1880, under his personal supervision. They proved of inestimable value to business men. As Evarts explained, "This step was taken in response to the wishes of the leading commercial communities of the United States as expressed through the chambers of commerce."[40]

On the whole, Evarts, assisted as he was by a return of prosperity, met some success in his efforts to develop trade. He informed Thurlow Weed in the summer of 1879 that there was a large increase of manufactured exports and that competition with the British in Latin-American markets was increasing. The following summer he reported that the increasing export of foodstuffs was exciting the wonder of the world, and that American manufacturers had a solid foothold everywhere. Steam transport and depots in all the chief trade centers of the world were still needed.[41] T. J. Barnett, consul at Ottawa, wrote Evarts toward the close of his term, "A world-wide feeling exists that the State Department is in wise, temperate, and honest hands. . . . Through you we have added to our wealth an unprecedented wealth of commercial intelligence and founded a system which will bind us in detail to all the world."[42]

Despite disappointments and defeats, Evarts' general policy in Latin America was an improvement upon antecedent conditions. The troubles with Mexico were largely ironed out; the American position on an Isthmian canal was vigorously stated; our principles of neutrality were reiterated and defended; the rights of Americans were upheld; mediation and arbitration were encouraged; and trade was given a distinct impetus. Well might William Trescott declare that the marked feature of Evarts' work was the closer diplomatic relations established with Latin America, and the prestige given to the United States as head of the Pan-American system.[43]

25

A Friendly Hand in the Far East

In after years, when Evarts thought of China, two unhappy memories must have come to mind: the troubles he had experienced as Secretary of State at the height of the Chinese exclusionist agitation, and, even more poignant, the loss of a son.

His fourth son, William M. Evarts, who closely resembled him in looks and manner, a young man of promise, left Harvard to go to China in 1874 to enter business. Bearing letters of introduction from Hamilton Fish to diplomatic and consular officers, he found a place in the offices of Russel & Company. But during the next three years his health declined, a serious illness finally overtook him, and he started home in the spring of 1878. His father and mother, hastening westward to meet him, found him almost too feeble to travel. He was taken to Windsor, where he soon afterwards died, aged only twenty-seven. Neither parent could attend the funeral because the serious illness of another son, Allen, required their immediate attention in New York. Laconically Evarts telegraphed the President, "We are summoned from the unfinished burial of one son to attend the sick bed of another whose condition the physicians pronounce extremely critical."[1]

The credit for the gradual solution of the problem of Chinese immigration belongs in no small part to Evarts' persistently friendly attitude toward China. From 1848 to 1870 Chinese immigrants had received a welcome on American shores. The California gold rush first brought them, offering higher wages and better conditions;

and between 1852 and 1860 their numbers in California increased from ten to forty thousand. They worked long hours for low pay, engaged in cooking, laundering, mining, railroad building, and miscellaneous occupations. They were respected for their dignity, industry, cleanliness, and unobtrusiveness. Cheap labor was needed in California, and they filled the need.

In 1869 the Burlingame Treaty encouraged immigration and established relations with China on a cordial footing. Anson Burlingame, after resigning his post as minister to China, headed a Chinese delegation to the United States to negotiate a treaty. Evarts presided at a banquet given him in New York and spoke highly of the Chinese. Under the treaty, free entry was granted the Chinese, and citizens of both nations were to enjoy the same privileges, immunities, and rights of travel as people of the most-favored nation. Upon his return to China, Burlingame told the Chinese in Pekin that there was "room for a million Chinese laborers on the Pacific coast."[2] The country then contained sixty-three thousand Chinese, of whom fifty thousand were in California.

But a violent antipathy, based on race prejudice and economic difficulties, flared on the Pacific Coast during the next decade. Unemployment after the completion of the Central Pacific Railroad started the trouble and the panic of 1873 accentuated it. By 1877 the long-continued depression had produced a serious situation. San Francisco was filled with unemployed, who blamed their plight on the Chinese and raised ever more bitter complaints, with "cheap labor" as the chief grievance. Blaine denounced the Chinese for "their blighting system of labor," their "impure and lewd" women, their unassimilability, and their religious ideas. In California the masses showed a grim determination to oust the Chinese. Leaders of both parties, competing for the labor vote, denounced the unresisting aliens, and made no effort to spare the feelings of a friendly nation. The legislature enacted discriminatory laws, some of which were declared unconstitutional by the Supreme Court. In 1879 a state constitutional convention proposed severely repressive measures, quite un-American in their flagrant violation of human rights.

Dennis Kearney, leader of the "Sandlotters," gave currency to the slogan, "The Chinese must go."[3]

The issue first became of national importance in the campaign of 1876. Hamilton Fish discreetly did nothing about it, for his policy was one of concerted action with the European powers in Far Eastern affairs. But Congress soon rushed into action. A committee in February, 1877, reported upon the evils of Chinese immigration. More impartial was the posthumous report of Senator Morton, who concluded that the Chinese were industrious and of great value to California; but the Democrats were determined upon a modification of the Burlingame Treaty. Senator Sargent of California introduced a resolution requesting the President to enter into negotiations with China with a view to limiting Chinese immigration.[4]

This was the situation facing Evarts in 1877. Chinese appeals for justice quickly began to reach him from many quarters. One significant letter from certain Chinese companies in San Francisco pointed out that, while China had largely indemnified the United States for outrages committed upon American citizens, not one outrage in fifty on Chinese by Americans had been properly punished.[5] From a representative of the Chinese in California he received the following telegram in January, 1878: "I am requested to convey to you the following suggestion which, if carried out by this government, will most assuredly meet their views and quite effectually stop further immigration. First, that Congress may enact a law entailing a tax of one hundred dollars upon each subject of China landing in the United States. Second, that the money so collected may be used to return their indigent countrymen to China with such other restrictions as may seem best. . . . They are entitled to indemnity for past outrages and those that are here full protection for their lives and property in the future. They desire to express to you that they are perfectly aware of their utter weakness to defend themselves where other foreign residents boldly demand and receive protection from the authorities. Hence it was that they, after long suffering, asked that protection of the National Government a short time since which they supposed solemn treaty obligations entitled them to and most particularly do they wish to convey to you the highest respect they entertain now and will always cherish for the kindness they have invariably received at the hands of American born citizens with a few exceptions."[6]

There arrived in Washington in September a picturesque mission from China headed by Chin Lan Pin, the first minister to the United States since Burlingame. Evarts conducted the delegation in several carriages to the White House, where curious bystanders gathered to watch the delegation march inside, two by two. Evarts, thin and gaunt, dressed in a plain evening suit, seemed insignificant beside the robust, grandly dressed Chin Lan Pin, with his bowl-shaped hat and scarlet plume, his flowing silk garments, his lavender blouse covered with ornaments, and his short sword in a jewelled scabbard. The President and Cabinet met them in the Blue Room, with Evarts introducing the guests. Chin produced his credentials, drawing them from an elaborate bamboo sheath three feet long. They were read in Chinese, not one word being understood by the Americans, and then read in translation, after which Hayes responded with a few words of welcome.[7]

But Congress was not thinking of the courtesies of diplomacy or the feelings of a sensitive people. Statesmanship yielded to politics and in January, 1879, the "Fifteen-Passenger Bill" was passed. This act prohibited any shipmaster from bringing to the United States more than fifteen Chinese on one voyage, and provided a penalty of one hundred dollars a head and six months' imprisonment for exceeding that limit. The advocates of the act contended that a repeal of the Burlingame Treaty was necessary for self-preservation; that no mere technical consideration should intervene to prevent action, and that state laws had failed. Blaine justified the abrogation of the Burlingame Treaty on the ground that China had violated its spirit by permitting coolie immigration. With a dramatic flourish he said, "We have this day to choose whether we will have for the Pacific Coast the civilization of Christ or the civilization of Confucius." A small group of senators, however, fought the bill as a serious breach of treaty obligations toward a friendly nation. Senator Hamilton, chairman of the Foreign Relations Committee, argued for equal rights for the Chinese and asked that the ultimate decision be left to the President. Though Conkling's proposal that the President be instructed to abrogate the Burlingame Treaty directly was rejected, the Fifteen-Passenger Bill passed by a margin of two votes in the Senate. Thus did Congress slaughter the principle of racial equality in the house of its friends.[8]

Hayes recorded in his diary, "Our treaty with China forbids me to give it my approval. . . . No change in facts has occurred since the treaty was made. . . . No new and sudden emergency has arisen." Evarts was alarmed and angered. To him the Burlingame Treaty was a sacred obligation. He agreed with the Chinese minister that the act was "offensive" and "insulting."[9]

The President prepared a veto message and asked Evarts to write another. Deciding that Evarts' was the better, he transmitted it to Congress, the only veto he sent not written by himself. In this important state paper, manifestly the work of a legal mind, Evarts directed his main attack at the method rather than the purpose of Congress. He admitted that the Burlingame Treaty needed change to prevent too rapid an ingress of cheap Chinese labor, yet insisted that it contained "important advantages which once relinquished cannot easily be recovered." Above all, the change should not be accomplished by a blunt abrogation of the treaty. "This ancient Government," he wrote, "ruling a polite and sensitive people, distinguished by a high sense of national pride, may properly desire an adjustment of their relations with us, which would in all things confirm, and in no degree endanger, the permanent peace and amity. . . . A denunciation of a treaty is, confessedly, justifiable only upon some reason both of the highest justice and of the highest necessity. . . . No circumstances can tolerate an exposure of our citizens in China, merchants and missionaries, to the consequences of so sudden an abrogation of their treaty protections."[10]

No act of Hayes was more to his credit than the approval of this veto message, and nothing more to Evarts' credit than the writing of it. In the face of violent opposition in California and stern hostility in Congress, both showed an unflinching courage. They were determined that the good faith and honor of the nation should not be impaired. The message did much to moderate anti-Chinese sentiment in and out of Congress, and the necessary two thirds to override the veto could not be mustered.

Following up his victory, Hayes sought a modification of the Burlingame Treaty by direct negotiations with China. Undertaking the task, Evarts found that the Chinese representatives in Washington lacked authority to negotiate. He instructed George F. Seward, American minister to China, to gather information regarding contract labor, to inform the Emperor of the difficulties arising under the treaty, to sound out the Chinese government on the possibility of a change, and to allay the irritation that had arisen.[11]

The minister, however, proved a hindrance to Evarts. A son of William H. Seward, he had served as consul for fifteen years and had been appointed minister in 1876. Although an able man, he was overconfident of his abilities and inclined to act as he pleased. He did not agree with Evarts' policy, and so completely lacked faith in the Chinese government that he felt coercion necessary. He believed in a united front by all nations represented at Pekin, and always consulted these representatives before taking action. He became pessimistic over Evarts' proposed revision of the treaty; and while reporting that the Chinese government was willing to discuss immigration restriction, he did not press the issue.[12]

One reason Seward disliked Evarts' policy was that the Secretary took an absolutely impartial attitude in the war then looming up between China and Japan over the possession of the Loo Choo Islands. Seward believed the United States should support China; but Evarts knew that China was the aggressor and, backed by Great Britain, was making heavy war preparations. John Russell Young, who was well informed on the situation, advised Evarts to assert a principle in Far Eastern affairs which might be known as the "Evarts Doctrine," but of course Evarts dismissed this idea.

He would have welcomed any opportunity for mediation, but war was happily averted.[13]

Seward's activities became increasingly embarrassing to Evarts. His demands for extortionate fees compelled an investigation by the State Department, and brought him much adverse publicity in the American press. Worse still, he became involved in the building of the Woosung Railroad and other financial schemes. Learning that Evarts was about to send a diplomatic mission to China, he made the absurd charge that this body was being appointed at the instigation of an Irish mob, and advised the Chinese government to pay no heed to it. He spoke disrespectfully of Hayes and "that man Evarts." The Secretary ordered him to come home and bring all his papers, books, and accounts. Although a House committee recommended that he be impeached for irregularities in accounts, fraudulent dealings with the Chinese, and arbitrary administration, the evidence was not clear and Congress dropped the subject. But Evarts reluctantly removed Seward.

Frederick Seward was greatly embarrassed by the situation. But after his brother's dismissal he said to Evarts, "You should know how the two brothers received the news, and that one regards it at least with philosophy and the other with approval." Some light is thrown upon Seward's misconduct in China by a letter of Consul-General Denny of China to Trescott, in which he wrote: "Seward has stepped down and out—glad of it—for the interests of both governments it ought to have been thus years ago. You will find that his stupendous diplomatic blotching has increased your labors. He has damned Mr. Evarts up hill and down for being, as he says, a party to his downfall."[14]

With Seward eliminated, Evarts proceeded with his plan for sending a special mission to China to settle the immigration problem. Republicans saw in it an opportunity to deprive the Democrats of a possible campaign issue. But great care had to be exercised, for the friends of Seward in China were troublesome, while it was known that Li Hung Chang, the Chinese Viceroy, had been angered by the treatment of Chinese in California. In February, 1880, Evarts sent for James B. Angell, President of the University of Michigan, whom Senator Edmunds had recommended as an able diplomatist. Angell was delighted by Evarts' charming manner and the humor which "ran through his gravest talk like a vein of silver through the rock." They discussed the Chinese situation at length. Evarts offered him the leadership of the commission, at the same time emphasizing the need of a careful approach. "We had better not despise a government," he said, "which for thirty centuries has ruled a nation now numbering three hundred millions, while we have only fifty millions."[15]

Angell, after pondering the matter for a time, wrote in March that if direct prohibition of Chinese immigration were the goal, he would not accept the task; but if a mere "correction of abuses" was desired, he would try. Evarts accepted the qualification, and Angell was appointed minister to China as well as head of the commission. It was understood that his appointment was only temporary. The two other commissioners were William H. Trescott, so often useful to Evarts, and, since California insisted that the views of the Pacific Coast be represented, John F. Swift, a prominent California lawyer. The New York *Times* called his selection an "act of deference to the senseless clamor of a small section of the country."[16]

Evarts did not give the commission detailed instructions, thinking it wiser to leave much to their discretion. He did prepare general instructions, stressing the importance of a definite American policy rather than a united front with Great Britain. The rights of Chinese already in the United States were not to be discussed; a settlement of commercial and extraterritorial questions was to be sought, despite the fact that these were special problems requiring long study. Evarts intended that these instructions should overtake the commission at San Francisco, but he sent them too late for that.[17]

Upon arrival Angell was distressed to find the American legation inadequately furnished to meet his needs and regretted having brought his family. For a time the commission also lacked funds, but Evarts soon provided these. Disagreement arose between Swift and the other two commissioners. He wanted a definite restriction of Chinese immigration; Angell and Trescott were more considerate of the Chinese and preferred an arrangement whereby Congress might regulate immigration as the need arose. Swift thereupon became angry and refused to live in the same quarters with the other two; but he finally gave way, though insisting that his protest should be placed on record.[18]

The commission found that the visit of General Grant had done much to smooth the way for their introduction to the Viceroy. Nevertheless, Li Hung Chang showed his anger at the treatment of Chinese in California, striking his fist on the table. The actual negotiations were conducted by two Chinese commissioners, Pao Chun, an aged man of high repute, and Li Hung Tsao, a prominent scholar, who showed a fair and friendly spirit. That the discussions were completed in the astonishingly short time of forty-eight days was proof that the course of diplomacy had run smoothly.[19]

The Chinese proposed that immigration should be "regulated" by the United States subject to the approval of the Chinese government; that "laborers" should include artisans; and that there should be a definite limit on the time and number to be affected by the regulation. The American proposals were more restrictive. They suggested that there be a reciprocal most-favored nation provision for those engaged in trade, travel, temporary residence for teaching, study, or curiosity; that whenever the migration of Chinese laborers threatened to affect American interests, the United States might regulate, limit, suspend, or prohibit such coming after due notice to the Chinese; and that all Chinese residents in the United States should be protected under existing treaties.

For a time after the two plans were submitted the negotiators were at a deadlock. Trescott became pessimistic and wrote Evarts that he doubted whether a settlement could be reached. The controversial point in the American plan was the word "prohibit," which might be taken to mean an absolute limitation of immigration. Finally the American commissioners agreed to strike out the word in return for concessions on other points. The Chinese waived their demands that American immigration to China should require Chinese approval and that Chinese in America be given special protection against maltreatment. An agreement was finally reached on November 7, 1880. With relief, Trescott wrote Evarts: "At last I can draw a long breath, for yesterday after a two-hour final discussion the treaty with the Chinese commissioners was agreed to. . . . I think it ought to be satisfactory to the country. The right of the Govmt. of the U. S. 'to regulate, limit, or suspend' the immigration of Chinese labourers according to the requirement of its own social and political interests, has been recognized without condition except the general and proper one that this power shall be used reasonably and in a friendly spirit. The Chinese are unwilling that immigration should be absolutely and perpetually prohibited and I believe the traditional policy of our own people would have opposed such an extreme demand."[20]

The treaty embodied most of the American demands. Article I declared that "whenever in the opinion of the United States" the coming of Chinese laborers should "affect or threaten to affect" the interests of the country, the United States might "regulate, limit, or suspend" such coming or residence but could not absolutely prohibit it. Such limitation must be reasonable. Article II exempted "teachers, students, merchants, or travellers from curiosity, together with body and household servants, and Chinese laborers who are not in the United States" from such suspension and granted them most-favored nation status. By Article III the United States promised to give protection to the exempted classes. China was to be informed of all laws on the subject, and if they worked hardship, a mutual consideration of the problem was to take place.

Almost equally important was the commercial treaty made at the same time. Evarts had instructed Angell to seek an end to the discriminatory duties laid upon American goods entering Chinese ports, as well as the more burdensome internal transit duties. It was during the deadlock over the immigration treaty that the Chinese first suggested a trade with each other—fix tonnage and import duties on the same scale, prohibit the opium trade, and establish extra-territorial courts for Americans in China. The prohibition of the opium trade was especially important, and was greatly appreciated by the Chinese government. It was a bold and righteous step for the United States to take, but other nations did not follow the example.[21]

The agreement to establish extra-territorial courts was also a step forward. Evarts had experienced difficulties with both China and Japan over this problem. He had insisted that Americans could not be tortured or intimidated for refusing to testify in Chinese courts. In mixed cases he had insisted that the trial be held in the court and under the laws of the defendant's country, and in cases not of mixed nature he refused to recognize a submission to Oriental courts, except in land questions or infractions of the press regulations.[22]

Evarts was greatly pleased by the work of the commissioners. In transmitting the two treaties to the President, he declared that one of them settled questions in an "honorable and satisfactory" manner, while the second supplemented the "incompleteness of some of the provisions in former treaties." But the people of California were discontented. In San Francisco the *Examiner* expressed disappointment and declared the question to be as far from settled as ever, and the *Post* insisted that more should have been obtained from China. The California legislature protested against the treaty. Eastern journals, on the other hand, were quite uniform in approval. The New York *Herald* hailed the settlement of "one of the gravest questions that ever menaced our own civilization"; the *Times* regarded the surrender of the Chinese government as the most complete ever obtained by a civilized government.[23] The Senate ratified both treaties overwhelmingly. Indeed, they may be regarded as Evarts' outstanding diplomatic achievement; and the ease with which he settled this long-vexed question can be attributed to the straightforwardness of his dealings with China.

His diplomacy reached its full fruition, soon after he left office, in the Chinese Exclusion Act of 1882. The treaty had permitted exclusion, but had not defined its extent; Congress decided that it permitted the ten years, and periodic reënactments followed. Evarts might well feel proud of his work. A problem that had grown to alarming proportions had been speedily settled, and the legal right of Congress to make a unilateral abrogation of a treaty was definitely denied.

While Evarts was striking out upon a policy in China independent of the European powers, he was following the same course toward Japan. In 1866 Japan had been forced to subordinate its tariff system to that of the European powers. Evarts agreed that the United States would recognize Japan's tariff autonomy if she could persuade the other powers to do the same. Japan could not secure the desired concessions, but appreciated Evarts' good will. Trescott congratulated the Secretary, declaring, "The establishment of American influence in the East on independent grounds and opening a certain prospect of large increase: this, I think you can fairly claim to have effected." A larger trade with Japan ensued. On the other hand, when the Navy Department dispatched Commodore Robert W. Schufeldt in the *Ticonderoga* to seek trade concessions in Korea, Evarts was pessimistic of success. Japan temporarily blocked the purpose but a treaty was made soon after he left office.[24]

The possibility of gaining a foothold in the Samoan Islands, whose people seemed ready for annexation, did not escape Evarts. President Grant had striven to acquire the islands despite the opposition of the Senate; but the notorious manipulations of the self-seeking Colonel Steinberger upset his plans.[25] In November, 1877, there entered Evarts' office a tall, swarthy-complexioned, handsome minister of foreign affairs from Samoa—La Mamea, known as the "Tatooed Prince." In fluent English he talked first with Frederick Seward and then with Evarts, pleading for annexation of Samoa or at least the establishment of a protectorate. He argued that the increasing intrigues of the British and Germans, who were interested in trade, made some such step indispensable to Samoan peace and safety. He was ready to accept a treaty in almost any form, and proposed that the harbor of Pago-Pago be given the United States. It seemed likely that the Senate might accept such an offer, and the Secretary began negotiations.

A treaty of commerce and friendship was finally signed by Evarts and La Mamea in January, 1878. They agreed, first, that Pago-Pago should become an American naval station, a provision that remained ineffectual till 1899. They agreed, second, that in cases of difference between Samoa and other governments, the United States would "employ its good offices for the purpose of adjusting these differences upon a satisfactory and solid foundation." The Senate made some objections but finally ratified the treaty. It did not arouse public interest, and some of the diplomatic corps were amused and puzzled by it. Actually the United States already held Pago-Pago, and thus in return for something already possessed the United States acquired the problem of mediating to protect Samoa from forces without and conflicting factions within. But in time the treaty proved its value in preventing the islands from falling completely into the hands of another power.[26]

Though Evarts assured Great Britain and Germany that the United States was seeking not a protectorate, but merely trade opportunities, they were unconvinced and took advantage of intertribal wars to obtain concessions from rival factions. Evarts sought to work out an agreement with them, and a joint statement was finally issued by the three powers declaring they were not seeking to appropriate the islands. This virtually meant a three-power joint protectorate over the islands, but by the close of his term Evarts was unable to secure the actual legalization of such a protectorate.[27] The Samoan problem continued to vex later administrations till 1900, when the United States received Tutuila with its harbor of Pago-Pago, and Germany obtained the rest of the Samoan group.

Evarts' policy in Samoa sought commercial expansion; but, discovering that he would have to abandon it or coöperate with the other powers, he became more imperialistic. As in China and Japan, he pursued a strictly American policy, unshackled by European ties; but the intrigues of the natives frustrated him. Although his diplomacy seemed dubious to his contemporaries, he secured a naval station which has been of value ever since. Political penetration in the Far East was never in his mind. Evarts continued the policy of non-intervention, laying a basis for cordial relations between the United States and the Far East.

26

Relations with Europe

Evarts wished the United States to maintain friendly relations with Europe, and particularly with Great Britain. In his four visits to England he had learned to like English life and people, and had made a wide circle of acquaintances among persons of rank and influence. With Sir Edward Thornton, who had represented the British government at Washington for a decade, he was on intimate terms. Thornton visited him at Windsor and always acknowledged Evarts' "kindness and indulgence."[1]

In London, Edwards Pierrepont served as minister during Evarts' first year in office. When Pierrepont resigned, Don Cameron brought pressure upon Hayes for the appointment of his father Simon to the post. Evarts, who had not forgotten how Simon Cameron had tried to defeat his own appointment, opposed it. When the whole Pennsylvania delegation in Congress petitioned Hayes in Cameron's behalf, there were rumors that the "old weasel" was about to take vengeance on Evarts; but the appointment went to John Welsh.[2]

This wealthy Philadelphia merchant served creditably till 1879. Difficulties with Great Britain had then become so serious that it was rumored that Evarts himself might resign to become minister. He offered the vacancy to John Jacob Astor, who declined because of the shortness of the unexpired term. Senator Hoar likewise refused, but recommended the transfer of James Russell Lowell from Madrid to London. Evarts hesitated, and Hoar believed that his reluctance was due to the historic Harvard-Yale rivalry, Lowell being a Harvard man. More probably, however, he hesitated because of the contrast between the solemn Baptist-deacon Welsh and the charming and brilliant, but highly individual Lowell.[3]

The appointment of Lowell proved wise. He was handicapped by an invalid wife and lack of financial means, but his personal charm and literary and oratorical powers soon captivated Englishmen high and low. He wrote Evarts just after his arrival: "I have learned here that, provided a man be otherwise acceptable, there is no need of his making any great display, so far as his usefulness is concerned. It impresses the vulgar, no doubt, and gets into the corners of the newspapers, but does not add in the least to his influence in essential matters. It is perfectly well known in England that I am neither a duke nor a millionaire."[4]

First among the questions to be settled with Great Britain was the problem presented by the predatory Indians on the Canadian border. It arose at the close of the Grant administration, when Thornton reported that Sitting Bull had taken his Sioux tribe into Canada after the slaughter of Custer's men, and was encamped near the border. The Canadian authorities asked Evarts to bring back the Sioux, who were stealing from the peaceable Canadian Indians and causing general disorder. Thornton besought Evarts to find some way to rid Canada of the nuisance. But there was no precedent or treaty providing the return of trespassing Indians. It was not a question of the reciprocal crossing of the border to punish raiders, as in the case of Mexico; it was rather a question of which country had jurisdiction over the Indians. Evarts at first held that the Indians had voluntarily emigrated from the United States, and had not invaded Canada; and that therefore the responsibility was not upon the United States. He was willing, however, to negotiate with the Indians for their return to an American reservation.[5]

In 1879 the problem became more serious. Sitting Bull crossed southward into Montana, encroaching upon the lands of peaceful American Indians, stealing horses and scattering buffalo herds. Regarding Sitting Bull as a British subject, Evarts declared: "It is the duty of the British Government to take such supervision of belligerent Indians as may prevent them from using British territory for purposes hostile to the United States." Thornton replied that hunger was the cause of the migrations, and that the best solution would be to induce the Indians to return peaceably to American soil.[6] Evarts had food sent to Indians on the American side of the border, and set free some of those arrested who were found innocent. Like his father years before, he did what he could for the suffering red man, in one instance liberating three hundred families that were found innocent of wrong-doing.[7]

But Evarts rejected the Canadian proposal that all Sioux refugees be induced to return to American soil or that reciprocal hunting rights be given along the border. At the close of his term the situation had been greatly improved by the coöperation of Canadian frontier officials, but the Sioux still crossed restlessly from one side to the other. The problem continued to vex the next two administrations.[8]

Evarts' controversy with Great Britain over the North Atlantic fisheries, one phase of the longest diplomatic dispute of American history, was far more serious. As a New Englander, he was sympathetic with the difficulties of the Yankee fishermen, some fifteen thousand of whom earned their livelihood on the Canadian coast.

The historical background is too long, too involved, and too dull to give in detail. After the American Revolution the privilege of fishing within and without the three-mile limit of the Canadian coast was given the New England fishermen. But in 1818 the United States acquiesced in a convention renouncing the inshore fisheries except at specified places on the coast of Newfoundland and Labrador. Difficulties at once arose in determining the location of the three-mile limit. For thirty-six years there were vexatious seizures of American fishing vessels. In 1854 a reciprocity treaty restored to the fishermen the inshore fishing privilege on any part of the coast in return for reciprocity of trade in specified products which favored Canada. In 1866 the United States refused to renew the treaty; and the situation thus reverted to the unsatisfactory status of 1818, with New Englanders again deprived of the inshore fisheries. They suffered greatly because three fourths of their mackerel catch, valued at six million dollars, came from within the three-mile limit. Clashes became more frequent, and New Englanders grew angrier. Under the Treaty of Washington in 1871 a solution was found. Great Britain agreed to restore the inshore fisheries in return for partial Canadian free trade in the United States, and the payment of a lump sum to Great Britain, the amount to be determined by a Mixed Commission. The fisheries issue was therefore in a quiescent stage just before Evarts took office. The Gloucester men now enjoyed legally what they had determined to take by force if necessary: the inshore fisheries and rights of trade, repair, recruitment, and transshipment.[9]

The Mixed Commission had not begun its work at Halifax when Evarts took office. Grant's choice as American commissioner, E. H. Kellogg, contrasted dubiously with the able British commissioner, Sir Alexander Galt. The selection of M. Maurice Delfosse, Belgian minister to the United States, unquestionably favored Great Britain, for Belgium wished to remain on the good side of England. The commission met in June, 1877, to consider the evidence before it and hear arguments by counsel. Evarts selected Trescott and Dana as counsel, this proving to be Dana's last public service. Hundreds of Canadians appeared before the commission to testify to the value of the inshore fisheries, and an equally large number of American witnesses maintained that the fishing privilege would gladly be renounced if the tariff on Canadian fish entering the United States were reimposed. Galt displayed a judicious temper, but Kellogg kept to himself, sometimes fell asleep, sometimes appeared intoxicated, and finally declared the award would never be paid.[10]

As Delfosse held the balance of authority, it was a foregone conclusion that the decision would favor Great Britain. But it was not anticipated that the commission would award Great Britain five and one-half million dollars. Evarts had expected an award of one million, two hundred thousand dollars, that is, a hundred thousand dollars for each of the twelve years comprised in the period from 1873 to 1885 under the Treaty of Washington. Greatly chagrined, he wrote Fish that he had spared no pains or expense in having the case well presented at Halifax, that he feared the United States had been "overmatched," and that the award at Geneva doubtless had something to do with the excessive amount in the present case.[11]

In reporting the result to the President in May, 1878, Evarts praised the work of the counsel, the agent, and Professor Baird, Commissioner of Fisheries, who had given valuable scientific information. But he protested against the award on two grounds: first, that precedent required a unanimous decision; second, that it was incompatible with the facts submitted to the commission. With elaborate statistics, he showed that the sum granted was out of all proportion to the supposed benefits of the fisheries. Furthermore, he contended, if the grounds for the award were not clarified, a perplexing situation would arise in 1885 when the terms of the treaty expired.[12]

Evarts' well-reasoned report was forwarded to Congress and became public. Of course he was accused of haggling with Great Britain, of sinking to the level of "bargaining" instead of paying the award immediately, and of seeking a tariff union with Canada as a make-weight for the payment of the award. These charges Evarts publicly denied. He had taken no steps to negotiate for a customs union, and was surprised at the widespread rumor in London upon the subject. Doubtless he did desire a customs union, but he did not wish to mix the subject with the question of the Halifax award. Probably his innocent statement to the National Board of Trade that he had "no objection to business men putting their heads together" was the cause of the false rumor.[13]

As the award was not payable for a year, Congress decided to follow Evarts' suggestion, appropriating the money, but making its payment contingent upon the President's discretion after further negotiations with Great Britain. It was no easy task to reopen the question. Evarts went to Windsor to ponder the matter. "I have found it very hard to begin," he wrote Hayes, "and I fear I shall find it still harder to end—to my satisfaction."[14]

The battle of notes immediately opened between Evarts and Lord Salisbury, the British foreign minister. On September 27 Evarts dispatched a long, carefully prepared argument. He made it clear that he was not seeking to avoid payment or to deny the validity of the award. He was merely looking to the future and to the principles upon which the award was made. "If this Government," he said, "by silent payment of the award, should seem to have recognized the *principles* upon which it proceeds, . . . it will at once have prejudiced its own rights, when it shall become necessary to insist upon them." In a dispassionate tone he argued the injustice of the award, declaring the value of the inshore fisheries could not be more than one and a half million dollars.[15]

Salisbury waited till the month the award was due before replying. In a terse note he denied that any rule required unanimity or that the award was excessive. He considered the matter closed except for the payment of the money. There was some reckless talk in Congress of refusing payment, but the amount was handed over on time, though under protest.[16] Fish, who was amazed at the amount of the award, wrote Evarts: "I am very glad that you saw your way clear to the payment of the 'award,' extortionate and irrational as it was. . . . The U. S. can far better afford to have paid it, than Great Britain to have received it."[17]

In 1880 charges of deliberate falsification of the evidence by the agents who presented the Canadian case at Halifax were published by Henry Y. Hind, the compiler of the index of the documents and proceedings of the commission. He had made his discoveries in 1878, but was not allowed to present them to the British Foreign Office till after the award was paid. He wrote Evarts, "When [the facts are] known, it will be found a most disgraceful sale of honor and interests for pecuniary recompense." Evarts was urged to investigate, but decided to ignore the charge.[18]

Meanwhile the fisheries problem took a more serious turn. A fleet of some fifteen Gloucester schooners were at Fortune Bay,

Newfoundland, waiting anxiously the arrival of herring. When the fish struck, the fishermen began to fill their vessels. On the next day, which happened to be Sunday, two schooners began making a sweep with seines attached to each vessel, the ends being secured on shore. The seines were soon filled and the catch was estimated at three thousand barrels. But the local inhabitants gathered on the shore, seized the ends of the seines, and dragged them in, destroying them and releasing the whole school of fish. The fleet was compelled to return home empty-handed, suffering a heavy loss. Angered by the outrage, the citizens of Gloucester petitioned Evarts for relief.[19]

A new battle of notes began. Evarts demanded an explanation. After a long delay Salisbury sent the report of Captain Sullivan, a British officer entrusted with the investigation of the affair. The blame was laid upon the fishermen for ignoring local regulations by fishing on Sunday and using seines prohibited at such seasons. Evarts saw at once the crux of the matter: local provincial regulations were being given precedence over international treaty rights. He sent a rejoinder to Salisbury in which he made no attempt to conceal his irritation. Refusing to accept the British explanation, he questioned the right of a mob to enforce local law. Of what use, he asked, was the Treaty of Washington if it could be annulled by local regulations? Was the United States to pay an exorbitant sum for the right to catch fish, and then be told that it could fish only in such manner as local authorities might permit? A more definite understanding was needed. Such was Evarts' protest. It was an able reply, but might well have been more vigorous. George Bancroft called it "a faultless state paper . . . made with the utmost delicacy and force."[20]

Salisbury astutely evaded the issue, denying that there was any inconsistency between the local regulation and the treaty, and placing the burden of proving such inconsistency upon Evarts. Evidently the treaty of 1871 was a bad bargain. Senator Edmunds rose in Congress to speak in favor of its annullment and the Gloucester fishermen petitioned Evarts for abrogation. He questioned a delegation of fishermen on the conditions of their industry, and promised to do what he could for them.[21]

Negotiations lapsed for a time, leading to charges that Evarts was dilatory; but the fact was that the Senate was trying to take matters out of his hands. In August, 1879, however, he sent another skillfully drafted note to Salisbury, repeating that a mob could not enforce a law and adding that no protest against American fishing methods had been made at the time of the Halifax award, although the methods were then well known. He demanded an indemnity of one hundred thousand dollars for the fishermen.[22]

In September Evarts made a short visit to Toronto, which did much to offset the growing friction. He found Princess Louise, wife of the Governor-General, an engaging personality, as popular with the Canadians as Mrs. Hayes was with Americans. He visited the Exhibition with the Governor-General and the Princess, and attended a reception to the Governor-General at the University. In reply to a complimentary address by the Chancellor, he said that no group of American lawyers had ever accorded him such kind treatment. At a reception by the American residents of Toronto, he was enthusiastically applauded when he spoke of the generosity of Great Britain in submitting to the Geneva arbitration, and recommended that free trade be promoted between the two countries. Evarts always played the diplomatic game best under such circumstances. The President pronounced his speech "capital" and the eminent free trader, Goldwin Smith, was encouraged to seek reciprocity with the United States.[23]

After an exasperating delay, Salisbury replied to Evarts' note in April, 1880. He asserted that Great Britain owed no indemnity, that the Halifax commission was not concerned with local fishing regulations, and that such regulations were binding on American fishermen. In an elaborate report to the President, Evarts showed that Salisbury was trying to make old provincial regulations, enacted before 1871, binding under the treaty. "The proposition of Lord Salisbury," wrote Evarts, "reduces the grant of the fishery from the dimensions . . . as Great Britain had power to convey it . . . to the fishery as it had been trimmed and curtailed by local legislation. . . . I respectfully advise that it be recommended to Congress to reimpose the duties upon fish and fish-oil . . . as they existed before the Treaty of Washington. . . . I respectfully advise, also, submitting to the consideration of Congress the propriety of authorizing the examination and auditing of the claims of our fishermen for injuries."[24]

Evarts' report was forwarded to Congress. Just as this body was about to act, the fall of Disraeli brought in Earl Granville as foreign minister and gave hope of adjustment. Indeed, Granville admitted that mob violence was unjustified, that the injured fishermen should be indemnified, and that Americans were subject only to those provincial regulations which did not conflict with treaty rights. Evarts accepted Granville's proposal to pay an indemnity of fifteen thousand pounds. But a difficulty arose: Granville wanted it understood that the indemnity was to cover "all claims arising out of any interruption of American fishermen on the coast of Newfoundland and its dependencies." Evarts rejected this alteration in Granville's original offer because he did not wish to prejudice the rights of other fishermen who might have claims against Great Britain. Thus no agreement was reached by the time he left office.[25]

Blaine agreed to Granville's terms, but outrages did not end. After the expiration of the treaty in 1885, the situation grew worse nor did a plan for licensing American fishermen in Canadian waters improve matters. A settlement was not reached till 1910, when the Hague Tribunal held that the Canadian Provinces had the right to make fishing regulations, thus overthrowing one of Evarts' main contentions; but, on the other hand, declared that a permanent commission should be established to decide the fairness of such regulations, thereby vindicating Evarts' argument that Great Britain alone could interpret such regulations.[26]

Evarts' difficulties with Salisbury may have been due in part to the British desire to court the friendship of Newfoundland and induce it to join the Dominion, and a desire to offset the agitation for Canadian annexation to the United States by a conciliatory policy toward Canada.[27] Although Evarts did not settle the fisheries problem, he helped to build a basis for a future solution.

Living in a century of wars and abhorring them, Evarts encouraged arbitration and the friendly discussion of international problems. He realized that the United States was not ready to adopt a general measure submitting to arbitration all disputes arising under any particular treaty; but much, he believed, could be accomplished by such means.[28]

A deep conviction inspired his remark to a friend in later years on the problem of war: "The only way to stop war is to stop it. World control by nations means simply self-control. We shall never have another war with England. She and we are alike—in law, in morals, and in spiritual aspirations. Our disputes will be family quarrels. We can for that reason, by arbitration and adjustment, settle all questions with her, because we understand one another and know how to arrange matters on a common basis. Not only so, but we can go further—England and we alone, with France, with whom there will always be a good understanding, can keep the peace of the world until other nations gradually get ready to join us in due course of natural development."[29]

Non-intervention in European affairs was one of the keynotes of Evarts' pacific policy. It was good American doctrine. When hostilities broke out between Russia and Turkey in 1877, he found himself again enunciating the familiar rules of neutrality. Making it clear that the United States had no interest in the Near-Eastern struggle, he warned Russia against fitting out privateers in American waters and cautioned both belligerents to protect Americans.[30]

Indeed, the second keynote of his policy was the protection of American lives and property in Europe. As each problem arose, he took his position cautiously, first ascertaining the facts and then seeking reparations without bluster. He regarded this as the primary function of his office. Such protection often raised questions of maritime law and jurisdiction, a subject with which he was very familiar. The Anderson Case offers a good illustration. The British authorities at Calcutta claimed jurisdiction over a British seaman named Anderson who had killed an American officer aboard an American ship. Anderson was in the custody of an American consul and Evarts refused to deliver him to the British authorities, claiming that jurisdiction belonged to the nation under whose flag the ship was registered. When the British authorities seized Anderson and gave him a trial and punishment, Evarts protested vigorously. Anderson was not restored to American jurisdiction, but the British government offered a disavowal and an apology.[31]

American rights in Turkey especially needed protection, for the Porte had long sought to abridge the privileges granted under the treaty of 1830. Evarts admitted that the English translation was erroneous, but insisted that since it was the one agreed upon, it should be recognized till a new one was made. The main problem related to the Turkish courts. Evarts denied their jurisdiction over Americans because they did not meet the proper standards. The murder of a distinguished Turkish lawyer by an American named Mirzan brought the controversy to a focus. Evarts instructed Maynard, the American minister, to try the case at Alexandria and furnished him with a full statement of American extra-territorial rights in Turkey. Mirzan was sentenced to death, but Hayes commuted the sentence to life imprisonment. It was not till after Evarts left office that Turkey finally accepted the American interpretation of extra-territorial right, which Evarts' legal skill had done much to clarify.[32]

Protection of American rights in Germany proved a complicated task, for in its dealings with the United States the new-born German Empire stood upon the principle, "Once a German, always a German." Bayard Taylor, the American minister at Berlin during the first half of Evarts' term, was greatly troubled by the problem, and Andrew D. White, who succeeded him, continued to experience difficulties.[33] Especially serious was the question raised by Germans who became naturalized American citizens and returned to the Fatherland to find themselves subject to military conscription. The State Department was flooded with complaints from

German-Americans. There could be no doubt that many of them had become naturalized in order to avoid military service. According to the treaty of 1868 an American forfeited his citizenship if he returned to the country of his birth and remained more than two years. Evarts held that those returning for business or pleasure incurred no liability of allegiance unless they remained beyond two years. In reply to the flood of requests he sent a stereotyped answer that he would seek the release of such citizens as were arrested or coerced; but he tacitly recognized that in many instances he was helpless.[34]

The most widely discussed of Evarts' efforts to protect citizens abroad was the case of Edward O. Condon, who was given a life sentence by a British court for the murder of a constable during the Fenian disturbances in Ireland. Lowell was annoyed by the problem of Irish Nationalists who obtained American citizenship and returned to Ireland to engage in agitation against England. Evarts asked clemency for Condon and upon refusal sent an agent abroad to seek a new trial if the evidence warranted. The question was happily settled when Condon was pardoned and returned to the United States at British expense.[35]

The third keynote of Evarts' diplomacy in Europe was his oft-reiterated demand for religious and racial toleration. It was an era of persecution for Jews in Eastern Europe, and Evarts received many petitions from Jewish-American organizations. It was chiefly in Russia that the Jews ran afoul of intolerant laws. When Foster left Mexico to take up his duties at the Russian court, he was informed by his predecessor that about all he would have to do would be to go to the Foreign Office once a month to get a poor American Jew out of trouble. But Foster found the problem one of great difficulty. The cases of two naturalized Americans named Wilczynski and Pinkos were especially heartrending. Evarts sought a definite remedy in all grievances, but the best he could do was obtain a promise that American Jews would receive the same privileges as all other foreigners in Russia.[36]

The fourth keynote of Evarts' policy was international coöperation. He believed in the solution of international problems by conferences. He invited the nations to a monetary and a sanitary conference; he favored participation in the Madrid Conference of 1880 upon the status of Morocco, insisting that the question of Jewish toleration be brought before it; he reversed Fish's policy by coöperating with the Egyptian debt commission; and he agreed to a mixed commission to settle Franco-American claims.[37] Coöperation was furthered also by extradition agreements, treaties being concluded with Holland and Colombia.[38] Evarts' negotiations with Denmark failed because the Danish government wanted an arrangement that would place the burden of expense upon the United States, while Congress blocked his extradition treaty with Greece.[39] Evarts laid before Sir Eward Thornton the draft of a new extradition treaty with Great Britain. A special British commission, including Cockburn, Palmer, and Harcourt, approved it and even proposed a more liberal plan, but the British government rejected both plans.[40]

Coöperation was also furthered by the encouragement of trade. Consular conventions were made with Belgium, the Netherlands, and Italy. Evarts showed great care in the wording of these conventions and they proved practical. With Great Britain, Italy, and Brazil he negotiated trademark conventions.[41] George W. Curtis interested him in international copyright, which would benefit authors and publishers; but his efforts in this direction were to come later.[42] Not without difficulty he secured a commercial treaty with Rumania. Congress delayed necessary appropriations and Eugene Schuyler, the American representative, found difficulties with the Rumanian government. The commercial treaty included most-favored nation treatment to Americans in Rumania.[43]

In Mexico he was driven from one concession to another and forced to change his policy; but he did protect American life and property, laid the basis for the later use of the doctrine of pursuit, and kept the country out of war. In the Caribbean he strengthened the Monroe Doctrine, and asserted more strongly than any predecessor the doctrine of paramount interest in an Isthmian canal. Although irked by Spanish policy in Cuba, he refused to be dragged into any serious difficulties. As pacificator between Chile and Peru he failed, but in this war he ably asserted neutral rights. As never before, Latin America recognized the leadership of the United States in American affairs. Trade reached an unprecedented peak, and a new system of consular reports was inaugurated.

In the Far East Evarts laid a basis for Chinese exclusion, and simultaneously allayed a growing race hatred. He struck out independently of European nations. In Samoa he secured a valuable naval station. He left the Canadian Indian and fisheries problems unsettled, and was outmanoeuvred by Salisbury. But he cultivated good relations with Canada, defined American fishing rights more clearly, prepared the way for the Fortune Bay indemnity, and placed the whole controversy in better posture for final settlement. In European relations he stood for the principles of non-intervention, protection of American life and property, toleration, international coöperation, and commercial development. He improved the tone of the diplomatic and consular service and made valuable extradition and commercial treaties.

This record falls below that of Seward and Fish, who faced more significant problems and had eight years in which to solve them. It was not so spectacular as the diplomatic career of Blaine under Presidents Arthur and Harrison; for the path of good will is seldom spectacular. But it was nevertheless highly creditable to Evarts and to the country.

27

For Garfield and Blaine

WHILE EVARTS had no desire to continue in public office himself, he felt it incumbent upon him to assist in the Republican campaign of 1880. He feared that Grant would win the prize again, and he watched anxiously as the national convention assembled at Chicago.[1] It proved a grim struggle between the Stalwarts behind Grant and the Half-Breeds supporting Blaine, and the deadlock between them was broken by a final stampede for James A. Garfield. The New York delegation was divided, though a majority supported Grant. The Stalwarts were furious over the result, but partly pacified by the nomination of Arthur as vice-president.

Evarts was pleased because the selection of Garfield promised party unity, and Bundy was elated. "My cup of joy is full," he wrote Evarts. "Conkling humiliated and compelled to grace the triumph of the one man he said he would not support. . . . The Republican party has proved its ability and will choose freely a good man. It has not risen far enough to recognize its great men." He was right. Neither Garfield nor Arthur was a great man, and the latter was especially displeasing to the reform element. With the gallant but inexperienced General Hancock as their standard-bearer, the Democrats hoped to discredit both Republican candidates.[2]

Evarts was pressed into service for Garfield. When the Chinese issue was raised, the candidate sought his advice and incorporated in his acceptance speech ideas from the Secretary which were calculated to win the California vote. Henry C. Bowen of the *Independent* tried to induce Evarts to speak at a great meeting at Woodstock, Connecticut, but he was unable to leave Washington. Though Garfield urged him to go to Indiana, where the political battle was close, he confined his speech-making to New York as usual. Bundy assisted him to prepare two addresses, declaring: "You can drive home the wedge that may split the Democracy in the East. You will be able to touch the pocketbooks of our capitalists—which no 'waving of the bloody shirt' will reach."[3]

The first speech was delivered at the Academy of Music, where Conkling had spoken a few nights before. With flashes of wit and telling illustrations, Evarts addressed a crowded hall and a sympathetic audience. Surveying party history with his usual clever analysis, he concluded that the Republicans were entitled by their defense of the Union, by their prosecution of the war, by their abolition of slavery, and by their management of public finance to the renewed confidence of the people. Although acknowledging Hancock's worth as a soldier, Evarts insisted that Garfield stood "upon a plane of longer and more varied experience, of better proved capacity, of larger benevolence, of more comprehensive mind and tenderer heart . . . than any candidate . . . since Henry Clay." He denounced the Democratic proposal to pay the national debt in greenbacks. Criticizing Southern Democrats for depriving the Negro of the ballot while professing to stand for equal suffrage, he asked if it were not like the man who beat his wife over the head with the framed motto, "God Bless Our Home." "I find nothing," concluded Evarts, "in the politics of the Democratic party that proposes anything. It is to undo everything. It is to fight the war back from Appomattox to Bull Run. It is to unravel the fabric of noble and expanded nationality that the Republican party has woven for this people."[4]

The second speech, at the Brooklyn Academy of Music, was given before an overflow audience, with Seth Low, Beecher, and other dignitaries on the platform. Lashing at the Southern Democrats again, he said: "The Republican blacks pick all the cotton of the Democratic whites, and the Democratic whites pick all of the votes of the Republican blacks. . . . To take the suffrage from them cannot be respectable in the contemplation of God or man." Ridiculing the Democratic party, he continued, "The American people would rather keep their prosperity in the hands of the Republican party and Providence, rather than give it into the hands of the Democratic party and take their chance of what Providence might do." He derided Hancock's shiftiness on the tariff issue, saying, "It is true you can shift from one leg to the other, but still it is not graceful and it is very tiresome."[5] Evarts also contributed five hundred dollars to the campaign at a moment when funds were low.[6]

Garfield won by a popular majority of less than nine thousand. Undoubtedly his victory was due in part to the failure of the Democrats to present a program, and in part to widespread bribery by the Republicans. Evarts' friends credited him with a large share of the victory in New York and Brooklyn, while Barnett, the consul at Ottawa, wrote that "New York turns out to be the pivotal state this time and it is saved at the point of Mr. Evarts' labor."[7]

Immediately after the election Garfield came to Washington to plan his Cabinet. He dined with Hayes and Evarts, but apparently did not offer Evarts a Cabinet post. John Hay, who was intimate with Garfield, urged the appointment of Blaine to the State Department, declaring that he knew no one better qualified except Evarts.[8] Blaine was chosen, and became politically active even before Evarts left office.

Evarts' friends hoped in the spring of 1881 that he would be elected to the Senate. Tom Platt, the machine candidate, was none too popular with the legislature; but the opposition was so divided between Depew, S. S. Rogers, Hitchcock, and Evarts that the machine carried the day. Conkling took great delight in the one vote cast for Evarts, and when a pile of telegrams announcing the result was handed him at a dinner, he read aloud patronizingly: "Evarts one vote. A tear for the departing administration."[9]

On March 7 Evarts retired from office. From Pekin, Trescott wrote: "It will scarcely do for me to tell you how sorrowfully I look forward to your giving up the Department just when you have . . . put into practice principles so broad, so beneficent, and so genuinely patriotic." Sir Edward Thornton wrote, "I trust indeed that the cessation of our official intercourse will not prevent our meeting socially, and I can assure you that we shall all deeply regret that you and your charming family are leaving Washington where we have so much enjoyed their society." Still more prized was the letter from Garfield, which read: "Your countrymen bear testimony to the ability and patriotic fidelity with which you have discharged the duties of your office; and I cannot permit your retirement without adding the assurance of my personal respect and regard."[10]

Evarts was really glad to be free. Noting his relief, Mrs. Henry Adams confided to a friend, that he was "evidently gay at the sight of the end of [his] tether with no scandal to blush for and no newspapers to make [him] afraid." More than a hundred prominent New Yorkers invited him to a testimonial dinner, but he declined.[11]

The day after leaving office Evarts wrote Garfield, "The appointments for the Paris [Monetary] Conference will naturally come up for your action. . . . My estimate of the importance of this Conference and my interest in the subject to be considered by it, the attractive circumstances under which I might take a brief recreation in Europe, and my hearty desire to undertake any public services which are consistent with other obligations, have all combined to favor my taking this position if you should wish it."[12] Garfield could scarcely refuse such a modest request, which may have forestalled a higher appointment that Garfield had in mind. Even Conkling approved, doubtless glad to have Evarts out of the country.[13] But Evarts was not an expert on currency problems, and adverse comments came from part of the press. On the other hand, he had taken the initiative in bringing about the conference of 1878, which failed, and had joined the French in bringing about this conference of 1881.[14] He received his commission from Blaine with a letter informing him that his compensation would be five thousand dollars plus "reasonable expenses." It was his fifth transatlantic voyage. With him went his wife and several of his children. He renewed friendships in England and then joined the other commissioners, Allen G. Thurman, Timothy O. Howe, and Dana Horton, at Paris.[15]

The conference of fifteen nations met on April 19, held thirteen sessions, and adjourned July 8. The French and Italian delegates agreed with the Americans in favor of a bimetallic international ratio for gold and silver; but more than half of the nations, including Great Britain and Germany, stood solidly for the gold standard.

Evarts' chief contribution was a speech on "What America Asks of Other Nations," a theoretical treatment of the case for international bimetallism. America, he said, was not seeking a market for its silver but the improvement of world commerce and the service of both metals in the place of the mastery of one. An international ratio, he declared, was not unnatural; it would be a progressive step made by "the wit of man."[16] Philosophically his argument was excellent, but it made little impression upon the British and German delegates.

During a six-week adjournment he sought permission from Blaine to visit England and Germany to influence public opinion; but Blaine opposed this, fearing that it would give the impression that America was seeking bimetallism as a favor. Evarts therefore went to England for pleasure. Among others he met Bancroft Davis, who cynically wrote Fish: "Evarts talks largely of what he did as Secretary but does not mention his silver business." While in London Evarts was alarmed to learn that political bickering and scandals had already clouded Garfield's administration. He remarked to Whitelaw Reid, "It used to be thought safer in politics to talk than to write, but in the present outbreak of perfidy in politics it is safer to be in London."[17]

The conference had scarcely reassembled when news that Garfield had been shot reached Paris. The attitude of Great Britain and Germany made further proceedings futile. Returning to New York, Evarts told the press that the European powers had recognized the unselfish purposes of the United States, and that progress had been made, but the future depended on continued interest.[18]

When Garfield died, Evarts was asked to deliver a memorial address at a meeting of the New York Historical Society. "It has been my fortune," he said, "to be acquainted for many years with James A. Garfield. . . . With the masses, even the most ignorant, he was loved and respected for the self-education he had acquired and the position he had made for himself. . . . Two of these [Presidents] have been plagued to death by the importunities of office-seekers. . . . Let us consider whether all this plague of patronage, the placeman's pride, the statesman's scandal and the Nation's shame, cannot be averted in the future. It is a disgrace that must be exterminated."[19]

The year 1882 was so occupied with law cases that Evarts scarcely noticed politics, though he did write some letters upon public affairs to Hayes.[20] He also appeared at Cooper Institute in defense of a constitutional amendment to abolish tolls on New York canals, arguing that canal policy should be based upon service rather than revenue; and his audience gave him a warm welcome.[21] In the state campaign that fall he was merely an interested observer. Governor Cornell had broken with Conkling and was now supported by the Half-Breeds. The Stalwart candidate was Judge Folger and the Democratic standard-bearer was Grover Cleveland. Evarts knew that Folger, backed by a corrupt machine, was certain of defeat and refused to speak for him, writing the candidate that he "might as well address a snow-storm with a view to stopping it."[22] The result proved a veritable blizzard for the Republicans, Cleveland sweeping into office by an unprecedented majority. Evarts was still regarded by the public as an Independent Republican, though actually he was becoming a Half-Breed; but, he proposed to keep out of active politics.

Early in 1883 he consented to speak on the tariff issue at Cooper Institute. A tariff commission created by Congress had recommended a heavy reduction in the high Civil War rates and Congress hesitated. Evarts took a highly conservative stand. As Secretary of

State he had sought the expansion of commerce and had shown no interest in a protective tariff; but now he was ready to speak for the protected interests. He was plainly becoming more "regular" in his party attitude. The audience he faced contained a conspicuous number of men of wealth, who heard from him just what they wanted to hear.

He was frequently interrupted by applause. He began with an appeal to individualism in business. "As far as I have observed," he said, "the rich men of the country—nine-tenths of them, started in life as poor men supportng themselves by their labor." Admitting that the protective tariff enriched the capitalist, he insisted that it likewise benefited labor. He denied that it tended toward monopoly. One feature of his speech was an ingenious comparison with the position of Great Britain. "When," he said, "we possess our own markets and the growth of our own industry enables us to compete with foreign nations; . . . when . . . we have made ourselves as great as England . . . so that we can see that a proclamation of free trade to all nations of the world means that every nation shall buy everything of us and nothing of them—then we shall be free trade."[23]

Evarts deserved to be sharply criticized for this speech. To be sure, as a lawyer he had naturally always been on the side of wealth and conservatism—he never abandoned that side. But his political popularity in New York had always been due to his independence. Furthermore, he was no tariff expert and had never spoken publicly on the subject before. Professor William Graham Sumner of Yale denounced his "antiquated" arguments, asserting that his views were on a level with those of "the vulgar protectionist" and quite lacking in an understanding of free trade. The *Tribune* came to Evarts' rescue with a counterattack upon Sumner, ridiculing him as "unworthy of Yale" and even urging his dismissal from the faculty.[24] Evarts was unabashed, and during the fall campaign of 1883 he spoke again at Cooper Institute on the tariff.[25]

On the other great issue of 1883, Civil Service reform, Evarts showed a more liberal spirit, heartily endorsing the Pendleton Act.

As newly elected president of the Union League Club he made his first address a few weeks after the passage of this law. The club had been a pioneer in reform, and the two great reformers, Dorman B. Eaton and John Jay, were prominent members. Evarts made an excellent speech, in which he spoke with pride of the efforts for reform. "We went on and on," he exclaimed, "with line upon line and precept upon precept, here a little and there a good deal, until we have lived to see greater unanimity among the parties and in Congress on that subject than on any other. . . . All at once, as it were, it was found that the breath of future campaigns was to be the will of the people, without regard to political relations, race, color, or previous condition of *political* servitude. . . . There are no institutions in which it is easier to be slaves and poltroons than under free institutions." He recommended three improvements: appointment under the merit system for all but the more important officers, honest performance of public duties, and respectful treatment of those in authority. With his recent experience in the Hayes administration in mind he said, "There is no human nature that can long stand the wear and tear of promotion in the good opinion and the suffrage of the people, being merely an elevation to a perpetual public pillory."[26]

There was no doubt of Evarts' sincere interest in Civil Service and civic reform. A few weeks later he accepted the chairmanship of a nonpartisan Citizens' Committee of Fifty-three for the reform of the municipal government of New York. Having headed a similar committee in 1877, he was well acquainted with the problem. The new committee was the fruit of a great mass meeting to support the Roosevelt bill, which aimed to deprive the aldermen of the power to confirm the mayor's appointments. Cooper Institute was jammed to the doors to hear Evarts' report for the committee. He was wildly cheered when he declared that the legislature had agreed to pass the Roosevelt bill and was considering a general plan for the improvement of city government.[27]

In the election of 1884, Evarts supported Blaine. In fact, he faced a capacity audience at the Grand Opera House in July to make the principal speech in support of Blaine's nomination. Hamilton Fish, who was to have presided, mistrusted the Maine leader and asked to be excused. When Evarts rose to speak, the five hundred on the platform and the huge audience rose to applaud. They did not know the misgivings of the speaker as to the candidate and the impending election.[28]

His speech was decidedly partisan. He had little to say of Blaine, devoting his attention to the Mugwumps, who bolted the party, and the Democrats. The former he called "political marsupials," carried about in the Democratic pouch. To be sure, they had a right to their own judgment; but with the hungry Democratic party sneaking back for spoils and plunder, it was their duty to stand by the party and its candidate. He pictured Cleveland as a "swaddled, a rocked, a dawdled legislator over night"; Blaine as a man who had "over and over again proved in the face of a great people, his right to the honor of being useful to his country."[29] Evarts was right on the need of party unity if the Republicans were to win; but he was unfair to Cleveland and his support of Blaine was hardly creditable.

He demonstrated his thick-and-thin partisanship again in October in an effective speech at the Brooklyn Academy of Music. Waving the "bloody shirt" in Blainesque manner, he called the Democratic party the "party of rebellion and disloyalty." He referred to Blaine as an "accused" man who was not proven guilty of misusing public office. It was a clever plea, which brought thunders of applause from Blaine admirers; but nowhere in the speech did Evarts openly avow a belief in Blaine's honesty. The *Times* declared next day that "in making light of Blaine's vices, he made a fool of himself"; and Carl Schurz asserted that such "post-prandial statesmanship and patriotism" should not be taken too seriously.[30]

The climax of the campaign was the famous "millionaires' dinner" at Delmonico's, given in Blaine's honor at the close of his Western tour. It was planned by some two hundred business men who signed the invitation, with Evarts' name at the head of the list.

Never was there greater excitement around Delmonico's than that evening of October 29. Blaine spent the afternoon reviewing a great parade and came to the dinner weary and tired. As he entered the banquet hall with Evarts on one arm and Cyrus Field on the other, he was given three rousing cheers. In front of Blaine's seat stood a magnificent array of flowers lettered with his initials; in the center of the table was an artistic representation of the White House and a plumed knight. Among those at the table were such party leaders as Levi Morton, Noah Davis, Alonzo B. Cornell, Tom Platt, and Whitelaw Reid. The presence of such millionaires as Russell Sage, Jay Gould, Henry Clews, Henry Rogers, Jesse Hoyt, and John Jacob Astor gave the dinner a plutocratic flavor.

Evarts presided and spoke cautiously in introducing the "plumed knight." He touched on a question that had arisen during the campaign, criticized the Mugwumps again for their "transcendental politics," and lauded Blaine as a leader. Blaine rose and turning to Evarts said, "It is a great reversal of positions, Mr. President, that makes me hear you ascribe leadership to me. For it has been my duty and my pleasure in these long years to follow you; to learn from your wisdom in public affairs, and to join with my countrymen in ascribing to you not merely the great merit of leadership in the noblest of professions, but to yield our admiration for the singular success which has given you the opportunity to lead in the three most important cases ever pleaded by a member of the American bar."[31]

In emphasizing prosperity under Republican rule before a group of millionaires at a time when the country was suffering from a depression and thousands were unemployed, Blaine made a mistake. Indeed, the whole affair was ill-conceived. McDougall's cartoon in the *World* next day depicted "Belshazzar Blaine and the Money Kings" with blazing diamonds in their shirt fronts, seated at a sumptuous feast, while a poor fellow with shivering wife and starving child begged for crumbs which fell from the table. Even more unfortunate was the speech earlier that day by the Rev. Samuel D. Burchard, whom Blaine later dubbed as "an ass in the shape of a preacher," and who referred to the Democratic party as "the party whose antecedents have been rum, Romanism, and rebellion."[32]

Evarts' prophecy that New York would be the pivotal state proved true. The returns showed that Cleveland had carried it by the slender margin of 1,149 votes and had won the presidency by one electoral vote. Although fearful of a return of the Democrats, Evarts was perhaps not keenly disappointed.

28

Finishing with the Law

After leaving the State Department Evarts was more active in non-political than in political affairs. In fact, partisan activities occupied but a small part of his time. His profession and numerous non-political speeches kept him very busy despite advancing age. He was more sought after than ever as a speaker. He responded often, perhaps too often for the good of his law practice. His keen understanding, philosophic mind, and aptness of expression had earned him a wide reputation as an oracle of wisdom. His non-political speeches varied from solemn historical or dedicatory addresses to phosphorescent flashes of witty nothingness.

His reputation for wit was greater than ever, bceause the stories he had told while in office had been given a wide publicity. At a New England Society dinner in Brooklyn in 1882, with Mayor Seth Low present, he complimented the Brooklyn citizens upon following Milton's admonition: "What is *low* raise and support." At a Yale alumni dinner in 1883 he declared that he felt toward his Alma Mater as the French bishop did toward the strawberry when he said, "God Almighty might have made a better berry, but doubtless he has not."[1] At a Delmonico dinner in honor of Dr. Oliver Wendell Holmes, who was retiring from the Harvard Medical School, he said, "How much pleasanter it is to be asked to meet three hundred doctors than to ask one to meet me." And in his inimitable way he contrasted the professions of law, medicine, and the clergy—estate, body, and mind, as he called them—all three hunting the human race by different paths and all three sure to be in at the death. In the hunt the doctor had the advantage; for everybody had a body, but all did not have mind and estate. The popular belief that lawyers and doctors were wolves and the clergy were sheep was inaccurate; the clergy were wolves in sheep's clothing.[2]

Most of Evarts' speeches, however, were serious. In 1882, at a mass meeting at Chickering Hall to protest the persecution of Jews in Russia, he denounced intolerance, as he had done when Secretary of State. "Are we our brother's keeper?" he asked. "If the ancient test of the hatred of the Jew is to be the encomium and pride of our Christianity, it may be admitted that some Russians may be very good Christians, and very bad men."[3]

Within a year he spoke three times at the reception of eminent British visitors. In November, 1882, he presided at a dinner at Delmonico's in honor of Herbert Spencer, who had been lecturing in America and was about to return home. Spencer was at the peak of his fame. But he was tired and not well. He begged Evarts to limit the conversation and expect meager replies. Evarts was not acquainted with his works, but with a lawyer's facility for getting up an unfamiliar subject, he looked over some of his books and, as Henry Holt said, "Pulled it off very handsomely, of course, with a slip here and there, much to the amusement of those 'inside.'" Declaring that the guest had been chosen by a process of "natural selection," Evarts turned to Spencer with the compliment, "We recognize in the breadth of your knowledge . . . a greater comprehension than any living man has presented to one generation."[4]

Evarts presided again at Delmonico's two months later at a dinner to Sir Edward M. Archibald, British Consul-General at New York, who was retiring after fifty years' service. Evarts had been associated with him as a referee in the case of the *Magicienne* at the close of the Civil War. After several neatly worded compliments, Evarts turned to him and said, "Our nation has the reputation of getting in somebody's way; but your nation is not so much better off in its international reputation, for your nation has the reputation for never getting out of anybody's way. Now, to be a consul and to go off without ever having allowed us to get in your way, nor allowed your nation to get out of our way, and yet have the respect and affection of the community in which you have lived, I am sure is great praise."[5]

The most distinguished visitor to America in 1883 was Lord Chief Justice Coleridge, who came at the invitation of the Bar Association of New York State. He received a great welcome and was feted everywhere. He liked America and came often enough to receive the title of "advance agent of Henry Irving and Ellen Terry." There are several stories told of Evarts and Lord Coleridge, but there is one so well known and so often attributed to other persons that it may be called Evarts' most enduring pun. They took a trip to Mount Vernon and as they stood on the lawn in front of the mansion, Lord Coleridge said, "I have heard that he [Washington] was very strong physically, and that, standing on the lawn here, he could throw a dollar right across the river to the other bank." Evarts measured the distance with his eye and looked doubtful. "Don't you believe it?" asked Coleridge. "Yes," replied Evarts, "I think it is very likely to be true. You know a dollar would go further in those days than it does now."[6]

At the formal reception to Lord Coleridge at the Academy of Music—a grand affair with two military bands, the judges of the state and local courts, and numerous dignitaries on the stage—Evarts was the principal speaker. His slight figure contrasted markedly with the massive frame of the British jurist. Evarts' remarks proved another hilarious introduction. "The glory of the American lawyer," he said, "is the poverty of himself and the wealth of his client. . . . There be these three estates in law: the judges and the lawyers and the clients, but the greatest of these is the clients. . . . We [lawyers] are accused of fleecing them, but we never flay them." At a reception which followed at the Union League Club Evarts and Lord Coleridge both spoke again in the auditorium. Picturing America as it might seem to Coleridge, Evarts said, "Our faults can be seen three thousand miles off; as a modest retiring people our public and private virtues need to be closely inspected to be seen." Soon after

Lord Coleridge's arrival home in England, he sent Evarts a copy of a rare book with the comment, "I will not try to say how grateful I feel to America and Americans and amongst Americans most particularly to you."[7]

One of Evarts' best addresses was made the same year at the laying of the cornerstone of Sherred Hall at the General Theological Seminary in New York. As his son Prescott was studying there for the ministry, he had a special interest. He spoke with unusual frankness and candor for a layman addressing the clergy. He urged a practical type of education for theological students; polemics, church history, and the lives of the saints, however valuable, could not be the staple of sermons. A clergyman should preach as if he knew that another clergyman was to follow him with a sermon of opposite opinion. He suggested that sermons deal less with denominational doctrines and more with "faith in God and faith in man." Evarts' address revealed more clearly than any previous public utterance the depth of his religious thought. Declared one religious journal, "None of the Yale lectures on preaching have contained sounder or more necessary counsel than this address of the pew to the pulpit." Greatly pleased, the Rector of St. George's Church said, "You stated with rare force what some at least of us clergy feel must be said."[8]

The same year Evarts shared in the impressive ceremonies near Helena, Montana, which marked the completion of the Northern Pacific Railroad. To attract attention Villard invited government and state officials to be present at the driving of the last spike. Four special trains brought guests from the East. Evarts, in company with General Grant and other notables, rode in a private car. At Bismarck he saw Sitting Bull, who had been released for the occasion with two thousand of his warriors. At the ceremonies at Mullen Pass Evarts spoke briefly and again at the dinner given Villard.[9]

A marked feature of Evarts' later life was his interest in historic monuments and commemorations. He found it easy to express the sentiment and philosophy appropriate for the occasion.

At Delmonico's he spoke at a banquet given by the Chamber of Commerce to a delegation of some thirty eminent Frenchmen who came as guests of the nation to participate in the Yorktown Centennial. Never was Delmonico's in more patriotic setting: flags and shields everywhere and the orchestra regaling the guests with selections from English, French, and German operas. Speeches were made by a descendant of Rochambeau and of Steuben; spokesmen for America were Evarts, Schurz, Cornell, and Mayor Grace, who made short addresses.

Evarts spoke of the French alliance of 1778. In a clever introduction he said, "I speak French and German equally well, but I thought it would be a poor compliment after all. . . . They surely hear enough of that at home. . . . I do not know that the 6th of February has anywhere been honored . . . but, for myself, as an humble individual, from the earliest moment, I have done all in my power to show homage to that day, for on that day I was born." Becoming serious, he said, "It was a great thing for France to make the Treaty of Alliance . . . with a nation that, as yet, had received no acceptance from the Powers. . . . Here were we, a young, growing, self-conscious, self-possessed damsel, just peeping from our mother's apron, when there comes a gallant and a noble friend, who takes up our cause, and that, too, at a time when it was not quite apparent whether we should turn out a beauty or a hoyden. . . . If we could take some of the moral sunlight which shines upon that nation; if we could be more cheerful, more gay, more debonair; and they could take from us some of the superfluous ice which we produce, . . . we have no tariff on either side that would interfere with the blending and intercommunication of the moral resources of both nations."[10]

The best of all of Evarts' orations, with the possible exception of the Centennial speech of 1876, was delivered at the Centennial celebration of Washington's Headquarters at Newburgh in October, 1883. In planning the celebration, the New York legislature first took action and then Congress appropriated money for the monument to mark the site of Washington's Headquarters. A congressional committee decided upon the style of monument and the plan of dedication and invited Evarts to deliver the dedicatory address. Hamilton Fish wrote John Schuyler, "These 'Centennials' have become a nuisance. They have been gotten up for the notoriety of some few persons, and for the pecuniary benefit of a few others. . . . I believe that my friends, Bayard of Delaware and Evarts of N. Y., are in training for this 'Newburgh' occasion. Don't tell anyone that each is to make a bid on the occasion for the Presidency. . . . Evarts will be there as 'Champion orator of the United States,' the successor of the eloquence of Patrick Henry, John Adams, Henry Clay, Daniel Webster, and of all others [whose] 'gift of gab' [has] transmitted their name and fame to the present age. But, this too, is 'strictly confidential' and must not be repeated, for it might touch W. Evarts' proverbial and well known modesty and diffidence. He will make a good speech. He would do so were the occasion the centennial anniversary or the bicentennial anniversary of John Hancock's tom cat."[11] Evarts did make a good speech, but he made no bid for the presidency.

It was a great day at Newburgh. There were probably fifty thousand visitors in town. Governor Cleveland arrived in coach-and-four and reviewed the great parade. The exercises were held in the afternoon on the beautiful site of Washington's Headquarters overlooking the Hudson. On foot Cleveland led a distinguished group of dignitaries up the hill. As they reached the top, the caretaker, recognizing Cleveland, opened the gate to allow him to pass, but shut it with a bang upon the rest. "The band goes up the other way," he said, pointing out to Evarts, Depew, and the other notables a dusty path, much to Cleveland's amusement. A program of martial music, a military drill, singing by a chorus of five hundred voices, an introductory address by Senator Bayard, and the climax—Evarts' oration—all ran off smoothly.[12]

Evarts' speech was hardly an oration; it was rather an historical study and philosophical reflection—a delineation of that period of suspense which followed Yorktown and a tribute to the exalted patriotism of Washington. He first pictured the "ordeal of virtue," the eighteen months after Yorktown while the soldiers awaited a peace settlement, months of anxiety and perplexity. They felt that the people had forgotten their sacrifice and that a neglectful Congress was about to repudiate its obligations to them. Washington's pleas accomplished nothing. There seemed but one hope: make Washington king. It was a rash move, but based only on love of country and safety of the people. But "those modest headquarters were no Lupercal, . . . the ragged army that lay here encamped, were not the Roman legions or the Roman mob—and Washington was not Julius Caesar." He refused the crown. The soldiers proposed to coerce Congress. Washington alone could still this mutiny. He addressed and mastered his troops "by the power of his reasons, the earnestness of his expostulations, and the authority of his presence." They disbanded and he bade them farewell. Had he never given further service, "his face would have shone to all the people, as did the face of Moses to the children of Israel when he delivered the tables of law. . . . Such was the immortal name of Washington."[13]

Judge Noah Davis wrote Evarts, "I have read your oration at Newburgh with immense satisfaction. It is entitled to take rank with the patriotic efforts of Ames, Webster, and the great English orators."[14] Eloquent teachers of Evarts' type are rare in any generation. Whatever criticism one may level at his politics, there can be no doubt of his elevated patriotism.

To celebrate his sixty-fifth birthday in 1883 Evarts' law partners gave him a dinner at Pinard's on East Fifteenth Street. The table was set for fifty-two. A birthday cake, surrounded by sixty-five candles, stood at Evarts' place and the menu bore the appropriate sentiment: "Age cannot wither or stale his infinite variety."[15]

The same year the Column Club, that early organization of young lawyers which Evarts had joined during his apprenticeship, celebrated its fifty-eighth anniversary at Pinard's. There were fourteen present, including Augustus Schell, the archon; Evarts, the premier, Hamilton Fish, John Bigelow, Edward S. Van Winkle, and Parks Godwin. The silver column was brought from Tiffany's and the Etruscan lamp, emblematic of the inextinguishable life of the club, was lighted. In the course of time Evarts became archon with Bigelow and Godwin the only other surviving members.[16]

The law firm experienced changes in the seventies and eighties. Although Charles E. Butler returned to the firm, it still went under the name of Evarts, Southmayd, and Choate. In 1874 Charles H. Tweed, Prescott Hall Butler, and Allen W. Evarts became members. In 1879 Charles C. Beaman also joined. In 1882 Charles E. Butler again retired, and in 1883 Treadwell Cleveland became a member.

Probably the important case of Evarts' later life was the defense of the constitutionality of the Tenement House Cigar Law in the Court of Appeals in 1884. The law provided: "The manufacture of cigars or preparation of tobacco in any rooms or apartment which in the city of New York are used as dwellings for the purpose of living, sleeping, or doing any household work therein, is hereby prohibited." It was the first deliberate attempt of the New York trades unions to coerce capital by prohibitory legislation. Defeat meant injury and possible ruin to the trades unions; defeat to the cigar makers meant a comparatively small pecuniary loss, but the loss of what seemed to them a lawful, inoffensive occupation. It was a question whether the weight of numbers and influence of politics could win for the trades unions.

The cigar manufacturers, knowing they had the support of the Health Department, which had repeatedly declared that cigar-making in the home was not detrimental to health, decided to test the law in the case of David C. Paul. The Paul family occupied rooms on the fourth floor of a house on East Eighth Street and Paul used the front room to make cigars. He was arrested and carried his case to the Court of Appeals. Evarts appeared as senior counsel for the cigar manufacturers with A. J. Dittenhoeffer as junior counsel. They conducted their case with great skill. There were two questions at stake: first, was the refusal of a writ of habeas corpus to Paul an illegal restraint; second, was the act of 1883 unconstitutional?

Evarts' argument was truly remarkable. The state could not, under the pretense of a police regulation, encroach upon the personal freedom and private property of individuals. However valuable might be the police power, it had limits and was not as boundless as infinite space. The law was a subversion of the freedom of labor under the guise of a health measure; it was an interference with the right of every man to labor; it was a local measure applying only to New York City; it was an impairment of the obligation of contracts. At one blow it deprived three hundred and seventy thousand cigar-makers of their means of livelihood and forced them to seek employment in cigar factories where health and moral conditions were worse.

The court did not render a clear-cut decision. But meanwhile another case had arisen which became the real test. Peter Jacobs made cigars on the first floor of a tenement house, using one of seven rooms for that purpose. Evarts was pitted against Attorney General Olney. Interest had become keen and many lawyers and politicians were present at the trial.

Evarts won a great victory, repeating much of his former argument. Olney was quite taken aback when Evarts described tobacco as a form of fumigation. The court declared the law unconstitutional as an unreasonable use of the police power, holding that the act was not a health law and had no relation whatever to public health.[17]

This case, like some that have preceded it, illustrates that Evarts was usually ranged on the side of capital rather than labor. The same could be said of most illustrious lawyers of his time. He had been interested in political reform and in good government, but he had little knowledge of or connection with economic and social reform. This does not mean, however, that he had no interest in the welfare of the common man.

The retirement of Southmayd in 1884 was a great loss to the firm. His inspiration and indefatigable labors had contributed much to its success. He retired at sixty, being afraid, as he afterward told Choate, that he might spoil his work by a mistake. His work had been his hobby. He had no outside interests and few friends, although he was genial toward those he had. He led a solitary life and refused to marry, declaring half-seriously to his partners, "Your women folks will be the ruin of you yet." He had a summer home in Stockbridge, Massachusetts, upon which he poured money lavishly; but he became increasingly penurious in his habits.[18] He likewise became apprehensive of his health and more conservative in his views, distrustful of all innovations. He rode the four miles from his Forty-Seventh Street home to the office in a horsecar, till one cold morning he saw a stove under the car seat and immediately got off. Later, when the trolleycar replaced the horsecar, he got off and took a cab. He had an excellent pair of horses, but seldom used them, declaring, "If I hire a cab and an accident occurs, I incur no liability."

He was a match for Evarts in repartee, and when there was nothing else to do, it was a treat for the junior partners to hear them chaffing each other merrily. Southmayd had a slight lisp and a habit of innocent swearing. Not long before his death, when his memory was failing, a former employee who took care of his personal affairs called to see him on business. His sister told him that Mr. Rowe was waiting to see him. "Mr. Rowe," queried Southmayd, "who is Mr. Rowe?" "Why you surely know Mr. Rowe," replied his sister. "Oh yes," responded Southmayd absent-mindedly, "hell and damnation, show him up." Truly Southmayd was an interesting lawyer, reminiscent of the old-type English solicitor. "Take him all in all," said Choate, "we ne'er shall look upon his like again—an absolutely unique character—an honor to our profession."[19]

Choate's reputation as a lawyer was becoming almost as great as Evarts'. In earlier life he had been chiefly a jury lawyer but was now appearing often in the appellate courts. He could present a case with such ease and simplicity that there seemed to be but one side to it. He always gave the impression that a case was not difficult. He never dealt sledge-hammer blows and seldom wrangled with an adversary. He took an independent, nonchalant attitude, omitting technicalities and fine-spun theories, and appealed to reason, justice, and a comprehensive view of the law and the facts. His versatility in the different branches of the law was unusual.

Nature was kind to Choate in giving him a sound body, an attractive appearance and personality, and a temperament which spared him from worries or regrets. He was quick-witted and met emergencies in the courtroom intuitively. Best of all, he was optimistic and unafraid. He had a fresh, original way of looking at life; the eternal boy in him lightened his whole spirit. Although his power of satire and ridicule was a terrible weapon, he did not use it often against fellow lawyers. In fact, it was difficult to pick a quarrel with him. He was elected president of the Bar Association in 1888 at an earlier age than any of his predecessors. He did not have the good fortune to serve in as many great cases as Evarts, but after Evarts retired, James C. Carter was the only other lawyer who could dispute Choate's leadership of the bar.[20]

The passing of O'Conor in 1884 was a blow to the profession. From Evarts it brought a sincere expression of regret. O'Conor was seldom seen in court after the war, confining his practice mainly to written opinions. His prosecution of Tweed added to his fame, but his refusal to enter public life prevented distinction such as Evarts obtained. His acceptance of a forty-thousand-dollar fee from Mrs. Forrest in the famous Forrest divorce case injured him for a time. He welcomed the investigation by the Bar Association and explained that the greater part of the fee covered expenses and loans to Mrs. Forrest. The investigating committee, including Evarts, Choate, Bosworth, Parsons, and Silliman, reported that O'Conor's word was sufficient and the Association heartily approved.[21]

There is no biography of O'Conor, only brief accounts. But his cases in the law reports are a permanent monument to his work. He had the papers bearing on his principal cases brought together in expensively bound volumes, numbering over a hundred, which he bequeathed to the New York Law Institute.[22]

He had the satisfaction of knowing that he had, without the advantages of social position, attained the highest pinnacle of his profession. But years of hard labor undermined his health, accentuating his caustic temperament and making him overcritical. He was always perverse and seemed to delight in austerity to confound his adversaries. But he was generous to his friends. Indeed, he was of mixed character, cold in professional life and warm in private life. He was not an orator and could not win popular applause. He had little outward charm and his manner was scholastic, with few gestures, and a hard, rasping voice. His mind was analytic, not imaginative; in this respect he differed from Evarts, who combined the power of analysis with a broad background of a liberal education and philosophic mind. O'Conor always went straight to the heart of a problem. He once said, "The great lawyer is not the one who knows the most law, but who understands what point is involved. I have known many cases to go to the Court of Appeals where neither party knew what the real point was."[23] Unlike Evarts, he was never a great constitutional lawyer. He showed lack of judgment in insisting upon carrying his point, and seldom undertook a case unless reasonably certain that the law was on his side. This undoubtedly explains why he lost so few cases.

His last years were spent as a recluse at "The Cliff," a house which he built in Nantucket in 1882. On this isolated, rock-bound northern shore of the island he spent many hours writing legal opinions for his colleagues on knotty problems. Here he stored his large library of some eighteen thousand volumes in a brick, fireproof building twenty feet from the house. Here in 1884 he died.[24]

The New York Bar Association, representing state and federal courts, met solemnly in the General Term Court room to pay respects to his memory. Evarts had known O'Conor longer than anyone else present. He spoke of him in the highest terms, paying tribute to his skill, courage, and learning, and to the open, manly conduct of his cases. O'Conor was absolutely without vanity, said Evarts, hostile to all humbug, a self-made man, and a believer in "an upright judiciary and an intrepid and independent bar."[25]

After the passing of O'Conor, perhaps the ablest of Evarts' rivals were the veteran David Dudley Field and the much younger James C. Carter. One of Evarts' last clashes with Field was his opposition to Field's Civil Code. Field had been fighting for simplification and codification of the laws of New York since 1839, giving tremendous effort and time to it without recompense. He had induced the legislature to approve a Code of Civil Procedure but could get no further action for many years. In 1879 the legislature adopted his Civil Code but the governor vetoed it. By 1882 the Criminal and Penal Codes were adopted, but the Civil Code was still the object of controversy. It was this code which brought the blast from Evarts in 1882.[26]

Although Evarts appreciated the desirability of ending the overrefined technicality of the law and boiling down the myriad of precedents to a systematic form, he disliked the principle of codification. For four hours he argued against it before the Judiciary Committee of the legislature. He could see no general demand for it by the bar or the people. "I have never known," he said, "so vast an innovation, so untried an experiment." It would be replacing the old common law with methods of legislation; the whole bar would be occupied with trying to get justice under the code instead of by precedent or equity. Revision of the statutes and common law was doubtless needed, but codification was a quite different thing. The code was fragmentary and incomplete, a mixture of treatise, digest, law dictionary, and compilation. It was unwise to change the wording of laws upon which the courts had long rested. At least, concluded Evarts, it would be best to submit Field's "hobby" first to the study of a committee of lawyers. The hostility of the Bar Association proved the deciding factor in defeating the code.[27]

Like O'Conor, James C. Carter had an uphill fight to fame.

Without intellectual brilliancy, genius, or attractive social qualities, he won his way by hard work. Coming from Harvard over a decade after Evarts, he entered a law office which developed into the great firm of Scudder and Carter. He aided O'Conor in the prosecution of the Tweed Ring and served on the Evarts Commission to devise a plan of municipal government. He worked with O'Conor in the famous Jumel case and broke down under the strain, retiring for several years; but returned to attain greater distinction.

Carter was learned, resourceful, and versatile. Unlike O'Conor he was approachable, unassuming, and courteous; but like him, he lacked humor and dealt sledge-hammer blows calculated to compel rather than persuade. He had strong convictions and was unyielding. He was a good speaker and a power for good in the profession, always at Bar Association meetings, and like Evarts, five times elected president. Cleveland considered him for Chief Justice to succeed Waite, but the uncertainty of Carter's health prevented the appointment. Carter had absorbed so much from O'Conor that his conduct and style in the courtroom bore a resemblance to O'Conor's. His mode of thought, thoroughness of research, style of speech, and even his manner suggested his great mentor.[28]

Carter was Evarts' rival in the famous case of *Post* v. *Weil,* which reached its climax in 1889 and proved the last of Evarts' cases. There was nothing dramatic about this final legal battle in the Court of Appeals, but it raised a vital question of law and has proven an important precedent.

The facts were complex. In 1807 Michael Hogan, owner of two twenty-acre farming estates known as Claremont and Monte Alta, located near the present Columbia University on Riverside Drive, conveyed Monte Alta to his trustees to be sold under the special condition that "no part of the land or buildings shall ever be used or occupied as a tavern." In 1811 Jacob Marks purchased Monte Alta with the condition attached; in 1812 Claremont was sold without the conditional clause; in 1816 all parties to the sale of Monte Alta endorsed a release of the condition, but the release was never recorded. In 1821 both estates fell to the possession of Joel Post and by subsequent conveyances to John Post in 1873. He offered the lands for sale at auction in lots and Max Weil bought certain lots at the corner of Claremont Avenue and 122nd Street, paying ten per cent of the price, but refusing the balance when he discovered the condition in the deed.

Post sought Evarts' opinion and was told that the condition ended when Hogan disposed of the property. Thereupon Post sued Weil to compel a completion of the purchase. The case was first heard at Special Term with Evarts and Carter as opposing counsel. Evarts argued that Hogan's conveyance to Marks and the uniting of the two estates extinguished the condition and that a condition in a deed was only for the benefit of the grantor (Hogan) and not for those who subsequently acquired the property. The court agreed and Evarts won the first round.[29]

In 1876 Weil appealed to General Term. Again Evarts insisted that a perpetual condition could not exist in equity. He recalled the similar situation in the will case of *Stanley* v. *Colt*. Such a perpetual condition, when applied to a valuable tract in a growing city, was intolerable and contrary to public policy. The condition in the deed was a covenant, not a condition requiring forfeiture if broken. But the court reversed the decision and upheld the condition as a defect of title which entitled Weil to refuse the purchase.[30]

The finding of the lost release, together with a new suit brought against Bernheimer, another purchaser at auction in 1873, brought the issue to its second phase. Knowing that O'Conor had given Bernheimer an opinion that the condition was a defect in the title, Evarts was all the more anxious to prove otherwise. To his disgust the Special Term held that the discovery of the release of a condition years after did not perfect the title. But at General Term in 1883, the court gave some hope by an equivocal decision.[31]

The last stage of this protracted struggle was in the Court of Appeals in 1889. The two cases of Weil and Bernheimer were combined. Evarts was anxious for a vindication. Many years had passed and advanced age had come upon him, taxing his strength and weakening his eyesight. He knew the decision was vital to real estate law and was determined to go through with it. He bore up remarkably well, showing signs of physical but not mental weakness. There was a striking contrast between his frail, emaciated form and the ponderous frame and heavy face of the much younger Carter.

Evarts knew the case thoroughly. "I have seven points, one for each judge," he said. His elaborate brief, written in his own hand, was proof of his industry and, in view of his failing eyesight, quite an achievement. There was little that was new in his argument. He repeated that the condition in the deed was a covenant, driving home point after point to prove it. The court vindicated him completely, holding that the condition was simply a covenant running with the land for the benefit of the adjoining estate and was extinguishable by the union of the two estates.[32]

The death of Waite in 1888 was another loss of a colleague. Evarts presided at the proceedings in his memory in the Supreme Court, and at a later meeting of the bar paid tribute to Waite. He recalled the fifty-five years of "unbroken friendship and unbroken respect," the comradeship at Yale, and the close intimacy at Geneva. He described Waite as a mild, gentle, courteous, but immovable judge; one who faced great problems on the bench, but proved himself "adequate in intellect, integrity, and in the firmness to maintain and administer the law of the land."[33]

There is no more alluring hoax in the history of the American bar than the narrative of Captain Kidd and the Astor fortune, which was supposed to include Evarts and Elihu Root. According to this amazing tale, oft-repeated with added embellishments, even appearing as a feature article of the *Liberty* magazine in 1934, Frederick L. Olmsted is supposed to have found one of Captain Kidd's treasure chests on his estate on Deer Island, Maine, and to have traced the contents by the most elaborate, painstaking research to the original John Jacob Astor, who disposed of its contents in England and so laid the basis for his fortune.

In 1893 Olmsted is supposed to have completed the chain of evidence, to have sought Evarts' advice, and on being assured that he had good grounds for a lawsuit, to have gone with Evarts to face Astor's heirs with the facts. This concluded Evarts' connection; but a suit is supposed to have followed, with Choate acting as Olmsted's counsel, for the payment of five million dollars. Elihu Root is supposed to have defended Astor, but secured a settlement out of court. The records of the case are supposed to have disappeared except the account published by Franklin H. Head in 1898 and preserved in the rare book department of the Library of Congress. The story is a fable fabricated by Head. Olmsted specifically repudiated it; there is no mention of it in the recent authoritative life of Root; and Evarts was too old in 1893 to have participated in it.[34]

Evarts' last professional service was an opinion rendered to the High Court of Chancery of England in its capacity as guardian of infants.[35] Actually he appeared in very few cases after 1885 because the political bee had stung him again.[36]

29

The Return to Public Life

STRANGE THINGS happen in politics. It would be strange, indeed, if Evarts should take the seat in the Senate made vacant by Roscoe Conkling. In a bitter feud with President Garfield over certain appointments Conkling had resigned, expecting vindication from the legislature. To his mortification Eldridge G. Lapham was chosen to complete his term, which expired March 4, 1885. During the presidential campaign of 1884 Evarts' candidacy to succeed Lapham became popular; but it was doubtful whether he could carry the legislature without a following.

Evarts' efforts for Blaine pleased the "regulars" of the party, while his reputation as a reformer still made him acceptable to many of the left wing. But he had no intention of seeking the senatorship, nor was his support of Blaine motivated by a desire for the office. He knew few members of the legislature intimately and had little part in state party councils.[1] But Whitelaw Reid again went to work for him, declaring him to be superior to most senators and sufficiently independent to represent all wings of the party. Letters begging him to run began to reach him, one enthusiastic college professor prophesying that the senatorship would lead him to the presidency in 1888.[2] These appeals kindled his interest. Twenty-five years had passed since Greeley and Harris defeated him for the Senate. He was much stronger now than then, but again it was a question whether the party would recognize ability or bow to political finesse.

Levi Morton was the candidate of the Republican machine, with Tom Platt, upon whom Conkling's mantle had fallen, as his chief supporter. Morton was disturbed by the rumors that Arthur was also a candidate and was hampered by being absent from the scene of battle, serving as minister to France. He was an able man, wealthy, generous, shrewd, and tactful. He hoped to revive the Stalwart machine, which had fallen with Conkling.[3]

The manner in which Evarts acquired supporters without effort on his part was miraculous. First, the Arthur delegates, who knew that their candidate would not run, threw their votes to Evarts as a compromise a week before the caucus.[4] Second, he had the aid of George B. Sloan, who took the lead in his behalf. Again, the politicians at Albany were able to get a look at Evarts in action by visiting the Court of Appeals where he happened to be engaged in the Tenement House Case and their impression was favorable. Furthermore, Senator Arkell took up his cause, being interested in the tariff and feeling it would be the great issue in the coming Congress. Even the usually hostile *Times* admitted that Evarts was qualified and that his independence would be an advantage.[5] Evarts protested that he lacked financial means. He knew the Senate was rapidly becoming a plutocratic chamber. He spoke so frankly of his lack of qualifications that Hayes, who was watching closely, feared he would ruin his own cause.[6]

He had not yet declared that he would run. But when he heard that the chairman of the Republican National Committee supported him, he announced his candidacy in the *Albany Evening Journal*. He was careful to avoid the tariff issue and make no promises. But he refused to go to Albany to solicit votes. He simply said, "I'm in it to beat or be beaten. It's the thing I've been doing all my life, and the result never disturbs me."[7] Since he would not go to Albany, a group of legislators went to New York in early January to see him. Failing to obtain promises from him, they offered the nomination to Chauncey Depew, but Depew declared himself for Evarts.[8]

Morton was favored to win by reason of superior resources and the backing of the machine. Platt was his generalissimo and Cornell his lieutenant. Evarts' campaign was managed from the Delevan House at Albany by Arkell and H. E. Tremaine, with Theodore Roosevelt as one of his most energetic supporters. By the second week in January the campaign grew hot and petitions for one candidate or the other poured in upon the legislators. The Evarts boom grew surprisingly. By January 9 it became clear that Morton's victory was not assured, although Evarts had definitely only thirty-one of the ninety-two votes to be cast at the Republican caucus.[9] At a great Republican rally in Brooklyn the next day the enthusiasm for Evarts was unbounded, with speeches by Stewart L. Woodford, Joshua Van Cott, Judge Noah Davis, and some others. By the 14th deputations were arriving in Albany to work for him.[10]

But his enemies were not asleep. The dairymen denounced him for having given a professional opinion favorable to the oleomargarine manufacturers and declared that he had better remain in private life for representing such "steer-grease-hog-fat-cotton-seed-oil-bosh-butter interests."[11] The *Times* accused him of "utter lack of courage and conscience" in public affairs, of joining "a progressive and reforming movement only when the majority swing to that side," and of being a lover of the "sunshine." This reference to Evarts' growing conservatism brought Senator Miller into the fray. Miller declared Evarts was needed in the Senate because an "unswerving party allegiance" was the only way to check a Democratic administration. Cornell, who supported Morton, retorted that Evarts had never been in full sympathy with the party. Evarts was angered by Cornell's accusation that he had betrayed Folger in 1882. He insisted that his letter to Folger, showing why he had refused to speak for him, be published. Roosevelt came to Evarts' rescue by charging Cornell with bad taste, considering that Evarts had supported him for governor.[12]

The caucus met on the night of January 19. Evarts remained at home receiving telegrams from Albany. An early one from Roosevelt assured him that he would win. The Morton men called for a secret ballot, partly to avoid public responsibility and partly to permit a shift to Depew. But the Evarts men replied that it would be unfair and cowardly and by a vote of sixty-four to twenty-eight the open ballot was approved.[13] Evarts' name was presented by Assemblyman Howe of New York City. On the final ballot Evarts received sixty-one votes, Morton twenty-eight, and Depew three. The nomination was equivalent to an election.[14]

The Evarts men were jubilant. They had experienced some anxious moments. The victory was due partly to Evarts' popularity, partly to the factionalism in the party, but mainly to the unexpected weakness of the Platt machine. The legislature was virtually forced into virtuous action. But it later proved that Evarts' victory postponed the unity of the party in New York. To be sure, Republicans might rejoice in the election of a senator who called himself neither Stalwart, Half-Breed, nor Reformer, but simply Republican, a man who had been a charter member of the party. They also might rejoice that his election left so few wounds and gave such promise of the future. But could he go far in the Senate without a machine behind him or would he join that machine?

Evarts was at home in the library when the good news arrived. He was in a jovial mood and asked eagerly for the details. The next day was occupied in meeting the stream of visitors who came to his office to congratulate him. A flood of telegrams covered his desk. He picked up one from Murat Halstead. It read: "The morning light is breaking in the Imperial State." Another from Arkell declared: "Public sentiment tells after all if the right kind of man is behind it." Hayes was greatly pleased, regarding Evarts' victory as a vindication of his administration and a defeat for the Stalwarts.[15]

He was soon made to feel the responsibility of his office. William E. Dodge told him that his election was "a large promise of better things and purer government"; Thurlow Weed's daughter wrote him, "Your influence and voice will strengthen our party and protect and defend Republican Government." General Sherman's comment was most significant: "Were I to be guided solely by my own convictions, I would be doubtful of the wisdom of one occupying so prominent a place in the Bar of New York City changing it for a seat even in the Senate of the United States. But you yourself told me you wanted it and surely you know your own interests and business best. . . . I will be prepared to see you take a leading rank in it from the day you take your seat."[16]

The Forty-ninth Congress would not meet till December. Evarts therefore had a year to prepare for a readjustment and continue his profession. During the months succeeding his election, however, much time was given to a gay round of dinners and receptions.

He declined the impressive invitation signed by J. P. Morgan, Whitelaw Reid, Hamilton Fish, and numerous others to be guest of honor at a public reception at the Academy of Music. But he did appear at an elaborate reception given him at the Union League Club.[17] A throng of Yale men, from gray-bearded alumni to dapper youths, welcomed him at the University Club. Chauncey Depew presided and Evarts' wit flashed exuberantly.[18] Notwithstanding the excitement and round of honors, Evarts looked well and spoke vivaciously everywhere, carefully refraining, however, from politics.

He went to Albany and was met by Arkell and other political friends. He called upon President-Elect Cleveland and they chatted for a time, both doubtless wondering to what extent they would be political enemies at Washington. A reception was given him by Governor Hill in the executive chamber, attended by the legislature; another held at the Fort Orange Club was attended by the Court of Appeals and many state officials.[19]

He visited Boston in April as guest of the Middlesex Club. It was expected that he would assert political leadership, but he contented himself with one of the wittiest and most informal talks he had ever made. He touched on politics only incidentally, describing the Democrats as fish who had gotten into the water again after a long refrigeration, jumping and flopping about aimlessly. His best story related to a case in which he was pitted against George T. Curtis. Indulging in extravagant rhetoric, Curtis reached the climax of his peroration, shouting, "Six men would be worth more than six babies"; whereupon Evarts interrupted with the interjection, "Six babies are something in a squall." Evarts was in fine fettle that evening, many remaining after the speech-making to listen to his brilliant conversation. But Senator Hoar, who was present, was disappointed by Evarts' frivolous air. "I felt as though a pail of ice-water had been poured down my spine," said Hoar, "but modesty and disinterestedness are qualities that are so infrequent among public men that we may as well pardon this bright and delightful genius for that fault."[20]

Soon after at Delmonico's, Evarts presided at a dinner given to the famous English actor, Henry Irving. It was a gathering of intellectuals and literary men, among them Mark Twain, Holmes, Howells, Beecher, and Edwin Booth. Describing himself merely as a "scene-shifter," Evarts introduced Irving with his usual felicity. After the dinner two actors accosted him to remind him of a transatlantic voyage they had made on the same ship with him. Evarts did not recall them. "In what ship was it?" asked a bystander. "I don't know," replied Evarts, "I only know we were all in *transports*."[21]

Evarts could not evade politics indefinitely. In October he appeared at the Brooklyn Academy of Music at a great rally. The hall was crowded from floor to dome and he was the principal speaker. A few Democrats were on hand to heckle him, but were soon silenced. It was a partisan speech, touching upon party unity, Civil Service reform, the tariff, shipbuilding, the currency, and good government. He seemed most interested in the Southern question and waved the "bloody shirt" with unbecoming emphasis. He believed Cleveland had already committed errors as President. This speech, together with another political address soon after at a dinner of the Boston Merchants' Association at the Hotel Vendome, was not a very promising start.[22] Instead of asserting leadership, he gave evidence of being a follower—a loyal partisan.

He went to Washington as the first senator from New York City since 1863. He had to find quarters and sought out Henry Adams to see if his house was available. He finally found a house at the corner of Eighteenth and I streets, where he lived two years. In 1887 he moved to No. 1519 K Street and in 1888 to No. 1601 K Street, where he remained for the rest of his term.[23]

Although he wanted the senatorship, he took it with misgivings. He was sixty-eight years old and would be in his middle seventies by the close of his term. He hoped that he might have a part in ending the protracted period of bitter party politics. But he was not at all sure he would enjoy the life of a senator. "I have lived so independent a life," he told Robert C. Winthrop, "that I am not sure I should altogether like the bonds of Senatorial responsibilities."[24] After all, he was a lawyer, not a politician. He found the senatorship a costly luxury. A salary of five thousand dollars did not even cover the rent upon the large house and stable on K Street. He told Cyrus Field that he found a salary very different from being paid "by the job."[25] He expected to continue law practice, but really had neither time nor energy for it.

In appearance Evarts had changed little since the day he defended Andrew Johnson. The lines about his eagle-like face had deepened, the hair was much grayer, and the shoulders more stooped. He was the thinnest man in the Senate and weighed only one hundred and twenty-five pounds. As a rustic from Vermont said, on catching sight of him for the first time, "Well, I declare, why he looks as though he boarded."[26] But he was wiry and unusually active for his age. He did not pay great attention to dress. The trousers were invariably baggy at the knees and his coat too loose. He clung to the old style, with big, rambling, turned-down collar and cravat and with old top hat jammed down close to his ears. In speech he was more deliberate than ever, lacking perhaps some of the old fire, but still with perfect rhetoric and powerful logic. Age had not dulled his intellect.

Three tragedies darkened the Senate years. His oldest son, Charles B. Evarts, who managed the Windsor estate, was stricken with paralysis in 1886, recovered almost completely, and then died suddenly in 1891 at the age of forty-six.

An accident at Windsor during the summer of 1886 nearly cut

short his senatorial career. He went for an afternoon drive with Charles C. Perkins, father-in-law of his daughter, and Jeannie Matthews, daughter of Stanley Matthews. One of the horses became restive and when the coachman reined him in, the bit broke and the bridle came off, causing both horses to break into a run. The coachman tried to stop them but was thrown. Running madly, the horses turned a sharp corner, throwing the three occupants from the carriage. Perkins was hurled against a stone embankment and killed, Evarts escaped with a sprained ankle and slight scalp wound, Miss Matthews was badly bruised. Within a week Evarts recovered, despite the fact that he had been thrown head-first. Describing the accident, Evarts said, "The light phaeton, which had been the favorite carriage of pleasure drives for thirty years, will never carry any laughing guests again. It went to pieces after the upset. . . . The horses were neither fractious nor untrustworthy, the harness was strong, the coachman competent and faithful and brave, and we all met the dangers we were suddenly thrust into without a sense of alarm or discomposure. The broken bit discloses a secret and undiscoverable flaw and from that cause the whole tragedy. . . . My escape was wonderful."[27]

The third tragedy was Evarts' declining eyesight, which sounded its warning especially during his last two years in the Senate. Prior to 1889 he was remarkably free from bodily ills, drolly attributing his good health to the fact that he rose late in the morning and that he had never taken any exercise.[28] But after 1889 he found reading increasingly difficult and finally reached the point where he could not read at all. He bore the calamity cheerfully at first, but increasingly chafed under this greatest of physical handicaps. Senator Hoar said it was due to overwork in the preparation of law cases.[29] In an estimate of his work in the Senate this handicap must be borne in mind.

Evarts was not by nature a legislative leader. His life had been given to arguing causes, not originating policies or playing the political game. As Senator from New York he was in a position to become a party leader, but he had neither the taste nor adaptability for political management. He was bored by the work of the committee room, the incessant pursuit of patronage, and the work of compromise. He appeared to best advantage when stimulated by a worthy cause. Occasionally he disappointed his New York business friends by his seeming timidity or indifference and likewise disappointed the Independents by his over-regularity in party matters, following the lead of men much smaller than himself. With the same easy-going attitude toward routine work that he had evinced in the State Department, he now refused to be unduly troubled with details. In exasperation Hoar met him one day in the corridor of the Capitol and said, "By the way, Evarts, when you report that bill of mine, just notify my executors." To which Evarts retorted, "They will be gentlemen whom I shall be delighted to meet."[30] He regarded Congress as a debating body rather than a law-making body. He thought there were altogether too many laws already and that a session of Congress might well be confined to the discussion of a few outstanding questions.[31]

He held some important committee assignments. Throughout his term he was member of three committees: the Judiciary, Foreign Relations, and Privileges and Elections. During his last four years he was chairman of the Committee on the Library. He served a short time on the Committee on Private Land Claims and the Committee on Immigration.

The Senate represented plutocracy more than democracy. Half of the seventy-six senators were wealthy and represented large vested interests, among them such men as Dolph, Jones, Brown, Allison, Cameron, Aldrich, Sewall, Spooner, and Sawyer.[32] The prestige of the Senate had waned since the war. It had overreached itself by insistence upon senatorial courtesy and disposition to hamper the President; moreover, it treated the new economic problems with an all-too-evident sectional spirit. The number of senators who, like Evarts, owed their seats to intellectual eminence or political experience was growing smaller. But there were some able members: Cullom, Dawes, Hoar, Edmunds, Sherman, Spooner, and Teller.

A month after taking his seat, Evarts made it clear that he was going to be a loyal party man. "I believe," he declared in the Senate, "that steadfast and intrepid adhesion to a party is a merit, and I believe that political contests fail much of their service to the country when steadfast and intrepid adherence to political leaders is neglected on the part of the mass of the party."[33] He was not thinking of blind partisanship as much as the need of Republican unity to meet the immediate situation. The Democrats held the presidency and a fair margin in the House; in the Senate the Republicans had a bare majority. A bitter partisan deadlock existed and was to last throughout Cleveland's term. Evarts, doubtless to his disgust, was necessarily drawn into the political feud between the President and the Senate.

Senator Edmunds, whom Evarts greatly admired, was the leader of the senatorial cohorts in this bitter fight. Edmunds had few friends in the Senate but his colleagues had a healthy respect for his virtue and sarcasm. He had a profound contempt for humbug and hypocrisy and probably did more than any other senator to maintain the integrity of the Senate. He precipitated the struggle with Cleveland, determined to curb his power of appointment and removal and elevate the prestige of the Senate. The battle began when Edmunds demanded that Cleveland transmit to the Senate papers concerning the suspension of George M. Duskin, a district attorney of Alabama, and the appointment of John D. Burnett to succeed him. Cleveland admitted the right to request public documents dealing with an appointment, but refused any paper bearing upon a removal or confidential papers dealing with an appointment.

Evarts watched the struggle with dismay, not participating in it till toward the close. He was interested because the issue centered upon the Tenure of Office Act of 1867. He had not openly asserted his belief that the act was unconstitutional at the impeachment trial of Johnson, but he undoubtedly thought so at the time. A later act of 1869 had not repealed it, but permitted the President to suspend officers during a recess on condition that he restore them at the end of the recess unless the Senate affirmed the suspension.

At all events, Evarts felt the President should submit the papers to the Senate and joined the majority of the Judiciary Committee in signing a report affirming the right.[34] But the President refused and appealed for popular support. Edmunds slapped back by recommending a resolution censuring the President. During the month of debate that followed Evarts spoke on the legal and constitutional aspects of the issue.

He debated the question vigorously with Senator Voorhees, insisting that the President must submit *all* papers and that the Senate, in secret session, could decide which were confidential. Apparently he visioned the Senate as a secret "star-chamber" where appointments and removals were concerned. He admitted that the removal power vested solely in the President and that the Tenure of Office Act was unwise; but the Duskin Case was a suspension and hence only the act of 1869 applied. That act did not allow the President to suspend an officer and appoint his successor simultaneously.[35]

However accurate might be Evarts' argument, popular opinion was distinctly with Cleveland, and the Senate, after passing the vote censure, beat a hasty retreat. Hoar introduced a bill for the repeal of the Tenure of Office Act and the whole Judiciary Committee, except Edmunds, signed it. Evarts gladly spoke in favor of repeal. He still refused to hold it unconstitutional, but called it "inexpedient and improvident" to divide the removal power and place the President in a "strait-jacket." The repeal was a victory for Cleveland and a vindication of his power of removal. Had not Edmunds burned his personal papers before his death, more light might be thrown upon Evarts' share in this unfortunate feud.[36]

The tariff was expected to be the great issue before the Forty-ninth Congress. Undoubtedly one strong reason for Evarts' election was the belief that he would fight strongly any attempt by the Democrats to lower it. The Morrison bill, proposing a general reduction, was never reported from committee in 1886; but in 1887 a great struggle again loomed between the President and the Senate. Cleveland had decided to make it the leading issue.

Evarts spoke in Utica and at Cooper Institute in favor of the protective system. The surplus in the treasury, he argued, was no reason for lowering the tariff; it was only a "flea-bite" and could be spent for pensions, internal improvements, and payment of the national debt. The country had recovered from the depression of 1884 and could stand high taxes and a high tariff; indeed, it was the best guarantee of prosperity.[37] Except for these two speeches, Evarts did little about the tariff. The fact was that the real tariff struggle was postponed till the next Congress, by which time the Republicans were stronger.

Deadlocked as it was, the Forty-ninth Congress found it difficult to make headway. But there were several important nonpartisan measures before it which greatly interested Evarts. One of these was the Electoral Count bill of 1886, which aimed to prevent a recurrence of the dangers arising from the disputed election of 1876. The original bill in the Senate provided that when the two houses of Congress disagreed over the election returns from a state, such state should lose its vote. Evarts insisted that a state should not be deprived of its vote and that the best rule to follow would be the one he advocated in 1876: count the returns certified by the governor. The final act so provided and Evarts was given credit for contributing a valuable idea.[38]

The death of Vice-President Hendricks not only brought a fine eulogy in the Senate from Evarts, but roused his interest in the problem of presidential succession.[39] Who should become president if Cleveland died? The act of 1792, providing that the President *pro tempore* of the Senate and Speaker of the House should succeed in order, was unjust to the party in power, unwise in placing a legislator in the executive office, and insufficient in leaving a contingency in which there still might be no president.

Evarts spoke at length in favor of Hoar's well-devised bill providing succession by Cabinet officers in order of their rank. The framers of the Constitution, he said, never intended Congress to control the election of the President. Under the act of 1792 it might impeach a President in order to elevate one of its own members.

This and other evils could be remedied by the Presidential Succession bill. He had the satisfaction of seeing this measure become law.[40]

As a member of the Committee on Privileges and Elections, Evarts spoke on several interesting problems in the Forty-ninth Congress. His indignation was aroused by a bill to prohibit members from acting as attorneys to railroads which held charters or received aid from the government. Of course his own law practice was affected. But he felt it a reproach to the legal profession and an insult to the Senate, where sixty-five of the seventy-six members were lawyers. Never before, he said, had he known the need of penal legislation to secure the proper conduct of lawyers in the Senate. No grave situation had arisen requiring such a measure; bribery was already penalized; and lawyers should not be singled out for discriminatory legislation. Senator Beck replied to Evarts with an attack so bitter that he later regretted his words and apologized. But the passage of the bill proved the need for a curb on railroad senators.[41]

Evarts had quite a battle with Beck on another question of privilege. Beck had presented a bill forbidding members of Congress to practice law in the Supreme Court. Condemning Beck and his bill, Evarts referred to lawyers whose practice was limited to specialties as "unilateral lawyers." Beck misunderstood Evarts' meaning, became angry, hurling epithets at Evarts, and shouted that a unilateral lawyer from Kentucky was more respected than a "quadrilateral pettifogger" from New York. It was some time before Evarts could pacify Beck.[42] They later became good friends.

The most unpleasant duty of the Committee on Privileges and Elections is to decide the disputed elections of senators and report its findings. Senator Henry B. Payne, wealthy Democratic politician from Ohio, had dubious connections with the Standard Oil Company. The Ohio legislature charged that he had purchased his seat and asked an investigation. He offered his books and accounts to the committee, which meant nothing because the corruption came from others. He made no explanations and produced no witnesses. The committee acquitted him for lack of evidence, but the decision was not popular. Hoar and Edmunds ridiculed the verdict. Whether Evarts believed Payne guilty cannot be said, but he defended the report of the committee. He explained the committee had only meager evidence. If it was to be regarded with suspicion, the whole Senate might as well be held unworthy. All the evidence came from Payne's political enemies, mostly editors. "These editors," said Evarts satirically, "decided they would hold a crow carnival. If anybody has ever observed the proceedings of that most extraordinary concert among the birds, he will find that their parliamentary system is extremely simple. They all speak at the same time, and they all say the same thing. They have a great power of voice but a very limited vocabulary. They have great energy of assertion, but great poverty of argument." He appealed for an abandonment of the investigation till new evidence appeared and the Senate approved. It proved later, however, that the suspicions concerning Payne were well grounded.[43]

The question of greatest future importance in the Forty-ninth Congress was the regulation of interstate commerce. It offered Evarts an opportunity to express again, as he had done in the granger cases, his views on regulation of the railroads. The debate upon the famous Interstate Commerce bill of 1887 was one of the best ever heard in the Senate.[44] In 1884 the Reagan bill had passed the House prohibiting some of the abuses of the railroads, but the Wabash decision of the Supreme Court in 1886, forbidding state regulation, opened the door to further abuses and made some action by Congress imperative. Senator Cullom presented his famous bill for the creation of a commission to regulate the railroads and it passed the Senate with Evarts voting for it.[45]

Thus there were two measures, the Reagan and Cullom bills, of widely different character, before Congress. The Democratic House disliked the idea of a commission; the Senate disliked the antipooling clause of the Reagan bill, upon which the controversy seemed to center. A compromise bill finally emerged, the House accepting the plan for a commission in return for Senate acquiescence on pooling and the regulation of long and short hauls. A great, spontaneous, rapid-fire debate followed upon this compromise bill and all of the strong men of the Senate were heard from.

In opposing the pooling and long-and-short-haul clauses of the bill, Evarts voiced not only his own opinion but that of the New York Chamber of Commerce. He favored a commission, but not the two clauses in question. The long-and-short-haul clause, he argued, "will unsettle all business interests throughout the West; will depreciate the value of all farming lands west of the Middle States; will work directly in the interest of lake ports, lake transportation lines, Canadian roads, and the Eastern farmer." The clause would create lawsuits enough to keep the lawyers at work for twenty years and placed too great a burden of enforcement upon the commission. Substantially Evarts' contention was that commercial development should not be disturbed by regulation. He asked that the bill be recommitted for amendment of the two clauses in question.[46]

Provoked by Evarts' opposition, Senator Cullom exclaimed, "I have no disposition, God knows, to interfere with the commerce of the country, properly conducted, but I do say that it is the duty of the Congress of the United States to place upon the statute book some legislation which will look to the regulation of commerce."

The Senate finally gave way on the two clauses and the opposition led by Sherman, Evarts, Hoar, and Spooner was defeated by a vote of thirty-seven to twelve. The act forbade rebating, various discriminatory practices, and pooling; it contained the long-and-short-haul provision; it created the Interstate Commerce Commission.[47]

Evarts had approved the commission, objecting mainly to problems of enforcement that would arise under the act. In view of the difficulties the commission experienced during the first decade of its existence, his objections were not without point.

It was appropriate that Evarts should be a member of the Foreign Relations Committee, for which few senators were better fitted. John Sherman, who was also a member, said, "I learned from my intimate association with him in the cabinet, and subsequently as a member of the committee on foreign relations, to respect and love him."[48]

Old age and long experience in international affairs had not dampened his respect for international law and peace. He secured the purchase and distribution of some four thousand copies of Francis Wharton's *Digest of International Decisions*. He told the Senate of his long acquaintance with Wharton and defended him against criticism for using his time as a government employee in the State Department to compile his valuable treatise. When Wharton died before completing his work, Evarts prevailed upon the Senate to have it completed by John Bassett Moore.[49]

Evarts believed the foundations of peace lay in international law, which would gradually supplant war. "As law enters the door," he declared to a friend, "war flies out of the window. Some way must be found to nourish and fertilize international law, to the end that the world may have law, adjudication, and order, in place of war, reprisal, and anarchy. We must have periodical conferences of the nations at short intervals, to thresh out the public opinion of the world and to promote the growth of international law. . . . Long after I am gone, the world will have to wake up and watch the Germans and set barriers, as you would against a wild bull until he is tamed. That will probably be the special work of England and America." A world order, concluded Evarts, should include an effective police to enforce judicial decisions. America must lead in the peace movement and assume the burden for calling the nations to make agreements.[50]

As Secretary of State, he had stressed the improvement of the foreign service. As Senator, he renewed the attack, urging better salaries and the creation of ambassadorships. He pointed out that Sir Edward Thornton had been withdrawn because the United States did not send a representative of equal rank to London. But it was not till 1893, just after Evarts left the Senate, that Congress established ambassadorships in the leading countries of Europe.

He may, however, be fairly credited as a pioneer in this reform.[51]

Evarts' main contribution to the Forty-ninth Congress was his speeches on the fisheries problem. No senator could speak with more authority. In 1885 the arrangement with Canada under the Treaty of Washington terminated, reviving the unsatisfactory status of 1818. Canada was indignant when the United States refused to renew the treaty. The question now was whether a new treaty should be sought or the treaty of 1818 enforced. If the latter alternative was adopted, where was the three-mile limit? Did it follow the sinuosities of the coast, as the United States had always contended, or was a line drawn from headland to headland, as Great Britain had long contended? If the British view prevailed, a large share of the inshore fisheries were denied Americans. This was the crux of the controversy.

Evarts opposed Cleveland's plan for the creation of a commission to settle the problem and felt it inconsistent to seek a new treaty when one had just been abandoned. The Senate approved this view by a resolution in April, 1886.[52] The "Retaliation bill" then emerged from the Foreign Relations Committee, empowering the President to prohibit the entry of Canadian fish or vessels whenever American fishermen were harassed. Evarts did not agree with the extreme position taken by Edmunds on this bill; nevertheless he spoke for it, insisting that its object was not retaliation but a demonstration to Canada of our interpretation of the treaty of 1818.[53] Evarts agreed with John Jay's suggestion that the treaty of 1818 might well be abrogated, restoring the original situation at the end of the Revolution.[54] The Retaliation bill passed overwhelmingly in both houses. Cleveland reluctantly signed it with no intention of using the power it conferred.

The President, taking a more tolerant view, sought a new treaty with Great Britain. Politics entered the picture, the Senate Republican leaders seeking to curb the President's treaty-making power. Cleveland went ahead with his plan, and the Bayard-Chamberlain negotiations for a new treaty ensued at Washington. Upon Joseph Chamberlain's arrival, Evarts was present at a dinner given him by

John Hay and as usual lent the light touch with his amusing stories.[55] A fair treaty was agreed upon providing for the creation of a mixed commission to decide all territorial rights of fishermen, recognition of the British headlands theory, and the right of American fishermen to necessary operations on the Canadian coast if the United States removed its duty upon Canadian fish.

Republican senators pounced upon this treaty, and party lines were closely drawn. Evarts, Edmunds, Frye, Sherman, and Dolph were the five majority members of the Foreign Relations Committee who fought ratification. Evarts spoke against the treaty at great length despite excessive heat which overtaxed his strength and caused him obvious difficulty. He asked the indulgence of the Senate toward his infirmities; only the importance of the subject could induce him to speak.

His speech was not as partisan as those of his colleagues, although he accused the Democrats of a friendliness to Great Britain that was "redolent with the odor of denationality." He believed public opinion averse to the treaty. He denied that its defeat would lead to war or to the collapse of the New England fisheries. "My proposition is this," he declared, "that the object of the Canadians has always been not to observe the treaty of 1818, . . . but to make a persistent encroachment on those liberties and produce, at least, an irritation." The object was to "worry" the United States into a commercial treaty "by indefatigable teasing." On a large map which hung in the Senate chamber Evarts pointed out the absurdities of the headlands theory and asserted that Great Britain could not make a bay by calling it a bay. He called the Bayard-Chamberlain treaty "a diplomacy of surrender," which gave away forever what we had sturdily refused to concede in the past. It meant a multiplication of regulations; it was an abandonment of claims for insults and damages; it was an acceptance of the absurd headlands theory. The best solution would be the creation of an international patrol to prevent clashes, not the sacrifice of American rights under existing treaties.[56] He would risk embroilment with England rather than make further concessions, but did not believe it would come to war.

As was anticipated, the treaty was defeated, more because of political considerations than the weaknesses of the proposed treaty. Evarts joined his colleagues in blocking all amendments to the treaty so as to insure its defeat before the presidential election. But the Republicans overshot the mark and were dumbfounded when Cleveland called for wholesale retaliation against Canada. The Senate dared not approve the new course and thus inconsistently opposed retaliation after having introduced it. Evarts had no comment to make on this masterstroke.[57]

Fortunately the Bayard-Chamberlain negotiations had provided a way out if the treaty failed. The Canadian authorities offered licenses to American fishermen who accepted their terms. To Evarts and many New England fishermen this was an acceptable arrangement, certainly preferable to the concessions of the proposed treaty. It did not, however, secure a permanent settlement of the problem, nor was there one till 1910.

Evarts might have been more active during his first two years in the Senate if a party deadlock had not existed. His record was undoubtedly a disappointment to his friends. He unquestionably had become more partisan than ever and could no longer be called an Independent. But he was still popular in New York and still had some real contributions to make as senator.

30

Breaking the Deadlock

THE GREAT PARTISAN issues which agitated the Fiftieth Congress were the tariff, the silver question, and the Southern problem. Upon these issues there was a deadlock till 1890. Evarts had a part in all three, taking a strong partisan stand.

Cleveland had devoted his entire annual message in December, 1887, to the tariff, denouncing the protective system as class legislation at the expense of the taxpayer and consumer. The Democrats in Congress rallied to his support and a great battle ensued in 1888. They brought forth the Mills bill for drastic reduction and it received the blessing of the President. It became the chief issue of the campaign of 1888.

That summer Evarts attended the state convention at Saratoga to urge protection. He was a stranger to state conventions but received a cordial welcome. The hostile *Evening Post* declared that the delegates were so glad to behold his "lean, Cromwellian visage" that they rose and applauded for several minutes, but cared little for what he said; indeed, his speech was "a chronicle of reflections on ancient history as far as he had progressed with it." The "ancient history" was Evarts' survey of the tariff and the story of George Washington's insistence upon wearing a suit of domestic manufacture at his inauguration. While speaking, Evarts noticed that the rain was dripping through the roof into his top hat, which he had placed in a chair. He deliberately removed it to a safer place, remarking that his head could take care of itself but his hat needed "protection." He ridiculed Cleveland's tariff message and read extracts from the British press to prove that the President was a free trader.[1]

As a challenge to the Mills bill there appeared the Allison bill in the Senate, frankly protective in its provisions, yet cleverly designed to win some of the farmer element. At an informal caucus at Evarts' house on the night of July 25 Aldrich and Evarts persuaded the majority to accept the Allison bill. To this crack of the party whip the Republican senators promptly responded.[2]

The presidential campaign grew hot by September. Evarts accepted an invitation by Henry C. Bowen (prominent in the Beecher-Tilton scandal), to speak at Roseland Park in Woodstock, Connecticut. Evarts, Senator Hawley, and several other speakers arrived to find that large crowds from surrounding towns had gathered, some bringing bands with them. Evarts adapted his speech cleverly to the mind of his rural audience, keeping them laughing continuously. Tariff reducers, he said, would let England produce American food and clothing and keep the Southerner always from "half a crop to a crop and a half" behind the English manufacturer. They seemed to think that "if you have a small price for a small crop of wool, from small sheep, and then bought small clothes and few of them of a lasting or durable nature that would carry you through a year or two with a suit, you would be the happiest people in the world." England would enjoy seeing us adopt a low tariff so as to make all Americans tillers of the soil, receiving, like the laborers of India, ten cents a day.[3] Evarts' speech was shrewdly conceived, but the anti-British appeal smacked strongly of James G. Blaine.

By the end of October Evarts had made no other speech. The *Times* ridiculed his inactivity and also charged him with abusing the franking privilege to circulate campaign material, portraying the facsimile of two signatures that he was supposed to be using to defraud the mails.[4] This charge, of course, was never proved. He soon set at rest the other criticism by appearing at Cooper Institute before a large, enthusiastic audience. Again the tariff was the main theme. He cleverly reversed Cleveland's well-known admonition, calling Cleveland's conception of it "a theory and not a condition." He condemned the administration for its conduct of foreign affairs; he prophecied a Republican victory.[5]

The Republicans carried the election. Harrison became President, although his popular vote was less than Cleveland's. On the other hand, Hill, a Democrat, carried New York by more than eighteen thousand. Evarts rejoiced in the national victory. It was rumored that Harrison intended to appoint Evarts minister to Great Britain, but the post went to Robert T. Lincoln.[6] The election had a decisive effect upon Congress. For the first time in fifteen years, a Congress assembled which had in both houses a clear majority in support of the administration. In the Senate the Republican majority was ten; in the House it was seven. The long deadlock seemed broken at last; legislation might be expected.

Regarding their victory as a popular mandate for protection, the Republicans, notwithstanding the grave misgivings of some leaders, presented the McKinley bill for increasing the rates. McKinley boasted that it was "protective in every paragraph and American in every line and word." It passed the House in May, 1890, but ran into obstacles on reaching the Senate. Apparently a new deadlock appeared in the form of concerted action by its enemies, who succeeded in holding it up five months. The resistance came from Secretary of State Blaine, who wanted a clause giving him power to negotiate reciprocity treaties with South America; from Western senators who wanted a new silver act; and from Southern senators who objected to the proposed Force bill.

While these questions pended, Evarts became much interested in a less controversial aspect of the tariff, the Custom Administration bill, which aimed to eliminate fraud in the collection of duties and to create a board of appraisers to hear appeals. Evarts had appeared in dozens of revenue cases and was thoroughly aware of the need of these reforms; he had also read the evidence of the Jay Commission after its investigation of the New York customhouse. He heartily favored the bill but opposed certain provisions handicapping the importer. He felt the appraisers should not have final decision, preferring a separate court of customs appeal, such as was later created in 1909. Failing that, he advocated that appeals should go to the circuit courts and the Senate adopted his suggestion.[7] The act was passed and saved the government millions of dollars. Also, his persistent petitions for a new customhouse, to replace the old inadequate building on Wall Street, met with success, as did also his petitions for an appraisers' warehouse in New York.[8]

To return to the deadlock, one question was: How much must be done for silver? Evarts had always supported sound money. Could the representative of the wealth of New York City do otherwise? Yet, in speaking at Paris and elsewhere for international bimetallism, he seemed friendly to silver. The *Times* might well complain of his indefiniteness and declare that he was "playing the sphinx." The *Commercial Gazette* went so far as to demand his resignation.[9] As long as Cleveland was in office he was only one of many senators who kept silent to avoid the appearance of coöperating with him in his stand for sound money.[10] In the one speech Evarts made on silver during Cleveland's term he disappointed those who came to hear him in the Senate. He devoted his attention almost exclusively to the need for another monetary conference to establish an international bimetallic ratio; but he did convey the impression that he was hostile to silver.[11]

The silver issue reached a climax in June, 1890. Senator Plumb of Kansas presented a bill for free coinage in the ratio of sixteen to one. A similar bill had already passed the House. It was the bugbear which sound money advocates had long dreaded, and a heated debate ensued. Evarts rose to speak. For over two hours he interested a large, attentive gallery. Using no notes and talking in a conversational manner, he treated the subject with a wit and piquancy quite in contrast to the heavy style that had thus far marked the debate.

He turned his fire upon the pending silver bill. "When the apostles Peter and John stood at the gate of the Temple called Beautiful, and looked with pitying eyes upon the cripple who lay there hopeless and helpless, asking alms, they required him to fasten his eyes upon them, and then in the faith of their Master they bade him rise and walk, and he arose and walked and leaped, and went into the Temple walking and leaping for joy. If I could attribute to these my friends [silverites] on my right here that apostolic grace and endowment that belongs to these apostles, speaking in the name of authority that could accomplish it, I, too, would like to see the limping silver leg on the march of money metal in the world thus raised and exhibited in the Temple, walking and leaping for joy. . . . But if we ask a cripple to throw away his crutch and break his broken limb again, what shall happen to the hapless victim of faith without a miracle to reward his faith!" The bill, continued Evarts, would hinder international parity; as America increased its silver, it would become more difficult for Europe to open its mints to the ratio of fifteen and a half to one. "I cannot tolerate," he concluded, "this idle talk of the separation of this country from the money of the world."[12]

The free silver bill failed; but something had to be done to win the silverites. The Sherman Silver Act was a compromise and like most Republican senators, Evarts voted for it, undoubtedly with reluctance.[13] The compromise proved inexpedient and further deranged national finances.

In the second obstacle, the Force bill, Evarts had a deeper interest. This Republican measure, which proposed to enforce the Fourteenth and Fifteenth amendments, seemed an act of justice to the disenfranchised Negro of the South. Senator Edmunds was its most vigorous sponsor and was extremely vindictive toward the South.[14] Ever since the war Evarts had pleaded for a square deal for the Southern voter. Threats against the purity of elections always disturbed him. At Cooper Institute in 1879 he had prophecied, "Hereafter if there should continue to be a permanent and serious threat on a large scale in this country against the integrity and freedom of the suffrage, this people will not hesitate to accord the full executive authority of their government to that citizen who best understands and can best maintain the power of the people on election days."[15]

But the Force bill sought more than the purity of elections. The Republicans wished to cut the over-representation of the South in Congress by enforcement of the amendments. The Force bill passed the House in July by a narrow margin. It provided that, on petition of five hundred voters of any election district, a bipartisan board of federal supervisors should be appointed to decide the legitimacy of ballots rejected by local officials in national elections. Southern senators angrily denounced the bill, refusing to support the McKinley tariff till it was withdrawn.

The bill went to the Senate Committee on Privileges and Elections, of which Hoar was chairman. Room 17 on the top floor of the Capitol, where the committee met, was the scene of serious consultation. Both Hoar and Evarts, while approving the bill in principle, feared it would create sectional bitterness and might even divide the Republicans. Evarts afterward told the following story to illustrate the reluctance with which he joined the majority of the committee in approving the bill. "I spent Sunday with Judge Hunt on the Hudson a good many years ago with several New York lawyers. We all went to the Episcopal Church in the forenoon and dined with the Judge after church. During the service one of the company kept far behind in the response, which annoyed the Judge a good deal. At dinner he broke out, 'Davis, why can't you descend into Hell with the rest of the congregation?' I will descend into Hell with the rest of the congregation."[16]

A deadlock followed the report of the bill. It was finally decided to postpone action on the Force bill—an expedient move but disappointing to those wishing to restore Republican influence in the South.

The track was now cleared for action on the McKinley bill and in September the bill was debated at great length in the Senate. Evarts' eyesight and health were none too good. He proposed to keep out of the debate, but Democratic appeals to class strife, and charges that the protectionists were "robbers," sulking behind "evasions, prevarications, and fraud," brought him into the fray.[17]

He defended the tariff with some of his old-time fire. Denouncing the appeal to class strife, he said, "The so-called millionaires of this country are but the gilded fringe upon the garment with which the body of our people are clothed. . . . This idle talk about poverty on the one hand and wealth on the other . . . is a new doctrine and . . . seems to be the woof and warp of the politics of the Democratic party." Industry and labor alike need protection and the Republican party intended no distinction between them. To open our markets to competition with foreign labor would be to reduce our standard of living; to drain our manufactures to Europe would be to "kill the goose that laid the golden eggs." Like Henry Clay, he stood for the American system. "What shall it profit this nation," he asked, "to join the whole world of commerce and lose its own soul?" He would, however, approve reciprocity trade agreement. He told the Senate of his own attempts while in office to make such agreements. But he believed they should be made by Congress, not by the President. Closing his long speech, which had occupied several hours on two different days, he exclaimed, "Make your tariff as you think right. And when you reach, as England has reached, the position where you can devour the substance by tariff legislation, then change your laws."[18]

Evarts treated the tariff as a national question and not, like some of his colleagues, as a matter of special privilege. The McKinley bill passed, but proved a disappointment and a political blunder. Two months later it brought the Democrats back into power in the House.

It was under this adverse condition that the Republicans, facing a new deadlock, revived the Force bill. Evarts spoke twice for it. He defended the clause which prescribed a house-to-house canvass in each election district to check registrations. There had been strong criticism of this clause as an interference with personal liberty and the sanctity of the home. Speaking with great difficulty, his opponents heckling him and talking loud to drown out his voice, he stubbornly persisted. He described the registration laws in New York; he accused the Democrats of seeking to overthrow the purity of elections.[19] The bill was temporarily sidetracked by the deciding vote of Vice-President Morton.

A month later, Evarts made a four-hour speech on the Force bill—one of his longest. It was intended as the closing argument of the debate and a final estimate of the constitutionality of the bill. He spoke before a large gallery, using no notes because of blindness and speaking with more force than seemed possible under such handicap.

"A vote honestly ascertained and counted" was his objective. The Fifteenth Amendment, he declared, took precedence over the right of the states to regulate national elections. "Away with this notion that local communities are to be let alone when we are regulating our elections under the Constitution." He made a dispassionate examination of the situation in the South, pointing to Mississippi as an illustration of the subversion of the Negro vote. Senator Walthall of Mississippi, who seldom took part in debate, challenged Evarts at every step. Walthall asked whether there was any constitutional reason why the people of the state should not protect themselves against the Negro and whether the Force bill would end arbitrary apportionment of representation. Evarts made no reply to the first question and to the second retorted that Mississippi could do so by example. He appealed to the Senate to take a broad view of the problem.[20]

The indefinite postponement of the Force bill was a foregone conclusion. Enough Republicans joined the Democrats to kill it, ending a futile twenty-year attempt to enforce Negro suffrage in the South.

Evarts' share in the political struggle over the tariff, silver, and the suffrage was secondary. In no sense was he a leader but rather a follower. Most valuable was his contribution to the Customs Administration bill. If his record in the Fiftieth and Fifty-first congresses had been confined to these major political problems, it would have been drab indeed.

With the famous Sherman anti-trust law of 1890 he had slight connection. The framing of this act long remained a mystery. Sherman submitted one bill, but it was the bill of the Judiciary Committee which became law. Edmunds wrote five of its eight sections; Ingalls, George, and Hoar wrote one each; Evarts wrote the eight words in the first section: "In the form of a trust or otherwise." He took no part in the debate, but there is no doubt that he favored the bill.[21]

The temporary break of the deadlock in 1890 permitted the passage of several other measures with which Evarts was connected. One of these was the curbing of the liquor traffic. Two years before, at the Saratoga convention, as member of the committee on the platform, Evarts used his influence to seek the defeat of the New York liquor interests. The legislature had just enacted the Crosby bill, granting local option and requiring high licence fees, but Governor Hill, a leader of the liquor interests, had vetoed the bill. Evarts' committee produced a plank which went further, providing local option and permitting restriction by taxation. He raised a laugh in the convention by reminding it that "the power to tax was the power to destroy." The plank was accepted, but the Crosbyites accused him of "spitting on the bait" to catch the votes of the Prohibitionists.[22]

The following year he attacked the liquor interests before a large audience at the Philadelphia Academy of Music. With striking illustrations and scathing tone, he denounced the influence of the saloon upon children. In Boston alone, he said, rum was sold to fifteen thousand children. The *Times* accused him of not daring to discuss the issue in his own state. But soon after, he spoke even more frankly at Cooper Institute, condemning Governor Hill as sponsor of the saloon and prophesying the downfall of the liquor interests.[23] In Congress he presented numerous petitions for curbing the liquor traffic.[24]

Most important was his share in the debate on the Wilson bill in 1890. In the so-called "original-package case" the Supreme Court had held that the police power of a state could not prevent the shipment of liquor into the state if sent in the original package; but the court intimated that Congress could modify this rule where a state had enacted prohibition laws. Taking the hint, the Judiciary Committee presented the Wilson bill, proposing to prohibit liquor importations into a dry state.

When Evarts rose to defend the bill, he said he would detain the Senate only a few minutes, not feeling well enough to speak at length; but becoming interested in his subject and urged on by questions from the floor, he went on with a long, forceful, constitutional argument. As he got deeper into the subject, the others who expected to speak became impatient and went out in the coatroom to confer. It was planned that one of them should gain the floor after Evarts finished, declare that he felt too ill to speak, and then proceed with his speech; but an adjournment after Evarts' speech prevented the rebuke.[25] Evarts had discussed the Wilson bill fully in committee and was anxious to make his position clear to the Senate. His chief point was that the original-package rule, laid down in the famous case of *Brown* v. *Maryland,* could not be used to subvert the police power of the states and thereby produce "an enormous fraud upon the whole system of importation."[26] The Wilson bill passed, protecting the dry states, and the Supreme Court sustained its validity.

Evarts was not carried away with the pension craze like many of his colleagues. During the Forty-ninth Congress he had submitted very few bills or petitions for pension aid. But after Cleveland's successful veto of the Dependent Pension bill, he became more active. He sought to frame a new bill, offered numerous petitions seeking a general law based upon the *per diem* service of veterans, and submitted numerous private pension bills.[27] After the Dependent Pension became a reality under Harrison, he felt the pension system had gone far enough and submitted relatively fewer petitions. Among other aids to veterans he sought preference in Civil Service appointments, land grants and bounties, the honorable discharge of certain soldiers, and vindication against charges of desertion.[28]

Of scores of instances in which he sought aid to other individuals, two of special interest deserve mention. When it was proposed that Francis Hunter, the aged Assistant Secretary of State, had outlived his usefulness and should be retired, Evarts hastened to his defense. He was fond of Hunter and knew his value. He became angered by Senator Cockrell's description of Hunter as a superannuated clerk. He described Hunter's sixty years of service and declared that he deserved more respect than some senators. Cockrell apologized and Hunter was continued in service.[29]

The other case concerned an appropriation of fifty thousand dollars to the family of Spencer F. Baird for his sixteen years of service as commissioner of fisheries. To keep the office out of politics Baird had performed its duties without pay in addition to other work. Indeed, he had overworked, giving time, health, and money in an extraordinary voluntary service. Well aware of his service at Halifax and elsewhere, Evarts urged the appropriation, showing that the government was deeply indebted to him and that he had died leaving his family almost penniless. He ridiculed the objection that it would be unconstitutional to appropriate a salary after the death of an officeholder. Congress finally appropriated twenty-five thousand dollars for Baird's family and made the office thereafter a salaried one.[30]

As a member of the Committee on Privileges and Elections Evarts encountered further problems. Curiously enough, the question how long a President *pro tempore* of the Senate should serve had never been answered. The Constitution was vague on the point. Evarts disagreed with the interpretation that a new *pro tempore* chairman should be chosen daily in the absence of the Vice-President. He presented a resolution: "Resolved, that it is competent for the Senate to elect a President *pro tempore* who shall hold the office during the pleasure of the Senate and until another is elected, and shall execute the duties thereof when the Vice-President is absent." This would avoid past evils and give permanent tenure to the presiding officer. The Senate adopted the resolution and the rule is still in operation.[31]

Evarts became involved in two other troublesome cases of disputed senatorial elections. Three Texans filed a petition, complaining they were deprived of voting at congressional elections by lawless ruffians who destroyed the ballot boxes. The Committee on Privileges and Elections had scarcely begun its investigation when news of a cold-blooded murder of a Republican tax-collector of Texas named Hoffman reached Washington. The blame appeared to rest upon Ku Kluxers. Evarts demanded a new investigation, but Senators Reagan and Coke of Texas denounced him for meddling in a matter that was beyond the jurisdiction of Congress. Evarts was unquestionably wrong on the Hoffman case. But this did not apply to the election disorders. Five months later, Evarts presented the following resolution: "Resolved, that the Committee on Privileges and Elections be directed carefully to revise the existing laws regulating the election of members to Congress, with a view of providing for the punishment of offenses against it." The resolution was adopted and thereupon Evarts submitted the seven-hundred page testimony that had been taken in the Texas investigation. In his report he insisted upon connecting the election disorders with the Hoffman Case and demanded action. But the Senate, well aware of the political implications, did nothing.[32]

In the case of a disputed election in Montana the question was whether five Republicans or five Democrats had been properly elected to the legislature from Silver Bow County. Evarts defended the committee's findings in favor of the Republicans. Harking back to the principle for which he had pleaded in 1876, he said the committee had refused to go behind the returns of the state canvassing board. "We cannot purge the ballot-box," he said, "because we have not the ballot-box to purge." The Senate approved the report.[33]

In retrospect, it again appears that Evarts had asserted no great leadership in these problems of liquor control, pensions, or senatorial privileges and elections. Again he seemed to be a follower; not a leader. But the record is not yet complete.

31

Senatorial Highlights

Evarts might play a secondary rôle in the political issues of the day, but he found a less fretful realm in which to be useful. The Committee on the Library was not of first-rate importance, but as chairman he did some interesting things. It may be doubted whether any senator ever contributed as much as he to matters of historic interest.

First, there was his connection with historic centennials. In July, 1888, his address at the Centennial in Marietta, Ohio, was the feature of a celebration which commemorated the inauguration of General St. Clair as first governor of the Northwest Territory. Governor Foraker met Evarts at the train and introduced him to an audience of some five thousand. Evarts spoke without manuscript and was frequently applauded. He emphasized the part played by the Northwest in national development, particularly in checking slavery. "Each generation," he concluded, "must understand its duties and its share in the great progress by which Providence leads us onward, or we shall not long be actuated by a higher and nobler civilization."[1]

Evarts presented a resolution for celebrating in New York the centennial of the inauguration of George Washington as president and was a member of the conference committee to arrange for it. He attended the great dinner at the Metropolitan Opera House where President Harrison, the Cabinet, the Supreme Court, congressmen, governors, diplomats, and scores of other notables formed an imposing array. In a brief speech he exalted the judiciary as protector of the Constitution and safeguard of liberties.[2]

He had a part in initiating the movement for a World's Fair in 1893. He wished the fair to be held in New York and presented petitions for it. When Boss Platt blocked the plan, Evarts had Elihu Root read an explanation at a Cooper Institute mass meeting, showing New York would have been preferred to Chicago but for political dissensions. He was invited to serve on the advisory council for the fair but refused.[3]

Evarts was likewise interested in historical societies. He introduced the bill for the incorporation of the American Historical Association.[4] He advocated the incorporation of the Sons of the American Revolution. Several senators, amused at what seemed to them a waste of time on petty matters, began to tease him about his historical hobbies, but unperturbed he stoutly insisted upon the importance of historical societies and the preservation of records.[5]

While in the State Department, he had opened the archives to James Schouler, the historian, and with the aid of Senator Hoar had induced Congress to purchase from Benjamin Stevens the Franklin Papers, consisting of some three thousand manuscripts. As Senator, he got Congress to buy the *Townshend Records of the Civil War,* a complete collection in eighty-eight volumes.[6] He also secured the purchase of portraits of John Rutledge, Oliver Ellsworth, and Morrison Waite, to be hung in the anteroom of the Supreme Court.[7] He argued the importance of a safe repository for historical manuscripts, showing that owners of private collections would be more willing to donate them to the government if assured of a safer care. Congress responded with an appropriation for such a repository.[8]

As chairman of the Library Committee, Evarts supported the international copyright bill, designed to protect foreign authors against piracy. The United States was the only nation which had persistently refused to do justice to writers of other lands. Labor unions, particularly the typographical union, had long opposed international copyright as a deterrent to American printing. Evarts had received protests against the selfishness of these labor interests when in the State Department. Congress tried to pass a bill several times. In 1891 Evarts entered the debate on the Simonds bill. "The sole question," he said, "is what shall we do concerning something which is the essential nature of copyright and patent protection, namely, monopoly." He favored the bill, especially as it would lessen plagiarism. A compromise was finally reached and the measure passed under great pressure on the last day of the session.[9]

Evarts was equally active in securing the erection of monuments. He had much to do with the placing of the Lafayette monument in Washington on its present site. This equestrian statue, a gift from France, arrived in 1890 and Congress authorized the Library Committee to spend fifty thousand dollars for a pedestal, half of which was to be paid the builders before the work began. A difference of opinion arose in Congress over the proposed site on Pennsylvania Avenue because it obstructed the view of the Jackson statue. Evarts was disgusted when several Democratic senators exploded with fervid oratory against the slight to Old Hickory, and Bartholdi, who had designed the statue in France, was likewise upset by the delay. Evarts strove to untangle the matter and finally got approval of a new site near the Treasury Building.[10] He induced Congress to complete the Newburgh memorial at Washington's Headquarters, to raise a monument to mark the Revolutionary battle at Stony Point, and to erect one at Fort Greene Park in Brooklyn in memory of the prison matyrs of the Revolution.[11]

Though an address on Garibaldi deserves mention,[12] the best of Evarts' speeches while senator—indeed, the last of his so-called orations—was his eulogy of William H. Seward at Auburn in November, 1888. Twelve years before, he had dedicated the Seward statue in Madison Square. The Auburn statue was the gift of friends and admirers of Seward. It stood in a small park adjoining the Seward estate and was about eighteen feet high. The great statesman seemed in the act of pronouncing his "higher law," with right arm raised and forefinger pointing upward. Despite the rain, a large crowd was assembled to witness the unveiling. The exercises were then adjourned to the Opera House, where Evarts delivered his oration. He touched upon the three phases of Seward's life: as senator, in the war Cabinet, and in Johnson's Cabinet. His whole public career, said Evarts, displayed "a calm judgement, a penetrating forecast, an intrepid courage, a fervid spirit, unfailing patience, and the largest charity. . . . He betrayed no trust, he deserted no duty, he quailed before no danger, he recoiled from no labor, he broke no friendship, he rose on no man's fall, he gained by no man's loss, he fed no grudges, nor raised his repute by defaming others."[13] In selecting Seward's virtues, Evarts revealed those which he most admired.

Evarts played a conspicuous rôle in the hectic history of the Statue of Liberty. For nine years he was connected with this undertaking. Laboulaye, the eminent French historian, was the originator of the idea and Bartholdi its chief executor. The statue was to be made in France and sent to the United States as a gift of the French people. In 1875 the Franco-American Union was organized in France to sponsor the project and raise funds. The French people responded and Bartholdi went to work on the statue.

In 1876 Bartholdi came to New York to participate in the dedication of his statue of Lafayette, which was erected in Union Square—a gift of the French government to the city. At the same time Evarts was chosen chairman of a citizens committee of twenty-one to arouse national interest in subscription for a pedestal for the Statue of Liberty. Clubs, societies, chambers of commerce, and individual subscriptions from ten cents to one hundred dollars were solicited. Evarts' committee included Edwin D. Morgan, John Jay, William Cullen Bryant, Parke Godwin, and Theodore Roosevelt. Congress approved and designated General Sherman to select a site for it. Bedloe's Island in New York Harbor was chosen. Evarts' committee, now increased to sixty, set to work in earnest to raise the needed funds. By 1880 Bartholdi had nearly completed his work as sculptor, and the Franco-American committee informed Evarts that France had raised the money for the statue.[14]

But an exasperating series of delays followed. There was an avalanche of criticism: editors, architects, and art critics declared the project ridiculous or impossible; experts said the statue would blow over in the first storm; there were uncertainties whether the gift was to the United States, to New York State, or to the city; it was complained that the enterprise was to subserve some private interest. Other cities became jealous. In alarm Bartholdi wrote Evarts expressing the anxiety of the Franco-American committee. Evarts replied that America would do its part.[15]

The real drive for funds did not get started till the fall of 1882. At a great patriotic mass meeting in the Academy of Music on November 28, Evarts, Choate, and others made a strong appeal. A new committee, less local in composition but with Evarts still its head, was put in charge. This committee, with the help of Joseph Pulitzer of the *World,* did much to dispel the feeling that the statue was a gift to New York City alone.[16]

By 1883 Bartholdi had completed the statue, but the pedestal on Bedloe's Island was hardly started. The death of Laboulaye was another blow and Evarts wrote Bartholdi a letter of sympathy. The American fund was not increasing as it should. The New York Board of Education refused to allow the schools or school children to be utilized in concerts to aid the fund. The state would not grant desired help. Congress made an appropriation, but it failed because the expenditure was not inserted as an item in the budget. Evarts' committee resorted to the sale of statuettes, photographs, and pamphlets, but the returns were meager and the committee became discouraged. An attempt to make up the deficit by one-dollar subscriptions resulted in a wrangle with the Sons of the American Revolution. A point was reached in the spring of 1885 where something had to be done by somebody. Pulitzer launched a subscription campaign of his own with the result that the one hundred thousand dollars was oversubscribed. Evarts sent to him the sincere thanks of the committee.[17]

The statue arrived on the French man-of-war *Isère* in June, 1885, and the Chamber of Commerce gave a dinner to the ship's officers to celebrate the arrival. In paying tribute to the commander of the *Isère,* Evarts said, "He has done what in the history of the world no nation, no ruler has successfully attempted; he has kept 'Liberty Enlightening the World' under the hatches for thirty days."[18]

The erection of the pedestal was hastened in 1886. As senator, Evarts did not hesitate to ask Congress for a fifty-thousand-dollar appropriation for the improvement of Bedloe's Island. Congress had already given that amount for the inauguration expenses and hesitated to spend more. But Evarts finally got most of what he asked. Writing the secretary of the committee, he said, "It will seem . . . that *everything* asked for by the committee, for the purpose of expenses . . . are included in the sum allowed in the Senate Bill, except the sum of $2,500 for Refreshments. . . . The Bartholdi appropriation is safe, the President having signed the bill."[19]

In October the French delegates who had come to attend the dedication were given a reception at the Academy of Music. Amid unbounded patriotic fervor, the orchestra playing, Evarts led the French delegation to the platform with De Lesseps and Bartholdi in the van. Frederic R. Coudert gave the French a stirring welcome and Evarts concluded with his usual cleverness, "What these two great nations have joined together, let not the malice of men nor the virulence of the elements put asunder."[20]

October 28 was a great day in New York and never was there a gayer scene in the harbor. After a great parade in the city, two steamers carried the notables—President Cleveland, the Cabinet, and dozens of others—to Bedloe's Island. Thousands came out in boats, and other thousands lined the shores. It was a foggy, rainy day; but enthusiasm was high. Above towered the Goddess of Liberty some three hundred feet. On the platform sat the notables: Cleveland, Evarts, Bartholdi, and others.

Evarts made the presentation address. Unaccustomed to such conditions and interrupted by noise in the harbor, his voice could not be heard well. He lauded all who had a share in the final result, especially the French people who "contributed from many slender means and of their own free will, . . . from their hearts as well as from their purses, and all for the love of liberty." As he paused for a moment in his address, the young man near him who was to signal the men above when to release the veil, believing Evarts had finished, gave the signal prematurely. A tremendous burst of steam whistles from the ships in the harbor drowned his closing words. He had the presence of mind to sit down. It was some fifteen minutes before quiet was sufficiently restored for the President to make the acceptance speech. An oration followed by Chauncey Depew. Again the whistles blew and the guns roared and Liberty was inaugurated.[21]

As senator, Evarts showed great interest in education. In a public address he said, "It is by education that I learn to do by choice what other men do by force."[22] He was one of the most loyal and esteemed alumni of Yale and a favorite at class reunions. Henry Holt declared, "I think I saw him at every Commencement I went during his active years. The Yale Alumni Association was founded during the sixties and used to meet monthly during the season at Delmonico's. . . . A good shepherd he was. One night he talked to us of what a young man beginning in New York ought to know. I remember two things he said—You can't expect much help from friends; but you can expect that any good thing you do will be recognized."[23] Three of his sons went to Yale. In the seventies he was elected a trustee of the college. At a Harvard dinner James C. Carter once compared Evarts to a ship launched at Yale, but fitted at Harvard. "Yes, gentlemen," agreed Evarts, "it is true that I got my *education* at Yale, and took my *brass* at Harvard."[24]

Evarts presided at his class reunion in 1887. Twenty-eight members were there, including Waite and Pierrepont. When the class of 1857 came to serenade them, Evarts went out on the veranda to address the visitors. At the dinner that evening Evarts was called upon by the president of the college to "say a single sentence"—a jibe at his involved rhetoric. "If I were to take you at your word," responded Evarts, "it would be a source of grief for the rest of the course of your natural life. Why should I have such a bad reputation? What fault of mine is it that the intelligence of my hearers has been short and their ears long?"[25]

During the Senate years there was one educational project with which Evarts' name will ever be connected, the law school of Howard University in Washington, which opened its new building in October, 1892. It was the only law school for Negroes south of Mason and Dixon's line. The school had outgrown its old quarters and a new three-story edifice on Fifth Street was made possible through the generosity of Evarts, Collis P. Huntington, John W. Ambrose, Cephas Brainerd, and other members of the New York bar. Over the door of the new building was engraved in large letters "William M. Evarts Hall," in recognition of his services in procuring funds. Professor W. W. Hart of the faculty wrote Evarts, "The authorities of the University and friends of the cause of educating colored youth owe you and Senator Allison much for magnanimity and measureless service in this behalf." Evarts not only gave money, but was active in getting appropriations from Congress for endowment and gifts of duplicate law books for the library.[26]

One of the most important educational measures ever presented to Congress was the Blair Common School bill. It contemplated an expenditure of nine and one-half million dollars annually for eight years with a view to giving every child equal educational facilities. Of course the danger lay in federal control of schools; but such was not the aim of the bill, nor was it designed to be permanent aid to the states, which would receive the funds in proportion to their illiterate population, for elementary schools. Necessarily its chief benefit would go to the South. Evarts had become interested in it even before entering the Senate. Blair had written him in 1884, "If after the country has been fully advised by three weeks of debate in the Senate, the American People will not push it through the popular branch of Congress, it is proof that they are unfit to receive the benefits of the measure."[27] Blair's fears proved true; the House rejected the bill.

When the bill reappeared in the Senate, Evarts gave it cordial support, refuting constitutional objections to it. He justified the appropriation under the power of taxation and the general welfare clause. When Senator Morgan chided him for speaking as if constitutional questions had never before been debated in the Senate, he replied tartly that he had long debated in a "forum more accurate than the Senate." He secured two important amendments to the bill: that it should apply only to non-sectarian schools and that a grant refused by a state should be redistributed among the other states.[28] Again the bill passed the Senate but failed in the House. In 1888 it likewise met the same fate, with Evarts again speaking for it.[29]

When the bill was revived in 1890, Evarts made his best plea. He realized however that there was little hope because the Republicans were in full power. Constitutional objections, he charged, had been used as a stalking-horse to conceal personal or local opposition. Rivers, canals, roads, arts, and manufactures could all be developed under the Constitution; but "this primal and universal interest of education was buried so deep in the clauses of the Constitution that the country could not unearth it." Should the richest people in the world hesitate to spend fifteen cents per capita for our common schools?[30] But the Republicans were unwilling that the lion's share of the subsidy should go to the South.

Evarts' interest in the Blair bill was doubtless due to the understanding he had acquired of Southern conditions as trustee of the Peabody Education Fund. He had served as trustee since 1867. By 1880 there was no more able group of men than this self-perpetuating body, including Hayes, Evarts, Grant, Fish, Waite, and Winthrop. Its meetings were business-like: Hayes testified to Evarts' efficiency. Once a year a dinner was held in New York. Fish grumbled when it was held in Washington in 1880, writing Davis, "Winthrop always wants some excuse to get a smell of the old fleshpots and wander about in the regions of departed greatness. They [Winthrop and Evarts] will both be prepared for the occasion, the one bland, magniose, and grand: the other, as ever full of wit, *et produi nil.*"[31]

When Evarts entered the Senate, he and Fish, Hayes, and Winthrop, were the only survivors of the original sixteen trustees; indeed, Evarts proved the last. During the Senate years he continued to be active. Whatever he may have thought of Grant politically, he praised him warmly as a Peabody trustee. Speaking in the Metropolitan Church in Washington at a service in memory of Grant, he described him as "the most modest of that body" and an "obedient servant of that trust."[32]

In advancing commercial interests Evarts was fairly active in the Senate. As representative of New York, much of course was expected of him, more undoubtedly than he accomplished. Just before entering the Senate he had advocated a simple, inexpensive bankruptcy plan which would do justice alike to debtor and creditor and give as little as possible to lawyers. In the Senate he supported the Torrey bill and presented numerous petitions for its passage. The bill failed because it too closely resembled a penal code upon debtors; but it became a law in modified form some years later.[33]

Persistently Evarts strove for the improvement of the Harlem River in New York. Finally Congress approved a two-million-dollar contract to dredge the river and connect North and East rivers by canal. Evarts sought additional expenditure and was irritated by the opposition of Hoar and Reagan. Although failing to get the additional funds, he secured appropriations for bridges across Arthur Kill to New Jersey and across East River to Long Island.[34] Evarts did not indulge in the scramble for "pork-barrel" legislation; he did support worthy improvements.

His petitions for the improvement of the postal system were numerous, including a reduction of postal rates, better postal facilities for New York, and shorter hours and higher pay for employes. One day he rose to object to the building of post offices of more than seven floors. The skyscraper had not yet lifted itself on the skyline, but Evarts saw it coming and objected to a "cell system of architecture."[35]

The improvement of foreign commerce of course interested him.

As member of the Committee on Immigration he again sought cordial relations with China. The killing of twenty-eight Chinese by a mob in Rock Springs, Wyoming, angered him and led to a strenuous appeal for indemnity to the Chinese, which Congress granted. When Congressman Scott introduced a bill to prohibit Chinese laborers in America from returning to their homeland, the intent being to discourage further emigration from China to America, Evarts attacked it as an affront to China and a violation of the treaty he had negotiated in 1880. But the bill passed in plain violation of treaty stipulations.[36]

When Congress proposed to cut off the annual appropriation for support of the international bureau of weights and measures at Paris, Evarts explained the value of the bureau in preventing the undervaluation of imports. The appropriation was continued. On several occasions he worked for the improvement of the ocean mail service.[37]

In two interesting cases he sought relief for marine inventors: most persistently, for Joseph Francis, inventor of the life car for use of the coastguard. Francis, a man over eighty, was the real father of the modern life-saving service. He had been recognized abroad but neglected at home. He had received patents long before his rival, Dr. Ottinger, and was supported by the New York Chamber of Commerce and the American Institute. Evarts was not satisfied when Congress gave him a medal and vote of thanks. He insisted upon the recognition of Francis' prior right as inventor, arguing that Ottinger had received ten thousand dollars for improvements upon Francis' work whereas Francis received nothing. The Senate approved recognition but the House refused to concur.[38]

The second case, that of John Roach, builder of naval craft, was more tragic. He had acquired virtual monopoly of government shipbuilding, but the inferior quality of one of his ships brought him financial ruin. Evarts felt he had been treated unjustly and had spoken of his case to sympathetic audiences before entering the Senate. When Roach died, broken and humiliated, in 1887, Evarts tried unsuccessfully to secure relief for his family.[39] It was later discovered that Roach was not to blame for the defective vessel.

During these years Evarts deplored the weakness and inefficiency of the navy and supported Secretary Whitney's plan for improvement, presenting bills for a new cruiser, ten large ships for harbor defense, and the purchase of Ericsson's destroyer. He secured the erection of a marine hospital at Middlesex, New York. By the close of his term, however, when the beginnings of a modern navy were apparent, he opposed further increase.[40]

Although a gentleman-farmer himself, Evarts had little to say of agriculture in the Senate. The dairymen of New York had opposed his election because he had acted as attorney for the oleomargarine interests. As Senator, however, he defended the dairymen and vigorously attacked the oleomargarine makers. He spoke in favor of a tax of two cents a pound on oleomargarine, approving its constitutionality. A tax prohibiting oleomargarine as a fraud, he said, would be lawful; but one prohibiting it as an honest product would be void. Plainly, oleomargarine sold as butter was a fraud, and since the states had proved themselves incapable of dealing with the fraud, Congress should act. When it appeared that the Supreme Court would void a tax on oleomargarine, he urged a new law which would meet legal requirements.[41] Such a law, however, did not become a reality till 1902.

Evarts was at his best when dealing with a legal problem. As a member of the Committee on Private Land Claims he shared in the solution of some difficult problems. Both parties had promised for years to reclaim the national domain for actual settlers, but little had been done. Vast areas had been granted to railroads under conditions which had never been fulfilled, and legally such lands should have been forfeited to the government. By 1885 an area equal to that of New York, New Jersey, Pennsylvania, Delaware, Maryland, and Virginia was subject to forfeiture, but no action was taken.[42]

To compensate for past extravagance a bill appeared early in

Evarts' term to tax lands sold by railroads to private persons. Evarts was sympathetic with the purpose, but he foresaw legal difficulties and proposed changes. The Senate sustained his objection that the tax should not apply to unsurveyed lands, but his recommendation that no one should be allowed to buy more than one square mile was rejected. It was mainly the idea of forfeiture to which he most objected. He had a heated controversy with several senators over the point. "The law," he said, "abhorred forfeiture, placed the government in the position of a feudal lord, and created a defect in land titles." Forfeiture became, however, the keynote of congressional policy.

Of a different nature was the Des Moines River bill, which had been before the Senate for years and sought to untangle a dispute over lands on the Raccoon River in Iowa. Congress had granted the lands to Iowa, which in turn granted them to the Des Moines Navigation Company and others. But settlers had entered and set up adverse claims, and in 1873 Congress had recognized nearly all of these three hundred-odd adverse claimants. Evarts had a special interest because some of the original holders under the Iowa grant were New Yorkers. He opposed the proposal of Congress to recover the lands and give the settlers new titles, calling it an invasion of private property rights and not a solution that could be permanent. Nevertheless the bill passed the President's veto by the margin of one vote, although it failed in the House. The reappearance of the bill at the next session brought another blast from Evarts. He complained that it would unsettle titles and bring an avalanche of lawsuits. "If you pass such a law as this," he warned, "who can complain that rights are insecure, that courts are untrustworthy and the serene majesty of the Supreme Court of the United States is whistled down the wind in the Senate of the United States?" He presented a substitute bill, proposing to indemnify all claimants for damages. He felt it better to compensate than disturb titles. Again the Senate overrode the President's veto.[43]

Evarts himself became a land owner in Washington during the Senate years, adding to the properties he already held in New York and Vermont. Indeed, one of the most surprising real estate transactions in Washington in 1887 was his purchase of a three-hundred-acre tract, known as Mount Beverly farm, some twelve miles south of the city on the Potomac branch called Swan Creek, just above Fort Washington. All around it, extending up and down the river, were manor houses of old lordly Maryland domains. Directly across the river was Mount Vernon. Many wondered why Evarts bought the tract since there were no improvements upon it. Evidently he intended it for a country home near the Capitol, but soon found a new use for it. It proved to be the heart of a rich marl district and the valuable fertilizer was found to lie close to the surface.[44]

It was only natural that Evarts' chief contribution as Senator should have been in the field of judicial reform. It was here that his legal knowledge showed to best advantage. As member of the Committee on the Judiciary, he not only gave expert advice, but took the lead in a reform which bears his name today. This committee, which met in Room 29 in a corner of the lower floor of the Capitol, was one of the busiest and most prominent. Evarts often shed a brightness on its prosaic work. One day objections had been filed with the committee to a certain appointment on account of the dissolute habits of the candidate. Some evidence to prove these objections had already been found in the files, but a new search was made, resulting in new documentary evidence against the candidate. "The papers in this case," remarked Evarts, "appear to be more dissipated, if possible, than the candidate."[45]

Evarts was active in the minor improvements of the judicial system. The drawing of judicial districts, determining places for court sessions, creation of new judgeships, questions of jurisdiction, and the increase of judicial salaries—all of these problems interested him.[46] He urged a bill granting the owners of ships and cargoes the right to sue the government for damages resulting from collisions caused by official negligence; but his recommendation did not succeed. He did secure a measure providing *per diem* compensation of federal attorneys, clerks, and marshals.[47]

His greatest legacy as Senator was the Court of Appeals Act of 1891, otherwise known as the Evarts Act. His hard work upon this important reform, despite bedimmed eyesight which almost precluded reading, accomplished a noteworthy improvement in the federal court system. The reform grew out of the enormous increase of judicial business which crowded the docket of the Supreme Court after the Civil War. The whole judicial system gave signs of collapse under the weight of accumulating cases. Attorney General Garland begged that "something be done," declaring, "Almost every mail brings me one or more letters about this matter from the people."[48] Bench and bar urged reform. By 1889 over sixteen hundred cases awaited a hearing and it would take the court over four years to clear its docket even if no new cases arose.

Methods of relief had long been discussed. One plan was to increase the pecuniary amount necessary for a case to reach the Supreme Court. Another suggestion was to divide the court into quorums for the decision of most cases and leave a full court for important constitutional questions, thus enabling the court to dispose of two or three times as many cases. A third plan was the creation of a new intermediate court of appeals to relieve the Supreme Court by final decisions in certain types of cases.

In 1881 Evarts had been appointed a member of a committee of the American Bar Association to report on a method of relief. The committee divided: five approved the intermediate court plan and four, including Evarts, preferred the division of the Supreme Court into quorums. At the meeting of the association in 1882 Evarts took the lead for this plan, fearing that an intermediate court might delay appeals and that two courts with power to render final decisions might be dangerous and of doubtful constitutionality. But the association approved the intermediate court plan by a vote of thirty-nine to twenty-seven.[49]

Congress had taken no action by the time Evarts entered the Senate. He felt something must be done, but was convinced Congress would never accept the quorum plan. Rather than have no reform, he shifted to the plan of an intermediate court, thereby of course incurring some criticism. In April, 1890, the Rogers bill passed the lower chamber by an overwhelming approval. It provided for the creation of nine new intermediate courts with final jurisdiction in certain kinds of cases. When the bill reached the Senate Judiciary Committee, Evarts took the lead in framing a new bill, which differed materially from the Rogers bill.

He made an exhaustive study of the laws and decisions bearing upon the jurisdiction of the federal courts and then drafted in outline his new bill. He submitted it to the justices of the Supreme Court and several Circuit Court judges for criticism and suggestion. He then dictated to his secretary, Henry Satterlee, at one sitting, the so-called Evarts bill. It provided for nine intermediate courts of appeal of three judges each, to be known as the Circuit Courts of Appeal, to receive appeals in many kinds of cases from the district and circuit courts. Although certain cases would go directly to the Supreme Court from the lower courts, particularly questions of constitutionality, the bulk of appealed cases, especially that numerous class of cases involving diversity of citizenship, would receive final consideration in the nine new courts.[50]

The majority of the committee favored the bill, while the minority, led by Edmunds, favored the quorum plan. Thus there were three bills in Congress, one each by Evarts, Edmunds, and Rogers. Evarts sought support for his measure. To an influential member of the American Bar Association he wrote, "If the profession will give a united support at the meeting at Saratoga for the bill I reported, I feel confident that the bill will pass both houses of this Congress." His appeal met favorable response and the association approved the bill.[51]

Three weeks later he defended his bill in the Senate. Unable to read, he spoke from memory, calling on the clerk to read portions of the bill when needed. Having previously advocated the quorum plan, he knew its merits and now, curiously enough, found himself refuting those arguments which he had formerly approved. As for the Rogers bill, he believed it gave too much finality and too little flexibility to the decisions of the intermediate courts. He showed that his bill worked out a reasonable compromise between finality and flexibility. An interesting phase of the debate was the question whether cases of conviction for high crime should go on appeal to the Supreme Court. Public opinion was swinging decidedly toward leniency and some senators urged that the door of appeal be opened wide. Evarts suggested that the right of review be extended to all cases of "infamous" crime. His suggestion was approved but had the unfortunate result of adding greatly to the number of cases that would otherwise be shunted to the new courts.[52]

Except for minor alterations and amendments, the Evarts bill passed the Senate in the form in which he had drafted it.[53] It made important changes in the Rogers bill, especially by dividing the stream of appellate cases and sending the more important to the Supreme Court. Of course Evarts did not escape criticism for contradicting his former preference for the quorum plan. "The Senator from New York," said Senator Vest sarcastically, "with his great ability and great experience, championed for a long time the very system which I stand here honestly to advocate as the best relief." Evarts replied that only two members of the American Bar Association now favored the plan.

The Evarts bill passed the Senate by a vote of forty-four to six. A conference committee, with Evarts as chairman and Hoar and Pugh as other senatorial members, went to work with the House members. To confer with it was another committee of ten representatives of the American Bar Association. Evarts' judgment dominated the conferences, and the Rogers bill was abandoned in favor of his. The bill finally became law on March 2, 1891, two days before Evarts left office.[54] In 1911 the Evarts Act was carried to its logical conclusion by the abolition of the ordinary circuit courts. His reform therefore still endures.

The ingenuity of the reform lay in giving relief to the Supreme Court while retaining as much of the traditional court structure as possible. Evarts did not satisfy the extremists, like Edmunds and Vest, who felt that the Supreme Court should retain its touch with the people by continuing on circuit. But the benefits of the act were decisive and immediate; a flood of litigation was shut off and the number of appellate cases dropped remarkably. Considering the handicap under which Evarts labored, it is not to be wondered that his secretary regarded his preparation and conduct of the bill as an extraordinary achievement.[55] It was appropriate that his last and greatest service in the Senate should be in the furtherance of justice.

32

"Full of Honor and Years"

THE DARKNESS CREEPING over his eyes reminded Evarts that his career was drawing to a close. In 1889 his physicians felt they could do little for him and suggested that he go to Europe for the relaxation of the journey and for further medical advice. But his physicians in Paris told him there was not the slightest hope that his gradual blindness could be cured. Evarts received the news with composure and declared that he had long wished to see Raphael's famous Virgin in Dresden and that he would do so before the night set in.[1]

Not realizing his handicap, Evarts' friends worked vigorously for his reëlection. But Governor Hill, by his manipulations at Albany, won eighty-one votes to Evarts' seventy-nine. Rockwood Hoar wrote Evarts, "It is a pity that your successor [Hill] could not have been on hand . . . to mark the contrast which darkness furnishes to a setting luminary."[2] Two weeks before his term expired, Evarts was given a farewell dinner at the Arlington Hotel in Washington. President Harrison, Vice-President Morton, twenty-three senators, and other notables attended. Harrison spoke highly of his "long and honorable service" to the country and soon after offered him an appointment as delegate to another monetary conference abroad. In refusing Evarts wrote: "I am afraid we cannot neglect the Scriptural warning, the light of the body is the eye, and that missing, the whole body is full of darkness." Harrison replied: "If I remember the Scripture correctly, it is when the eye is *evil* that the body is full of darkness, and I do not think you mean to admit that to be your state."[3]

During the year after he left Washington, Evarts continued his interest in the law and politics and still appeared at public functions. But his genial wit was no longer uppermost. Soon after his return he spoke at the Grant birthday dinner at Delmonico's, an event of unusual impressiveness because of the recent laying of the cornerstone of Grant's tomb. Evarts' speech was solemn in tone. "It is difficult to understand," he said, "until the work is completed, how the fabric of great men's lives is woven, for much of the plying of the loom is unnoticed until the conciliated colors are united and presented as the complete fabric of their lives." And of Grant he said, "It is the great satisfaction of my life that whatever there might have been of difference at one or another stage of public affairs on public questions between us, I had the pleasure of knowing that in a contest—and I certainly had a great contest—the methods and the result of which made me Senator, General Grant heartily participated in my behalf."[4]

Still keenly interested in the Republican party, Evarts prophesied success in 1892. He was quite disgusted with the manipulations of Governor Hill. Not satisfied with seizing the senatorship, Hill attempted to undermine Cleveland and get the presidency for himself. To succeed Hill as governor, Lee Crandall, editor of the Washington *National Leader,* believed Evarts to be the only man who could "lead the united opposition to a Bourbon Democracy to victory." But Evarts knew that he had finished with public office.[5]

He hoped to see Harrison elected again. In September the President and his party visited Windsor, spending more than an hour at Runnemede. Evarts played host to twenty-four guests. An outdoor meeting had been planned for the villagers, but a heavy rain caused it to be moved to the town-hall. A week after Harrison's nomination, Evarts published in the *Vermont Journal* a statement of his faith in the party and its candidate. He wanted to speak for Harrison, but his strength would not permit. He also had to decline an invitation to the Chamber of Commerce dinner in honor of Whitelaw Reid, the vice-presidential candidate. "I regret," he wrote, "to feel that the impaired condition of my eyesight precludes me from taking part in public assemblages."[6] But as the campaign grew close and exciting that fall, he could not resist an invitation from the Brooklyn Republican Club, which read, "It is due to our Democratic fellow citizens to say that we believe they also would welcome an address from you."[7] Evarts hesitated, but more petitions reached him. Perhaps it was the urging of James C. Carter, chairman of the Republican National Committee, that induced him to make the last political speech.

He appeared at the Clermont Rink before an enthusiastic audience. In a long, black ulster reaching to his feet, and wearing his silk hat and kid gloves, he stood waiting some minutes for the applause to cease, his face pale and wrinkled, his eyes wandering nervously over the crowd. He spoke for nearly an hour, but his voice was too weak to carry more than a dozen rows from the platform. He criticized the Democratic candidate and platform, argued for a protective tariff, and prophesied unprecedented prosperity if Harrison were elected. It was a great effort,[8] but it proved futile. The Democrats swept Cleveland into office again.

A few months later he attended his last political function, a dinner given to retiring Vice-President Morton by some twenty senators. The invitation to attend came from Senator Manderson: "All of your associates in the Senate, who hold you in dear remembrance, want to hear your voice again."[9] Evarts appeared at the Arlington Hotel and was warmly greeted by his old colleagues. Something of his old-time humor came back. He started the fun by declaring it to be a privilege to address so *full* a Senate, and the jollity lasted till a late hour. It was a fitting close to his political career, surrounded as he was by admiring friends and political leaders.

On August 30, 1893, Evarts and his wife celebrated their golden wedding anniversary at Windsor, the crowning event of the mellow autumn of two well-spent lives. The day before, guests began to arrive from New York, Boston, and more distant points. Festivities began that night with a dinner at which twenty were seated around a long table, including Senator Hoar, Mrs. Hoar, Joseph Choate, Evarts' sons Allen, Sherman, and Prescott, and his daughter, Mrs. Perkins.

The next day was ideal. Evarts rose early, declaring that he wished to make use of the whole day, since he did not expect another golden anniversary. Runnemede was in gala attire. After breakfast the company assembled in the library and read in turn from the Psalms. Then sons, daughters, and others presented their gifts to the aged couple. There followed a general reunion of friends and relatives, some of whom had been thousands of miles apart and had not seen each other for years.

At eleven the villagers came to offer congratulations and were met in the garden-house by the genial host. In the afternoon the grandchildren, seventeen in number, met for a salutation from their grandparents, who enjoyed this part of the reunion most of all. A photograph of relatives and guests was taken on the lawn, and another of Evarts and his wife, seated with a beautiful garden for a background. Mrs. Evarts wore a white silk dress and over her head was the lace veil she had worn when married. Evarts, dressed in black, with eyes bedimmed, sat pensive, his thoughts going back over the years. They were an extraordinary couple, with qualities of almost indefinable impressiveness and charm.

The dinner that evening was full of gaiety and fun. Prescott Evarts read a poem of his own composition, while Evarts B. Greene, the oldest nephew, delivered a sonnet dedicated to the occasion:

"All life's rewards are won by strenuous toil,
And of its progress no small part is due
To him whose great powers, greatly used 'mid the turmoil
Of courts and parties, rescued from despoil
Endangered rights, and so his honors grew.
But 'tis the home life that we now review—
A happy life, whose brightness few griefs soil;

Of father wise and faithful, mother true,
Ruling her house with dignity and grace;
Of many sons and daughters, strong and fair,
Who will maintain the honor of your race.
Morning's bright hopes never more fairly shone
Than the sweet sunshine of life's afternoon."[10]

Evarts responded with a brief speech. Healths were drunk from the golden loving cup, and the day closed with a dance at the garden-house, under the light of hundreds of Chinese lanterns, and a great display of fireworks attended by the townspeople.

Most of the guests stayed over till the next day, many of them going to Beaman's estate at "Blow-Me-Down" only two miles away, where a reception was given to Evarts. As visitors entered the grounds, they saw the initials W. M. E. and H. W. E., made of new-mown hay, raked up in this form by workmen. Evarts and his wife, who did not seem tired, received the guests in the parlor and then went out on the piazza to watch the gay scene on the lawn, where couples were dancing to music furnished by a band from Claremont. The whole three-day celebration was a memorable event for all who attended and one of the brightest episodes in Evarts' life.

Evarts attended the annual meetings of the Peabody trustees to 1896, and from 1896 to 1898 was chairman despite enforced absence from all meetings. At the meeting in 1893 he spoke in memory of Hayes and Fish, who had just passed away. The death of Robert C. Winthrop the following year brought another tribute from him. Only a few months before, Winthrop had sent him a copy of his *Reminiscences* and a commentary on Daniel Webster.[11] By 1898 Evarts was the sole survivor of the original board of trustees, but he was too feeble to attend meetings.

On February 15, 1895, the New York Bar Association celebrated its twenty-fifth anniversary. As one of its founders and its first president, Evarts felt he must make the effort to appear. It brought together some five hundred members of bench and bar in a social, informal affair. The former presidents—Nash, Coudert, Peckham,

Butler, and Carter, with Evarts in the center—formed the receiving line. Evarts did not appear fatigued and at dinner stood erect and spoke for nearly three quarters of an hour. In reminiscent mood, he reviewed the early conditions which led to the forming of the association. "The two hundred lawyers," he said, "who signed the first call for the meeting . . . should be regarded with veneration as the founders of this great society. Lawyers have ever been the men who have made the revolutions in this country. . . . At the time of the formation of this association I had observed the course of affairs, and I felt that the alternative was either to be gloriously successful or gloriously beaten in our opposition to a great evil. We realized the importance of organization. But it was a question whether we should bow our heads to the petty tyrants on a corrupt bench, and the association took up the gage of battle and won the victory."[12]

During these last years Evarts still took an interest in his farm at Windsor. When "Coxey's Army" gathered in 1894 to march on Washington, the town was infested with vagabonds. Through Evarts' generosity a water supply was placed at their disposal, and a site for encampment. After the death of his son Charles, the estate was managed by another son, Maxwell.[13] Evarts also had real estate in New York and Brooklyn, which his son Allen looked after. Mount Beverly farm near Washington was under the care of Professor Hart of Howard University, an efficient gentleman, but somewhat frank in asking favors for himself and the university. Evarts' property during these last years was estimated as worth three hundred and fifty thousand dollars and his interest in the law firm at twenty-five thousand a year.[14] When in town he saw much of two of his sons. Sherman lived near by on East 13th Street and Allen on West 12th Street. Prescott was winning distinction as an Episcopal clergyman in Cambridge. All were bringing credit to their father in their chosen professions.

Almost to the last, Evarts' mind was active and alert, but this only made it the more difficult for him to endure the life of a recluse. He drove a great deal, slept much, talked much, and often had his wife read to him. His blindness made him restless and sometimes irritable. One day, while calling on Gail Hamilton with his daughter as a guide, he exclaimed, "How much better than if I were led around the street by a dog with a little string." His family agreed not to mention his blindness in his presence.

He was deeply attached to his quiet, comfortable home on Second Avenue. The neighborhood was no longer fashionable, and the more pretentious families had long since moved uptown; but he refused to leave this mansion so full of memories, with its shuttered windows and great willow tree sweeping its branches over the eastern portico. After 1894 he seldom left it.[15]

He would not write anything about himself. When given a large new blank book especially adapted for recording memoirs, he opened it, noted its clean white pages, and said they should be left so.[16] A reporter came one day in 1894 to induce him to tell something of himself. After a long wait, he saw Evarts with feeble step shuffling down the stairs, shoulders stooped and face pale. His eyes wandered dreamily around the room. Finally seeing the reporter, he asked abruptly, "What do you want?" The reporter stated his purpose. Evarts fingered his dressing coat but he did not reply. The reporter became nervous, feeling like an intruder. Finally Evarts rose, shook his head, and said he had "nothing for the public." Then bowing low, he turned abruptly and went upstairs.[17]

He still enjoyed the visits of his friends and retained his interest in world affairs, on which his comments were often vivacious and pungent. From Washington he had Hart send him copies of the *Congressional Record*. But early in 1897 he grew worse, and an attack of grippe in April left him in weakened condition. His spirits began to flag and his melancholy troubled his family, but he recovered.[18]

On February 6, 1898, his eightieth birthday, he enjoyed a quiet reunion in his New York home. Sons, daughters, and grandchildren came to see him. But there was no celebration, for he was unable to share in one. Growing weaker during the year, he spent much time in bed. Benjamin Silliman, who was celebrating his ninety-fourth birthday in Brooklyn, wrote him, "I hope you are comfortable and doubt not that you are serene and firm as ever."[19]

Surprisingly, his health improved the following year, and he was no longer confined to his room. But his helplessness preyed upon his mind. Choate, just before embarking for England to take up his duties as ambassador, called to say farewell. Evarts congratulated him upon his appointment and prophesied for him a brilliant diplomatic career. Choate reminded him of their forty years of congenial partnership and expressed a hope that it might be renewed upon his return. But Evarts shook his head and said, "When I think what a care I am to my people, lying so helpless here, and that I can do nothing any more to repay their kindness, or to help in the world, I feel like the boy who wrote home from school to his mother a letter of twenty pages, and then added: 'P. S. Dear Mother, please excuse my longevity.'"

He was no longer able to make the trip to Windsor, which was a great disappointment. But on a sunny day he might go out to the park near by, where he sat, his eyes dreamily looking far away, while around him on the grass the children romped and played. But he rarely left the house, which now gave the appearance of being deserted. The shutters were invariably closed; but if a passer-by chanced to watch a certain window at certain hours of the day, he would see them open and the sharp features of the old man peer out for a moment and then disappear. He was willing that one last portrait should be painted. Augustus Franzer, well-known artist, came to his house to do the work. Evarts, too feeble to pose, was propped up in bed. The portrait was a success, one of the most notable paintings on exhibition at an art gallery soon after.[20]

As he grew weaker, Evarts lost interest in events of the day. Not even the exciting issue of imperialism in 1900 could arouse him. When Thomas B. Reed called to try to interest him in the Philippine question, he listened patiently but finally said: "Reed, I don't think I care to hear more about the Philippines. I'm not going *there* anyway." He was thinking much of the future life and talked much of it, showing a strong religious faith.[21]

The law firm still carried on business under the name of Evarts, Choate & Beaman. When Beaman died in 1900, Allen Evarts became head, since Choate was abroad. Other active members of the firm were J. Evarts Tracy, Treadwell Cleveland, and Prescott Hall Butler. Allen ultimately became the head, and the firm name was changed to Evarts, Tracy, and Sherman. In 1900 some sixty lawyers, who at different times had been associated with Evarts, formed the Evarts Club, and at frequent intervals the older members dined together and exchanged reminiscences of him.[22]

On February 6, 1901, Evarts reached his eighty-third birthday. Out of respect to Beaman's memory there was no celebration. Several friends called to congratulate him and he was able to recognize them. Two weeks later, February 20, he was stricken with pneumonia and his condition became critical. For a time he rallied and was believed out of danger. His vitality was remarkable. But at four o'clock on the morning of the twenty-eighth he began to sink rapidly and death came five hours later. His wife, four sons, and four daughters were at his bedside. Messages of condolence poured in from hundreds of friends. Mayor Wyck directed the lowering of the flag at City Hall, declaring that one of the greatest men in the history of New York had passed.[23]

There was an elaborate public funeral at Calvary Church, with Bishop Potter of New York, Bishop Leonard of Ohio, and the Rector, James L. Parks, presiding. The pallbearers included J. Pierpont Morgan, William Allen Butler, Whitelaw Reid, Carl Schurz, and Thomas P. Reed. Delegations from the Bar Association, the Union League Club, the Chamber of Commerce, the New England Society, and other organizations were present. Another service was held in St. Paul's Church in Windsor. The townspeople realized they had lost a friend, and with the passing of Mrs. Evarts a year later they lost another.

Evarts was laid to rest in Ascutney Cemetery in Windsor. On a high knoll, shaded by pine trees, somewhat apart from the rest of the cemetery, is a simple grave, marked by a small, old-fashioned stone, with merely the name and dates inscribed upon it.

No man in the history of American jurisprudence holds a more eminent position than Evarts. He will be remembered first of all as a lawyer. Distinguished as were his other services, they only accentuate his eminence at the bar. As a lawyer he was an original thinker who for sheer intellectual power had few equals. No other American attorney has ever had the good fortune to serve in so many conspicuous cases.

He will also be remembered as an eloquent orator and a great wit. His orations, addresses, and after-dinner speeches were admirable. They had wisdom, sparkle, literary charm, and elevation. His flow of anecdotes, his inimitable manner as a *raconteur,* his timely puns—at the after-dinner gathering, on the public platform, or in private conversation—earned him a national reputation. His was a natural wit, bubbling up refreshingly and without effort from an overflowing mind. He deserves equally to be remembered for his diplomatic services during the Civil War and as head of the State Department—the best type of leader in foreign relations, cultivated, high-minded, alert, a gentleman whom America could depend upon for dignified representation in international affairs. He performed difficult tasks in diplomacy and performed them with a grace all his own.

Finally, he will be remembered for the numerous public services he performed outside of his profession or public office. Whether pronouncing a eulogy of a departed statesman or fighting the spoilsman in New York City, he gave of his powers lavishly. His generous service in time, talent, and money for public causes, for his friends, and for his family were exemplary. He performed these unselfish tasks with apparent ease. Throughout his career he illustrated the possibilities of a public life without soiling of hands. As an independent in politics during most of his career, he did not seek office, but let it seek him. He deserves some criticism for his excessive regularity in party matters during the later years, but while living in a sordid political era, he clung to high ideals of citizenship. He was different from most politicians, if he could be called a politician at all. His comprehensiveness of view, his ethical habit of mind, his appreciation of governing principles, his vision of national development and responsibilities, and his acquaintance with other nations and peoples—all this set him apart as a distinguished American.

Notes

Bibliography

Index

Notes

CHAPTER I

1. 127 U. S. 1.

2. *New England Historical and Genealogical Register,* January, 1907, 25-31; Looseleaf notebook entitled Evarts Genealogy in the possession of the Evarts family.

3. E. C. Tracy, *Memoir of the Life of Jeremiah Evarts, Esq., passim.*

4. G. F. Hoar, *Autobiography of Seventy Years,* I, 17; H. Beckley, *The History of Vermont,* 278.

5. *American Quarterly Register,* November, 1831; G. Spring, *A Tribute to the Memory of Jeremiah Evarts, Esq.;* L. Woods, *Sermon of Rev. Leonard Woods on Death of Jeremiah Evarts.*

6. W. D. Lewis, ed., *Great American Lawyers,* VII, 209-210.

7. Tracy, *Jeremiah Evarts,* 113.

8. W. M. Evarts, *Address on the Victories of Protection;* E. S. Martin, *Life of Joseph Hodges Choate,* I, 33.

9. R. Carver, *History of Boston,* 124-127.

10. *Catalogue of the Boston Latin School . . . 1835-1885,* 305; Lewis, *Great American Lawyers,* VII, 212.

11. Hoar, *Autobiography,* I, 8.

12. E. E. Hale, *A New England Boyhood, passim.*

13. *New York Herald,* March 25, 1888.

14. *Catalogue of the Boston Latin School . . . 1835-1885.*

15. Evarts Papers, Journal of My Readings, 8; A. H. Thorndike, *Modern Eloquence,* II, 142.

16. S. E. Baldwin, *Life and Letters of Simeon Baldwin,* 477.

17. Evarts Papers, T. M. Day to S. Evarts, November 24, 1903.

18. E. Baldwin, *Annals of Yale College,* 229-230.

19. J. A. Porter, *Sketches of Yale Life,* 4-5.

20. B. Dyer, *The Public Career of William M. Evarts,* 6.

21. Evarts Papers, T. M. Day to S. Evarts, November 24, 1903.

22. *Record of the Class of 1837, in Yale College,* 14-15.

23. A. P. Stokes, *Memorials of Eminent Yale Men,* II, 270.

24. W. H. Yeager, *Chauncey Mitchell Depew,* 19-20; *Record of the Class of 1837,* 194.

25. Evarts Papers, Journal of My Readings, 11, 24, 37, 52, 97-98.

26. *The Yale Literary Magazine,* February 1836.

27. *Ibid.,* April, 1837; Stokes, *Memorials,* II, 269.

28. Evarts Papers, Journal of My Readings, 4-5.

29. *Catalogue of Connecticut Alpha of Phi Beta Kappa, August, 1838.*

30. Evarts Papers, Journal of My Readings, 57-58.

31. *Memorial Biographies of the New England Historic Genealogical Society,* III, 105-125.

32. *Catalogue of the Officers and Students of the Law School of Harvard University, 1817-1887;* Hale, *New England Boyhood,* 66.

33. W. W. Story, *Life and Letters of Joseph Story,* II, 35-39; Hoar, *Autobiography,* I, 130.

34. C. F. Adams, *Richard Henry Dana,* I, 23.

CHAPTER II

1. H. H. Hagan, *Eight Great American Lawyers,* 257; *The Green Bag,* VIII, 95.

2. S. Evarts, ed., *Arguments and Speeches of William Maxwell Evarts,* III, 187-188. Hereafter cited as *Arguments and Speeches.*

3. L. B. Proctor, *The Bench and Bar of New York,* 641-671; *Arguments and Speeches,* III, 183-193, 431-432.

4. Hoar, *Autobiography,* I, 15; Dyer, *Evarts,* 12.

5. Evarts Papers, Anniversary Poem, 1835, by Edgar S. Van Winkle; B. J. Lossing, *History of the City of New York,* II, 436-437.

6. Speech at the Astor House, November 17, 1868.

7. *Arguments and Speeches,* III, 277.

8. *The Green Bag,* VIII, 95.

9. *Arguments and Speeches,* II, 407-410; I, Introduction, xvi; Dyer, *Evarts,* 22-23.

10. *New York Tribune,* October 31, 1845.

11. *The Green Bag,* VIII, 95.

12. Evarts Papers, Evarts to Butler, January 26, 1842; T. G. Strong, *Joseph H. Choate,* 156-157.

13. C. Coleman, *The Life of John J. Crittenden, With Selections From His Correspondence and Speeches,* I, 97; *New York Herald,* June 7, 1842.

14. F. L. Wellman, *The Art of Cross-Examination,* 189-191.

15. A. Nevins, *The Diary of Philip Hone, 1828-1851,* 606; *Memoirs of Philip Hone,* XIX, 190-192.

16. *Life and Adventures of the Accomplished Forger and Swindler, Colonel Monroe Edwards, passim; Morning Courier and New York Enquirer,* June 10, 1842; *New York Herald,* June 7-15, October 18-23, 1842.

17. *Arguments and Speeches,* III, 178.

18. Coleman, *Life of Crittenden,* I, 97-98.

19. Martin, *Life of Choate,* I, 185-186; Don C. Seitz, *Horace Greeley,* 332.

20. W. Barrett, *The Old Merchants of New York City,* I, 93, 95.

21. G. B. Wells, *Life and Career of Samuel Rossiter Betts,* 33-34.

22. Olcott's Reports, 140.

23. *Ibid.,* 246, 388; 1 Blatchford 211.

24. 4 Edwards' Chancery Reports, 412.

25. 3 Sandford 5, 11, 518.

26. 4 Sandford 221, 414.

27. L. B. Proctor, *Lawyer and Client,* 299-304; *New York Legal Observer,* VI, 345-348.

28. 4 Sandford 48; 1 N. Y. 433.

29. Alden Chester, *Legal and Judicial History of New York,* III, 54-55; *The Green Bag,* IV, 401-402: *New York Legal Observer,* III, 318-326.

30. 1 Sandford 297; 2 Sandford 263; 3 Sandford 176, 311.

CHAPTER III

1. D. A. H., Smith, *Commodore Vanderbilt,* 145; Nevins, *The Diary of Philip Hone,* II, 866.

2. *Official Opinions of the Attorneys General of the United States,* V, 92; State Dept. Archives, Notes to German States, VI, 214, Clayton to Von Roenne, April 10, 1849; Miscellaneous Letters, Hall to Clayton, May 8, 12, 14, 17, 25, 1849; *American Whig Review,* X, 98-99.

3. L. N. Feipal, "The Navy and Filibustering in the Fifties," *United States Naval Institute Proceedings,* XLIV; State Dept. Archives, Miscellaneous Letters, Hall to Clayton, September 15, 1849, June 28, 1850; *New York Herald,* September 22, 1852.

4. *New York Herald,* April 27, 28, 1851; L. M. Perez, "Lopez Expeditions to Cuba, 1850-1851," *Publications of the Southern History Association,* X, 345-362; R. G. Caldwell, *The Lopez Expeditions to Cuba, 1848-1851;* State Dept. Archives, Miscellaneous Letters, Hall to Webster, April 22, 24, 1851; Evarts to Webster, April 26, 28, 1851; Hall to Webster, April 26, 1851.

5. *New York Herald,* May 19, June 13, 19, 28, July 17, 1851; March 6, 1852.

6. *The Green Bag,* VIII, 96.

7. *New York Herald,* March 6 to April 5, 1852.

8. State Dept. Archives, Miscellaneous Letters, Hall to Clayton, May 30, June 7, 1850.

9. *New York Herald,* May, 1, 1851; *New York Times,* October 7, 1852.

10. C. Edwards, *Pleasantries About Courts and Lawyers of New York,* 164-165; *Arguments and Speeches,* III, 180.

11. 2 Blatchford 207; *New York Herald,* May 6, 8, 11, June 3, 1851.

12. Lossing, *op. cit.,* II, 437.

13. *New York Herald,* October 30, 1850.

14. *Proceedings of the Union Meeting, Held at Castle Garden, October 30, 1850.*

15. *The Green Bag,* VIII, 98; *New York Herald,* October 31, 1850.

16. C. F. Adams, *Richard Henry Dana,* I, 176; *New York Herald,* December 24, 1850; *The Green Bag,* XII, 319.

17. Barrett, *The Old Merchants of New York City,* II, 166; *New York Herald,* March 6, 1852; *Arguments and Speeches,* II, 439

18. 2 Blatchford 563; *New York Times,* October 28, 1852.

19. *Statistics of the Class of 1837 from 1837 to 1850, With A Notice of Their Meeting at Yale College, August 15, 1850.*

20. W. M. Evarts, *An Oration By William Maxwell Evarts, and A Poem, by Francis Miles Finch, Delivered Before the Linonian Society of Yale College, at Its Centennial Anniversary With An Account of the Celebration.*

21. Evarts Papers, R. H. Dana to Evarts, December 14, 1853; G. S. Hilliard to Evarts, November 19, 1853.

22. C. and E. Brainerd, *New England Society Orations,* II, 236.

23. *New York Herald,* December 23, 1854.

24. W. M. Evarts, *An Oration Delivered Before the New England Society of the City of New York, in Celebration of the Two Hundred and Thirty-Fourth Anniversary of the Landing of the Pilgrims.*

25. *Independent,* February 8, 1855.

26. Lossing, *op. cit.,* II, 651-652; Dyer, *Evarts,* 29.

27. *New York Tribune,* March 8, 1901.

28. E. Thayer, *A History of the Kansas Crusade,* 203.

29. Evarts Papers, Thayer to Evarts, June 26, 1879.

30. *New York Evening Post,* April 30, 1856; *New York Tribune,* April 29, 30, 1856; *Arguments and Speeches,* II, 442-444.

31. M. Storey and E. D. Emerson, *Ebenezer Rockwood Hoar,* 117-118.

32. *New York Herald,* May 30, 1856.

33. Dyer, *Evarts,* 33; *New York Tribune,* October 23, 1856; *Arguments and Speeches,* II, 457.

34. *Arguments and Speeches,* II, 463-467, 471.

35. Dyer, *Evarts,* 34.

CHAPTER IV

1. *The Green Bag,* VIII, 96.

2. *The Yale Review,* October, 1920.

3. S. E. Baldwin, *The Young Man and the Law,* 46.

4. T. G. Strong, *Landmarks of a Lawyer's Lifetime,* 457.

5. *Arguments and Speeches,* III, 372.

6. F. C. Hicks, *Arguments and Addresses of Joseph H. Choate,* 144; A. O. Hall, "The Ghost of Nisi Prius," *The Green Bag,* VII, 346-347; Strong, *Joseph H. Choate,* 159-162, 171.

7. J. Choate, *American Addresses,* VI.

8. *Arguments and Speeches,* III, 365.

9. Martin, *Life of Choate,* I, 93-94, 103, 112-113; F. L. Stetson, *Joseph Hodges Choate,* 3.

10. Strong, *Joseph H. Choate,* 30-33, 59-66, 89.

11. W. A. Butler, *A Retrospect of Forty Years, 1825-1865,* 231.

12. *New York Tribune,* September 2, 1876.

13. *Annual Report of the American Historical Association For the Year 1918,* II, 537.

14. H. S. Wardner, *The Birthplace of Vermont: A History of Windsor to 1781,* I, 384-385.

15. 4 Blatchford, Appendix; 13 Blatchford, Appendix; *New York Herald,* March 22, 1860.

16. Strong, *Landmarks of a Lawyer's Lifetime,* 37-38, 234-235, 240; A. Chester, *Courts and Lawyers of New York,* II, 803 n., 808; *The Green Bag,* II, 277-291.

17. 13 Blatchford, Appendix.

18. 5 Howard IV.

19. 20 Howard 583.

CHAPTER V

1. S. W. Fisher, *William Curtis Noyes; The Green Bag,* VI, 545-551; Butler, *A Retrospect of Forty Years,* 321-322; 43 Barbour 649; *New York Times,* December 26, 1864.

2. H. T. Cheever, *Memorial Address Given in the First Congregational Church Washington, D. C., December 13, 1891;* 32 Barbour 55.

3. Fisher, *Noyes,* 28; Lewis, *Great American Lawyers,* VI, 232-234; 38 Barbour 534; *New York Herald,* March 22, July 3, 1860.

4. 4 Abbott's Court of Appeals 108; Fisher, *Noyes,* 28.

5. T. F. De Voe, *The Market Book,* I, 447-453; *New York Herald,* January 12, 1860.

6. J. L. Blundell, *Arguments of Counsel in the West Washington Market Case; New York Times,* July 13, 1860.

7. *New York Times,* December 26, 1864; Fisher, *Noyes.*

8. H. M. Field, *The Life of David Dudley Field,* 99-106; Lewis, *Great American Lawyers,* V, 125-174; *The Green Bag,* III, 49-55, VI, 209-213.

9. 29 Barbour 552.

10. *New York Herald,* May 31, June 1, 15, 1860.

11. Evarts Papers, manuscript copy of Evarts' argument; 32 Barbour 102.

12. Evarts Papers, points for the Respondent; *New York Herald,* February 28, 1860; 30 Barbour 24; 21 N. Y. 517.

13. 30 Barbour 537; *New York Times,* February 16, November 12, 14, 1859; J. G. Wilson, *Memorial History of the City of New York,* IV, 205-206.

14. *New York Herald,* January 10, 13, 14, 17, 22, 1860.
15. *New York Legal Observer,* XI, 263; 3 Blatchford 305; 4 Blatchford 28.
16. 3 Blatchford 77.
17. 4 Duer 234; 21 N. Y. 378; 19 N. Y. 272.
18. 1 Wallace 456.
19. 1 Bosworth 520; 17 N. Y. 194.
20. 1 Robertson 194; *New York Times,* July 20, 1860.
21. 6 Duer 176; 26 Barbour 202; 19 N. Y. 19; 1 Duer 707.
22. Strong, *Landmarks of a Lawyer's Lifetime,* 282-285.
23. 5 Duer 106.
24. 10 N. Y. 579.
25. 25 N. Y. 577.
26. 30 Barbour 471.
27. 5 N. Y. 320; 19 N. Y. 207; 41 Barbour 237.
28. David McAdam *et al., History of the Bench and Bar of New York,* II, 6; 6 Bosworth 520; 2 Bosworth 485.
29. 11 Barbour 485; *New York Legal Observer,* VIII, 354.
30. 3 Bosworth 321; Evarts Papers, Evarts to Man, December 10, 1859.
31. 8 Bosworth 415.
32. 1 Robertson 340.
33. 1 Robertson 489; 8 Bosworth 538.
34. 32 Barbour 121; Evarts Papers, points for Mrs. Atterbury and Olivia Phelps; 23 N. Y. 69.

CHAPTER VI

1. *In Memory of Charles O'Conor. Report of A Meeting of the Bar of the Courts of the State and of the United States, for the Second Circuit, Held in the City of New York, on Friday, May 23d, 1884.*
2. C. B. Daly, "Charles O'Conor," *Magazine of American History,* XIII, 513-535.
3. Charles O'Conor Papers, Tilden to Bigelow, January 15, 1853.
4. J. C. Walsh, "Charles O'Conor," *Journal of the American Irish Historical Society,* XXVII, 285-313; J. Bigelow, "Some Recollections of Charles O'Conor," *Century Magazine,* March, 1885; *The Green Bag,* VII, 1-12; Strong, *Landmarks of a Lawyer's Lifetime,* 217-219; Lewis, *Great American Lawyers,* V, 85-93.
5. *In Memory of Charles O'Conor. . . .*
6. 2 Duer 139.
7. O'Conor Papers, pamphlet on "The Disputed Comptrollership—Giles v. Flagg."
8. 5 Bosworth 538; 35 Barbour 340; 4 Blatchford 262; 5 Duer 310; 21 N. Y. 36.
9. 6 Bosworth 76.
10. 6 Bosworth 245.
11. *New York Times,* January 7, 1859.
12. Evarts Papers, points for the defendant; 37 Barbour 357; 27 N. Y. 188.
13. M. Smith, *Sunshine and Shadow,* 174-177
14. Hayes, *Diary,* IV, 96.
15. Lossing, *op. cit.,* II, 665-667; Wilson, *Memorial History of the City of New York,* III, 456-457.
16. 24 Barbour 187; 25 Barbour 344.
17. *The Green Bag,* VIII, 98-99; Evarts Papers, Evarts' Brief; 15 N. Y. 532.
18. C. F. Adams, *Richard Henry Dana,* II, 159.
19. Evarts Papers, opinion dated November 19, 1857.
20. Evarts Papers, brief for defendants; 19 N. Y. 188.
21. Strong, *Landmarks of a Lawyer's Lifetime,* 198.
22. *The Parish Will Case.* Vols. I-V.

23. Surrogate's Court of the County of New York, in the Matter of Proving the Last Will and Testament of Henry Parish.

24. *The Parish Will Case,* V, 803.

25. 1 Redfield 1.

26. *The Parish Will Case. Mr. Evarts' Brief For Opening Argument:* Evarts Papers, Evarts' Argument in Reply.

27. Evarts Papers, argument of John K. Porter; *The Green Bag,* IV, 353-367.

28. 25 N. Y. 9.

29. 5 Sandford 681; *New York Times,* April 16, 1860.

30. G. F. Howe, *Chester A. Arthur,* 13-15; Lewis, *Great American Lawyers,* VII, 222-223.

31. *Speech of Charles O'Conor, Esq., at the Union Meeting at the Academy of Music, New York City, December 19th, 1859.*

32. *State of New York. Court of Appeals. Jonathon Lemmon vs. The People of the State of New York. Statement and Points for the Plaintiff and Appellant.*

33. *The Illustrated Pilgrim Memorial, 1866,* 28-32; *New York Times,* August 3, 1859, November 4, 1859, December 2, 1859.

34. *New York Herald,* January 27, 30, 1860.

35. *Arguments and Speeches,* I, 14-90.

36. *N. Y. Court of Appeals. Report of the Lemmon Slave Case,* 107-109, 114-115, 120.

37. 20 N. Y. 562.

CHAPTER VII

1. *Arguments and Speeches,* II, 479-487; *New York Herald,* February 22, 24, 1860.

2. Seward Papers, undated clipping.

3. Smith, *Sunshine and Shadow,* 317-322; A. Nevins, *Hamilton Fish,* 34-35.

4. F. Bancroft, *The Life of William H. Seward,* I, 373-374; H. Greeley, *Recollections of a Busy Life,* 315, 319.

5. *History of the State of New York,* Vol. VII; *Modern Party Battles,* 104; *New York Herald,* March 2, 1860.

6. *New York Herald,* May 19, 1860.

7. Bancroft, *Seward,* I, 332; M. L. Bonham, "New York and the Election of 1860," *New York History,* April, 1934; C. M. Feuss, *Carl Schurz, Reformer,* 70-71; *New York Herald,* May 16, 1860.

8. *New York Herald,* May 16, 1860: Winters Collection, III, undated clipping by A. Oakey Hall.

9. *Michigan History Magazine,* XIX, 96; Field, *The Life of David Dudley Field,* 137-138; F. B. Carpenter, "How Lincoln Was Nominated," *Century Magazine,* January, 1882.

10. J. G. Blaine, *Twenty Years of Congress,* I, 166.

11. *Proceedings of the Republican National Convention Held at Chicago,* 113-117: Winters Collection, III, undated clipping.

12. *Proceedings of the Republican National Convention,* 119-120.

13. Bancroft, *Seward,* I, 539.

14. D. S. Alexander, *A Political History of the State of New York,* II, 289.

15. *New York Herald,* May 22, 1860.

16. *Ibid.,* June 8, 9, 1860.

17. *Ibid.,* August 9, 1860.

18. *Arguments and Speeches,* II, 488-528.

19. *New York Herald,* November 3, 1860.

20. *Ibid.,* December 13, 19, 1860; Dyer, *Evarts,* 48-49.

21. *New York Herald,* December 24, 1860.

22. Storey and Emerson, *Ebenezer Rockwood Hoar,* 126-127; Dyer, *Evarts,* 42.

23. F. R. Stark, "The Abolition of Privateering and the Declaration of Paris," *Columbia University Studies in History, Economics and Public Law,* XXXIX, No. 2, 300-306, 331-332; *New York Herald,* January 12, 23, 1861.

24. *New York Tribune,* February 4, 1861.

25. T. Weed, *Autobiography,* II, 323-324; Alexander, *Political History,* II, 363.

26. *The Green Bag,* VIII, 98; *New York Herald,* January 30, February 1, 1861.

27. *New York Herald,* February 1, 2, 3, 5, 1861; H. B. Stanton, *Random Recollections,* 218.

28. Seitz, *Horace Greeley,* 186; *New York Herald,* February 5, 1861.

29. Dyer, *Evarts,* 46.

30. *New York Herald,* February 23, 1861.

CHAPTER VIII

1. *Arguments and Speeches,* II, 612-613.

2. *New York Times,* April 16, 1861.

3. Quotation from Henry S. Wardner; Rev. Morgan Dix, *Memoirs of John A. Dix,* II, 10; *Leslie's History of Greater New York,* I, 399-400.

4. *New York Herald,* April 18, 19, 1861; *New York Times,* April 21, 1861.

5. *New York Times,* April 24, 1861; J. A. Stevens, *The Union Defence Committee of the City of New York, Minutes, Reports, and Correspondence; Arguments and Speeches,* II, 529-530; Lossing, *op. cit.,* II, 725-726.

6. F. W. Seward, *Seward at Washington As Senator and Secretary of State,* II, 551; *Record of the Class of 1837 in Yale University, With a Notice of Their Meetings in 1877, 1882, 1887.*

7. Nevins, *Hamilton Fish,* 82, 90, 103; Fish Papers, Evarts to Fish, June 17, 22, 1861; Fish to Evarts, June 26, 1862.

8. *New York Herald,* June 16, 17, 20, 23, 26, 1861.

9. Stark, "The Abolition of Privateering," 367-376; *New York Times,* May 11, 1861; *Charleston Mercury,* June 12, 1861.

10. W. M. Robinson, *The Confederate Privateers,* 139-140; *New York Herald,* July 30, 1861; *New York Times,* October 24, 25, 28, 30, 1861.

11. *The Green Bag,* XV, 396.

12. Smith, *Sunshine and Shadow,* 538-539; H. W. Scott, *Distinguished American Lawyers,* 64-74; *The Green Bag,* July, 1891.

13. *Trial of the Officers and Crew of the Privateer Savannah,* 236-237, 258-259, 270, 273, 279, 283.

14. *The Yale Review,* October, 1920.

15. *Arguments and Speeches,* I, 98-99, 108-109, 120, 137, 168-169, 172, 185, 189-196, 213.

16. *Trial of the Officers and Crew of the . . . Savannah,* 368-373; *New York Times,* October 31, November 1, 1861; *New York Herald,* November 9, 14, 18, 1861; *Charleston Mercury,* November 10, 1861.

17. *Arguments and Speeches,* I, 92; Evarts Papers, Evarts to E. D. Smith, November 25, 1861.

18. Martin, *Life of Choate,* I, 235.

19. *New York Herald,* December 24, 1861.

20. Bancroft, *Seward,* II, 360.

21. *Ibid.,* II, 360-361; Dyer, *Evarts,* 52.

22. T. W. Barnes, *Memoir of Thurlow Weed,* 410-411; Dyer, *Evarts,* 52.

23. *New York Times,* February 24, 1862.

24. E. M. Coulter, *William G. Brownlow,* 225-226; *New York Times,* May 16, 1862.

25. Evarts Papers, Evarts to Marble, May 27, 1862; *New York Times,* June 22, 1862.

26. Wilson, *Memorial History of the City of New York*, III, 493-494; *Arguments and Speeches*, III, 366.

27. *New England Soldiers' Relief Association, No. 194 Broadway, New York, Minutes of the Organization and of Meetings Held in April, 1862; Reports of the Superintendent and Treasurer of the New England Soldiers' Relief Association, 194 Broadway, New York, November, 1863;* Evarts Papers, Evarts to H. W. Bellows, March 1, 1867.

28. H. W. Bellows, *Historical Sketch of the Union League Club of New York;* E. P. Oberholtzer, *Jay Cooke, Financier of The Civil War*, I, 344-347.

29. Evarts Papers, Evarts to Bates, November 23, 1861.

30. Evarts Papers, Evarts to Seward, November 23, 1861; Seward to Evarts, November 26, 1861; Bates to Evarts, February 1, March 11, 1862.

31. *Arguments and Speeches*, I, 214-215, 226-227.

32. *Supreme Court—The Prize Cases—Mr. Evarts' Brief For the United States.*

33. *Arguments and Speeches*, I, 225, 245, 256, 263, 266-275, 285, 288-289, 293.

34. 2 Black 635; *New York Times*, March 11, 1863.

35. Evarts Papers, Taylor to Evarts, June 6, 1863.

CHAPTER IX

1. J. H. Kiger, "Federal Government Propaganda in Great Britain during the American Civil War," *The Historical Outlook*, XIX, 204-208; E. W. Emerson, "John Murray Forbes," *Atlantic Monthy*, September, 1899; J. P. Baxter, "The British Government and Neutral Rights," *American Historical Review*, XXXIV, 26.

2. *Massachusetts Historical Society Proceedings*, XIII, 193.

3. Bancroft, *Seward*, II, 386.

4. State Dept. Archives, Domestic Letters, Seward to Evarts, April 12, 1863; Instructions, Great Britain, Seward to Adams, April 13, 1863; Bancroft, *Seward*, II, 387.

5. Evarts Papers, small diary in Evarts' handwriting with brief entries from May 1 to 19, 1863, and list of addresses; Evarts to Bancroft, April 15, 1863; E. L. Pierce, *Memoir and Letters of Charles Sumner*, III, 136.

6. State Dept. Archives, Dispatches, Great Britain, April 30, 1863, No. 395; Adams to Seward, May 8, 1863, No. 411; Evarts to Seward, May 1, 1863, No. 411.

7. Evarts Papers, Journal of My Readings, 12-13; Diary entry, May 7, 11, 14, 15, 18, 19, 1863; J. A. Hobson, *Richard Cobden*, 373-374.

8. E. H. Coleridge, *Life and Correspondence of John Duke Lord Coleridge*, II, 26, 119-120.

9. H. Adams, *The Education of Henry Adams*, 197; W. C. Ford, *A Cycle of Adams Letters*, I, 297.

10. Ford, *A Cycle of Adams Letters*, II, 18-19.

11. C. F. Adams, *Charles Francis Adams*, 354-356; C. F. Adams, *Studies Military and Diplomatic*, 363.

12. J. Bigelow, *Retrospections of An Active Life*, I, 637-638.

13. State Dept. Archives, Dispatches, Great Britain, Evarts to Seward, June 10, 1863.

14. E. D. Adams, *Great Britain and the American Civil War*, II, 136; E. P. Oberholtzer, *A History of the United States Since the Civil War*, II, 406-407; Bancroft, *Seward*, II, 386-387.

15. State Dept. Archives, Dispatches, Great Britain, Adams to Seward, July 3, 1863, No. 447.

16. *New York Tribune*, December 8, 1883.

17. Evarts Papers, Evarts to Bancroft, August 18, 28, 1863.

18. *Ibid.*, Holland to Evarts, October 27, 1863.

19. *Ibid.*, Holland to Evarts, November 7, 1863.

20. State Dept. Archives, Dispatches, Great Britain, Evarts to Seward, January 15, 1864.

21. Bancroft, *Seward,* II, 395-396.

22. Bigelow, *Retrospections,* II, 113, 134-135, 147, 156.

23. State Dept. Archives, Dispatches, France, LIV, Dayton to Seward, January 15, 1864; Bigelow, *Retrospections,* II, 129-130; *American Historical Review,* XXXIV, 89-91.

24. *New York Tribune,* November 10, 1877; State Dept. Archives, Dispatches, Great Britain, LXXXV, Evarts to Seward, February 12, 1864.

25. State Dept. Archives, Dispatches, Great Britain, LXXXV, Evarts to Seward, February 12, 1864.

26. Bancroft, *Seward,* II, 397.

27. State Dept. Archives, Dispatches, Great Britain, LXXXV, Evarts to Seward, February 12, 19, 1864; Evarts to Seward, February 26, 1864; Dyer, *Evarts,* 72.

28. *Hansard's Parliamentary Debates.* Third Series, Vol. 73; State Dept. Archives, Dispatches, Great Britain, LXXXV, Evarts to Seward, March 4, 5, 1864; LXXXVI, Evarts to Seward, April 8, 16, 1864; *London Times,* April 7, 1864; E. D. Adams, *Great Britain and the American Civil War,* 196 n.

29. State Dept. Archives, Dispatches, Great Britain, LXXXVI, Evarts to Seward, April 16, 22, 1864.

30. *Report of the Proceedings at the Inauguration Banquet, Given By Mr. Cyrus W. Field,* 13-15.

31. *New York Tribune,* May 13, 1864.

32. *Proceedings of the Massachusetts Historical Society,* XLVIII, 466; *Arguments and Speeches,* III, 254.

33. Evarts Papers, Receipted bill, dated September 1, 1864; H. Adams, *The Education of Henry Adams,* 148.

34. *New York Tribune,* May 21 1864.

CHAPTER X

1. Evarts Papers, Evarts to Brent, October, 1864; *New York Times,* October 24, 1864.

2. Evarts Papers, outline of Evarts' speech; *New York Times,* October 22, 1864.

3. *New York Herald, New York Times,* November 5, 1864.

4. *New York Tribune, New York Herald,* November 24, 1864.

5. G. Smith, *Reminiscences,* 327; *Welcome to Godwin Smith,* etc. November 12, 1864; *New York Tribune,* November 13, 1864.

6. W. E. Smith, *The Francis Preston Blair Family in Politics,* II, 297-298.

7. Lewis, *Great American Lawyers,* VII, 241.

8. Dyer, *Evarts,* 156-157.

9. A. B. Hart, *Salmon Portland Chase,* 320-321.

10. Storey and Emerson, *Ebenezer Rockwood Hoar,* 141-144.

11. G. Welles, *Diary of Gideon Welles,* III, 182-183; *Arguments and Speeches,* III, 460; C. Warren, *The Supreme Court in United States History,* III, 122.

12. *New York Times,* February 23, March 7, 1865.

13. *Summary of Class Meetings and the Biographical Record of the Class of 1866, Yale University,* 151-152.

14. Evarts Papers, manuscript of Evarts speech at Grant anniversary dinner, April 26, 1891; *New York Tribune,* April 16, 26, 1865.

15. *Addresses and Proceedings, Including the Oration Pronounced by Rev. Dr. Bushnell at the Commemoration Celebration, Held July 26th, 1865, In Honor of the Alumni of Yale College;* E. Eliot, *Yale in the Civil War,* 29; *New York Tribune,* July 26, 27, 28, 1865; *New York Herald,* July 27, 28, 1865.

16. *Arguments and Speeches,* III, 368-370.

17. *Ibid.,* III, 264-274.

18. H. B. Learned, *The Attorney-General and the Cabinet,* 460-461.

19. *New York Herald,* May 18, 19, 20, 21, 22, 29, 1864; *New York Tribune,* May 20, 31, 1864; 5 Blatchford 222.

20. *New York Herald, New York Tribune,* July 10, 11, 1864.

21. *The Great Libel Case. Opdyke vs. Weed. A Full Report of Proceedings,* 6-8; Weed, *Autobiography,* I, 528-529.

22. *New York Herald,* December 14, 15, 17, 18, 21, 22, 24, 28, 29, 30, 1864.

23. A. Nevins, *Frémont, the West's Great Adventurer,* II, 671; H. M. Field, *Life of David Dudley Field,* 101; *The Great Libel Cases,* 57-64, 148-149.

24. *The Great Libel Case,* 135-137, 140, 141.

25. *The Opdyke Libel Suit. A Full Metrical, Juridical, and Analytical Report . . .,* 45.

26. Weed, *Autobiography,* I, 59.

27. *New York Tribune,* May 24, 1865; A. Nevins, *The Evening Post,* 427-429.

28. Evarts Papers, "In the Matter of Benjamin W. Perkins against the Russian Government"; Nevins, *Hamilton Fish,* 503-504.

29. *New York Herald,* October 28, 1865.

30. 2 Wallace 350, 366; H. L. Carson, *The History of the Supreme Court of the United States,* II, 413.

31. Evarts Papers, Evarts to F. de Lisardi & Co., June 15, 1867; 5 Wallace 170, 517.

32. Evarts Papers, Seward to Evarts, November 16, 1863.

33. 5 Wallace 630; 7 Wallace 542.

34. 5 Blatchford 336; Evarts Papers, Evarts to Eames, February 11, 1867; S. L. Barlow to Evarts, February 22, 1871; Evarts to Robinson, May 21, 1867; 6 Blatchford 138; 5 Blatchford 231; 12 Wallace 130.

35. S. F. Hughes, *Letters and Recollections of John Murray Forbes* II, 71-72; R. B. Forbes, *Personal Reminiscences,* 304-308; *New York Herald,* January 24, 1866.

36. F. V. Balch, *Report of the Case of the Steamship Meteor,* I, vii-ix, xii-xiii; *New York Herald,* January 25, 26, 1866; Forbes, *Personal Reminiscences,* 309.

37. Balch, *Report of . . . Meteor,* I, 10-27.

38. *Ibid.,* 48, 53, 55, 68-70, 81, 83, 85, 98-101; *United States Circuit Court—Case of the "Meteor,"* 22-241; R. H. Dana, ed., Wheaton's *Elements of International Law,* 536 note.

39. Balch, *Report of . . . Meteor,* II, 229-283; R. H. Dana, Jr., "The Present Aspect of International Law," *North American Review,* October, 1866.

40. C. G. Fenwick, *The Neutrality of the United States,* 50-51.

41. Balch, *Report of . . . Meteor,* I, xiv-xv; II, 7-8, 201-202.

42. R. B. Forbes, *Personal Reminiscences,* 312-313.

CHAPTER XI

1. L. P. Stryker, *Andrew Johnson;* R. W. Winston, *Andrew Johnson;* D. M. De Witt, *The Impeachment and Trial of Andrew Johnson;* G. F. Milton, *The Age of Hate;* C. Bowers, *The Tragic Era.*

2. *New York Herald,* October 17, 1867.

3. *Trial of Andrew Johnson . . .,* II, 362-363; *Congressional Globe,* 40 Cong., 2 Sess., 3-5.

4. Welles, *Diary,* III, 300.

5. Lewis, *Great American Lawyers,* V, 450, 453; O. H. Browning, *Diary of Orville Hickman Browning,* II, 183.

6. W. N. Brigance, "Jeremiah Black and Andrew Johnson," *The Mississippi Valley Historical Review,* XIX, 205-218.

7. G. Hunt, "The President's Defense," *Century Magazine,* LXXXV, 432-433; Browning, *Diary,* II, 185; Welles, *Diary,* II, 307-308.

8. Evarts Papers, undated clipping from *Independent.*

9. *The Nation* (New York), May 21, 1868; *Harper's Weekly,* May 16, 1868.

10. Evarts Papers, Stanbery's balance sheet.

11. S. S. Cox, *Three Decades of Federal Legislation, 1855-1885,* 589.

12. *New York Herald,* March 13, 1868.

13. *Trial of Andrew Johnson,* I, 19, 21, 33-34.

14. *New York Herald,* March 24, 1868; W. G. Moore, "Notes of Col. W. G. Moore . . .," *American Historical Review,* XIX, 129.

15. *Trial of Andrew Johnson,* I, 68-82; M. A. D. Howe, *Portrait of an Independent: Moorfield Storey,* 84.

16. John B. Henderson, "Emancipation and Impeachment," *Century Magazine,* LXXX (December, 1912), 204; B. F. Butler, *Autobiography and Personal Reminiscences of Benjamin F. Butler,* 929.

17. *Trial of Andrew Johnson,* I, 87-154; *New York Herald,* March 31, April 3, 1868.

18. *Arguments and Speeches,* III, 84-85.

19. *Trial of Andrew Johnson,* I, 185, 258-259, 268, 424, 598-599; E. R. Wheeler, *Sixty Years of American Life,* 71-72.

20. Howe, *Portrait of an Independent,* 91; *Trial of Andrew Johnson,* I, 377-414; *New York Herald,* April 10, 11, 1868.

21. *Trial of Andrew Johnson,* I, 440-490.

22. *Ibid.,* I, 485.

23. *Ibid.,* 538; *New York Herald,* April 13, 14, 15, 1868.

24. De Witt, *op. cit.,* 447; *New York Herald,* April 16, 1868.

25. *Trial of Andrew Johnson,* 538; *New York Herald,* April 18, 1868; Hoar, *Autobiography,* I, 343.

26. *Trial of Andrew Johnson,* I, 636-637; Welles, *Diary,* III, 371.

27. *New York Herald,* April 19, 1868; Dyer, *Evarts,* 88-89.

28. J. M. Schofield, "Controversies in the War Department," *Century Magazine,* August, 1897; Milton, *The Age of Hate,* 568-570.

29. *Trial of Andrew Johnson,* II, 116-217; *New York Herald,* April 23, 24, 25, 26, 1868.

30. *Trial of Andrew Johnson,* II, 219, 224; S. W. McCall, *Thaddeus Stevens,* 343; *New York Herald,* April 28, 1868.

31. *Trial of Andrew Johnson,* II, 230-249; *New York Herald,* April 28, 29, 1868.

32. R. Cortissoz, *The Life of Whitelaw Reid,* I, 127-130.

33. J. F. Rhodes, *History of the United States,* VI, 135; *Cincinnati Daily Gazette,* May 5, 1868.

34. *Arguments and Speeches,* I, 355-356.

35. *Ibid.,* 359-362, 368; Evarts Papers, Ketchum to Evarts, March 24, 1868.

36. Lewis, *Great American Lawyers,* VII, 233; *New York Tribune,* April 29, 1868.

37. *Arguments and Speeches,* I, 369, 371; *New York Herald,* April 30, 1868.

38. *Arguments and Speeches,* I, 398; *New York Herald,* April 30, 1868.

39. G. S. Boutwell, *Reminiscences of Sixty Years in Public Affairs,* Chap. XXXII; *New York Tribune,* April 30, 1868.

40. Evarts Papers, Adams to Evarts, July 24, 1868; *Arguments and Speeches,* I, 385-396.

41. *New York Herald,* May 1, 1868.

42. *New York Tribune,* May 1, 1868; *Arguments and Speeches,* I, 462-463.

43. Welles, *Diary,* III, 342.

44. *Arguments and Speeches,* I, 481-491.

45. *Ibid.,* 519-521, 525; *New York Herald,* May 2, 1868.

46. *New York World,* May 4, 1868.

47. *New York Tribune,* May 2, 1868; *The Nation* (New York), May 7, 21, 1868; Ford Collection, undated clipping from *Independent; Harper's Weekly,* May 16, 1868.

48. G. E. Baker, *The Works of William H. Seward,* V, 23; Evarts Papers, Curtis to Evarts, May 8, 1868; Adams to Evarts, July 24, 1868; Tiffany to Evarts, May 4, 1868.

49. Cox, *op. cit.*, 589-590; *Trial of Andrew Johnson*, II, 359-389; *New York Herald*, May 2, 3, 1868.

50. *Trial of Andrew Johnson*, II, 395; Stryker, *Andrew Johnson*, 702-704.

51. Hunt, "The President's Defense," 208; Dyer, *Evarts*, 98.

52. H. White, *The Life of Lyman Trumbull*, 318; W. Salter, *The Life of James W. Grimes*, 337-357; F. Fessenden, *Life and Public Services of William Pitt Fessenden*, II, 239-273; Hunt, "The President's Defense," 204.

CHAPTER XII

1. Evarts Papers, Stanbery to Evarts, June 30, 1868; Blaine, *Twenty Years of Congress*, II, 384; B. R. Curtis, *A Memoir of Benjamin Robbins Curtis*, I, 419; Welles, *Diary*, III, 390, 410.

2. *Journal of Executive Proceedings of the Senate*, XVI, 269-270, 292, 301, 308, 313.

3. *New York Herald*, June 16, 1868; *The Nation* (New York), July 2, 1868; Welles, *Diary*, *III*, 247; Storey and Emerson, *Ebenezer Rockwood Hoar*, 149-150.

4. Martin, *Life of Choate*, I, 281-283; Dyer, *Evarts*, 112.

5. Browning, *Diary*, II, 240; *New York Herald*, July 21, 22, 1868.

6. *Arguments and Speeches*, III, 247; Welles, *Diary*, III, 468; Browning, *Diary*, II, 226-227; *New York Herald*, November 18, 19, 1868.

7. *Arguments and Speeches*, III, 247-258.

8. *The Green Bag*, VIII, 139; Winston, *Andrew Johnson*, 449 n.

9. Welles, *Diary*, III, 409-410, 446, 451-452, 480.

10. J. M. Schofield, *Forty-Six Years in the Army*, 22, 419; Browning, *Diary*, Introduction.

11. Welles, *Diary*, III, 409; G. E. Baker, *Works of Seward*, V, 34, 589-592.

12. *New York Herald*, January 21, February 2, 1869.

13. *New York Herald*, February 22, 1869.

14. Howe, *Portrait of An Independent*, 129.

15. H. Adams, *The Education of Henry Adams*, 244-245; W. C. Ford, *Letters of Henry Adams, 1858-1891*, 147-148, 151; J. T. Adams, *Henry Adams*, 114-120.

16. J. M. Schofield, "Controversies in the War Department," *Century Magazine*, August, 1897; Welles, *Diary*, III, 504; *New York Herald*, August 1, 1868.

17. Welles, *Diary*, III, 504-505.

18. Blaine, *op. cit.*, 384; *The Nation* (New York), August 13, 1868; *New York Herald*, August 1, 13, 1868.

19. L. M. Short, *The Development of National Administrative Organization in the United States*, 330; *New York Herald*, November 3, 1868.

20. *The Green Bag*, V, 308.

21. *Official Opinions of the Attorneys General of the United States*, XII, 530-536; *The Nation* (New York), December 3, 1868; Welles, *Diary*, III, 471.

22. *Opinions*, XII, 472-474, 443-449; *New York Herald*, July 29, August 1, 7, 10, 13, 19, December 1, 1868; *The Nation* (New York), August 20, 1868.

23. *Opinions*, XII, 449-457, 468-470.

24. *Ibid.*, XII, 555-557.

25. *Ibid.*, XII, 470-471, 494-496, 504-508, 541-544, 559-562, 510-511, 528-529, 547-549, 544-546, 511-514; Browning, *Diary*, II, 242; *New York Herald*, September 9, 11, October 23, 1868; *New York Times*, August 27, 1868; Welles, *Diary*, III, 431; Evarts Papers, Evarts to Magruder, August 20, 1868.

26. R. F. Nichols, "United States vs. Jefferson Davis," *American Historical Review*, XXXI, 266-275; J. G. Randall, *Constitutional Problems Under Lincoln*, 111.

27. Evarts Papers, Stanbery to Evarts, October 25, 1867; Chandler to Evarts, October 19, 1867; Nichols, 276.

28. Evarts Papers, Stanbery to Evarts, November 4, 1867; Evarts to Stanbery, November 2, 1867; *New York Herald,* November 6, 25, 27, 1867; Evarts Papers, Evarts to Chandler, February 18, 1868.

29. R. H. Dana, "The Reasons For Not Prosecuting Jefferson Davis," *Proceedings of the Massachusetts Historical Society,* LIV, 201-209.

30. Evarts Papers, Evarts to Wells, February 24, 1868; J. C. Walsh, "Charles O'Conor," *The Journal of the American Irish Historical Society,* XXVII, 298; Nichols, "United States vs. Jefferson Davis," 279-280.

31. Dana, "The Reasons For Not Prosecuting Jefferson Davis," 205, 208; Browning, *Diary,* II, 225-226; Nichols, *op. cit.,* 281-282.

32. *New York Herald,* January 13, 1869.

33. Nichols, *op. cit.,* 282-284.

34. 7 Wallace 32; *New York Herald,* January 15, 1869.

35. 7 Wallace 354, 454.

36. *New York Herald,* February 8, 9, 1869.

37. 7 Wallace 122, 347, 580, 666, 743; 3 Court of Claims 10; *New York Herald,* March 10, 1869.

38. H. Adams, *The Education of Henry Adams,* 249-250.

39. *American Law Register,* XVII, 194-197.

40. *Arguments and Speeches,* I, 534-545.

41. *Ibid.,* I, 556-579.

42. 8 Wallace 603.

43. *Arguments and Speeches,* I, 527-528.

44. Welles, *Diary,* III, 533, 537-538, 541-542; Stryker, *Andrew Johnson,* 770-772.

45. *New York Times,* March 13, 1869.

46. Evarts Papers, manuscript copy of speech on April 26, 1891; Dyer, *Evarts,* 112; *New York Herald,* January 10, 11, 1869.

47. Evarts Papers, Hoar to Evarts, August 30, 1868.

CHAPTER XIII

1. Bellows, *Historical Sketch of the Union League Club of New York,* 86; A. D. White, *Autobiography of Andrew Dickson White,* I, 142; Alexander, *A Political History of the State of New York,* III, 184; *Harper's Weekly,* September 14, 1867.

2. C. L. Lincoln, *Constitutional History of New York,* II, 248; *The Green Bag,* II, 248.

3. A. Chester, *Courts and Lawyers of New York,* II, 704-705; A. Chester, *Legal and Judicial History of New York,* III, 179, 181, 184; *New York Times,* December 6, 1867.

4. *Arguments and Speeches,* III, 225-226, 230-236.

5. *Ibid.,* III, 241-244.

6. *Proceedings and Debates of the Constitutional Convention of the State of New York,* IV, 2635-2636; *Harper's Weekly,* September 21, 1867; Lincoln, *Constitutional History,* II, 256; Ford Collection, Evarts to Greeley, January 7, 1868.

7. E. A. Merritt, *Recollections,* 76-77.

8. *Proceedings and Debates,* I, 95, 365, 555, 563; II, 943, 982, 1112; IV, 2634.

9. Strong, *Landmarks of A Lawyer's Lifetime,* 159; *North American Review,* CV, 150, 155; *New York Times,* December 2, 1865.

10. *Arguments and Speeches,* III, 365-366, 372-373.

11. Association of the Bar of the City of New York, *Constitution and Address,* 6; Bar Association Proceedings, *Reports,* I, No. 1; Strong, *Landmarks of a Lawyer's Lifetime,* 161-162.

12. *New York Times,* February 2, 1870; Association of the Bar of the City of New York, *Report for 1902,* 110-111; *Report of the Proceedings of the Bar Association of the City of New York,* 25-29.

13. *New York Times*, February 16, 1870.

14. Strong, *Landmarks of a Lawyer's Lifetime*, 163-164; *Bar Association Proceedings, Reports, 1870-1876*, I, 23; II, 41, 45.

15. H. C. Lodge, *Early Memories*, 255; Strong, *Landmarks of a Lawyer's Lifetime*, 72.

16. *Arguments and Speeches*, III, 358.

17. *Ibid.*, III, 544-557; *New York Times*, April 7, 1871; *The Nation* (New York), April 13, 1871; *North American Review*, CXXI, 146.

18. *New York Times*, May 5, 13, 1871; *American Law Review*, V, 761-766; S. J. Tilden, *The New York City "Ring,"* 30-31.

19. M. Breen, *Thirty Years of New York Politics*, 335-340.

20. Evarts Papers, invitations signed by Allen Evarts.

21. *Arguments and Speeches*, II, 557-569; *New York Times*, October 26, 1871.

22. O'Conor Papers, O'Conor to Tilden, January 4, 1875; D. Seitz, *The Dreadful Decade*, 181-186; C. O'Conor, *Peculation Triumphant*, 29-31.

23. *New York Times*, November 3, 1871; *Arguments and Speeches*, II, 570-573.

24. *New York Tribune*, November 2, 1872; Strong, *Landmarks of a Lawyer's Lifetime*, 84.

25. Breen, 445-448.

26. *Constitution, Rules, Officers, and Members of the Union Club*, 1875; Lossing, *op. cit.*, II, 434-435.

27. 53 Barbour 513; *New York Times*, January 7, February 7, 8, 13, 1868.

28. Evarts Papers, Evarts to Eldridge, September 25, 1868; *New York Times*, March 8, 1877; E. H. Mott, *Between Ocean and Lakes*, 142-143.

29. A. Nevins, *Abram S. Hewitt*, 261.

30. 8 Blatchford 347, 413, 536; *New York Times*, April 29, 30, 1871.

31. 9 Blatchford 226, 316; Evarts Papers, Choate to Evarts, August 26, 1871.

32. *New York Herald*, March 11, 1874; Mott, *op. cit.*, 227-229.

33. Strong, *Landmarks of a Lawyer's Lifetime*, 191-192; *North American Review*, CXXI, 146-149.

34. J. B. Bishop, *A Chronicle of One Hundred and Fifty Years: The Chamber of Commerce of the State of New York, 1768-1918*, 182-185; *New York Times*, May 2, 1873.

35. *New York Times*, April 9, 10, 1874; Alexander, *Political History*, III, 323-324.

36. *Report of the Commission to Devise A Plan For the Government of Cities in the State of New York*, 1-29, 41-45, 72; *New York Tribune*, April 15, 1876, March 7, 1877.

37. J. Bigelow, *The Life of Samuel Tilden*, I, 266; *New York Tribune*, April 9, 1877.

CHAPTER XIV

1. Welles, *Diary*, III, 470.

2. C. C. Beaman, *The National and Private "Alabama Claims" and Their Final and Amicable Settlement.*

3. Fish Papers, Davis to Fish, May 29, 1871; Nevins, *Fish*, 511-512.

4. Fish Papers, Davis to Fish, August 24, 1871; *The Green Bag*, IV, 1-13.

5. Fish Papers, Evarts to Fish, March 12, 1869; Fish to Schenck, October 13, 1871; Schenck to Fish, September 28, 1871; Davis to Fish, October 18, 1871; Evarts Papers, Hoar to Evarts, October 29, 1871.

6. Nevins, *Fish*, 513; *The Green Bag*, XIV, 257-262; Evarts Papers, Waite to Evarts, December 1, 1871; B. R. Trimble, *Chief Justice Waite*, 90.

7. F. W. Hackett, *Reminiscences of the Geneva Tribunal*, 126; Evarts Papers, Johnson to Evarts, October 29, 1871; Ashton to Evarts, November 4, 1871.

8. Hackett, *Reminiscences*, 105 n.

9. Evarts Papers, Dana to Evarts, November 3, 1871; Nevins, *Fish*, 521.

10. Fish Papers, Evarts to Fish, December 2, 1871; Fish to Evarts, December 23, 1871; Evarts to Fish, December 25, 1871; Trimble, *op. cit.*, 94.

11. *Papers Relating to the Treaty of Washington*, II, 414-416.

12. Evarts Papers, Blatchford to Evarts, December 13, 1871; *Arguments and Speeches*, III, 374-377.

13. Evarts Papers, Schenck to Evarts, November 14, 1871; Hackett, *Reminiscences*, 104; C. M. Feuss, *The Life of Caleb Cushing*, II, 334; T. W. Reid, *The Life of the Right Honourable William Edward Forster*, II, 25-26.

14. Dyer, *Evarts*, 122.

15. Fish Papers, Fish to Loring, March 11, 1872; Fish to Schenck, March 18, 1872.

16. *Ibid.*, Hoffman to Fish, March 22, 1872; Hackett, *Reminiscences*, 104; *Papers Relating to the Treaty of Washington*, IV, 550.

17. Hackett, *Reminiscences*, 101-102 n., 103 n.

18. *Papers Relating to the Treaty of Washington*, I, 429-856; II, 1-196; IV, 6.

19. *Ibid.*, II, 203-410; IV, 6; C. Cushing, *The Treaty of Washington*, 38.

20. Fish Papers, Fish to Schenck, April 26, 1872; Fish to Washburne, April 30, 1872; Fish to Schenck, May 7, 1872; Nevins, *Fish*, 538-542, 556. Fish Papers, Fish to Schenck, June 4, 1872; S. Walpole, *The Life of Lord John Russell*, II, 365.

21. Feuss, *Caleb Cushing*, II, 334; *Papers Relating to the Treaty of Washington*, IV, 6, 17-18.

22. Fish Papers, Fish to Ullman, July 2, 1872; Fish to Davis, July 19, 1872.

23. *Ibid.*, Fish to Davis, July 19, 1872; Hackett, *Reminiscences*, 266-269; Nevins, *Fish*, 556.

24. *Papers Relating to the Treaty of Washington*, IV, 24-26; Hackett, *Reminiscences*, 266-269.

25. W. Theron, *The Letters of Mrs. Henry Adams*, 28 n.; Trimble, *Chief Justice Waite*, 102.

26. *Harper's Weekly*, February 3, November 2, 1872.

27. *The Green Bag*, I, 45-47.

28. *Arguments and Speeches*, I, 582.

29. *Argument of the United States Delivered to the Tribunal of Arbitration at Geneva, June 15, 1872*, 3, 13, 18, 320, 330, 345-346; *Papers Relating to the Treaty of Washington*, III, 153.

30. Hackett, *Reminiscences*, 125 n.

31. *Papers Relating to the Treaty of Washington*, IV, 26-29; Lord Edmund Fitzmaurice, *Life of Granville George-Gower, Second Earl of Granville*, II, 102.

32. *Papers Relating to the Treaty of Washington*, III, 384-441; IV, 7, 30; C. Cushing, *The Treaty of Washington*, 122-123.

33. *Papers Relating to the Treaty of Washington*, IV, 31.

34. *Arguments and Speeches*, I, 586-593.

35. *Ibid.*, I, 596-628.

36. *London Times*, August 8, 1872; Trimble, *Chief Justice Waite*, 102.

37. *Arguments and Speeches*, I, 635-664.

38. Nevins, *Fish*, 588; Trimble, *Chief Justice Waite*, 107.

39. *Papers Relating to the Treaty of Washington*, III, 520-549.

40. *New York Herald*, August 26, 1872.

41. *North America. No. 1 (1873) Papers Relating to the Proceedings of Arbitration at Geneva*, 367; *Papers Relating to the Treaty of Washington*, IV, 43-46; Hackett, *Reminiscences*, 322.

42. *North America. No. 1 (1873) Papers . . .*, 378; *Harper's Weekly*, November 2, 1872.

43. *New York Times*, October 3, 1872; *Papers Relating to the Treaty of Washington*, IV, 8, 545.

44. E. S. Martin, *Joseph Hodges Choate*, I, 117-118.

CHAPTER XV

1. R. Palmer, *Memorials, Personal and Political,* I, 247-248, 285-286.

2. Bigelow, *Retrospections,* V, 134.

3. *New York Times,* October 31, 1872.

Times, December 10, 1872.

4. C. Warren, *The Supreme Court in United States History,* II, 536 n.; *New York*

5. *New York Times,* December 5, 1872.

6. *Arguments and Speeches,* III, 378-382; Fish Papers, Davis to Fish, December 24, 1872; Nevins, *Fish,* 564-565 n.

7. 17 Wallace 29.

8. Fish Papers, Davis to Fish, December 24, 1872.

9. Evarts Papers, Printed folder by Cushing entitled "Distribution of the Alabama Claims."

10. *Cong. Globe,* 42 Cong., 3 Sess., 1178-1183; Evarts Papers, Evarts to Edmunds, December 24, 1872; "Memorandum: The Sum Awarded by the Tribunal at Geneva."

11. *Cong. Globe,* 42 Cong., 3 Sess., 1219-1230, 1754, 1927, 2164, 2170, 2210; 17 Statutes-at-Large 601; Dyer, *Evarts,* 138.

12. W. M. Evarts, *Arguments of Mr. Evarts Before the Judiciary Committee of the House of Representatives at Washington; New York Herald,* January 28, 1874.

13. *Cong. Rec.,* 43 Cong., 1 Sess., 3688, 3753-3762, 3786-3790, 3811, 3863.

14. 18 Statutes-at-Large 245; J. B. Moore, *A History and Digest of International Arbitrations,* V, 4639, 4648, 4652; *North American Review,* CXXXIV, 76-96.

15. E. C. Stowell, and H. F. Munro, *International Cases,* II, 381-392; C. J. Colombos, *A Treatise on the Law of Prize,* 173.

16. *Papers Relating to the Condemnation of the British Barque "Springbok" and Her Cargo By the District Prize Court of New York, U. S., With the Opinions of the Press Thereon,* 7, 16-89; 5 Wallace 1; F. Wharton, *A Digest of International Law,* III, 404 n.; W. E. Hall, *A Treatise on International Law,* 720-721; *The Journal of the United Service Institution,* December, 1902; J. B. Moore, *Digest of International Law,* VII, 723.

17. Evarts Papers, Evarts to D. F. Campbell, May 6, 1873.

18. T. Twiss, *A Juridical Review of the Case of the British Barque "Springbok,"* 36-40.

19. W. M. Evarts, *Brief on Behalf of the Owners of the Cargo of the British Barque "Springbok," As Submitted on the 18th August, 1873, to the Mixed Commission on British and American Claims Under the Treaty of Washington,* 14-15.

20. *Ibid.,* 16-49.

21. *Arguments and Speeches,* I, 667.

22. *Parliamentary Papers. North America, 1873, No. 2,* 146; Evarts Papers, Evarts to Campbell, October 31, 1873.

23. W. E. Hall, *A Treatise on International Law,* 695 n.: *Johns Hopkins University Studies in Historical and Political Science,* XLIV, No. 2, 73-77; *New York Herald,* November 5, 1877.

24. T. Twiss, *The Doctrine of Continuous Voyage;* Evarts Papers, Antwerp Conference resolution; Moore, *Digest of International Law,* VII, 731-732; C. C. Hyde, *International Law Chiefly as Interpreted and Applied by the United States,* II, 619-620, 625; Colombos, *A Treatise on the Law of Prize,* 174-175.

25. *New York Herald,* June 18, 1869; Nevins, *Fish,* 186.

26. Nevins, *Fish,* 667-675.

27. Evarts Papers, Hoar to Evarts, November 28, 1869.

28. *New York Tribune,* November 18, 1873; *New York Times,* November 18, 1873; *New York Herald,* November 18, 1873; *The Nation* (New York), November 20, 1873.

29. Fish Papers, Evarts to Fish, November 30, 1873.

30. Dyer, *Evarts,* 159; Storey and Emerson, *Ebenezer Rockwood Hoar,* 234-235.

31. Fish Papers, Fish to Crosby, January 17, 1874; T. C. Platt, *The Autobiography of Thomas Collier Platt*, 67-68; Strong, *Landmarks of a Lawyer's Lifetime*, 212-213.

32. *Independent*, January 8, 1874.

33. Trimble, *Chief Justice Waite*, 128-129 n.

34. Strong, *Landmarks of a Lawyer's Lifetime*, 213-214.

35. *New York Times*, February 22, 1874.

36. Hicks, *Arguments and Addresses of Joseph H. Choate*, 1140.

CHAPTER XVI

1. *Proceedings of the Bench and Bar of the Supreme Court of the United States in Memoriam Morrison R. Waite*, 29.

2. H. R. Phelps, *The Albany Hand-Book*, 47-48; *The Green Bag*, II, 321-341.

3. 35 N. Y. 559; Evarts Papers, Mrs. Tyler to Evarts, November 16, 1877; April 9, June 1, October 11, November 16, 1879; January 29, October 25, 1879.

4. 35 N. Y. 617; *In the Court of Appeals—Robert Lovett, Executor, Against Augusta Gillender—Appeal Book*.

5. 5 Wallace 119; *Supreme Court of the United States. December Term, 1866. Ezra S. Stanley et al. vs. Elizabeth H. Colt. Brief of Counsel For Stanley Heirs;* Evarts Papers, Manuscript memorandum.

6. 43 Barbour 147.

7. *Arguments and Speeches*, III, 187-193.

8. 40 Conn. 250; *Harriet A. Phelps et al. vs. Mary A. Robbins and Horace W. Robbins, Jr. Brief of Counsel for Defendants;* 127 U. S. 300.

9. 28 Hun 564; *Argument in the Stokes Will Case on Behalf of the Proponents, Before the Hon. Daniel Rollins, Surrogate, Delivered on the 3d, 4th, and 5th Days of March, 1884, By William M. Evarts; New York Times*, March 5, 1884; A. P. Stokes, *Stokes Records*, I, Part 2, 247-248; *New York World*, June 10, 1888.

10. P. C. Jessup, *Elihu Root*, I, 97; II, 156; *Hoyt Will Case*, 1-101; 5 Demarest 284; 12 N. Y. 493.

11. 76 N. Y. 475; *The People ex rel. Henry C. Murphy v. John Kelly; New York Herald*, March 26, 1879.

12. 10 Wallace 339; 17 Wallace 417; 6 Blatchford 14. Other contract cases can be found in 5 Blatchford 285; 45 Barbour 657; 54 Barbour 191; 37 N. Y. 106; 1 Wallace 298; 8 Wallace 292; 10 Wallace 604; 17 Wallace 123; 92 U. S. 412; 94 U. S. 207.

13. Hicks, *Arguments and Addresses of Joseph H. Choate*, 145; 8 Wallace 276; Evarts Papers, Brief and Points for the Defendant.

14. 1 Lansing 381; 45 Barbour 560.

15. 52 Barbour 581; *Supreme Court. Francis B. Carpenter against George H. Danforth and Another. Propositions of Law and Fact.*

16. 93 N. Y. 162; *Argument of Evarts Before the Senate Committee.*

17. 92 U. S. 618. Other bankruptcy cases may be found in 16 Wallace 610; 3 Benedict 360; 95 U. S. 3.

18. 45 Barbour 327; 51 N. Y. 639; 103 N. Y. 341; 89 N. Y. 559; 7 Wallace 44, 53; 9 Wallace 161; 12 Wallace 389; 15 Wallace 664; 16 Wallace 378; 19 Wallace 640; 92 U. S. 439; 107 U. S. 485.

19. 4 Wallace 411; Warren, *The Supreme Court in United States History*, III, 137.

20. *N. Y. Court of Sessions Before City Judge. The People vs. Robert Murray and Others. Points For the Motion;* J. B. Moore, *A Treatise on Extradition and Interstate Rendition*, I, 33-35; Baker, *Works of Seward*, V, 19-20.

21. Nevins, *Fish*, 642-646; *The Case of General J. Watson Webb, Late U. S. Envoy Extraordinary to Brazil vs. Hamilton Fish and E. R. Hoar, February 12, 1875.*

22. 5 Wallace 599; Evarts Papers, Brief in Evarts' handwriting.

23. 9 Wallace 187; Evarts Papers, Brief in Evarts' handwriting and letter to Evarts, May 11, 1877. Another land case may be found in 110 U. S. 471.

24. 48 Barbour 522; 9 Wallace 788; *Supreme Court, City and County of New York, Charles Goodyear, Jr. against The Phoenix Rubber Company.*

25. 11 Blatchford 552; *United States Circuit Court. Before Hon. J. T. Nixon, The Rumford Chemical Works vs. George V. Hecker. Report of Argument of William M. Evarts, Esq.*

26. 19 Wallace 287; *Argument of Mr. Evarts and Opinion of the Court in the case of the Amoskeag Manufacturing Company vs. William T. Garner et al. in Special Term of city and county of N. Y. in Supreme Court;* 105 U. S. 580; Evarts Papers, E. S. Higgins to Evarts, January 7, 1882.

27. 15 Blatchford, 349; 109 U. S. 633.

28. 1 Benedict 241; 2 Benedict 249; 3 Benedict 536; 6 Blatchford 71; Various letters in Evarts Papers.

29. 104 U. S. 694; *Supreme Court of the United States. Edwin A. Merritt vs. Samuel Welsh. Brief of Defendants in Error in Reply.*

30. *The Daily Graphic,* June 10, 1875; 13 Blatchford, 178; Jessup, *Elihu Root,* I, 103-104; *In the Circuit Court of the United States, For the Southern District of New York. The United States of America vs. Horace B. Claflin et al. Argument of Mr. Evarts.*

31. Evarts Papers, plan of Evarts' argument; R. Topp to Evarts, October 28, 1871.

32. *Opinions of Charles O'Conor, William M. Evarts, and Grosvenor P. Lowry, Given to the Pacific Mail Steamship Company and the Central American Transit Company;* 42 N. Y. 374; 3 Wallace 441, 445; 10 Wallace 58; 107 U. S. 59; 118 U. S. 445.

33. 114 U. S. 270; Warren, *The Supreme Court in United States History,* III, 392.

34. 2 Wallace 200.

35. 3 Wallace 573; *Argument of William M. Evarts, Esq., Before the United States Supreme Court, Also the Decision of the Court, and the Opinion of Chief Justice Chase and Justices Wayne and Swayne; The Supreme Court of the United States. G. Clarence Churchill v. The City of Utica, Mr. Evarts' Brief;* 35 N. Y. 423; 4 Wallace 244; Evarts Papers, Evarts' outline for summary; Evarts to the Executive Committee, March 14, 1867.

CHAPTER XVII

1. 3 Blatchford 366.

2. 6 Blatchford, 487; W. T. Reeves, *The First Elevated Railroads in Manhattan and the Bronx of the City of New York,* 6-9.

3. *Great Speech of Hon. William M. Evarts on Rapid Transit;* 9 Hun 303; 70 N. Y. 361; *New York Tribune,* June 10, 1876; *New York Herald,* April 28, 1877.

4. 11 Daly 373; Evarts Papers, Evarts' argument for the defendants.

5. *Opinion of Hon. William M. Evarts as to the Validity of the Charter and Franchises of the New York Cable Railway Company; New York Supreme Court. The New York Cable Company vs. The Second Avenue Railway Company: Points For the Plaintiff;* 40 Hun 1; 104 N. Y. 1; Evarts Papers, statement in the Matter of the New York Cable Railway Company.

6. 90 N. Y. 122; *Court of Appeals. Rufus Story against the New York Elevated Railroad Company: Supplemental Brief;* Strong, *Landmarks of a Lawyer's Lifetime,* 208.

7. 3 Robertson 411. Evarts Papers, Pleadings and Evidence.

8. Evarts Papers, Evarts' argument for the plaintiff; *American Law Register,* V, 733-745.

9. 3 Wallace 275. Another Ohio and Mississippi case is in 37 N. Y. 218.

10. Strong, *Landmarks of a Lawyer's Lifetime,* 201-202.

11. *Legal Opinion of the Hon. D. H. Chamberlain and Hon. William M. Evarts Sustaining the Validity and Constitutionality of Loans by the State of South Carolina;* Simkins and Woody, *South Carolina During Reconstruction,* 212-214.

12. *Minnesota State Bonds Issued to Railroads. Case, or Statement of Facts, With Accompanying Documents . . . and Opinions of the Hon. Benjamin R. Curtis and Hon. Wm. M. Evarts.*

13. 92 U. S. 299; W. W. Folwell, *A History of Minnesota*, III, 428-430, 439.

14. 42 N. Y. 217; 12 Wallace 384. Another Ogdensburgh Railroad case may be found in 4 Hun 268, 712.

15. *Arguments Before the Hon. S. F. Phillips, Solicitor-General of the U. S. on Behalf of The Central Branch Union Pacific Railroad Company, by Eff'm H. Nichols, Esq., Hon. B. R. Curtis, and Hon. Wm. M. Evarts, December 12, 1872.*

16. 11 Blatchford 385; *The Nation* (New York), December 11, 1873; 98 U. S. 569; *Supreme Court of the United States. The United States against the Union Pacific Railroad Company and Others. Brief on the Question of Jurisdiction.*

17. 18 Wallace 5; 20 Wallace 36; *Central Law Journal*, I, 3-4.

18. *Laws of Wisconsin, Iowa, and Minnesota. Affecting Railroad Service in Those States, Passed 1874.*

19. *Ibid., opinion of Mr. Evarts.*

20. 94 U. S. 113.

21. 94 U. S. 164, 179, 180, 183.

22. 107 U. S. 147; *Supreme Court of the United States. The Inhabitants of the Township of Montclair vs. Thomas Ramsdell;* E. B. Godell, *Montclair*, 54, 113-114.

23. Evarts Papers, Evarts to Villard, April 18, 1882; February 5, 1883.

24. *Argument of Hon. William M. Evarts Before the Committee on Public Lands of the U. S. Senate, Saturday, February 23, 1884; New York Tribune*, February 24, 1884.

25. 110 U. S. 667.

26. J. G. Pyle, *The Life of James J. Hill*, I, 168-173; 120 U. S. 303; *Supreme Court of the United States. Jesse P. Farley vs. Norman W. Kittson, James J. Hill, and the Manitoba Railway Company. Brief For Respondents on Re-argument;* Folwell, W. W., *A History of Minnesota*, III, 465; J. B. Bishop, *Notes and Anecdotes of Many Years*, 180; 150 U. S. 572.

CHAPTER XVIII

1. J. C. Carter, "Memorial of William M. Evarts," *Report for 1902* of the Association of the Bar of the City of New York, 107; *Brooklyn Eagle*, May 28, 1875.

2. P. Hibben, *Henry Ward Beecher*, 136-137, 167-170, 184-185; W. C. Beecher and S. Scoville, *A Biography of Rev. Henry Ward Beecher*, 488-490.

3. C. M. Rourke, *Trumpets of Jubilee*, 192; Beecher and Scoville, *Beecher*, 491-492; Hibben, *Beecher*, 201-203, 218-221.

4. *Sixty-Fourth Anniversary Celebration of the New England Society in the City of New York at Delmonico's, December 22, 1869.*

5. *New York Sun*, July 22, 1874; *Independent*, July 14, 1870.

6. Beecher and Scoville, *Beecher*, 501.

7. A. F. Warburton, *Uncontradicted Testimony in the Beecher Case*, 3-4, 6-7; Hibben, *Beecher*, 223, 242-258; Beecher and Scoville, *Beecher*, 494; Rourke, *op. cit.*, 215-218.

8. *The Nation* (New York), February 25, May 13, 1875; Beecher and Scoville, *Beecher*, 496-498, 505, 508-515; Hibben, *Beecher*, 264, 267-298; Rourke, *op. cit.*, 199-211.

9. Hibben, *Beecher*, 303-309; Beecher and Scoville, *Beecher*, 528-533; Rourke, *op. cit.*, 211-214; *Letter-Missive, Statement, and Documents,—The Brooklyn Council, 1874;* E. B. Fairchild, *Wickedness in High Places—A Review of the Beecher Case;* R. R. Raymond, *The Case of the Rev. E. B. Fairchild.*

10. *Brooklyn Eagle*, January 7, 8, 1875; *The Daily Graphic*, January 13, 30, 1875.

11. Winters Collection, V, press clipping.

12. *Brooklyn Eagle*, January 5, February 9, 1875.

13. Hibben, *Beecher*, 303, 311.

14. *The Green Bag,* II, 509-521; *Brooklyn Eagle,* January 5, 1875; Strong, *Landmarks of a Lawyer's Lifetime,* 285-288.

15. *Brooklyn Eagle,* January 5, 1875; Winters Collection, V, press clipping.

16. T. W. Knox, *Life and Work of Henry Ward Beecher,* 403; Hibben, *Beecher,* 313.

17. *Theodore Tilton v. Henry Ward Beecher. Action for crim. con. Tried in the City Court of Brooklyn,* I, 16-17; Hibben, *Beecher,* 303; *Brooklyn Eagle,* January 14, 1875.

18. *Brooklyn Eagle,* January 15, 1875; *Harper's Weekly,* June 5, 1875; Rourke, *op. cit.,* 218-219; T. v. B., I, 72-73, 122, 150-151, 174-175.

19. T. v. B., I, 52.

20. T. v. B., I, 259; J. H. Dougherty, *William M. Evarts,* 23; *Brooklyn Eagle,* January 19, 1875.

21. *Brooklyn Eagle,* January 7, February 9, 1875; Strong, *Landmarks of a Lawyer's Lifetime,* 207-208.

22. T. v. B., I, 341-342, 364-365.

23. Evarts Papers, Undated clipping in the *Independent; Sixty-Fourth Anniversary Celebration of the New England Society.*

24. *Brooklyn Eagle,* February 5, 9, 1875; B. v. T., I, 436-437, 459-460.

25. T. v. B., I, 501-502, 525-526, 575-576; M. Van Doren, *An Autobiography of America,* 648; *Brooklyn Eagle,* February 16, 1875.

26. T. v. B., I, 719-720; Hibben, *Beecher,* 316-318.

27. T. v. B., II, 93, 123-124, 153, 158-159, 191, 290-291, 322-323, 354, 610, 723-724, 775-777, 825-826, 876-877; *New York Tribune,* April 2, 3, 7, 1875; *Brooklyn Eagle,* April 9, 1875; Rourke, *op. cit.,* 215.

28. Strong, *Landmarks of a Lawyer's Lifetime,* 286; Hibben, *Beecher,* 314.

29. T. v. B., II, 876-877; III, 119-120.

30. T. v. B., III, 421, 478, 507; *The Nation* (New York), March 4, 1875; *Brooklyn Eagle,* May 3, 1875; Van Doren, *op. cit.,* 648-660.

31. Van Doren, *op. cit.,* 648-660; *New York Sun,* July 5, 1875.

32. T. v. B., III, 556-557, 592, 603-604; *Brooklyn Eagle,* May 28, 1875; *The Daily Graphic,* May 27, 1875.

33. *New York Herald,* May 28, 1875; *New York Tribune,* May 28, 1875; T. v. B., III, 653.

34. *Arguments and Speeches,* II, 7-10, 19-25, 32, 35, 39, 41; *New York Herald,* May 28, 1875.

35. *Brooklyn Eagle,* May 28, 1875; *New York Herald,* May 29, 1875; *New York Tribune,* June 2, 3, 1875; *Arguments and Speeches,* II, 54-56, 64-70, 81-86, 98-99.

36. *Arguments and Speeches,* II, 98-99.

37. *Ibid.,* II, 162-172, 177, 180-182, 199; T. v. B., III, 703.

38. *Arguments and Speeches,* II, 234, 237-245; III, 872; *New York Tribune,* June 5, 8, 1875; *The Daily Graphic,* June 8, 1875; *New York Herald,* June 9, 1875.

39. T. v. B., III, 813-814, 872, 875, 895, 917, 953, 977-978, 998-999; *Albany Law Journal,* March 19, 1887; *New York Herald,* June 24, 1875.

40. *New York Herald,* June 20, 1875; *Albany Law Journal,* July 3, 1875.

41. T. v. B., III, 1025-1026; L. Abbott, *Henry Ward Beecher,* 295.

42. *New York Sun,* June 26, 1875.

43. *Daily Argus,* June 25, 1875; *The Nation* (New York), July 8, 1875; *Brooklyn Eagle,* June 26, 1875; Knox, *Beecher,* 404.

44. Evarts Papers, Beecher to Evarts, March 10, 1877; *The National Baptist,* July 8, 1875; *New York Tribune,* July 3, 1875.

45. Hibben, *Beecher,* 314; *Windsor Journal,* July 10, 1875.

CHAPTER XIX

1. Martin, *Life of Choate,* I, 116.
2. *Arguments and Speeches,* III, 182.
3. *Ibid.,* III, 92.
4. Hoar, *Autobiography,* II, 348-349.
5. T. C. Smith, *Life and Letters of James Abram Garfield,* I, 639.
6. *Boston Daily Globe,* November 9, 1876; *New York Times,* November 11, 1876.
7. H. W. Bowen, *Recollections Diplomatic and Undiplomatic,* 67-68; Hoar, *Autobiography,* II, 17.
8. Lodge, *Early Memories,* 256; *Arguments and Speeches,* I, 20.
9. Cortissoz, *The Life of Whitelaw Reid,* I, 234-235; Howe, *Chester A. Arthur,* 34.
10. *The Green Bag,* X, 83.
11. P. Godwin, *A Biography of William Cullen Bryant,* II, 214, 220.
12. *New York Tribune,* December 30, 1868.
13. E. L. Morse, *Samuel F. B. Morse, His Letters and Journals,* I, 86-87; *New York Tribune, New York Times,* December 30, 1868.
14. H. Holt, *Garrulities of an Octogenarian Editor,* 185-186; *New York Times,* June 2, 1875; *New York Sun,* January 30, 1887.
15. Lodge, *Early Memories,* 254-255; Winters Collection, V, press clipping.
16. *New York Herald,* June 25, 1874; *Arguments and Speeches,* III, 66-91.
17. *New York Tribune,* June 25, 1874, March 1, 1901; Storey and Emerson, *Ebenezer Rockwood Hoar,* 242-243.
18. *Harper's Weekly,* October 14, 1876; Fish Papers, Fish to Evarts, September 2, 13, 1876; *New York Tribune,* September 28, 1876; *Harper's Weekly,* October 21, 1876.
19. *New York Herald,* November 26, 1876; *New York Tribune,* November 27, 1876; *Arguments and Speeches,* III, 275-283.
20. Evarts Papers, outline of address with excerpts in Evarts' handwriting.
21. *New York Times,* May 23, 1875; *New York Tribune,* May 24, 1875; *Arguments and Speeches,* III, 93-94.
22. *New York Herald,* July 3, 1876; *Arguments and Speeches,* III, 95.
23. *New York Herald,* July 4, 5, 1876; *New York Times,* July 4, 5, 1876; *Harper's Weekly,* July 26, 1876; W. W. Tucker, *His Royal Highness Prince Oscar At the National Celebration of the Centennial,* 62-66.
24. *Arguments and Speeches,* III, 97-98.
25. *Ibid.,* III, 105-128.

CHAPTER XX

1. E. Lonn, *Reconstruction in Louisiana in 1868,* 295-299; *New York Times,* January 12, 1875; *Arguments and Speeches,* II, 577-583.
2. *New York Tribune,* April 28, 1875.
3. *North American Review,* October, 1876; *New York Trade Reporter,* June 3, 1876; Ford, *Letters of Henry Adams,* 297; *New York Tribune,* March 4, 25, June 10, 1876; *New York Times,* June 12, 1876; March 8, 1877.
4. H. J. Eckenrode, *Rutherford B. Hayes,* 115-116; *New York Times,* August 23, 1876; *New York Tribune,* August 23, 25, July 14, 1876; Alexander, *A Political History of the State of New York,* III, 336-338; Merritt, *Recollections,* 31-32; *New York Tribune,* September 2, 1876.
5. *Harper's Weekly,* September 9, 1876.
6. Cortissoz, *The Life of Whitelaw Reid,* I, 350.
7. Dyer, *Evarts,* 169.
8. *New York Tribune,* November 2, 1876; *New York Times,* November 1, 2, 1876; *Arguments and Speeches,* II, 585-616.

9. *Harper's Weekly*, November 18, 1876.

10. Dyer, *Evarts*, 172 n.

11. Cortissoz, *The Life of Whitelaw Reid*, I, 358-359; *New York Herald*, January 26, 1877; Smith, *Garfield*, I, 629-630; *New York Tribune*, January 25, 1877.

12. Evarts Papers, Dennison to Evarts, January 26, 1877; Sherman to Evarts, January 27, 1877; Z. Chandler and others to Evarts, January 28, 1877.

13. *Cong. Rec.*, 51 Cong., 1 Sess., 3282.

14. *Proceedings of the Electoral Commission*, 31-32, 75-76.

15. Evarts Papers, J. P. Root to Evarts, January 30, 1876; *Proceedings of the Electoral Commission*, 81-82.

16. P. L. Haworth, *The Hayes-Tilden Disputed Presidential Election of 1876*, 231.

17. Eckenrode, *Hayes*, 214; *New York Herald*, February 7, 1877.

18. *New York Times*, February 6, 1877; *Magazine of American History*, February, 1892.

19. *Arguments and Speeches*, II, 270, 273; Evarts Papers, notes on argument.

20. *Proceedings of the Electoral Commission*, 113-124; *New York Times*, February 6, 1877.

21. *New York Tribune*, February 6, 1877; Smith, *Garfield*, I, 643.

22. *New York Tribune*, February 10, 1877.

23. *Proceedings of the Electoral Commission*, 139.

24. *Arguments and Speeches*, II, 276-278; *New York Tribune*, February 9, 1877; *Proceedings of the Electoral Commission*, 147.

25. *Arguments and Speeches*, II, 283-286; Evarts Papers, notes on argument.

26. *New York Times*, February 16, 1877; Evarts Papers, notes on argument.

27. *Arguments and Speeches*, II, 319-320, 326-327, 329, 333-334.

28. *Proceedings of the Electoral Commission*, 419-421; *New York Times*, February 16, 1877.

29. *Arguments and Speeches*, II, 340, 342-343, 347-348, 359-361; Evarts Papers, notes on argument.

30. H. Watterson, *"Marse Henry," An Autobiography*, I, 308-311; Lonn, *Reconstruction in Louisiana*, 509; Eckenrode, *Hayes*, 216-218; *House Misc. Doc. No. 31*, 45 Cong., 3 Sess., 883, 976.

31. Address at Cooper Institute, October 24, 1876.

CHAPTER XXI

1. C. R. Williams, *The Life of Rutherford Birchard Hayes*, II, 24 n.; R. B. Hayes, *Diary and Letters of Rutherford Birchard Hayes*, III, 402; C. Schurz, *Speeches, Correspondence, and Political Papers of Carl Schurz*, III, 395.

2. *New York Tribune*, *New York Herald*, February 28, 1877; Williams, *Hayes*, II, 24.

3. Hoar, *Autobiography*, II, 12.

4. *New York Herald*, March 7, 8, 1877; *New York Tribune*, March 8, 1877.

5. *New York Herald*, March 9, 10, 13, 1877; Williams, *Hayes*, II, 27-28.

6. Evarts Papers, the original commission; *New York Tribune*, March 13, 1877.

7. Evarts Papers, Dana to Evarts, March 27, 1877; *The Nation* (New York), March 8, 1877; *New York Herald*, March 19, 1877.

8. *New York Tribune*, March 2, 1877.

9. Dyer, *Evarts*, 188; Statements from members of the Evarts family.

10. Smith, *Garfield*, II, 664.

11. Fuess, *Carl Schurz*, 239.

12. M. S. Gerry, *Through Five Administrations, Reminiscences of Colonel William H. Crook*, 224; Eckenrode, *Hayes*, 320-321; Howe, *Chester A. Arthur*, 74.

13. Evarts Papers, Weed to Evarts, March 11, 1877; Hayes, *Diary*, III, 412; Nevins, *Fish*, 857-859.

14. Evarts Papers, Haskell to Evarts, March 3, 1877; W. Allen, *Governor Chamberlain's Administration in South Carolina,* 469-470.

15. D. S. Muzzey, *James G. Blaine,* 131-132; Simkins and Woody, *South Carolina During Reconstruction,* 539-540; Evarts Papers, Chamberlain to Evarts, March 11, 1877; Allen, *op. cit.,* 471; *New York Tribune,* March 13, 1877.

16. *New York Herald,* March 30, 1877; E. L. Welles, *Hampton and Reconstruction,* 193.

17. *Letters and Messages of Rutherford B. Hayes,* 22-25; Evarts Papers, Evarts to the Commission, April 13, 1877.

18. *New York Tribune,* April 16, 1877.

19. Evarts Papers, the Commission to the President, April 21, 1877.

20. *New York Times,* June 7, 1877; *New York Herald,* March 27, 1877.

21. *Meetings of the Yale Class of 1847 on June 27, 1877; New York Herald,* June 26, 27, 1877.

22. *New York Herald, New York Tribune,* August 17, 1877.

23. Hayes Papers, Evarts to the President, August 25, 1877; *Vermont Journal,* August, 1877; *New York Herald,* August 18, 19, 1877.

24. *New York Herald,* August 23, 24, 1877.

25. *Ibid.,* September 16-26, 1877, October 31, November 1, 2, 1877.

26. *Ibid.,* October 31, November 1, 2, 1877.

27. *New York Tribune,* September 21, 1877.

28. G. F. Howe, "Extracts from the Hayes Papers," *American Historical Review,* January, 1932.

29. Evarts Papers, undated argument.

30. Hayes Papers, Evarts to the President, August 6, 1877; *New York Herald,* June 26, 1877.

31. *New York Herald,* October 24, 1877.

32. Eckenrode, *Hayes,* 295; Hayes, *Diary,* III, 461-462; IV, 257; *New York Herald,* March 16, 1878.

33. *New York Herald,* October 24, 25, 1878; *New York Tribune,* October 25, 1878; Evarts Papers, notes on speech.

34. M. M. Miller, *Great Debates in American History,* IX, 133.

35. *Letters and Messages of Rutherford B. Hayes,* 98-99; *New York Tribune,* October 22, 25, 1879.

36. *New York Tribune,* April 5, 1879; White, *Autobiography,* 528-529.

37. Williams, *Hayes,* II, 172-173, 173 n., 204, 205 n.

38. Hayes Papers, Evarts to the President, August 20, 1878.

39. Bigelow, *Retrospections,* V, 318-319; *New York Tribune,* April 27, 1877; *New York Herald,* May 16, 1877.

40. *New York Herald,* April 20, 30, 1877.

41. Evarts Papers, Bundy manuscript; *Evening Mail,* March 24, 1877; Evarts Papers, Bundy to Evarts, March 7, 1877.

42. Evarts Papers, Bell to Evarts, November 11, December 10, 1877; Bundy to Evarts, May 29, June 18, 1877; Hayes Papers, Evarts to the President, December 8, 1877.

43. Dyer, *Evarts,* 240.

44. Cortissoz, *Life of Whitelaw Reid,* I, 393-394; II, 4-5; G. S. Merriam, *The Life and Times of Samuel Bowles,* II, 423.

45. D. B. Chidsey, *The Gentleman from New York: Life of Roscoe Conkling,* 239-240; *The Daily Observer,* August 18, 1877.

46. Eckenrode, *Hayes,* 270-271; Chidsey, *Conkling,* 245-250.

47. *New York Herald,* August 26, November 9, 1877.

48. *New York Herald,* November 10, 1877; C. M. Depew, *My Memories of Eighty Years,* 103.

49. Howe, *Chester A. Arthur,* 20 ff., 48, 289; Chidsey, *Conkling,* 244; *New York Herald,* April 26, 1877; D. B. Eaton, *The "Spoils" System and Civil-Service Reform in the Custom-House and Post-Office at New York,* 36; 45 Cong., 1 Sess., *House Ex. Doc., No. 25,* 7-16; *North American Review,* CXXVII, 280-285; J. D. Richardson, *Messages and Papers of the Presidents,* VII, 450.

50. J. D. Platt, *Autobiography,* 97; Cortissoz, *Life of Whitelaw Reid,* I, 382; Dyer, *Evarts,* 191; *New York Tribune,* August 31, 1877; *New York Herald,* December 14, 1877.

51. *Journal of Executive Proceedings of the Senate,* XXI, 98-99, 112, 144, 159-160, 162, 169-172; Eckenrode, *Hayes,* 273-274; *New York World,* December 13, 1877; Chidsey, *Conkling,* 253-254.

52. Hayes Papers, Evarts to the President, July 13, 1878; *Journal of Executive Proceedings of the Senate,* XXI, 378-379, 502-503; Eckenrode, *Hayes,* 274-277; Chidsey, *Conkling,* 268-270; *Evening Mail,* July 17, 1877; Hayes, *Diary,* III, 519-520.

53. Evarts Papers, Bundy to Evarts, August 1, 3, 1879; Evarts to the President, August 24, 1878.

54. G. F. Howe, "The New York Custom-House Controversy," *Mississippi Valley Historical Review,* XVIII, 354-355; J. Sherman, *Recollections of Forty Years,* II, 681.

55. Evarts Papers, Bundy to Evarts, January 9, April 15, 17, May 7, June 20, November 21, December 2, 30, 1878; January 2, February 28, March 29, April 2, 1879; Field to Evarts, May 10, 1880.

56. J. G. Blaine, *Political Discussions,* 210, 214; *New York Times,* December 24, 1878; *Arguments and Speeches,* III, 391-397; Evarts Papers, Bundy to Evarts, October 18, 19, 30, 1878.

57. Evarts Papers, Bundy to Evarts, April 28, 1879; *New York World,* March 9, 1880; *New York Tribune,* August 11, 1879; Evarts Papers, Evarts to Curtis, August 29, 1879.

58. Evarts Papers, Curtis to Evarts, September 5, 1879; Alexander, *A Political History of the State of New York,* III, 413, 416; Evarts Papers, Bundy to Evarts, September 5, 1879.

59. Cortissoz, *Life of Whitelaw Reid,* II, 11.

60. Evarts Papers, Dorsey to Evarts, October 19, 1879; Bowker to Evarts, October 16, 1879.

61. Evarts Papers, Hoar to Evarts, October 18, 1879; Sherman to Evarts, September 14, 1879; Hayes Papers, Evarts to the President, September 25, 1879; *Arguments and Speeches,* II, 621-622.

62. Evarts Papers, Morton to Evarts, October 10, 1879; Arthur to Evarts, October 21, 1879; Hall to Evarts, October 21, 1879; *New York Tribune,* October 22, 1879.

63. *New York Tribune,* October 22, 1879.

64. *New York Herald,* October 22, 1879; Ford, *Letters of Henry Adams,* 319; D. B. Eaton, *The Independent Movement in New York,* 41; Alexander, *Political History,* III, 425; *Harper's Weekly,* November 8, 1879; Hayes Papers, Evarts to the President, August 10, 1879.

65. Evarts Papers, Cole to Evarts, June 14, 1880.

66. Hayes Papers, Evarts to the President, March 29, 1881.

CHAPTER XXII

1. Evarts Papers, Hutchinson to Evarts, no date; *New York Tribune,* September 25, 1877.

2. H. Adams, *History of the United States,* I, 98.

3. *New York Herald,* June 15, 1877; Evarts Papers, C. B. Evarts to Evarts, October 2, 1877.

4. Evarts Papers, Evarts to Bancroft, January 18, 1876.

5. *New York Tribune,* March 3, 1901.

6. Martin, *Life of Choate,* I, 314-317.

7. H. St. Gaudens, *The Reminiscences of Augustus St. Gaudens,* I, 113, 123, 129, 143; II, 178; *The Augustus Saint-Gaudens Memorial, passim.*

8. Ford, *Letters of Henry Adams,* 303; Gerry, *Through Five Administrations,* 240.

9. Evarts Papers, numerous invitations to White House; H. Nicolay, *Our Capital on the Potomac,* 404-405; Gerry, *Through Five Administrations,* 239-240; *New York Herald,* April 19-23, 1877.

10. W. Maycock, *With Mr. Chamberlain in the United States and Canada,* 147.

11. *New York Herald,* January 21, 1878.

12. Ford, *Letters of Henry Adams,* 309; Nicolay, *op. cit.,* 407; G. M. Towle, *American Society,* I, 49, 81.

13. Bishop, *Notes and Anecdotes,* 61; Gerry, *Through Five Administrations,* 249.

14. Sherman, *Recollections,* II, 749; Hayes, *Diary,* II, 630; III, 507.

15. *New York Herald,* July 19, 1877.

16. Winters Collection, XVI; *Modern Eloquence,* XIII, 20; White, *Autobiography,* 528-529.

17. *New York Herald, New York Tribune,* November 26, 1879; Interviews of author with Henry S. Wardner.

18. *Proceedings of the Maryland Historical Society, in Connection With the Proceedings of the One Hundred and Fiftieth Anniversary of the Settlement of Baltimore, October 12, 1880;* Evarts papers, Latrobe to Evarts, November 3, 1880.

19. Bowen, *Recollections Diplomatic and Undiplomatic,* 313-314.

20. *New York Tribune,* November 18, 1879; *Arguments and Speeches,* III, 398-400.

21. *New York Herald,* October 14, 1877; *New York Tribune,* October 15, 1877.

22. *New York World,* November 11, 1879; Evarts Papers, undated letter of Hurlburt to Evarts; *New York Tribune,* February 23, 1881; *Arguments and Speeches,* III, 292, 294.

23. Nevins, *Fish,* 140.

24. *Register of the Department of State,* 1880.

25. L. Sears, *John Hay,* 59-60; T. Dennett, *John Hay,* 126-128; W. R. Thayer, *Life and Letters of John Hay,* 433-436; Evarts Papers, Hay to Evarts, August 19, 1880; Hayes to Evarts, August 21, 1880; Nevins, *Fish,* 863.

26. Williams, *Hayes,* II, 76; Evarts Papers, Weed to Evarts, March 11, 1877; Fish Papers, Fish to Davis, March 22, 1877; *Arguments and Speeches,* III, 389-390.

27. Feuss, *Carl Schurz,* 246-248.

28. Hayes Papers, Evarts to the President, August 29, 1877; Evarts' address at Cooper Institute, October 24, 1878.

29. Evarts Papers, Evarts to Smith, July 4, 1878; *New York Times,* March 26, July 9, 1877; August 9, 1878.

30. *Arguments and Speeches,* III, 415; Lodge, *Early Memories,* 257.

31. Hayes, *Diary,* III, 469; Hayes Papers, Evarts to Edgerton, July 10, 30, 31, August 5, 14, 28, September 10, 19, 1878; Evarts to the President, July 31, August 20, 1878; Edgerton to Evarts, September 17, 20, 1878.

32. *Albany Law Journal,* LXIII, 111; *New York Tribune,* June 14, 1900, March 3, 1901.

33. *Register of the Department of State, 1880,* 10-11; *New York Herald,* February 15, 1879; *New York Tribune,* March 15, 1878.

34. B. Perry, *Richard Henry Dana,* 95-96.

35. London *Pump Court,* August, 1883.

36. Hoar, *Autobiography,* II, 17.

37. J. W. Foster, *Diplomatic Memoirs,* II, 261; Nevins, *Fish,* 140; Cortissoz, *Life of Whitelaw Reid,* I, 392; Lodge, *Early Memories,* 257-258.

38. White, *Autobiography,* I, 257-258.

39. Information given by Professor Allan Nevins.

40. Fish Papers, Davis to Fish, May 15, September 26, 1877.

41. *Ibid.,* Evarts to Fish, June 15, 21, 1877; Fish to Davis, March 8, 1881.

42. *Ibid.*, Fish to Davis, April 23, 1877; Evarts Papers, Evarts to Ward, December 27, 1879; *New York Herald*, March 29, April 3, 1877, June 2, 1878.

43. Dyer, *Evarts*, 187.

44. *Arguments and Speeches*, III, 416-417.

CHAPTER XXIII

1. Wharton, *Digest of International Law*, I, 232, Evarts to Foster, August 13, 1878.

2. D. Hannay, *Diaz*, 167.

3. Nevins, *Fish*, 912-913; *For. Rel., 1877*, 376-396, 410, 412: *House Report No. 701*, 45 Cong., 2 Sess., Appendix C, 316.

4. F. W. Seward, *Reminiscences of a War Time Statesman and Diplomat*, 436; State Dept. Archives, Instructions, Mexico, XIX, Evarts to Foster, March 27, 1877; *For. Rel., 1877*, 405.

5. *House Ex. Doc., No. 13*, 45 Cong., 1 Sess., 4-5, Shafter to the Assistant Adjutant-General; Nevins, *Fish*, 912-913.

6. S. D. A., Instructions, Mexico, XIX, 328, No. 379, March 3, 1877; *House Report No. 701*, 45 Cong., 2 Sess., Appendix B, 235-238; *For. Rel., 1877*, 400-401, Foster to Evarts, March 31, 1877; *House Ex. Doc., No. 13*, 45 Cong., 1 Sess., 13-14.

7. Nevins, *Fish*, 912; Foster, *Diplomatic Memoirs*, I, 92.

8. J. M. Callahan, *American Policy in Mexican Relations*, 372.

9. S. D. A., Instructions, Mexico, XIX, No. 390, May 16, 1877, Evarts to Foster; Evarts Papers, Journal, I, 64.

10. Evarts Papers, Journal, I, 64; *House Ex. Doc., No. 13*, 45 Cong., 1 Sess., I, 12.

11. *Message of the President of the United States, . . . 1877-1878*, 12.

12. Evarts Papers, Hertz to Evarts, June 19, 1877; *New York Herald*, June 2, 1877.

13. *House Ex. Doc. No. 1*, 45 Cong., 2 Sess., I, 411; *House Ex. Doc.*, 45 Cong., 1 Sess., I, 20-27, Foster to Evarts, June 22, 1877; *New York Herald*, June 9, 1877; Hannay, *Diaz*, 194; C. L. Jones, *Mexico and Its Reconstruction*, 281.

14. Foster, *Diplomatic Memoirs*, I, 93-94; Callahan, *Mexican Relations*, 376-377.

15. Callahan, *Mexican Relations*, 379-381; *New York Herald*, July 2, 3, 1877.

16. *New York Tribune*, July 6, 1877; S. F. Bemis, *American Secretaries of State*, VII, 240-241.

17. Wharton, *Digest*, I, 32, Evarts to Foster, August 2, 1877; Jones, *Mexico*, 281.

18. S. D. A., Instructions, Mexico, XIX, 354-358, No. 407, August 2, 1877; *House Ex. Doc., No. 701*, 45 Cong., 1 and 2 Sess., III, 451, Evarts to Foster, August 2, 1877; *House Report No. 701*, 45 Cong., 2 Sess., XXXIX; S.A. D., Despatches, Mexico, LX, Nos. 597 and 598, September 4, 1877; J. F. Rippy, *The United States and Mexico*, 304; Foster, *Diplomatic Memoirs*, I, 94.

19. Evarts Papers, Journal, I, 148, 155; Jones, *Mexico*, 281-282.

20. *House Report No. 701*, 45 Cong., 2 Sess.; Callahan, *Mexican Relations*, 391; *New York Herald*, December 12, 1877; S. D. A., Despatches, Mexico, LXI; *House Misc. Doc.*, No. 64, 45 Cong., 2 Sess.

21. *Letters and Messages of Rutherford B. Hayes*, 69-70; *New York Daily Mail*, December 24, 1877.

22. Callahan, *Mexican Relations*, 392; Evarts Papers, Journal, I, 179-181; Foster, *Diplomatic Memoirs*, II, 261-262.

23. *For. Rel., 1878*, 543-544, Foster to Evarts, March 23, 1878; Priestley, *The Mexican Nation*, 377; *House Ex. Doc.*, 45 Cong., 3 Sess., 543-544; *House Report No. 701*, 45 Cong., 2 Sess., April 25, 1877; *The Southwestern Historical Quarterly*, July, 1924, 52-53.

24. Evarts Papers, Journal, I, 148; Cortissoz, *Life of Whitelaw Reid*, I, 373.

25. S. D. A., Despatches, Mexico, LXII, No. 708, April 28, 1878; No. 714, May 30, 1878.

26. *New York Herald,* July 8, 1877; Callahan, *Mexican Relations,* 397; Wharton, *Digest,* I, 57-58, Evarts to Foster, September 30, 1878; 59-60, Evarts to Zamacona, October 30, 1878; Foster, *Diplomatic Memoirs,* I, 101-103.

27. Rippy, *U. S. and Mexico,* 309-310; Callahan, *Mexican Relations,* 400.

28. Callahan, *Mexican Relations,* 402; Wharton, *Digest,* I, 436, Evarts to Foster, March 26, 1879.

29. *New York Herald,* February 25, 1879; Wharton, *Digest,* I, 513-514, Evarts to Foster, February 20, 1880; 519, Evarts to Foster, July 10, 1879; 499-500, Evarts to Morgan, December 8, 1880; Moore, *Digest,* VI, 917, Evarts to Scott, April 4, 1879; Bemis, *Diplomatic History,* VII, 242.

30. *The Southwestern Historical Quarterly,* October, 1920, 152; H. H. Bancroft, *History of Mexico,* II, 446; Priestley, *Mexican Nation,* 377.

31. S. D. A., Despatches, Mexico, LXIX, 1078-1079; *For. Rel., 1880,* 726; Evarts Papers, Foster to Evarts, April 21, 1879. Marginal notes in Evarts' handwriting approve Foster's work. Foster, *Diplomatic Memoirs,* II, 263.

32. *For. Rel., 1880,* 781, Evarts to Zamacona, March 1, 1880; *House Ex. Doc.,* 46 Cong., 3 Sess., 735; Rippy, *U. S. and Mexico,* 313.

33. *For. Rel., 1880,* 764, 768; Callahan, *Mexican Relations,* 403.

34. *New York Herald,* November 14, 1877; Wharton, *Digest,* II, 552-557, Evarts to the President, April 13, 1880; Evarts Papers, Trescott to Evarts, March 13, 1879; Hay to Evarts, August 16, 17, 1880; Moore, *Digest,* VII, 63-65; Stowell and Munro, *International Cases,* 75-78.

35. *For. Rel., 1881,* 751-752, Evarts to Morgan, December 8, 1880; S. D. A., Despatches, Mexico, LXXI, No. 125, October 27, 1880; No. 133, November 13, 1880.

CHAPTER XXIV

1. E. T. Parks, *Colombia and the United States,* 356; Nevins, *Fish,* 914.

2. J. C. Rodrigues, *The Panama Canal,* 53-59; Parks, *Colombia,* 357-359.

3. Evarts Papers, King to Evarts, January 23, 1880; Williams, *Hayes,* II, 218.

4. Hayes, *Diary,* III, 588; Williams, *Hayes,* 221 n.

5. *Senate Ex. Doc., No. 112,* 46 Cong., 3 Sess.

6. *Senate Misc. Doc., No.* 42, 46 Cong., 3 Sess.; Rodrigues, *Panama Canal,* 67-68; *Milwaukee Sentinel,* March 10, 1880; Evarts Papers, J. E. Russell to S. Ward, June 8, 1880.

7. *For. Rel., 1880,* Outrey to Evarts, March 22, 1880, 385; March 25, 1880; Bemis, *Diplomatic History,* VII, 238; Parks, *Colombia,* 360.

8. Wharton, *Digest,* II, 106-107, Evarts to Dichman, April 19, 1880.

9. *Ibid.,* II, 12-15, Evarts to Arosmena, June 5, 1880.

10. Evarts Papers, Williamson to Evarts, March 5, 1880; *Senate Ex. Doc., No. 12,* 46 Cong., 2 Sess., 7; Wharton, *Digest,* II, 107, 209, Evarts to Logan, March 4, 1880; Evarts to Dichman, July 31, 1880.

11. Evarts Papers, S. Ward to Evarts, June 8, 1880; Williams, *Hayes,* II, 223-224; Evarts Papers, W. C. Wickam to Evarts, December 19, 1880.

12. Evarts Papers, Eads to Evarts, January 17, 1881; Bemis, *Diplomatic History,* VII, 238.

13. *For. Rel., 1881,* 361-388; *Senate Ex. Doc., No. 237,* 56 Cong., 1 Sess., 473 ff.; Parks, 367-368.

14. Wharton, *Digest,* II, 108-109, Evarts to Dichman, February 18, 1881.

15. Fish Papers, Fish to Anthony, November 28, 1881.

16. *New York Herald,* November 26, 1877; Moore, *Digest,* VI, 539, Evarts to Comanche; Bemis, *Diplomatic History,* VII, 234-235; Dyer, *Evarts,* 225.

17. Moore, *Digest,* VI, 246; VII, 234, 247; Bemis, *Diplomatic History,* VII, 234; Muzzey, *Blaine,* 207.

18. *New York Herald,* April 1, July 10, 1877; Moore, *Digest,* I, 152; IV, 555-556; Wharton, *Digest,* I, 548-549, Evarts to Baker, June 14, 1879; 628, Evarts to Comanche, April 20, 1880; Muzzey, *Blaine,* 207.

19. F. Greenslet, *James Russell Lowell,* 186-194; H. E. Scudder, *James Russell Lowell,* II, 224-235.

20. Moore, *Digest,* II, 65, Evarts to Adee, May 29, 1877; *For. Rel., 1878,* 800-801, Evarts to Lowell, September 12, 1878; Callahan, *Cuba and International Relations,* 449.

21. *Correspondence Between the Spanish Minister and Secretary of the United States,* etc., i-xi, 1-38; E. H. Strobel, *Mr. Blaine and His Foreign Policy,* 2; *New York World,* April 30, 1881; Moore, *Digest,* III, Evarts to White, December 10, 1878; Wharton, *Digest,* II, 354, Evarts to Durant, March 7, 1879.

22. Moore, *Digest,* II, 913, Evarts to Lowell, November 13, 1877; *For. Rel., 1878,* 784, Evarts to Lowell, February 25, 1878.

23. Moore, *Digest,* VII, 1020-1021; *New York Herald,* December 6, 8, 17, 1877.

24. Hayes Papers, Evarts to the President, November 15, 1879.

25. Evarts Papers, Dean to Evarts, August 10, 1880.

26. *Senate Ex. Doc., No. 79,* 47 Cong., 1 Sess, 27, Evarts to Christiancy, June 18, 1879; Wharton, *Digest,* III, 619-621, Evarts to Christiancy, June 18, 1879; Wharton, *Digest,* II, 666-672, Evarts to Christiancy, May 8, June 20, December 26, 1879.

27. Dyer, *Evarts,* 230; Wharton, *Digest,* III, 381-382, Evarts to Christiancy, January 25, 1881; S. D. A., Instructions, Bolivia, I, No. 12, 248, Evarts to Pettis, June 23, 1879; Wharton, *Digest,* III, 515, Evarts to Sherman, November 14, 1879.

28. Moore, *Digest,* VI, 508-509, Evarts to Christiancy, March 9, 1880.

29. H. Evans, *Chile and Its Relations With the United States,* 101.

30. S. D. A., Instructions, Bolivia, I, 248, No. 12, Evarts to Pettis, August 8, 1879; 262, No. 26, Evarts to Pettis, October 1, 1879; 323, No. 24, Evarts to Adams, December 14, 1880; *Senate Ex. Doc., No. 79,* 47 Cong., 1 Sess., 6-9, 18; W. H. Hurlburt, *Meddling and Muddling—Mr. Blaine's Foreign Policy,* 44-46.

31. Hurlburt, *Meddling and Muddling,* 46-47.

32. *Senate Ex. Doc., No. 79,* 47 Cong., 1 Sess., 147-148; Hurlburt, *Meddling and Muddling,* 47-48; Parks, *Colombia,* 104.

33. *For. Rel., 1881,* Evarts to Osburn, February 10, 1881; Evarts Papers, Suarez to Evarts, February 1, 1881; W. H. Trescott to Evarts, undated; Hurlburt, 48-53.

34. *Chamber of Commerce of the State of New York—One Hundred and Ninth Anniversary Banquet at Delmonico's, May 14, 1877,* 10-14.

35. *New York Press,* July 16, 1877; *Arguments and Speeches,* III, 396-397.

36. *New York Times,* February 17, 1878; Evarts Papers, G. Smith to Evarts, September 17, 1879; G. Hunt, *The Department of State,* 148-150.

37. *Letters and Messages of Rutherford B. Hayes,* 125-128; Evarts Papers, Evarts to Velasquez & Co., August 7, 1880.

38. Nevins, *Fish,* 654-655; *Register of the Department of State, Corrected to December, 1880,* 12-36; *North American Review,* April, 1876, 309-337.

39. Evarts Papers, Schultz to Evarts, June 17, 1878; Hunt, *The Department of State,* 150-151.

40. Hunt, *The Department of State,* 148; *Report of the Consuls of the United States, No. 1.*

41. *New York Tribune,* August 11, 1879; *New York Times,* August 8, 1880; Evarts Papers, J. Codman to Evarts, May 7, 1880.

42. Evarts Papers, T. J. Barnett to Evarts, August 21, 1880.

43. Evarts Papers, W. H. Trescott to Evarts, undated.

CHAPTER XXV

1. Evarts Papers, E. R. Hoar to Evarts, November 7, 1868; Fish Papers, Evarts to Fish, April 30, 1874; Fish to Evarts, April 30, 1874; Hayes Papers, telegram, April 29, 1878; *New York Times*, April 13, 1878.

2. M. R. Coolidge, *Chinese Immigration*, 23; J. F. Rhodes, *History of the United States From Hayes to McKinley*, 181.

3. *New York Tribune*, February 24, 1879; Coolidge, *Chinese Immigration*, 119.

4. Nevins, *Fish*, 915; Williams, *Hayes*, II, 212; Coolidge, *Chinese Immigration*, 132.

5. *New York Herald*, December 2, 1877.

6. Evarts Papers, Bee to Evarts, January 16, 1878.

7. *New York Herald*, September 29, 1878.

8. *Cong. Rec.*, 45 Cong., 3 Sess., 793, 1303, 1383 ff.

9. Williams, *Hayes*, III, 524; Dyer, *Evarts*, 221; *New York Tribune*, January 4, 1879.

10. Williams, *Hayes*, I, 257, 257 n. Original draft in Evarts Papers; *Letters and Messages of Rutherford B. Hayes*, 145-148.

11. S. D. A., Instructions, China, III, 19-23, Evarts to Seward, April 23, 1879.

12. *Pacific Historical Review*, December, 1933, 402-404; S. D. A., Dispatches, China, Seward to Evarts, August 1, September 9, 1879; *New York Herald*, May 2, 1878.

13. Evarts Papers, J. R. Young to Evarts, March 4, 25, 26, 1880; Bemis, *Diplomatic History*, VII, 232-233.

14. *New York Herald*, December 21, 1878; Evarts Papers, F. W. Seward to Evarts, April 16, 1880; Trescott to Evarts, September 4, 1880.

15. *Outlook*, April 23, 1904; J. B. Angell, *Reminiscences of James Burrill Angell*, 129-132.

16. Evarts Papers, Angell to Evarts, March 17, 1880; telegram, Angell to Evarts, March 18, 1880; Angell to Evarts, March 11, 1880; *New York Times*, April 6, 9, 1880.

17. *Outlook*, April 23, 1904; Angell, *Reminiscences*, 132; Bemis, *Diplomatic History*, VII, 255-256.

18. Evarts Papers, Angell to Evarts, August 2, 5, 1880; Trescott to Evarts, August 15, 1880; Trescott to Evarts, October 10, 1880; J. B. Angell, *Reminiscences*, 142; S. D. A., Dispatches, China, LV, the commissioners to Evarts, October 26, 1880.

19. Evarts Papers, J. R. Young to Evarts, March 26, 1881; *New York Herald*, January 15, 1881; *New York Times*, January 11, 1881.

20. Evarts Papers, Trescott to Evarts, November 8, 1880; *For. Rel., 1881*, 177-178, 186-187.

21. Wharton, *Digest*, I, 462, Evarts to Angell, June 7, 1880; Evarts Papers, Trescott to Evarts, August 15, November 8, 1880.

22. Wharton, *Digest*, I, 810, Evarts to Bingham, October 7, 1880; II, 666, Evarts to Seward, May 6, 1879; *For. Rel., 1880*, Evarts to Seward, January 22, 1880; Moore, *Digest*, II, 665, Evarts to Bingham, January 3, 1881.

23. *New York Times*, January 14, 18, 31, 1881.

24. Moore, *Digest*, V, 751-753; T. Dennett, *Americans in Eastern Asia*, 456-457, 517-520; Bemis, *Diplomatic History*, VII, 256-257; Evarts Papers, W. H. Trescott to Evarts, undated; *Political Science Quarterly*, September, 1910, 470-499.

25. S. F. Bemis, *A Diplomatic History of the United States*, 454-455; Wharton, *Digest*, I, 437-438, Evarts to Van Thielmann, June 15, 1878.

26. Seward, *Reminiscences*, 438-440; Bemis, *Diplomatic History*, 455-456.

27. Wharton, *Digest*, I, 438, Evarts to Welsh, May 15, 1879; Bemis, *Diplomatic History*, 457; G. H. Ryden, *The Foreign Policy of the United States in Relation to Samoa*, 265-266.

CHAPTER XXVI

1. Hayes Papers, Evarts to Hayes, August 20, 1879; Evarts Papers, Thornton to Evarts, March 5, 1881.

2. Hayes, *Diary,* III, 466; Evarts Papers, Byland to Evarts, November 3, 1877; *New York Herald,* October 31, 1877.

3. Evarts Papers, Bundy to Evarts, October 15, 1879; Evarts to Astor, December 25, 1879; Astor to Evarts, December 27, 31, 1879, January 3, 1880; W. Theron, *The Letters of Mrs. Henry Adams,* 164.

4. Evarts Papers, Lowell to Evarts, January 21, February 23, 1880; Hoar, *Autobiography,* II, 294-295.

5. *New York Herald,* June 23, 25, 1877; J. M. Callahan, *American Foreign Policy in Canadian Relations,* 388.

6. Wharton, *Digest,* I, 51-54, Evarts to Thornton, March 15, May 27, 1879; Moore, *Digest,* II, 439.

7. Evarts Papers, Woodbridge to Evarts, October 12, 1878; Callahan, *Canadian Relations,* 390; *For. Rel., 1881,* Evarts to Thornton, February 5, 1881.

8. Callahan, *Canadian Relations,* 390.

9. L. B. Shippee, *Canadian-American Relations, 1849-1874,* 472.

10. Hicks, *Arguments and Addresses of Joseph H. Choate,* 60; C. F. Adams, *Richard Henry Dana,* II, 377-378; Evarts Papers, Journal, I, 122-123.

11. Evarts Papers, Journal, I, 153-154; Fish Papers, Evarts to Fish, December 6, 1877; Nevins, *Fish,* 889.

12. *Letter of the Secretary of State on . . . the Fishery Commission.* The original is in the Evarts Papers.

13. *New York Times,* August 30, 1878; *New York Tribune,* August 29, September 4, 1878; *New York Herald,* September 6, 1878; Callahan, *Canadian Relations,* 357.

14. Hayes Papers, Evarts to Hayes, August 24, 1878.

15. *Cong. Rec.,* 50 Cong., 1 Sess., 7344-7347.

16. *For. Rel., 1878,* Salisbury to Welsh, November 7, 1878; *New York Herald,* March 8, 12, 1878.

17. Fish Papers, Fish to Evarts, November 25, 1878.

18. Evarts Papers, circular of Henry Y. Hind; Hind to Evarts, March 20, 1880; Wood to Evarts, January 13, 1881.

19. *New York Herald,* February 26, March 11, 1878.

20. *Cong. Rec.,* 50 Cong., 1 Sess., 7347-7348; Bancroft Papers, Bancroft to Evarts, October 31, 1878.

21. *New York Herald,* January 21, 30, 1879.

22. *New York Herald,* April 2, 1879; *Cong. Rec.,* 50 Cong., 1 Sess., 7351-7353.

23. Hayes Papers, Evarts to the President, September 19, 1879; *Toronto Mail,* September 12, 1879; Evarts Papers, Hayes to Evarts, September 22, 1879; G. Smith to Evarts, September 17, 1879; Callahan, *Canadian Relations,* 360-361.

24. *For. Rel., 1880,* 570-573, Salisbury to Hoppin, April 3, 1880; *Cong. Rec.,* 50 Cong., 1 Sess., 7348-7351.

25. *For. Rel., 1880,* 588-590, Granville to Lowell, October 27, 1880; 499-502, Evarts to Lowell, February 4, 1881; 509, Granville to Lowell, February 26, 1881; S. D. A., Instructions, Great Britain, XXVI, 62-64, Evarts to Lowell, March 1, 1881.

26. Muzzey, *Blaine,* 196; *Senate Ex. Doc., No. 870,* 61 Cong., 3 Sess., I, 247.

27. Evarts Papers, Barnett to Evarts, August 21, 1880.

28. Moore, *Digest,* VII, 75.

29. *New York Herald,* October 31, 1920.

30. *New York Tribune,* April 17, 1877; *New York Herald,* June 3, 1878; Wharton, *Digest,* III, 619, Evarts to Aristarchi Bey, May 3, 1877; 375, Evarts to Shishkin, June 12, 1877; 588, Evarts to Sullivan, February 21, 1878; Moore, *Digest,* VII, 896, Evarts to Park, October 9, 1877; S. D. A., Instructions, Turkey, III, 246, Evarts to Maynard, June 18, 1877.

31. Wharton, *Digest,* II, 123-125, Evarts to Welsh, July 11, 29, 1879; *For. Rel., 1880,* 479-481, Lowell to Evarts, June 16, 1880.

32. Wharton, *Digest,* II, 293, Evarts to Aristarchi Bey, December 18, 1877; 623, Evarts to Aristarchi Bey, December 8, 1877; 294, Evarts to Aristarchi Bey, May 14, 1880; Moore, *Digest,* V, 684; Bemis, *Diplomatic History,* VII, 248-249.

33. R. C. Beatty, *Bayard Taylor,* 352; *New York Herald,* December 20, 1878; Evarts Papers, Reid to Evarts, December 30, 1878; Bemis, *Diplomatic History,* VII, 248.

34. A. H. Smyth, *Bayard Taylor,* 283; White, *Autobiography,* I, 534-535; Wharton, *Digest,* II, 391, Evarts to Williams, February 5, 1879; Moore, *Digest,* III, 748, Evarts to Luxon, November 21, 1878; *New York Tribune,* November 22, 1880; *For. Rel., 1880,* Evarts to White, December 1, 1880; 223-232, Evarts to Taylor, September 27, 1878; Taylor to Evarts, October 19, 1878.

35. Greenslet, *James Russell Lowell,* 195-196, 203-204; Wharton, *Digest,* II, 623-625, Evarts to Welsh, July 1, 21, 1878; *For. Rel., 1878,* 285-286, Welsh to Evarts, August 27, 1878.

36. Wharton, *Digest,* I, 253, Evarts to Foster, June 28, 1880; Moore, *Digest,* IV, 115, Evarts to Foster, September 4, 1880; Wharton, *Digest,* I, 253-254, Evarts to Foster, March 3, 1881; A. F. Tyler, *The Foreign Policy of James G. Blaine,* 272-273.

37. *For. Rel., 1880,* 5-6, Circular No. 4, July 30, 1880; Wharton, *Digest,* II, 240-242, Evarts to Drummond, July 30, 1880; Moore, *Digest,* V, 584; *Rules of the French and American Claims Commission.*

38. S. D. A., Notes to the Netherlands Legation, VII, 470-471, 490, 503, 542, 544, 553-554, 557-559; VIII, I, 4-7; Wharton, *Digest,* II, 818, Evarts to Dichman, November 12, 1879; *For. Rel., 1879,* Evarts to Dichman, May 12, 1879.

39. *New York Herald,* January 23, 1879; Moore, *Digest,* IV, 872, Evarts to Read, June 18, 1878; S. D. A., Instructions, Denmark, XV, 206-209; Instructions, Greece, I, 185-187.

40. Fish Papers, Cadwallader to Fish, May 22, 1878; Fish to Cadwallader, July 2, 1878; S. D. A., Notes to the British Legation, XVII, 389-390, 433, 455; Nevins, *Fish,* 870-871; *New York Herald,* July 2, 1878.

41. Bemis, *Diplomatic History,* VII, 249-250; Wharton, *Digest,* II, 325-326, Evarts to Fish, November 12, 1879; Moore, *Digest,* III, 717, Evarts to Fish, October, 1880; III, 320, Evarts to Stoughton, October 23, 1878.

42. S. D. A., Notes to the Belgian Legation, VII, 117; Notes to the Italian Legation, VII, 359; Notes to the Netherlands Legation, VII, 475; Instructions, Netherlands, XV, 312-349; Instructions, Brazil, XVII, 92.

43. Evarts Papers, Schuyler to Evarts, November 23, 1880; February 5, 1881; Moore, *Digest,* I, 114-115; IV, 443-444; *For. Rel., 1879,* July 13, 30, 1879.

CHAPTER XXVII

1. *New York Tribune,* September 5, 1878.

2. Evarts Papers, Bundy to Evarts, June 8, 1880; Cole to Evarts, June 14, 1880.

3. Evarts Papers, Garfield to Evarts, July 14, 1880; Weed to Evarts, July 17, 1880; Bowen to Evarts, September 11, 1880; Garfield to Evarts, September 15, 20, 1880; Bundy to Evarts, September 22, 1880.

4. *New York Tribune,* September 30, 1880; *Evening Mail,* September 30, 1880; *Great Republican Speeches of the Campaign of 1880,* 20, 22, 27, 30.

5. *New York Tribune,* October 21, 1880; *Evening Mail,* October 21, 1880; *New York Times,* October 21, 1880; *Great Republican Speeches of the Campaign of 1880,* 43-46, 49, 50.

6. Evarts Papers, Crandall to Evarts, October 30, 1880; Hubbell to Evarts, October 28, 1880; *Evening Mail,* September 30, 1880.

7. Evarts Papers, Barnett to Evarts, November 6, 1880.

8. Evarts Papers, Nye to Curtis, November 11, 1880; Dennett, *John Hay,* 169; Chidsey, *Conkling,* 315.

9. Evarts Papers, Forster to Evarts, November 5, 1880; Webster to Evarts, December 24, 1880; Theron, *The Letters of Mrs. Henry Adams,* 255-256.

10. Evarts Papers, Trescott to Evarts, November 8, 1880; Thornton to Evarts, March 5, 1881; Garfield to Evarts, March 7, 1881.

11. Theron, *The Letters of Mrs. Henry Adams,* 261; *New York Tribune,* March 28, 1881; Evarts Papers, Parkman and others to Evarts, March 8, 1881.

12. Evarts Papers, Evarts to Garfield, March 8, 1881.

13. Evarts Papers, Hayes to Evarts, March 10, 1881; Chidsey, *Conkling,* 329.

14. *New York Times,* March 13, 16, 1878; March 10, 1881; *Speech of Mr. Evarts, A Delegate of the United States at the International Monetary Conference;* Evarts Papers, Weed to Evarts, September 11, 1879; Evarts to Belmont, December 11, 1880.

15. Evarts Papers, Blaine to Evarts, March 31, 1881; Cortissoz, *Life of Whitelaw Reid,* II, 74.

16. *Speech of Mr. Evarts.*

17. Dyer, *Evarts,* 244; Fish Papers, Davis to Fish, June 21, 1881; Cortissoz, *Life of Whitelaw Reid,* II, 74.

18. *Proceedings of the International Conference,* 446-521; *New York Tribune,* September 5, 1881.

19. Evarts Papers, manuscript copy of Evarts' speech.

20. Hayes Papers, Evarts to Hayes, February 11, 1882.

21. *New York Tribune,* November 2, 14, 1882.

22. *New York Tribune,* September 22, 1882; *New York Nation,* January 22, 1883.

23. *New York Tribune,* February 2, 1883; *Proceedings of the Great Mass Meeting Held at Cooper Institute, February 1, 1883.*

24. *New York Times,* February 6, 1883; H. E. Starr, *William Graham Sumner,* 273-283.

25. *New York Times, New York Tribune,* November 4, 1883.

26. *Proceedings of the Twentieth Anniversary of the Union League Club, February 6, 1883.*

27. *New York Tribune,* February 15, March 28, 1884.

28. Fish Papers, Fish to Evarts, July 10, 1884; Evarts to Fish, July 9, 1884.

29. *New York Tribune,* July 16, 1884.

30. *New York Tribune,* October 24, 1884; *New York Times,* October 25, November 3, 1884.

31. T. B. Boyd, *The Blaine and Logan Campaign of 1884,* 186; *New York Tribune,* October 30, 1884.

32. Muzzey, *Blaine,* 316-317, 319; Rhodes, *History of the United States,* VIII, 228.

CHAPTER XXVIII

1. *New York Tribune,* December 8, 1883; February 1, 1885.

2. *Arguments and Speeches,* III, 419-424.

3. *New York Tribune,* February 2, 1882.

4. Holt, *Garrulities of an Octogenarian Editor,* 51; H. Spencer, *Autobiography,* II, 478; *Arguments and Speeches,* III, 411-413.

5. *Arguments and Speeches,* III, 414-418; *New York Tribune,* January 30, 1883.

6. *The Green Bag,* VI, 305-308; VII, 41.

7. *Proceedings of the Special Meeting . . . to Receive the Lord Chief Justice; New York Tribune,* October 26, 1883; Evarts Papers, Coleridge to Evarts, December 8, 1883.

8. *Arguments and Speeches,* III, 420-424; Evarts Papers, Ramsford to Evarts, May 10, 1883.

9. H. Villard, *Memoirs of Henry Villard,* II, 309-311; Evarts Papers, Sims to Evarts, August 16, 1883; printed program of the itinerary.

10. Bishop, *A Chronicle*, 186-187; *New York Tribune*, November 6, 1881; *Arguments and Speeches*, III, 404-410.

11. *Arguments and Speeches*, III, 130-131; *House Misc. Doc., No. 601*, 50 Cong., 1 Sess; Fish Papers, Fish to Schuyler, September 29, 1883.

12. A. Nevins, *Grover Cleveland*, 134; *New York Tribune*, October 19, 1883.

13. *Arguments and Speeches*, III, 139-151.

14. Evarts Papers, Davis to Evarts, October 21, 1883.

15. *New York Tribune*, February 11, 1883.

16. Evarts Papers, Edict No. 1 of the Column Club, March 8, 1883; Lossing, *History of New York City*, II, 478; Bigelow, *Retrospections*, I, 45-47.

17. *Tenement House Cigar Law. Argument of Hon. William M. Evarts;* 98 N. Y. 98; 33 Hun 374.

18. Evarts Papers, Choate to Evarts, August 26, 1871.

19. Strong, *Joseph H. Choate*, 165-171; Strong, *Landmarks of A Lawyer's Lifetime*, 200.

20. Hicks, *Arguments and Addresses of Joseph H. Choate*, 8-12; Strong, *Joseph H. Choate*, 138-154.

21. *New York Times*, April 12, 19, 1876.

22. Lewis, *Great American Lawyers*, V, 83-84.

23. *Magazine of American History*, XIII, 513-535.

24. J. Bigelow, undated manuscript in New York Library entitled "Some Recollections of the Late Charles O'Conor."

25. *Arguments and Speeches*, III, 199-206.

26. *The Green Bag*, III, 49-55; VI, 209-213; Lewis, *Great American Lawyers*, V, 125-174.

27. Evarts Papers, argument of Evarts in manuscript and Memorandum of the Reply of Mr. Field.

28. Strong, *Landmarks of A Lawyer's Lifetime*, 276-281; Lewis, *Great American Lawyers*, VIII, 3-21; Choate, *American Addresses*, 266-267; J. C. Welsh, "Charles O'Conor," 285-313.

29. *Supreme Court, John A. Post against Adolph Bernheimer. The Same Against Matilda Weil and Others. Opinion of Mr. Evarts*, 21-29, 42-48.

30. 8 Hun 418; *Supreme Court. General Term. Winifred Post vs. Max Weil. Points For the Plaintiffs and Respondents.*

31. 31 Hun 247.

32. J. C. Carter, *Memorial of Evarts*, 107; *Arguments and Speeches*, I, XIII; Evarts Papers, original of the brief; 115 N. Y. 361.

33. *Proceedings of the Bench and Bar of the Supreme Court of the United States in Memoriam Morrison R. Waite.*

34. *The Forum*, LXXXVI, 56-64; *Liberty*, February 24, March 3, 10, 1934.

35. Hicks, *Arguments and Addresses of Joseph H. Choate*, 164.

36. *New York Tribune*, February 25, 1890.

CHAPTER XXIX

1. *Utica Morning Herald*, December 12, 1884; Alexander, *Political History of the State of New York*, IV, 47.

2. *New York Tribune*, December 11, 1884; Evarts Papers, Mead to Evarts, December 2, 1884; Hayes to Evarts, December 18, 1884.

3. R. McElroy, *Levi Parsons Morton*, 160-161; Alexander, *Political History*, IV, 47-48.

4. C. F. Howe, *Chester A. Arthur*, 278-281.

5. *New York Times*, December 16, 17, 1884.

6. Hayes, *Diary*, IV, 179-180.

7. *New York Times*, December 23, 1884; Howe, *Chester A. Arthur*, 279-281; Alexander, *Political History*, IV, 49.

8. Depew, *My Memories of Eighty Years*, 104-105.

9. *Albany Evening Journal*, January 10, 1885; Evarts Papers, Ingalsbe to Evarts, January 9, 1885; *New York Tribune*, January 10, 1885.

10. *An Address of Chief Justice Noah Davis and Letter of Rev. R. S. Storrs to Republicans of Brooklyn.*

11. *New York Tribune*, January 10, 15, 1885; Alexander, *Political History*, IV, 50.

12. *New York Times*, January 12, 1885; *New York Tribune*, January 15, 17, 1885.

13. *New York Tribune*, January 17, 1885; Alexander, IV, 51-54; Evarts Papers, Roosevelt to Evarts, January 19, 1885; *New York Times*, January 20, 1885.

14. Evarts Papers, original tally-sheets.

15. Evarts Papers, Arkell to Evarts, January 19, 1885; *New York Tribune*, January 21, 1885; Hayes, *Diary*, IV, 185-187.

16. Evarts Papers, Sherman to Evarts, January 25, 1885.

17. Evarts Papers, the original petition, dated January 22, 1885; *New York Tribune* February 14, 1885.

18. *New York Tribune*, February 21, 1885; Lodge, *Early Memories*, 255.

19. *New York Times*, February 22, 25, 26, 1885.

20. Lodge, *Early Memories*, 256; *New York Tribune*, April 19, 1885; *New York Times*, April 20, 1885; Hoar, *Autobiography*, II, 18-19.

21. Lodge, *Early Memories*, 255; *Arguments and Speeches*, III, 425-429; A. Brereton *The Life of Henry Irving*, II, 68-70.

22. *New York Tribune*, October 31, 1885; Evarts Papers, memoranda of speech.

23. Ford, *Letters of Henry Adams*, 364.

24. Winthrop Papers, Evarts to Winthrop, February 9, 1885; *Harper's Weekly*, January 31, 1885.

25. Evarts Papers, Evarts to S. Evarts, August 16, 1889; *New York Tribune*, March 2, 1886.

26. *Harper's Magazine*, January, 1878.

27. Evarts Papers, several telegrams; *New York Tribune*, August 26, 1886; Evarts Papers, Evarts to G. W. Curtis, September 27, 1886; Evarts to G. Bancroft, September 13, 1886; Hayes Papers, Evarts to Hayes, September 18, 1886.

28. *Albany Law Journal*, LXIII, 112.

29. Hoar, *Autobiography*, II, 19.

30. Lodge, *Early Memories*, 258.

31. *New York Tribune*, March 2, 1886.

32. Nevins, *Grover Cleveland*, 343-344.

33. *Arguments and Speeches*, III, 216.

34. Hoar, *Autobiography*, II, 137-141; Nevins, *Grover Cleveland*, 256-265.

35. *Cong. Rec.*, 49 Cong., 1 Sess., 2742-2746.

36. *Ibid.*, 2 Sess., 216; A. Nevins, *The Gateway to History*, 171.

37. *New York Herald*, October 18, 1887; *New York Tribune*, October 23, 28, 1887.

38. *Cong. Rec.*, 49 Cong., 1 Sess., 820, 1057-1058, 1062; *New York Tribune*, February 4, 1886.

39. *Arguments and Speeches*, III, 210-217.

40. *Cong. Rec.*, 49 Cong., 1 Sess., 248-250; *New York Tribune*, December 18, 1885.

41. *Cong. Rec.*, 49 Cong., 1 Sess., 6043-6045; 2 Sess., 1314-1320; N. W. Stephenson, *Nelson W. Aldrich*, 68; *New York Times*, December 16, 17, 1886.

42. *New York Tribune*, March 3, 1901.

43. H. D. Lloyd, *Wealth Against Commonwealth*, 374-385; *Cong. Rec.*, 49 Cong., 1 Sess., 7352-7359, 7361; S. M. Cullom, *Fifty Years of Public Service*, 184-185.

44. Miller, *Great Debates in American History*, X, 321-346.

45. *Cong. Rec.*, 49 Cong., 1 Sess., 4423.

46. Cullom, *Fifty Years,* 321-322; *Report of the Inter-State Commerce Bill; Cong. Rec.,* 49 Cong., 2 Sess., 603, 606-609, 664.

47. Cullom, *Fifty Years,* 325; *Cong. Rec.,* 49 Cong., 2 Sess., 326-327.

48. Sherman, *Recollections,* II, 749.

49. *Cong. Rec.,* 49 Cong., 1 Sess., 2866, 3463-3465, 5450-5452; 2 Sess., 1393; 51 Cong., 1 Sess., 633.

50. *New York Herald,* October 31, 1920.

51. *Cong. Rec.,* 50 Cong., 2 Sess., 1247-1248, 1250; 51 Cong., 2 Sess., 2776, 2778; Maycock, *With Mr. Chamberlain in the United States and Canada,* 66.

52. *Cong. Rec.,* 49 Cong., 1 Sess., 3435-3440.

53. *Ibid.*

54. J. Jay, *The Fisheries Dispute, etc.*

55. Nevins, *Grover Cleveland,* 406-410; Maycock, *Chamberlain,* 64-66.

56. *Cong. Rec.,* 50 Cong., 1 Sess., 7325-7328, 7331, 7335-7339, 7729-7732.

57. *Ibid.,* 7605, 7766; Nevins, *Grover Cleveland,* 412-413.

CHAPTER XXX

1. *New York Tribune,* July 12, 1888; *New York Evening Post,* July 13, 1888.

2. *New York Herald,* July 26, 1888; Nevins, *Grover Cleveland,* 432.

3. W. Bowen, *History of Woodstock, Connecticut,* I, 498-499; *Independent,* September 13, 1888.

4. *New York Times,* October 20, 1888.

5. *New York Times, New York Tribune,* October 31, 1888.

6. *New York Times,* March 16, 20, 1889.

7. *Cong. Rec.,* 50 Cong., 1 Sess., 702-708, 2059-2060, 2061-2067, 2104-2106; 51 Cong., 1 Sess., 4006-4007, 4013, 4015, 4019, 4069-4071, 4075-4082, 4119-4121.

8. *Cong. Rec.,* 50 Cong., 1 Sess., 4207; 51 Cong., 1 Sess., 1270, 7229; 2 Sess., 2849-2850.

9. *New York Times,* January 1, 26, 1886; February 28, 1886; *New York Tribune,* December 31, 1885; March 2, 1886.

10. E. P. Oberholtzer, *A History of the United States Since the Civil War,* II, 374.

11. *Cong. Rec.,* 49 Cong., 1 Sess., 7847-7848; *New York Tribune,* August 3, 1886.

12. *New York Tribune,* June 13, 1890; *Cong. Rec.,* 51 Cong., 1 Sess., 5970-5976.

13. *Cong. Rec.,* 51 Cong., 1 Sess., 6183, 7109.

14. S. Adler, *The Senatorial Career of George Franklin Edmunds,* 5.

15. Speech for Cornell, October 21, 1879.

16. Hoar, *Autobiography,* II, 151-152, 165.

17. *Cong. Rec.,* 51 Cong., 1 Sess., 5068, 5272, 5418, 5607, 6078.

18. *Ibid.,* 657-662.

19. *Ibid.,* 414-419, 475, 504, 506-507.

20. *New York Times,* January 16, 1891; Hoar, *Autobiography,* II, 189-190; *Cong. Rec.,* 51 Cong., 2 Sess., 1358-1363, 1367-1368.

21. J. B. Foraker, *Notes of A Busy Life,* II, 163-164; *Cong. Rec.,* 51 Cong., 1 Sess., 3152-3153.

22. Alexander, *Political History,* IV, 94-95.

23. *Address of the Hon. William M. Evarts, LL.D., . . . at the Seventh Annual Meeting of the Law and Order Society of Philadelphia, February 21st, 1888; New York Times,* February 22, 23, 1888; October 31, 1888.

24. *Cong. Rec.,* 49 Cong., 1 Sess., 1553, 1984, 2081; 2 Sess., 1603; 50 Cong., 1 Sess., 689, 784, 857, 964, 1039, 1251, 1488, 1531, 1617, 1723, 2281, 3548; 51 Cong., 1 Sess., 3134, 3375.

25. *New York Tribune,* March 3, 1901.

26. 12 Wheaton 419; *Cong. Rec.*, 51 Cong., 1 Sess., 5086-5088.

27. *Cong. Rec.*, 49 Cong., 1 Sess., 1232, 1985, 2940, 3302, 3303, 3535, 4302, 4942, 5548, 6105; 2 Sess., 101, 871, 1123, 1393; 50 Cong., 1 Sess., 1328, 1401, 1488, 1500-1501, 1531, 1579, 1617, 1723, 1809, 1846, 1940, 2090, 2202, 2244, 2284, 2327, 2390, 2427, 2542, 2794, 2895, 3381, 3768, 3867; 50 Cong., 1 Sess., 256, 617, 860, 1073, 1530, 1729, 1940, 1941, 2244, 2285, 3002, 3074, 4741, 5611, 5997, 9467; 2 Sess., 272.

28. *Ibid.*, 49 Cong., 1 Sess., 1120; 50 Cong., 1 Sess., 3674; 51 Cong., 1 Sess., 102, 121, 964, 2290, 2829, 3053, 3279, 3594, 5068-5069, 6078; 2 Sess., 707, 1535, 2371.

29. *Ibid.*, 49 Cong., 1 Sess., 6277-6278.

30. *Ibid.*, 50 Cong., 1 Sess., 6976-6977.

31. *Ibid.*, 51 Cong., 1 Sess., 46-47, 1717-1718, 2144, 2152.

32. *Ibid.*, 50 Cong., 2 Sess., 1782-1783, 1819-1856.

33. *Ibid.*, 51 Cong., 1 Sess., 3280-3285.

CHAPTER XXXI

1. Foraker, *Notes of a Busy Life*, I, 297-299; Evarts Papers, manuscript copy of speech and outline.

2. *Cong. Rec.*, 51 Cong., 1 Sess., 58, 64; Evarts Papers, manuscript copy of speech; *New York Times*, May 1, 1889.

3. *Cong. Rec.*, 51 Cong., 1 Sess., 137, 142; *New York Times*, February 19, 1880; Evarts Papers, Evarts to Butterworth, October 1, 1891.

4. *Cong. Rec.*, 50 Cong., 2 Sess., 338.

5. *Ibid.*, 51 Cong., 1 Sess., 3936-3937, 3703.

6. Evarts Papers, Beaman to Evarts, March 15, 1880; Hoar, *Autobiography*, II, 87-88; *Cong. Rec.*, 51 Cong., 1 Sess., 10075-10079.

7. *Cong. Rec.*, 50 Cong., 1 Sess., 7116.

8. *Ibid.*, 7116-7117.

9. *Ibid.*, 51 Cong., 2 Sess., 2387-2388, 2392, 2394-2395, 2667, 3885-3888; R. R. Bowker, *Copyright, Its History and Its Law*, 353-354.

10. Richard Butler Papers, Bartholdi to Butler, March 10, 1886; *Cong. Rec.*, 51 Cong., 1 Sess., 9197-9198, 9241-9242, 9248, 10117-10118.

11. *Cong. Rec.*, 49 Cong., 1 Sess., 3537; 50 Cong., 1 Sess., 3548, 7114-7115.

12. *Arguments and Speeches*, III, 436.

13. *The Unveiling of the Seward Memorial Statue . . . November 15, 1888.*

14. *New York Herald*, February 6, 1877; Evarts Papers, Franco-American Committee to Evarts, July 1, 1880.

15. Richard Butler Papers, Bartholdi to Butler, October 31, 1882; Evarts Papers, Bartholdi to Evarts, October 31, 1882; Evarts to the Franco-American Union, November 17, 1882.

16. R. C. Stone, *The Statue of Liberty Enlightening the World*, 36-39.

17. Richard Butler Papers, Bartholdi to Evarts, August 3, 1883; Evarts to Butler, July 23, 1885; Evarts Papers, Evarts to Cleveland, May 20, 1884.

18. Bishop, *A Chronicle of One Hundred and Fifty Years*, 189-190.

19. Richard Butler Papers, Evarts to Butler, July 27, August 5, 1886; *Cong. Rec.*, 49 Cong., 1 Sess., 7456-7457.

20. *New York Times*, October 27, 1886.

21. *Inauguration of the Statue of Liberty Enlightening the World; New York Times*, October 29, 1886.

22. Address at the Metropolitan Methodist Church, April 27, 1886.

23. Holt, *Garrulities of An Octogenarian Editor*, 185-186.

24. *The Yale Review*, October, 1920.

25. *Record of the Class of 1837 in Yale University, With a Notice of Their Meetings in 1877, 1882, 1887;* Ford Collection, undated clipping in 1887.

26. Evarts Papers, Hart to Evarts, July 9, 1892; *Cong. Rec.,* 51 Cong., 1 Sess., 3341, 10399.

27. Evarts Papers, Blair to Evarts, April 29, 1884.

28. *Cong. Rec.,* 49 Cong., 1 Sess., 1635-1640, 2083, 2085.

29. *Ibid.,* 50 Cong., 1 Sess., 835-839.

30. *New York Times,* March 19, 1890; *Cong. Rec.,* 51 Cong., 1 Sess., 2385-2389.

31. Hayes, *Diary,* IV, 343-344; Fish Papers, Fish to Davis, February 4, 1880.

32. *Celebration of the Sixty-Fourth Anniversary of the Birthday of Gen. Ulysses S. Grant . . . April 27, 1886.*

33. *Cong. Rec.,* 51 Cong., 1 Sess., 6653; 2 Sess., 499, 850, 904, 1945, 2045, 2129, 2222, 2535, 2662, 3519; Hoar, *Autobiography,* II, 300-303.

34. *Cong. Rec.,* 49 Cong., 1 Sess., 1553-1554; 2 Sess., 2; 50 Cong., 1 Sess., 1809, 2542; 51 Cong., 1 Sess., 96, 1792, 2875, 5919, 6736, 7081, 7171, 8487, 8611-8616, 8667-8672.

35. *Ibid.,* 49 Cong., 2 Sess., 2054; 50 Cong., 1 Sess., 256, 2824, 4207; 51 Cong., 1 Sess., 200, 299, 5918, 5920, 6368, 10781; 2 Sess., 359, 2136, 2222, 2480.

36. *Ibid.,* 49 Cong., 1 Sess., 5196-5198, 5235; 50 Cong., 1 Sess., 8452-8456; R. Jones, *The American Standard of Living,* 100-101.

37. *Cong. Rec.,* 49 Cong., 1 Sess., 5238-5239; 51 Cong., 1 Sess., 256, 2824; 2 Sess., 2480.

38. *Ibid.,* 49 Cong., 1 Sess., 448, 1232, 6372-6373; 2 Sess., 1607.

39. Nevins, *Grover Cleveland,* 217-218, 222 n.; *Cong. Rec.,* 51 Cong., 1 Sess., 102.

40. *Cong. Rec.,* 49 Cong., 1 Sess., 4075; 2 Sess., 201, 477, 1237, 1308, 1990; 51 Cong., 1 Sess., 1670, 1988, 2067, 2142, 2375, 2427, 2828, 3053, 3594, 4111.

41. Nevins, *Grover Cleveland,* 224.

42. *Cong. Rec.,* 49 Cong., 1 Sess., 5144-5152, 5191-5192.

43. *Ibid.,* 6208-6211, 6258-6261, 6265; 50 Cong., 1 Sess., 4745-4747, 4759-4761; 2 Sess., 1642-1643.

44. *New York Times,* August 8, 9, 1887.

45. *The Green Bag,* XII, 319.

46. *Cong. Rec.,* 49 Cong., 1 Sess., 7628, 7727; 2 Sess., 1177, 1220, 2468; 50 Cong., 1 Sess., 27, 1251, 2204, 2796, 3268, 6499; 51 Cong., 1 Sess., 102, 3434, 3459, 3482, 8133; 2 Sess., 2899.

47. *Ibid.,* 49 Cong., 1 Sess., 3419, 5454-5455; 2 Sess., 209, 1233-1234.

48. F. Frankfurter and J. M. Landis, *The Business of the Supreme Court,* 95-97.

49. *American Bar Association. Report of the Fifth Annual Meeting,* 64-79, 101, 343-384.

50. *Cong. Rec.,* 51 Cong., 1 Sess., 3398-3410, 3425, 10217-10223; *New York Tribune,* March 8, 1891; *Arguments and Speeches,* III, 323-324.

51. Evarts Papers, E. O. Hinkley to Evarts, August 29, 1890.

52. *Cong. Rec.,* 51 Cong., 1 Sess., 10217-10223; Frankfurter and Landis, *Supreme Court,* 109-110.

53. *Cong. Rec.,* 51 Cong., 1 Sess., 10278-10279, 10282-10283, 10297, 10314.

54. *Ibid.,* 2 Sess., 3583-3587.

55. *Arguments and Speeches,* III, 324.

CHAPTER XXXII

1. Hoar, *Autobiography,* II, 19.

2. Evarts Papers, E. R. Hoar to Evarts, April 11, 1891; Alexander, *Political History,* IV, 145-146.

3. *New York Times,* February 23, 1891; Dyer, *Evarts,* 262.

4. Evarts Papers, manuscript copy of Evarts' speech, April 26, 1891.

5. Evarts Papers, Evarts to Thurston, April 17, 1891; Crandall to Evarts, August 24, 1891.

6. Evarts Papers, Evarts to Horton, September 4, 1892; *Vermont Journal,* June 18, 1892; Winters Collection, undated clipping.

7. Evarts Papers, Brooklyn Republican Club to Evarts, October 13, 1892; Bentley to Evarts, October 19, 1892.

8. *Brooklyn Eagle,* October 30, 1892.

9. Evarts Papers, Manderson to Evarts, February 24, 1893.

10. *An Account of the Golden Wedding of Mr. and Mrs. Wm. M. Evarts at Runnemede, Windsor, Vermont, August 30, 1893.*

11. Winthrop Papers, Evarts to Winthrop, February 7, May 1, 1894; *Proceedings of the Trustees of the Peabody Education Fund, 1893-1894,* 45-47, 123-126, 191, 251, 311, 365; Evarts Papers, remarks at meeting of Peabody Trustees, September 25, 1895, illegibly written in Evarts' hand.

12. *New York Times,* February 15, 1895.

13. *Vermont Journal,* undated clipping for 1894.

14. Evarts Papers, Hart to Evarts, February 5, March 25, 1897; *New York Times,* August 12, 1901.

15. Martin, *Life of Choate,* I, 429-430; G. Hamilton, *Life and Letters,* III, 1012; Anecdote to author by Henry Wardner.

16. Anecdote to author by Mrs. Elizabeth Perkins.

17. Winters Collection, XVI, undated clipping; Evarts Papers, Hart to Evarts, December 6, 1895, January 1, 1896; *New York Tribune,* March 10, 1897; Carter, *Memorial of Evarts,* 111-112.

18. *New York Tribune,* February 6, 1898.

19. *Independent,* CVIII, 187; Evarts Papers, Silliman to Evarts, September 13, 1898.

20. *New York Tribune,* August 11, 1900; Winters Collection, XVI, undated clipping; *New York Herald,* March 1, 1901.

21. Bishop, *Notes and Anecdotes of Many Years,* 181; *New York Tribune,* December 9, 1901.

22. *New York Tribune,* March 5, 1901. In 1919 the law firm took its present name of Evarts, Choate, Sherman, and Léon.

23. *New York Times,* March 1, 1901.

Bibliography

1. Manuscripts

Evarts Papers. Papers, documents, letters, law briefs, and memoranda preserved by the Evarts family and temporarily in the possession of the author.

Winters Collection. William H. Winters, former librarian of the New York Law Institute, collected pamphlets, clippings, and sources relating to Evarts, which he brought together in fourteen volumes, 8 vo. sheep. Winters died before using the collection as a basis for a biography of Evarts. The collection was sold in 1923 to Allen W. Evarts, who placed it at the disposal of the author.

Hayes Papers. Some fifty letters of the great collection in the Spiegel Grove Memorial Library, Fremont, Ohio.

Hamilton Fish Papers. Columbia University. Some seventy-five letters of this large collection bear upon Evarts. It is of especial value upon the Geneva Tribunal.

Ford Collection. New York Public Library. A few of Evarts' letters and miscellaneous clippings.

Charles O'Conor Papers. New York Public Library. A few letters and clippings.

Seward Papers. New York Public Library. A few letters.

Richard Butler Papers. New York Public Library. Especially valuable on the Statue of Liberty.

Evarts Genealogy. A loose-leaf notebook, giving in detail the genealogy of the Evarts family from early Welsh beginnings.

State Department Archives. Abundance of material bearing upon Evarts' diplomacy as Secretary of State, his services as Assistant District Attorney, as government agent abroad during the Civil War, as counsel at the Geneva arbitration, and as delegate to the International Monetary Conference of 1881.

Massachusetts Historical Society Papers. A few of Evarts' letters.

Bancroft Papers. A few of Evarts' letters.

2. Government Publications

Concession From the Mexican Government to James B. Eads For the Construction of a Ship Railway Across the Isthmus of Tehuantepec. Washington, 1880.

Congressional Directory. 1885 to 1892. Government Printing Office, Washington.

Congressional Globe. 42nd Congress, 3rd Session.

Congressional Record. 45th, 49th, 50th, 51st Congresses.

Correspondence Between the Spanish Minister and Secretary of State in Regard to the Powers of the Spanish and American Commission, Under the Agreement of February 12, 1871, to enquire into the Citizenship of Native-Born Spanish Subjects claiming to be American Citizens by Naturalization. Washington, 1882.

Hansard's *Parliamentary Debates.* Third Series. Volume 173.

House Executive Documents.

House Miscellaneous Documents.

House Reports.

Journal of Executive Proceedings of the Senate, XVI, XXI.

Letters and Messages of Rutherford B. Hayes, President of the United States, Together With Letter of Acceptance and Inaugural Address. Washington, 1879.

Letter of the Secretary of State on the Subject of the Result of the Fishery Commission Appointed Under Certain Provisions of the Treaty of Washington. Washington, 1877.

Letter of the Secretary of State on the Subject of the Result of the Deliberations of the Fishery Commission Appointed Under Certain Provisions of the Treaty of Washington. Washington, 1878.

Moore, John B. *Digest of International Law.* Government Printing Office, Washington, 1906. Eight volumes.

——. *A History and Digest of the International Arbitrations to Which the United States has been a Party.* Washington, 1898. Six volumes.

Official Opinions of the Attorneys General of the United States. Volume XII. Washington, 1870.

Official Records of the Union and Confederate Navies in the War of the Rebellion. Series 1, Volume 2.

Papers Relating to Foreign Affairs. Especially the volumes for the period 1877 to 1881.

Papers Relating to the Treaty of Washington. Volumes I to IV. Washington, 1872.

Parliamentary Papers. North America, 1873, No. 1; *1874,* No. 2; *1863,* No. 1; *1873,* No. 2. London, 1873-1874.

Proceedings of the Bench and Bar of the Supreme Court of the United States in Memoriam Morrison R. Waite. Washington, 1888.

Proceedings of the Electoral Commission of the Two Houses of Congress in Joint Meeting Relative to the Count of the Electoral Votes Cast December 6, 1876, for the Presidential Term Commencing March 4, 1877. Washington, 1877.

Proceedings of the International Monetary Conference . . . in Paris. Washington, 1887.

Register of the Department of State. For the years 1877 to 1881. Government Printing Office, Washington.

Report of the Consuls of the United States. No. 1. Government Printing Office, Washington, 1880.

Richardson, J. D. *Messages and Papers of the Presidents.* 10 vols. Washington, 1903.

Rules of the French and American Claims Commission With the Convention Establishing the Commission. Washington, 1880.

Senate Executive Documents.

Senate Miscellaneous Documents.

Statutes at Large of the United States of America.

Trial of Andrew Johnson, President of the United States, Before the Senate of the United States, on Impeachment by the House of Representatives for High Crimes and Misdemeanors. Washington, 1868.

Wharton, Francis A. *A Digest of the International Law of the United States.* 3 vols. Washington, 1887.

3. Law Reports and Briefs

United States Supreme Court Reports: Over a hundred cases reported in Howard, Black, Wallace, and the United States reports.

Federal Circuit Court: Over twenty-five cases reported in Blatchford's reports for the Circuit Court of the Southern District of New York.

Federal District Court: About ten cases reported in Olcott and Benedict's reports for the District Court for the Southern District of New York.

Court of Appeals of New York: Over sixty cases reported in the New York reports.

Supreme Court of New York: Over forty cases reported in Barbour, Hun, and Lansing's reports.

Superior Court of New York: Over forty cases reported in Sandford, Duer, Robertson, and Bosworth's reports.

Court of Chancery of New York: Five cases reported in Sandford's Chancery Reports.

Court of Common Pleas of New York: Three cases reported in Daly and Smith's reports.

Surrogate's Reports. A few cases reported in Redfield and Demarest's reports.

The New York Legal Observer. Reports of a few of Evarts' early cases.

State courts outside of New York: A few miscellaneous cases reported.

Briefs: Over seventy printed briefs and arguments of counsel in Evarts' cases, most of them in the Evarts Papers.

4. Semi-Official Publications

An Account of the Golden Wedding of Mr. and Mrs. Wm. M. Evarts at Runnemede, Windsor, Vermont, August 30, 1893. Privately printed.

Addresses and Proceedings, Including the Oration Pronounced by Rev. Dr. Bushnell at the Commemoration Celebration, Held July 26th, 1865, In Honor of the Alumni of Yale College. New Haven, 1866.

An Address of Chief Justice Noah Davis and Letter of Rev. R. S. Storrs to Republicans of Brooklyn in Support of Hon. William Evarts for the Senate, January 10, 1885.

Address of the Hon. William M. Evarts, LL.D., U. S. Senator from New York, at the Seventh Annual Meeting of the Law and Order Society of Philadelphia, February 21st, 1888.

American Bar Association. *Report of the Fifth Annual Meeting Held at Saratoga Springs, New York.* Philadelphia, 1883.

An Appeal to the People of the United States in Behalf of the Great Statue, Liberty Enlightening the World. New York, 1882.

Argument of the United States Delivered to the Tribunal of Arbitration at Geneva—June 15, 1872. Paris, 1872

Association of the Bar of the City of New York. *Annual Report, 1902.*

Association of the Bar of the City of New York. *Constitution and Address.* New York, 1870.

Association of the Bar of the City of New York. *Report of the Proceedings.* New York, 1871.

Association of the Bar of the City of New York. *Reports, 1870-1876.*

Balch, F. V. *Report of the Case of the Steamship Meteor, Libelled for Alleged Violation of the Neutrality Acts.* Two volumes in one. Little, Brown, & Co., Boston, 1869.

Beaman, Charles C. *Chief Justice Waite—Memorial Before the Association of the City of New York.* 1890.

Catalogue of the Boston Latin School With an Historical Sketch, 1635-1885. Boston, 1886.

Catalogue of Connecticut Alpha of Phi Beta Kappa, August, 1838. New Haven, 1838.

Catalogue of the Officers and Students in Yale College, 1835-1836.

Catalogue of the Officers and Students in Yale College, 1836-1837.

Catalogue of the Officers and Students of the Law School of Harvard University, 1817-1887. Cambridge, 1888.

Celebration of the Sixty-Fourth Anniversary of the Birth of Gen. Ulysses S. Grant in the Metropolitan Church, Washington, D. C., Held Under the Auspices of Grant Memorial University, of Athens Tennessee, April 27, 1886. Washington, 1886.

Commemorative Celebration Held at Yale College, Wednesday, July 26, 1865. New Haven, 1866.

Constitution, Rules, Officers, and Members of the Union Club, 1875. New York, 1875.

Chamber of Commerce of the State of New York. One Hundred and Ninth Anniversary Banquet at Delmonico's, May 14, 1877. Toasts and Speeches. New York, 1877.

Correspondence Between the Spanish Minister and Secretary of the United States, in Regard to the Powers of the Spanish and American Commission, Under the Agreement of February 12, 1871, to enquire into the Citizenship of Native-Born Spanish Subjects claiming to be American Citizens by Naturalization.

Evarts, Sherman, ed. *Arguments and Speeches of William Maxwell Evarts.* Three volumes. Macmillan Company, New York, 1919.

Evarts, William M. *Address on the Victories of Protection.* Woodstock, Conn., 1888.

———. *Argument of Mr. Evarts Before the Judiciary Committee of the House of Representatives at Washington.* 1874.

———. *An Oration by William Maxwell Evarts, and a Poem, by Francis Miles Finch, Delivered Before the Linonian Society of Yale College, at its Centennial Anniversary. With an Account of the Celebration.* New Haven, 1853.

———. *An Oration Delivered Before the New England Society of the City of New York, in Celebration of the Two Hundred and Thirty-Fourth Anniversary of the Landing of the Pilgrims.* New York, 1855.

Fifty-Fourth Annual Report of the New England Society in the City of New York. New York, 1859.

Fifty-Sixth Annual Report of the New England Society in the City of New York. New York, 1861.

The Great Libel Case. Opdyke vs. Weed. A Full Report of Proceedings. New York, 1865.

Great Republican Speeches of the Campaign of 1880. Stapleton, New York, 1881.

Great Speech of Hon. William M. Evarts on Rapid Transit. New York, 1876.

Inauguration of the Statue of Liberty Enlightening the World by the President of the United States on Bedloe's Island, New York, Thursday, October 28, 1886. New York, 1887.

In Memory of Charles O'Conor. Report of A Meeting of the Bar of the Courts of the State and of the United States, for the Second Circuit, Held in the City of New York, on Friday, May 23d, 1884.

Letter-Missive, Statement, and Documents—The Brooklyn Council, 1874.

Meeting of the Yale Class of 1837 on June 27, 1877.

Minutes of the Organization and Proceedings of the New England Soldiers' Relief Association. New York, 1862.

Mixed Commission on British and American Claims. Claim No. 316. Cargo of Barque "Springbok." Correspondence between Mr. D. Forbes Campbell and the Foreign Office and between Mr. D. Forbes Campbell and Mr. Henry Howard.

The Opdyke Libel Suit. A Full Metrical, Juridical, and Analytical Report of the Extraordinary Suit For Libel of George Opdyke "versus" Thurlow Weed. New York, 1865.

The Parish Will Case. New York, 1864. Five volumes.

Papers Relating to the Condemnation of the British Barque "Springbok" and Her Cargo By the District Prize Court of New York, U. S., With the Opinions of the Press Thereon. London, 1864.

Proceedings and Debates of the Constitutional Convention of the State of New York, Held in 1867 and 1868 in the City of Albany. Albany, 1868. Five volumes.

Proceedings of the Great Mass Meeting Held at Cooper Institute, February 1, 1883. Document No. 2. American Association for the Protection of American Industry.

Proceedings of the Maryland Historical Society, in Connection With the Celebration of the One Hundred and Fiftieth Anniversary the Settlement of Baltimore, October 12, 1880. Baltimore, 1880.

Proceedings of the Republican National Convention, Held at Chicago, May 16, 17, & 18, 1860. Albany, 1860.

Proceedings of the Second Annual Dinner of the Republican Club Held at Delmonico's on the Seventy-Ninth Anniversary of the Birthday of Abraham Lincoln. New York, 1888.

Proceedings of the Special Meeting of the New York State Bar Association Held at the Academy of Music, New York, Thursday, 11th October, 1883, to Receive the Lord Chief Justice of England.

Proceedings of the Trustees of the Peabody Education Fund. Boston, 1875 and 1900. Volumes I to VI.

Proceedings of the Twentieth Anniversary of the Union League Club, February 6, 1883. New York, 1883.

Proceedings of the Union Meeting, Held at Castle Garden, October 30, 1850. New York, 1850.

Record of the Class of 1837 in Yale College, With Notices of Their Meetings in 1862 and 1867. New Haven, 1868.

Record of the Class of 1837 in Yale College, With a Notice of Their Meeting in 1872 and Personal or Biographical Notices of Each Member By the Secretary. New Haven, 1873.

Record of the Class of 1837 in Yale University, With A Notice of Their Meetings in 1877, 1882, 1887. Springfield, 1887.

Report of the Commission to Devise a Plan for the Government of Cities in the State of New York, Presented in the Legislature March 6, 1887. New York, 1877.

Report of the Proceedings at the Inauguration, Given by Mr. Cyrus W. Field, of New York, at the Palace Hotel, Buckingham Gate, on Friday, the 15th April, 1864. London, 1864.

Report on the Inter-State Commerce Bill, Pending in the United States Senate, by a Committee of the Chamber of Commerce of the State of New York. New York, 1887.

Reports of the Superintendent and Treasurer of the New England Soldiers' Relief Association, 194 Broadway, New York, November, 1863. New York, 1864.

Reports, Resolutions, and Documents of the Union Defense Committee of the Citizens of New York. New York, 1862.

Rowe, William V. *World Peace As Seen by William M. Evarts and Joseph H. Choate.* Reprint from *New York Herald,* October 31, 1920.

Seventy-Eight Anniversary Celebration of the New England Society in the City of New York at Delmonico's, December 22, 1883.

Silliman, B. *Records from 1837 to 1857, of the Class Graduated at Yale College in 1837, With A Notice of Their Fourth Meeting Held at Yale College, July 29, 1857.* New Haven, 1858.

Sixty-Fourth Anniversary Celebration of the New England Society in the City of New York at Delmonico's, December 22, 1869.

Some of the Papers Laid Before the Governor in Support of the Petition for the Commutation of the Sentence of William Foster to Imprisonment for Life.

Speech of the Hon. William M. Evarts, LL.D., U. S. Senator from New York, at the Seventh Annual Meeting of the Law and Order Society of Philadelphia, February 21st, 1888.

Statistics of the Class of 1837; from 1837 to 1850, With a Notice of Their Meeting at Yale College, August 15, 1850.

Stevens, John A., Jr. *Proceedings at the Mass Meeting of Loyal Citizens, in Union Square, New York, 15th Day of July, 1862.* New York, 1862.

———. *The Union Defence Committee of the City of New York, Minutes, Reports, and Correspondence, With an Historical Introduction.* New York, 1885.

Summary of Class Meetings and the Biographical Record of the Class of 1866. Yale University. Hartford, 1917.

Theodore Tilton vs. Henry Ward Beecher, Action for Crim. Con. tried in the City Court of Brooklyn. New York, 1874. Three volumes.

Trial of the Officers and Crew of the Privateer Savannah on the Charge of Piracy, in the United States Circuit Court for the Southern District of New York. New York, 1862.

Unveiling of the Seward Memorial Statue With the Oration by Hon. William M. Evarts, at Auburn, New York, November 15, 1888. Auburn, 1889.

Welcome to Goldwyn Smith, Regius Professor of Modern History in the University of Oxford, England, by Citizens of New York, Saturday, November 12, 1864. New York, 1864.

5. Articles in Periodicals

Albany Law Journal, March 19, 1887.

American Law Register, XVII (April, 1869).

American Law Review, July, 1871; January, October, 1872.

American Quarterly Register, November, 1831.

American Whig Review, X (July, 1849).

Baker, J. F. "James Topham Brady," *The Green Bag,* III (July, 1891), 305-309.

Baxter, James P., 3rd. "The British Government and Neutral Rights, 1861 to 1865," *American Historical Review,* XXXIV (1928).

Beale, Howard K. "The Diary of Edward Bates, 1859-1866," *Annual Report of the American Historical Association, 1930,* IV.

Beers, Henry A. "Yale College," *Scribner's Magazine,* April, 1876.

Bigelow, John. "Some Recollections of Charles O'Conor," *Century Magazine,* March, 1885.

Bonham, Milledge L. "New York and the Election of 1860," *New York History,* April, 1934.

Brandeis, Louis A. "The Harvard Law School," *The Green Bag,* I (January, 1889), 10-25.

Brigance, William N. "Jeremiah Black and Andrew Johnson," *The Mississippi Valley Historical Review,* XIX (September, 1932), 205-218.

Browne, Irving. "The New York Court of Appeals," *The Green Bag,* II (July, 1890), 277-291.

———. "David Dudley Field," *The Green Bag,* III (February, 1891), 49-55.

———. "Charles O'Conor," *The Green Bag,* VII (January, 1895), 1-12; VII (February, 1895), 85-89.

Brummer, Sidney D. "Political History of New York State During the Period of the Civil War," *Columbia University Studies in History, Economics and Public Law,* VIII, No. 3.

Carman, Harry J. "The Street Surface Railway Franchises of New York City," *Columbia University Studies in History, Economics and Public Law,* LXXXIX, No. 1.

Carpenter, Frank B. "How Lincoln Was Nominated," *Century Magazine,* January, 1882.

Carter, James C. "Memorial of William M. Evarts," Association of the Bar of the City of New York, *Report for 1902.*

Chittenden, L. E. "Legal Reminiscences," *The Green Bag,* V (July, 1893), 308.

Clyde, P. H. "Attitudes and Policies of George F. Seward, American Minister at Peking, 1876-1880," *Pacific Historical Review,* II (December, 1933), 387-404.

Coale, George B. "The Geneva Award and the Insurance Companies," *North American Review,* XXXIV (January, 1882), 76-96.

Cobb, John S. "Lord Coleridge," *The Green Bag,* VI (July, 1894), 305-308.

Daly, Charles B. "Charles O'Conor," *Magazine of American History,* XIII (June, 1885), 513-535.

Dana, Richard H., Jr. "The Present Aspect of International Law," *North American Review,* October, 1866.

———. "The Reasons for Not Prosecuting Jefferson Davis," *Proceedings of the Massachusetts Historical Society,* LIV (1930-1932), 201-209.

Dunning, William A. "The Impeachment and Trial of Andrew Johnson," *American Historical Association, Papers,* IV, Part IV, 145-177.

Emerson, Edward W. "John Murray Forbes," *Atlantic Monthly,* September, 1899.

Evarts, William M. "Mr. Webster's Position," *The New World,* October 2, 1841; "Mr. Tyler and the Whig Party," *The New World,* October 16, 1841.

Feipal, Louis N. "The Navy and Filibustering in the Fifties," *United States Naval Institute Proceedings,* XLIV, 1918.

Forum, LXXXVI (July, 1931) 56-64. "Captain Kidd and the Astor Fortune," anonymous.

Green Bag, The, II (1890), 156-157; IV (September, 1892), 401-402; VIII (1896), 382; IX (February, 1897), 49-54; XIII (October, 1901), 500; XV (August, 1903).

Hackett, Charles W. "The Recognition of the Diaz Government by the United States," *The Southwestern Historical Quarterly,* XXVIII (July, 1924).

Hale, Charles. "The Consular System of the United States," *North American Review,* CXXII (April, 1876), 309-337.

Hall, A. Oakey. "Ogden Hoffman," *The Green Bag,* V (July, 1893), 297-300.

———. "Reminiscences of David Dudley Field," *The Green Bag,* VI (May, 1894), 209-213.

———. "The Ghost of Nisi Prius," *The Green Bag,* VII (July, 1895), 346-347.

———. "William M. Evarts," *The Green Bag,* VIII (1896), 93-99.

Harper's Weekly. Miscellaneous articles between the years 1868 and 1879.

Henderson, John B. "Emancipation and Impeachment," *Century Magazine,* LXXX (December, 1912), 196-209.

Holcombe, Chester. "The Restriction of Chinese Immigration," *Outlook,* LXXVI (April 23, 1904), 971-977.

Howe, George F. Extracts from the Hayes Papers. *American Historical Review,* January, 1932.

———. "The New York Custom-House Controversy, 1877-1879," *The Mississippi Valley Historical Review,* XVIII (December, 1931), 350-363.

Hunt, Gaillard. "The President's Defense: His Side of the Case as Told by His Correspondence," *Century Magazine,* LXXXV (1913), 422-434.

Illustrated Pilgrim Memorial, The, 1866.

Ingalls, John J. "The Stormy Days of the Electoral Commission," *Saturday Evening Post,* March 24, 1900.

Jones, Francis R. "Morrison Remick Waite," *The Green Bag,* XIV (June, 1902), 257-262.

Kiger, John H. "Federal Government Propaganda in Great Britain During the American Civil War," *The Historical Outlook,* XIX (May, 1928), 204-209.

Knickerbocker, The. January, 1839, "The Civil Administration of Justice." December, 1856, "American Student Life."

Leech, A. G. "The Doctrine of Continuous Voyage," *The Journal of the United Service Institution,* December, 1902.

Lewis, William R. "The Hayes Administration and Mexico," *The Southwestern Historical Quarterly,* XXIV (October, 1920).

London *Pump Court,* August, 1883.

Lowry, G. P. "John K. Porter," *The Green Bag,* IV (August, 1892), 353-367.

McGrath, P. T. "The Atlantic Fisheries Question," *Atlantic Monthly,* (December, 1902), 741-748.

Magazine of American History, XXVII (February, 1892). Article on the Electoral Commission.

Marsh, Allen. Article on the Olmsted-Astor case, *Liberty,* February 24, March 3, 10, 1934.

Moore, W. G. "Notes of Col. W. G. Moore, Private Secretary to President Johnson, 1866-1868," *American Historical Review,* XIX (1913), 98-132.

Nation (New York), *The.* Miscellaneous articles between the years 1868 and 1885.

New England Historical and Genealogical Register, January, 1907.

Nichols, Roy F. "United States vs. Jefferson Davis, 1865-1869," *American Historical Review,* XXXI (1926), 266-284.

Paullin, C. O. "The Opening of Korea by Commodore Schufeldt," *Political Science Quarterly,* XXV (September, 1910), 470-499.

Perez, L. M. "Lopez Expeditions to Cuba, 1850-1851," *Publications of the Southern History Association,* X (1906), 345-362.

Proceedings of the Massachusetts Historical Society, XLVIII (October, 1914 to June, 1915). Extracts from the Diary of Benjamin Moran.

Russell, Horace. "William Augustus Beach," *The Green Bag,* II (December, 1890), 509-521.

Schofield, John M. "Controversies in the War Department," *Century Magazine* (August, 1897).

Sears, E. S. "Charles O'Conor," *North American Review,* June, 1865.

Shores, Venilla L. "The Hayes-Conkling Controversy, 1877-1879," *Smith College Studies in History,* IV (1919), No. 4.

Stark, Francis R. "The Abolition of Privateering and the Declaration of Paris," *Columbia University Studies in History, Economics and Public Law,* XXXIX, No. 2.

Stebbins, Homer A. "A Political History of the State of New York, 1865-1869," *Columbia University Studies in History, Economics and Public Law,* LV, No. 1.

Tansill, Charles C. "The Canadian Reciprocity Treaty of 1854," *Johns Hopkins University Studies in Historical and Political Science,* XL, No. 2.

Thomas, Harrison C. "The Return of the Democratic Party to Power," *Columbia University Studies in History, Economics and Public Law,* LXXXIX, 184-261.

Thompson, Isaac G. "Three Great Advocates," *Albany Law Journal,* XII (July 3, 1875).

Todd, William C. "Caleb Cushing," *The Green Bag,* IV (January, 1892), 1-13.

Walsh, J. C. "Charles O'Conor," *Journal of the American Irish Historical Society,* XXVII (1928), 285-313.

Wilkinson, William C. "That Famous Hole in the Sky," *Independent* (July 18, 1907).

Wingate, Charles F. "An Episode in Municipal Government," *North American Review* (July, 1875); "The Judiciary of New York City," (July, 1876); "The Shattering of the Ring," (October, 1872).

Yale Literary Magazine, The, Volumes I and II (1836-1837).

Yale Review, The, October, 1920.

6. Newspapers

Extensively used:

New York Herald, 1842 to 1901.

New York Times, 1852 to 1901.

New York Tribune, 1842 to 1903.

Scrap-Book of Newspaper Clippings on the Tilton-Beecher Scandal. 8 vols. New York Library.

Incidentally used:

Albany Evening Journal
Boston Daily Globe
Boston Statesman
Brooklyn Eagle
Cincinnati Daily Gazette
English Independent
Independent
London Daily Telegraph
London Times
Milwaukee Sentinel
Morning Courier and New York Enquirer
National Baptist.
New York Daily Graphic.
New York Evening Mail
New York Evening Post
New York Commercial Advertiser
New York Sun
New York Trade Reporter
New York World
San Francisco Evening Evening Bulletin
St. Louis Republican
Toronto Mail
Utica Daily Observer
Utica Morning Herald
Vermont Journal

7. Autobiographies and Memoirs

Adams, Henry. *The Education of Henry Adams, An Autobiography.* Boston and New York, Houghton Mifflin Company, 1930.

Adams, James T. *Henry Adams.* New York, Albert and Charles Boni, 1933.

Angell, James B. *Reminiscences of James Burrill Angell.* New York, Longmans, Green and Company, 1912.

Baker, George E. *The Works of William H. Seward.* 5 vols. Boston, Houghton, Mifflin & Company, 1884.

Baldwin, Simeon E. *Life and Letters of Simeon Baldwin.* New Haven, Tuttle, Morehouse and Taylor, 1919.

Bigelow, John. *Retrospections of An Active Life.* New York, Baker and Taylor Company, 1909. 3 vols; Vols. IV and V, Garden City, Doubleday Page & Company, 1913.

Bishop, Joseph B. *Notes and Anecdotes of Many Years.* New York, Charles Scribner's Sons, 1925.

Blaine, James G. *Political Discussions: Legislative, Diplomatic, and Popular, 1856-1886.* Norwich, Conn., H. Bill Publishing Company, 1887.

——. *Twenty Years of Congress.* 2 vols. Norwich, Conn., 1884.

Boutwell, George S. *Reminiscences of Sixty Years in Public Affairs.* McClure. 2 vols. New York, Phillips and Company, 1902.

Bowen, Henry C. *Recollections Diplomatic and Undiplomatic.* New York, Frederick H. Hitchcock, 1926.

Browning,. Orville H. *Diary of Orville Hickman Browning.* 2 vols. of the Illinois State Historical Society, Vols. XX, XXII, 1925-1933.

Butler, Benjamin F. *Autobiography and Personal Reminiscences of Benjamin F. Butler.* Boston, 1892.

Butler, William A. *A Retrospect of Forty Years, 1825-1865.* New York, Charles Scribner's Sons, 1911.

Coleman, Mrs. Chapman. *The Life of John J. Crittenden, With Selections From His Correspondence and Speeches.* 2 vols. Philadelphia, J. B. Lippincott & Company, 1871.

Conkling, Alfred R. *The Life and Letters of Roscoe Conkling.* New York, Charles L. Webster and Company, 1889.

Cullom, Shelby M. *Fifty Years of Public Service.* Chicago, A. C. McClure and Company, 1911.

Curtis, Benjamin R. *A Memoir of Benjamin Robbins Curtis, LL.D. With Some of his Professional and Miscellaneous Writings.* Boston, 1897.

Davis, J. C. Bancroft. *Mr. Fish and the Alabama Claims. A Chapter in Diplomatic History.* Boston and New York, Houghton, Mifflin & Company, 1893.

Depew, Chauncey. *My Memories of Eighty Years.* New York, Charles Scribner's Sons, 1922.

Dix, Morgan. *Memoirs of John A. Dix.* 2 vols. New York, Harper & Brothers, 1883.

Dougherty, J. Hampden. *William M. Evarts, Lawyer and Statesman.* An address read before the Law Department of Brooklyn Institute, October 28, 1901.

Foraker, Joseph B. *Notes of A Busy Life.* 2 vols. Cincinnati, 1916.

Forbes, Robert B. *Personal Reminiscences.* Boston, Little, Brown, and Company, 1878.

Ford, Worthington C. *A Cycle of Adams Letters, 1861-1865.* 2 vols. Boston and New York, Houghton, Mifflin & Company, 1920.

———. *Letters of Henry Adams, 1858-1891.* Boston and New York, Houghton, Mifflin & Company, 1930.

Foster, John W. *Diplomatic Memoirs.* New York, Houghton, Mifflin & Company, 1909.

Gerry, Margarita S. *Through Five Administrations, Reminiscences of Colonel William H. Crook.* New York and London, Harper and Brothers, 1910.

Gouverneur, Marian. *As I Remember.* New York and London, D. Appleton & Company, 1911.

Greeley, Horace. *Recollections of a Busy Life.* New York, J. B. Ford and Company (Boston, H. H. Brown and Company), 1868.

Hackett, Frank W. *Reminiscences of the Geneva Tribunal of Arbitration, 1872: The Alabama Claims.* Boston and New York, Houghton, Mifflin & Co., 1911.

Hamilton, Gail. *Life and Letters.* 2 vols. Boston, Lee and Shepard, 1901.

Hayes, Rutherford B. *Diary and Letters of Rutherford Birchard Hayes.* 5 vols. Ohio State Archeological and Historical Society, 1922-1926.

Hoar, George F. *Autobiography of Seventy Years.* 2 vols. New York, Charles Scribner's Sons, 1903.

Holland, Sir Henry. *Recollections of Past Life.* London, Longmans, Green, and Company, 1872.

Holt, Henry. *Garrulities of An Octogenarian Editor.* Boston and New York, Houghton, Mifflin Company, 1923.

Hone, Philip, Memoirs of, Vol. XIX. (No publication facts.)

Hudson, William C. *Random Recollections of an Old Political Reporter.* New York, Cupples and Leon Company, 1911.

Hughes, Sarah F. *Letters and Recollections of John Murray Forbes.* 2 vols. Boston and New York, Houghton, Mifflin & Company, 1899.

Johnson, Robert U. *Remembered Yesterdays.* Boston, Little, Brown, and Company, 1923.

Lodge, Henry C. *Early Memories.* New York, Charles Scribner's Sons, 1913.

Merritt, Edwin A. *Recollections, 1828-1911.* Albany, 1911.

Morse, Edward L. *Samuel F. B. Morse, His Letters and Journals.* 2 vols. Boston and New York, Houghton, Mifflin & Company, 1914.

Nevins, Allan. *The Diary of Philip Hone, 1828-1851.* 2 vols. New York, Dodd, Mead and Company, 1927.

Palmer, Sir Roundell. *Memorials, Personal and Political, 1865-1895.* 2 vols. London, The Macmillan Company, 1898.

Platt, Thomas C. *The Autobiography of Thomas Collier Platt.* New York, B. W. Dodge and Company, 1910.

Rowland, Dunbar. *Jefferson Davis, Constitutionalist, His Letters, Papers, and Speeches.* Mississippi Department of Archives and History. Jackson, Mississippi, 1923. Volume VII.

Saint-Gaudens, Homer. *The Reminiscences of Augustus St. Gaudens.* 2 vols. New York, The Century Company, 1913.

Schofield, John M. *Forty-Six Years in the Army.* New York, The Century Company, 1897.

Schurz, Carl. *Speeches, Correspondence, and Political Papers of Carl Schurz.* 6 vols. New York and London, G. P. Putnam's Sons, 1913.

Seward, Frederick W. *Reminiscences of a War Time Statesman and Diplomat.* New York and London, G. P. Putnam's Sons, 1915.

Sherman, John. *Recollections of Forty Years.* 2 vols. New York, The Werner Company, 1895.

Spencer, Herbert. *Autobiography.* 2 vols. New York, D. Appleton and Company, 1904.

Spring, Gardiner. *A Tribute to the Memory of Jeremiah Evarts, Esq.* New York, 1831.

Stanton, Henry B. *Random Recollections.* New York, Harper and Brothers, 1887.

Stetson, Francis L. *Joseph Hodges Choate.* Memorial read at Saratoga, September 4, 1917, at the request of the Committee of Obituraries.

Story, W. W. *Life and Letters of Joseph Story.* 2 vols. Boston, 1851.

Strong, Theron G. *Landmarks of A Lawyer's Lifetime.* New York, Dodd, Mead, and Company, 1914.

Theron, Ward. *The Letters of Mrs. Henry Adams.* Boston, Little, Brown, and Company, 1936.

Villard, Henry. *Memoirs of Henry Villard, Journalist and Financier, 1835-1900.* 2 vols. Boston and New York, Houghton, Mifflin & Company, 1904.

Watterson, Henry. *"Marse Henry," An Autobiography.* 2 vols. New York, George H. Doran Company, 1919.

Weed, Thurlow. *Autobiography of Thurlow Weed.* 2 vols. Boston, Houghton, Mifflin & Company, 1883.

Welles, Gideon. *Diary of Gideon Welles.* 3 vols. Boston and New York, Houghton, Mifflin Company, 1911

White, Andrew D. *Autobiography of Andrew D. White.* 2 vols. New York, The Century Company, 1905.

Woods, Leonard. *Sermon of Rev. Leonard Woods on the Death of Jeremiah Evarts.* Andover, 1831.

8. Biographies

Abbott, Lyman. *Henry Ward Beecher.* Boston and New York, Houghton, Mifflin & Company, 1903.

Adams, Charles F. *The Memorial Address of Charles Francis Adams, of Massachusetts, on the Life, Character, and Services of William H. Seward. Delivered by Invitation of the Legislature of New York, in Albany, April 18, 1873.* New York, 1873.

———. *Charles Francis Adams.* Boston and New York, Houghton, Mifflin & Company, 1900.

———. *Richard Henry Dana, a Biography.* 2 vols. Boston and New York, Houghton, Mifflin & Company, 1890.

Adler, Selig. *The Senatorial Career of George Franklin Edmunds, 1866-1891.* Urbana, Illinois, 1934.

Alexander, De Alva S. *Four Famous New Yorkers.* New York, Henry Holt and Company, 1923.

Bancroft, Frederic. *The Life of William H. Seward.* 2 vols. New York and London, Harper and Brothers, 1900.

Barnes, Thurlow W. *Memoir of Thurlow Weed.* Boston, Houghton, Mifflin & Company, 1884.

Beatty, Richard C. *Bayard Taylor.* Norman, Okla., University of Oklahoma Press, 1936.

Beecher, William C., and Scoville, Samuel. *A Biography of Rev. Henry Ward Beecher.* New York, Charles L. Webster Company, 1888.

Bigelow, John. *The Life of Samuel J. Tilden.* 2 vols. New York, Harper Brothers, 1895.

Brereton, Austin. *The Life of Henry Irving.* 2 vols. New York, Longmans, Green, and Company, 1908.

Caldwell, Robert G. *James A. Garfield, Party Chieftain.* New York, Dodd, Mead and Company, 1931.

Cary, Edward. *George William Curtis.* New York and Boston, Houghton, Mifflin & Company, 1894.

Chidsey, D. B. *The Gentleman From New York: Life of Roscoe Conkling.* New Haven, Yale University Press, 1935.

Coleridge, Ernest H. *Life and Correspondence fo John Duke Lord Coleridge, Lord Chief Justice of England.* 2 vols. New York, D. Appleton Company, 1904.

Cortissoz, Royal. *The Life of Whitelaw Reid.* 2 vols. New York, Charles Scribner's Sons, 1921.

Coulter, E. Merton. *William G. Brownlow.* Chapel Hill, N. C., University of North Carolina Press, 1937.

Dennett, Tyler. *John Hay.* New York, Dodd, Mead and Company, 1934.

Dyer, Brainerd. *The Public Career of William M. Evarts.* Berkeley, Cal., University of California Press, 1933.

Eckenrode, H. J. *Rutherford B. Hayes, Statesman of Reunion.* New York, Dodd, Mead and Company, 1930.

Fessenden, Francis. *Life and Public Services of William Pitt Fessenden.* 2 vols. Boston and New York, Houghton, Mifflin & Company, 1907.

Feuss, Claude M. *Carl Schurz, Reformer.* New York, Dodd, Mead and Company, 1932.

———. *The Life of Caleb Cushing.* 2 vols. New York, Harcourt, Brace and Company, 1923.

Field, Henry M. *The Life of David Dudley Field.* New York, Charles Scribner's Sons, 1898.

Fisher, Samuel W. *William Curtis Noyes.* Utica, New York, 1865.

Fitzmaurice, Lord Edmund. *The Life of Granville George-Gower, Second Earl of Granville.* 2 vols. London, Longmans, Green and Company, 1905.

Foulke, William D. *Life of Oliver P. Morton, Including His Important Speeches.* 2 vols. Indianapolis, The Bowen-Merrill Company, 1899.

Gillett, Frederick H. *George Frisbee Hoar.* Boston and New York, Houghton, Mifflin Company, 1934.

Godwin, Parke. *A Biography of William Cullen Bryant, With Extracts From His Private Correspondence.* 2 vols. New York, D. Appleton and Company, 1883.

Gorham, George C. *Life and Services of Edwin M. Stanton.* 2 vols. Boston and New York, Houghton, Mifflin & Company, 1899.

Greenslet, F. *James Russell Lowell.* Boston and New York, Houghton, Mifflin Company, 1905.

Hagan, Horace H. *Eight Great American Lawyers.* Oklahoma City, Harlow Publishing Company, 1923.

Hale, E. E. *A New England Boyhood.* Boston, Little, Brown, and Company, 1928.

Hart, Albert B. *Salmon Portland Chase.* Boston and New York, Houghton, Mifflin & Company, 1899.

Hibben, Paxton. *Henry Ward Beecher: An American Portrait.* New York, George H. Doran Company, 1927.

Hobson, John A. *Richard Cobden, the International Man.* New York, Henry Holt and Company, 1919.

Howe, George F. *Chester A. Arthur.* New York, Dodd, Mead and Company, 1934.

Howe, M. A. DeWolfe. *Life and Letters of George Bancroft.* 2 vols. New York, Charles Scribner's Sons, 1908.

———. *Portrait of An Independent: Moorfield Storey, 1845-1929.* Boston and New York, Houghton, Mifflin & Company, 1932.

Jessup, Philip C. *Elihu Root.* 2 vols. New York, Dodd, Mead and Company, 1938.

Knox, T. W. *Life and Work of Henry Ward Beecher.* Hartford, Hartford Publishing Company, 1887.

Lewis, William D. *Great American Lawyers.* 8 vols. Philadelphia, The John C. Winston Company, 1907-1909.

McCall, Samuel W. *Thaddeus Stevens.* New York, Houghton, Mifflin & Company, 1899.

McElroy, Robert. *Levi Parsons Morton.* New York and London, G. P. Putnam's Sons, 1930.

Martin, Edward S. *The Life of Joseph Hodges Choate.* 2 vols. New York, Charles Scribner's Sons, 1920.

Merriam, George S. *The Life and Times of Samuel Bowles.* 2 vols. New York, The Century Company, 1885.

Muzzey, David S. *James G. Blaine.* New York, Dodd, Mead and Company, 1934.

Nevins, Allan. *Abram S. Hewitt With Some Account of Peter Cooper.* New York and London, Harper and Brothers, 1935.

———. *Grover Cleveland, A Study in Courage.* New York, Dodd, Mead and Company, 1932.

———. *Frémont, the West's Great Adventurer.* 2 vols. New York and London, Harper and Brothers, 1928.

———. *Hamilton Fish.* New York, Dodd, Mead and Company, 1936.

Oberholtzer, Ellis P. *Jay Cooke, Financier of The Civil War.* 3 vols. Philadelphia, George W. Jacobs and Company, 1907.

Ogg, Frederic. *Daniel Webster.* Philadelphia, George W. Jacobs and Company, 1914.

Perry, Bliss. *Richard Henry Dana, 1851-1931.* Boston and New York, Houghton, Mifflin & Company, 1933.

Pierce, Edward L. *Memoir and Letters of Charles Sumner.* 4 vols. Boston, Roberts Brothers, 1894.

Proctor, L. B. *The Bench and Bar of New York.* New York, Diossy & Company, 1870.

Pyle, Joseph G. *The Life of James J. Hill.* 2 vols. Toronto, 1936.

Reid, T. Wemyss. *Life of the Right Honourable William Edward Forster.* 2 vols. London, Chapman and Hall, 1888.

Robins, Edward. *William T. Sherman.* Philadelphia, George W. Jacobs and Company, 1905.

Salter, W. *The Life of James W. Grimes.* New York, D. Appleton and Company, 1876.

Scott, Henry W. *Distinguished American Lawyers.* New York, Charles L. Webster and Company, 1891.

Scudder, Horace E. *James Russell Lowell.* 2 vols. New York, Houghton, Mifflin and Company, 1901.

Sears, Lorenzo. *John Hay: Author and Statesman.* New York, Dodd, Mead and Company, 1914.

Seitz, Don C. *Horace Greeley.* Indianapolis, Bobbs-Merrill Company, 1926.

Seward, Frederick W. *Seward at Washington As Senator and Secretary of State.* 3 vols. New York, Derby and Miller, 1891.

Smith, Theodore C. *The Life and Letters of James Abram Garfield.* 2 vols. New Haven, Yale University Press, 1925.

Smith, William E. *The Francis Preston Blair Family in Politics.* 2 vols. New York, The Macmillan Company, 1933.

Smyth, Albert H. *Bayard Taylor.* Boston and New York, Houghton, Mifflin and Company, 1896.

Starr, Harris E. *William Graham Sumner.* New York, Henry Holt and Company, 1925.

Stephenson, Nathaniel W. *Nelson W. Aldrich.* New York, Charles Scribner's Sons, 1930.

Stokes, Anson P. *Memorials of Eminent Yale Men.* 2 vols. New Haven, Yale University Press, 1914.

Storey, Moorfield, and Emerson, Edward D. *Ebenezer Rockwood Hoar.* Boston and New York, 1911.

Strong, Theron G. *Joseph H. Choate.* New York, Dodd, Mead and Company, 1917.

Stryker, Lloyd P. *Andrew Johnson—A Study in Courage.* New York, The Macmillan Company, 1930.

Thayer, William R. *Life and Letters of John Hay.* Boston, Houghton, Mifflin Company, 1915.

Tracy, E. C. *Memoir of the Life of Jeremiah Evarts, Esq.* Boston, Crocker and Brewster, 1845.

Trimble, B. R. *Chief Justice Waite.* Princeton University Press, 1938.

Walpole, Spencer. *The Life of Lord John Russell.* 2 vols. London and New York, Longmans, Green and Company, 1889.

Wells, Georgiana B. *Life and Career of Samuel Rossiter Betts.* New York, Maurice Slogg, 1934.

White, Horace. *The Life of Lyman Trumbull.* Boston and New York, Houghton, Mifflin and Company, 1913.

Williams, Charles R. *The Life of Rutherford Birchard Hayes.* 2 vols. Boston, Houghton, Mifflin & Company, 1914.

Yeager, Willard H. *Chauncey Mitchill Depew.* Washington, D. C. The George Washington University Press, 1934.

9. Other Secondary Works

Adams, Charles F. *Studies Military and Diplomatic.* New York, The Macmillan Company, 1911.

Adams, Ephraim D. *Great Britain and the American Civil War.* 2 vols. London, Longmans, Green and Company, 1925.

Alexander, De Alva S. *A Political History of the State of New York.* 3 vols. New York, Henry Holt & Company, 1906-1909.

Allen, Walter. *Governor Chamberlain's Administration in South Carolina.* New York and London, G. P. Putnam's Sons, 1888.

Atherly-Jones, L. A., and Bellot, H. H. L. *Commerce in War.* New York, D. Appleton and Company, 1907.

Bagg, L. H. *Four Years at Yale.* New Haven, 1871.

Balch, Thomas W. *The Alabama Arbitration.* Philadelphia, 1900.

Baldwin, Ebenezer. *Annals of Yale College.* New Haven, 1838.

Barrett, Walter. *The Old Merchants of New York City.* 5 vols. New York, Thos. R. Knox & Co., 1885.

Beaman, Charles C. *The National and Private "Alabama Claims" and Their Final and Amicable Settlement.* Washington, 1871.

Beckley, Hosea. *The History of Vermont.* Brattleboro, 1846.

Belden, Ezekiel P. *Sketches of Yale College.* New York, Saxton and Miles, 1843.

Bellows, Henry W. *Historical Sketch of the Union League of New York, . . . 1863-1879.* New York, 1879.

Bemis, Samuel F. *The American Secretaries of State and Their Diplomacy.* New York, Alfred A. Knopf, 1928. Vol. VII.

———. *A Diplomatic History of the United States.* New York, Henry Holt and Company, 1936.

Bernard, Montague. *A Historical Account of the Neutrality of Great Britain During the American Civil War.* London, Longmans, Green and Company, 1870.

Bishop, Joseph B. *A Chronicle of One Hundred and Fifty Years: The Chamber of Commerce of the State of New York, 1768-1918.* New York, Charles Scribner's Sons, 1918.

Bowers, Claude G. *The Tragic Era.* Boston and New York, Houghton Mifflin Company, 1929.

Bowker, Richard R. *Copyright, Its History and Its Law.* Boston and New York, Houghton Mifflin & Company, 1912.

Boyd, T. B. *The Blaine and Logan Campaign of 1884.* Chicago, 1884.

Brainerd, Cephas and Eveline W. *New England Society Orations.* New York, The Century Company, 1901.

Breen, Matthew P. *Thirty Years of New York Politics.* New York, 1899.

Caldwell, Robert G. *The Lopez Expeditions to Cuba, 1848-1851*. Princeton, The Princeton University Press, 1915.

Callahan, James M. *American Foreign Policy in Canadian Relations*. New York, The Macmillan Company, 1937.

———. *American Foreign Policy in Mexican Relations*. New York, The Macmillan Company, 1932.

———. *Cuba and International Relations*. Baltimore, The Johns Hopkins Press, 1899.

Callender, James H. *Yesterdays in Little Old New York*. New York, Dorland Press, 1929.

Carson, Hampton L. *The History of the Supreme Court of the United States*. 2 vols. Philadelphia, 1902.

Carver, R. *History of Boston*. Boston, 1834.

Centennial Memorial of Windsor, Vermont, July 4, 1876.

Chadwick, French E. *The Relations of the United States and Spain, Diplomacy*. New York, Charles Scribner's Sons, 1909.

Chapman, Charles E. *A History of the Cuban Republic*. New York, The Macmillan Company, 1927.

Chester, Alden. *Courts and Lawyers of New York*. 3 vols. New York and Chicago, The American Historical Society, 1925.

———. *Legal and Judicial History of New York*. 3 vols. National Americana Society, 1911.

Choate, Joseph. *American Addresses*. New York, Century Company, 1911.

Clews, Henry. *Fifty Years of Wall Street*. New York, 1908.

Colman, Edna M. *White House Gossip, From Andrew Johnson to Calvin Coolidge*. Garden City, New York, Doubleday, Page and Company, 1927.

Colombos, Constantine J. *A Treatise on the Law of Prize*. London, Sweet and Maxwell, 1926.

Cox, Samuel S. *Three Decades of Federal Legislation, 1855-1885*. Providence, J. A. and R. A. Reid, 1886.

Crawford, Lewis A. *A History of North Dakota*. 3 vols. The American Historical Society, Chicago and New York, 1931.

Cushing, Caleb. *The Treaty of Washington*. New York, Harper Brothers, 1873.

Demarest, Theodore F. C. *The Rise and Growth of Elevated Railroad Law*. New York, 1894.

Dennett, Tyler. *Americans in Eastern Asia*. New York, The Macmillan Company, 1922.

De Voe, Thomas F. *The Market Book*. 2 vols. New York, 1862.

De Witt, David M. *The Impeachment and Trial of Andrew Johnson*. New York, The Macmillan Company, 1903.

Eaton, Dorman B. *The Independent Movement in New York*. New York, G. P. Putnam's Sons, 1880.

———. *The "Spoils" System and Civil Service Reform in the Custom-House and Post-Office at New York*. New York, G. P. Putnam's Sons, 1882.

Edwards, Charles. *Pleasantries About Courts and Lawyers of New York*. New York, Richardson and Company, 1867.

Eliot, Ellsworth. *Yale in the Civil War*. New Haven, Yale University Press, 1932.

Evans, Henry C. *Chile and Its Relations With the United States*. Durham, N. C., Duke University Press, 1927.

Fairchild, Rev. Edmund B. *Wickedness in High Places—A Review of the Beecher Case*. Mansfield, Ohio, 1874.

Fenwick, Charles G. *The Neutrality of the United States*. Washington, D. C., 1913.

Folwell, William W. *A History of Minnesota*. 4 vols. Minnesota Historical Society, St. Paul, 1926.

Foster, J. W. *American Diplomacy in the Orient*. Boston and New York, Houghton, Mifflin & Company, 1903.

Frankfurter, Felix, and Landis, James M. *The Business of the Supreme Court*. New York, The Macmillan Company, 1927.

Gessner, Louis. *A Juridical Review of the Case of the British Barque "Springbok."*

Gibson, A. M. *A Political Crime: the History of a Great Fraud*. New York, Wm. S. Gottsberger, 1885.

Gosnell, Harold S. *Boss Platt and His New York Machine*. Chicago, The University of Chicago Press, 1924.

Hall, William E. *A Treatise on International Law*. London, 1917.

Halstead, Murat. *A History of the National Political Conventions of the Current Presidential Campaign*. Columbus, Ohio, 1860.

Haworth, Paul L. *The Hayes-Tilden Disputed Presidential Election of 1876*. Cleveland, Burrows Brothers Company, 1906.

Hicks, Frederic C. *Arguments and Addresses of Joseph H. Choate*. St. Paul, West Publishing Company, 1926.

———. *High Finance in the Sixties*. New Haven, Yale University Press, 1929.

Hill, Frederick T. *Decisive Battles of the Law*. New York, Harper Brothers, 1907.

Hunt, Gaillard. *The Department of State: Its History and Functions*. New Haven, Yale University Press, 1914.

Hurlburt, William H. *Meddling and Muddling—Mr. Blaine's Foreign Policy*. 1884.

Hyde, Charles C. *International Law Chiefly as Interpreted and Applied by the United States*. 2 vols. Boston, Little, Brown and Company, 1922.

Jay, John. *The Fisheries Dispute—A Suggestion For Its Adjustment by Abrogating the Convention of 1818, and Resting on the Rights and Liberties Defined in the Treaty of 1783*. New York, Dodd, Mead and Company, 1887.

Jenkins, Stephen. *The Greatest Street in the World*. New York and London, G. P. Putnam's Sons, 1911.

Jones, Chester L. *The Consular Service of the United States*. Philadelphia, 1906.

Leslie's History of Greater New York. 2 vols. New York, Arkell Publishing Company, 1898.

Life and Adventures of the Accomplished Forger and Swindler Colonel Monroe Edwards. New York, H. Long & Brother, 1849.

Lincoln, Charles L. *Constitutional History of New York*. 5 vols. Rochester, New York, 1905.

Lonn, Ella. *Reconstruction in Louisiana after 1868*. New York, G. P. Putnam's Sons, 1918.

Lossing, Benson J. *History of the City of New York*. 2 vols. New York, The Perine Engraving and Publishing Company, 1884.

McAdam, David, and others. *History of the Bench and Bar of New York*. 2 vols. New York, New York Historical Company, 1897.

Maycock, Willoughby. *With Mr. Chamberlain in the United States and Canada*. London, Chatto and Windus, 1914.

Memorial Biographies of the New England Historic Genealogical Society. Boston, 1883. Volume III.

Miller, Marion M. *Great Debates in American History.* 14 vols. New York, 1913.

Milton, George F. *The Age of Hate; Andrew Johnson and the Radicals.* New York, Coward-McCann, 1930.

Mott, Edward H. *Between Ocean and Lakes: The Story of Erie.* New York, Tucker Publishing Company, 1908.

Myers, Gustavus. *The History of Tammany Hall.* New York, 1901.

New York State Historical Association. *History of the State of New York.* New York, Columbia University Press, 1934. Vols. VI and VII.

Oberholtzer, Ellis P. *A History of the United States Since the Civil War.* 4 vols. New York, The Macmillan Company, 1917.

O'Conor, Charles. *Peculation Triumphant, Being the Record of a Four Years Campaign Against Official Malversation in the City of New York, 1871-1875.* New York, 1875.

Parks, E. Taylor. *Colombia and the United States, 1765-1934.* Durham, N. C., Duke University Press, 1935.

Phelps, Henry R. *The Albany Hand-Book.* Albany, 1884.

Proctor, L. B. *Lawyer and Client.* New York, S. S. Peloubet & Co., 1883

Randall, James G. *The Civil War and Reconstruction.* New York, D. C. Heath and Company, 1937.

———. *Constitutional Problems Under Lincoln.* New York, D. Appleton and Company, 1926.

Reeves, William T. *The First Elevated Railroads in Manhattan and the Bronx of the City of New York.* New York, The New York Historical Society, 1936.

Rhodes, James F. *History of the United States From the Compromise of 1850.* 7 vols. New York, The Macmillan Company, 1893-1906.

Rippy, J. Fred. *The United States and Mexico.* New York, Alfred A. Knopf, 1926.

Robinson, William M. *The Confederate Privateers.* New Haven, Yale University Press, 1928.

Rourke, Constance M. *Trumpets of Jubilee.* New York, Harcourt, Brace, and Company, 1927.

Ryden, George H. *The Foreign Policy of the United States in Relation to Samoa.* New Haven, Yale University Press, 1933.

Schouler, James. *History of the United States of America.* New York, Dodd, Mead and Company, 1899.

Seitz, Don C. *The Dreadful Decade.* Indianapolis, The Bobbs-Merrill Company, 1926.

Sherman, Thomas T. *Sherman Genealogy.* New York, Tobias and Wright, 1920.

Simkins, F. B., and Woody, R. H. *South Carolina During Reconstruction.* Chapel Hill, N. C., The University of North Carolina Press, 1932.

Smith, Matthew H. *Sunshine and Shadow.* Hartford, J. B. Burr and Company, 1868.

Stanwood, Edward. *A History of the Presidency from 1788 to 1897.* 2 vols. Boston and New York, Houghton Mifflin Company, 1928.

Stone, R. C. *The Statue of Liberty Enlightening the World.* New York, Bullion Publishing Company, 1887.

Stowe, Lyman B. *Saints, Sinners, and Beechers.* Indianapolis, The Bobbs-Merrill Company, 1934.

Stowell, Ellery C., and Munro, Henry F. *International Cases.* Boston and New York, Houghton, Mifflin Company, 1916.

Strobel, Edward H. *Mr. Blaine and His Foreign Policy.* Boston, 1884.

Taussig, F. W. *Tariff History of the United States.* New York and London, G. P. Putnam's Sons, 1892.

Thacher, Thomas. *Yale In Its Relation to Law, An Address Delivered at the Bi-Centennial Celebration at New Haven, October 21, 1901.*

Thorndike, Ashley H. *Modern Eloquence. A Library of the World's Best Spoken Thought.* 15 vols. 1928.

Tilden, Samuel J. *The New York City "Ring"; Its Origin, Maturity, and Fall.* New York, 1873.

Tucker, William W. *His Royal Highness Prince Oscar at the National Celebration of the Centennial Anniversary of American Independence.* Boston, 1876.

Twiss, Sir Travers. *The Doctrine of Continuous Voyages, As Applied to Contraband of War and Blockade, Contrasted With the Declaration of Paris of 1856.* London, 1877.

Tyler, Alice F. *The Foreign Policy of James G. Blaine.* Minneapolis, The University of Minnesota Press, 1927.

Van Doren, Mark. *An Autobiography of America.* New York, Albert and Charles Boni, 1929.

Warburton, A. F. *Uncontradicted Testimony in the Beecher Case, Compiled From the Official Records.* New York, D. Appleton and Company, 1876.

Wardner, Henry S. *The Birthplace of Vermont: A History of Windsor to 1781.* New York, Charles Scribner's Sons, 1927.

Warren, Charles. *History of the Harvard Law School and of Early Legal Conditions in America.* 3 vols. New York, Lewis Publishing Company, 1908.

——. *The Supreme Court in United States History.* Boston, Little, Brown, and Company, 1932.

Weise, Arthur J. *The History of the City of Albany.* Albany, 1884.

Welles, Edward L. *Hampton and Reconstruction.* Columbia, S. C., 1907.

Wellman, F. L. *The Art of Cross-Examination.* New York, The Macmillan Company, 1923.

Wheeler, Everett P. *Sixty Years of American Life.* New York, E. P. Dutton and Company, 1917.

Williams, Mary W. *The People and Politics of Latin America.* Boston, Ginn and Company, 1938.

Wilson, James G. *Memorial History of the City of New York.* 4 vols. New York, New York History Company, 1893.

Winters, William H. *Report of an Early Alumni Association of Harvard Law School.* July 15, 1868.

Index

Vita

Chester Leonard Barrows was born November 25, 1891, in Wareham, Massachusetts. He was graduated from Boston University in 1916, and, after teaching a year at Vermont Academy, enlisted in the army and saw service in the Argonne Forest campaign as a machine-gunner. In 1919 he was given six months' free tuition in the University of Edinburgh by the government. Returning to the United States, he became a teacher of history in the high school of Danielson, Connecticut, for one year and then took a similar position in the Marquand Preparatory School in Brooklyn, New York, where he became headmaster in 1923. In 1925 he became instructor in history in Adelphi College, Garden City, New York, and was promoted to head of the History Department in 1935, a position which he now holds. He is a member of a number of historical societies and of the Sigma Alpha Epsilon fraternity.

www.ingramcontent.com/pod-product-compliance
Lightning Source LLC
LaVergne TN
LVHW090254210926
848480LV00001B/17
* 9 7 8 1 4 6 9 6 1 3 0 6 2 *